D0840719

EXPENDABLE ELITE

ONE SOLDIER'S JOURNEY INTO COVERT WARFARE

Lieutenant Colonel Daniel Marvin

United States Army Special Forces (Retired)

Trine Day

EXPENDABLE ELITE
One Soldier's Journey into Covert Warfare
Copyright ©2003/2006 Daniel Marvin

Marvin, Daniel.
    Expendable Elite / Daniel Marvin
        p.   cm.
    Includes bibliographic references.
    ISBN 0-9777953-1-4
    1. Vietnamese Conflict, 1961-75—Special Forces   2. Counter insurgency—Vietnam 3. Assassination attempt—Cambodian Crown Prince Norodom Sihanouk
I. Title
959.704'3373-dc21
DS558.Ma
Victory Edition (Second Edition)

This manuscript recounts many conversations held over a long period of time and reconstructed from notes, letters, records, reports, audiotapes and memory.
In each instance the substance and tone of these conversations is accurate; the dialogue is as precise as the notes, letters, records, reports, audiotapes and memory permit.

Library of Congress Control Number: 2003103612

Printed in the United States of America.

DISTRIBUTION TO THE TRADE BY:
Independent Publishers Group (IPG)
814 North Franklin Street
Chicago, Illinois 60610
www.ipgbook.com

DEDICATED TO:

My wife, *Katherine Ann*

Former ARVN Lieutenant General *Quang Van Dang*

Former ARVN Lieutenant Colonel *Phoi Van Le*

All those American and South Vietnamese Special Forces, civilian employees and the estimated 64,000 residents whom I had the pleasure to serve and to serve with from December 1965 to 2 August 1966 in An Phu District, South Vietnam

Pastor *William C Calabretta* and his wife, *Jeanne*

Kathryn Carlyle Burns

Kris Millegan

THIS BOOK OF TRUTH WAS BEGUN IN 1984,
THE YEAR I ACCEPTED THE LORD JESUS CHRIST AS MY PERSONAL SAVIOUR

TABLE OF CONTENTS

TABLE OF CONTENTS *(CONT.)*

To Every Thing There Is A Season ...

W hat is it about a book? Why do they excite such passions—burn them, ban them, read them, write them, venerate them. We kill for them. We construct rooms around them. We mold lives around them. They are sacred. They are profane. Books are powerful. A book presents focused thought, the codified word that may burn one's soul. A book may change your life. A book is where the rubber hits the road: it takes conscious decisions, concerted effort and determined dedication to bring forth thoughts and ideas into something that you may hold in your hand. It is, at day's end, an act of creation. And as with any creature, a book may have a life of its own. Maybe even a soul.

This book, a modest venture, the simple telling of a soldier's war story—something as old as the campfire, where the young warriors learn from the victories and failures of yore—has become something more than what it began as.

A crusade, and a catharsis, a healing for souls ravaged from war, hiding from the savagery and brutal inhumanity behind a shield of camaraderie, loyalty and bravado. A journey of truth hitting many rocky shores along the way, finally making its way to the ocean of common discourse only to be challenged and set upon by lawyers, the seemingly preferred profession for 21st century book-burners.

You shall, hopefully, read the whole story in the pages that follow, and be able to make-up your own mind. Included in this book are the documentation, photos, etcetera that display the forthrightness of this tale.

Although it does have the elements, this not an action story, it is a story to learn from, to learn the courage, the sacrifice and the unheralded civic actions of our Special Forces, to learn the tenacity and beauty of the Hoa Hao people and culture, to learn that war is more than what is presented in history books. To learn that a country and our fighting men and women may be mislead by our political leaders.

Those who have been to war, to kill or be killed—sometimes simply for an ideal—are truly the only ones who understand the actual reality of war, the decisions that must be made, the burdens that must be borne, the shock, the terror, the blood, the guts, the adrenaline … the smell. They understand the hypocrisy, the insanity of war that allows death and destruction to fester. That the lies told by far-removed leaders may result in misery, mayhem and murder for many.

Was it just because LTC Marvin let the air out of an old lie? Was that the reason for the attack on this book? Or was it more endemic to the Special Forces and their values and sensibilities? Or was there something deeper, a systemic avoidance of the truth, a routine obfuscation of past misdeeds, a sacrifice to the god of plausible deniablity, secrecy for secrecy's sake?

Federal District Court is no free lunch, and the SFA hired lawyers playing hard-ball till the end, even demanded a unanimous verdict. After we won, one of plaintiffs' attorneys puts me on notice … threatening to sue us again, using other members of Dan's team.

What is going on? Speaking from experience, litigation in Federal District Court *is not cheap.* It cost Dan and I over $150,000 for the privilege of defending ourselves successfully (and for which we still have years of payments left). We just had ourselves, a pair of lawyers and the … truth. "They" had seven people and three lawyers, They had several paid witnesses. Their costs may even be higher than ours. The "financial" backer of the lawsuit, the Special Forces Association had in 1998 a total annual operating budget of only $146,000.

Which may lead one to wonder, who is really paying the bills? And what is so threatening about this book, a Vietnam-era memoir of covert warfare? There are hundreds, even a coffee-table book, a slick photo history. Are there deeper threads to this story, or deeper secrets of Special Forces experiences that the "talkative" Dan may reveal? Is that why? Who knows? There may be many reasons. That isn't what concerns me here.

Where does the SFA claim this right to "bully" our history. Where in our federal Constitution is a semi-military organization appointed to serve as the thought police, the monitor of the "official" record? For our "trouble" was not a first for the SFA. Except that we went beyond their bluster, under their influence, over their hurdles, actually defending ourselves in court, and … prevailing. For it seems that even in these jaded times, our legal system, justice by the people, still stands.

So, yes, dear reader, you get the opportunity to read or not read this book. Just a book, like many others. A labor of love, a precious thing you may hold in your hand, your heart, your mind … your soul. Having withstood the fires of Federal District Court, this book, *Expendable Elite,* forges anew.

Will it help us to examine ourselves and our actions, as Colonel Dan would like? We shall see. For in the beginning they're just … words.

Peace,
Kris Millegan
06/20/2006

ONE MAN WHO WASN'T

*E*xpendable Elite *tells of how, as a Special Forces captain, Daniel Marvin almost became an assassination-team leader for the United States Government. That experience has affected him for the rest of his life. The book is* also a fascinating glimpse into the early years of the Vietnam War, offering a very human story about a man who struggled under perilous circumstances, and his quest to find peace of mind.

The tale begins at Christmas 1965, when Dan found himself commanding a Special Forces A-Team in the district of An Phu on the Cambodian border. The war had just heated up, and few Americans knew how to fight a counterinsurgency. The United States Army was looking for the Special Forces to show the way. Dan was in charge of a unit that controlled the civilian irregular troops of the militant Buddhist Hoa Hao sect. Dan formed close personal relationships with many of the Hoa Haos, but as commanding officer, he found it necessary to maintain more of a distance from his own men, to avoid any chance or appearance of favoritism in assigning the often-highly-dangerous missions.

Dan's "voluntary" assignment included cross-border operations that would extend up to three kilometers into Cambodia to seek out and destroy the Viet Cong in their sanctuaries. He also ran intelligence networks inside Cambodia with multiple female agents. At this point in the war, intelligence gathering was an overriding concern—especially to the Central Intelligence Agency.

In June 1966, CIA officer Walter MacKem visited Dan at his camp in An Phu. MacKem asked Dan to develop and execute a plan to assassinate Cambodian Crown Prince Norodom Sihanouk. It was a proposition that would change Dan's life.

The pivot point of *Expendable Elite* is that Dan did not unequivocally accept this request to kill Prince Sihanouk. Captain Marvin put a condition on his acceptance of the mission: that the President of the United States would have to tell the American people that he would allow US forces to attack the Viet Cong in what had been its sanctuaries in Cambodia, such as the one from which the VC had attacked An Phu with impunity before the A-Team's secret assignment. To this point, and in the face of news reports to the contrary, the Johnson administration had insisted that Cambodia's official neutrality was marked by its refusal of sanctuaries to the Viet Cong, a bald-faced lie.

Why did the CIA want the Prince assassinated? The CIA's plan was to have the Prince killed inside Cambodia, west of the Viet Cong safe havens, and to make it appear that he was killed by Communist forces. Blaming the Viet Cong was expected to make the people of Cambodia look to South Vietnam and the Americans for help in ridding their nation's eastern border area of the Viet Cong and the North Vietnamese Communists. Cambodia would be transformed from a Communist-leaning "neutral" into an active ally.

Lest this seem far-fetched, let me hasten to add that documentation exists that provides details of "Operation Cherry," a three pronged CIA effort to find and assassinate Prince Sihanouk, activated in 1967, after Dan left Vietnam. This and the revelations from the 1975-76 United States Senate Select Committee to Study Governmental Operations with Respect to Intelligence Activities, generally known as the Church Committee, demonstrates the fact that assassination was, in 1966, official CIA policy.

Special Forces got this type of job because, as part of its "special" capabilities, the "Sneaky Petes" do things that regular Army outfits cannot. One of these talents is to make an assassination look as if the enemy had done it.

Dan's A-Team got the job because their camp was the closest to the possible ambush sites on the road Prince Sihanouk would travel on his annual visit to Buddhist temples southwest of Skoun, Cambodia. The Hoa Hao fighters were well suited to passing themselves off as Viet Cong soldiers. On his second visit in June of 1966, Walter MacKem came to meet with Dan and his Hoa Hao counterpart, bringing topographical maps showing the route the Prince would take, along with the date the kill would have to take place. The Hoa Haos would take a captured barge up the Bassac River into Cambodia and then on up the Mekong River to a location near the ambush site.

The situation came to a climax when Walter MacKem came back to Dan's camp just two days before Dan's group of 42 irregular fighters were to go into Cambodia, and Dan had not yet heard from his contact at Fort Bragg, who was to confirm that President Johnson had met the conditions of Dan's quid pro quo. Dan immediately confronted MacKem with that fact, and MacKem refused to even answer, asking Marvin instead if his people were ready to go across the border.

Dan, barely able to control himself, ordered MacKem out of camp. And as MacKem was escorted to his white Air America helicopter he turned, looked at Dan and shouted, "You can't fight the system, Captain—because you can't win."

What happened next proved MacKem to be absolutely right. Dan became expendable for not following what he believed were illegal orders. He, his men and the Hao Hoa "strikers" then became the enemy, and except for Dan's courage and convictions, and the timely intervention of a high-ranking South Vietnamese general, would have surely paid the ultimate price.

Special Forces people often find themselves caught between the rock of unconventional warfare and the dictates of their conscience. They have a dirty job to do, and they are supposed to provide the CIA with plausible deniability, which means they have to carry the secrets for the rest of their lives.

In this case, Dan Marvin chose conscience.

Decades later, when Dan broke ranks with Special Forces in order to reveal the truth, he suffered the wrath of the Special Forces Association. It's hard to imagine just how much misery the SFA put Dan, his family and his publisher through. When Dan published the facts of the CIA assassination mission, some of the men who were formerly under his command disavowed him, and some, perhaps acting under duress, even went so far as to bring a libel case against him.

The SFA-inspired libel case is but one example of the fail-safe mechanisms that are built into the system to assure that whistleblowers like Dan Marvin do not tell the truth about America's counter-terror war. As in Southeast Asia in 1966, such dishonorable covert tactics are employed in today's warfare, and this is what spurred Dan and publisher Kris Millegan to bring *Expendable Elite* to print.

The US government also pressured Dan's former team members to turn against him. According to scuttlebutt, some were threatened with the loss of their retirement pay if they so much as spoke with Dan. Other pressures were also brought to bear. One of the individuals told Dan that the act of simply speaking with Dan, by itself, would derail any chance his son had of being Regular Army. Careers were at stake, and these men were told so.

For Dan the price went way beyond his career. His entire livelihood was put at risk. The Special Forces Association, in its quarterly publication, *THE DROP*, said it would provide the attorneys and pay the expenses of the plaintiffs who would take Dan to Federal Court. Why would the Special Forces Association, nominally a fraternal organization, go to this extent? The answer is that they wanted to hide the facts of what Special Forces are really involved with in their day-to-day operations as counter-insurgents, terrorists, assassins and saboteurs.

And this is why Dan Marvin's story is so important. It dispels decades of disinformation about the Vietnam War, and it cuts through all the layers of plausible deniability to tell the unsettling truth about how our own government resorts to these methods, not only in its foreign affairs, but in how it will attack an honorable veteran here in the United States in order to preserve the "official" story.

In *Expendable Elite* you will learn about unbelievable things that were not only possible but were routine in the Vietnam War. Many men that have been through these conditions are afraid to come forward with the truth. Well, here is the true story of one man who wasn't.

Douglas Valentine
Author of *The Phoenix Program, TDY, The Hotel Tacloban* and *The Strength of the Wolf: The Secret History of America's War on Drugs*

12 Jan 66 — LTC Martha Raye and Captain Daniel Marvin in Camp Dan Nam.

FOREWORD

Throughout American history, patriotism has always been an honorable estate. In times of peril, deserters were vilified as cowards, and the cream of our youth were willing to lay down their lives for their country.

The Vietnam era ended that tradition. It was the only time in American history that patriotism was unpopular. Draft dodgers were exonerated, cowards were applauded as they deserted, and the underprivileged were called to arms while the cream of our youth was deferred from service.

It was the first and only time in American history our flag was bloodied on the field of defeat and almost drowned in the sea of shame.

Time will sort out the right and wrong of it all... as it always does. But just as history soon forgets cowards, it also honors the valiant who stood up and were counted. Those who fell will be remembered along with the founders of our country who taught us that liberty is not an abstract term, and America's willingness to insure freedom in the world is something of which we must be manifestly proud.

I met Lt. Col. Daniel Marvin when he was still a Green Berets Captain in command of a Special Forces "A Team" camp called An-Phu. It was located in an area known as a *Purple Zone* which signified a place of high enemy activity. Just before landing, our Huey was hit twice with groundfire from a .50 cal. machine gun. As we touched down, I remember thinking, so this is where Dangerous Dan lives. It figures.

That he was expert at his job was evident even then. Among the 26 medals and commendations he received he was later to become the only American upon whom the gallant South Vietnamese Hoa Hao Forces had conferred their famous insignia, the Purple Scarf.

The men and events recorded by him in the following pages give the reader a true overall picture of both conventional and unconventional warfare in overt as well as covert situations carried out by U.S. Special Forces Teams.

Lt. Col. Marvin has reduced the war to a single unit and recalls his response to a complex hierarchy of authority often issuing conflicting, almost frivolous commands upon which hundreds of lives depended.

You are the judge of the value of it all.

Lieutenant Colonel Martha Raye, Honorary
20 February 1988

Major Phoi Van Le and Captain "Dangerous Dan" Marvin
Comrades-in-Arms who introduce cross-border operations.

INTRODUCTION

By Jacqueline K. Powers

Y ou would have to know Lieutenant Colonel "Dangerous Dan" Marvin as I know him to understand just why he has devoted eighteen years to his single-minded crusade to see the truth published as it unfolds in this book. A retired Special Forces officer who began his military career as an infantry recruit in June 1952, Dan is still a Clint Eastwood kind of guy. He even looks a little like the actor, all sinew at 68 with a square jaw and steely eyes.

Dan's a grandfather and loves his eleven grandchildren, three daughters and his wife, Kate. But in his heart Dan is and always was a soul-fired crusader. Had he been born centuries ago he would have been a knight in armor searching for the Holy Grail.

I first met Dan in the Fall of 1990 when I was managing editor of the Ithaca Journal, a daily with a circulation of 20,000 in upstate New York. Dan literally invaded my office to confront me and convince me that it was my duty to investigate what had happened to former ARVN Lieutenant General Quang Van Dang, a man who had saved Dan's life and those of the men in his Green Beret A Team, their South Vietnamese Special Forces counterparts and hundreds of South Vietnamese irregular fighters who had worked and fought together to defeat the Communist Viet-Cong invaders and insurgents to keep their area secure.

Dan told me something that day that I'll never forget. It was a matter-of-fact statement that triggered my intense interest in what he had to say and opened the door to my appreciation for the real danger posed to a man who joins the Special Operations Forces. It was a sobering introduction to a staggering reality. "We don't fear the enemy we are trained to defeat," he told me, "We fear what may happen to us should those in power decide that our nation would be better served if we were no longer available for question or comment." Dan then told me without any outward manifestation or trepidation "other volunteers, trained and dedicated as we were would be asked to 'dispose' of us. It was as simple as that."

In this book, Dan provides an insight into a little known and perhaps the most dangerous aspect of covert operations. It is the secrecy that enshrouds the mission and its players that renders them easy victims for those who would deny its very existence.

A bizarre chain of events brought ARVN Lieutenant General Quang Van Dang to rescue Dan, his A Team and his irregulars from the deadly wrath of our own government when so-called "friendly" forces sent to destroy Dan's camp by the CIA were turned back by General Dang. It happened in June of 1966 in a remote area of South Vietnam along the Cambodian border and is grim testimony to why the CIA and the White House wanted General Dang kept in virtual exile, effectively silenced and unable to tell the truth of his rescue of our men and their irregular forces from certain death at the hands of a US advised and heavily armed ARVN Regiment.

Dan was born in Detroit, Michigan, in 1933, into poverty and injustice; it was the injustice that lit a fire in his soul. His father, a vain, inglorious womanizer, left his wife when Dan was born. It was that abandonment that led Dan to become a crusader. At age eleven he formed his first gang, the Blue Jackets, to protect little old ladies on South Side Chicago's mean streets. Today he is still crusading and the object of his crusades is; to honor the courage of those South Vietnamese he and his team of Green Berets fought alongside in the Bassac River Delta; to pay tribute to Lieutenant General Dang; to unmask the abuse of power and the tendency to engage in subterfuge and personal gratification at the expense of the mission that is inherent with independent unconventional warfare and covert operations.

He does this while giving recognition to the importance of what the men in the US Army's Special Forces, the men who wore the Green Beret, did in civic action, psychological operations and military government aspects of unconventional warfare that would help to win the hearts and minds of the people. Dan grinned from ear to ear with pride as he told me that his team spent 60 percent of their effort in these noncombat functions. In his words, "It was our goal to instill loyalty to the government among the Hoa Haos by acting on behalf of that government to secure the area for the people. What we did for the people during the day gave us the edge we needed for victory in the many battles, most of which were fought during hours of darkness."

Dan came to love and admire the people he was there to help. The vast majority of whom were members of the Hoa Hao Sect of the Buddhist religion. They were, in his words, "the finest, bravest, most caring people" that he'd had the good fortune to come to know. Dan was 32 years old when he became intimately aware of the true character of the Hoa Hao people.

Dan takes you there, gets your feet wet, and introduces you to the people, the places and the hard truth of what he experienced. He makes you keenly aware of the powerful forces that existed in the American political, military and intelligence systems, forces he ran afoul of when fighting to do his job — to protect the people and secure the area, forces Dan says still exist and whom he battles in the halls of Congress via the US Mail, and his facsimile machine. To this day he continues an almost single-handed struggle with the bureaucracy in the pursuit of truth and justice on behalf of those brave South Vietnamese of An Phu District and their betrayed democracy,

From his experiences as commander of Special Forces Team A-424, living and serving among the 64,000 people of An Phu, he understood what the United States should have done militarily and politically throughout South Vietnam in order to deny the Communists a fertile ground for a successful insurgency. Dan sincerely believes if we had helped shape a government that truly served the best interests of its diverse population, thereby gaining their loyalty while building a military force to secure its borders, we would have charted an almost certain course to victory. Dan has cause to state that unequivocally as he points out rather proudly and accurately that it "worked in An Phu".

Dan writes in vivid detail how the military was shackled by the dictates of a White House concerned with popular opinion, a State Department leaning toward "global impact" control and particularly anxious to appease Hanoi and Peking, and a military command structure all the way to the Joint Chiefs of Staff who despised the elite Special Forces men and their methods. It was those methods that inspired President John F. Kennedy to expand that elite organization and to send it in sufficient numbers to South Vietnam to do what they knew best. "To win the hearts and minds of the people so as to win the war was key in everyday planning and action," Dan told me, but in the end the military command was married to a failed conventional strategy that proved ineffective in the long struggle with Hanoi.

Dan challenges the reader to judge the propriety of General William Westmoreland's confessed failure to reveal the truth about the enemy's Cambodian sanctuaries, and to demand the right to take the war into those safe-havens where the enemy hid. In Dan's area alone, more than 200 people were killed by the enemy attacking out of those sanctuaries. Strategic blunders, precipitated by Political expediency born of a lack of resolve and integrity, led to America's betrayal of the South Vietnamese people. Those brave people who had trusted us to save them from the Communist threat were abandoned on the field of battle by a cowardly White House and Congress.

Dan quit school when he was sixteen to help support his mother, he worked in the student union building at Cornell University as busboy, janitor and short-order cook for the next two and a half years. Sensing a need to be a part of the military effort in Korea, he enlisted in the US Army at age eighteen as a recruit, and within four months was an acting Sergeant in charge of training infantry recruits at the Indiantown Gap Military Reservation in Pennsylvania.

Dan is a man of strength and character and he is without a doubt fearless. Though his relationship with wife and family suffered, Dan put the Army ahead of everything, and in his single -mindfulness and determination, excelled. He was promoted time and again. In February 1964, then Captain "Dangerous Dan" Marvin, as he'd come to be known, donned the Green Beret personally authorized for the elite Special Forces by the late President John F. Kennedy.

In 1984 Dan was born again, and became a soldier in Christ's Army. Dan now campaigns vigorously against government-sponsored terrorism and assassination, spending hours every day, usually late into the night, writing, mailing articles, reviewing and correlating newly acquired documentation or corroboration of what he reveals in the pages of this book. He has had to come to grips with the unfortunate reality that, in Dan's words, "there are few who possess the courage to put their voice or their signature on the line as testimony regarding illegal, immoral or unsound actions ordered and/or perpetrated by the CIA or other agencies within the Washington establishment."

Dan has taken years to collect, compile, and correlate information received in writing or on audio tape from former CIA Saigon Station Chiefs Theodore Shackley and Thomas Polgar, LTG Quang Van Dang, LTC Phoi Van Le, members of his Green Beret A Team, interpreters and others. He also uses researched facts gleaned from historical documents, books, letters and articles to corroborate his work.

What follows is the whole truth, the good, the bad, and the ugly of what took place during his tour of duty in South Vietnam, beginning in late December, 1965.

For any person who believes in this great nation of ours and understands the need for the truth, this is a must read.

Jacqueline K. Powers
Ithaca, New York

ACRONYMS, TERMS & ABBREVIATIONS
with pronunciation aide

A Detachment: See A Team

A Team: Basic 12 man Special Forces Unit (Green Berets)

Agency: Central Intelligence Agency

Air America: A proprietary air arm of the CIA

AKA: Also known as

APC: Armored Personnel Carrier

ARVN: Army of the Republic of Vietnam (South Vietnam)

ASA: Assorted small arms (does not include automatic weapons)

ASAP: As soon as possible

B Detachment: See B Team

B Team: Command & Control SF unit responsible for a number of A Teams

Bac-si (bach sea): Vietnamese for doctor

Bangalore Torpedo: Demolition device for breaching wire obstacles.

BAR: Browning Automatic Rifle

Battalion: A military organizational unit comprised of two or more companies

Berm: The path inside and just below the top of the earth mound inside a defensive perimeter

Bivouac: A temporary encampment with no fixed facilities

Black Pajamas: An all-black, loose fitting, cotton uniform with wide-brimmed, soft hat worn for night combat patrols and ambush operations

C Detachment: See C Team

C Team: Command & Control SF unit responsible for a number of B Teams

C4: Plastic, moldable explosive

CA: Civic Action

Cache: A safe place (covered hole, cave, etc.) to store items

Cao Dai (cow die): A Buddhist religious sect in Vietnam

Chams (chaams): People of Malaysian/ Polynesian extraction

Chao (chow): Vietnamese for greetings

CHICOM: Chinese Communist

Chieu Hoi (chew hoy): "Open Arms" program under which GVN offered amnesty to Viet Cong defectors

Chung-si (choong see): Vietnamese for Sergeant

CIA: Central Intelligence Agency

CIB: Combat Infantryman's Badge

CIDG: Civilian Irregular Defense Group - Irregular forces employed in Special Forces unconventional warfare program. Funded by the CIA.

CISO: Counterinsurgency Support Office - A logistical base in Okinawa that supports unconventional Special Operations

Civic action: The use of American and local military, paramilitary, or irregular forces on projects useful to the local population in such fields as education, training, public works, agriculture, transportation, communications, health, sanitation, and that contribute to economic and social development, which would also serve to improve the standing of the government with the population

Clicks: Term for kilometers

CO: Commanding Officer

Company: A military organizational unit comprised of two or more platoons - also slang for the CIA

CONUS: Continental United States (excludes Hawaii & Alaska)

Counterinsurgency: Military, paramilitary, psychological warfare, political, economical, and civic actions taken by a government to defeat a subversive insurgency

Cultivator: Farmer of a small parcel

Dai-uy (Die wee): Vietnamese for Captain

Division: A military organizational unit comprised of two or more regiments and/or separate battalions

District Chief: Governor of a county-sized territory (in SVN: normally an ARVN Captain or Major)

Dog Lab: That part of Special Forces medical training that was conducted in secret at Fort Bragg, North Carolina, using medically muted dogs instead of human patients in the surgical procedures training part of the course.

EE-8: WWII vintage hand-crank battery operated telephone

ETA: Estimated time of arrival

FAC: Forward air controller

Field Grade Officer: An officer of the rank of Major or higher

FOB: Forward operations base. Fortified position from which combat operations are conducted.

G-1: Military personnel staff at Division level or higher

G-2: Military intelligence staff at Division level or higher

G-3: Military operations staff at Division level or higher

G-4: Military logistics staff at Division level or higher

G-5: Military CA/PsyOps staff at Division level or higher

GEN: General

Grease Gun: .45 caliber sub-machine gun.

Green Berets: Members of US Army Special Forces

Green Zone: Code to indicate that an area is relatively secured and that an unarmed helicopter may enter and land without armed helicopter escort

Guano: Bat manure

Guerrillas: Fighters in a resistance movement who are organized on a military, paramilitary, or irregular basis

Guerrilla warfare: Combat operations conducted in enemy-held or hostile territory by irregular, predominantly indigenous forces

H&I Fire: Harassing and interdicting fire

Hamlet: A small rural village

Hoa Hao (wha how): Buddhist religious sect

HE: High explosive

HQ: Headquarters

HT-1: Hand-held portable, battery operated radio used by CIDG

Huey: Short for HU1 series of helicopters

KIA: Killed in action

Insurgency: A condition resulting from insurrection against a constituted government that falls short of civil war

Irregular forces: Armed individuals or groups hired and paid to perform as military units under direction of allied and/or American Special Forces units.

IV: Intravenous

Johns: Toilets

KKK: Khmer Kampuchea Krom. A Cambodian Sect whose members are employed in CIDG & Mike Force units

LCU: US Navy Landing Craft Utility

Leg: Disparaging term used by airborne qualified personnel to describe non-airborne soldiers

LLDB: Luc-Luong-Doc-Biet (Look Long Dock Be-yet) - Vietnamese Special Forces

LMG: Light Machine Gun

LTC: Lieutenant Colonel

LTG: Lieutenant General

M-79: 40MM hand-held grenade launcher

MACV: Military Assistance Command Vietnam

MAJ: Major

Mess: The dining area where meals are served and eaten

MIA: Missing in action

Mike Force: Irregular special reaction type units commanded by USSF and employed to aid outnumbered CIDG camps.

Modus Operandi: Method of operation

MOPSUM: Monthly Operational Summary - A well-defined and detailed report of one month's events and statistics

Mustang: An officer who had prior enlisted service

Nantucket: Code word for an official complaint from Cambodian authorities of a border violation.

NCO: Noncommissioned Officer

Need to know: A security procedure that requires recipients of classified information prove their need to know by position or mission.

NLT: No later than

Nungs: People of Chinese descent used in Mike Force units.

NVA: North Vietnamese Army

NVN: North Vietnam

OCS: Officer Candidate School

Ong: Vietnamese for mister

Paramilitary forces: Locally raised, commanded and assigned defensive company or platoon size units. (See RF and PF)

PF: Popular Forces. Paramilitary units used to defend their own hamlets comprised of part-time volunteers, normally platoon size units.

Platoon: A military unit comprised of two or more squads

P.O.L.: Petroleum, oil, and lubricant

POW: Prisoner of War

Prefix 3: Indicates, as part of the Military Occupational Specialty numerical code, that the individual has successfully-completed Special Warfare training and is authorized to wear the distinctive Green Beret.

Province Chief: Governor of a state-sized territory (in SVN: normally a high ranking military officer)

PUFF: Short for "Puff the Magic Dragon," a term used for aircraft armed with Gatling guns for close support of ground combat operations

PsyOps: Psychological Operations

PsyWar: Psychological Warfare

Purple Zone: Code indicating specific area is controlled by or imminently threatened by the enemy. Armed helicopter escort required for unarmed helicopters entering area

RF: Regional Forces - Full time paramilitary fighters in company size units at district and province level and under the authority of the chief of that territory

S-1: Military personnel staff at Regimental level or below

S-2: Military intelligence staff at Regimental level or below

S-3: Military operations staff at Regimental level or below

S-4: Military logistics staff at Regimental level or below

S-5: Military CA/PsyOps staff at Regimental level or below

SADM: Special Atomic Demolition Munition - A low yield, man-portable, atomic demolition munition that is detonated by a manually set timing device

Sappers: Demolition personnel

SF: US Army Special Forces (AKA Green Berets)

SITREP: Situation Report - A report on a specific combat action, normally submitted with overlay and details ASAP after action

Slick: A helicopter without pilot actuated weaponry. Door gunners sometimes part of crew of a slick.

SLR: Side Looking Radar - Method used to obtain infrared intelligence photos during hours of darkness using fixed wing aircraft

Smoke Bomb Hill: Slang term for U.S. Army Special Forces and John F. Kennedy Center for Special Warfare training and cantonment (barracks) area at Fort Bragg, North Carolina

SOI: Signal Operating Instructions. System of codes and frequencies used in radio communications

Special Forces: US Military forces highly trained in counter-guerrilla and other unconventional warfare techniques

Spooky: Another term for Puff the Magic Dragon gunship

SPOTREP: Spot Report - A radio message sent to summarize critical intelligence of an urgent nature or an action involving contact with the enemy that may be continuing or may impact on a neighboring SF camp area of operations

Squad: Smallest standard military organizational unit, normally between 10-15 men

SS: Sub Sector

Striker: Slang term for CIDG fighters

Sub Sector: Synonymous with "District."

SVN: South Vietnam

Thieu-ta (Tuuu-tah): Vietnamese for Major

TS: Top Secret

USAID: United States Agency for International Development

USOM: United States Overseas Mission

VC: Short for Viet Cong

Viet Cong: Vietnamese Communist forces

VIS: Vietnamese Information Service

VNAF: Vietnamese Air Force

VT: Variable time (fuse)

WIA: Wounded in Action

WP: White Phosphorus

XO: Executive Officer, second in command

Z: Greenwich Mean Time (AKA Zulu)

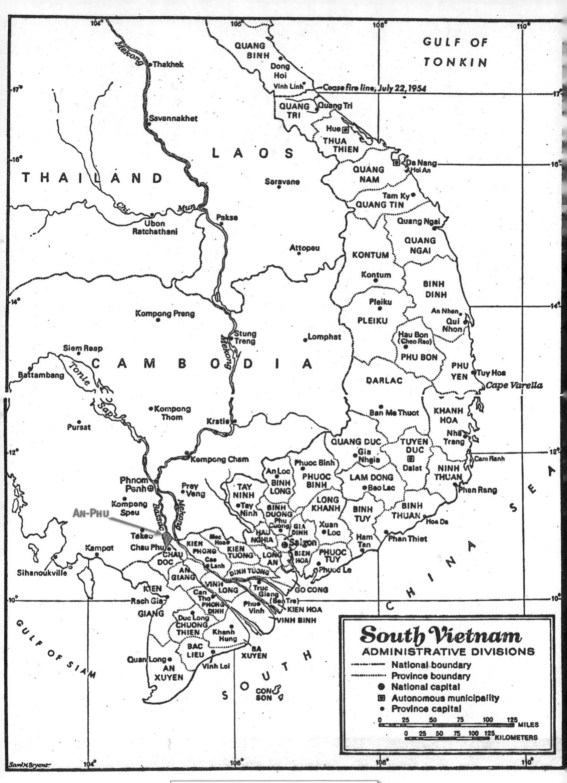

SPECIAL OPERATIONS MAP #1

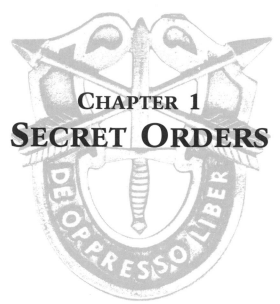

CHAPTER 1
SECRET ORDERS

Lieutenant Colonel Tuttle, the commander of all Special Forces in the IV Tactical Corps of South Vietnam, spoke in a whisper, "Dan, if you take command of A-424 and accept this TOP SECRET mission, you'll be on your own. When you leave this room, it will be as if we never met. We can't and won't stand behind you if you are caught doing what I am about to tell you to do. Got it, Captain?"

It was a sobering moment as together we looked out across the border from our command bunker toward the enemy's Cambodian Sanctuary. There a 2,400 man Viet Cong Regiment stood poised to attack our irregular forces who manned outposts and ambush sites all along that common border. It was 18 June 1966. Though outnumbered and outgunned by the Communists, we knew from past victories that we could defend the thirty kilometer stretch of border and maintain a secure area for our 64,000 people — if the enemy were our only concern.

Major Phoi Van Le and I, emotions temporarily masked, stood silent on either side of the .50 Caliber machine gun whose octagonal barrel pointed out over the defenses of our special operations camp and toward the Cambodian border.

Today was profoundly different from the previous times, ushering in an experience that would be forever seared into the very fabric of our wartime recollections. Major Le, my Vietnamese counterpart, was a courageous and truly stoic leader of men and a veteran of eighteen years in combat. I held him up as a five foot five equal to my film hero, John Wayne. "For the first time," he told me, "I fear what might happen in An Phu."

1

It was a fact he was not proud of, but it was the truth that he shared unashamedly with me as he would a brother. We had achieved that degree of closeness. Major Le was one of those rare leaders who had always stood tall, had never wavered from honorable conduct nor backed away from danger. He had always led his men into battle and was known for doing what he could to safeguard noncombatants whenever possible who had trusted him for their safety and security. For a brief period he was understandably unsure and perhaps most distraught by the thought he might no longer be capable of protecting the people of An Phu.

Why such a momentous shift in confidence? Just two days prior I had ordered CIA Agent Walter MacKem to leave my camp and he had left showing his anger at what I'd done, even threatening retribution, shouting "You can't fight the system, Captain, because you can't win."

It was the 20th of June 1966 when Major Le and I together pondered the situation and our alternatives. Only moments before we had received word from one of our agents in the Province Capital of Chau Doc that a heavily armed 1500 man ARVN Regiment with US advisors was being assembled immediately in front of our B Team compound in preparation for an attack on our camp. US Navy LCUs that would bring them, with their massive firepower, up the Bassac River to attack our camp, formed what seemed an endless line of vessels waiting their turn to load their deadly cargo. Major Le turned toward me, reached out and we shook hands. Both of us were very much aware that our time together could now be short. It was time for a miracle and I prayed for just that. Major Le looked into my eyes as he liked to do when he was real serious. "I hope our emissary from the Hoa Hao people reaches General Dang in time to stop the slaughter." Tears welled in his eyes. I'd never seen Major Le cry, but I knew he loved his men and that his real concern was that others would suffer, even die at the hands of the ARVN troops.

"And I hope General Dang is on our side," I returned, not knowing the General or his loyalties as well as Major Le. As military advisor to the Hoa Hao Central Council, he had coordinated with General Dang on military matters in the past.

Major Le glanced at me, smiling weakly, "Of that I have no doubt, Dai-uy. No doubt at all."

I would never have believed that when I gave my oath to defend our country, the US bureaucracy would turn full-force and order the death of my team and those whom we were there to help. It was shocking testimony to what can be a hidden danger in covert operations. What appeared to be truly catastrophic events threatening to engulf and destroy us came to pass because I stood my ground for what I truly believed to be the right and honorable course of action while going against the unconscionable dictates of the CIA. Those final, tense days now seem almost unreal, but they were indeed real and are relived in these pages as I unfold the truth I experienced as a 32 year old Green Beret Captain in Vietnam.

Secrecy was demanded during the many months of rigorous guerrilla and counter-guerrilla warfare training. Once we'd passed the acid test and had earned the right to wear the coveted Green Beret, we discussed little of what we'd learned with family or friends. That secrecy fostered strained relations within family, non-SF friends and wives. When Kate and I exchanged vows in October 1956, I was a 23 year-old Sergeant First Class and a paratrooper in the 82nd Airborne Division at Fort Bragg, North Carolina. We'd first met some seven years earlier at a square dance in Enfield Center, New York. I was sixteen, the stepson of a farmer who had bought a horse from her father when she was 13 years old.

The day President Kennedy was assassinated we were stationed at Yuma Proving Grounds in Arizona. I immediately volunteered for Special Forces, my passion being to earn and wear the Green Beret he had personally authorized. I wanted more than anything to be one of those unconventional warriors he considered as the "elite" within our military.

As the wife of a Green Beret, it would be psychologically heart-wrenching for Kate to be ready at a moment's notice to bid me good-bye, not knowing where the mission was taking me, how long I'd be gone, or what danger was involved. Duty demanded I tell her only superficial "fluff." If and when I could write, those letters were void of even the smallest detail of covert activities, code names or reference to unconventional warfare.

Though Kate knew in general terms where I was during my entire career, it would be twenty years after I earned the Green Beret before I shared with her what I'd actually experienced of an unconventional nature. I hadn't considered the negative mental effect telling the truth would have on her, thinking she would be happy to at last be aware of what being a Green Beret truly meant in all aspects of its secret, unconventional nature. After learning of the dark side of guerrilla warfare, special demolitions, interrogation methods and operations that ignored, even defied the International Law of Land Warfare, particularly assassination and terrorism, Kate was emotionally blown away. One day in the Spring of 1984 she blurted out, "You are **not** the man I married!" and she had never been so right. This way of life, though foreign and distasteful to most, was what made my adrenaline flow as nothing else could.

On 22 December 1965, 64 of us who wore the Green Beret arrived over South Vietnam at 10,000 feet, anxious to get on the ground and join in the counterinsurgency we'd all asked to be a part of. As we approached Saigon's Tan Son Nhut air base in a plush Southern Air Transport jet, we peered out cabin windows and saw flashes of artillery and rocket explosions in the distance, too far to disturb a perfect, though hurried, landing. As the big jet rolled to a stop, we gathered our gear, deplaned and were instantly introduced to the reality of 100 degree heat and high humidity.

A young sergeant from 5th Special Forces Group met us and led with quickened strides for 100 yards to a waiting Army Caribou aircraft. Its two propeller-driven engines were kept running as a load master motioned us up the ramp to the deck where we were told to stow our gear and strap ourselves into the canvas seats. In a few minutes we were airborne and on our way to Group headquarters at Nha Trang, situated 215 miles northeast of Saigon on the South China Sea coast.

Two days earlier I'd said good-bye to Kate and our three girls at the airport outside of Ithaca, New York. I'd also said good-bye to several inches of snow, a bitter wind and 25° temperature. I'd wanted to wave good-bye from my window seat but the swirling snow made it impossible to see the terminal where I knew they would be standing. I hoped that Kate would be safe driving our new Volkswagen Beetle home, some three miles distant, and I knew in my heart that she would take our separation and all that went with it in stride. Ithaca, after all, was where she was born, where we met and were married. If any problems arose while I was away, all of her family lived in the area and I was confident they would look out for her and the girls. The flight from Ithaca to the municipal airport in Fayetteville, North Carolina, was uneventful and the taxi trip to Pope Air Force Base, adjacent to Fort Bragg, quick and pleasant. Base operations personnel at Pope checked me in and quickly led me on board a large Southern Air Transport jet, its engines running and 63 other Green Berets already on board. The CIA played a big part in clandestine activities worldwide and Green Beret troops were routinely flown to various destinations in one of their proprietary airlines' aircraft. It was indeed a plush ride, with gorgeous stewardesses, free drinks, good hot food and a seemingly endless assortment of John Wayne movies.

We landed at Nha Trang Air Base, parked on the blacktop and deplaned into the midst of a scene of furious activity. It was immediately evident, even to the casual observer, that logistical support of all Special Forces (SF) camps in South Vietnam was a demanding and consuming task.

We were shown the mess hall on the way to our transient quarters which weren't fancy but good enough for some shuteye.

At 0700 the next morning, with a hearty breakfast to sustain us, three other officers and myself reported to the briefing room and attended a series of orientations by the Group Commander, Colonel William McKean, and his staff.

We were briefed on logistical support, including emergency air re-supply operations and channels of communication for ordering critical ammunition and other combat support needs by radio to the Logistical Support Center. 5th Group parachute riggers, commanded by First Lieutenant Peter Teasdale, using the SF bundle code[1] system, would drop desperately needed ammunition into the requesting camp's drop zone within a few hours of their request.

Lieutenant Teasdale had served as my assistant S-4 at Fort Bragg and was familiar with the early development of the bundle code system. The code grouped common items such as weapons, ammunition, medical supplies, communication equipment, demolition material, petroleum, rations, and other supplies critical to the mission. Pre-rigged quantities of each bundle were then placed in isolated storage areas with parachutes attached. Each bundle's three digit code, readily transmitted by Morse code or using one time message pads, made it simple and quick to get the right thing to the right place at the right time.

The Intelligence Officer (S-2) was the next briefer. Beginning with a summary of significant activity that had affected SF camps in South Vietnam for the preceding 24 hours, he went on to give us an overview of intelligence operations, a synopsis of the current enemy situation and an experience-based look into anticipated enemy activity. He made us acutely aware of the need for a good intelligence network using local assets available to each SF Camp. He warned us of the danger of buying intelligence based on the numbers reported as potentially rewarding agents for providing useless, even dangerous, exaggerations of enemy location, strength and weaponry.

The S-3 followed. Using a long, wooden pointer with a shiny brass tip, he directed our attention to the locations of SF Camps posted on a floor to ceiling map of South Vietnam. The security classification SECRET was stamped at the top and bottom in big, bold, red letters. He pointed out the seventy-eight CIDG camps, beginning in the north at Khe San, and moving southward. Many camps were located on or near South Vietnam's border with Laos and Cambodia and a lesser number in the interior, extending south to a former French customs outpost at Ha Tien, separated only by a narrow inlet from Cambodia in the Gulf of Siam.

Counting us there were 1,592 SF in country, with most advising approximately 28,200 Civilian Irregular Defense Group (CIDG) fighters. Others were leading those 2,300 irregulars assigned to Mike Force units. The CIDG were trained, equipped, and led by Vietnamese Special Forces A Teams, but were paid, housed, fed, supplied and advised by American SF A Teams. Most CIDG personnel, he said, were recruited from local areas to protect and defend their own homes and lands, fighting the Viet Cong insurgents and North Vietnamese regular forces that attacked their area. The program included ethnic Cambodians, members of the Buddhist Hoa Hao and Cao Dai sects, ethnic Chinese and the mountain tribal warriors known collectively as Montagnards. He took the time to tell us of the unique nature of the Mike Force. They were equipped as a mobile reaction force with certain of their units on stand-by and available around the clock to go to the aid of SF camps in real danger of being overrun. All Mike Force units were commanded by American Green Berets. In addition, a total of 28,800 Regional Force and Popular Force paramilitary soldiers operating in certain areas under Group control were advised by SF personnel. He stressed the importance of reports: The Monthly Operational Summary (MOPSUM), Situation Reports (SITREPs) and Spot Intelligence Reports (SPOTREPs). Every report was reviewed at Group headquarters to make sure that Group staff knew what was going on out in the field. Timely and accurate reports were essential to the task of developing sound plans for logistical support of unconventional operations in the field throughout South Vietnam. By pin-pointing enemy activity in each team area they could better place close air support and medical evacuation resources on stand-by at locations within range of those camps most likely to require emergency assistance.

He paused to sip from a glass of water on the podium, asked that we hold our questions until the briefing was over and told us he'd then be in the back of the room to answer any questions that remained. The Civil Affairs Officer (S-5), responsible for civic action and psychological warfare operations, was next to brief. He engaged us in an energetic, challenging and thought-provoking mental walk through those areas his office managed and supported, with particular emphasis on the importance of winning the hearts and minds of the people. He inspired with his enthusiasm and helped us to understand why at least half of our team effort on the ground must involve civic action projects and psychological warfare activity if we were to succeed. "For many years," he told us, "the Saigon government had been insensitive to the needs and aspirations of the Montagnards, Hoa Hao and Cao Dai Buddhist Sects and ethnic Cambodians. As a result, little if any loyalty to the Saigon regime existed among the people in these groups. All together," he explained, "they made up the majority of the rural population, but lacking a patriotic spirit, were fair game for Communist propaganda." One of our major challenges would be to help lessen and gradually set aside government apathy, and in some cases, open hostility toward these groups. He explained how most civic action programs would be developed by our A Team members working with their South Vietnamese Special Forces (LLDB) counterparts, local village leaders and district officials. They would initially determine the realistic needs of the people and assess the capability of local government and SF to satisfy those needs determined to be critical. Programs included bridge, school and dock construction, road building and medical patrols. SF medics were easily the most appreciated men in the operational A teams because they were out in the district on a daily basis, even into the smallest hamlets, easing pain and suffering among the local people, particularly children and the aged. All of what the teams did for and with the people helped to develop trust and foster the loyalty needed to count them as our friends in the struggle against the Communist insurgency. "Trust is earned and loyalty follows," he emphasized, "An important function of each A Team member is to then attempt to redirect that loyalty to the Vietnamese government. No easy task," he concluded, "but you best keep that first and foremost in your minds. We will all be gone back home some day and the worst thing we could do would be to leave a vacuum." He then introduced the Adjutant and stepped down.

The man each of us was anxious to hear from and who would tell us where we were going — now stood facing us, smiling and holding a number of personnel folders in his hand. Every SF Captain worth his salt hoped to command an A Team and I was no exception! At the same time, I thought my fate was sealed, that I'd have to stay in Nha Trang and work in the LSC due to my logistics background. At 32, I was the oldest Captain in this group, and I was pleasantly surprised when he called me up front, handed me a set of orders, and informed me I'd be going to Can Tho in the IV Corps Tactical Zone. He told me to report to Colonel Tuttle, the C Team commander. He directed me to the flight operations center where I was to ask for the earliest flight to Can Tho.

As I was leaving the briefing area I could hear him tell the remaining officers that they would probably get an A Team if they had combat experience. Knowing

I'd served as a combat engineer Lieutenant during the final days of the Korean War, I sensed that I might yet realize my dream of commanding an A Team.

The flight to Can Tho in an Army Caribou aircraft didn't get off the ground until shortly after lunch on Christmas Eve. Four of us strapped ourselves in canvas seats behind the cockpit, looking out over a cargo compartment loaded with supplies destined for Saigon and Can Tho. My three companions were Green Beret Sergeants on their way home and anxious to share with me some of what they'd experienced. I was treated to personal accounts of the many battles, triumphs and tragedies they'd each survived. They gloried in recounting in vivid word pictures many of the battles they'd fought alongside their irregulars, always emerging victorious, yet bloodied with many combat losses. One sergeant spoke with a slight tremor in his voice of Viet Cong "phantom warriors" who would suddenly appear, as if out of thin air, attack where and when least expected, and then disappear back into a jungle area. He was familiar with the region where he'd wait in ambush for our expected counterattack into the unknown. He was quick to point out that his team was ready for the enemy, the guerrilla warfare training he'd received on Smoke Bomb Hill had paid off. He looked at me, smiled and said, "Dai-uy, we got the job done and we made believers of those Cong."

Dai-uy, pronounced "die wee" was Vietnamese for Captain. I'd better get used to that, I thought.. It was now second nature to these men as were other Vietnamese words and expressions they'd picked up working with and fighting alongside the people in their area. I listened intently, wanting to absorb as much as I could to help me get off on the right foot when I got to where I was going.

They each expressed regrets that most of the men coming to Vietnam were conventional soldiers who arrived in country lacking proper training. Because of that, they didn't stand a chance against an elusive, well armed, combat-experienced enemy. Conversation ceased as we began our descent on the approach to Saigon's Tan Son Nhut airport. They were eager to get on the ground and it showed. From Saigon they'd board an aircraft for the final leg of the journey home to the States. We taxied to the passenger terminal, allowed the sergeants to deplane, then rolled on to a warehouse area where a pallet load of supplies was quickly pushed down the rear ramp's roller conveyors and on to the ground by the crew.

In less than 20 minutes we were back in the air and flying south over the rice paddy rich Delta area toward Can Tho. By early evening we were descending along a glide path that crossed the mighty Mekong River before touching down on the C Team landing strip. We taxied to a stop. Immediately the rear cargo ramp was lowered and the hot, humid air rushed in. I picked up my gear, walked out on the blacktop and was greeted by the C Team Sergeant Major. A big, burly man with huge, blacksmith-like arms, he grabbed my duffel bag like it was filled with feathers, strode through the main gate, led me past the mess hall and on to the transient barracks. With his free arm he pointed to a two-story wooden building with a metal roof. "That's headquarters, Dai-uy. Colonel Tuttle's office is up there. The map room and briefing area are just outside his door. The 'old man' will see you at 0800 hours sharp," he shouted.

After leading me through a door into the north end of the transient quarters, he showed me to a small cubicle where he set my duffel bag down just inside. No door to the cubicle, just a bamboo curtain for privacy. Pointing down the hall he told me where to find the shower and latrine. He let me know that the mess hall started serving supper at 1700 hours and that they might have some warm chow left over, suggesting that I'd better "hustle" if I wanted any. He turned to leave, hesitated a moment, stared at me and asked if I was the "Dangerous Dan" he'd heard about from the Group Sergeant Major. I said nothing, just smiled. He scratched his head, grinned, turned and ambled out, muttering something under his breath.

Muffled sounds of distant artillery and rocket fire were audible but the atmosphere in and around the compound was festive, as if there were no war. It was, I remembered, Christmas Eve!

I hurried over to the dining room and arrived in time to be served a hot roast beef sandwich, mashed potatoes, peas and black coffee. It was cooked just the way I liked it, bringing back memories of many similar meals I'd eaten in a Howard Johnson's Restaurant. On our trips home from various stations in the United States Kate and I would stop at Howard Johnson's whenever possible. I always enjoyed their hot roast beef or hot turkey sandwiches and seldom ordered anything else, except for breakfast.

Christmas decorations, including a six foot tree with all the trimmings, made memories of home surface. One of our favorite family things was to cut our tree. The camp kitchen and dining hall doubled as a bar and game room for any American Green Beret that happened by, regardless of rank.

I decided to get a good night's rest before my morning meeting with Colonel Tuttle. Three cups of coffee later, I made my way back to my cubicle. Within minutes I was in between the sheets, the mosquito net tucked securely under the thin mattress, and sound asleep.

I woke at 0700 hours on Christmas Day, sweat oozing from every pore of my body and soaking the flimsy cotton sheets and foam rubber pillow as the penetrating heat and high humidity challenged my entire system.

My mind had embraced the culture, the climate and the time zone change several days before, when I was yet back in the States. It was time now for my body systems to catch up with my thinking. I'd asked to come here. I wanted to be where the action was and I'd heard from others who'd already been down this road just how much the Vietnamese appreciated that we had volunteered to come here to help them. Being flexible and possessing the ability to adjust to changing situations with an open mind and a willing spirit were part and parcel of being a good Green Beret.

A bare light bulb dangling from a rafter just above me came to life and stirred me from sleep. The gruff voice of a duty sergeant reminded me of my early morning meeting with Colonel Tuttle. "He wants you to join him for breakfast in 30 minutes, Dai-uy," he shouted as he turned and walked out, not waiting for a response.

"Merry Christmas to you too, Sarge," I hollered out as he left the building and headed back to his duty desk. He's not in a real Christmas spirit, I thought to myself.

Colonel Tuttle greeted me as I entered the dining area. I echoed his "Good morning" and glanced around. Not another soul was in sight except for kitchen staff. I thought that odd until I noticed the sign above the bar that read "Christmas Breakfast: 0900." I knew then that Colonel Tuttle wanted privacy for our first face-to-face meeting. We shook hands. I sat down and a young, quite attractive Vietnamese waitress, wearing a spotlessly clean white dress and apron, placed a mug of hot, black coffee on the table in front of me and took my breakfast order: bacon, two eggs over medium, pancakes and toast. I was hungry. Colonel Tuttle had ordered prior to my arriving and was finishing a mug of black coffee. The inviting aroma of bacon filled the room.

I took a moment to study this intense man whom I'd been told was a good field commander. He was lean, stood tall in his chair, appeared stern, and was bald as a ping-pong ball. About an inch shorter than I and somewhat slimmer, his penetrating stare and powerful presence left no doubt that he was in charge here.

I sensed him giving me a similar once-over as the waitress walked away, leaving us to ourselves. Apparently my reputation had preceded me. He said he'd been with Special Forces since 1953 and was surprised our paths had never crossed. He let me know that an old friend of his, Colonel C.W. Patten, had told of my serving as his S-4 in the 6th Group at Fort Bragg. "Said you were tough as nails, could work out of your hip pocket and that you got the job done no matter who or what tried to get in your way." Having said that, Colonel Tuttle leaned across the table, lowered his voice, grinned and told me that Colonel Patten had told him candidly that I could be very devious if that's what it took to accomplish a mission.

I knew then and there that he had discussed my modus operandi with Colonel Patten. In Patten's final written evaluation of my performance as his chief logistics officer in 1965, he used almost those exact words in discussing my attributes that were, as he wrote in the formal report, "well suited for unconventional warfare."

Looking unflinchingly into my eyes, he let me know that he'd been through my file and that he felt like he knew me, my strengths, my weakness, and where I could best serve him. He said he needed a man like me to command Team A-424 in Camp Dan Nam, northwest of Can Tho in An Phu District. "I'll fill you in when we get to the secure briefing room after breakfast." The clatter of plates being placed on the table in front of us signaled the end of conversation.

We ate in silence as my thoughts went back in time to those days I served under Colonel Patten in the 6th Group at Fort Bragg. We had to be devious to provide adequate logistical support to our many Mobile Training Teams deployed in far off countries on secret missions whose very identity and location had to be masked by subterfuge. When using the international mail system or the Embassy and CIA courier services to ship important supplies, even ammunition and demolition materiel, we would list the contents of boxes and cartons to indicate that something relatively bland and harmless, such as canned goods, foul weather clothing, etc. were being sent. There was also the mid-1964 excitement and challenge of my assuming command of a six man team of Green Berets with TOP SECRET contingency missions.

My thoughts returned to the reality of the moment as Colonel Tuttle finished his breakfast, cleared his throat, and asked, "Thinking about home?"

"No Sir," I answered, "just another time, another place."

We filled our mugs with fresh coffee and then he led me out of the dining room and across the compound to his office. As we entered, Colonel Tuttle told the duty sergeant that he wanted total privacy. We were not to be disturbed. The duty sergeant nodded, got up from behind his desk and secured the entrance door. Using a map with several overlays showing friendly and enemy positions, a brass-tipped pointer and a few aerial photos, Colonel Tuttle briefed me on the tactical situation in and around An Phu District. He began with the Phu Hiep Forward Operations Base (FOB) located eleven kilometers northeast of Camp Dan Nam and two kilometers south of the Cambodian border. He pointed out a large enemy support base under construction three kilometers north of the FOB just inside Cambodia. It included a 50 bed field hospital, ammunition and gasoline storage pads, warehouse buildings and sufficient barracks to house a battalion of 400+ men. The "Bung Ven Secret Base," as it was called, was supplied with construction material and war goods through South Vietnam and into Cambodia via the Mekong River on ships of international registry. In Phnom Penh the cargo would then be put on smaller ships headed south on the Bassac River to Prek Chrey where they would enter the Bak Nam River and off load their cargo inside the secret base onto recently constructed docks.

"Within the last six months," he explained, "the VC have taken and occupied an area 1,500 meters deep and 3,000 meters wide between Phu Hiep FOB and the border. It was, in reality, an enemy-controlled buffer zone meant to protect the secret base. More than 5,000 pipe mine booby traps had been set in the dense thickets between the FOB and the Cambodian border. A VC security battalion of an estimated 400 men was quartered in that area to defend water and land approaches to the safe-haven. An NVA antiaircraft gun platoon was recently attached to the battalion to guard against aerial surveillance."

"Why is the enemy allowed to occupy and control that area?" I asked.

He explained that Major Le wisely chose not to clear the area and suffer the loss of many CIDG to booby traps and sniper fire so long as he lacked authority to pursue the enemy into Cambodia where he could force a fight and destroy him. "That's where you come in Dangerous Dan. I'd like you to take command of Camp Dan Nam and A-424 as an independent operation. Your primary mission will be to take the war into Cambodian territory. You will be the first to do so." He went on to explain that this was something the CIA had cooked up with Premier Ky. "What we discuss must never leave this room," he cautioned. I was to give only those specific details to my team that were necessary to accomplish the mission. It would be a "compartmentalized" operation and the B Team would not be privy to any aspect of it. How I handled that situation with the B Team CO would be mine to decide. Keeping distance between us and the use of subterfuge would have to suffice. "If you accept, you are on your own," he emphasized, "Once you walk out that door, it will be as if we never met. Understand?"

"Yes sir. What about combat support?" I asked.

He went on to let me know what he meant by the fact that I would be on my own. "When you cross that border you lose all support. No air, artillery or reinforcement. Not even medical evacuation. Nothing." He said.

He went on to describe Major Phoi Van Le, the LLDB Camp Commander, as being "tougher than nails" and a Hoa Hao first and foremost.

I'd read about the Hoa Hao Sect[2] of the Buddhist religion and had spoken to other Green Berets who had fought alongside the Hoa Haos. They were known to be brave fighters and honorable people.

In a serious tone, Colonel Tuttle told me, that at Major Le's request, Major Chuan, the LLDB C Team CO met with him and asked that the American Captain commanding the A team in An Phu be sent packing. Tuttle said he referred the matter to Major Arnn for action and Major Arnn reassigned the team leader, bringing him out of An Phu the very next day. "A-424 has been without a commander ever since," he admitted.

He handed me a copy of the last monthly report from A-424. I saw that the Hoa Hao CIDG consisted of five 132 man companies. Under District Chief control for close fire support was an ARVN 155mm howitzer platoon. Two Regional Force (RF) companies were located in close proximity to the camp and reported to Captain Tuoi, the District Chief who was responsible for governing and protecting the 64,000 citizens of An Phu, who were mostly Buddhists of the Hoa Hao sect.

Thirty kilometers of common border and the Bassac River entry into Cambodia required security. The new TOP SECRET mission would be a real test for all of us. How we handled it, how successful we were in turning the tide of the war in our small area, could make a difference in all of Vietnam.

Colonel Tuttle explained that Major Le, who was also the Military advisor to the Hoa Hao central council, convinced Council Chairman Luong Trong Tuong to meet with Lieutenant General Quang Van Dang, the commander of Military Region IV, and secure the right to hit back at the enemy inside Cambodia. Mr. Luong met with

General Dang who took his request to the Minister of Defense, who then worked out a compromise with Premier Ky and the CIA Station Chief. This resulted in a TOP SECRET independent operational mission status for An Phu. It would be a test case. Major Le had even acquiesced to allow the American Team Leader to be Camp Commander which then gave them the right to pursue the enemy into neutral Cambodia. An Phu would be the first border district to deny the VC their safe havens.

I asked, "Why the secrecy?"

"Politics," he told me. "It seems the White House's official position is that there are no enemy sanctuaries in Cambodia." Without a doubt we both knew that to be a lie. Prince Sihanouk broke diplomatic relations with the US on May 3, 1965, but our State Department was not anxious to do anything that would give Communist China reason to enter the fray.

Ridiculous, I told him. They've been in the fray since day one, supplying weapons to the Viet Cong and the NVA regulars, weapons that were superior to what we provided the CIDG, RF, PF and even ARVN units. There was no argument from Colonel Tuttle. Instead, he looked me in the eye and asked if I had made a decision.

"I want An Phu, Colonel." I knew in my own mind that I'd work out the command relationship with Major Le. His men needed him as their leader, someone they could trust who had proven himself in many battles. It would be stupid of me to disturb that trust.

I asked if combat activity on our part inside Cambodia, including indirect fire missions, were to be recorded or reported?

"Anything to do with the covert mission must not be reported or recorded. No SITREPs, SPOTREPs, or reports of any action that violates international borders or airspace. It will be as if nothing happened," he emphasized, asking me, "Do you still want An Phu?"

I told him yes, but with one condition. The serious tone of his voice told me he didn't like demands coming from junior officers. "What condition, Captain?"

"I want to hand pick my team, no questions asked." "You've got it." I could keep any or all of the team already in An Phu. He would replace any I sent out as soon as possible. "Fair enough?" he asked.

I reached out my hand and we shook to seal the deal. "Be ready to go in the morning, Dangerous, and good luck."

After weighing everything Colonel Tuttle discussed about the independent operation, the risks involved, and the complete lack of protection from my own government, I decided on a covert plan that would guarantee protection of the truth of what happened under my command, no matter if I lived or not. I would document all that happened of significance during my command and send it to a trusted friend in the States for safekeeping. If something were to happen to me, he would take all I'd sent him to a lawyer we trusted who would then unseal the envelopes and take that truth to the families of my men, to Congress, and to those in the media he trusted. Fortunately, I made it back, gathered the sealed envelopes and included pertinent details gleaned from those papers in the first draft of this book. I then mailed copies of the book draft to those team members whom I had located, asked for and received their corroboration, comments and additions to the text which have been incorporated.

On Christmas Day I stuffed myself with the traditional turkey dinner and thought of the many Christmas dinners Kate spoiled me with, especially with mincemeat pie, my favorite. After dinner I took a quick shower and then, pen in hand, I wrote and told her where I was going, what I had learned about the situation on the ground in An Phu and about the courage of the Hoa Hao fighters. "Not to worry," I wrote, "because I am with good people." I said nothing that would alarm her or cause her any concern and let her know how much I missed her. Once I got settled under the mosquito net and closed my eyes, even the heat of the night did not deter me from sleeping well, very well.

I was where I wanted to be.

* * * * *

Chau Doc River

Camp Dan Nam — View toward the west. 28 Dec 65

An Phu Village

CHAPTER 2
MASSACRE WEST OF RACH GIA

"What's going on, Colonel?" I shouted angrily to the helicopter pilot, "Your men just gunned down unarmed peasants, even women and children. Are you crazy? " "Calm down, Captain," he retorted, "they're just a bunch of gooks and we need body count!"

Shortly before 0900 the day after Christmas I reported to the operations center with my gear and was immediately ushered to a waiting helicopter where a young Lieutenant was already on board and strapped in, his back against the rear bulkhead. I stowed my gear next to his on the deck. After an exchange of thumbs up, the right door gunner signaled to the pilot and we lifted off of the landing pad and headed west across the Delta area. "I'm going to Ha Tien, Dai-uy. I'll be team XO," the young Lieutenant shouted in my ear, the smile on his smooth, unblemished face mirroring his excitement.

The roar of the engine and the deafening sound of rotors biting into the air at full torque drowned out my congratulations as we climbed rapidly to an altitude of 2,000 feet out of enemy small arms range. Our first check point would be the CIDG camp at Rach Gia, 70 air miles from Can Tho located just north of the city of the same name, a coastal municipality of 100,000 people. Two helmeted door gunners, fingers ready at the triggers of their .30 caliber machine guns, scanned the ground below for any sign of VC activity. Several metal canisters containing machine gun ammunition lay within easy reach of the gunners.

We flew over a number of large, forested plantations, each resembling a lush green carpet with a centrally located landscaped manor house encircled by a network of paths and dependencies. Once the pride of French colonialism, and later used in the early 1960s as "protected" relocation camps within the CIA's failed strategic

15

hamlet program, they were now for the most part occupied and controlled by the VC. We were then treated to a panoramic view of the rice paddy and small hamlet areas that dominated the Mekong River and Bassac River Delta regions. These green, patchwork-quilt-like expanses stretched out below as far as the eye could see, with the morning sunlight casting long shadows along the scenic tree-lined dikes that paralleled countless small canals criss-crossing the area. Narrow roads could be seen leading from one small hamlet to another sitting atop dikes. Scattered groups of peasants labored below, appearing to ignore the peculiar buffeting sound of our helicopter's approach. Sure-footed water buffalo yoked to plows or two wheel carts worked in harmony with the rice farmers. It seemed altogether peaceful and serene.

I began to view the Gulf of Thailand and the sprawling city of Rach Gia from my vantage point when, without warning, we suddenly plummeted in a steep dive at breakneck speed. I braced for the anticipated crash, the ground rushing up to meet us, hoping we'd survive. Instead of crashing, our chopper shuddered violently with the strain of being forced out of its dive and into low level flight not more than six feet above and paralleling the east-west rice paddy dikes at a rapid pace.

The Lieutenant leaned toward me and shouted in my ear, "What's going on, Sir?" I just shook my head, not knowing but thinking we were taking combative action, hoping to attack and kill the enemy. Get them before they get us, I thought. I noticed when I boarded that our pilot was a full Colonel. Unusual, I thought. Normally it would be a Warrant Officer flying a whirlybird.

The chopper groaned, creaked and shuddered from the strain of continued violent maneuvering as we careened along, just above the landscape, barely missing trees and thatched roof homes on either side of the main canal. Like an unyielding warrior bent on finding and destroying the enemy, we continued at full throttle, buzzing the Rach Gia Special Forces camp at such speed that all I got was a glimpse of it. I turned to see how the Lieutenant was holding up. His face was ashen and puffed. He looked to me like someone who'd not yet experienced anything even close to this and who was ready to puke his guts out. I hoped he wouldn't.

The Colonel changed course, heading in a northwesterly direction towards the SF camp at Ha Tien, another 55 miles as the crow flies, skimming the rice paddies at high speed. The young Lieutenant's face remained ghostly white and sweat dripped from his nose and chin despite the rush of cold air through the open sides of the chopper. I squeezed his right arm firmly, smiled at him in an attempt to comfort him and then shouted into his ear that we'd be OK. He responded with a weak smile and turned as if to view the terrain below. About that time we were taken up in a power climb to about 1,000 feet, and just as abruptly we descended in a stomach-wrenching dive only to level off approximately 100 feet above the ground and then slowing to about 80 miles an hour.

I'd flown in and parachuted from many different Army helicopters since my maiden flight in a "bubble" chopper under the Han River Bridge in Seoul, Korea, in early 1954. Why this Colonel was flying at tree top level, over an area controlled by the VC and within range of their small arms fire, I could not fathom. I would soon learn our pilot had a terrible and deadly agenda.

I leaned out the door to see what was ahead on the ground. No sign of VC, just a bunch of unarmed peasants working their rice field. Men, women and children, maybe 20 in all with two water buffalo, were toiling away and showing no outward sign of concern about our approach. Suddenly both door gunners began firing their machine guns at the people on the ground, spraying the area with hundreds of deadly rounds. I watched helplessly as some of the peasants were hit and spun around or knocked down by the force of the bullets, to fall in grotesque heaps in the shallow water below. Others, attempting vainly to outrun the hail of machine gun fire, were hit in the back and propelled forward by the impact to fall face down in the paddy. I asked myself, "What in the blue blazes is going on? Why are they killing these people?" I gripped the edge of the door with one hand and took hold of a tie down strap dangling from inside the fuselage and leaned out far enough to search the scene of carnage for weapons. There were none!

We began to circle. Convinced they'd knowingly killed innocent people, I wondered if they were going back to make certain there would be no witness to the carnage. Looking far ahead as the chopper slowed to about 40 miles per hour and dropped closer to the ground, I saw only motionless bodies scattered about in the bloodstained rice paddy. The water buffalo had somehow survived the attack and stood secure in their yoke, waiting for direction from their now lifeless handler, lead ropes still clenched in his fist. Horrified, I jabbed the lieutenant with my elbow and asked if he'd seen any weapons down there.

He just shook his head. His face was white as a ghost and he appeared to be in shock, perhaps from witnessing the slaughter, although I wasn't certain due to his silence.

I lunged forward, grabbed both door gunners by their shoulders and ordered them away from their weapons and back up against the ship's bulkhead. With the din of the engine I doubt either heard my voice, but each saw the set of my jaw, sensed the outrage in my eyes and hurriedly got out of my way, plunking their butts down on the deck. I reached out to both machine guns and, one at a time, opened their covers, jerked the ammunition belts out, threw them on the deck and rendered both temporarily harmless.

I motioned for a helmet with its headset from the nearest gunner and it was handed me without hesitation. I used it to shout my message to the pilot. "What's going on, Colonel? Your men just gunned down unarmed peasants, even women and children. Are you crazy?" His arrogant response crackled over the small receiver in the helmet. "Calm down, Captain." He said, "They're just a bunch of gooks and we need body count." I let him know I'd seen it all and that he had killed unarmed peasants.

He let me know that one "gook" was the same as another in his book and that its the "brass" that made him fly these taxi missions. As long as I live I won't forget his next words to me: "General Westmoreland wants body count and when I can log some body count, I figure to shoot first and I don't ask any questions."

Reaching forward with my right hand, I grabbed a handful of his shoulder at the collar bone and squeezed until the veins stood out on the back of my hand. I leaned forward and shouted in his ear, warning that one more try at anything like that and I'd grab hold of whatever I would need to grab to take his chopper right down to the ground. I tightened my vise grip on his shoulder one more time and hollered, "I mean it, stupid!"

Without another word, he changed course, took us up to cruising altitude and headed for Ha Tien at normal speed. I asked him for his name, but he wouldn't answer. I then asked his Warrant Officer copilot, who also paid no heed, just sat there, rigid and silent. I forced my way up between them, wanting to see their name tags, but found none.

I was disgusted with my inability to discern the Colonel's name to include in the incident report I would file when I arrived at the B Team in Chau Doc.

Angered that anyone would take innocent lives for the sake of a higher body count, but lacking what I needed for a comprehensive report, I searched for a way to make that crew, especially the Colonel, answer for what they'd done. I returned the one gunner's helmet, saw that neither of them had a visible name tag, motioned both back to their posts and then moved close to the still quaking Lieutenant. I needed his corroboration, yet I knew we'd reach his camp within minutes and this was neither the time nor the place to put together a written deposition.

I'll never forget seeing those innocent victims gunned down in cold-blooded murder. No other words sufficed. More than a dozen South Vietnamese had been killed. Peaceful farm families one moment, dead and dying men, women and children the next, a blood stained rice paddy silent witness to their fate. I had heard stories from Vietnam vets telling of General Westmoreland's fascination with body count and how his staff used those numbers to gauge the success of a mission, even to the extent of comparing the number of rounds of ammunition expended with the number of the enemy killed by body count.

I had hoped they were exaggerating the truth, but I would learn again in An Phu of the horror, death and destruction that could, if the officer in command permitted, result solely for the purpose of appeasing higher headquarters. As I write this account some 36 years later, I hope and pray that one man in that chopper crew acquiesced to his conscience and possessed the integrity and courage to report that incident in detail. It was a war crime and that Colonel should have answered in a court of law for his actions. Too late for the victims but not too late for surviving family members to learn that just punishment had been meted out.

The Lieutenant was all bent over, sweating profusely, and obviously sick to his stomach. I grabbed hold of his shoulders to help steady him as he leaned out into open space to get some fresh air and revive him sufficiently so that I could glean what he remembered about the incident near Rach Gia. Little time remained as I could tell from glancing down and seeing the picturesque city of Ha Tien, with its tree-lined streets, sandy beaches and beautiful parks overlooking the pale blue waters of the Gulf of Thailand. The beaches and docks were protected from the effects of violent storms by a wide inlet angling in from the gulf. A great place to vacation had there been no war.

We followed a flight path above a road leading out of the city and above a flat piece of grassed terrain void of homes or rice farms. It was a kind of buffer zone between the city and the island-like fortress that was home to the Ha Tien SF Camp. The camp itself was situated on a high, oval plateau that jutted out into the Gulf much like a giant thumb. The terrain around the camp dropped off on three sides to a mixture of rocky beaches and steep cliffs. We approached, flying above a road that wound gracefully along a series of switch backs, from just above sea level to the summit of what had been a French customs fort and now answered the needs of our A Team with their counterparts and irregular fighters.

Recalling Group intelligence briefings, I recognized the Kompong Trach VC sanctuary located in a mountain chain due west of the camp just inside Cambodia. Used by the VC as a training and staging area for a battalion, it was ideally located to conduct raids from and to withdraw into when the battle began to turn against them. There they would be safe from counterattack. It made me angry to think our government would permit the enemy his sanctuaries. I hoped even more that what we would do in An Phu would be the way of the future up and down the entire border, but with combat support provided whenever called for, even inside Cambodia.

As we neared the helicopter pad I glanced at the Lieutenant and saw that some color had returned to his face. He appeared more alert and smiled as he locked the safety on his rifle, grabbed his rucksack and prepared to join his team on the ground. I leaned over and spoke into his ear, wanting to be heard above the sound of the rotor. I asked if he'd seen any weapons in the rice paddy back there.

He appeared puzzled by my question and asked "Back where?"

I reminded him of the action that had taken place this side of Rach Gia. He shook his head and told me he didn't know what I was talking about. All he remembered was getting sick as a skunk. I knew then that any hope for justice to prevail in this tragedy was slight at best. The helicopter's skids came to rest momentarily on the pad and the Lieutenant grabbed his gear, scooted out quickly and ran over and jumped into a waiting jeep, waving to us as we flew up and out of his camp. The 60 mile flight to Chau Doc was both direct and uneventful. The Colonel flew a path east of the Cambodian border, flying high over the SF Camp at Vinh Gia, a square camp that was well situated for defense against a ground attack. Its western side of the defensive perimeter was butted up tight against the border canal. A lone hill inside Cambodia jutted up from the surrounding rice paddies and looked out across the border at Vinh Gia Camp only a short distance away. The young Captain I made mention of to Colonel Tuttle was the one who went to prison for returning fire on a VC battalion. The enemy had viciously attacked his camp with rockets from a vantage point on that very hill, inflicting numerous casualties. I remembered that Tuttle didn't want to talk about that incident.

The final leg of the flight took us over the Seven Mountains area, an enemy stronghold west of Chau Doc where our forces controlled the roads by day and the VC controlled everything at night. We continued over the city of Chau Phu, the capital of Chau Doc Province, where our B Team was located.

Coming in low and fast to a clearly marked chopper pad located in a soccer field, I had a gut feeling that I'd better be ready to clear the deck of that chopper with all my gear in hand the second it touched down or I'd get tossed out end over end. One thing for certain, there was no love lost between that Colonel and me. I believe he would have liked to have dropped me into the Gulf of Thailand, hoping I couldn't swim with all my gear. Sure enough, the skids barely stirred the dirt when he put the chopper in an on-the-ground tail spin, pivoting the chopper 180 degrees and then taking off full throttle, more forward then up, its nose nearly touching the ground. The skid nearest me missed by a fraction of an inch, but snagged my jungle fatigue shirt and spun me to the ground. My rucksack was torn from my grip and tossed about 20 yards, but I managed to keep hold of my M-16 and my brown leather bag.

From behind me I heard someone shout, "Welcome to B-42, Captain. What was that all about? If you'd been just a hair slower getting out of there you'd of been tossed the length of the field."

Not wanting to get into details at the moment, I only told him that it was a long story. "I guess he just didn't like my attitude." We both laughed at that but then his tone turned serious as he clued me in on what was going on in the B Team. Introducing himself as the personnel sergeant, he leveled with me, "It's been a bad day here, Dai-uy. Major Arnn and Sergeant Torello were both killed by VC snipers early this morning out near the foot of the Seven Mountains. Major Williford is out with half our team looking to get the snipers. He expects to be back at 1600 hours and will be ready to see you in his office at 0800. He wants you briefed by 0900 because two men from your team will come up river to take you to your camp at that time.

"I don't mind telling you, Dai-uy, that Major Arnn was none too happy yesterday when Colonel Tuttle told him you'd be going to An Phu and taking over A-424. That's moving fast, Captain. Our CO has always made those kind of decisions. This is a first, at least since I've been here. Anything you want to tell me, Sir?"

He was right and I knew it but I couldn't tell him why I was being treated different from routine. As personnel sergeant, he'd have access to the CO on matters like this, and he felt proper in hinting for an explanation. I'd have to act unawares, pretend to just accept an unusual set of circumstances, and perhaps steer him in a different direction. The fact that Major Arnn had been killed and could no longer state his case made it easier for me to mask the truth and not compromise my mission.

I let him know how sorry I was that Major Arnn and Sergeant Torello had gotten killed and how I hoped they'd get the VC who ambushed the CO and Operations Sergeant. I asked if that wouldn't be difficult in the Seven Mountains area where I'd been told the VC had control.

He told me how they would call in a B-52 strike to soften up the area before the men went in on foot.

After telling him that sounded like a good idea to me, I told him that I did remember overhearing a conversation at the C Team in Can Tho that probably had something to do with my going to An Phu. "Major Chuan was telling Colonel Tuttle, maybe demanding is the better word, that he'd like the next Captain to go to An Phu. Something about the fact they'd been out of action too long without a CO."

I could sense the wheels turning in his head as he thought over what I'd said. Before he could say anything, I told him to show me to my quarters and to point me to the toilet and showers so I could get squared away before supper. I was also anxious to write the incident report while my memory was fresh. We got in the jeep and he drove toward the B Team compound located just a few hundred yards down the road. Considerable activity was taking place as their reaction force prepared to deal with the enemy snipers who had ambushed and killed their CO and operations sergeant. Trucks were positioned on the gravel road in front of the former hotel that now served as the main B Team building and soldiers of all descriptions were milling about in the courtyard.

Parking his jeep near the sandbagged front entrance, the sergeant grabbed my rucksack and led me through the massive door and into what had once been the lobby and lounge. A wide, curving mahogany bar with a dozen tall stools took up a third of the area. A refrigerator and large, upright freezer occupied the corner behind the bar and a wide array of liquor bottles stood on a mirror-backed shelf that extended the length of the bar. A large, pedestal mounted fan on low setting stirred the air and a number of overstuffed chairs and lamp tables were scattered about the lobby.

He turned to go up a wide stairway to the second floor, and pointed in the direction of the dining room and explained that the toilet and shower were at the far end of that same hall. He continued on to a room at the front of the building, dropped my rucksack on the floor next to one of two steel Army cots in the room. I thanked him and he turned and left the room, walking in the direction of the stairs.

The room itself was long and narrow with a large window at the far end that overlooked the courtyard. From that vantage point, I could view the same tree-lined road I came in from the chopper pad on. Through the well guarded entrance gate I could see the B Team's boat dock where it jutted out into the busy Chau Doc River. Two light globes hung from the ceiling on long stems reminiscent of a Humphrey Bogart movie set in Casablanca. A ceiling fan was centered between them. Mosquito nets hung from steel frames on the two cots set up on either side of the room. Between the cots and the window were a folding chair, a small writing table, and a metal wall locker for those who were quartered here.

I sat down at the table and began the laborious task of putting together an incident report that I hoped would stand up in a court martial. Without another witness it was doubtful that anything would ever come of the report. Sad, but I tried my best to write it up, knowing it would at least have been reported. I found that I couldn't concentrate due to all the commotion in the courtyard just below my window. Quiet was needed to do it right if it were to be used as evidence.

Noise from outside my window, with trucks and troops coming and going, was distracting. It was too hot to close the window and shut out the noise so I set my notes aside and took time out for a much needed shower, hoping all would be quiet when I returned.

As I was toweling myself dry, I remembered what the Sergeant Major in Can Tho had said about it being too hot and muggy in the Delta to wear underwear. He'd been kicking around Special Forces for a lot of years, knew the area like the back of his hand, and was the kind of man I'd pay attention to. I took his advice and stuffed all of my shorts and tee shirts into my brown leather satchel and then dressed with clean socks, jungle fatigues and nothing else. It felt strange at first, but I knew I'd get used to it and it did feel cooler.

By the time I got back to my room all was quiet in the courtyard below. I sat down with pen in hand and wrote every detail of the killing of those unarmed peasants, including my attempts to obtain the pilot's name. I wrapped it up by telling of my brush with serious injury upon exiting the chopper at the soccer field.

On my way to the dining room for dinner I stopped by the communications center and saw behind the well secured lower portion of a Dutch door a room that was wall-to-wall radio equipment. As the heartbeat of communications to and from Can Tho and all A Teams, it was the vital link in their lifeline. A sign above the door in large, bold, red letters read "COMCTR - AUTHORIZED PERSONS ONLY." Sergeant Jonathan McCants, the communications supervisor, labored over a single side band radio console, turning knobs this way and that until the static was barely discernible. Sitting on Sergeant McCants' right was a soldier sending Morse code with a standard key faster than I'd thought possible. He introduced himself as Sergeant Melmot Smalls, and asked if he could help me.

"Yes," I told him, "but first, I want you to know that's as fast a key as I've ever seen or heard. Who's on the other end?"

He thanked me and told me the man on the other end was Sergeant John Eleam, the commo man in An Phu. "He's actually faster than me," Sergeant Smalls confessed, "so I set the pace whenever I'm communicating with John."

"Good to hear, Sarge." As I handed the incident report to Sergeant Smalls, I asked that he make certain Major Williford got it first thing in the morning"

"Sure thing, Dai-uy and good luck to you in An Phu. You've got a tough cookie to deal with there."

"He's talking about Major Le, Dai-uy," Sergeant McCants chimed in. "Your counterpart has gone through A Team leaders like salt through a sieve. You'll need all the luck you can muster."

I thanked him for the warning and let him know that I was anxious to get my feet on the ground in An Phu."

Major Le must be one tough customer, I thought. From what I've gleaned thus far, he single-handedly forced approval of the independent operation at An Phu with a TOP SECRET mission to engage in covert operations inside neutral Cambodia. The South Vietnamese military hierarchy surely holds him in high regard and their American counterparts must be equally enchanted or they wouldn't have gone along with his plan. Removing one Captain at Major Le's request in Camp Dan Nam and then sending me in there to command and control all forces with a no-holds barred mission to take the war across the border would, in my judgment, have a two dimensional effect on the conduct of the war, at least in that one area. Perhaps, seeming to acquiesce to Major Le, the CIA would, using this covert mission, gain a foothold in the CIDG program which would then allow the "Company" to again control powerful military, paramilitary and irregular forces and again shape battle strategy. If successful, would the CIA move to recapture the quasi-military leadership role it once had, using Special Forces and armed indigenous personnel in overt and covert operations to affect the future in all of Southeast Asia? Only time would reveal the true result of that equation. It was certain in my mind that the next 12 months would be an experience I'd never ever forget. I hoped more than anything that I would earn the respect of Major Le and his people.

I slept undisturbed and unaware of the return of Major Williford and the reaction force sometime during the night. I awoke at daybreak to the sound of different, peaceful activity drifting in through my open window. Looking out and past the entrance gate, I watched as hundreds of Vietnamese made their way by foot, bicycle, and two wheel cart along the narrow, gravel and dirt road that paralleled the Chau Doc River. I would learn that most were headed to the early morning market in the center of Chau Phu. Just beyond the road, the river itself teemed with boat traffic as merchants hauled rice, fish, hogs, watermelon and other wares to that same open-air market located but a few blocks from where I stood.

After a huge breakfast of pancakes smothered in honey with bacon and eggs on the side, I returned to my room, got my gear together, and then waited downstairs in the lobby for the expected tactical and intelligence briefing. Within a few minutes Sergeant Major Marshall Lynch came into the lobby, introduced himself, and asked me to follow him to Major Williford's office where he and his staff were seated and waiting. The mood from the beginning was not at all cordial. I walked past the many charts and maps and reported to Major Williford.

He stood, returned my salute, reached out and we shook hands. He was tall, maybe six feet and a few inches, big-boned and black. Partially bald and smooth-shaven, he made me think of him as a West Pointer. After introducing his staff, he motioned me to sit down. He did not appear pleased as he told me, "Captain Marvin, I received a message from Colonel Tuttle last night, directing that you assume command of A-424. He said he'd briefed you in detail and that he wanted you on the ground in Camp Dan Nam ASAP. Arrangements have been made as you know."

He then asked me if I knew why normal procedures had been set aside in my case and why I was briefed in detail and assigned directly to A-424 by the C Team Commander.

"No, Sir," I replied, "I had just arrived in country, and not knowing any different, I assumed that to be his way of doing things." Though contrived by me, that sounded logical and Major Williford had no choice but to accept my response.

Major Williford then began the briefing, telling me that A-424 had one officer and six enlisted men assigned with Lieutenant John T. Kallunki as XO. He lauded Kallunki for his excellent work in civic action, having also achieved excellent rapport with the district chief, Captain Tuoi Van Nguyen. "Unless you have questions for me," he stated rather tersely, "I'll turn the briefing over to Sergeant Major Lynch. He will acquaint you with your team's enlisted men."

"I have no questions, Sir."

Sergeant Major Lynch then took the floor. "You're lucky to get a team like A-424, Dai-uy." He told me how active they'd been in projects that helped win the hearts and minds of the people. "There's a lot of civic action work in progress with daily medical patrols and an almost superhuman effort to get schools, bridges and boat docks built and the road system improved."

I could tell he respected the men in that team.

"Master Sergeant Canuto Valenzuela is your team sergeant, Dai-uy, and he's as good as they come." He let me know that "Val" would take up the slack for me until I got my feet on the ground, if I let him. "I recommend," he added, "that you rely on his advice and ask for it when you get in a jam."

He seemed pleased to tell me that Specialist William Menkins had remembered me from the 6th Group at Fort Bragg. He told me that Menkins was now an E6 and team intelligence honcho for A-424. Recently, with the team more or less excluded from combat operations, Menkins was helping the Team XO in civic action projects. "He's done a super job and Val says he gets along famously with the District Chief's people." He also let me know that Menkins would be rotating back to the States in early February. The senior medic was Staff Sergeant Santos D. Tenorio. "Most everyone who knows him calls him 'T.' The other medic, and T's right hand man, is Staff Sergeant George Kuchen." He told of how they ran medical patrols every day out into every corner of the district and that the people love them, especially the kids. "They both rotate in early March and we're trying to get replacements in time for T to show them the ropes."

He began to tell me about Sergeant John Eleam. I interrupted to let him know that Sergeant Smalls had told me a little about John and that it was all good news to me. "I know that Eleam's a fast man on the key!"

"True enough," Sergeant Major Lynch commented, "and he's good at anything he sets his mind to." Eleam was studying hard, Lynch told me, so he could apply for appointment as a warrant officer in the communications field.

Sergeant Major Lynch wasn't familiar with the Vietnamese Special Forces team (LLDB) he advised, except to know that Val thought of them as being "top notch."

"That's good enough for me." As strong a man as Major Le was, I felt certain that he'd have carte blanche on who he wanted on his team.

"Anything else you'd like from me, Dai-uy?"

"Just one answer, Sergeant Major. How is the team's morale?"

"Not good, Dai-uy." He went on to let me know that the B Team didn't know what was going on in An Phu since the team leader came out. Major Le hadn't shared any intelligence or tactical information with A-424 and the team had been shut down except for medical patrols and civic action projects. "It's impossible to keep up morale under those circumstances."

Major Williford squelched any further discussion about the situation in An Phu by getting up out of his chair and telling me that the rest of the briefing would be conducted by the S-2 in the operations and intelligence center. I thanked Major Williford and Sergeant Major Lynch for their briefing and followed the S-2 Captain to the center. Nothing showy or frivolous there, only a very functional space adapted with ingenuity to meet the needs of both staff sections while providing an efficient joint briefing area. One wall contained a recessed map and chart display system with perhaps twelve tracks that would permit any one chart or map to be pulled for briefings while maintaining others, particularly those containing information of a classified or sensitive nature, secure and available only to those who were authorized access. Numerous charts displayed at eye level on the other three walls portrayed the status of various logistical, administrative, and civic action functions including the all important status of ammunition stocks at all the camps under their control.

A large ceiling fan made the room bearable, drawing the hot air up to the high ceiling while tightly closed shutters kept the heat of the morning sun at bay, allowing cooler air to enter through a vented doorway.

After scanning the map displayed for my benefit containing the current enemy and friendly orders of battle, I asked the S-2, "How close do An-Phu and Tan Chau work together on border security operations?"

"They don't," was his quick reply. He explained that Tan Chau was unusual, with three CIDG companies. Two were in the main camp and the third at an FOB a thousand meters from the Cambodian border on the west bank of the Mekong River. There has been little VC activity along the border above Tan Chau. "We don't know for certain, but we believe it has something to do with their not wanting to interfere with shipping activity on the river."

"Why not?" I asked, "We don't allow weapons to go into Cambodia on the Mekong, do we?" The S-2 smiled, "Wish it was that way, Dangerous, but it's not that simple. We're told that an agreement between Cambodian hierarchy and the White House permits ships, even ocean going vessels, to carry cargo into Cambodia while limiting our ability to inspect the ship's cargo." It seems they have to honor the ship's manifest. If it does not list war goods neither our people nor the Vietnamese Police are permitted to inspect the actual cargo, even if they think it suspicious. It seems the VC don't want the war to get too close to the river and scare off the merchant ships from other nations or cut off their global resupply channel. The situation allowed weapons and ammunition to be shipped right under our noses to our enemy who used the sanctuaries just across the border to rearm and re-group. Our forces were not allowed to stop the ships or attack the sanctuaries. Did they know for certain that military weapons and ammunition were getting to the VC via the river? I asked. "Judge for yourself, Dan. One day last month, the Tan Chau A-Team's men with Vietnamese police went aboard a large cargo ship and inspected the manifest. It read something like 10,000 tons of children's toys! He knew better, but was not allowed to inspect the cargo, nor was his National Police counterpart permitted to physically determine what was on board. The ship sailed on into Cambodia and our team dispatched a patrol to observe the off-loading of the ship's cargo not more than 1,000 meters inside Cambodia. They took pictures of some of the hundreds of cases of weapons and ammunition that were unloaded in broad daylight and put on NVA trucks. Probably headed for Bung Ven."

"What did Major Arnn do about that?" I asked.

"There was nothing he could do." The S-2 confessed to me, "We have to put up with a lot of stuff. It's enough to make a man puke. Oh, we did report it, but nothing came of it, and nothing changed; I can tell you that."

I let him know in a loud voice that I thought it was just plain rotten that our government agreed to conditions that favored our enemy. "It has to change, don't you agree, Dai-uy?"

"Sure do, Dangerous."

I thanked him and told him that I now felt like I knew enough now to get my feet on the ground in An Phu without making a fool of myself. "If you get a chance," I told him, "come on out and I'll give you a personal guided tour." With that I left his office.

How could a President, or any other official of our government, agree to anything that would place American troops or the people we are here to support in jeopardy and would aid and abet the enemy? Americans, and even a greater number of Allies and innocent men, women and children had and would yet be killed or wounded grievously because our leaders collaborated with the enemy. They allowed them safe havens to operate from and to return to with impunity along with a protected international waterway at their beckon call for resupply of essential war goods, even weapons and ammunition. As I left the operations and intelligence center I thought how fortunate I was to be the first to take the battle to the enemy in their so-called sanctuaries. There would be no safe havens across the border from An Phu. The shame of it was that I had to keep it secret and had to, with Major Le and our men, venture into Cambodia against formidable odds, knowing our headquarters would provide no support whatsoever once we were inside that "neutral" nation. We were, for the first time in the war, doing it right, fighting a war to win with no holds barred and we had to do it on our own. There would be no support and no reports, and in my mind because we were doing it right and honorably, I would have no regrets.

In An Phu we would operate in an honorable way.

* * * * *

A Tiger Named Le

ARVN Special Forces Major Phoi Van Le

"The most courageous, honorable and compassionate military leader I have known."

LTC (RET.) DANIEL MARVIN

CHAPTER 3
A TIGER NAMED LE

"It is time we send a message to the Viet Cong inside Cambodia, telling them we no longer recognize their sanctuaries. On the stroke of midnight on the first day of January 1966 we will rain rocket and mortar rounds with high explosive warheads into those places where they sleep. There will no longer be a safe haven in Cambodia for our enemy."
Major Phoi Van Le

Rucksack on my back, M-16 rifle slung comfortably on my right shoulder and my leather AWOL bag in my left hand to free my right hand for saluting, I walked out of the B Team compound, anxious to get my feet on the ground in An Phu. It was 0857 hours and it seemed years had passed since Christmas morning. What had been but two days with a secret and sober mission briefing and a tragic purposeful killing of innocents would live in my mind's eye forever. Returning the gate guards' salute, I wished them a good day and crossed the dirt road, narrowly avoiding a collision with a fast moving two wheel cart drawn by a muscular young man taking two ladies toward the downtown Chau Phu marketplace.

Though there but a few days, I had come to admire the quiet and courageous nature of the people, particularly the children. As muffled sounds of distant artillery and mortar fire reached their young ears, a reminder that others had fought and died to protect the freedoms they enjoyed, the children went about their day as if there were no war. They too had to be brave and shoulder their youthful burden with a positive, even optimistic view of the future. That attitude was certainly reflected this morning in the walk and talk of school children on their way to classes. Each carried books of one kind or another and walked briskly by but not too hurried to look up, smile and say hello to this American stranger. I returned the smile and greeting of each one, hoping in my heart that some day, with our help, they would live in complete peace. I crossed the road and walked to the far end of the boat dock with its unhindered view of the Chau Doc River and caught my first glimpse of An Phu District on the other side. Fifty meters from where I stood was the tree-lined hamlet of Da Phuoc with its many bamboo houses set back a short distance from the river. Village homes in the Delta area were engineered simply but uniquely centuries ago. Built to survive the challenges that monsoon rains would bring their way, the floors could be elevated as the waters rose and lowered as the waters receded. While standing there waiting, I was treated to a welcomed glimpse of village life. Women, squatting on their haunches, washed clothes in the shallow area of the river in front of their homes while children bathed and frolicked nearby. In many of the yards facing me chickens were pecking and scratching as chickens do while small pigs strained at the end of tethers, rooting in the dirt and mud at river's edge.

A number of idle sampans were pulled up on shore. Nearby, people hustled about in and around larger fishing vessels, repairing nets and pulling them aboard in readiness for the day's fishing. Barge and sampan traffic on the river was continuous with most on a down-river course.

Downstream, where the Chau Doc River flowed into the Bassac I noticed three assault boats rounding the sharp bend and heading toward me. Each of the 14 foot olive drab, fiberglass boats carried four or five camouflage-clad men with most wearing wide, floppy brimmed hats. Of the three who wore green berets, I saw that two were Americans and the third was one of their LLDB counterparts. The lead boat was guided skillfully by its operator, weaving through mostly opposing river traffic, while the others followed in its wake.

The first eased up to the dock in front of me and Master Sergeant Canuto Valenzuela sprang up onto the dock, saluted and welcomed me to the team.

I returned his salute and let him know how pleased I was to be there. "I've got good news for the team," I shouted over the noise of the assault boat's 40HP Johnson outboard motor, "I'll tell you all about it as soon as we get the team together for a briefing in camp."

"We could use some good news, Dai-uy," he replied, a generous smile on his face. The other American Green Beret, stood for a moment in the second boat, hollered out, "Good to see you, Dangerous Dan, Sir!"

"Good to see you too, Menkins. It's like old home day. You don't look any different than I remember you from our time together in the Sixth. Menkins was lean, about 5'10" tall and wore glasses.

Sergeant Valenzuela, a Mexican-American, was just a little shorter than I, very muscular, barrel chested and a master parachutist. "Team Sergeant," I asked, "Okay to call you Val?"

"Okay by me, Dai-uy."

Tossing my rucksack and leather bag into the boat, I followed Val, got aboard, and was introduced to Map Map, the man who kneeled in the stern of the boat with the forty horsepower outboard motor control stick in his left hand, an M-2 semi-automatic carbine in his right hand and a .45 caliber pistol holstered on his cartridge belt.

"Map Map is your chief bodyguard and the leader of all of your boat operators. Map Map smiled and we shook hands. He had a strong, firm grip. His face was rounder, his eyebrows thicker, and he had more meat on his bones than the others in the boat. I learned that "Map Map" was Vietnamese for "fat" and was pronounced "Mop Mop." He was far from fat according to our measure. I liked him from the beginning.

As we pulled away from the B Team dock, Val pointed to a tall, sharp looking Vietnamese with a green beret cocked over his left eye, standing in the lead boat. "That's LLDB Team Sergeant Hung. His full name is Hung Doan Nguyen and he's as tough as they get. He carries that strange looking Thompson sub-machine gun everywhere he goes. He got rid of the stock and he probably sleeps with the gun. Hung is Major Le's right hand man and when there's a job to be done that involves both teams, I find Hung, tell him what needs doing, and together we see it through." Sergeant Hung, seeing us looking at him, smiled and put up his right hand with fingers extended in a "V for victory" sign.

We boated east on the Chau Doc River about 400 meters and then turned north into the Bassac. It was about 125 meters across where we entered and heavily trafficked with sampans, barges, house boats and all sizes and shapes of fishing boats. They were all moving slowly and smoothly along on the gently flowing waters, respectful of each others' space.

Map Map steered a course that kept our boat about 15 meters back from and to the left of the lead boat with Sergeant Hung at its helm. "Val," I hollered out, so as to be heard above the motor's sound "tell Map Map to take us in the lead. Tell him we will always be the lead boat when I'm aboard, no matter where or when."

Val grinned, gave the order to Map Map, and we quickly captured the lead. The river banks boasted tree-lined villages with narrow dirt roads, most often separating two rows of thatched-roof bamboo homes built side-by-side along the length of the river with but a few gaps between. People, especially young children, waved and shouted greetings to us from the river banks and from the many boats and sampans we passed. I noticed that Map Map was careful not to speed and cause a wake that would upset the smaller sampans and he gave wide berth to anchored fishing boats with their clusters of nets set in the water between long poles driven into the river bottom. Simple courtesies such as that helped to win and keep friends.

"We are coming to Vinh Thanh Island, Dai-uy. It will be quiet from here to camp. The Hoa Haos tightly control the Bassac for two kilometers in either direction from Camp Dan Nam. We're less than a click from home now.

"Look up ahead and on the left about two kilometers ahead, Dai-uy, and you'll see a tall tree with a straight, clean trunk and a small crown of branches at the very top. It's a kind of landmark that tells us where our camp's water entrance meets the Bassac." "I see it, Val. Can't miss it, must stick up at least 20 meters above anything else. It's a good landmark for certain!"

As we continued on the Bassac toward camp, Val reached into his jungle fatigue pocket, pulled out a three by five card, and handed it to me. "You'll want to read this and stick it in your pocket, Dai-uy, you'll be needing it."

It contained the SOI[1] (signal operating instructions) for our radio net between camp and the FOBs (Forward Operations Bases). It included radio call signs, frequencies and contact time schedule. A very necessary card for a newcomer like myself in particular. A good thing to memorize because until you did you know you'd have to eat it if you got captured. The first thing that struck me was that the code name assigned me as the commander was "Thunderbolt." I told Val I'd keep that same code name for the duration. He let me know it was 5th Group policy to change the code name frequently and at random in case the enemy intercepted a call while having an SOI taken from a prisoner or off the field of battle. "It's best that Charlie doesn't know where you are, Dai-uy, or he'll make getting you top priority. If you don't want your head paraded around on a bamboo stick on their side of the border, you'd best let the SOI work like it's set up to work."

"I understand, Val, but I've got my own strategy or psychology or whatever you want to call it. I may be crazy, but I want Charlie to know where I am, and knowing he knows where I am, we can draw him out when we want to and where we want to and get him when he's trying to get me. I want to strike fear in his heart, by making him believe we aren't afraid of him." Val didn't appear persuaded by my argument if I read the expression on his face right.

I explained how I looked at fear. It was simple and something I learned on the mean streets and alleys of south side Chicago when I was just 12 years old. I was leading five or six other boys my age, protecting old ladies from a high school gang out to steal their money and groceries, even hurting them if it took that. The way I figured it, if the older and bigger guys thought we weren't afraid of them, then they would be at least a little bit frightened of us. So, I led my little gang into the streets and alleys to find the bad guys and we never once ran from them. Instead, we ran toward them or waited in ambush on the edge of rooftops on two, three, even four story tenement houses with rocks, rotten eggs, or whatever else we found to throw down at them. We never got beat and the only reason we didn't was because they thought we weren't afraid of them and it gave us the edge. They were older and bigger and there were more of them, but we showed no fear of them. "That's exactly what we'll do here too, Val. Exactly!" "Airborne, Dai-uy," he shouted. "I believe you mean what you say and that you can back it up. I know something else for sure, Dai-uy."

"What's that, Val?"

"You and Major Le are going to get along just fine. Yes, sir, just fine."

I shared my boyhood memories with Val because I didn't want him to think I was just mouthing what I'd said about having no fear. I could have told him a lot more about my days in Chicago, but I thought what I'd said was enough so that he'd know I was serious and that I'd had a real life experience to back it up. In a nutshell, I'd been there.

I would be privileged some 30 years later to address the 36 New York State Troopers, who together made up their two Mobile Response Teams (MRTs), on the subject of "How to control Fear." The MRTs are similar to military SWAT teams. An all-volunteer highly motivated force, they too are trained in all sorts of special tactics with unconventional weapons and equipment and are on call 24 hours a day to respond at a moment's notice to any kind of crisis. Often-times facing a numerically superior foe, they are the elite whom we depend upon in New York State to quell the most dangerous situations, in what most would consider next-to-impossible scenarios. My primary caution to them was to be honest with themselves. "You can't pretend to be unafraid," I warned. "Your foe will sense your real fear, and you'll be dead. You either build up your self-confidence and your ability to control fear, or you do your best to hold the line and maintain the status quo until back-up arrives on the scene."

As we passed to the west of Vinh Thanh Island, Sergeant Valenzuela told me, "Just ahead on your left is the village of An Phu. Captain Nguyen's district headquarters and two Regional Force companies are located in the village. Our on-call ARVN 155 howitzer platoon is north of the village about 200 meters. A public marketplace is set up in the center of the village. You'll like that, Dai-uy. That's where we get our hair cuts too."

"How far to the Cambodian border, Val?"

About 3600 meters due west of camp, he explained, and went on to tell me that two PF Outposts stood between our camp and the border and each was manned by Hoa Haos. Pulling a map out of his right trouser pocket, he pointed to the locations of the two outposts near the hamlets of Phu Hoi and Vinh Hoi. One was west of the Chau Doc River and the other to the east. Val told me that Major Le would be taking me all around the district in the morning so I could see first hand where the FOBs and PF Outposts were located.

Ahead and to the left I could see where other assault boats were tied up. Not a dock, it was just a muddy bank, but easy to get in and out of.

Map Map let up on the throttle and eased along on what was now a river virtually teeming with river craft of all kinds converging on the village of An Phu, center of trade in the district. I also noticed that the thatched-roof houses got closer together as we neared town's center. Women were outside and many were sweeping front yards, washing clothes or preparing chickens, snakes, field rats and even squid for the noon meal. Seeing our boats, they stood and waved a friendly greeting as we waved back. I knew then that the men on our team had established a good rapport with the people of An Phu.

Bicycles, tricycles, carts, and foot traffic shared the district road. It was the only land connection between An Phu District and the Chau Doc Ferry. I watched as two Army trucks moved slowly northward, politely respecting the rights of non-vehicular traffic. "Those ours?" I asked.

"No, Dai-uy, they belong to district. Probably headed toward the Regional Forces (RF) barracks."

Being careful to avoid any contact with walkers or bike riders, the drivers of those big trucks displayed excellent driving acumen and common courtesy, traits I had not expected to witness. "They're really good," I told Val. He let me know that the two Regional Force companies in our district were all Hoa Haos, even kin to some of the villagers. "Our drivers are Hoa Haos too," Val told me, "All of us try hard to show our high regard for the people. How could we ask them to respect us, if we didn't show our respect for them?"

I told Val that made good sense. I would learn that An Phu was a special place and it was because all but 200 of 64,000 plus people in An Phu were Hoa Haos. The other 200 were Chams who lived in a really quaint hamlet named Phu Hoa, located less than 300 meters south of the Phu Hiep FOB.

Val told me that the Hoa Haos rely on Major Le, Captain Nguyen and our team to protect them and their property. "I believe we can trust each and every one of them," he bragged, "I don't think there is an enemy spy among them. They're just good people wanting to fish, farm and live in peace."

Just before we reached the boat dock, we turned left into a narrow canal and under the low concrete bridge that supported the district road. We then traveled but a short distance, passing by more of the villagers' homes, before reaching the defensive perimeter of Camp Dan Nam.

Before we docked I told Val that I'd like to meet the rest of the team before I meet with Major Le. "Is he in camp?" I asked.

Val answered, "For certain. He told the XO that he wanted you to meet with him at 1500 hours in the briefing room. It's just around the corner from your office. As far as our team goes, Tenorio and Kuchen are out on medical patrol in the hamlet of Vinh Phu. It's just north of here on the west bank of the Bassac. They'll be back in camp by noon. I'll get them all together and then let you know. Okay, Dai-uy?"

"Sounds good, Val"

Passing through the outer perimeter of the camp, we entered the camp moat. I learned from Val that Dan Nam was built by the Seabees in 1963. It was 180 meters square with excellent defenses against a direct assault. Except for the canal and the main entrance gate, the perimeter defenses were tight and formidable. Triple concertina, double apron barbed wire, tanglefoot, and claymore mines were sufficient to cause the VC heavy casualties should they try to come at us on the ground. The moat was another deterrent over and above the many machine guns, BARs, rifles and carbines in the hands of the Hoa Hao defenders. There seemed enough firepower to mow down just about anything that would come our way.

I asked Val "Got a drop zone close by?"

"Got the smallest one in Vietnam right in our camp, Dai-uy. Its about 60 meters wide and a little less than 180 meters long, and they manage to get the bundles in it most of the time!" He told me that almost everything came to us by air drop and mostly using Army Caribou aircraft. There was no way into the district by truck except for a slow ferry that Val admitted he wouldn't risk putting a deuce and a half on, thinking it might sink. "We do get some medical supplies and other light stuff plus all of our mail by chopper," he added.

We pulled up to a narrow wooden dock set on thick bamboo piles, extending halfway out into the moat, debarked and walked past a large ammunition bunker on the way to the headquarters building. Val explained that it was one of two bunkers that together held a 15 day stock of ammunition and explosives. He said they were made of reinforced concrete with three feet of sandbags covering all exposed surfaces. They were designed to survive a direct hit from a 250 pound 155mm howitzer HE projectile. Another three days stock for machine guns and mortars was stored in the bunkers or pits with the weapons.

"Up ahead, Val, is that wooden tower with the rubber tank our water treatment tower?"

"Yes, Dai-uy. It uses a standard diatomite number 2 system with a charcoal filter." The treated water was piped to the dispensary, kitchen and the shower, sink, and toilet facility we shared with Major Le and his team. A big problem, he said, was that the moat around the camp was our source of water and it was used as a toilet by the Strikers. "They wash clothes, bathe and whatever in it. But, they have no choice. They have nothing to use except the moat."

"Nothing?" I asked.

"Nothing, Dai-uy, and I don't think that's right."

"I agree, Val. I'll discuss it with Major Le."

We walked past other camp buildings and went into the inner perimeter through a barbed wire gate past the triple concertina barrier and an empty machine gun bunker. I asked Val why it wasn't manned.

He told me the Navy Seabees had built this camp like many others, including an inner compound with machine gun bunkers and barbed wire to house and protect the American and Vietnamese A Teams if their own CIDG turned against them. "We're not worried about the Hoa Haos turning against us, Dai-uy, so we maintain the inner perimeter defenses as a second line of defense against the VC if they attack and manage to penetrate the outer perimeter."

Ahead was the headquarters building, with the flag pole and the South Vietnamese National Colors fluttering in the morning breeze.

> *As an unconventional warfare unit we were there at the invitation of the South Vietnamese government and we did not fly the American flag out of doors. It was their sovereign territory, and we accepted that fact, flying a small American flag inside our team room. In that way, we could honor our nation's standard in an area used exclusively by our team while respecting their colors flying in its place of rightful prominence.*

Protection for those inside the headquarters building against direct ground fire was provided by an encompassing, waist-high concrete block wall. Half of our men and half of the LLDB were quartered in this building. Val led me through a screened-in porch into our team's kitchen. Pointing upward to an access hole in the ceiling he showed me the two layers of sandbags that protected against indirect fire from enemy mortars or rockets. He told me, "We have the same protection in the building that houses our dispensary and quarters for the rest of our team."

The philosophy behind providing direct and indirect fire protection in only those buildings housing American and South Vietnamese A Team personnel and the medical and operational facilities was simple and honest. Should the camp be attacked, the CIDG, whom we counted on to defend the camp, would be less likely tempted to remain in an unprotected barracks, and therefore highly motivated to move to their protected perimeter positions or mortar pits where they could engage the enemy. The two protected buildings permitted essential command, control, medical and logistical support functions to continue, even during an attack.

I was greeted with a smile and a salute by the team XO as I entered the hallway that would lead to my office, the quarters area and briefing center. "Lieutenant John T. Kallunki, Sir. Welcome to Camp Dan Nam." John was slim, about six foot tall and had large ears and a big nose.

I returned his salute, shook his hand, and then reminded Val to let me know when the team was together in camp so we could have our meeting.

Instead, Val suggested that we all come to the mess for lunch at noon, get to know each other as we eat, and have the meeting afterwards over a cup of hot coffee.

"Good idea, Val. See you at lunch,"

I then followed John down the hall and into the briefing center. It was brightly painted with a podium, five CIDG Company flags and a Camp flag made of blue colored silk with a white looped fringe. At the center was a sliding map case similar to what I'd seen in the B Team's briefing center.

He led me then to my small cubicle, adequate for what little time I would spend there. A folding chair and a steel cot with a pillow, sheets, and mosquito net seemed adequate to satisfy my needs for creature comforts. An Ithaca 12 gauge shotgun hung on the bamboo mat-covered wall as a useful reminder of where I came from and what our being here was all about.

If the enemy were to attack and fight their way through the concertina, tangle-foot, and claymore mine obstacle belt and threaten the inner perimeter defenses, we would be better able to defend in close quarters with our 12 gauge shotguns and double aught buckshot. The Ithaca Gun Company made the best of what-ever weapon the Army purchased using Ithaca Gun Company as one of the manufacturers. Wherever I went in the Army I would look first for an Ithaca .45 Caliber pistol. Once in Special Forces I also sought the Ithaca shotgun over any other make. The machined tolerances of moving parts were superior in an

Ithaca weapon and therefore more trouble-free and dependable, particularly important in a weapon you turn to when the war at a given moment in time is close up and personal.

A 60 watt bulb in a pull-chain socket dangled from a rafter to light up the cubicle. Nails were located in the wall below the shotgun to hold my rucksack, field cap, M-16, flashlight and bayonet.

John stepped back, gave me maneuvering room and pointed to a closed door directly across the hall from where we stood, "Your office, Dai-uy."

I stepped across the hall and into what would be my command post for the next seven months. It was furnished with a small wooden typing desk, manual Royal typewriter, oak desk chair, small table, three drawer steel file cabinet and two folding chairs.

I sat down behind my desk and asked John to join me. "How's the team's morale, John? What's happened the last few weeks that I should know about?"

"The morale has been slipping, Dai-uy. From what I have heard about you and how you'll get along with Major Le, the morale should start picking up once you meet with the team. Menkins told us all he remembers about "Dangerous Dan." Said he served with you in the 6th at Bragg and that you weren't afraid of anything or anyone. He also said that you got the job done no matter what it took to do it and that you were loyal to your men."

He went on to tell me that we had a good team but that the past couple of weeks had been rough on them. Major Le didn't confide in John, said he was waiting to talk to the new team CO about changes in war strategy. "He wouldn't discuss it with me. We don't know why we've been put in neutral since the old team leader was sent packing. But, with you here we should get right back into business." John informed me that Major Le had only let them out of camp on Civic Action[2] projects and medical patrols. "He left camp for two days, went to Hoa Hao Village where his family lives, and then on to meet with Major Chuan Nguyen, their C Team CO in Can Tho. He hasn't spoken to me since returning to camp."

Major Arnn had instructed the team to avoid any talk about their team leader's early and sudden departure. It seemed like somebody was trying to cover something up. "Do you know what's going on?" John asked.

"Yes, and I'll tell you when we're all together at the team meeting. Anything else you'd like to discuss right now?"

He went on to tell me that he had a hard time dealing with the issue of our men smoking, drinking beer, even drinking coffee and associating with the local girls. "I'm a Mormon and getting those things right are important to me."

"Drinking coffee and smoking bothers you?" I asked.

"Yes, Sir, it sure does, I'm a Mormon."

I looked John in the eyes and told him I wanted to get a few things straight between us. In the future, starting today, he was not to let anyone know that their smoking or drinking coffee bothered him. If anything else the men did or didn't do bothered him, I told John he'd have to stifle it until he talked to me about it. "If it's something serious in my judgment and my judgment only, I will deal with it and let you know. Understand?"

"Yes, Sir, I'll do my best."

I told John that he was right about it not being good for our men to associate with local girls and that I also agreed that beer drinking could be bad if it affected any man's performance of duty. "I'll discuss all of these matters at our team meeting."

"Thank you, Dai-uy."

Shortly before noon I acquainted myself with the dining area, kitchen and the screened-in porch at the south end of the building. The dining area also acted as information center, mail room and a place for meeting, planning and study. Two walls had screened openings, one looking out on the porch to the south and the other on the drill field to the east. Hinged bamboo shutters could be dropped in short order to repel monsoon rains or ward off a hot afternoon sun. Six wooden, four-man tables were set with plastic table-cloths, eating utensils, napkins, sugar dispensers, salt and pepper.

An interior partition on the west side was covered with charts, calendars and a bulletin board with papers posted in four categories: Current, Permanent, Team Status, and Interpreter Status. A 48 star American Flag hung on a staff at one end of the partition, while individual mail bins and distribution boxes occupied the other end.

In the far corner and adjacent to a large, screened-in porch was our kitchen. A young Vietnamese woman stood over a charcoal burning stove preparing a lunch of pancakes, bacon, and eggs for our team. The aroma was inviting. A small, two burner canned heat stove sat nearby under a kettle of water coming to a boil for the brewing of fresh coffee. Looking around, I noticed there was no refrigerator. Where one would logically be, there stood a good-size corrugated can full of ice inside a larger can with sawdust separating one from the other for insulation. Shelves covered two walls of the kitchen and contained canned vegetables, soups, and other commissary type foods, such as spaghetti and spaghetti sauce, sliced Dole pineapple, and all kinds of fruit juice. Some boxed pasta and cookies were on the top shelf. Very little fresh food was visible. Watermelon, potatoes, eggs and other fresh vegetables waited cooking on a preparation table. I exchanged greetings with the cook and continued my impromptu survey, ending on the screened-in porch with a view of the inner perimeter area. To my far right was the east end of the second building that housed the other half of our team plus the dispensary which had a rear door that opened onto the landing zone, permitting quick and easy transport of wounded in and out of the treatment area on stretchers.

Our 4.2" mortar pit was just a short distance away from the porch. Directly in front of me were the toilets, wash basins and showers in one covered building that served the two Green Beret Teams. Towering over and tight behind that was a substantial wooden tower with a large, rubber gravity storage tank and the camp's water purification equipment. Potable water was piped from the tank to the kitchen, wash basins, shower stalls and toilets.

What I had seen so far was neat and apparently well maintained. I went out, used the toilet, washed my hands in one of the sinks, told myself that I'd get used to washing and bathing in nothing but cold water, and returned to the dining area to find the team all there, except for John Eleam. Eleam was in the communications bunker, the one place that had to be manned 24 hours a day without exception.

"Please excuse the pancakes," Kallunki asked of me, "we haven't made a commissary run in a while and we're short of the good stuff."

I told him that was no problem, that pancakes were one of my favorite things, so long as I had lots of syrup or honey to pour on them. I told them to go ahead and eat and when we were enjoying our coffee after lunch, I'd talk to them.

Specialist Menkins hurriedly ate his meal, took a full mug of coffee with him and left to relieve Eleam in the commo bunker. After our hunger was satisfied, we pulled two tables together and the seven of us sat down, coffee in hand, for our first team meeting.

I waited until everyone had settled down in their chairs and then let them know how I stood on the military courtesy matter. "Each of us has a job to do here and I'm sure you all know who is in charge here." Looking across the table at Team Sergeant Valenzuela, I continued, "Val has already given me good advice that I'll share with you. First off, there won't be any saluting in camp, in the FOBs, or out in the district. No need to call me 'Sir.' Call me 'Dai-uy.' I like the sound of it. Call Major Le 'Thieu-ta' or 'Major Le', whichever comes easiest to you, and treat him with the respect due the leader of our Hoa Hao fighters and a veteran of 18 years of combat. "If a field grade officer or a General visits, or if Major Chuan or Major Re stops by, show them the respect due them and salute them." I paused to drink a little coffee. I told them Lieutenant Kallunki and I had met and talked over a few matters that would affect each of us in one way or another. "About coffee," I told them, "you drink coffee if you choose to." I let them know that I drink a lot of coffee and that I have since I was 11 years old. I also let them know that they could smoke if they wanted except when out in an ambush position, night or day. "You all probably understand that better than I do since you've been down that road more recently than me."

After another sip of coffee I briefed them on the three hard and fast rules that we must adhere to as long as I am their commander. There would be no drinking of any amount of hard liquor, even medical alcohol. One sip and I'd send them packing to the B Team. That was a promise.

"I understand that you drink quite a bit of Cambodian beer here in camp because the water gives you dysentery." I let them know, without question, if they were to just one time drink so much that it impaired their judgment in my opinion alone, they would be past history in A-424.

I spoke loud and clear to them about rule number three, telling them to pay close attention to what I was about to tell them whether they agreed or disagreed. No one, including me, who is assigned or attached to this team would be authorized to have any, "and I mean ANY," I emphasized, personal relations with any female in the entire district of An Phu. "There will be no exceptions, period. Any questions so far?"

"We're with you, Dai-uy," volunteered Team Sergeant Valenzuela. The others remained silent, apparently accepting the fixed rules of behavior as law.

I also briefed them on the fact that I would ask Major Le to meet with Captain Nguyen and establish a law in An Phu that would have any man who rapes or personally assaults the wife or daughter of a Striker to be brought into this camp and be summarily executed within twenty-four hours of his being apprehended, preferably with his victim as a witness to the execution.

"That's pretty heavy, Dai-uy" Kallunki offered. "No doubt," I told him, "but effective." I let the team know that I'd been protecting women as my "thing" since I was old enough to understand how much my mother suffered when my father deserted her, leaving her to fend for herself, my brother and me during the dark days of the Depression. We were truly dependent on the welfare system, a Catholic Church and a local Salvation Army soup kitchen for survival.

"Women whose men are at war must be protected. I depend on the police back home in Ithaca, New York, to watch out for my wife and children while I'm gone. The wives of Strikers should feel they can depend on us. It is as simple as that."

Val spoke up, asking me to talk about our new mission.

Looking around to make certain there were no civilians within earshot, I began by telling them it was a TOP SECRET mission. "Colonel Tuttle offered me this command and briefed me on Christmas Day in Can Tho. Major Le fought a long, hard battle, going all the way up to the Minister of Defense to obtain approval for this camp to be the first to attack VC targets inside Cambodia."

I sat quiet for a moment, letting that sink in.

Cheers of "Airborne" and "All the Way, Dai-uy" erupted around the table. "What does that mean, Dai-uy?" Sergeant Kuchen asked. "Do we invade Cambodia?"

"Major Le and I will work out the details. We have to be tight-mouthed about our mission inside Cambodia and our role as an independent team. I don't answer to B-42 or anyone else." I explained that we couldn't tell anyone, "I mean ANYONE outside of our team, or they'll go bananas." I let them know there would be problems dealing with the B Team because they were not to know what our new role was. "When we fire a mission into Cambodia or we attack, probe or even follow the VC in hot pursuit across the border, we don't tell anyone anything. As far as the B Team or C Team are concerned, it will be as if it never happened."

"What about reports?" Kallunki asked.

"None," I answered. "No entry in MOPSUMs, no SITREPs or SPOTREPs, not even if we have friendly losses."

"If one of us is killed or wounded?" asked John Eleam.

"No, John, not even then. That's the way it has to be. You each must volunteer to stay in A-424. Now you understand why. Think about this as you make up your mind whether you want to stay with me or not. We will be refused combat support anytime we are inside Cambodia: no artillery, no med-evac, no close air support, not even Puff.

"Colonel Tuttle told me flat out that if he were asked, even by the CO or anyone else in B-42, any of his own people in C-4 or 5th Group headquarters, he would deny the mission and deny knowing me. This must be a tightly compartmentalized CIA operation. It's yes or no for each of you. That simple."

Sergeant Tenorio asked if that was a good position for us to be in. "Kind of like sending us to do their dirty work and leaving us to suffer the consequences alone. What happens if we get caught on the other side?" Of Mexican heritage, Tenorio was dark skinned and about five nine with strong features, coal black hair and normally a broad smile. No smile for the moment. "Colonel Tuttle told me he would deny any connection, call us a renegade team if necessary," I answered. "The reason I volunteered for An Phu is that I wouldn't want to be in any other camp, witness my men being killed or wounded and be forced to look the other way when the enemy crossed back into Cambodia. We're on our own. If any of you or even all of you think I'm crazy to want to head this thing up and want no part of it, you're free to go. No one will hold anything against you. It's that simple. We'll fire our first mission into Cambodia as soon as I get the details worked out with Major Le. I'm gearing everything for New Year's Day, figuring that's a good day to celebrate our new mission."

Everyone smiled, most shouted "Airborne!"

I told them it was stupid to have to hide the fact that we would be taking the war to the enemy, no matter where that took us. We'd do it right for the first time in the war and have to be secret about it. "It's ridiculous." I told them. "It is hard for me to understand how these people have lived and fought with one hand tied behind their back for so long. It would be like letting an enemy of yours come across your property line from your neighbor's land, rape your wife, steal whatever he wanted, burn your house down, step back into the land next door and stand there laughing at you, knowing you couldn't do anything about it. If you called the police, they'd tell you the Mayor had given him sanctuary on your neighbor's property." I told them how anxious I was to meet Major Le, the man who had put his own career and perhaps his life on the line to demand the right to fight the enemy wherever he went and to protect his people from an unfair war policy.

"Why does General Westmoreland or anyone up the line allow the enemy his safe-havens?" I asked out loud, knowing I'd not get an answer.

"I hate politicians running a war," Val said.

Kallunki smiled and said, "Within a few days our people will know what Major Le has done, because there will be no safe havens for the enemy across the border."

In his book, A Soldier Reports,³ General Westmoreland writes about a quotation of Napoleon Bonaparte that he kept under a panel of glass on his desk during his entire tour of duty in South Vietnam. In effect, Napoleon said that a military commander cannot use as an excuse for his mistakes in warfare an order given by his superior when the person giving the order is not in the war theater, is imperfectly aware or wholly unaware of the latest state of affairs. He went on to state unequivocally that any military commander who undertook to carry out a plan which he considered defective is at fault, if when he had made his objections known, was denied the proper change, "should tender his resignation rather than be the instrument of his army's downfall."

With that in mind, it is impossible for this writer to understand why General Westmoreland would state rather matter-of-factly in that same book that the enemy used Cambodia as a sanctuary while the White House and the Congress refused to allow him to do anything about it and then not resign in a very public way to protest our government's aiding and abetting the enemy. He went on to write of his own lack of courage and integrity, telling that he was refused the right to tell the world press about the Cambodian sanctuaries, yet did nothing about it. It wasn't until late 1967, after the Associated Press and United Press International revealed the location of an enemy camp inside Cambodia, that the world knew the truth. Westmoreland admitted how his own contingency plans that would allow hot pursuit of the enemy into Cambodia and the military blockade of the Mekong and Bassac Rivers was opposed by the State Department and rejected by President Johnson. In my opinion, General Westmoreland and every person above him in the chain of command aided and abetted the enemy by providing a refuge for those in the enemy ranks who would use those same sanctuaries as a base of operations where they could return to after killing and wounding our forces and those of our allies, knowing we were not permitted to pursue.

Interestingly enough, in the district of An Phu, during my seven months in command, we did not permit the enemy safe havens in the immediate proximity of the 30 kilometers of Cambodian border area we secured. And, we effectively blocked any shipments of war goods on the Bassac River that would have gone to the enemy in Cambodia.

I told my men that we had to be prepared to deny having taken any action that would have been the basis for reports we would receive coded "Nantucket," the code word for all reports relating to the violation of neutral territory, and we would have to deny them fast. "I'll prepare some canned responses and give them to Eleam to keep handy in the commo bunker. Eleam, I want you to make sure our commo men know where they are."

"Will do, Dai-uy," Eleam answered.

"Unless you want to go to Leavenworth," I warned, "and take me with you, you'll all keep quiet about everything we do here except civic action and medical patrols. That way you aren't apt to slip and say the wrong thing."

I told them I wouldn't allow what happened at Vinh Gia Camp to happen here. They probably knew the team leader was relieved, but didn't know he was serving time in Leavenworth Penitentiary because he was honest. He admitted firing HE rounds into the VC base in Cambodia in retaliation for their rocket attack from that same base earlier in the day that killed or wounded some of his Strikers. Sergeant John Eleam told how he'd heard about that while monitoring B Team radio channels. "Did they really put him in prison for firing on the enemy, Dai-uy?" John had handsome features, stood about five seven, was black and slight, but muscular.

"That's what I was told, and when I confronted Colonel Tuttle with it, he neither affirmed nor denied it, wouldn't even talk about it. We can't do anything about it, but maybe someone will, some day. We've got to watch out for each other and help protect our people." I told Eleam how pleased I was to hear from Sergeant Smalls that he was studying to apply for a communications' Warrant. Val had told me Eleam didn't tire easily and that he was cool under pressure. "I'll be counting on you in that commo bunker, Eleam. When do you rotate?"

"The 30th of May, Dai-uy, and I won't go a day earlier."

"Good, John, I need you."

I explained the new plan would work, beginning with the fact that Colonel Tuttle had sent me here to command Camp Dan Nam, the CIDG and Major Le's LLDB. But, I let them know, I wasn't stupid. I knew that Hoa Haos didn't take orders from anyone but a Hoa Hao and I recognized that Major Le was a far better judge of what to do in combat situations, whether offensive or defensive, then I would be.

"I will meet with Major Le at 1500 hours and I will tell him what my instructions are and let him know right off that I would trust his experience and his judgment. I want us to work as a team. If there is any disagreement between him and me, nobody will know except him and me. He knows my word will be the final word, but I will make certain he knows I will rely almost exclusively on his combat experience and knowledge of the enemy to guide us in planning our joint actions." I did not have much infantry experience so I let Val know that I'd be counting on him to help me get my feet on the ground.

Val smiled and asked when we'd get current intelligence from Major Le's people. "We need to update our situation maps, Dai-uy."

"After I meet with Major Le," I answered.

Staff Sergeant George Kuchen asked, "Can we get a refrigerator, Dai-uy? We need one for medical supplies, especially to store the better drugs for pain." George was about five eight, had a light complexion and a high forehead. He let me know that Kuchen was his right arm, not only in the dispensary, but on medical patrols too.

I turned to Lieutenant Kallunki, "John," I said, "do whatever you have to do to get us a kerosene refrigerator."

"Yes, Sir. I'll take care of that."

I asked Val to brief Menkins on all that we had discussed, especially the new mission concept." "Will do, Dai-uy."

I looked at each man sitting at that table, sat back in my chair and spoke to them as a stranger wanting to be one of them and to be known by them. "Sergeant Major Lynch told me a little about each one of you and I've learned more about you since meeting you. You should know a little about me so you know where I've been and where I'm headed.

"I was born in Detroit, Michigan, in 1933. My dad deserted my mom the day I was born and went running off with some young girl and ended up in prison for a spell, so I was told. Mom raised my older brother Bill and me through the Great Depression, sticking by us when the going was really rough for her. We moved to Chicago when I was five years old. I was only nine when I saw a dead Negro man dangling from the end of a rope inside a garage on Snake Alley. Snake Alley separated the blacks from the whites along a four block-long stretch between 43rd and 47th streets on the south side of Chicago, maybe four blocks from Lake Michigan. By the time I'd walked to the end of the alley, found a policeman, told him what I'd seen, and led him hurriedly back to the garage the only thing left was a piece of that rope, still dangling from the rafter where I'd seen him hanging, along with a few spots of blood on the concrete floor directly below.

"After taking down my name and address, the officer told me the Negro was probably the one that white people along the alley had accused of killing their dogs by hanging them in that same garage. 'If the dog killing has stopped in this alley, we'll know they got their man.' That was my first taste of people's inhumanity toward their fellow man.

"I've already told Val about the years that followed when I had my own gang and when the gangster Al Capone was my hero. Val knows my philosophy on how to control fear. He'll tell you about that when I'm done. Okay, Val?"

"Sure, Dai-uy."

"For now let it suffice that my Mom moved us to a little town named Mokena, southwest of Chicago, where she bought a one acre lot just across the road from the New York Central railroad tracks. We first lived in an old 28 foot long house trailer without an inside toilet. The move to Mokena was precipitated by Mom catching me trying to hide a homemade crossbow I'd put together to give my small gang of 11 and 12 year boys an edge on the high school thugs we were going up against.

"I then went to work on a large Hereford beef cattle and Poland China hog farm near New Lennox, Illinois, owned by Daniel T. Walker. I rode my bike the eight miles each way to the farm on a gravel road. Mr. Walker was a good farmer and a real man among men. His wife Lila was a remarkable woman. Seemingly tireless and God-fearing, she was honest and humble and they both treated me like another son, even paying for my first trips ever to a dentist. Lila tended a large garden, raised chickens, cooked, ironed, and kept a large home for her husband, three sons and her father-in-law, Daniel T. Walker Sr. I never once heard her complain, even on those hot summer days when she would be cooking two large meals for her family plus six or eight hired men. "A stern disciplinarian, honest and fair in all his dealings, Mr. Walker was an excellent example to follow. I learned from him the direction a good man should take in life, though I can't honestly say I always followed in his footsteps. He introduced me during dinner table conversation to men who became my new heroes, men like General Douglas MacArthur, Field Marshall Montgomery, Winston Churchill, and my favorite war hero, General George S. Patton, Jr.

"I quit school the day I was 16 to help out on the 100 acre hilltop farm my mother and new step-father had bought eight months earlier. It was 14 miles from Ithaca, New York. When I was $18^{1}/_{2}$ I enlisted in the US Army. I'm here today because this is exactly where I want to be and I'm doing exactly what I want to do. Any questions?"

Tenorio asked, "Why do they call you Dangerous?"

I answered with a serious expression on my face, "Because I am." That response brought on some good natured laughter from the whole team.

It's not a nice story. The truth can be ugly at times. Early in the Spring of 1958 I was the Division Supply Operations Sergeant for the 82nd Airborne Division at Fort Bragg, North Carolina and a Company Platoon Sergeant. I'd earned a reputation in earlier assignments for being able to 'straighten out' any man who had been a constant discipline problem and a very ineffective soldier.

The company commander asked that I take this one soldier under my wing and, as he put it to me, "either make a soldier out of him or drive him so hard that he'll desert." That particular soldier had a bad attitude and just didn't want to obey authority, no matter how simple or necessary the order was. I tried my best for two weeks to convince that soldier that he should change his attitude and perform like a paratrooper or, if he couldn't take it - get out. Finally, one morning, the soldier didn't show up for the reveille formation, could not be found in the area, and was officially recorded as being AWOL. After a few days had passed and the soldier had not returned, the company commander thanked me for getting the "dud" off his hands, and I went about my duties.

We assumed that the young private would be apprehended near his home out West and that he would be picked up on that garrison's morning report, discharged for unsuitability and we'd be done with him. We assumed wrong. His body was found next to that of his girl friend in a remote lover's lane near Fayetteville, North Carolina, just outside of Fort Bragg. He had killed his girlfriend with a single pistol shot between the eyes and then turned the gun on himself. He had left a suicide note on the dashboard of his old car.

Military Police investigators from Fort Bragg Post stood in front of my desk the next day, questioned me and told me that the suicide victim had left a long letter telling of how his company commander didn't like him and that he had been used and abused by me on orders from the Captain. He ended his letter asking that the company commander be relieved of command and asking that

I be "removed from the United States Army" because I was "too dangerous."
Neither the company commander nor myself was found responsible or negligent,
but I was from that day forward known as "Dangerous Dan."

I recognized the fact that we had a huge job to do and few men to do it. "We'll just have to work longer and harder during daylight hours on civic action projects and medical patrols. Though we're few in number we'll have to be ready to help defend the camp against enemy action, get out on night ambush operations and daytime combat patrols whenever possible."

I'd seen in the B Team briefing center that we were authorized four officers and 20 NCOs because we had the dual mission of CIDG operations and Sub-Sector advisory. "So," I told them, "it boils down to the fact that seven of us have to do the work of 24 men. I can't promise we'll get any more men, but I'll try my best. In the meantime, we've really got our work cut out for us.

"I'm not a sleeper, and never have been," I explained. "I'll sack out between 0330 and 0600 and again from 1300 to 1400. Woe be the man who bothers me when I'm sleeping if we're not under attack!"

We discussed the need to continue to maintain a healthy rapport with the people of An Phu while we encouraged them to place their trust in the Saigon government."

"Of course, Dai-uy, but we have to understand if they are cautious about the latter." Kallunki offered, "Until it embraces the Hoa Haos as a South Vietnamese religious sect and not as an enemy of the government, we'll have a tough time building a bridge of loyalty between the Hoa Haos and Saigon."

Sergeant Val reinforced what I'd been told at Nha Trang. "The Hoa Haos are good night fighters," he said, emphasizing our need to "take advantage of darkness and the fear that most men have of moving around in blackness."

I thanked Val for his input and let them know this had to be a team effort if we were to succeed. "Every one of you around this table has more experience with the Hoa Haos and the local situation than I have and I'll be picking your brains. Just make real sure that you let me know if you think I'm headed in the wrong direction. Whether it be tactics, civic action programs, psy-war operations, even rudimentary camp functions. "It's very important," I added, "If you've got something to say, say it, and don't wait for a good time to say your piece, because it may never come. I'll take what you say into account before I decide on a course of action. But I will decide and you will follow." I explained that the same rule applied to questions. If they had a question, ask it. They might not like my answer, but they could be sure to get one. Lieutenant Kallunki and Val then gave me a run-down on our South Vietnamese colleagues. Three interpreters were now with us. Lo Lap Co, who went by the nickname "Flash" was senior and would go with me when I was not with Major Le who spoke fluent English. Flash was fluent in Vietnamese, Chinese, and English. Quang and Tony spoke Vietnamese and English. Tony was usually with the medics in the dispensary and on medical patrols. Quang was perhaps the busiest of all the interpreters because he filled all the other needs of the team.

A 42 man reconnaissance platoon was augmented by 10 bodyguards. The recon platoon's weapons included six M-1D sniper rifles. Map Map headed the boat operations with 14 assault boats and a larger boat with a $2^1/_2$ ton truck engine as it's inboard motor. "It's our quick reaction boat, Dai-uy; it'll take a whole platoon, an 81mm mortar, ammo, light machine guns, the works," bragged Sergeant Val.

Major Le and his entire LLDB team, particularly Lieutenants Ba and Hanh, Sergeants Hung Nguyen and Chet, were said to be exceptional. They were praised by team members for excellent discipline, courage, and efficiency.

Win, the house boy was a 70 year old, stooped-over Cambodian, infrequently called on to translate Cambodian language radio broadcasts and propaganda leaflets dropped along the border by the enemy.

Serving in different aspects of the camp's operation were six cooks, six laborers, two mechanics, four boat operators and two nurses. Tenorio spoke out, saying, "We provide medical supplies and training to six midwives who work out of maternity houses scattered around the district that we helped build and also to public health nurses who work in the USOM health center. It's just 80 meters or so from our front gate, on the right side of the road, almost in An Phu Village."

Lieutenant Kallunki advised that the midwives and USOM nurses were paid by Sub Sector. "We do provide intelligence funds to Major Le to support his efficient and critically needed network of agents and handlers who work both sides of the border to keep us informed." Kallunki reported. "We can depend on what they tell us about enemy strength, weapons, and location inside Cambodia."

Val told me that we had five CIDG companies, with three housed in the main camp, one at the Khanh Binh FOB and one at the Phu Hiep FOB. Four LLDB were at each FOB, but no Americans. "There's just not enough of us to go around." I reiterated that I'd do my best to get more men, thanked them for their input and told them we'd get together again in the morning after breakfast. By then I'd have met with Major Le and would have had a chance to put together a new mission and forces paper. "Val," I added, "I'd like numbers on the LLDB team and the CIDG later tonight."

"Will do, Dai-uy."

As I rose to leave, Lieutenant Kallunki leaned forward in his chair, clasped his hands in front of him on the table and spoke out in a low, but serious tone, "There's something you might want to discuss with Major Le, Dai-uy. There's an undercurrent among the CIDG. If you approach a group of them talking together, and get close enough so they think you can hear what they're saying, they quit talking and take off in all directions. That happened to me a few times in recent days since our last team leader left.

"When I asked Flash what was wrong, he refused to say anything except that I should talk to Lieutenant Ba. So I got Ba off to the side and asked him to level with me.

"He told me that most of the Strikers are worried about going to prison when the CIDG is converted to Regional Forces. From what we've been told through the B Team, that's supposed to happen this summer and we're to be one of the first camps to convert."

The others' faces mirrored his concern. I told them I'd heard mention of the conversion program but nothing about any thought of our Strikers going to prison. "Why should they? They'd done a great job securing the border, why would anyone want to put them in prison?" With that I eased back down into my chair, wanting to learn more about this situation.

Lieutenant Kallunki related how Ba had told him that almost half of our Strikers had deserted from ARVN or dodged military service. "They didn't want to serve in a unit that wasn't all Hoa Hao and they wouldn't take orders from anyone but a Hoa Hao. They've proved themselves in combat but Saigon is worried that they'll try to take over the central government. Nothing official, Dai-uy, but a lot of scary talk that's filtered down from Group. B-42 has at least two camps with all Hoa Hao CIDG. If something isn't done, the Strikers will suffer, or just take off and leave us holding the bag. Who would blame them?"

As it stood, any Striker could quit the CIDG whenever he wanted to. There was no service obligation with the CIDG. They were volunteers and the only requirement was that they turn in all issued weapons and equipment when they chose to leave. Our Strikers had remained loyal because they were with their own people, protecting family, neighbors and friends from a common enemy. An A Team's first and foremost challenge when it went into an area to organize a CIDG operation was to gain rapport and earn their respect and loyalty. In reality, that is the true test of a Green Beret in unconventional warfare situations such as we faced in South Vietnam.

"So," I chimed in, "with CIA backing, Saigon gives the OK for TOP SECRET operations inside Cambodia when pressured by Major Le, and backed by General Quang Van Dang, the IV Corps Commander. At the same time they make plans to retaliate against the Hoa Haos by way of military tribunal action. In either instance, only the Hoa Haos can get hurt, along with anyone who stands with them."

General Westmoreland, if he was aware of the plan, would likely go along with it due to his intense dislike for General Dang, who consistently blocked Westmoreland's attempts to position conventional American units in the IV Corps area, known as 'The Delta.' It was General Dang's belief, as proved by facts available to General Westmoreland, that of the four corps areas, in South Vietnam, the IV Corps was the most secure and that security was due to the courage and capability of South Vietnamese forces. There were ARVN, Regional Forces, Popular Forces and the CIDG. In An Phu and neighboring Tan Chau Districts, all CIDG, RF and PF were Hoa Hao. General Westmoreland would have to have known from routine field reports that it was the Hoa Haos, backed by ARVN Forces, that were continuously victorious against a VC force four times their strength and armed with superior weapons. They maintained security in those two critical border area combat zones with no support from US conventional forces.

"Val, you take over here. Lieutenant, I'll let you know as soon as my meeting with Major Le is over." As I got up to go, I looked each of my team in the eye and told them I was proud to be there with them in An Phu.

At precisely 1500 hours on 27 December 1965, I entered the briefing area and was greeted by Major Le. "Good afternoon, Dai-uy," he said in perfect English, "Welcome to An Phu and Camp Dan Nam." Standing in the center of the room with a smile on his face he reached out and shook my hand in a firm, but friendly manner.

"Thank you, Major Le," I answered. "I'm proud to be here. I've been anxious to meet you. I've been hearing much about you and the Hoa Haos of An Phu and it is all good."

Major Le stood about 5'-5", with neatly combed black hair and cool, dark brown eyes. He wore jungle fatigues that looked tailor made, were freshly laundered and pressed, with only a cloth name tag sewn over his right chest pocket and the insignia of a major on both sides of his collar. No leather belt, just the standard black issue belt. He had a rather pleasant face, with the jaw set of a very resolute man, one I'd like on my side when the going got tough.

To Major Le's right was the briefing area, but it was to his left where he motioned me to go. A small table, covered with an embroidered cloth, was set with the delicate amenities of an afternoon tea, including teapot, cups, saucers, a bowl of sugar cubes and other delicacies. Two chairs were set, one on each side of the table.

"We have much to talk about, Dai-uy. Please join me." A pleasant surprise, tea in a combat zone! Once seated, Major Le poured and suggested I try the sugar wafers laid out on a delicate china plate in the center of the table. The tea was excellent and the wafers sweet and crunchy. Major Le sat back in his chair and smiled as I helped myself to seconds on both.

"I received word from Major Chuan in Can Tho about your coming to An Phu. Colonel Tuttle told him of your record and great enthusiasm about working with the Hoa Haos. He also told me about our new TOP SECRET mission and I was pleased to know you volunteered to come here."

I told Major Le how proud I was to be there and that I'd also heard about his many years of fighting for his people. "Major Le, I know that you risked everything to convince Saigon of the need to oppose the sanctuary matter."

"Please call me Thieu-ta. We will be working very closely, Dai-uy. It is better."

"I agree, Thieu-ta. I am here to help you in any way that I can. I have met with my team and will meet again with them in the morning to discuss tactical plans. We will rely very much on your experience to develop the new tactics and the overall strategy to plan our new, exciting mission."

Major Le was smiling, but intent, advising that we "must devise our strategy quickly, that time was running out. We must go quickly on the offensive now that we have the green light."

"I agree. We must act soon. I think it would be good psychology to make our first strike into Cambodia on New Year's Day. Use mortar fire only this time so that we do not expose the Strikers to unnecessary danger. Then we'll make our plans to attack into Cambodia where the enemy is, using short, stabbing actions that will make the VC nervous. Without artillery or air support and with no helicopters available, not even for medical evacuation, we have no choice. Do you agree, Thieu-ta?"

"I believe we see eye to eye on these matters. Do you have a plan?"

"Only for the first shots on New Year's Day. I want to attack them with our mortars from here in the main camp, from Khanh Binh and from Phu Hiep also. We should target every VC location inside Cambodia that we can reach with our mortars and fire the first round from each position at exactly the same time. We will then catch them in their sleep and turn their dreams into nightmares. Then, I think we should harass them with nightly fire missions. Never the same time, never the same place. What do you think, Thieu-ta?"

"It is a good plan. Yes, Dai-uy, it is time we send a message to the Viet Cong inside Cambodia, telling them we no longer recognize their sanctuaries. On the stroke of midnight on the first day of January we will rain rocket and mortar rounds where they sleep. There will no longer be a safe haven in Cambodia for our enemy.

"All we can do for certain is to drive them deeper into Cambodia, beyond our mortar range. It will mean they have to come farther to attack us and they cannot just step across the border to kill our people. They will have no place close to the border to go to treat their wounded, to rest or re-group after an attack on An Phu. It is a good plan we have, Dai-uy."

I told him that we would need the latest intelligence reports to know where the enemy is located. "We must try to plan so that we do not kill or injure any Cambodian civilians."

"Your team sergeant will have a copy of the latest intelligence before we are done here. We know where the VC are allowed to camp and move around. The Cambodian people have a curfew, the same as our people, and they will not leave their homes during the hours of darkness. They are friends of the Hoa Haos and we respect those people in the hamlets that are across the border from An Phu.

"It is the Communists who collaborate with your leaders in Washington to give the enemy a safe place, and my leaders in Saigon are forced to say or do nothing because the United States pays all the bills. I don't understand it, Dai-uy, why your President lets the enemy have places of safe refuge when they are killing our people from those places?"

I told Major Le it was a terrible policy and that I was very happy that we did not have to honor their sanctuaries across from An Phu.

He then stood, asked that I join him in the briefing area, and led the way, mo-
tioning for me to take a seat. He slid the unclassified map of Vietnam aside and
pulled out a tactical map marked SECRET showing both friendly and enemy orders
of battle. "Sergeant Nguyen will carry the latest intelligence summary[4] to your team
sergeant after I have briefed you, Dai-uy. Pointing to the map, he continued, "As
you can see, the 261st VC battalion is now west of our FOB at Khanh Binh, and
the 267th VC battalion northwest of the same FOB. They have a strength of 950
VC with 81mm mortars, 57mm recoilless rifles, 3.5 rocket launchers and other
smaller mortars. Machine guns are in position and they are making preparations
to attack our 132 Strikers at Khanh Binh who have only 60mm mortars and .30
caliber machine guns, besides BARs, rifles and carbines to repel the invaders.

"North and northeast of Phu Hiep we have the 367th VC battalion with 400
men and the 260th VC heavy weapons company with 150 men which are in
position to attack our 132 man CIDG company in that FOB. Again, the VC
have vastly superior weapons and are located just inside Cambodia, except for one
infantry company belonging to the 367th that is now dug in above Phu Hiep just
inside our area behind a defensive minefield. They have placed thousands of pipe
mines and many poisoned punji traps among the groves of small trees and tall
bushes near the border. Between our FOB and the area the VC now occupy is a
flat, wide open space of tall grass maybe 400 meters in depth that we must cross
to attack them. The grass is not tall enough to conceal our advance, so it is a very
dangerous situation when we do not have supporting artillery or air power near
the border." "The VC have a foot hold in our area, Thieu-ta?" "Yes, it is not good.
Allow me to finish, please."

"Yes, Thieu-ta, and then I'd like to talk more about the situation north of
Phu Hiep."

"Sure, Dai-uy. I too want to discuss that problem. Looking toward the far north
tip of our district, we have, for the first time, gotten reports from our agents that
tell of a new threat in our area. It is the 512th VC heavy weapons battalion with
320 men and at least two anti-aircraft .50 caliber machine guns in addition to an
81mm mortar and 3.5 rocket launchers. The 512th is now located inside Cambodia north of the Bassac River from Khanh An and Khanh Hoa Villages in an area
never before used as a sanctuary.

"All of these units have been drawn together to form what they call the 'Southward Regiment' with over 1800 men. We are told that it is their plan to prepare
for an all-out attack on our northern areas. That is our report, Dai-uy. What do
you think about Phu Hiep?"

I told him that I wanted to lead an operation that would take back the area
north of Phu Hiep FOB and destroy the mines and punji traps.

Major Le agreed but thought it very risky with so many mines and the VC dug
in near the border. "But, it is perhaps more of a danger to do nothing." He asked
when I thought would be a good time to do such a plan. "After I know the area
and your men a little better." I told him, "I'd like to meet each of your company

commanders, visit the FOBs and the PF outposts on the border, meet the District Chief, and get acquainted with the lay of the land in the entire district before I lead the attack." I asked him if we could begin the next day.

Major Le smiled. "I will take you around camp this afternoon and you will meet three of our company commanders. We will begin the tour of the district at 1030 hours. As we go around the area in my jeep we will talk about what needs to be done in our civic action program and how important it is to the people of An Phu and to victory. The value of good psychological operations is something else we can discuss while we are between stops. Okay, Dai-uy?"

I nodded agreement. "Tell me about the intelligence net here in An Phu. How many men do the dangerous work of spying across the border?"

"No men, just 12 women. I train them personally."

"Why women?" I asked.

He told me of an informal agreement between the officials on both sides of the border near Khanh Binh that permitted women to cross the border in either direction during the daylight hours. "It is for shopping and also for visiting in the interest of good will between the neighboring peoples. When our women spies go across the bridge, they do much shopping to help conceal their real purpose for being there. They buy the ice, fresh fruit and vegetables we use in the FOB at Khanh Binh and bring it to our friends in the village marketplace where it is kept for us by the local people. They go back across the bridge in the afternoon and disappear into the sanctuaries where they spy on the VC units and make notes to report what is useful to us in our planning for both defense and offense. When they come back the next day they shop again for paper and other things like cooking oil for the FOB and return across the bridge."

"Sounds good, Thieu-ta. They must be very brave, these women. How do you get the reports from them?"

"Yes, they are very bold and we owe very much to their courage. When they return with the things they buy they hide the reports inside the bags or sew them into their clothing. They also stop and shop at the marketplace on our side of the border in Khanh Binh Village where our agent-handlers keep an eye out for them. From the marketplace to the FOB is a short distance with much cover and concealment that is needed to avoid detection by the VC who spy from their nearby Cambodian outpost. Very simple, Dai-uy. We have 12 good women who do this dangerous duty."

"It is very perilous work, Thieu-ta. Not for the timid or fearful. It must be particularly risky and take much longer to obtain information in the area north of the Bassac River and above Phu Hiep. Once our agents cross the bridge over the Binh Ghi Canal and are in Cambodia they must also cross the Bassac River. Is that a problem?"

"No, Dai-uy. There are no restrictions once they are safely inside Cambodia to keep them from going from one side of the river to the other and there are many ferries daily. Their National Police only watch the river for contraband and such."

"Good. Please tell me, Thieu-ta, how do you pay them? When I was in training I heard many bad stories about agents being paid by the number of enemy they report and giving false information to get paid more. Their reports were of no good use."

"Very simple, Dai-uy. We have 12 agents and six agent handlers. All of these people are paid a wage they can live on. The agents get paid a bonus that I determine on a case for case basis. If they give us reports that result in victory for us or allow us to better prepare for an attack we would not have otherwise known about, I reward them. I also take into consideration examples of extreme bravery, as when an agent is wounded in the act of getting a report to us that tells of an imminent attack."

"Sounds like you're doing it right and that our money is well spent. Speaking of doing it right, Lieutenant Kallunki has spoken to me about the serious situation involving your Strikers and the possibility of military tribunal action against them. How serious is the situation, Thieu-ta, and what can we do to resolve it and protect the CIDG?"

"It is very serious, Dai-uy, and I have asked to meet with the Minister of Defense to request amnesty for all Hoa Haos serving in the CIDG program."

"What do you think of their chances, Thieu-ta?"

"I believe we will win the amnesty. They have proven themselves in battle and have made the Province of Chau Doc a very secure province for all the people who live there. We also have a friend in IV Corps, Lieutenant General Quang Van Dang. I asked for his support in this matter of amnesty and he said he would speak with the Minister of Defense before my meeting with him in Saigon. We can trust General Dang. He is a friend of the Hoa Haos.

"When is your meeting?"

"At 1100 hours on 10 January in the Minister's office in Saigon. Will you come with me, Dai-uy?"

Feeling honored to be asked to go with him on such an important issue, I answered, "I will be proud to go with you, Thieu-ta. Let me know when we will leave camp and I will be ready."

"That is good, Dai-uy. That is good. Now it is time to show you our camp. Unless you have questions about what we have discussed, please follow me."

Pausing for a moment, he then led me through the back door of the building, out two paces and on up a set of seven concrete steps and into the command bunker. It was an impressive concrete block structure with a heavy wooden roof overlaid with two layers of sand bags to protect from incoming artillery rounds. A .50 caliber machine gun was positioned on the west wall, aimed toward Cambodia. This was where Major Le and I would come when there was trouble anywhere in An Phu. He pointed out that our communications bunkers were back-to-back and just below where we stood. He showed me two telephone handsets, located in wooden boxes with hinged doors on a narrow wall built into the center of the bunker. Those phones were our link to the outside world through the radio facilities in our respective commo bunkers.

"My communications supervisor is Tao and he works close with your man Eleam to keep all the radios and antenna systems working for us." Major Le advised, "It is what I call the 'heart beat' of our operation." He showed me how to access the handset.

I pointed to a third wooden box located between the phone boxes but different from the others in that it was secured by a heavy lock. "What's in that box?" I asked.

"When the American Seabees built this camp they placed demolition charges in each of the outer perimeter automatic weapons positions. He pointed out the positions we could see from where we stood. "In some CIDG camps they worry about the Strikers turning on the Green Berets. If a man turns his machine gun or BAR around and begins to shoot at us, we can blow him up at the pull of a switch." Pulling his key ring from a secure place on his belt, he unlocked it and opened the door. Inside were 28 switches. "Each one will blow up a machine gun or BAR position. It isn't something we need in Dan Nam because we are all Hoa Haos and the Hoa Haos do not attack each other or the American Green Berets.

"Look there, Dai-uy, between us and the outer perimeter, you will see all around us another 'inner perimeter' with 10 automatic weapon bunkers and barbed wire defenses. Only our two teams, our civilian workers and those whom we invite are permitted inside the inner compound.

Major Le then explained what comprised our 60 meter wide obstacle belt around the camp. There were five belts of triple concertina, four belts of double apron barbed wire, one belt of tanglefoot wire, a belt of claymore mines and a moat that was eight meters wide.

I was impressed and I told him so. "Thieu-ta, it would be tough fighting for even two battalions of VC to get through to us without losing most of their men to our fire." Major Le smiled, and then led me back down the steps and past the many buildings in camp, stopping near the moat where two Strikers were relieving themselves. That prompted me to ask Major Le, "Why don't your CIDG have a toilet and shower like we have?"

"Because the past team leaders of your team would not give me the money to build it, Dai-uy. I have the plans to build the tower, the toilet and the shower rooms. Will you approve the money I need?"

"Yes, Thieu-ta, and as a high priority. When you build it, have clean water piped to the new water tower from our tower. I don't want your people to think that we believe we deserve anything better than they do."

A broad grin now framing his face, Major Le said to me, "I know we will do good together, Dai-uy. I believe that you care about the Hoa Haos and that is a good thing. Please join me for dinner at our mess. When I return from subsector, I will call you."

With that, he turned and got into a waiting jeep and left camp through the front gate that opened onto a road leading directly to An Phu Village.

Strolling leisurely back to the front entrance of our camp headquarters, I noticed for the first time that the large cement planters situated on either side of the base of the camp flag pole had small topiary yew shrubs in them. Trimmed and trained to look like miniature deer with antlers, they were beautiful examples of someone's handiwork. From my position near the flagpole I could see climbing roses scrambling up latticework installed between the awnings along the front of the CIDG mess. The cascading beauty of the red roses and the delicate perfection of the topiary somehow seemed in harmony with the fact that we were there to win the peace, to provide a secure environment for the people and to enjoy the beauty as we now saw it.

Lieutenant Hanh, the LLDB administrative officer, noticed my interest in the roses as he was walking across the compound and he stopped to tell me, "The deer and the roses are the work of Major Le, Dai-uy. Do you approve?"

"Yes, Lieutenant Hanh, I approve and enjoy it. You?"

"Yes, Dai-uy, I like them very much."

"Lieutenant, would you tell me what CIDG companies are here in camp? Major Le has invited me to dinner and I would like to know more about the camp before I sit down with his officers in the mess."

He told me that the 441st with Lieutenant Thuan Hieu Nguyen commanding, the 443rd with Lieutenant Triet Van Tran, the 445th under Lieutenant Hong Khanh Luong, and the Recon Platoon with Sergeant Dung commanding, were in camp. Hanh added, "You should also know that Lieutenant Luong Hoang Le has his 442nd Company at the Khanh Binh FOB and Lieutenant Ang Ngoc Nguyen commands the 444th at Phu Hiep."

I wrote everything down on 3x5 cards as he spoke, and when we were done, thanked him for the information.

I was ready now for my first experience in a Hoa Hao mess and I was prepared mentally for anything they might serve this now hungry man. At least I thought I was!

* * * * *

Looking out over inner perimeter machine gun bunker, drop zone, and at outer perimeter corner machine gun bunker. Cambodia is behind tree line.

CAMBODIA

4.2" Mortar & ammo. Taken after first fire mission into VC Sanctuaries in Cambodia. Note large cracks in concrete base.

CHAPTER 4
TAKING THE WAR TO CAMBODIA

At five minutes past midnight on 1 January 1966 the deafening roar of a maximum powder charge hurling the first of ten 4.2" high explosive rounds more than 5000 meters into what had, until this moment, been the enemy's safe-haven in Cambodia, signaled the beginning of our new TOP SECRET initiative that would deny our enemy its heretofore unjust and deadly tactical advantage. "It is good, Dai-uy," shouted Major Le, as we all savored the moment, "It is very good."

At 1830 hours on 27 December 1965 Major Le stopped by my office where I had waited his return from a meeting with Captain Nguyen at sub-sector. We then walked together across the drill field to join his men for dinner. Lieutenants Triet Tran, Hong Luong and Thuan Nguyen met us just inside the metal-roofed building that served as the mess hall and recreation center for the CIDG. The dining area covered the largest area with square-legged, rugged looking tables and checkered oilcloths that boasted a latticework and rose pattern. The most that could be seated at one time was 150, Major Le explained, and each of the three 132 man companies in camp were scheduled to eat in 30 minute shifts.

The kitchen was located in the rear of the building and opened out into a large lean-to where a variety of food was being broiled on the grate of a large, above ground barbecue pit. My stomach juices started flowing as the aroma of spicy barbecue sauce used in basting everything being prepared for dinner reached my nostrils. I watched as a large hog, maybe 70 pounds with head and innards removed, 50 chicken halves and a dozen snakes were being turned and basted with that sweet-and-sour sauce that I'd come to love. Cooked and dressed, and in trays placed on tables in a serving area between the kitchen and where we sat, was another pig, perhaps six dozen of what looked like squirrels, bowls of rice, greens, onions and sauces. Last, but not least, was a table covered with sliced watermelons.

I followed behind Major Le and filled my plate the same as he did his with a little of everything. Once seated with Major Le and his Lieutenants, I determined to do as they did. Eating everything with both hands like it was all finger food. As we ate, we tossed fat, scraps, even bones, on the floor for the dogs, their in-house cleanup crew, to eat or carry off. No knives or forks, only spoons were used during the meal. Everything tasted good. The barbecue sauce was especially zesty, making the pork, chicken and squirrel just that much better. As I ate the last morsel of what I thought to be squirrel, Major Le glanced across the table and asked, "Do you want more of that, Dai-uy?"

"The squirrel?" I asked. "There are no squirrels in An Phu, Dai-uy. What you eat is field rat we trap for food out in the rice paddies." They all sat there, listening, waiting my reaction, my response. When he said it was rat, I wanted to bolt from my seat, run outside and vomit. I knew better, and besides it had tasted good, real good. I smiled, nodded, and two more of the rodents were quickly placed on my plate. Finishing it as I would a squirrel, I noticed Major Le and his officers glance at each other and smile. I knew then that I'd just passed my first test!

As the weeks and months passed, Major Le and I would have a bit of fun with those few senior American officers who would visit by helicopter when there was a break in the local combat action. They would come for the sole purpose of getting their "out in the boonies with the Green Beret warriors" ticket punched. They would ask to tour the camp, eat with the Strikers, and have a picture taken with them in the command bunker, mortar pit, or machine-gun bunker to send home, pretending to have been here during a battle with the Viet Cong. Major Le or I would make certain, as they were in the middle of munching on what they too thought to be squirrel, that they learned what it really was. I can't recall any visitor of that nature that was able to maintain his composure when faced with that revelation. Instead, we would witness a desperate rush to exit the building and then hear the sound of those same visitors emptying their innards outside the mess. They would leave shortly thereafter - as soon as they could muster their chopper.

All of us in my A Team normally ate in our own mess in the team house, bought our own groceries, hired our own cook and pulled our own KP. It was always a special treat to eat in the CIDG mess, usually when celebrating a major victory or on those rare and wonderful occasions when we were invited, either individually or as a team, to join them in what was always a feast to remember!

At 0800 the next day, with a breakfast of eggs and toast smothered with honey filling my stomach cavity, I called my team together to discuss my meeting with

Major Le. I told Val to brief John Eleam, who was in the commo bunker, later. Before Lieutenant Kallunki sat down he handed me a ring of keys that fit the locks in the command bunker demolition switch boxes. "I'm glad to get these out of my hands," he told me. "Just the thought of pulling one of those switches and killing our own Strikers is enough to make me sick. It's up to you and Thieu-ta now. I'd rather have that decision in someone else's hands than mine."

I shared my thoughts regarding our Strikers, "You men know the Hoa Haos better than I do but I want to get to know them like the back of my hand. One worry we don't have is that our strikers will turn on us. We have a huge job to do there and we have to do 24 men's work with just the seven of us." Our challenge was to do our best with what we had. I asked Val to give me a run-down on our little "navy." He was ready. With a grin, he pulled a paper from his clipboard and pushed it across the table to me. The title read, "Facilities, Weapons, and Equipment Status: 28 December 1965."[1] It contained everything I needed to know about the physical assets of Camp Dan Nam and our two FOBs, including our "floating inventory." We had 14 Assault boats, seven of them with 25HP Evinrude motors and seven with 40HP Mercury motors; 50 Sampans with $7 1/2$HP Briggs & Stratton long stem motors which were parceled out ten per CIDG Company and 200 Sampans without motors with 40 in each company. We also had one Barge that had a $2 1/2$ ton truck motor with a six speed transmission as its inboard powerhouse. "The barge is our quick reaction boat" Val said. "We load on an 81MM mortar with two basic loads of HE and WP rounds, two machine guns with eight to 10 cans of metal-link-belt ammo and a dozen Strikers. Our barge can pass anything, even an assault boat, to get us where we're needed. Tell you the truth, Dai-uy, we've never put her in 5th gear yet!"

"Sounds like a real winner, Val. Where did you get it?" Val told me how an agent's tip gave Major Le cause to have his men, along with a national police officer, stop and board the barge on the Bassac River just east of Bac Nam Island in front of the Phu Loi PF outpost. "Turns out the owner had it loaded with food and medicine headed for the VC base at Bung Ven. The barge was confiscated and we just put it to good use." Val smiled.

"Nice going. It's good getting to know you and what we have to work with a little better. I want to talk things out as a team whenever time and circumstances permit. I'll always listen to what you have to say, then I'll talk over tactical matters with Thieu-ta to take advantage of his combat experience and wisdom. But when push comes to shove, I make the decisions. In 1956 I was a Sergeant First Class in the 82nd Airborne Division and worked for an officer by the name of Captain Harry Corkill. He was a mustang[2] and had seen a lot of combat in the Pacific as a Marine corporal in WW II. He called me Marv, and as a Captain he held down a Lieutenant Colonel's position as the Division Supply Officer. When he first called me into his office to brief me on his modus operandi, he spoke very matter-of-factly."

"Marv," he said, "when I call you in to give you direction and tell you what I want done, you tell me right then and there if you think you know of a better way. As we discuss the matter, if I raise my voice, you may raise yours in response. When I speak slow and lower the volume, you will do the same. Once the discussion is over I will excuse you. When you leave this office, no matter what the final decision is and no matter if it's my way, your way, or some place in between, you will act as if it were the only decision, the best decision, and get the job done. Is that understood?"

"Yes, Sir," I answered and I was a better soldier for having listened and learned that day. Once I'd proved myself to him, he saw to it that I had the opportunity to step up a notch to work under Lieutenant Colonel Helen Bouffier, the XVIII Airborne Corps G-4. That fine lady was an excellent logistician and leader. Within a few months she sent me to Third Army to work for the G-4. Shortly after having arrived I was told to report to the Commanding General of Third Army for an interview. Based on his recommendation I received a direct commission to First Lieutenant under a special program for a limited number of outstanding NCOs. "How Colonel Corkill handled our relationship is how I want things to function around here. I'll put together a new mission[3] and forces paper and post it on the bulletin board in the morning. Any questions?"

There were none so I asked Val to meet me in my office in an hour and walk me around the outer perimeter defensive mound, show me the ammo bunkers and supply room and tour the rest of the camp so I'd get a feel for what's out there. "It'll give me a good idea of what we've got to deal with on a day to day basis."

"Sounds good to me, Dai-uy. I'll brief John Eleam right away and see you at 0930."

On schedule Val stopped by and we headed out past the LLDB team house and onto the defensive earth mound that surrounded the camp. Just as we got started, a helicopter set down on our landing zone pad behind the aid station.

Sergeant Tenorio appeared out of the back door to the aid station, ran to the chopper and grabbed a bag handed him by the crew. "That's our mail run, Dai-uy, and once a week the PX chopper is sent our way. Can't come in if any of our area is under attack, but we're happy anytime it gets here. It just brings the essentials, Dai-uy: shaving cream, razor blades, deodorant, shampoo and all that kind of stuff." As we began our walk along the berm, a young Striker popped out of his sandbag and reinforced concrete machine-gun bunker, snapped to attention, smiled, saluted and said "Chao Dai-uy." I returned his salute and said "Chao Ong."

It was a beautiful day, the sun was shining, and I was impressed with the attitude and military bearing of each of the CIDG machine gunners, BAR men and riflemen as well. Looking out across the wide belt of outer defenses, including an eight meter wide moat and barbed wire obstacles of every description, I noticed something that hadn't been mentioned in the status report. It was "phugas," the common name for homemade napalm. The deadly mixture was positioned in 55 gallon drums every 25-30 meters around the perimeter in front of automatic weapons bunkers and snug up to the earthen mound. Detonated by the man in the position under attack, it would cover a large, fan-shaped area with molten spray that would burn through light clothing, adhere to the skin and critically injure anyone in its path. Like any other serious injury it placed a demand on others in the attacking force to remove those who were incapacitated from the scene for medical treatment.

> *The undated **Improvised Munitions Handbook** published by Frankfort Arsenal in Philadelphia, was used at the Special Warfare Center at Fort Bragg in the Spring of 1964 to train those of us who attended the Guerrilla Warfare course. We learned how to produce "jelled flame fuels" for use in close-in defense "phugas" systems such as we had at Camp Dan Nam.*

Val continued to guide me around the camp facilities including the CIDG barracks and supply room, finishing up in the camp aid station where we were greeted by Sergeant Kuchen. Sergeant Tenorio, our senior medic, was out on medical patrol. The aid station was well organized, clean and equipped with a sink, running water, two wooden operating tables, screened doors and two single pedestal instrument holding stands, a practical piece of equipment when tending the wounded.

Sergeant Kuchen, looking proud about what he was to say, told me, "One day each week we open the aid station to treat wives and children of our Strikers who are in camp."

"Good," I told him. "Whatever we can do to assist the people helps to build trust. Keep up the good work."

I turned to Sergeant Val, "Thanks for showing me around, Val. I'd better get ready for my tour of the district. Meet me in the operations center at 1025."

Major Le, a veteran of 18 years as a combat leader was as punctual as I thought he'd be. As Val and I stepped out of the front door of the operations center at exactly 1030 hours Major Le got in and sat behind the wheel of his Jeep, glanced at his watch, looked up at us and smiled.

I saluted, greeted him with, "Chao, Thieu-ta," and got in on the right side. A bodyguard and a radio operator with a PRC-10 radio were seated in the back. Major Le's Jeep was of Korean War vintage and looked to be well maintained, as were all camp vehicles, generators, boat motors and any other mechanical equipment I'd seen during my tour with Val. He told me that it was a father and son team who took care of all that "stuff."

Val followed in a ¾ ton truck with his friend, LLDB Team Sergeant Nguyen, standing next to the driver with his Thompson submachine gun at the ready. Eight well-armed Strikers rode in the back as a security force.

When we entered the village of An Phu, Major Le's popularity was evident as everyone who saw us coming, old and young alike, smiled and waved greetings to their military leader. Major Le looked almost regal in his starched and pressed tiger suit, green beret, polished leather shoulder holster and metal-framed sunglasses. We drove slowly and carefully past the busy marketplace. He held his head high, smiled and waved, especially to the children at their mother's side who were too young to be in school at that hour. Nothing staged here, just local people letting him know they admired and respected him.

Hundreds of people from all around the district mingled and shopped at the many tent stalls. It was a social event as well as morning market. There were men and women happily haggling with smiling vendors over fresh squid, chicken, snakes, pork, fish and even the rice-paddy rats. Others sold watermelon, a favorite of the Hoa Haos and us too, sugar beets, short stalks of sugar cane and bottles of homemade sweet drinks. Hot foods, from fried fish to sweet waffles, were hawked from three-wheeled vending carts, each with its own charcoal burner. The women wore full-length black pants and long sleeved blouses with their heads protected by large, conical rice-straw hats.

All ages of women were represented here, but most of the men were very old, except for the National Policemen with their distinctive white hats and snappy uniforms. There were also off-duty CIDG fighters enjoying the festive atmosphere of market. Still, everyone seemed to be going about their daily routine as if war were but a distant danger. "You will see, Dai-uy, as we go through all the villages in the area how the people respect the LLDB and the CIDG. They will always greet us warmly. It is because our men behave themselves as soldiers should among the people whom they are here to protect."

As he drove out of the market area, he turned south along the river and past the district headquarters building complex which included the barracks for two RF companies. "I am anxious for you to meet Captain Tuoi Van Nguyen, our district chief. He, his staff and the men in his two companies of Regional Forces are also highly regarded by the people and they too are all Hoa Haos."

Major Le then drove further south to where our boat dock was situated on the Bassac River and introduced me to Sergeant Dung, our reconnaissance platoon leader. Dung was in the middle of planning a river reconnaissance operation with Map Map, the leader of our assault boat and barge operators. We stopped only long enough to exchange handshakes and greetings, leaving them to finish their planning. "Sergeant Dung is a brave and loyal man who needs little supervision," Major Le advised, "It is good that he knows his business and how to lead men. It is a very important mission that he has and it takes a load off my back.

"So, you see, Dai-uy, we have good rapport with the people and because of that I have an excellent relationship with many old-aged men in the villages. Anytime, anywhere, they will give me information about the enemy activities around the border, even on the other side, because they are of such an age that they can go across the border to fish. Younger men, as you know, cannot cross the border into Cambodia.

"They also help me to maintain good relations with the people by giving me the 'most important information' about the behavior and activities of our Strikers in the villages, good or bad, so I can better handle the situation."

He went on to tell me, "The old-aged men do not get any pay. Now and then I offer them some small gift such as tea, sugar, or what they may need for basic survival. We have a deep respect for each other."

As we moved slowly north on the river road Major Le told me about the Hoa Haos. "About 90 percent of our people are cultivators. Growing rice is their main career, but every family has a mixed career. Besides rice, they can grow all kinds of vegetables and some have fruit trees, while others catch fish, raise beef cattle, pigs and chickens. Of course the cattle are raised to sell in the Chau Doc market only because the Hoa Hao does not eat beef.

"Each family in the countryside has a small piece of land around the house and they can make money selling what they grow or raise. There is also a small number of people who have built bat houses where they collect the droppings of the bats, dry it and sell it as a fertilizer we call 'guano.' It is very good fertilizer for growing many kinds of vegetables."

We turned around and headed north, back through the village and up a narrow tree-lined dirt road, their shade a welcome relief from the heat of the day. We passed through several hamlets of neatly kept, thatched-roof houses set on either side of the road alongside the gently flowing Bassac River. Boats of every shape and description were either navigating the river or pulled up to the shore near the homes of their owners, with men in and around them making repairs, mending nets, or loading goods. Most of these men, Major Le explained, were Popular Force soldiers who worked in the daylight hours and manned the local PF outposts and other local defenses during the night.

Children playing in the shaded yards waved as we drove by. Women were out sweeping the space between their homes and the middle of the road, smiling and apparently happy keeping their area neat and tidy. A tribute to their self-motivated efforts was the fact that I did not see a trace of litter or garbage anywhere we went that day.

About one and a half kilometers beyond the hamlet of Phuoc Khanh, Major Le pulled over to the side of the road and stopped, making room for animal drawn cart traffic to pass. Sergeant Nguyen's vehicle pulled in just behind us and he ordered his men to form a protective crescent between our Jeep and the river. Major Le pointed to a small outpost situated to our left and then located it for me on a tactical map he'd pulled from his shirt pocket. "This is the Dong Co Ki PF Outpost, Dai-uy. We are 14 kilometers from camp, and as you see, the only way we can re-supply or bring a reaction force to reinforce the FOB or counter an attack by the enemy from their safe-havens against the PF outpost at Khanh An and the FOB at Khahn Binh areas is on this road or by boat up the river." Pointing to the east and across the river to a second PF Outpost, he continued, "That is the Phu Loi PF Outpost. The river is very wide here, almost 500 meters, and these two outposts guard our critical approaches to the north."

"I understand, Thieu-ta." Looking northward up the river, I asked, "What is that island I see just up the river? Who controls it, us or them? I can understand how it could be a problem if it were in the enemy's hands."

"It is no-man's land, Dai-uy. My government and the government of Cambodia both claim it. Once there were many houses for fishermen and their families on

Bac Nam but it is now a dangerous place and nobody lives there." Pointing to a small island between Vietnam and Cambodia, he went on to tell me, "It is only maybe 20 meters from the Cambodian VC sanctuary area to that small island and then the same distance to Bac Nam Island. We are certain they move to Bac Nam at night from Cambodia to spy on us."

It was obvious that keeping this narrow but crucial corridor open and secure was a priority concern. The VC strategy to take An Phu would logically be an attack from the north against Khanh Binh, Khanh An and Phu Hiep. To keep us from sending a reaction force the VC would have to send a force to block our way north at where we now stood.

"You can see on the map that Lake Thien Lon is a large natural obstacle that runs from just north of this outpost west to the Cambodian border. It is an average of 500 meters wide. They would not dare to try to cross that wide open space where we could pick them off from trenches on the south side of the lake like they were sitting ducks."

"Very true, Thieu-ta. How strong are these outposts?"

"Maybe 40 men in each one, but they must send out three or four night ambush patrols of three men each to secure their area. That would leave no more than two dozen men to defend the outpost. They could defend longer and much better if they had the weapons they need.

"Why do you say that, Thieu-ta?"

"Because they have no real firepower, no mortars or machine guns. They have only old carbines. It is also very important that we keep the river and the road open for refugees. If the VC attack north of Lake Thien Lon, as many as 8,000 of our people will become refugees and they must have a way to move south to live by our camp where we can help and protect them."

I asked Major Le if he had the people to train the PF on mortars and machine guns if we could get some to them. "Yes, Dai-uy, to train is no problem."

"I'll do what I can." I made a few notes on a 3X5 card and stuffed it in my pocket. I'd tell Sergeant Val to get the weapons as soon as we got back to camp.

Major Le smiled, started his Jeep and we continued on north. I asked him about joint operations between our camp and the adjacent camp to the west at Tan Chau, near the Mekong River. "How do we coordinate border defense and intelligence?"

He glanced at me, his face expressionless. "We don't, Dai-uy. The VC do not bother our sister camp. We will visit them soon and you will then understand why that is true." After a brief pause, he added, "All Tan Chau intelligence reports go to your B Team in Chau Doc. If the B Team thinks we need to know what has been reported to them they will send it to you."

I thanked Major Le and then, as we were approaching the hamlet of An Thanh, I was suddenly overcome with the most foul odor I'd ever encountered. "What is that stink, Thieu-ta?" I asked.

He laughed out loud and stopped at the base of a few tall palm trees. "Look up there, Dai-uy, that is a bat house like I told you about before."

About 20 feet above the ground was a structure that was somehow attached to those trees. "I don't understand, Thieu-ta. How does it work?"

"You see the framework up there, Dai-uy. On top is a roof with a peak made of bamboo to protect the bats from the rain and to keep the sun from making it too hot inside. There is a closely-knit frame about three feet below the roof and they tie thousands of four foot long palm fronds for the bats to hang on as they sleep in the daylight hours." Then he pointed to what I'd noticed when we first stopped, a bamboo mat partially covered with the bat droppings. "The droppings fall onto these mats, are taken up, dried, packaged and sold in the market."

Having learned all I needed to know about guano and wanting fresh air, I told Major Le I was ready to go. He grinned, started his jeep, and within ten minutes we were in Khanh An Village where the Binh Ghi Canal joined the Bassac River. Major Le pointed to the bridge crossing the border canal where the women shoppers and the old fishermen were permitted to go across during daylight hours. Major Le stopped the Jeep and suggested that we walk through the village, meet some of the people and have tea.

As we slowly strolled down the street his Jeep followed with one of the bodyguards driving. Major Le told me that the National Police were tough and vigilant with the river traffic. The VC seldom tried to bring war goods into Cambodia on the Bassac. "But there are two areas we watch closely, Dai-uy. The canal in front of you winds like a snake from here all the way to where it goes into the Chau Doc River. There are more than seven good crossing sites between here and Lake Thien Lon and there are many houses and trees on both sides of the canal with dense undergrowth to mask any movement. The other bad area is the wetland area between Phu Hiep and Phu Loi, where three kilometers of deep grass could easily conceal hundreds of VC."

He told me about the curfew in effect during the hours of darkness and how it helped to secure the border. "We have many night ambush patrols, each is always in a different place, our CIDG are well disciplined for night operations, having no problem maintaining total silence. With binoculars we can detect any movement in the dark of the night if there is any part of the moon visible." I would learn on my first night ambush just how true that was.

We came to a small, open-front cafe. A neat place with a raised wooden floor, it boasted six small tables that sat four and an atmosphere of congeniality. We were served Oolong tea and sugar wafers by the owner who was a pudgy, happy sort. Sitting and sipping tea we could look out toward the west, across the nearby border canal, and see a Cambodian PF Outpost that was less than 400 meters distant. I wondered how the civilians on either side of the border could deal with the fact of the sanctuaries and of the potential danger they faced. It had to have been on their minds, yet to look at them and talk with them it was as if their trust in Major Le and his fighters allayed all of their fears. Major Le's face mirrored my concern as he told me, "I am afraid for our people on the border, Dai-uy. When the big attack comes this will be a dangerous place. They know the VC are across the canal to their west and across the Bassac River to the north and also to the east, but they trust us to protect them because we have done so in the past. We have to do what we can to secure the border, but we have never faced so many of the enemy. I think we will see the border canal flow red with blood before Spring season is past."

Now in a very sober mood, we finished our tea and drove on to the FOB, just two kilometers south on the road that paralleled the border canal. Lieutenant Hoang Luong Le, the FOB commander, met us at the entrance to the main building, a former Buddhist Temple. The western wall of the old temple was so close to the road, and beyond that the Binh Ghi canal and Cambodia, that it permitted only one belt of triple concertina and a four foot high woven barbed wire fence to be installed between the building and a would-be attacker. We toured the FOB and I found the spirit of the men to be very high. The defensive fortifications appeared adequate except for that area I'd first noticed. The weaponry, however, was inadequate, in my judgment. "Having no long range weapons here is bad in my judgment, especially knowing we can get no air or artillery support this close to the border," I told Major Le and the FOB Commander. "We should have an 81MM mortar up here." I asked Major Le, "Can you get a mortar crew together in the morning to man it?"

With a look of surprise that turned to one of delight, Major Le answered, "Yes, Dai-uy. I must tell you that I have asked many times in the past for this to take place but my request was always refused because there were not enough Americans to send a mortar crew to Khanh Binh and I was told that an 81MM mortar must be manned by Americans. Do you have more men coming to your team tomorrow?"

"I hope to get more some day, but I don't know when or how many for certain. One big change now, Thieu-ta, is that An Phu is now an independent operation and I make the decisions. I will give you an 81MM mortar for Khanh Binh if you provide the crew. Sergeant Valenzuela will train them. Okay, Thieu-ta?"

"For certain, Dai-uy. Sergeant Hung will coordinate with your team sergeant for the training. We should return to camp soon so we can make arrangements." With that we got back into the Jeep and returned to camp. On the way back we discussed the enemy situation, agreeing on the need for some depth in our fields of fire to force the enemy back farther from the border, and decided to also place an 81MM mortar with LLDB crew at the Phu Hiep FOB as soon as his men were qualified.

"Maybe tomorrow we can visit Phu Hiep and take them their 81MM mortar and crew and ask Sergeant Valenzuela to train them at the FOB. Okay, Dai-uy?"

"Good idea, Thieu-ta."

On the way back to camp I asked Major Le, "What are some of the things I should look out for or remember to do when I am out in the district? Are there any taboos or customs I should recognize and deal with so I do not hurt any Hoa Hao feelings?"

"Our customs are not much different from yours. I think you must have been taught at Fort Bragg to have good manners with the Vietnamese, because I have noticed in the past how most of your Green Berets try very hard to get along well with our people.

"As far as customs go, you should be especially kind to old people, women and children and you should always take your hat off when you go into a temple or into someone's home. Unless you have a weapon and are prepared for battle, you should also take your hat off and say hello to any old man that you pass by.

"If the people like you, and you will be invited into many of their homes to have some tea, maybe even some fruits. You should accept at least some of the invitations, Dai-uy. When you step inside you should not sit next to the most respectful ancestor table in the middle of the home. That is where the family worships their parents and ancestors. Then there is another place where you should not sit unless you are asked to. If they ask you to sit there, you will know that they have come to respect you. That place is in front of the ancestor table and is a plank bed or a round or rectangular table.

"There are two kinds of temples. Each village has a temple to worship a famous man whom they believe to be a genius. The temple in Chau Phu village is to honor General Nguyen Huu Canh, past advisor to the Cambodian King. It was General Nguyen who commanded the troops and the people who dug the Vinh Te canal in the 18th century. The other kind of temple is built for the people to worship a special genius or virgin who can take care of them about health matters."

"Thank you, Thieu-ta, I want to do right by you and your people. It is important to me, and what you've told me will help me to do better."

Back in my team dining area I gathered the men for a brief meeting about firepower in the FOBs and the PF outposts at Don Co Ki and Phu Loi. Both medics were out on a hamlet medical patrol and John Eleam was in the commo bunker, so I was joined by my XO, Team Sergeant and Specialist Menkins.

I told them of my decision to send 81MM mortars to Khanh Binh and Phu Hiep with LLDB crews. I also wanted to get at least one 60MM mortar and a .30 caliber machine gun to each of the two PF outposts that guarded our reaction force and resupply routes to the northern area. The 5th Group policy that required Americans man the 81MM mortars was mentioned and I quickly reminded them that we were now an independent operation and that I'd been told we would have no back up or fire support across the border. "We must do everything we can to build up our defenses. Even with what we are doing we'll have to rely more on courage and fighting skills than on what we have in crew-served weapons."

Menkins chimed in, "It makes me sick, Dai-uy. North of there and not more than two kilometers from the border are four VC battalions with eight 81MM mortars, a dozen 57MM recoilless rifles, five .50 caliber machine guns and 3.5 rocket launchers up the gazoo and they plan to attack us when they are ready. We should get whatever we can for those guys who'll be doing the fighting and the dying. Everyone on up the line all the way to Nha Trang knows we're outnumbered five to one in the north. They know the VC are setting back there safe and sound inside Cambodia building up for the day they'll swarm across that border and try to wipe us off the face of the map. I say let's do it, Dai-uy, let's give 'em some more muscle!"

"What if Major Williford inspects the district," Kallunki asked, "and sees those mortars without any Americans around?."

"I won't let him go near the northern area. You can count on that. Let me quote to you a few words I heard General Yarborough speak in April 1964 when he addressed my class in the Special Forces Officer's Course. He told us 'I don't want officers that have to follow regulations to get a job done. I want people who can operate from their hip pocket.' Listen up, men, it's hip pocket time in An Phu."

Lieutenant Kallunki spoke up, saying, "I'll take action on the 81s, Dai-uy. They'll be on the way in the morning." Menkins followed, saying, "I'll see what I can scare up for the PF outposts, Dai-uy. I'll need to see some friends of mine in the depot near Saigon."

"Tell Sergeant Nguyen what your mission is and ask him to get you a squad of CIDG and two assault boats to take you down to the Saigon depot. Make sure you take a radio and enough gas and chow to get you there and back. I'm sorry nobody else from our team is going with you, but we can't spread ourselves any thinner. Don't stop by or even radio the B Team or Can Tho. Just get there as fast as you can and bring back what you went for."

The meeting over, everyone went about doing what had to be done. Team Sergeant Val told me they'd gotten a John Wayne western movie along with the mail today. We'll be watching it tonight, just outside from you're sitting."

"What time, Val?"

"Soon's it gets dark, Dai-uy. Eleam will set it up. We all take our chairs and so do the LLDB. We put up a sheet on a frame made from 2x4s and set it up so we can all watch it from the inner compound and the Strikers can watch it from their side in the outer compound."

"They see it backwards?"

"Sure do, Dai-uy, and they love it."

At 2010 hours I watched as John Eleam waved the signal telling us that he was ready. He had the speakers set up so we'd hear best from our side. The Strikers didn't understand English and yet they still could hear the music good enough as background. Bac-si Tenorio watched the movie with the Strikers in the outer compound. He spoke enough Vietnamese to translate those parts when the action didn't necessarily help the viewer to understand what was being said. There was plenty of action on the screen to draw a flurry of excited uproars on both sides of the screen. Major Le sat next to me and let me know that western films were the favorite of the Strikers. "John Wayne, he is very special," Major Le commented.

I agreed.

At 0830 hours on 29 December, four LLDB NCOs with a security party of 30 Strikers headed north in a three vehicle convoy, carrying an 81MM mortar, a

14 day supply of ammunition, and all the gear they would need to set up in the Khanh Binh FOB.

At the same time, Major Le and I, with Sergeant Kuchen and nine Strikers in three assault boats departed the boat dock headed north toward Phu Hiep. Our barge had gone ahead, escorted by 12 Strikers from the recon platoon in three assault boats. The barge carried Phu Hiep FOB's new four man LLDB mortar crew, an 81MM mortar, a two week supply of ammunition and all the day-to-day needs to house and support the LLDB fire team.

Three kilometers north on the Bassac River we passed the Vinh Loi PF outpost that dominated the eastern bank. A solitary masonry building with a clay tile pagoda style roof stood in the middle of a square compound surrounded by a high stone wall. At the two corners of the compound overlooking the river, two large stone towers guarded the approach to this bastion of paramilitary strength.

When we were five kilometers further along we slowed and turned into the narrow Co Lau River, passing the Phu Huu PF Outpost located high on the south side of the river at a hairpin turn. Two PF fighters waved from atop a corner machine gun bunker. Another waved from his vantage point on the roof of the larger of two concrete buildings that comprised the outpost. Hundreds of sharpened bamboo stakes, firmly anchored in the ground at river's edge, formed an impressive first line of defense against would-be-attackers. Beyond that tight belt of punji stakes the bank rose almost straight up for about 3 meters to a $1\frac{1}{2}$ meter high fence of steel posts interlaced with barbed wire. It appeared to be impregnable from ground attack.

Map Map, on order from Major Le, slowed our boat to a stop and permitted it to drift in toward the punji staked area. "I will show you a defense that the outpost leader designed himself." Tapping me on the shoulder, he said, "Look close where I am pointing, Dai-uy and you will see something peculiar to this outpost."

I leaned over the bow, peered at the spot he was pointing to and saw the tips of huge punji stakes barely breaking the surface of the water. Continuing my gaze toward the center of the river I saw more punjis, now below the surface of the water. The design is meant to prevent VC from sneaking up close in sampans to surprise the sentinels. The fire-hardened bamboo would rip the bottoms of those lightweight boats.

"A tribute to the ingenuity of that outpost leader," I suggested.

"You will learn, Dai-uy, that each outpost has different defenses and each is a result of the thinking of its leader."

We turned onto the Co Lau River, a twisting tributary of the Bassac, and wound our way through eight kilometers of marsh and jungle to the FOB at Phu Hiep. Map Map piloted our lead boat, ever watchful for signs of enemy activity on either bank of the river. "Map Map has a good wife and eight children." Major Le told me, "He has led the boat operators with an iron hand, yet he has also seen to their welfare in good times and bad. He is a fine leader." Map Map opened the throttle and increased our speed as we entered a five kilometer uninhabited stretch of the river, an area ripe for ambush with heavy vegetation on either bank to conceal potential attackers. Fortunately, there were none that day.

Soon the most intriguing hamlet of Phu Hoa, a Cham settlement of about 200, appeared on our left. Jungle growth gave way to cleared fields. The unusual domed haystacks raised on stilts and thatched-roof dwellings joined to cattle shelters were symbolic of the unique culture of the Chams. The Chams once ruled here when this area was part of the Kingdom of Siam. A short-statured bronze-skinned people of Malaysian and Polynesian origin, their women were known for exceptional grace and beauty with long, flowing, black hair and delicate features. Major Le told me they were a hard working, honest people who kept to themselves. This was not surprising since they now lived in the midst of the Hoa Haos, a culture whose traditions were much different than theirs.

Lieutenant Ang Ngoc Nguyen, the commander of the 444th Company that now manned the FOB, met us at their boat dock. It was a rather flimsy-looking arrangement of bamboo poles tied to one another that somehow, as if by a miracle, bore the weight of our numbers with but a few creaks and groans.

Two separate bands of barbed wire obstacles were in place around the FOB, with the area between the barriers used as temporary shelters for Striker families. It was a bizarre sight: children playing and mothers hanging wash on the barbed concertina wire that hemmed them in as if they were prisoners and not the families of the defenders. An amazing people the Hoa Haos were, able to make the best of any circumstance so long as they were together as families and could feel the comfort and promise of the bigger family of Hoa Haos; all were smiling and waving to Major Le as soon as they were aware of his presence. Lieutenant Nguyen, noting my concerned expression, told me, "Do not worry, Dai-uy, at the first hint of an attack, the women and children come inside under safe cover of the buildings." He then told me with a proud smile, "many will join their husbands in the trenches and help them by loading ammunition into the clips of their weapons when we are under attack."

"You have brave women, Lieutenant," I remarked.

I would come to know the Hoa Haos as the most courageous, honorable, family-centered people I would ever meet, even to the time of writing this book. Their fierce determination and loyalty to each other and to their Hoa Hao heritage were unequivocal and indeed, admirable. Major Phoi Van Le, my counterpart and my hero, was and is yet the finest leader of men, the most courageous of soldiers and the wisest of military combatants and tacticians I'd ever been blessed to serve with.

A former PF Outpost, the FOB was an impressive, though small, low-profile defensive fortress. Six open-front, metal covered, pole buildings stood in the triangular compound. Each set of two buildings had direct access to the concrete block parapet built atop an earthen rampart. The parapets joined at each point of the triangle to form concrete machine-gun bunkers. The bunkers appeared as three tall sentinels, guardians of peace, with excellent fields of fire and a view to the north across wide-open vistas that any attacking force would need to cross if they were to achieve victory and take Phu Hiep. Like the wheat field at Gettysburg, any movement across that area would bring heavy casualties on any force foolish enough to attack, especially during daylight hours.

Major Le hadn't come here merely to show me around the area. It was close enough to the end of the month that I'd given him the funds to pay the Strikers in this least accessible of our FOBs. Each Striker had a pay card with his picture on the front cover, together with his name, rank, unit assignment, and serial number. Inside were two pay logs, each one covering a calendar year, where the amount paid and the initials of the Striker showing receipt of the money were entered. The back cover contained a certification of the man's assignment to Camp Dan Nam, signed by Major Le. A Striker would not be paid without a pay card.

The system was set up for the American officer to disburse the pay. I thought it best to enhance and further solidify Major Le's position with his troops if he were to do the paying and I were to oversee the procedure. I worked side-by-side with him to calculate the monthly payroll and then gave him the funds to disburse during the last three days of the month. My philosophy, which he shared, was to make certain they had their money in time, knowing the enemy might keep us on our toes defending the area on the last day of the month and cause a potential morale problem if their families did not have the funds they needed to survive.

The strikers and their families seemed in very high spirits, which spoke well of their loyalty and determination under the primitive living conditions imposed at Phu Hiep. We arrived back in camp near noon, in time for lunch. Relaxing with a cup of coffee after a hearty meal of chicken and rice, I noticed a small camera on the table in front of my XO. It was like I'd seen many of our Strikers with at Khanh Binh and Phu Hiep. "What kind of camera is that, John?"

"It's called a 'Pen double E', Dai-uy. The Counter-insurgency support Office in Okinawa had them made in Japan just for SF. It's what they call a half-frame camera and it is the most simple thing to operate that you've ever seen. All you do is point it and push the button! We issued one to each CIDG squad and encourage them to take pictures, with emphasis on any VC activity across the border, and send the rolls back to us for processing and review. We get some good photos for our intel files that way. After a battle is over, they take lots of pictures showing enemy casualties and the extent of damage done to our FOBs."

"Why do they call it 'half-frame', John?"

"Because we get two pictures in each frame. The printing is cheap through sub-sector and we reimburse them from our petty cash. Me, I mostly take pictures of civic action projects, and when I'm out and about I carry our team Polaroid along also. I take lots of pictures of children and give them the snapshots. You should see the smiles on their faces, Dai-uy!"

"Good going. Make a child happy and a family is at least a little happier. You've got your head on straight, John."

"The Hoa Haos are wonderful people, Dai-uy. They've invited me into their homes to show me they are thankful for what we do here. They don't have a heck of a lot, but what they have they share. They're very religious, but in a different way than we are. Every Hoa Hao house that I've been in has a simple altar, maybe just a board covered with a purple scarf and pictures of their ancestors on it. They kneel and pray in front of the altar every day. They are the salt of the earth, Dai-uy. They take care of their own, too. You won't see an orphanage or an old folk's home here, no Sir. Family is important to them. I think the whole bunch of Hoa Haos is just one big family."

On the 30th Major Le, Sergeant Valenzuela and I made a quick trip to Khanh Binh to pay the Strikers and inspect the 81MM mortar emplacement. On the way we discussed the upcoming first firing into the VC Sanctuaries. I suggested we fire the first salvo at 0005. "Five is my favorite number, Thieu-ta."

"Okay, Dai-uy, that's exactly what we'll do. They will get their first taste of death inside their safe havens at 0005 hours on the first day of January. No more safe havens near An Phu!"

I witnessed the paying of the 442nd CIDG Company as the Team Sergeant was inspecting the mortar pit. Val returned and told me they had done a good job and were ready to 'blast off' when Major Le gave them the order.

Upon return to camp we had lunch and I sacked out for an hour, went over some paperwork and then waited in my office for Lieutenant Kallunki to come so we could discuss civic action projects. He'd no sooner entered when he said, "Let's take your jeep and see what civic action we're talking about."

"Good thinking, John, let's go."

John introduced my jeep driver as we approached my WW II vintage jeep. "This is Hoang Vinh Tran, Dai-uy." He introduced me to Tran very simply as "The Dai-uy."

He instructed Tran to drive through the district village marketplace, take us north on the river road all the way to Khanh An and then return to camp the way we'd come. "You will see examples of many of our civic action projects as we go along this route."

I thought back to my training on Smoke Bomb Hill and, for some reason, the title of one block of instruction came into mind: Anti-Ethnocentrism. Simply stated, it meant how not to be an ugly American. Of the officers who began the Special Forces Officer's Course, only seventy percent graduated. I don't believe any field grade officer graduated. They were simply too full of themselves and unable psychologically to hack the humbling role of grass-roots diplomacy and hands-on assistance that was demanded of an officer, regardless of rank or position, who wore the Green Beret. Incapable of putting their pride in their pockets, they were clearly the transient egocentrics - the ugly Americans. In An Phu I would learn through experience that civic action is really caring and sharing in a multi-faceted business of the heart. Accomplished through sweat, kindness, and compassion it was the reality of schools, bridges, cures, and corn that made it a real blessing and a necessary ingredient in any recipe for victory in an unconventional war.

Lieutenant Kallunki was responsible for planning, coordinating and arranging monies and materials needed for various civic action programs and construction projects. No easy task. "Mostly," John told me as we drove past a new three-room school, "we are involved in replacing buildings destroyed by the VC. We also helped to determine the need for additional schools or room additions to existing schools to support school-age population growth."

"Sounds exciting, and it makes good sense, John."

"Yes, Sir. And we do it hamlet by hamlet. The local people really appreciate how quickly we replace what the VC have destroyed. We work with the people to provide funds and drawings to help them help themselves. Whether it be monkey bridges, school houses, boat docks or a complicated market building, I do what I can to help sub-sector come up with what the people need. The people are wonderful too. They pitch right in to do whatever has to be done and even old men and small children pick up a shovel or hammer when that's needed.

"I also worked together with our team medics and the USOM health specialists to come up with the number of maternity houses we need in the district. We've helped build four thus far and we'll continue building until we have our goal of eight maternity houses open, stocked with supplies and midwives on board to serve the women of An Phu."

"You sound like a good CA and PR person, Lieutenant."

"Thank you, Sir. I'd like to mention something that concerns me. When I first got here I learned that there were no doctors or dentists in An Phu. Can you believe that?"

"You're telling me, John, and I believe you. How do our medics make up for that? So, there are 64,000 people in the district and not one doctor?"

"That's the way it is, Dai-uy. Tenorio and Kuchen go out on medical patrols almost every day with at least one LLDB medic, an interpreter, one or two nurses and a security force of six or eight CIDG. The patrols are a most effective tool for winning the hearts and minds of the people. They cover 220 square kilometers of territory. They go by boat or truck, and even walk part way to some hamlets to treat the people. Looking at and treating from 60 up to 200 women and children of all ages and men too old to be in service is a huge job. They even pull teeth and teach people to understand the need for good personal hygiene if they are to be healthy.

"Sergeant Kuchen once said that every time they went into a hamlet they made a positive difference. 'It wasn't just the shots, bandages, pills or the pulling of teeth, it was the good feeling the people got from just knowing that we cared for them.' Kuchen proudly advised me. Dai-uy, they care for each other's needs like no other people I've known. Friendly, optimistic, family-oriented and as honest as the day is long, they are also brave beyond measure. Young and old alike are willing to put their lives on the line for family, neighbors and friends.

"Perhaps it is the precepts of their Sect and the fact that they pattern their lives to honor those canons that endear the Hoa Haos to me. They were to be thankful for and to honor their parents, to love their country, to respect Buddhism and its teachings, to love their countrymen and their fellow man regardless of race or religion. "In between treating the wounded during and after a battle, and preparing for and conducting the almost daily medical patrols, our medics placed a high priority on training CIDG medics, indigenous midwives and nurses to fill in and gradually take over the local people's needs when we are gone. We are, as you know, scheduled to convert this camp in a few months from CIDG to Regional Forces. They will have MACV advisors. No more medicine, medical treatment, training or assistance that they now get and have come to expect from our medics."

"God bless our medics, John. It would be nice if we could just stay here in An Phu until we've won the war with North Vietnam and their Chinese Communist friends."

"Sure would, Dai-uy. Sure would."

The second civic action project that we came to was a nicely engineered, covered boat dock that now served the village of Vinh Phu. "Our people are really proud of that one, Dai-uy, and most of the material was donated by local people. A bridge like the one ahead, made for vehicle traffic up to one of our 2½ ton trucks, is a different story. We got help from province engineers to design it. We provided the funds and hired a company to build the bridge using mostly local labor. Major Phoi was instrumental in getting that done and done right."

As we passed the village chief's house, just south of the bridge in Phuoc My, John pointed to two men installing a new bulletin board. "Another of our projects, Dai-uy." Just then we drove over the bridge, the wooden treads sounding like a washboard as we proceeded over the top of the arched structure and on down to the other side. "We just crossed the little river called Rang, Dai-uy. That bridge replaced one destroyed by VC sappers a few months ago, so its still fairly new."

"And, quite solid, John. A bit on the noisy side, but solid." I remarked.

A little ways farther we came to a brand new maternity house, painted white with a red tile roof and the midwife standing in the open doorway waving at her hero, Lieutenant Kallunki. "Number four, Dai-uy." He said with a broad grin. To the left of the maternity house was an arched foot, bicycle and motorcycle bridge made from local bamboo. "That's one we put in to make it easier for people to get to the school down the road and the maternity house we just passed."

Last, but not least, John stopped in front of a four-room school still under construction at Khanh An, just across the Bassac River from Cambodia. It was a long, one-room-deep building made of concrete block, wood poles, rafters and tin roofing, with a full-length covered entry porch. "That's our latest and our best. We plugged into USAID funds for this and all the other schools, even one-room additions and the maternity houses too. It's a team effort. We do what we can with the few people we have to help provide the people what they need and where they need it, then work with them to get the job done."

Except for Specialist Menkins, who was on duty in the commo bunker, our team gathered in the dining area for a meeting at 1800 hours.

Sergeant Kuchen mentioned that he and the XO had spent a lot of time out in the district and that one of the things they'd noticed was that field corn was not grown in the area. They thought it unusual because pork was the staple meat of their diet and the Hoa Haos raised a lot of hogs. Lieutenant Kallunki chimed in, saying, "I'd like to go to Saigon, meet a missionary friend of mine, bring back some corn seed and work with Mr. Duc, our district agricultural chief to get something new going that would really help the local farmers. What do you think, Dai-uy?"

"Excellent idea, John. When you meet with Mr. Duc, make certain you've got some good proof in your hands that corn-fed hogs are the greatest. I know it's true. I worked on a large farm in central Illinois in the mid-forties and they raised 400 head of Poland China hogs. Those hogs were fed mostly field corn right on the cob. If I remember right they would fatten those hogs up to between 400 to 800 pounds on the hoof."

"I'll talk to Mr. Duc and let you know what he says."

Sergeant Valenzuela got us back on the subject of our New Year's message to the Viet Cong, wondering if everything had been worked out with Major Le. "What's the plan, Dai-uy?"

"Tonight Thieu-ta and I will select the target areas for our four deuce and the 81MM mortars at Khanh Binh and Phu Hiep. Basically, we want to hit where the major VC units are, believing that they will be sleeping and unaware of what we're up to. This will be our only opportunity for complete surprise. We'll fire an arc shaped pattern with the first round to go out of the tubes at 0005 hours on New Year's Day and aimed to impact at the far left of the target arc. Gunners will then adjust right after each round for a total of 10 rounds of HE in each of the target areas."

John Eleam remarked, "That should stir 'em up a little, Dai-uy."

"Dead on, Eleam. You can expect a 'Nantucket' message coming your way after the shock has worn off and the Prince has decided how tough his message to Saigon should be. We are planning this and future attacks inside Cambodia to miss Cambodian hamlets and innocent people. By striking in the dark hours when the Cambodian curfew is in effect we hope to eliminate Cambodian civilian casualties. Prince Sihanouk may not get so tough in his rhetoric if we leave his people alone and limit the death and damage to Viet Cong and NVA forces and their facilities."

I explained in detail how serious we had to be in our dealings with others, especially the B Team, to make certain we didn't accidentally expose our TOP SECRET independent operational status. "Major Williford isn't to know about our mission, which sounds stupid, but that's the way it's got to be. It's called deniability by compartmentalization. As long as he has no knowledge of our independent status, he can back any denials we make in response to charges from Sihanouk. What happens when the first Nantucket message comes past the Major's desk? He'll demand that we respond and come visit us if he doesn't believe what I tell him. Eleam, I'll give you some 'stock' answers that we'll fire back when we receive a Nantucket.

"Another matter - We must keep reporters out of our area except for the VIS people whom Major Le trusts.

"If Major Williford comes up the Bassac to visit, I'll somehow take charge of his itinerary whether he likes it or not and make certain he doesn't see or hear anything that would let him know what we're doing in Cambodia."

Lieutenant Kallunki quipped, "That's not going to be easy."

"I know John, but it's something we've got to deal with. We'll handle it by doing what's got to be done and then blame Major Le when the B team makes a fuss. Remember, Thieu-ta reports to Major Chuan, CO of their C team in Can Tho, not to anyone in Chau Doc. Major Chuan knows what's going on and will allow any complaint funneled through Colonel Tuttle to him to bounce off his back like a rubber ball."

"With those thoughts in mind, Eleam, I want you to send a message to Major Williford from me, saying that An Phu is now off limits to outside reporters, even American, and that only the VIS people will be allowed to report on activities in our area. Make sure that goes out ASAP."

"Sure thing, Dai-uy."

"Whatever the VIS provides the Vietnamese media is fine with me. I'd like to blow this whole thing about enemy safe- havens sky high. At the same time I don't want to go to prison because the American press reported classified stuff they learned from one of us. It's a mess for sure. This should be told to the world, but we'll have to play their games for now. I don't like it any more than you do. And, remember, any time you want out, just let me know and you'll be on your way within the day, no questions asked. But remember, if and when you leave An Phu you are sworn to secrecy about our mission."

An uneasy quiet settled in as I stood to leave. The meeting was over, and the full impact of our new mission was beginning to register in their psyches. It would be a new way of life for all who stayed the course. An exciting, dangerous, and TOP SECRET part in the war is what each of them would have to volunteer for. It was an awkward and perhaps frightening challenge. We would be the first to take the war where no one had gone before and we would be doing the right thing while having to keep our mouths shut. Plans and actions could only be discussed in secret and with no one outside our small group.

The truth of what we had done as a team and as individual human beings would be swept under the "covert operations" rug, even sacrificed, if necessary to protect those in Washington, D.C. who lacked the courage to stand behind the men they'd sent to Vietnam to fight, even die.

In An Phu American and South Vietnamese alike would fight side by side against overwhelming odds, under threat of total annihilation by Viet Cong and

NVA forces, while knowing that US combat support would be denied due to the proximity of the battles to the border. We knew without question that the White House permitted the enemy safe-havens with the right to operate freely inside Cambodia. It was a terrible injustice to all allied fighting forces and the nation of South Vietnam. As we look back on it, the sanctuaries remained in place long enough to aid and abet our enemy sufficiently, in the final analysis, to win total victory.

The people at home would likely be kept in the dark as the news coming out of Vietnam was controlled to the extent of feeding blatant lies to the press. In July 1965, just five months earlier, Arthur Sylvester,[4] Assistant Secretary of Defense for Public Affairs, told the assembled American journalists, "If you think any American Official is going to tell the truth [about the war in Vietnam], then you're stupid. Do you hear that? Stupid!"

At 1920 hours Major Le, I and our two Team Sergeants met in the operations center to plan our first fire mission against the enemy's Cambodian sanctuaries.

Sergeant Nguyen and Master Sergeant Valenzuela had met earlier and prepared an overlay map showing the locations of enemy units threatening our forces from inside Cambodia and those situated in the entrenched positions straddling the border 1200 meters north of Phu Hiep FOB. We agreed on a pre-planned fire mission that would impact on enemy locations west of Camp Dan Nam, west and northwest of Khanh Binh FOB and north of Phu Hiep FOB. There would be 10 rounds of HE fired from each location which we posted on the overlay,[5] now marked TOP SECRET with target patterns as a guide. We would continue the attacks every day at different times during the hours of darkness, modifying the target patterns based on new agent reports and common sense.

The last day of 1965 was a day of heightened patrol activity, night ambush operations, training, reviewing latest agent reports on enemy troop movements, maintenance of all weapons and finally, the paying of Strikers in the three companies of CIDG now in Camp.

Nantucket report response messages were canned and ready in our commo bunker. Major Le and I visited the District Chief, briefed him on our new independent role and told him what we had planned for at 0005 hours on New Year's Day. Though we would have savored the inclusion of his two long range 155MM howitzers in our planned bombardment of the sanctuaries we understood that he was answerable to Province Chief Re and that what we were planning would not be made known to Province. Captain Nguyen could not commit his RF or the 155MM Howitzer Platoon without clearance from Province except for normal fire support of combat operations inside the district.

But, we did trust Captain Nguyen, and he trusted us. We certainly didn't want him waking at midnight to the sound of our four deuce hammering rounds into Cambodia and thinking An Phu was under attack. His forces weren't a part of our unconventional operations but his heart was with us all the way!

At exactly five minutes past midnight on the first day of January in 1966 we took the war to the enemy's sanctuaries inside Cambodia. With the joy of a fighter who

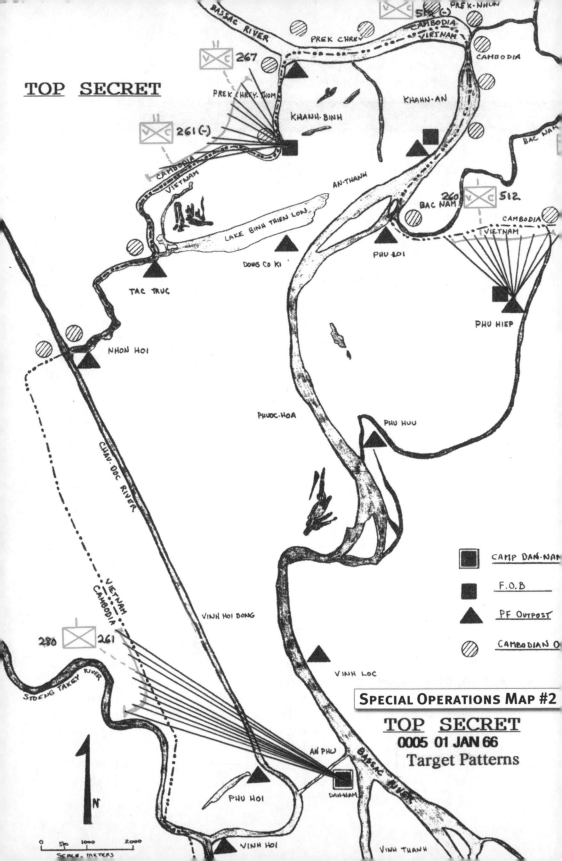

no longer had to face a two-fisted opponent while having one hand tied behind his back, we savored the deafening roar of a maximum powder charge hurling the first of ten 4.2" high explosive rounds more than 5000 meters into positions of the 280th VC Heavy Weapons Company. Bivouacked northwest of Camp Dan Nam, theirs was one of three enemy units to feel the death and destruction that signaled the beginning of our new strategy to deny the enemy its tactical advantage over the forces and people of An Phu. "It is good, Dai-uy," shouted Major Le, as we all relished the moment, "it is very good!"

Simultaneously 10 rounds of 81MM HE were sent hurling into positions occupied by the VC 367th Battalion and 260th Heavy Weapons Company north of Phu Hiep by FOB gunners, including strikes targeted on both sides of the border with Cambodia.

The third mortar, another 81MM with a target area north and northwest of the Khanh Binh FOB, lobbed its ten rounds of HE into nearby positions of the 261st and 267th VC Battalions.

Prince Sihanouk had broken diplomatic relations with the United States some eight months earlier (May 1965) and, as General William C. Westmoreland detailed in his published memoirs,[6] there was "conclusive proof" of at least seven major bases in Cambodia used by the VC and North Vietnamese. Bung Ven was one such base. General Westmoreland stated unequivocally that the enemy maintained base camps in Cambodia where they could "regroup, retrain, and mass [their] forces with impunity" for strikes against American and allied forces inside South Vietnam, "effectively circumventing [friendly force] efforts to forestall major attacks by preemptive strikes. " On 8 August 1965 Premier Nguyen Cao Ky, whose bark was obviously greater than his bite, threatened to attack Laos and Cambodia for harboring Viet Cong guerrillas, warning the US Ambassador that he would not submit to American dictation. However, Ky folded to US demands and acquiesced to those who would permit the enemy safe-havens inside Cambodian territory.

General Westmoreland, in that same book[6] went on to woefully complain that all they could do to the enemy in Cambodia was "drop propaganda leaflets on our side of the border whenever the wind was right to blow them across [into Cambodia]." Cowardly, I thought. I could imagine the enemy picking up leaflets that had been carried by the wind into their safe-havens, laughing at the American leaders who lacked the courage and loyalty to their troops to join them in open combat. The State Department reportedly based their provision of safe-havens to the enemy on an insane conclusion, as General Westmoreland writes, "...it is better to tolerate the enemy's use of Cambodia than to spark Sihanouk's open collaboration with the enemy."

It is interesting that the World Almanac and Book of Facts,[7] a publication considered a reliable source of factual information told that "US Forces began firing into Cambodia May 1, 66," yet, I know for a fact that our first fire mis-

sion into Cambodia was on January 1st, some four months earlier and it was accomplished by American and South Vietnamese Forces.

Secondary explosions in the area targeted by FOB gunners at Khanh Binh signaled a direct hit on an ammunition dump. Flames could also be seen high above the area in Chrey Tom where two VC battalions were located meaning those same gunners had hit a POL dump.

The impact fan above Phu Hiep and to the west of Camp Dan Nam would have gotten surprised VC caught above ground in their so-called "sanctuaries." It felt good just knowing we'd finally hit the enemy where he least expected it. It was a powerful way for us to let them know that they were no longer welcome anywhere within range of our mortars. It would have been a lot better if we could have sent in an air strike or been able to call on the two 155MM Howitzers in our area that, due to conditions dictated by the Johnson White House, could not fire support on the border much less inside Cambodia.

Major Le and I stood side-by-side in the command bunker looking toward the northwest where we had targeted the 280th VC Heavy Weapons Company to feel the wrath of our four deuce fire. They had set up camp east of the Cambodian Stoeng Takey River and we felt confidant, based on our latest intelligence, of their exact location. We wondered why there was no return fire from any of the VC units we had just surprised with a good dose of high explosive ordinance.

I believe Major Le hit the nail on the head when he turned to me and told me that he could almost see and hear the VC battalion and company leaders frantically calling the commander of their newly formed Southward Regiment asking for answers and direction. What happened? Were the rules changed? Was war declared on Cambodia? Was there reason to believe that a ground attack was imminent?

Needless to say we had good thoughts about their likely state of mental confusion and hoped it would continue. I got my early morning two and a half hours of sleep and felt great. Even knowing we were on our own, had no outside support and were facing an enemy force three or four times bigger and better armed, both of our teams felt encouragement from the fact that we could call the shots and that our Strikers were the best fighters in South Vietnam.

Along about mid-morning we received two very noisy and full grown white geese from the District Chief. Major Le, knowing that Captain Nguyen's aide had brought the geese into camp through the main gate, sent two of his men with needed materials, who promptly built us a fenced pen for them.

Major Le then stopped by my office and told me that it was traditional to give a new friend a pair of geese as a means to establish his own prosperous flock. After telling Val to have our new cook, Bon, care for the geese, I wrote a note thanking Captain Nguyen on behalf of the team and sent it on over to District Headquarters with my driver.

At 1210 hours that same day we received our first "Nantucket" message. Forwarded through the B Team, it read: "Intentionally firing hundreds of rounds of high explosive rockets into the sovereign territory of Cambodia along a distance of 20 kilometers and deep inside that nation, destroying the homes of innocent people and bringing death and injury to the defenseless Cambodian men, women and children, was the charge in an official diplomatic complaint we received at 5th Group Headquarters that demands immediate investigation and report. You are to submit report NLT 1200 hours, 2 January 1966 through channels."

My response was short and simple, telling of "an indefinite border, faulty ammunition and obsolete weapons," advising that "any actual border violation was unintended and that our agent reports tell of no civilian casualties."

Partial truths answering partial truths. We had fired only thirty rounds total and we did learn from our agents "that Cambodian civilians and their homes had been spared," one of our primary goals. Good news from that front!

The following night and every night thereafter for the next five months we fired missions into the enemy's staging areas and stockpiles, being careful to avoid death or destruction in the Cambodian civilian villages. There would be no safe-havens for the enemy within reach of our mortars. Nightly we sent high explosive reminders into whatever enemy positions we could reach inside Cambodia. Never the same place, same time or same number of rounds. Our main goal was to keep the VC wondering, moving and incapable of easily organizing an assault force on or near the border during the hours of darkness. There would be no lightning-speed surprise attacks against our FOBs or PF outposts.

At the same time, we increased our night ambush patrols from 12 to 16, wanting to cover the border areas wherever and whenever a possibility of invasion existed.

A vital bridge near Dong Co Ki, on our only north-south road that was used to supply and support the Khanh Binh FOB, along with that entire area of the district north of An Phu, was damaged on 3 January by a VC sapper squad. We were relieved that the bridge suffered only minor damage when the ineptly packed charge was triggered by a wandering water-buffalo. The animal was torn to pieces by the explosion and Major Le asked for funds to offset the farmer's loss of his water-buffalo. Lieutenant Kallunki and Specialist Menkins went by assault boat with a bodyguard escort in a second boat north to Dong Co Ki to investigate. A close inspection of the bridge showed it to be structurally sound and the remains of the water buffalo was all the proof we needed to honor Major Le's request for funds. I would soon come to know that his word was his bond and I would have no need to verify or corroborate what he had told me. After reporting back, Kallunki located Major Le and let him know that we would provide the funds to buy a new animal at a fair price.

Major Le was pleased and told Kallunki that he would send one of his officers "to make certain the farmer haggled over the price at Chau Doc marketplace as if it were his own money." Not many as honorable as Major Le in this tough world of ours, Americans, Vietnamese, or whomever, I thought.

My XO returned to explain how difficult it could have been to investigate the bridge mining incident without an interpreter. Fortunately it was straight forward and a rather simple situation. "All the hand and arm signals in the world wouldn't have helped me discuss anything intelligently with that farmer if there had been questions. "We need more interpreters. It's as simple as that." Kallunki told me.

I let him know he was right and that I was spoiled, being within earshot of Major Le most of the time that I was dealing with other Vietnamese. "He just steps right in to do the translating for me." I told him, adding that I figured we needed four more good interpreters. "Get with Lieutenant Ba," I directed, "and ask him to have his team recruit and clear four interpreters as soon as possible. Have them report to you at first so you and Quang can familiarize them with terms peculiar to us and what we do. Okay?"

"Will do, Dai-uy."

Early the next day, Major Le stopped by my office to let me know that he was taking action on my request for four interpreters. "It takes some time, Dai-uy. I have asked the Province Chief and the District Chief to send some men here for an interview. If I think they are okay I will give their names to the National Police who will do a background check. After each man is cleared he will be brought to you for your decision. Okay?"

"Okay, and thanks."

As he was leaving, he turned to ask, "Would you like to go with me day after tomorrow to visit Tan Chau Camp? I will leave here after breakfast."

"Yes, Thieu-ta. What time should I be ready?"

"The helicopter will come to pick us up at 0900 hours. We should be back by noon if all goes as planned."

"I'll be ready, Thieu-ta, thanks for asking me along."

An old, lumbering, ARVN H-34 helicopter arrived on schedule at 0900 on 5 January to take us to Tan Chau SF Camp. Tan Chau was southeast of our camp, near the Mekong River and 10 kilometers from the Cambodian border.

LLDB Captain Kich and his American counterpart, Captain Jim Miles, met us at the chopper pad inside their camp. Major Le and Captain Kich went their way and I followed Jim Miles to his office. Freshly brewed coffee now in hand, we agreed to share intelligence anytime either of us thought it could affect the other's camp. I learned first hand from Jim that there had been little enemy activity along the border in his area, and most of that was daylight reconnaissance patrolling and light probing actions.

I asked Captain Miles to explain how he worked with the National Police to control the Mekong River traffic to keep it from being used to ship arms into Cambodia.

"We don't," was his short and simple reply. He told how they were only permitted to board a ship with the National Police and inspect the ship's manifest. "If the manifest didn't list war materiel or other contraband, the ship is free to proceed up the river into Cambodia."

"You can only look at the manifest? You can't inspect the cargo holds?" I asked.

"We've got our orders, Dan. It doesn't make any sense at all. Just yesterday, two of my men and the National Police boarded a cargo ship. I think it was Lithuanian. The manifest that was shown them listed '10,000 tons of toys' as the entire cargo.

"I was born at night, but not last night, Dangerous. You know and I know there isn't even a remote possibility that there were 10,000 tons of toys on that or any other ship. But, if I'd taken men onto that ship and tried to force our way into the holds to inspect cargo, I'd have ended up on in Fort Leavenworth and behind bars. I can tell you this, Dan. I sent a patrol up river to where the Mekong enters Cambodia with high-powered binoculars to watch as barges pulled up alongside that same ship to off-load crates from the ship onto the barges which then continued up the Mekong River. The soldiers guarding the crates on those barges wore NVA uniforms. Now, I'm not naive enough to think they'd have soldiers guarding toys, would they, Dan?"

"Not hardly, Jim, not hardly." Out of the corner of my eye I spotted Major Le waving me back into the H-34. As we walked toward the waiting chopper, I told Jim I was glad not to be in his shoes because I'd probably have gotten myself into real trouble about that shipload of "toys," and I welcomed him to visit my camp when he got a chance. He nodded his head and smiled.

On the return chopper flight I told Major Le about my conversation with Captain Miles about ships being allowed to take war goods up the Mekong River into Cambodia.

"It is a very bad thing, Dai-uy. Your government and mine should demand that all ships be inspected by a boarding team to make certain that no weapons or ammunition reach the enemy through our area. By letting those war goods enter Cambodia on the way to their safe-havens we are arming and equipping our enemy. We are aiding and abetting his killing our people. It is a very stupid way to fight a war!" "My thoughts exactly, Thieu-ta. We'd better make certain nothing like that goes up the Bassac into Cambodia."

He then told me that it was not possible for large ships to come up the Bassac River and go into Cambodia. "The river is so shallow south of Vinh Thanh Island, near Phuoc My that ships would hang up on the bottom. Only flat bottom barges, fishing boats, sampans, and very shallow draft boats can navigate the Bassac, Dai-uy."

I told Major Le that we must make certain that none of the boats are allowed to go into Cambodia without being inspected. "If we have to we will close the river to all traffic going north."

Major Le laughed, told me that he now works with the National Police to inspect every boat that goes or comes at the border and he reminded me how they had confiscated the barge we now use as our quick reaction boat. "We discovered contraband and took his barge to make sure he could not do that again."

General Westmoreland, in his memoirs,[6] spoke of being frustrated that "some supplies were probably reaching the VC via international shipping passing through South Vietnam up the Mekong and Bassac Rivers," and yet, to the best of my knowledge, he did nothing to demand the authority to board and inspect the cargo in those ships. I knew too that whoever provided Westmoreland that information was unaware that the Bassac River was too shallow to permit navigation by deep draft ships. Incredible, I thought, with all the Special Forces generated intelligence provided MACV headquarters, they would be unknowing that weapons and other war goods were being shipped to the enemy on the Mekong into Cambodia and unaware that the Bassac River was only navigable by shallow draft boats.

We were back in our camp in time for lunch. I wrote what I'd learned at Tan Chau and what Major Le had told me about the Bassac River and put that in Lo Lap Co's mail box to go to my friend at Fort Bragg and then took my afternoon siesta.

SFC James A. Taylor arrived via assault boat at 1730 hours, a welcome addition to our camp. Team sergeant Val brought Taylor to my office after he'd gotten settled into his cubicle located next to the aid station. Jim was a heavy weapons man with almost a decade of service, and all but six months of that was on airborne status. He was lean, muscular, had an 'airborne' crew cut and looked tough as nails until he smiled. A ready smile, a good sense of humor and the ability to laugh when the going got tough were valuable assets in this kind of business.

I welcomed him aboard, told him he'd take over on the four deuce, would be responsible for maintenance of all mortars, training all crews, even at the FOBs. "I also want you to take over supply room activities. After Val shows you around camp and you begin to know where everything is, I want you to take a good inventory of our ammunition stocks. Order what we need to get up to snuff and scrounge up whatever extra mortar ammunition you can get your hands on to support our new TOP SECRET mission. We've been short of people and even shut down for too long. We have to be ready for whatever comes across the border.

"Yes, Sir, I'll do my best." With a questioning look, he asked, "but, what is the TOP SECRET mission and what did you mean when you said the team was 'shut down'?"

"I'll let Val explain all that. He was here for the shut down and knows about our new mission that will take a lot more mortar ammunition than the B Team is going to understand. Unfortunately, we can't tell them what our new mission is." I let Taylor know that I'd be counting on him to get the ammo we needed. "Got it, Sergeant?"

"Sure thing, Sir. Anything else?"

"Yes. You call me Dai-uy and I'll call you Jim. Val will tell you the rest about saluting and military courtesy with our counterparts. We shook hands and Val took over.

During my years of service as a commissioned officer in the US Army, I made it a practice to be somewhat distant, perhaps indifferent is the better word, from those whom I served with, whether senior or subordinate. I did not want friendship or concern for a particular individual to affect my ability to lead or to make tactical decisions. I knew an officer who sent a sergeant to lead a dangerous mission because the man was single; when there was another, more capable and experienced sergeant, a married man with children, whose turn it was to go on that patrol, a patrol that never returned. If that officer had sent the sergeant whose turn it was to go, would the patrol have returned? We will never know, but I do know that what he did was wrong. He was acting as God, and no man should try to be God. In 1988, after learning of the whereabouts of a few of those who served with me in An Phu, I asked each of them to provide background information and personal data that would most likely identify them to the reader. Jim Taylor was one of the first to respond. Jim was born in Beardstown, Illinois in 1938 into a large family that eventually included 15 brothers and sisters. He was raised in the city, played football, and had been in a few fist fights before enlisting in the Army in June 1955. He loved Special Forces and he was especially proud to have been in An Phu with the Hoa Haos.

The next two or three days flew by as I accompanied Major Le on his rounds of the district. I learned a lot just keeping my eyes and ears open, and for the most part my mouth shut, while witnessing his interaction with people from all walks of life and all parts of the district. Whether in rice paddy or hamlet, marketplace or fishing dock, he stopped and spoke with people and introduced me to them as their friend. It felt good just being with Major Le as I began the important task of building rapport with the Hoa Hao people of An Phu.

One of the facts about the Hoa Haos that fascinated me was the atmosphere of mutual trust and respect that permeated their society, existing between the military, paramilitary and the people as if it were born and bred in them. There was no hint of any displeasure or anger brought on by the imposition of martial law nor was there a climate of fear, though the very real and constant threat of more than 1000 Viet Cong, organized as an enemy regiment, lurking across the border and making preparations to attack An Phu was known among the populace.

The people of An Phu, predominantly farmers or fishermen with few worldly possessions, went about life in such a decent and honorable way as to be envied by all others. They were good neighbors, neither showing nor feeling hostility toward their Cambodian neighbors whose border they shared, and whose territory had been eroded by VC sanctuaries that protected their very enemies.

Major Le's attributes of integrity, loyalty and courage under fire were contributing factors to the almost pervasive feeling of serenity that overshadowed any negative feelings among the people. His words to me one evening, as we stood side-by-side in the command bunker, were like an echo from the past. It was as if my closest friend and long time Green Beret, Master Sergeant Gerard V. Parmentier, had spoken them. Almost word for word they conveyed the same message: a set of leadership standards to live by. "To be a real leader here, an officer must first be loyal to his men and his people and it will bounce back. He must earn their respect, not demand it, and he must be honest and admit to his own failings if he is to admonish others for theirs. If I take care of my men and our people," he concluded, "they will take care of me."

The 7th of January was a special day for agriculture in the Delta Region. Lieutenant Kallunki made a quick trip to Saigon by helicopter, met a Guatemalan missionary in a pre-planned rendezvous at Tan Son Nhut air base in Saigon, and received sufficient field corn seed to plant an acre. On return to camp, Kallunki took the corn to Mr. Duc at district headquarters and within days the Agricultural Chief had met with and convinced a local farmer to plant the corn as part of a test program that we funded.

Sometime after midnight on that same day, two newly installed bulletin boards were destroyed and a VIS Lambretta mobile speaker unit was pushed off the end of a dock into the Bassac River in An Thanh Hamlet. A CIDG patrol returning from an all-night ambush position on the river passed through the hamlet just before daybreak and spotted the Lambretta's loudspeakers sticking out above the surface of the river. They pulled the vehicle from the water and picked up many VC propaganda leaflets they found strewn on the main road nearby the remnants of the bulletin boards. The theme of the leaflets was "anti the American Imperialists."

Major Le and I discussed the incident and agreed it was likely the work of female saboteurs. The river entry into the area would have been impossible, given the moonlit night and the fact it was covered by National Police and our night ambush patrols. Agent reports had told of women being trained as terrorists and saboteurs at Bung Ven secret base, north of Phu Hiep and northeast of An Thanh. As was the case with our female agents, they could easily cross into An Phu posing as shoppers and hide in the heavy vegetation between Khanh Binh and An Thanh until nightfall. When all was quiet and the local people were within the confines of their homes to comply with the curfew, they could then venture forth to perform their mission of sabotage and return to Cambodia the next morning after doing some "cover" shopping in the Khanh Binh marketplace.

Those same agent reports included details of barges being off loaded in the Prek Chrey area inside Cambodia and across the Bassac River, north of Khanh Binh. Hundreds of clearly marked crates of weapons and ammunition were seen being transferred to smaller boats which took their war cargo eastward on the river, staying close to the Cambodian shoreline. Our Agent lost sight of the boats as they veered into the Mung Yu River, the river that flows to and through the Bung Ven secret base.

Major Le, believing as I did, that those crates of weapons were part of the so-called 10,000 tons of toys that Captain Miles had told me about, was visibly angered. "How could our leaders permit such things to happen? How many of our people must die from this act of cowardly stupidity? There can be no good reason for us helping to arm the enemy."

"I agree, Thieu-ta. It is this weakness in Saigon and in the White House that will lead to defeat on the battlefield unless they waken to recognize the evil of what they do and allow us to fight the war without restrictions and provide us needed combat support. I'm glad we no longer honor safe-havens across the border from us, but I am sad that the enemy is able, even today, to enjoy a safe haven beyond the reach of our mortars. They still have those sanctuaries because of the weakness of our leaders."

"It is sad, but we can do no more, Dai-uy."

I would learn, some 30 years later, from former Secretary of Defense McNamara's memoirs[8] published in March 1996, that General William E. DePuy, General Westmoreland's operations officer and principal planner from 1965-1968, said in a 1988 interview, "[We] eventually learned that we could not bring [the Viet Cong and North Vietnamese] to battle frequently enough to win a war of attrition. ... We were arrogant because we were Americans and we were Soldiers or Marines and we could do it, but it turned out that it was a faulty concept, **given the sanctuaries** *(emphasis mine), given the fact that the Ho Chi Minh trail was never closed. It was a losing concept of operation." Sad, I came to realize, that so many Generals and politicians allowed so many of ours to die while providing safe-havens for the enemy.*

Having boarded the ARVN H-34 helicopter a few minutes earlier, Major Le and I lifted off our Camp grounds at 0730 hours on 9 January 1966, and headed toward Saigon where we would meet with the Minister of Defense on the subject of amnesty for our Strikers. We refueled at Vinh Long, flew across the Mekong River Delta into Saigon and landed there at an ARVN heliport. On arrival we were whisked away to the South Vietnamese government complex in a military sedan.

The ride through the streets of Saigon was an experience I want never to repeat, but it gave me renewed appreciation for life among the Hoa Haos in An Phu. People and vehicles were everywhere on narrow streets and tree-lined boulevards. Military vehicles, cars, trucks, buses, pedicabs and motor-bikes fought for right-of-way on the roadways and the air was so foul with vehicle exhaust that a bluish haze filled the hot, sticky air and constricted our throats. Sidewalks were jammed with pedestrians and vendors selling everything imaginable. Beggars, prostitutes and petty thieves freely roamed the streets. Not where I'd take Kate strolling!

On arriving at the Defense Ministry, we were promptly ushered directly into the office of the Minister of Defense. It was an impressive office filled with teak furniture and plush carpets. The Minister, General Co Huu Nguyen, was a solid looking man, tall for a Vietnamese and younger than I'd imagined him to be. He stood behind his desk as we entered, framed by the silk colors of his nation and the banner of his office. There was no doubt in my mind that the skids had been greased by someone: the entire meeting lasted only a few minutes, not long enough to be seated.

Major Le introduced me to the General, we shook hands and the General smiled. I just stood there, listened and watched, oblivious to the content of their conversation, but I could sense by the tone that the discussion was a positive one. When the Minister handed Major Le a rather impressive looking document with the gold seal of his office affixed to it, shook his hand and smiled, I knew that Major Le had gotten what he'd come for. He now had the decree of amnesty for his Strikers, and I breathed much easier when General Nguyen reached across his desk, shook my hand and bid me courage for the coming battles.

Once we were outside, I congratulated Major Le on his victory. He smiled and thanked me for coming with him. "I think we are a good team, Dai-uy."

I wondered out loud, once we were back in the sedan, why he as a Major would be received personally by the Minister of Defense. "It is because I am military advisor to the Hoa Hao Central Council and it is my duty to represent all Hoa Haos in these matters. You see, Dai-uy I was charged to do so by Tuoug Trong Luong, the Hoa Hao Central Council chairman."

While we had some private time in the sedan without the day-to-day concerns of leadership, I asked Major Le to tell me a little about his background.

He smiled and told me that he was born in Sa Dec, on the south side of the Mekong River in 1930. "My parents were poor farmers who worked hard, saved some money and bought a piece of land. I was the only child in our family who was going to school for a very long time. I began school when I was seven years old and, after seven years of school, I went to the first year of courses at Can Tho College and that is when the Japanese made the coup in Vietnam in September 1945. I had to leave school to go back to my home and work with the family. At that time, in each village there were very few families who could afford to send their children to college. In 21 provinces of South Vietnam there were only three colleges. Later I studied at home by myself to finish education at college level which is like high school level in your country.

"In 1947 the situation in South Vietnam was very mixed up. The French came back and the Viet Cong harassed and killed many Hoa Hao people. One night I left my family and joined a Hoa Hao group of 20 people to fight against the VC and the French. We had only three shotguns and I was one of those who carried a shotgun. Then we joined the Hoa Hao forces. In May 1952 I was sent to a French military school in Bien Hoa, north of Saigon, for five months platoon leader's training. In October 1952 I was promoted to Second Lieutenant and I was very fortunate because I was one out of 88 who were in the course. Dai-uy, like yours, my military life is a long and special story that I will tell you at another time."

Lieutenant Colonel Tuttle told me that Major Le had proven himself in combat and as a leader of men in wartime for some 18 years when he was selected by Lieutenant General Quang Van Dang, IV Corps CG, to head up the CIDG in An Phu. Major Le told General Dang that he would rather be a commander and a "real fighter" than a district chief. General Dang's respect for the Hoa Haos and for Major Le as a 'total' leader, inspired him to obtain express permission for Major Le to attend Special Forces Camp Commander training at Nha Trang although he was not parachute qualified. "He is probably the only non-airborne LLDB Camp Commander," Tuttle suggested.

With time to spare, Major Le decided to touch base with some friends in Saigon. He had the driver stop and let me out at the Officer's Mess in the MACV compound, telling me he'd be back at 1400 hours to pick me up. It was 1130 when I thanked him, waved as the driver pulled away and decided to have lunch first and then see what the PX had to offer. I glanced around as I entered the dining room, didn't see any other Green Berets, and took a table in one corner, always liking to have my back to the wall in a strange place. I was grubby compared to the other officers, most of whom wore tailored, starched and pressed fatigues with glistening belt buckles and spit shined black-leather boots. There were a few who wore something I'd never seen or heard of before: patent leather boots! I thought to myself, "This is a combat zone?"

I laid my M-16 rifle across the table, draped the bandoleers across the back of an empty chair and put my beret across the chamber of my M-16. Wanting to savor the moment, I sat back in what was a comfortable dining chair, ordered a medium-well done broiled steak with all the trimmings, a piece of cherry pie and black coffee. It felt good to really relax while the cooks did their thing in the kitchen. When it was served, the steak was broiled to perfection, the rolls soft and warm enough to melt the butter and the mashed potatoes and peas done just right. With a fresh cup of coffee in hand, I turned my attention to the bits and pieces of conversation drifting my way from nearby tables. I learned just how bad life was treating these officers in the big city of Saigon. Poor maid service topped the list, with heavy traffic, bad tennis games and the long line at the telephone center main complaints relating to their desperate life in the big city. The most horrendous crisis of all was the complaint I heard from three officers not five feet from where I sat, who were sharing how they had to suffer an hour or so without air conditioning.

Never a word about the war, just endless drivel about girls, games, gags and keeping cool.

From there I strolled over to the base PX, the biggest I'd ever seen. I could hardly believe my eyes as I walked around and saw what was being sold. Most of what they had to offer was for girls, games, and partying. There was a small area devoted to military clothing, shoes, boots and other essentials, but in size it paled in comparison with the space and inventory dedicated to what I considered to be less than honorable pursuits of pure pleasure. The selection of women's bras, panties, watches, perfume, personal hygiene items, jewelry and clothing was enormous. I didn't buy a thing. It was a disgusting experience, even more so because I knew in my heart that every senior officer in MACV, generals included, and especially General Westmoreland, were well aware of what and who was being served by it. They did nothing to clean it up and place the conduct of the war at the top of their priority list." I was ready when Major Le's sedan pulled up in front of the Officer's Mess at 1400 hours to pick me up. I'd seen and heard enough in MACV's backyard to make me want to get back to An Phu as soon as possible.

"I'm happy to be here and I know you are very anxious to tell your people of the victory." I told Major Le after getting into the sedan.

"Yes, Dai-uy," he said, smiling. "We have good news for my people. I am glad you are with me. It is as if we were brothers."

On return to camp, I learned that Sergeant First Class Paul Bridgewater had reported earlier that day. Bridgewater was a heavy weapons man and I assigned him to work under Jim Taylor and help take up the slack in the team.

The level of activity across the border, including the movement of a VC heavy weapons company with anti-aircraft machine-guns to a location within striking distance of our main camp, prompted me to declare our area a purple zone which required armed escort for "slicks" (unarmed choppers) to enter the air space in our district.

Early the morning of 12 January we received word that Martha Raye would be visiting our camp. There's not a man who wears the Green Beret who wouldn't want Colonel Maggie, as we called her, to visit him no matter where he was. There was none other as brave and as loyal as she was to the Special Forces troops. She would regularly go to every SF camp, no matter how remote or dangerous, to visit her friends. She was an honorary Lieutenant Colonel and an honorary Green Beret. She always came with black bag in hand, ready to help out wherever there were wounded and whenever she was needed.

When we heard the familiar sound of a chopper's beating rotors, we looked up and saw a single Huey coming in toward our landing zone. I sent Menkins to the commo bunker to tell Eleam to make contact with the chopper and turn it away.

Though Eleam got through to the pilot, Colonel Maggie insisted she visit "her friends" and ordered him to land.

Assuming the chopper would turn back, I began to walk toward the operations center and glanced up to see the chopper circling toward the west, on a course that took it within range of that VC heavy weapons company. John Eleam came charging out of the commo bunker to tell us that Colonel Maggie had gotten on the radio herself and told him, "I don't care about purple zones. I TOLD THAT PILOT TO TAKE ME DOWN!"

We all watched as the chopper began its approach from the west and our worst fears were realized when we saw .50 caliber tracers arcing up from the other side of Phu Hoi PF Outpost, searching out Colonel Maggie's chopper. If one of those bullets were to hit in the right place that chopper would have become a ball of fire. The pilot saw what was coming at him and veered sharply toward our camp, gave the engine full throttle and came toward us like his tail was on fire.

We knew he may have been hit by the way he brought the chopper down kind of hasty-like, cut the engine and got everyone out real fast. The crew chief circled the ship quickly on foot, checking for smoke and ended up standing next to the chopper, looking at the two .50 caliber holes in the fuselage and scratching his head.

Colonel Maggie strode toward us, black leather nurses bag in hand, a Green Beret pulled down over her right ear, looking calm and cool in her Hollywood sunglasses. Unruffled by what had happened, she got within ten feet of us and shouted, "You really should do something about your neighbors. They're not very friendly!"

After glad handshakes all around, she asked if she could help out in the dispensary. I'm not usually at a loss for words, but Colonel Maggie had just flown through a steady stream of anti-aircraft machine-gun fire, her chopper had been hit twice and yet she walked up to us, smiled and talked as if nothing had happened.

I mumbled something unintelligible, and realizing I was making a fool of myself, told her to follow me and led her to our aid station. Once inside she saw Sergeant Tenorio leaning over an injured Striker with nurse Lau at his side, she opened her bag and asked "T" if she could help. I stood there for a moment watching Colonel Maggie, Sergeant Tenorio and Nurse Lau working together like a well-oiled machine tending the injured Striker and a civilian employee with a sebaceous cyst. The cyst, or carbuncle, was likely a result of Chinese needle therapy, using a dirty needle. Colonel Maggie didn't leave her sense of humor at the door. As I was leaving everyone was laughing and "T" looked like he was going to split a gut over something she'd said or done.

After the wounded were cared for she joined all of us in the team house. We just sat around talking and enjoying each other's conversation for about 40 minutes. She was a small woman with dark, curly hair and looked quite sassy in her Green Beret, fatigues and jungle boots. Most of all we thought of her as someone who really loved us and what we did. We knew she would go anywhere that we were to visit with anyone who wore the Green Beret. She was a patriot, entertainer, woman and nurse all rolled up into one lovely person dedicated to doing what she could do best.

After posing with the team for pictures near the command bunker, she grabbed her black bag and wished us God speed. Then she boarded her chopper and gave us a thumbs up as it lifted off and headed east to the Bassac River, then south to Chau Doc. We'd not soon forget Colonel Maggie's visit!

On 14 January Lieutenant General John Heintges stopped by for a whirlwind visit. General Westmoreland's deputy came in by helicopter. He was a tall, rather distinguished looking officer who nonetheless made me feel comfortable in his presence. He came to tell me that the CIDG of An Phu would be converted to Regional Forces before summer was over. He was counting on us to get the job done, to make it a smooth transition. He told me of "disastrous results from two previous attempts in other areas."

I told him, "I'm confident that Major Le is the one LLDB commander who can make it happen. I'm certain we can make it work together, but I think it best to keep An Phu in the CIDG program, General."

General Heintges told me he agreed and that he'd "rather see the SF presence doubled." He went on to explain that the SF expansion option was no longer on the table in Saigon. "I can't even guarantee you'll be staying here through the conversion, Captain."

I asked him to try, that if he were to check the records he'd learn that two other SF Captains before me didn't fare too well with Major Le and his Hoa Haos. "From what I understand, General, it wasn't Major Le's fault."

"I'll do what I can, Captain." He told me.

With that promise he boarded his waiting chopper, smiled and returned my salute as he was lifted out of our camp to fly on to his next stop.

General Heintges was not new to Special Forces or unconventional operations. In 1959, posing as the civilian director of a fictitious "cover" organization in Laos, known as the "Programs Evaluation Office," he oversaw US Army Special Forces unconventional operations in that country. My best friend, then Sergeant First Class Gerard V. Parmentier, who spoke French, was one of those 107 SF troops who were dropped from US Army rolls, slipped into Laos aboard CIA "Air America" aircraft wearing civilian clothes, and instructed to perform their Laotian Army training mission while pretending to be civilian evaluators in that country to assist their government. They were to be involved in developing intelligence and helping to build a base of Laotian troops trained in guerrilla warfare.

There were only a handful of senior officers who agreed with the employment of elite forces, such as the US Army's Special Forces, in unconventional roles as we were now engaged in throughout South Vietnam. General Heintges was one of our few friends. I knew he would be the only one with a ghost of a chance to convince General Westmoreland of the real need to expand the kind of effort we were involved in at An Phu. I briefed my team on General Heintges' visit with emphasis on our need to do all that we could to make the upcoming conversion to RF successful.

Major Le, after I'd covered the General's visit in detail with him, told me, "It is most important that we make certain the conversion plan includes having only Hoa Haos as company commanders and camp commander. If not, Dai-uy, it will surely fail."

"I agree, Thieu-ta. We must not fail. What we do here in this time together will be our legacy forever."

* * * * *

Proverbs 28:1 — *The wicked flee when no man pursueth:*
but the righteous are bold as a lion.

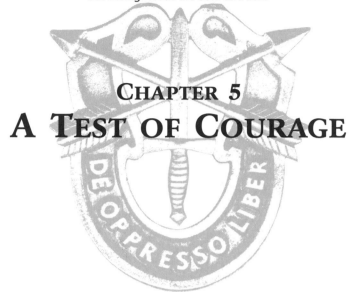

CHAPTER 5
A TEST OF COURAGE

"Dai-uy, the Strikers are no longer with us." Flash, my interpreter, told me
as we entered the flat, grassy area that lay between our force and the bamboo
thicket where some 200 deeply entrenched Viet-Cong waited with a clear
field of fire to defend against our attacking forces. "I will stay with you," he
bravely added. The air was suddenly filled with the "whooshing" and "crack-
ing" sound of incoming rifle and machine gun fire penetrating the air all
around us. "Don't look back," I shouted to Flash, as I began firing my M-16
at the muzzle flashes of automatic weapons pouring fire at us, "Just keep on
moving," all the while hoping that our Strikers would join us in the fight.

In mid-January Sergeant Val stood in my office doorway with a wide grin on
his ruddy face and motioned me to follow, saying "Come take a look, Sir."
    "What's up, Val?"
    "Our team flag, Dai-uy! We all decided to go with what you suggested. Two
weeks ago I gave the drawing to Sergeant Hung and asked if he could find someone
to make it for us. He brought it over a few minutes ago. I think Sergeant Chet did
the sewing, using Cambodian silk."
    It hung proud and beautiful in the briefing area next to the camp flag. "Thanks
Val, it's outstanding and two sided as I'd hoped it would be." I shook his hand in
celebration. "What are the two gold streams for?"
    "One for each year the camp has existed."
    "Thanks again," I offered, "and please pass on my thanks and compliments to
Sergeant Hung and Sergeant Chet."
    "Will do, Dai-uy." The grin on Val's face faded to a look of concern as he asked
how I felt as a Quartermaster officer leading men into actual combat.

93

"I understand why you ask that. I know where you're coming from. You were here when my predecessor dove under the truck in mortal fear when Dan Nam came under mortar attack. He was an Infantry officer. You think of Quartermaster officers as belonging in warehouses, depots, or possibly, giving them the benefit of the doubt, in parachute rigging outfits. I was Infantry before I was first commissioned an Engineer Officer when I graduated from OCS at Fort Belvoir, Virginia. I saw some combat at the end of the Korean War or I wouldn't have been accepted for Special Forces training. They weren't taking anybody for officer's training that wasn't a combat veteran.

"Val, I went through the same training that every other Green Beret officer did and I graduated among twelve who made it in a class that started with thirty-two. I told you a little about my background in the boat on the way to camp. Only time will tell, Sarge, but I'll do my best to make you feel good about this Quartermaster officer."

Val looked me in the eyes and told me that he thought I had my act together, adding that he'd heard Major Le had set some wheels in motion to test me under fire."

"Anything you want to tell me, Val?"

"No, Dai-uy. Let Major Le set the stage. I feel like you've come to respect him as we do. He's a giant of a man and I guess, when push comes to shove, we'd like to have someone like him leading us."

As Val walked away to go about his business, I couldn't help but think how fortunate I was to be here, to have the opportunity to learn from some one like Major Le, whom Val called "a giant of a man." Before we would part company I would come to know just how much of a fearless and courageous leader of men he really was.

Being in An Phu was an experience like nothing else on earth for me. If there was one thing I did pray about, it was that I would do my part and do it well. This whole notion of fear controlling a man should be foreign to a soldier or an officer in combat. When I've spoken with Vietnam veterans in the past, hardly a one mentioned fear, a fighting man's worst enemy and a continual element in the diet of war. The control of fear, the ability to function in the face of certain danger, is the beginning of courage. A man on patrol in enemy-held territory is a fool if he isn't constantly considering the relative probability of an ambush or of being taken unawares by a booby-trap or antipersonnel mine should he let down his guard. Fear pervades his being. A soldier charging his foe across an open field is alert to his circumstance and runs with fear as his constant companion. A soldier in a defensive position, waiting for the enemy to attack knows fear, but its impact on his psyche is lessened by the relative security of his protected position.

The men of Special Forces, those who wear the coveted Green Beret, stood out as being much different from conventional soldiers. A good many of my team, I would learn much later in life, were cut from a similar mold: poverty and other less-than-fortunate circumstance forced the role of survivor on each of us at an early age. Courage was a by-product of a continuing struggle. Without courage, most of us would not have survived the rigors or overcome the pitfalls we faced of one kind or another. Most conventionally-minded military brass seemed frightened by those of us who chose to become a part of the "elite" forces. They considered us "uncontrollable wild men." We were truly special people. Each of us was a three-time volunteer trained to work as a part of small teams doing special jobs, anywhere, anytime, and with little else than what we could carry on our backs, bonding us together in a way outsiders might find difficult to understand. Only the Navy SEALs, Air Force Commandos and other similar type units, regardless of country of origin know and appreciate what we were all about.

At 0800 hours on 16 January Major Le and I met in front of the new CIDG shower and toilet building. Major Le cut the ribbon and gave a short ceremonial speech. I spoke next, apologizing for their having to wait two years for what they should have had all along. It was a decent looking facility and we were able to pipe purified water from our tower to their shorter tower saving on the expense of the new facility, while providing them the same quality water that we enjoyed. "It's a real shame," I told Major Le after we'd returned to the Operations Center, "that your men were denied something as basic and necessary for their health and well being."

"We see eye to eye on that, my friend," he replied, smiling as he spoke. The men already feel a loyalty to you because they know you care about them.

At 1400 hours a squad from the 444th CIDG Company out of Phu Hiep FOB sighted an estimated 12 khaki-clad VC in the waist-high grass approximately 1,000 meters northwest of the FOB. They approached with due caution, wanting to get within easy small arms range before making contact. The lightly-armed Strikers in their tiger-striped fatigues approached within 300 meters before the enemy spotted them. A short fire fight ensued. It was the VC who broke contact and fled into that part of An Phu District they controlled due north of the FOB, disappearing into a dense stand of bamboo. One wounded VC was seen being carried away by two comrades as they fled. There were no friendly casualties. The squad leader wisely decided not to follow the enemy into the heavily mined bamboo thickets where the enemy would be waiting in ambush.

Later that same day Menkins stopped by my office to let me know that his trip had been a success. He didn't have to go any further than Can Tho where he visited a MACV Supply Point. "I scrounged two 60MM mortars and enough parts to assemble two light machine guns for the outposts at Don Co Ki and Phu Loi," he told me, a wide grin on his face. "I traded an authentic VC battle flag to a non-airborne ordinance sergeant. Of course I didn't tell him that 'authentic' was our code word for 'sewed together and stained with pig or chicken blood by the girls in our camp laundry." We both laughed.

Menkins concluded, "I'll get with Sergeant Hung and we'll make sure it's put together and tested. We'll take a 15 day supply of ammunition when we deliver them to the outposts. The LLDB gunners will be in the outposts in the morning, teach the PF to operate and maintain the weapons, and they'll all be back in camp before the day is out."

"Sounds great! Good job, Menkins. They need them badly and I know the Hoa Haos will appreciate what we've done."

We met at 2000 hours to plan the operation that would take back the area above Phu Hiep now occupied by the VC. The report of contact north of Phu Hiep early this afternoon spurred me to action. I asked Major Le to meet me in the Operations Center to discuss the situation. Paramount among Major Le's concerns was the likelihood of heavy casualties among his men because of the thousands of pipe mines and booby traps that had been set among the thick stands of bamboo in that area.

"There is another concern, Dai-uy." He said, "The 512th Heavy Weapons Battalion has moved into the Bung Ven secret base, about 2000 meters north of the area we plan to clear. If the news of our plans is known to them, they will reinforce the 260th Company that now defends that place and we would have to attack a larger force with heavy weapons."

I told him I agreed and that we would keep the ultimate objective of the plan secret between the two of us, take quick action and catch the VC unawares. "If our men believe it is to be a routine reinforced company operation in the area west of the FOB, we will have the element of surprise on our side." "When do you suggest we attack?" Major Le asked. "Tomorrow morning at first light."

"That is very soon, Dai-uy, but I agree it is important we take them by surprise. I must be at Province to meet with Major Re in the morning. Would you lead the operation, knowing it is possible my men may not follow you because I will not be there?"

With that comment I sensed I was being set up for a test of what I would do when faced with real danger. I understood why he would want to test me, given what another in my shoes had done before. But, I would not let on that I was suspicious of his words or his intent.

I looked him square in the eyes and told him, "If you tell them to follow, they will follow."

"Okay, Dai-uy. It is approved. Tell me your plan and I will get you what you will need."

I outlined my concept: To take a company from Camp Dan Nam to Phu Hiep and join with three platoons from the FOB. "We must, from the beginning, tell our men it is to be a search and destroy operation to clear the area west of the FOB, all the way to the hamlet of Phu Hung on the Bassac. Your LLDB will provide fire support with the 81MM mortar." I explained that it would be very important, because he would not be there, to give the LLDB mortar crew chief a sealed envelope containing the actual mission that he would open after our clearing force departed the FOB. One platoon of Lieutenant Ang Nguyen's 444th Company would remain in the FOB to provide security."

"And," Major Le suggested, "You will tell them of the real operation when they are formed up and ready to go on the dummy operation?"

"It must be that way, Thieu-ta. We will have to shuttle a company from here to Phu Hiep in two trips, using all available assault boats plus the barge. Sergeant Taylor, two interpreters and I will go with the lead elements and send the boats back for the remainder. Once we are all on the ground at the FOB and ready to move out toward Phu Hung, I will give them your written orders for the real mission." I explained that it would be important for him to prepare and sign duplicate orders to cover the real mission, place them in sealed envelopes for me to give to the two company commanders when I brief them using the tactical map for the clearing operation. "Then we'll conduct the operation to push the enemy back into Cambodia and clear all mines and booby traps from the area north of the FOB to the border."

"Sounds good, Dai-uy. I will tell Lieutenant Thuan Nguyen to move the 441st Company to Phu Hiep beginning at 0600 tomorrow. The envelopes with secret orders will be ready for you at that time. Okay?"

"Outstanding, Thieu-ta." I suggested that he send his LLDB team with the 60MM Mortars and the light machine guns up to Dong Co Ki and Phu Loi at 0600 also, using the 3/4 ton truck to take them to Dong Co Ki. From there to Phu Loi they would be transported by motorized sampans. "When they fire training missions with the mortars and machine guns, please tell them to aim all of their fire at uninhabited parts of Bac Nam Island. That may help to distract the attention of the VC at Bung Ven and mask our activities around Phu Hiep."

"It is a good plan, Dai-uy."

I called a team meeting as soon as I'd finished meeting with Major Le. I told them we would be conducting an operation out of the FOB at Phu Hiep and that Sergeant Taylor, myself, Flash and Quang would be going with the lead element at 0600. I also told them Major Le would be at Province in a meeting with Major Re and that I would be leading the operation out of Phu Hiep. "Everything is set for the movement by the LLDB of the mortars and machine guns to Dong Co Ki and Phu Loi outposts. Menkins, I want you to make sure they have a 15 day load of ammo plus whatever they need for weapons training at the outposts."

When asked about details of the operation out of Phu Hiep I told them they'd be told later. "Why all the secrecy, Dai-uy? You know you can trust us," Sergeant Valenzuela asked.

"Sure I trust you guys. Major Le trusts his men and commanders also, but certain details will be kept secret until the time is right. Details of what we are planning would lead to heavy casualties if the wrong ears heard them. Just trust me. The moment you get the word, you'll understand why I'm not sharing any details with you now."

At 0030 hours on the 17th I took my shotgun and binoculars and went up to stand watch in the command bunker. The VC preferred to attack during the dark phase of the moon and so did we if it gave us the tactical advantage for a specific operation. I tried never to miss our nightly mortar salvos into Cambodia. This was one of those moonless nights when the VC might be tempted to attack. It was the kind of night when a mortar round exploding on or near their positions might make the enemy think twice about a ground assault. Our mortar attacks were beginning to wear on the enemy's nerves, as they wondered where or when the next rounds of high explosive projectiles would drop in to kill or maim.

Most men would rather not venture out in total darkness to meet the enemy. Our CIDG were cut from a different cloth: unafraid, ready, willing and able to engage the enemy no matter what the circumstance, daylight or dark.

The only discernible light glimmered from the countless stars in the cloudless sky. It was a perfect night to spot VC mortar or rocket flashes, locate their positions inside Cambodia and return their fire.

A light breeze drifted across and through the bunker, bringing a breath of cooler air, a welcomed change from the heat of the day. The quiet suddenly gave way to the powerful blast of our four-deuce sending another deadly message to the VC inside Cambodia. As the fire mission continued, I scanned the length of the border, knowing our FOB mortars were in action also, pounding suspected enemy positions in our so-called "neutral" neighbor.

The enemy guns remained silent as stillness returned to An Phu. I made the rounds of the camp and found the Strikers on the perimeter alert and happy, knowing we'd just sent another deadly salvo of HE into the enemy camps.

With Major Le's secret orders' envelopes in my breast pocket, and Flash at my side, I joined Sergeant Taylor and Quang outside the operations center at 0600 sharp. We got into our jeep with gear in hand and Tran drove us to the boat dock where Lieutenant Thuan Nguyen waited our arrival. Half of his company had boarded the ten available assault boats and the barge. Four assault boats remained to permit a small reaction force capability should there be a need due to enemy action in another place.

Flash felt uneasy with Major Le absent from our operation until I explained my logic, thinking it to be a test of my ability to perform under fire. "Yes, Dai-uy, I think you are right. He has never missed an operation of company size before and he would have to have a good reason."

Sergeant Taylor, yet unconvinced, voiced his opinion, "I would still feel better if Thieu-ta were with us."

Wanting Jim Taylor to know that he wouldn't be in the dark much longer, before I turned to join Lieutenant Thuan Nguyen in the lead assault boat, I told Taylor "Time to go, Jim; you bring up the rear in the barge. I'll tell you the whole story when we get to Phu Hiep."

"About time" he said with a wide grin on his face.

On the way at 0605 hours, we soon passed the PF outposts at Vinh Loi and Phu Huu, and waved greetings to the local militia men as they prepared to return home after a night's watch and patrol activity. We arrived at the Phu Hiep FOB at 0710 hours. All the boats were quickly unloaded and sent back to our camp to bring the remaining fighters of the 441st company to join us.

As we waited, I quickly briefed Sergeant Taylor on our real mission. "When we have all the men here and are ready to move out of the FOB and towards Phu-Hung, we will then meet with the two company commanders. With Flash and Quang there to interpret, I'll give them the envelope from Major Le, wait until they have read and digested the secret orders and then go over the details on this tactical map,[3] finalize the plans and move towards the real objective." I explained how the LLDB mortar crew would learn of the secret plans.

"Sounds good to me, Dai-uy, but I'd still feel better if Thieu-ta were here."

I understood Sergeant Taylor's apprehension. After all, I was a Quartermaster officer, and who wanted a "bean counter" to lead them against a dug-in and defending enemy?

"I know what you're saying, Jim, and I understand, but try to remember I was an Infantry NCO and a Combat Engineer officer before I went Quartermaster to get back in the Army in 1959. The Engineer Branch wouldn't take me back because I didn't have a college degree. You know I had to prove myself to get to wear this Green Beret, Sarge. Just think of me that way. You can judge it for yourself. Okay?"

"Fair enough, Dai-uy, fair enough."

By 0920 boats had returned with the remaining platoons of the 441st company. After they formed up for the bogus operation west of the FOB, I called the commanders together and gave them the envelopes. After reviewing Major Le's secret orders, Lieutenant Thuan Nguyen spoke up. "It is a very dangerous mission, Dai-uy. There are many mines and booby traps and it is defended by a deeply entrenched heavy weapons company. Besides, Dai-uy, the new VC battalion is located in the Bung Ven secret base, very near and able to reinforce their company. Maybe we should have a battalion to attack?" Thuan was the oldest and most experienced of the company commanders.

Lieutenant Ang Nguyen chimed in, "We could lose many men if we did not do it right, Dai-uy." Ang was young and aggressive. He was also a little on the flamboyant side, with a wide-brimmed camouflage hat, chin strap drawn tight framing a solid jaw and firm mouth. His head had a jaunty tilt, and he sported a bright red silk scarf, embodying his company battle colors.

"Then we must do it right, Ang, and surprise them. We cannot allow them to occupy what is Hoa Hao land."

There were no further objections, but neither officer jumped up and down with joy at the thought of going against that formidable a target without Major Le in command.

The First Sergeant of the 444th company remained in the FOB with the first platoon of about 40 Strikers to defend the outpost and to maintain communications with Camp Dan Nam. Two LLDB manned the 81MM mortar in the FOB and were on call for tactical fire support and counter-fire if the VC fired at our men from inside Cambodia.

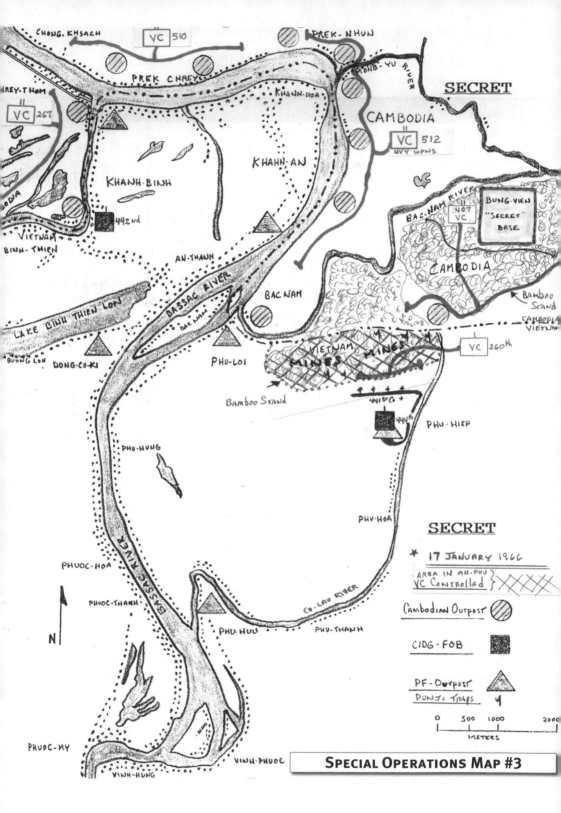

SPECIAL OPERATIONS MAP #3

100

"You will have 30 minutes to brief your men and check their equipment and ammunition here in the FOB," I explained to the two company commanders, Sergeant Hung Nguyen and Sergeant Jim Taylor, with Flash translating. "At 1030 hours we will form in a column of twos south of the FOB and north of Phu Hoa hamlet, using the large grove of trees as cover. From there we will proceed north along the Co Lau River for 500 meters. Lieutenant Thuan, you will lead with your company and Ang, you and your platoon will follow. Sergeant Hung will command the four 60MM mortar sections, laying in behind your platoon as a fire support unit. Sergeant Taylor and Sergeant Hung will work together with Quang there as interpreter to bridge the language gap as he is needed. The Sergeant leading the third platoon of the 444th will report to Hung and provide security for their fire base. If you have any questions, ask them as I tell you the plans.

"When we reach that point we will turn and head west in column until Ang's platoon has completed the turn to the west. Ang, you will radio your position to Thuan. Thuan, you tell Flash and he'll let me know. I will then move to the center of the column and lead the attack force north from there and make contact with the VC. Sergeant Hung, you will set up the fire support base due north of the FOB and immediately behind our line of departure. Start dropping HE into the VC positions as soon as they make their location known. We'll keep moving north until we've pushed the enemy across the border.

Sergeant Taylor suggested, "And maybe a little ways into Cambodia, Dai-uy?"

"That's the plan, Jim. I was given this command for the express purpose of denying the enemy sanctuaries across from An Phu. It was a political victory Major Le won in Saigon and one that we've GOT to win on the ground." Sergeant Hung asked for time to get his mortars set up. "You've got it, Sergeant Hung, bring your mortars and the security force up and to the left of Lieutenant Thuan's company. Their continued movement after you stop to set up your fire base will mask most of what you are doing. When the column halts on the line of departure for the attack, I'll give you more time by walking along the column slowly until I reach mid-point and we begin the attack."

All went as scheduled and I felt confidant, knowing the mortars were in place; the Strikers were lined up abreast at five meters apart with light machine guns on both flanks.

I reached the mid-point and looked out across the 500 meters that separated us from the enemy and could see nothing but waist-high grass all the way to the bamboo thickets where they lay in wait. I asked Flash if Lieutenant Thuan was ready.

"No word yet, Dai-uy," Flash told me, patting the stock of his M-2 Carbine and holding an HT-1 radio in his left hand.

"Tell him we are moving out now."

"Yes, Dai-uy." Flash gave the Lieutenant my message as I started forward, my M-16 at the ready and Flash at my side. I could sense forward movement of the line of

Strikers behind us, but only for a few moments. As we moved slowly and deliberately forward toward the tree line in the 90°+ heat, sweat soaking our tiger suits, the only discernible sounds being that of the dry grass crunching softly under our boots and my own labored breathing. We watched for signs of the VC ahead of us and listened for sounds of friendly movement behind us. Only our own trudging sounds broke the silence. Our slow, steady pace widened the gap between us and our Strikers. The agonizing loneliness of the moment weighed heavy on each of us. I glanced at Flash and laid my hand on his shoulder, as much to comfort me as him. He forced a smile, his M-2 Carbine at the ready, as we continued our trek toward the enemy.

"Sling your radio, Flash. I wouldn't have asked you to come with me if I'd known we'd be alone in danger for such a long time. I had an idea there would be some kind of test and I knew I would have to face that if I were to lead. Flash, you don't have to stay with me, but if you do, get ready to shoot, we're getting too close for comfort."

He slung his radio and turned to look back. "Dai-uy, the Strikers are no longer in sight." He reported. We were closing the gap between us and an estimated enemy force of 200 men deeply entrenched in front of the bamboo thicket ahead. "I will stay with you, Dai-uy," he bravely added.

The air was suddenly filled with the "whooshing" and "cracking" sound of incoming rifle and machine gun fire penetrating the air all around us.

"Don't look back," I shouted to Flash, and we began firing at the muzzle flashes of the many automatic weapons pouring their wrath upon us, "Just keep on moving," all the while hoping that our Strikers would join us in the fight. I fought a natural impulse to drop to the ground as the pfft, pfft, pfft sound of near misses caused goose bumps to flourish on my body and the rush of adrenaline to charge through my veins. The danger and even excitement of close combat caused my senses to become extra alert and quick to react to the stimulus.

I reached out, grabbed Flash's arm and pulled him down to his knees beside me to re-load. I rammed a fresh magazine into my rifle as Flash thrust a loaded banana clip into his carbine and we started back to our feet. Before we could squeeze off another round we heard a loud clamor behind us, turned and looked back to see Thuan, Ang and all the Strikers running and screaming toward us, letting loose a torrent of bullets as they closed the gap between us with lightning speed.

I dropped to the ground, yanking Flash with me to avoid becoming a casualty of friendly fire from our own men. Within seconds, 60MM mortar rounds arced over our heads and dropped into the enemy's positions with deadly accuracy raining death and destruction on the ranks of the VC's 260th Heavy Weapons Company.

The welcome sound of bullets from our rear screaming overhead to search out the enemy let us know in real terms that we were no longer alone in this fight. The sense of relief was almost overwhelming as we were joined by Thuan, Ang and the Strikers, who virtually surrounded me as I stood and joined in the renewed attack on our objective. An enemy bullet would have to have found my head to do me any damage because of the human shields I was now blessed with.

I halted the advance when we were within 200 meters of the enemy trench-line and ordered a heavy volume of mortar, machine gun and small arms fire on the now-fleeing Viet Cong, scurrying from their shallow trenches, retreating across the border into what they believed to be safe-havens. Not today!

Lieutenant Thuan, now standing beside me in the grass, radioed for fire support from the FOB. Within seconds, the first "marking" round of 81MM white phosphorous sprayed its own brand of death and misery in the midst of the now retreating and panic-stricken enemy. We stood watching as HE rounds from that same mortar found their target with Thuan acting as forward observer, giving excellent fire direction to the mortar crew. Numerous smaller, secondary explosions were heard as our shelling set off many of the booby-trapped mines in the thicket and followed the bolting enemy well into Cambodian territory.

The time had finally arrived. The VC must be shown that it would no longer be safe near the border with An Phu. I looked at Thuan and told him, "We must continue our operation into Cambodia and push the VC back from the border before dark. I would like to put fear in their hearts. Thinking we are not afraid of them, they will be afraid of us."

"Yes, Dai-uy, you are right. We will clear a path through the bamboo, and when we cross the border we will carry their dead and leave them inside Cambodia. Okay?" "Okay, Thuan." Encountering no resistance, we easily reached the enemy trenches and began the grim task of recovering two of our Strikers who'd been killed in action and searching the bodies of enemy dead. We found nothing of any importance, only a few snapshots of children that we returned to their pockets.

We lost two killed and two seriously wounded, while the VC suffered four killed, another 40 wounded and left two AK-47 assault rifles and two SKS carbines behind. We evacuated our dead and wounded back to camp by assault boat and sent orders with Map Map to bring three more assault boats back, leaving one for emergencies in camp. It had been a test and I now knew that Flash was a brave and willing, though initially unwitting, participant. His real name was Lo Lap Co and he would be by my side in and out of danger for the next seven months. I would learn to love him like a brother. I walked back with him to the fire support base and thanked Sergeant Hung and Sergeant Taylor for the excellent fire support they provided from their 60MM mortars. "What you did helped to make believers of them." Hung grinned from ear-to-ear. Jim Taylor, looking quite concerned, asked me to step away with him for a moment. Once out of earshot of Hung, Taylor asked me, "Did you know that this was coming down, Dai-uy?"

"I had an inkling, Jim. I was certain in my mind that Major Le would test me sooner or later. I'm glad it's done and behind me now. I wouldn't want to go through that again." "It sure put the fear of God in me, Dai-uy, and I was just back here watching. There was nothing I could do."

"What you guys did with those 60s once you got the green light was what routed the enemy. You dropped a couple of HE rounds into their laps and made them believe Cambodia had to be safer than that trench. You must of seen them run like their tails were on fire."

"Sure did. Thanks, Dai-uy. I feel better now, knowing that."

We replenished our ammunition and prepared to clear a wide swath through the bamboo thicket all the way to the border, removing or blowing in place all the mines and booby traps we would find.

At 1300 hours on 17 January, after a hot lunch of rice and chicken soup we relaxed for a half hour, savored the morning's victory and planned the next phase. I decided to intermittently shell the border area above the Phu Hiep FOB and inside Cambodia. The VC had most likely positioned snipers there to slow or stop our effort to remove mines and booby traps they'd set in place to protect the Bung Ven Secret Base from surprise attack.

On schedule we formed up and moved toward the north slowly, 150 men abreast with weapons at the ready, looking and feeling for trip wires and hidden punji traps. Most of the 700 pipe mines we disarmed or destroyed that afternoon were set at eye level in the thick bamboo with thin, barely distinguishable trip wires strung at varying distances from the ground. Each was positioned where it would inflict maximum casualties with serious head injuries. The 3/4 inch diameter iron pipe mine was stuffed with plastic explosive or dynamite that would be triggered by a pull-type or a pressure release-type detonator.

The Strikers had an uncanny ability to spot the trip wires and mines. Most were well experienced in disarming the pull type detonators, but when we knew or suspected a pressure release type was involved, we would blow it in place, using its own arming device.

The Viet Cong used several ingenious methods to put in place booby traps using hand grenades. The most common ones found in our sweep that day were dangerous to disarm. The safety pin had been pulled and the release handle held firmly as the hand grenade was slipped into a cardboard tube with one end closed. The tube was then placed in a bush or tree crotch and tilted toward the closed end. A wire was taped on the outside of the open end and stretched across a likely approach path. The slightest movement of the wire would pull the open end of the tube downward, allowing the grenade to fall from the tube, arm itself and explode. This was also a dangerous booby trap to deactivate. Tilt the tube in the wrong direction once the grenade was in place, and good-bye you! There were no second chances for care-less work. We uncovered camouflaged traps with punjis like we'd not seen before. Sharpened bamboo stakes set in the ground with water buffalo dung smeared on their tips to cause infection were what we'd been used to seeing. But these were made from steel rods about the diameter of a ten penny nail. Bent into a loop with a sharp spear-point hammered into one end, they were sharp enough and tough enough to pierce the steel insoles in jungle boots. The points were smeared with dung and the blunt ends were pushed into pre-drilled, fire-hardened bamboo in two or three rows of punjis four inches apart in all directions. Placed in trap holes about three feet wide by two feet across and a foot deep, they would seriously injure anyone stepping through the flimsy mat disguising the trap. We brought hundreds back to camp for our own use and set aside a pair of the punjis themselves for each man to take home as souvenirs. We captured or destroyed more than 700 pipe mines and brought back ten hand grenades that had been booby-trapped.

In warfare it was often more advantageous to seriously wound an enemy than to kill him. A dead man was no burden on a fighting force until the battle was over. A seriously wounded fighter required immediate treatment thereby creating a significant drain on the available fighting force as warriors were redirected to treat and evacuate wounded comrades. This reduced the combat capability of the unit as a whole at the very time it was most needed. The booby traps, mines and punji traps fit that psychology perfectly.

After shutting down our mortar fire into the area ahead of us, we carried four dead VC across the border and laid them on the edge of the main trail that crossed a footbridge spanning the narrow Co Lau River. From there the trail turned north and continued on to a Cambodian Outpost that stood as a sentinel on its east bank. I glanced at my watch. It was 0510 on 17 January and we had taken our first steps inside Cambodian territory. It felt good!

Our push due north took us about 100 meters inside the enemy's safe-haven, giving us a psychological victory that eclipsed even the taking back of the ground above Phu Hiep. We were actually standing where the VC had previously felt secure to attack us from without fear of retaliation.

"This is far enough, Thuan," I shouted, "Let's go home."

"I will not forget this day and this time, Dai-uy. Thieu-ta will be very pleased."

We crowded into our barge and 13 assault boats at the FOB, wanting to return before darkness had set in on the river. After a happy send-off by Lieutenant Ang Nguyen at 1800 hours, we moved quickly down the Co Lau, onto the Bassac and down river to Camp Dan Nam's boat dock. Major Le met us with congratulations and hardy handshakes. Smiling, he told me in front of Lieutenant Thuan and his men, "You are one of us, Dai-uy. You did well today."

I had passed the test!

When we arrived back in camp I asked Major Le what my team or I could do for the families of the two Strikers who were killed in action earlier above Phu Hiep.

"You are very kind, Dai-uy. You need do nothing, except perhaps you would like to go with me tomorrow when I visit the widow of one and the mother of the other. I will present them with the Cross of Gallantry their men earned in battle today. We will meet in front of the Operations Center at 0730 and go from there. Okay?"

"Okay, Thieu-ta. I would be honored to go with you. Are you sending a fresh company to Phu Hiep to clear the rest of the area of mines and booby traps?"

"Yes, it is good you asked. They will be on their way to the FOB before we leave in the morning. I am sending Lieutenant Hong Khanh Luong and his 445th Company, along with the reconnaissance platoon to finish the work you started."

The next day, with Flash in the back seat, we left at the appointed time in Major Le's jeep with a 3/4 ton truck bringing the security personnel following close behind. He told us that we would first see the widow and her three children. A simple, solid-looking bamboo house on stilts was their home that looked out over the Bassac River. Major Le consoled the widow and presented her husband's medal for bravery. It was a tragic, yet tender moment, as the three small children tugged at her long, black pants, tears streaming down their faces, not making a sound. She thanked Major Le for the Cross of Gallantry he had brought to her in recognition of her husband's courage in battle. Flash was moved with emotion, a fact borne out by the trembling in his voice as he translated for me. I bowed to show my respect for the widow as we turned and left.

The woman's display of personal courage and graceful acceptance of the tragedy in her time of grief stirred my emotions. Major Le's kind, comforting words to her were indicative of a true leader who could show compassion when needed and yet be an unshakable force in combat, a tiger who was courageous and unrelenting when facing the enemy.

Our visit to the second Striker's mother went as well as it could under the circumstances. Again, Major Le consoled, spoke of her son's bravery and soldiering accomplishments and then awarded the Cross of Gallantry to her that he had earned in battle. She was moved by Major Le's sincerity, his kind words and praise of her son's courage in battle.

By the time we left her home and were headed back to camp I could no longer hold back my emotions. My hand instinctively reached for the farmer's handkerchief I carried in my jungle fatigue pocket to quickly wipe the tears from my eyes. Upon regaining my composure, I asked Major Le what we could do to help the widow, now that she was alone with three children to take care of.

Major Le turned to look at me and said, "Thank you Dai-uy, but there is nothing you need do to help her. The Hoa Haos take care of their own. She and her children will be looked after. There is nothing to worry about, my friend."

"That sure speaks well of the Hoa Hao people. I tell you the truth, I've never met or even heard of people like the people of An Phu. You must be very proud to be their leader and protector."

He smiled and said nothing. He was a very different kind of military leader from those I had met in the past. A courageous and powerful leader, he was also humble and understanding of the needs of those whom he served. As we entered the front gate of Camp Dan Nam I knew I'd treasure every moment of my time with Major Le and the Hoa Haos. As the sun began to set in the west, Lieutenant Luong, his 445th Company and the Reconnaissance Platoon returned as heroes to camp, having disarmed or destroyed over 2000 mines and booby-traps, clearing another four large punji traps and recapturing all of their territory the VC had previously taken and controlled.

The combination of nightly mortar bombardment inside Cambodia and our successes above Phu Hiep began to take its psychological toll on the enemy. This was proven out as two young VC recruits crossed the border at 0030 on 19 January and turned themselves in at the Phu Loi PF Outpost northwest of our FOB at Phu Hiep. They carried Chieu Hoi program safe-conduct-passes we had dropped over their area. The pass guaranteed amnesty, good treatment and the opportunity to serve their country as repatriated civilians.

They wore new black uniforms and carried brand new Chinese AK-47 assault rifles that still had tell-tale traces of cosmoline from factory packaging. Information freely given by them verified our agents' reports about the Bung Ven secret base (for some time not so secret) citing morale problems among the VC who'd suddenly been subjected to our "invasion" of what had been considered their safe-haven.

They spoke of our having killed seven of their comrades in the recent operation to clear the minefields and take back our territory. Also, they said there was much talk about avenging their deaths. One of the men told of overhearing two of their officers talk about mounting a large attack to destroy Phu Hiep and kill all the "American Lackeys," as they referred to the CIDG.

In mid-morning of that same day, our reconnaissance platoon encountered a group of seven well armed black-pajama-clad men coming north towards An Phu village on a B Team 3/4 ton truck and stopped them at a point three kilometers south of the village. CIA paramilitary officer Walter MacKem, leader of the Vietnamese Counter Terrorist team, asked to be escorted to meet Tuoi Van Nguyen, the An Phu District Chief. Instead, Sergeant Dung brought them into Camp Dan Nam where Major Le and I met them at the main entrance gate.

> *"The Chau Doc province level CIA paramilitary officer responsible for promoting and organizing counter-terrorist (CT) teams was Walter MacKem. MacKem, who had arrived in Vietnam in early 1964 to organize the six man CT teams, would sometimes don black pajamas and accompany his teams on missions deep into enemy territory to snatch and snuff out Vietcong Infrastructure cadres," wrote Douglas Valentine in his book, THE PHOENIX PROGRAM.[1] Major Le knew of MacKem's CT teams and how they operated in other parts of Chau Doc province and wanted no part of that kind of activity in An Phu. It was, in Major Le's judgment, virtually impossible for the Vietcong to infiltrate Hoa Hao government or military organizations. The Hoa Haos ran a tight ship, and except for those Vietnamese civilians hired by the American A Team leader, a non-Hoa Hao would be foolhardy to so much as attempt to infiltrate the CIDG or the local populace.*

After we were introduced by Sergeant Dung, I explained the situation in An Phu and told Agent MacKem that we did not need nor want his team operating in An Phu.

"I report to a higher authority, Captain Marvin. It's my job to come into your area and help to find and eliminate VC who have infiltrated your CIDG," MacKem said in an annoyed tone.

"We'll take care of our CIDG, MacKem. Major Le knows each and every one of them and they are all Hoa Haos loyal to him. Check with your higher authority if you feel like questioning my right to control who comes and goes in An Phu."

"Who do you think you are, Captain, King of the Hoa Haos?"

Before I could respond, Major Le, sensing a real confrontation, broke in and told him, "Sergeant Dung will take you back to Chau Doc in our assault boats, Mister MacKem. What Dai-uy says is true. We do not need your expertise among the Hoa Haos. All the fighters in An Phu are Hoa Hao."

As they turned around and left back through our main gate, I let Major Le know he was a far better diplomat than me. He laughed and we went on with the day's routine activities.

I spent some time with Sergeant Tenorio, learning more about what an average day's work consisted of for our two medics. First thing I learned was that there was no such thing as an average day. The fact that there were no doctors in An Phu made it doubly difficult for our medics. If they had lacked the in-depth training they received in what is realistically called the "Dog Lab" at Fort Bragg, they would have been unable to cope with the demands of their job.

"I like going out in the small hamlets with my team and especially seeing the kids," Tenorio told me. "Anything I can do to make those kids happy makes me happy too." His team consisted of himself, Sergeant Kuchen, the LLDB medic named Chet, a Vietnamese nurse, an interpreter, future nurses or medics in training, and a security force. They would go by boat or truck, depending on which of the hamlets they would serve that day.

"Round worm is endemic here, been here forever, mostly due to the lack of pure water," he told me. "They've always had the worms and they always will until they start wearing shoes of some kind. Going barefoot, the spores get into the cracks of their feet and work their way up into their intestines. I go out into the hamlets and see kids throwing up those long, white worms. Or you see it in their stool. I help 'em the best I can, Dai-uy.

"Same goes for head sores. They wash in dirty river water and don't use soap. I'll give a mother a bar of soap, tell her how to use it, and the next time she sees me she'll smile and tell me how her kid's head sores cleared up in just three days. She's so happy, you'd think it was a miracle.

"I carry dental equipment too, Dai-uy, because the local habit of chewing betel nuts goes hand-in-hand with gum disease."

"Betel nuts?" I asked.

"You're new here. They come from the betel palm tree that grows all over Southeast Asia. The people chew the nuts, along with the leaf of the betel plant like we would chew tobacco."

Tooth extractions were done on an assembly line basis. Sergeant Chet would get the people in line, old and young alike and the nurse would inject the area around the bad tooth with Novocaine, using disposable, sterilized needles. Once the mouth was numb, Bac-si would pull the offending tooth and stuff treated cotton in the void. The other SF medic would be further along, dispensing toiletry kits and demonstrating tooth brushing techniques. When Kuchen smiled after brushing, his gleaming teeth were a shining example to everyone who'd gone through the painful extraction. At the very end of the line, another nurse or medic trainee would explain when they should take the cotton out and tell them how odd the cotton would feel for a while when they stuck their tongue in where the tooth used to be.

In a way it was like a traveling medicine show and a source of entertainment as well as a real help to the local people. A close circle of onlookers smiled, pointed and giggled at everything the medic did to someone else. That team never left a hamlet or village without feeling appreciated, maybe even loved.

Tending and treating Strikers, their families and as many of the local civilians as they could get to was an awesome task. I asked Bac-si how many they saw and treated for one thing or another every month on the average. "Somewhere between 4000 to 8000, Dai-uy. We use a lot of medical supplies. What makes it so tough is they don't have any real doctors in An Phu. There are some acupuncture nuts," he said, "Chinese style doctors, poking and infecting the people with dirty needles which just adds to our work. Maybe some day there will be Hoa Hao doctors, Dai-uy?"

"I just don't know, Bac-si, but I do know they'll have some good medics, nurses and midwives in An Phu when we leave because of what you, Kuchen and the others have done."

Later, I asked Major Le why there was such a shortage of doctors.

"Because there were so many years of war and there is only one medical university in South Vietnam. We do not have enough doctors in Vietnam for each district to have one. Mostly doctors are in big cities where there are more people to serve. Your medics are very good. They have done so much for all the people, even the children of this district. Of course we have those people who use the Chinese needle method of Chinese medications believing they could help. But, of course they did not. Because of infection they really make the situation much worse."

"Exactly what Sergeant Tenorio told me earlier today."

Specialist Menkins left on the 20th for a three day commissary run to Saigon. We were nearly out of strictly American food because the team had been shut down in December and couldn't make the run. Most of what we ate we bought in An Phu at the local marketplace. It is important to recognize that, as Green Berets, wherever we go we try to blend in and support the local economy. What we needed from Saigon were things we couldn't get at the local market, like canned soup, crackers, pizza mix, pasta and other back-home delights, maybe even some steak! We'd each chipped in and given Menkins the money needed to buy everything we wanted.

Menkins, with a four man security force and two assault boats, went down-river to Can Tho and from there he hopped a flight on a Caribou aircraft to Saigon. At daybreak he'd give our order to the commissary clerk, knowing it would be ready the next morning. They did a good job: meat was packed in dry ice to avoid spoilage in the hundred degree heat and everything was boxed and strapped to a pallet to load on the Caribou for the flight to Can Tho. They even trucked the pallet to the airport once it was paid for.

When he would arrive back at Can Tho, Menkins, with the Strikers' help, would move the boxes from the pallet into the waiting assault boats and retrace their way back up the Bassac River to our camp.

Early in the afternoon of 20 January I prepared to go on a CIDG night ambush operation out of the Khanh Binh FOB. Group policy and common sense prohibited any of my team from going alone on a combat operation with irregular troops. Easy to say, but not easy to do when your team had so few men as mine. There were only nine of us doing what 24 should be doing because of the sub-sector advisory mission. With Specialist Menkins on the commissary run we were really hurting for warm bodies. Lieutenant Kallunki would command in my absence, Sergeants Valenzuela and Taylor would man the four-deuce, Sergeant Bridgewater would back up Sergeant Eleam in the commo bunker and the two medics would continue to meet themselves coming and going on medical patrols and casualty tending.

It was not a good situation. We were so limited by our numbers that we seldom went on patrol or ambush operations with our Strikers. No lack of enthusiasm among my men, who would rather be out in the field with our Strikers on civic action projects, combat operations or medical patrols then be dealing with the routine of camp operation.

I stuffed my rucksack with a camouflage poncho liner, binoculars, water purification and salt tablets, a change of black pajamas, and extra ammunition. After cleaning my rifle and my forty-five, I secured three hand grenades, a canteen full of water, lensatic compass, and holstered pistol on my web belt. After securing two bandoleers of 7.62mm ammunition across my chest, I donned my rucksack, took my M-16 in my right hand and checked to make certain I had my flashlight with night filters in place clipped onto my harness webbing. The black-pajama night-fighting uniform I wore, along with a wide-brimmed floppy black hat was much the same uniform the VC wore and perfect for night ambush operations. There was no concern that we'd mistake one another for a VC which could lead to a disastrous conclusion. Once in place, after moving to the location at dusk, there would be no movement unless we made contact with the enemy.

The trip to the FOB was uneventful. It wasn't until we neared the border and were on the final leg of the trip to the FOB that I realized I'd come through the village of An Thanh with its many bat houses and had not even noticed the pungent odor of guano. I never thought that day would come, but it did and I was glad!

Flash and I were met at the FOB gate by Lieutenant Luong Hoang Le, commander of the 442d Company. He invited us to have tea and afterwards showed us around the FOB. The western part of the perimeter fronted on the road paralleling the border canal and included an old masonry building with its share of scars from the cross-border clashes of the recent past.

After a delicious dinner of soup, pit-barbecued fish and steamed rice, we joined the ambush platoon for a mission briefing. First thing I noticed was that the Strikers treated Flash as if he were one of them. Normally the interpreters were considered outsiders but Flash had proven himself when he stood his ground alongside me during the testing above Phu Hiep. The word had spread among the Strikers and the LLDB quickly, making him welcome in all corners of An Phu.

Shortly after the sun set behind the Cambodian outpost, a stone's throw across the border canal, our 42 black-clad Strikers silently filed out of the FOB. One carried a light machine gun and two toted BARs, adding clout to our force.

With Flash just behind me I followed the platoon leader as we moved south for about 200 meters, crossed the narrow dirt road that led to An Thanh, turned toward the southwest and moved towards AP III Hamlet.

The Strikers moved quietly and cautiously through the shadowless darkness of the moonless night. We remained close together in single file until we arrived at the ambush site, 500 meters east of AP III Hamlet. Silently we took our positions behind a slight hump in the terrain, faced to the south and spaced ourselves six feet apart. The machine gunner, flanked by Strikers with BARs, took center position as we carefully oriented our field of fire to avoid shooting in the direction of AP III.

Once in position it was a waiting game. We lay still, listened and watched. The waiting was always the hardest, not knowing when or if the enemy would enter our trap. We hoped our movement from the FOB to the ambush site went undetected. If we somehow were seen or heard, we would have given the enemy the advantage and unwittingly placed ourselves in his trap. The element of surprise was critical. Once in place, we would rely on a sixth sense to alert us to imminent danger from any direction, and hoped it would work. The minutes dragged into hours and our senses began to dull. Again and again I lifted my binoculars to my eyes and scanned the area to my front. Nothing, yet.

Scattered clumps of bamboo, visible about 200 meters distant, were silhouetted against a starlit sky. Without the aid of binoculars, I would have seen nothing. Just beyond the bamboo clumps, the six little lakes of Roc Dung formed a natural deterrent to flight should the VC attempt to escape our ambush in a westerly direction. Likewise, larger and deeper Thien Lon Lake stood as a barrier to their escape in a southerly or southeasterly direction. Villagers in AP III had reported to our men at Khanh Binh that the natural corridor which lay before us had been used recently by the VC to skirt the defenses of our FOB when conducting after dark incursions into An Phu. If they did so again this evening and if the ambush were triggered at the right moment, they'd have little choice but to attempt escape the way they had come, taking them through our killing field. In their rush to retreat through AP III and back across the border canal they would play into our hands.

The effectiveness of mosquito repellent, generously applied hours earlier, would wear off after a few hours in position, but it would prove unwise, and possibly deadly, to apply even a small amount with the ambush in place. The pungent aroma would carry a long ways on the slightest breeze, betraying our position. Malaria-carrying mosquitoes will cover any exposed areas of skin quickly once the repellent has worn off and a person is then forced to cope, hoping they will fly away. After an hour or two muscles begin to cramp and aches and pains tempt you to move as your body naturally wants to reposition itself to ease the situation. The physiological tug-of-war between a man's need to remain quiet, alert and still, and his natural tendency under those circumstances to succumb to sleep, demand extraordinary self discipline. A man had to maintain continuing control of his faculties so he could react instantly and with accuracy in what would suddenly be a kill or be killed situation.

At 0220 hours our long wait proved fruitful as 20 armed, black-uniformed VC were seen emerging from AP III hamlet and moving in an easterly direction in single file. Most likely they had crossed the border canal northeast of our Tac Truc PF outpost, quietly slipped through AP III, and believing they had gone undetected, were now proceeding toward An Thanh and directly into the killing zone for our ambush force, 100 meters distant.

Our ambush platoon leader exercised good judgment and patience, waiting until the last of the foe was clearly visible and directly to his front. The initial burst of semiautomatic fire from his rifle triggered a virtual hailstorm of bullets from our machine-gun, BARs, rifles and carbines. We filled the air with bullets, catching the enemy by surprise.

Not unprepared for an ambush, they immediately dropped to the ground and returned our fire with equal ferocity. Brilliant muzzle-flashes revealed each shooter's position as fiery tracers crisscrossed the pitch-dark of the no-man's-land, creating an eerie fireplay of night combat.

As suddenly as it had erupted, the exchange of fire ceased. In less than a minute the battlefield was momentarily still. I laid my M-16 aside and peered through my binoculars, focusing in on the location of the last muzzle flash I'd seen. Within seconds I observed a number of heads bobbing above the high grass as the enemy moved slowly towards AP III Hamlet, in the direction of the border canal and Cambodia. The slow pace of their retreat meant they were dragging dead or seriously wounded comrades.

I motioned to the Platoon Leader, then Flash hollered something in Vietnamese to the Sergeant and 42 weapons exploded into action, following my burst, using the path of my tracers to guide their aim. Our quarry then retreated in panic, leaving those bodies and disabled warriors who would slow their pace, this time not even stopping to return our fire, wanting only to escape into what they had known to be a safe-haven.

We continued to pepper their retreat route with machine-gun, rifle and carbine fire, ceasing when they reached the hamlet, not wanting civilian casualties. We moved into the hamlet cautiously. Once we felt confidant that they'd kept moving through the village and across the nearby canal into Cambodia, we closed on the border and directed mortar fire from the FOB on their suspected positions. We then witnessed some expert rapid-fire action by the FOB 81MM mortar crew as they lobbed ten rounds of HE, covering a wide span inside their former safe haven. We lacked knowledge of how many casualties we'd exacted, but felt certain the VC now knew that we meant business: there would be no safe place anywhere within range of our firepower. Two of our Strikers received minor injuries and were treated on sight by a CIDG medic our medic had trained. We found four dead VC, searched their bodies, and finding nothing of any use to us, carried their bodies to the near bank of the border canal. One of the villagers reported to the FOB within a few hours that their comrades had returned for them.

Coming back through the hamlet of AP III, I couldn't help but reflect on the caring nature of our Strikers and their LLDB leaders, particularly toward the local civilians. The people of AP III no doubt felt secure enough in the knowledge we would not intentionally allow the combat to reach into their homes, that they obeyed the dark to light curfew fervently. When the ambush patrol platoon leader signaled his men to cease firing, knowing that continued attempts to hit the enemy might cause civilians to be injured or killed, it proved to them just how much the CIDG cared for them.

Within minutes we were back at Khanh Binh FOB and I was sound asleep on a bamboo mat inside the command post, using my rucksack for a pillow.

We returned to camp, departing at 0700 after an early breakfast, wanting to get our vehicles back to accomplish the routine rotating of our companies. Major Le met us inside the gate to congratulate us on our victory. After dismounting from the trucks, Lieutenant Kallunki and our two Team Sergeants joined us and we stood around in a kind of circle discussing the previous night's ambush action. While we savored the sweet taste of victory, we heard the distant drone of an Army Caribou aircraft approaching our drop zone.

"Don't worry, Dai-uy, Jim Taylor has got it covered. He's out on the drop zone now, making certain the red target panel is located just right to compensate for wind drift." Our civilian workers had moved the cattle to the windward side of the drop zone. We didn't want any of them hit by an ammunition pallet weighing a 1000 pounds.

Four bundles slid out of the rear of the aircraft in rapid succession, their colorful, cotton parachutes popping open within seconds of deployment by the static line. I never tired of seeing the heavy bundles swinging like pendulums under their parachutes, stabilizing only moments before landing with a thud on the soft turf.

Ours was a small drop zone and a real challenge for the pilot and crew chief of that aircraft. Understanding the importance these drops of vital ammunition and medical supplies were to our mission was what kept them on their toes and normally very accurate. This day, however, was one of those days when everything didn't go as planned. The last bundle got caught in a cross wind gust and was swept out over the compound. It descended and crashed through the roof of a CIDG barracks building with a resounding crash, tearing a gaping hole in the corrugated tin roof and splintering the wooden roof trusses like so many toothpicks.

Major Le and I ran to the scene and saw that the building was empty and we knew then that we had just missed a major disaster. The heavy canvas bundle had ripped open on impact with the roof and its cargo of hundred pound boxes of mortar ammunition had been scattered out over half of the barracks floor, busting up metal cots and lockers on impact.

Both of our Team Sergeants were quickly on the scene, surveying the wreckage, discussing plans to repair the damage and to replace anything destroyed by the errant bundle of ammunition and ordering Strikers into action, all within a ten minute span of time. "We'll have it fixed up in three days time, Dai-uy," shouted Sergeant Valenzuela, just as I was heading back to the drop zone with Major Le.

"Sounds good to me, Val. We're sure lucky the barracks building was empty."

"Someone up there is looking out for us, Dai-uy." Major Le and his team coordinated the rotation of CIDG companies, using our trucks to shuttle Lieutenant Triet Van Tran's 443rd Company from Camp to the Khanh Binh FOB and returning to camp with half of Lieutenant Luong Hoang Le's 442nd Company each time.

Our boats and barge were used to shuttle Lieutenant Thuan Hieu Nguyen's 441st Company from Camp to Phu Hiep FOB, returning an equal number of men of the 444th each time with their commander, Lieutenant Ang Ngoc Nguyen, leading the first half back to camp.

Specialist Menkins returned from Saigon on the 22nd with all kinds of goodies he'd bought at the commissary. We celebrated that evening with huge charcoal-broiled steaks, fried potatoes, peas and local baked bread. For the next few days we ate our fill of perishable items, not wanting to lose anything due to lack of refrigeration. Meat could last just so long on ice.

The next days would be busy, especially for those in my team who worked with the LLDB inspecting, repairing or replacing weapons, radios, and other equipment as part of the regular rotating/refurbishing cycle for the two companies that had most recently arrived back in camp. Even uniforms, boots and other personal items were repaired or replaced, depending on their condition. Our goal with each rotation was to bring the units back to peak operational condition and then schedule some free time for the Strikers to have with their families, while making certain we had sufficient forces on call in camp to react to emergencies anywhere in the district.

Major Le appeared to be particularly pleased about something when he joined me just before midnight in the command bunker. "I would like you to go with me to Hoa Hao Village tomorrow. Will you meet me in my office at 0700?"

I was excited just to have the opportunity to go to Hoa Hao Village and quickly answered yes. I asked what the agenda for the visit was. He grinned widely and told me I'd know soon enough.

After breakfast, I donned my best jungle fatigues, Green Beret and pistol belt with a holstered .45 caliber pistol. I ordered Lieutenant Kallunki, who would assume command in my absence, to stay close to the flagpole. The trip to Hoa Hao Village took five hours by assault boat, going south on the Bassac River to Chau

Doc where the Bassac turned in a southeasterly direction and then on to Binh Long, where we entered a cross-channel that took us over to the mighty Mekong River. Going with the flow toward the South China Sea, we soon came upon Hoa Hao Village, located on the southeastern bank of the Mekong River, arriving just before noon. On the last leg of our journey, Major Le explained, "This is a special day for the Hoa Haos to celebrate the Hoa Hao religion foundation. Because of what you have done to help the Hoa Hao people in An Phu and because of your courage and excellent cooperation that led to successes in battle and in caring for the people, I have recommended you to be named an honorary Hoa Hao. When we get to Hoa Hao Village I will introduce you to the Mother of the Teacher of the Hoa Haos and also you will meet the Hoa Hao Central Council. As of this day," he said, looking at me, "You are the only American that has ever been recommended for this honor."

Speaking of Huynh Phu So, "He was our first prophet and teacher," Major Le explained. "He was murdered by the Communists."

After we had disembarked, Major Le led the way to an open courtyard in the center of Hoa Hao Village. There were no temples, pagodas, or statues within sight. We were greeted by the sight of perhaps 60 or more people standing shoulder-to-shoulder in a semicircle behind an elderly lady who sat in the only chair present in the courtyard. With the exception of two South Vietnamese in civilian suits and those of us in uniform, the Hoa Haos wore black, knee-length tunics over white trousers and small, black caps with narrow, turned-up brims. Whispering discreetly, Major Le told me that the seated lady was Madame Bo Huynh. Her chair was ornately carved with some gold leaf, but not ostentatious. She wore a long-sleeved black robe that revealed only her hands, face and the tips of her highly shined black shoes. Silver-gray hair drawn back in a tight bun topped a severely proud, age-wrinkled face. She watched the proceedings with the elegant composure of a queen, her hands cupped over the ends of the graceful mahogany arms of her chair. Behind her stood a younger woman, her personal assistant.

Major Le led me up to where I stood directly in front of Madame Bo Huynh, introduced me and I bowed as was the custom when greeting elders. She reached out with a frail but steady hand to shake mine and, as Major Le translated, I told her how honored I was to meet her and how proud I was to serve among the Hoa Haos. She smiled and told me they were pleased to have me among their people. Just before we were to pose for photos with Madame Bo Huynh, Major Le presented me with a scarf of purple silk as a memento from the Hoa Haos, tied it around my neck and tucked it under the collar of my jungle fatigues. "You are now an honorary Hoa Hao, and you should know that you are the only American who has been given this honor." Madame Bo Huynh smiled, and tears came to my eyes as I accepted the scarf and thanked Major Le and Madame Bo Huynh for such an honor.

When Sergeant Hung, Map Map and the bodyguards, waiting in the boats, saw the scarf, they eagerly reached out to shake my hand and offer their congratulations. I would always have a warm feeling in my heart for the Hoa Haos, their values and their friendship. I knew I would never forget them nor the honor they bestowed on me this day. At one point during the return trip I turned to Major Le and told him, "This is the greatest honor I have ever received, Thieu-ta. I hope I can live up to what it represents."

"That you have already done, Dai-uy," he said, smiling.

The border area was quiet for the remainder of January as is usually the case during the time of the full moon. Actual enemy activity was limited to minor harassment of PF border outposts with no casualties on either side.

During this period of relative peace, we were able to concentrate more effort on civic action projects, medical assistance, psychological warfare and military government activities. To my way of thinking, meeting the needs of the people was by far the most important work that we did to make it possible to win against the Communist forces, whether they be North Vietnamese regular forces or the guerrilla forces that we more typically fought against in An Phu.

Lieutenant Kallunki continued to work very closely with Mr. Minh, the District VIS officer, using all available resources to keep the people informed and to instill fear in the hearts of the enemy. The District newspaper glorified our recent victories and kept the people informed about the many civic action projects recently completed or in progress. Leaflets were designed, printed in the Cambodian tongue and, using a hired civilian aircraft, dropped out to drift and fall into hamlet areas on the Cambodian side of the border canal, describing our victories over the Communist invaders and asking them not to help the enemy, but to remain neutral.

At 0730 hours on 30 January, Kallunki came running into my office from the direction of the command bunker, all excited and out of breath. "An Air America chopper just landed," he shouted, "The pilot says he's here to take you on recon along the border."

Hurrying out to the landing zone, I hollered, "Thanks, John, I'll take it from here."

Earlier in January I had sent a message to Lieutenant Colonel Tuttle in Can Tho, asking for a helicopter to take me on reconnaissance along the border. I wanted to assess the effect our cross-border mortar fire was having on VC units inside Cambodia. Perhaps this CIA chopper was his answer. A shame, I thought, that our own helicopters or Air Force reconnaissance aircraft couldn't be used to search out enemy locations inside Cambodia and near the border.

The pilot was in his mid-forties, of medium build, and wore tan trousers, white shirt and a light blue cotton jacket. His only weapon was a .38 caliber pistol slung in a shoulder holster. During the short time he was on the ground he talked me into giving him an M-2 carbine with three full thirty round magazines to keep in his chopper. Made sense to me being he was risking his life to take me up over the VC safe-havens, especially with him knowing an enemy heavy weapons battalion lay in wait across the border with its .50 caliber antiaircraft machine guns pointed skyward.

Once we were airborne and out of range of enemy small arms fire, I guided him in a southwesterly direction toward the PF outpost at Vinh Hoi. From there we flew north directly above the border, following it up to the Khanh Binh FOB, around the Khanh An "thumb" and then in an easterly direction along the border to Phu Hiep where he circled the area we'd just taken back under our control. I had a good look at the VC trenches we'd overrun less than two weeks prior. Gave me goose bumps recalling that day!

"Now that you know the border, how about taking me inside Cambodia 1000 meters deep so I can see what damage we've done in their sanctuaries?" I asked the pilot.

"Sure thing, Captain," he spoke over the intercom, "I like excitement." He immediately maneuvered to a position approximately one kilometer inside Cambodia and headed back the direction we'd come.

Looking down, I could readily see that 29 nights of random mortar attacks had done their job. I saw no sign of enemy bivouac areas or emplacements within 2000 meters of the border itself. The evidence of deserted encampments and abandoned trenches, along with many small craters created by our mortar bombardment made it crystal-clear that what we were doing was having an impact on the Viet Cong the length of the border area with our district.

Prior to lifting off after he'd brought me back to camp, the Air America pilot told me he'd try to get back in three week's time. "Could you get me a VC battle flag to take home to show off to my kids when I come back?" He asked.

"You take me where you took me today and you can count on a VC flag with blood on it." I hollered back at him.

He lifted off, a smile on his face.

On 1 February I compiled the combat statistics report for the month of January and gave it to John Eleam to send to the B Team in Chau Doc. Our forces had killed 11 VC and wounded another 41. We captured four weapons, destroyed an ammunition dump and captured or destroyed 2700 pipe mines and hand-grenade booby traps. Our losses were four CIDG killed and four CIDG wounded in combat actions. "Not bad, Dai-uy," Kallunki remarked after reviewing our file copy.

Just before lunch on the 3rd, our team got a boost of added manpower when Sergeant First Class Edward P. Davis returned in the assault boat from Chau Doc with Lieutenant Kallunki. Davis was slender, stood about five feet nine, and had sharp facial features. "I'm glad to be here, Dai-uy," He told me, "But, I won't be here very long. My rotation date is the 28th of March. I'll do my best as long as I'm here."

Sergeant Davis was a weapons man with a strong interest in civic action and an engineering background. "We're happy to have you aboard," I told him. "As soon as you get your gear stowed, you'll be off out in the district with Lieutenant Kallunki. I want you to meet the people you'll be dealing with and helping and getting to know the area as soon as possible. You'll soon have no doubt in your mind that he needs help with the many projects we've got in the mill. No lack of work here, Davis, and I know you'll like the Hoa Haos."

117

Sergeant Davis smiled, said he'd already heard a lot about the Hoa Haos, and told me, "They call you 'King of the Hoa Haos' at the B Team, Dai-uy. I overheard two of the sergeants talking in the mess and it sounded to me like their CO hates your guts. Is it true what they said about you doing things the way you want to regardless of what the B Team tells you?"

"I won't go into that right now, but Sergeant Valenzuela will fill you in on our mission and he'll tell you why I'm not too popular with the B Team commander. Let me tell you about the Hoa Haos real quick-like. I doubt you got the real word about them from the B Team. Davis, you can go anywhere in this district and lose your wallet, in the middle of the road, path, or wherever, and you can be certain in your mind that it will be returned within a day with everything in it that was there when you dropped it. I've never met people like the Hoa Haos before. You'll get to know them quickly when you're out with the XO. Our philosophy of civic action is not anything new or radical. We learn from them what really needs doing and we help them to get the job done any way that we can. It's as simple as that. We don't force-feed anything. We want to be known by them as their helpers, friends who will go out of their way to do what is right for them, even to giving of ourselves personally. If there is one thing I am certain of, if your head is on straight, it's that you'll have good memories of your seven weeks here in An Phu helping the Hoa Haos. Any questions?"

"Not right now, Dai-uy. Sounds like I've got a lot to learn about An Phu, and I'm looking forward to it."

Team Sergeant Val showed Davis to his cubicle and gave him a thorough briefing in the Operations Center, high-lighting civic action programs as well as the tactical situation and latest intelligence. Lieutenant Kallunki then took him under his wing and toured the district showing Davis many of the completed CA/PSY OPNS projects and stopping by other projects yet in progress, including a three room school, maternity house and boat dock. He introduced Davis to the District Chief, VIS Chief and Agricultural Chief and took him to witness a typical loudspeaker appeal being made using their Lambretta powered system along the border area near Khanh Binh.

We'd no sooner finished lunch that day when a fire broke out in the nearby village of An Phu. A CIDG sentry at the front gate heard the explosion, saw the flames, ran into the mess area where we sat and motioned us outside in a hurry. As we stepped out we saw the fire. I left John Eleam to man the communications bunker, told Sergeant Tenorio to set up a mobile aid station near the village and treat victims of the fire and then led the rest of my men, running the 1000 meters to where the fire now raged out of control.

Recognizing within minutes that village fire-fighting gear was hopelessly inadequate to control the raging inferno, we organized bucket brigades to bring water from the nearby canal to wet down houses in the path of the conflagration, hoping it would slow or stop the fire.

Every fourth or fifth bucket was poured on those of us nearest the fire in each of the lines to keep the dangerously close flames from igniting our clothes. We labored feverishly alongside the villagers but soon saw that flames were racing along the rooftops, too high for us to quench with buckets of water.

I decided on a different approach, grabbed five of the strongest men I could get my hands on, and we literally tore two houses apart, piece by piece throwing their remnants over the bank and into the canal to form a fire break. We quickly stepped back and watched as the fire consumed the last house remaining at the edge of the newly created gap. Something within the last structure, perhaps a can of cooking oil, exploded and sent pieces of blazing bamboo and sparks flying in all directions, but failed to bridge the gap. Forty houses were saved from fiery destruction. We then turned our attention to a row of threatened shops that stood with their backs to the Bassac River, repeated the scenario, and saved ten shops. As we stood there, drenched with sweat and physically exhausted, four gasoline powered water pumps, borrowed from a nearby village arrived and were quickly placed in service, bringing the fire completely under control in a matter of minutes.

A 12 February 1966 article in The Observer,[2] an English language newspaper published in Saigon, told of the fire in vivid detail: "She had done it a thousand times before. She threw a handful of charcoal in the cooking urn, drenched it with gasoline and threw a match on the charcoal. Normally it lit with a 'whoosh' and burned down to a satisfactory glow.

"This time, the fumes exploded, and a sheet of fire shot up to the roof. In seconds the walls were ablaze, and the fire that eventually destroyed two-thirds of the town of An Phu had broken out.

"An Phu [Village] lies on the Bassac River in the Delta province of Chau Doc. Its 5,000 inhabitants are mostly members of the Hoa Hao Buddhist sect, and An Phu itself is an important marketplace and trading center.

" Special Forces team A-424 was just finishing lunch when the fire broke out, and the entire team rushed to the village to aid the people in removing precious belongings from threatened buildings. The fire, raging out of control as sparks began setting additional fires in other areas of the town threatened to wipe out the entire village.

"The blaze began in a row of buildings in the center of the village and quickly spread through the tinder-dry thatched roof houses. The only fire-fighting equipment available at the onset of the blaze were inadequate bucket brigades organized from the river to the fire.

"Special Forces team members began directing the destruction of houses in the path of the flames, pushing them into the river or a canal running laterally through the town. As the fire reached its height, four pumps from a settlement down river arrived, and progress toward control of the fire began.

"When the last embers had burned out, 108 families — nearly 2,000 people —were homeless. Fortunately, there were no fatalities.

"Within minutes after the Special Forces team arrived on the scene, SSGT Santos D. Tenorio, senior medic, had set up an aid station, although he received

little business. The team, as soon as the fire was under control, stripped its supply room, donating 100 blankets, 230 ponchos, 100 sets of black pajamas and 35 mosquito nets. Capt. Daniel Marvin, team chief, dipped into the team's emergency fund and turned over to the district chief 100,000 piasters for distribution.

"The fire, which broke out at 12:30 p.m., raged until 2 p.m. before it was extinguished, and by 4 p.m. the district chief was distributing money, clothing, salad oil and other necessities donated by the Special Forces team to the families who were wiped out by the flames.

"Early the next morning a convoy arrived from the B team at Chau Doc, with additional blankets, clothing and cooking utensils.

"At dawn, villagers were clearing away the still-smoldering debris, and with an emergency grant of 800,000 piasters from the Vietnamese government, were taking the first steps toward rebuilding their devastated homes."'

The caption under a photo showing the South Vietnamese National Colors being raised in An Phu village's center, read, "MORALE BOOSTER - The Vietnamese flag that flew over An Phu was turned an ugly brown by the heat and smoke of the fire, and from the Special Forces supply room this new flag was donated to the village. Capt. Daniel Marvin, right, A-424 team chief, helps two CIDG strike force soldiers run up the new flag."

The recovery and reconstruction effort was phenomenal. Our team, working with the LLDB, CIDG Strikers, Regional Force soldiers and people from all over the district gave of themselves, contributing money, labor or both to rebuilding the village. Within a period of seven days, under the caring and expert supervision of Sergeant Davis and his LLDB counterpart, a total of 97 thatched roof, bamboo-framed homes were built from scratch. At the same time, friends and neighbors pitched in to help repair hundreds of fire-damaged homes and shops, working at a feverish pace. If one had not believed that the Hoa Hao people were one big family who loved and cared for one another, one would only need to have been in An Phu during that week of destruction and renewal.

Leaving shortly after breakfast in his jeep on the 5th of February with a 3/4 ton truck carrying the security escort close behind, Major Le and I began an inspection tour of the FOBs. It was more a morale-boosting visit than anything else, but did include an inspection of weapons and facilities with emphasis also on making certain their ammunition stocks were adequate to hold out against a large scale attack. Two VC battalions were within small arms range of Khanh Binh. Major Le and I felt a lot better knowing the FOB had what they needed to defend themselves.

On the way back through the district village, we noticed the barber shop was back in business under a makeshift tent-like shelter. Major Le pulled over and stopped, knowing I was wanting to get a haircut and seeing there was no one in the barber's chair. "I will do some visiting and come back in 15 minutes, Dai-uy."

"Thanks, Thieu-ta, I need this." I sat down in the high and comfortable folding chair facing a four-legged work table with a large mirror at just the right height to let the customer see what the barber was doing. This was my second time in his shop and I enjoyed the extras: a head massage, eyebrows and ears clipped, and the "feather" treatment. When he finished cutting he'd hold a quill of a goose feather between his palms, stick the tip of the feather in each ear and twist it around so as to flick out the little pieces of hair he'd just clipped. It about drove me nuts the first time, this time it just tickled.

As I stepped down and paid the barber, Major Le started the jeep. I got in and he drove to the camp dock where we boarded a waiting assault boat with Map Map at the helm and two Strikers with M-1 rifles midship. Two assault boats with a total of eight well-armed Strikers joined us on our trip to Phu Hiep. We met with Lieutenant Thuan Nguyen and inspected the FOB and CIDG company as we had done at Khanh Binh earlier. Major Le told Lieutenant Thuan to be especially vigilant due to his concern that the VC would soon attempt to revenge their recent defeat and take back the territory north of Phu Hiep that we had recently liberated. "They have their 510th battalion on the border, along with the 260th heavy weapons company. We also have a report of another battalion now in reserve at Bung Ven. I believe it is the 407th VC battalion," he told Thuan. On our way back to camp we discussed the timing of the VC's expected revenge attack on Phu Hiep. I felt very strongly, as did Major Le, that it was already overdue. "They want us to become complacent because of our victory and let our guard down, Dai-uy."

"I think you hit the nail on the head, Thieu-ta."

We were certainly right when we speculated that an attack was overdue at Phu Hiep. The very next day, at 0200 hours, the time I usually sit at my desk and write home, I felt a conscious need to be in the command bunker. It was like a sixth sense tugging at me, telling me something was about to happen and that I had better be at my post. Though I tried to write Kate every day, even if just a few sentences letting her know I was Okay, I felt somehow the need to set that aside for the moment.

Neither the early morning quiet, nor the cooling breeze, nor the faint light of a first quarter moon and countless stars in the cloudless sky detracted from the sense of impending danger that seemed to permeate my being. I'd had this kind of strange feeling embrace me in other places and at different times in my life. Without exception, I heeded the summons to marshal my faculties and prepare as best I could for any eventuality. I was here now because I did take heed and averted becoming the victim of a situation that I could, in fact, stave off or control.

The calm was suddenly interrupted by the distinct staccato of multiple explosions in the west. Through my binoculars I saw flashes of enemy mortar fire, coming from locations north of the PF outpost at Phu Hoi and northwest of where I stood. A red glow shone in the sky above the outpost. I yanked the field phone off the hook, spun the crank, and when John Eleam answered, I told him to alert our team. "Phu Hoi is under attack." I said.

I looked to the north as Major Le joined me in the command bunker. We both heard the low, muffled sound of distant mortar and rocket salvos. "Phu

Hiep is under attack, Thieu-ta," I shouted. About that time Lieutenant Kallunki and Lieutenant Minh, along with Sergeant Taylor, came up the steps and into the command bunker.

Major Le's phone rang. Seconds passed like they were hours as my binoculars focused in on a virtual eruption of white flashes and red-hued rays shooting skyward above the FOB at Phu Hiep.

"That was Lieutenant Thuan from Phu Hiep, Dai-uy. They are receiving much mortar and rocket fire and are getting hit on all sides with heavy concentrations of machine gun fire. Many casualties already, even many of the men's families injured." Pointing at a tactical map[3] he also reported that "a platoon of about 40 VC are headed south of the FOB as if to attack Phu Hoa. Maybe it's to get into position to hit the FOB even harder from the South and to set up an ambush on the Co Lau River to prevent us from reinforcing our FOB. "They know we will send a relief force up the river." Lieutenant Minh interrupted. "Sub sector called to report that the VC attacked Tac Truc and Nhon Hoi PF Outposts with 60MM mortar fire and are now only harassing the outposts with small arms fire."

"Please tell Dai-uy Tuoi to help our FOB at Phu Hiep with the 155 howitzers." Major Le instructed Lieutenant Minh.

"Dai-uy Tuoi told me his Howitzer platoon leader is in communication with Thuan and he will direct their fire support of Phu Hiep."

Major Le, smiling, told Minh, "That is good, Minh."

Lieutenant Minh, now with the hand set in one hand and a pencil in the other, was busied writing down coordinates of VC mortar and rocket positions received from the PF Outposts West of us via the communications center below us. Minh then gave me the coordinates, I plotted the enemy positions on our four-deuce fire direction control map board, gave Kallunki the range and azimuth which he immediately relayed by a second telephone system to Specialist Menkins in the mortar pit. He, in turn gave the information to Sergeant Taylor. Taylor, assisted by Sergeant Bridgewater, set the elevation and direction on the four-deuce, attached the proper number of powder increments and fired the first round of white phosphorus to mark and adjust fire with. One more round of WP was on the way after Taylor made the adjustments radioed from the outpost, translated and relayed through the command bunker to his mortar pit via field telephone.

"On target," Minh hollered, after receiving word from the outpost. "Fire for effect."

The loud blasts of exploding powder increments that propelled the heavy high explosive projectiles almost 5000 meters in rapid-fire to support the PF outposts were quickly followed by the thunder-like percussion of the 155MM howitzers as they began to fire in tandem to support Phu Hiep FOB. The wooden structure supporting the sandbagged roof of our command bunker shivered with each re-sounding blast of the nearby guns firing at maximum range to impact between the FOB and the border. In less than a minute, they had adjusted their fire and were pounding the VC positions above the FOB with devastating fury.

Captain Tuoi Van Nguyen informed us that he'd moved two RF platoons into place to strengthen the defenses around the 155MM howitzer fire base. This action was prompted by discovery of a second VC fire base less than 4000 meters west of our camp which had begun to place mortar and rocket fire on the PF outposts of Phu Hoi and Vinh Hoi.

Our LLDB 81MM mortar crew went into action, and quickly zeroed in on the VC fire base. The enemy mortars and rockets ceased their bombardment of the PF outposts. They had either pulled up stakes and were moving to new positions to resume their attack or they had been taken out of action by the quick response and deadly accuracy of our LLDB mortar crew.

Major Le disappeared into the LLDB communications bunker for a few minutes and returned with bad news. "The situation at Phu Hiep is desperate, Dai-uy. Thuan told me it was the close support of the 155MM howitzers that saved the FOB from being overrun. They are now surrounded by more than 200 VC. He believes they will assault the FOB again soon, and will hit from all three sides.

"All the CIDG's families are now inside the compound, but there are many wounded among them, Dai-uy. He thinks they have only enough ammunition to last another three hours, maybe four at the most. We must go up to relieve them and take ammunition for their weapons. I will tell Lieutenant Hong Luong to prepare his company to move to Phu Hiep at 0430 hours."

"Good," I said, "We will use all the boats and take extra ammunition in each boat plus mortar and machine gun ammunition in the barge. I will leave Lieutenant Kallunki in command and Sergeant Taylor will go with us. Sergeant Valenzuela will work with Sergeant Hung to get the ammunition together at the boat dock."

I looked at my watch. It read 0320 hours. I briefed Kallunki, then sought out Val, asking that he help the XO get through the night and have Sergeant Kuchen help Eleam out in the commo bunker.

"Will do, Dai-uy. Don't worry about anything back here, just keep a watchful eye on the way to Phu Hiep."

I pulled Jim Taylor from the four-deuce, put Sergeant Bridgewater in charge with Sergeant Davis and Specialist Menkins as his crew. Jim Taylor and I got our gear together, including two M-79 grenade launchers and three bandoliers each of the 40MM HE grenades, and went in my jeep down to the boat dock, instructing the driver to report back to Lieutenant Kallunki.

When Major Le arrived at the boat dock, he told us that he'd gotten a call from the District Chief just as he was leaving the command bunker. "Captain Tuoi reported that the VC are now attacking the PF outposts at Phu Loi, Phu Huu, Khanh An and Dong Co Ki with mortar and machine gun fire. He is pulling his 155 howitzer support from Phu Hiep to help his outposts and to keep the VC from isolating the entire Khanh An and Khanh Binh areas. It's like a peninsula, as you know, Dai-uy."

He continued, "I asked Captain Tuoi if he would support our reaction force as we passed through the ambush corridor on the Co Lau River between Phu

Huu and Phu Hiep." A smile of relief on his face, Major Le added, "He said they would stand by with one of the big guns and establish radio contact with me so I can direct their fire."

I gave him the thumbs up signal and asked when it would be available.

"From 0440 to 0510. That should give us the support when we need it." Major Le told me that Captain Tuoi had just reported that the VC were now placing only small arms harassing fire on Tac Truc and Nhon Hoi PF outposts.

We discussed the tactical situation as the boats were readied. We agreed that the enemy battle plan was to destroy our FOB at Phu Hiep and the Phu Loi PF outpost and kill every man, woman and child, wanting to put fear into our hearts so they could take control of the entire area north of the Phu Huu outpost and east of the Bassac River. The attacks on our western outposts were probably ordered to give us reason to believe that their objective was the Howitzer fire base and our main camp. That would cause us to keep all the Strikers in camp and RF companies in the district compound to defend our southern and western outposts, the 155 fire base, district headquarters and our camp.

The enemy bombardment of all friendly positions in the vicinity of Phu Hiep and their setting of ambushes along the northern side of the Co Lau River, made clear their intent to isolate the FOB from support or reinforcement.

At 0430 we headed up river to Phu Hiep. Using the full thrust of our 25HP engines at maximum output to gauge our speed (wanting to keep our little reaction fleet close enough together to come to one another's aid should the need arise) our 40HP outboard was purring along at about two thirds throttle. Major Le and I were in the lead boat. A total of 13 assault boats of Strikers plus the barge with Sergeant Jim Taylor, Tony and Sergeant Hung aboard, were now headed north on the Bassac.

After turning into the Co Lau River we moved quickly until we approached the sharp bend in the river about 200 meters beyond the Phu Huu PF outpost. From that point on we moved slowly and cautiously as Major Le brought the howitzer fire base up on the radio. He called for a marking round to come in about 200 meters to our front. We soon heard the fluttering sound of the 155MM white phosphorus-arching overhead. We all flinched a bit as the round burst in the middle of the Co Lau River and right on target! That howitzer crew was as good as they get.

Major Le shouted adjustments for each round of HE as he directed a pattern of fire along the left bank of the river, dropping one round every 100 meters and coaching Map Map to keep a safe distance behind our artillery cover. The variable time fuses on the 155MM HE projectiles had been set to detonate about 50 feet above the ground to maximize the killing zone and disrupt any ambush that had been put in place along that dark, narrow stretch of the ever-dangerous river.

Thanks to our remarkably accurate artillery support paving the way for us, we received only light and sporadic small arms fire along the 2000-meter ambush danger zone. Major Le lifted the cover fire as we neared our pre-planned debarkation point just south of the Cham Hamlet of Phu Hoa. Our move ashore was partially masked by the 100+ Chams that had quickly abandoned their homes for fear of being caught in crossfire during the battle over Phu Hiep. It was a situation we used to our advantage while taking measures to assure their safety. Major Le instructed Map Map to move the Chams in our assault boats to the safety of Vinh Loc outpost. He was to wait there for further instructions.

With the Cham's homes deserted we used the hamlet to cover our move toward the enemy cordon.

Sergeant Hung, with one squad of CIDG, remained on the barge with its large cargo of ammunition, a .30 caliber machine gun and orders to move it to the friendly side of the river and stand fast. When called he would bring it to the FOB to off-load the ammunition. Sergeant Taylor and Tony joined the 445th commander in his assault boat. Lieutenant Hong was pleased to have them and the extra 60MM mortar they'd brought up river on the barge.

After establishing radio contact with the FOB and the 155 Fire Base, Major Le designated a target area 100 meters northwest of the FOB, hoping to distract the VC and make them think a relief force would be coming from the direction of the Phu Loi outpost.

Our two pronged assault plan to penetrate the VC encirclement was put into action. Lieutenant Hong, with Sergeant Taylor and Tony at his side, would take two platoons, circle around and attack from the west. I would go with Major Le and the remaining Strikers, work our way quietly through the hamlet, and prepare to attack the VC cordon from the south. Major Le instructed Lieutenant Thuan to redirect all defensive fire to the northwest and southeast when he saw two parachute flares pop to signal the beginning of our assault.[4]

Once our two attack elements were in position, Major Le called in the next howitzer mission, placing four more rounds of HE northwest of the FOB, followed by two parachute flares.

Our two attack elements fired a five mortar salvo of 25 rounds of 60MM HE into the enemy ranks and began our assault on their positions. Though we were outnumbered two to one we were confident that our strategy and the courage of the Strikers would give us the victory. An intense fire-fight ensued as we leap-frogged toward them, each attack force covering the advance of the other by kneeling and firing a steady rain of bullets at an enemy who lacked both cover and concealment.

As additional parachute flares lit the FOB we saw VC falling under the continuing crossfire. Others entangled themselves in the outer perimeter barbed-wire belt while FOB Strikers used their remaining ammunition to kill or injure the VC who had been caught unawares in the middle of working their way through the triple concertina, double-apron barbed wire, and tanglefoot obstacles. Their plan, had we not interrupted it, was to regroup at the base of the FOB parapet, storm the compound and complete their revenge by killing or capturing the remaining defenders and their families.

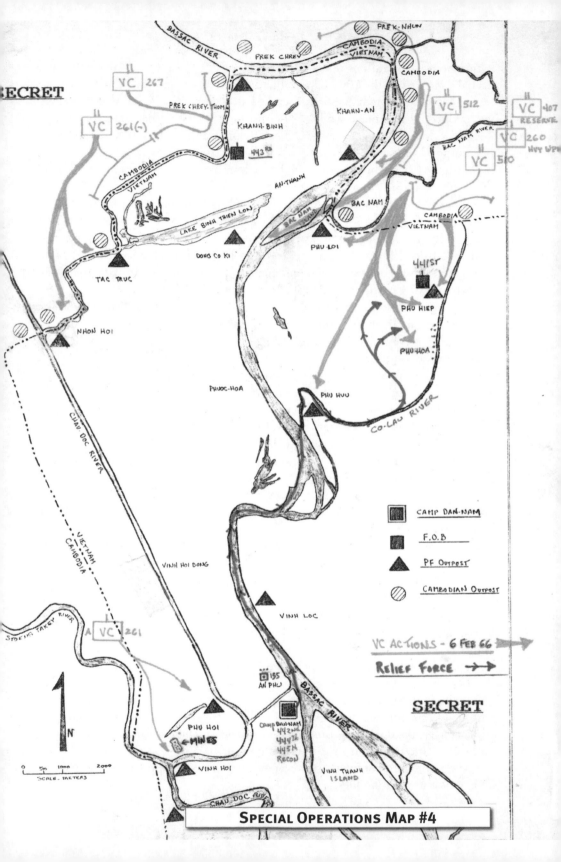

SECRET

BASSAC RIVER

PREK-NHUN

PREK CHREY

CAMBODIA-VIETNAM

CAMBODIA

VC 267

PREK CHREY. THOM

KHANH-AN

VC 512

VC 407
RESERVE

VC 261(-)

KHANH-BINH

443RD

BAC NAM RIVER

VC 260
HVY WPN

CAMBODIA
VIETNAM

AN-THANH

VC 510

LAKE BINH THIEN LON

DONG CO KI

BAC NAM RIVER

BAC NAM

CAMBODIA
VIETNAM

TAC TRUC

PHU LOI

441ST

PHU HIEP

NHON HOI

PHU HOA

PHUOC-HOA

PHU HUU

CO-LAU RIVER

CHAU DOC RIVER

VIETNAM
CAMBODIA

VINH HOI DONG

CAMP DAN-NAM

F.O.B

PF Outpost

Cambodian Outpost

STOENG TAKEV RIVER

VC 261

VINH LOC

VC ACTIONS - 6 FEB 66

RELIEF FORCE

1
N

155
AN PHU

SECRET

PHU HOI

MINES

CAMP DAN-NAM
442ND
444TH
445TH
RECON

VINH HOI

VINH THANH ISLAND

0   500 1000   2000
SCALE. METERS

CHAU DOC RIVER

BASSAC RIVER

SPECIAL OPERATIONS MAP #4

By 0605 hours we had successfully routed the enemy who fled into Cambodia in the direction of Bung Ven Base. Seven of the barefoot, black pajama-clad men were caught up in the trap formed between our two attack elements and captured unhurt. We would later learn from these prisoners that their commander didn't expect a relief force to come to Phu Hiep's rescue. He had believed their cunning plans to deceive were foolproof.

Lighting the area one more time with parachute flares, we searched the 22 dead VC that had been left behind, found no papers, but took up 19 weapons and 22 hand grenades. We estimated another 32 were wounded based on visual sightings of men being helped off the battlefield and evidence of blood on their paths of retreat.

A scene of almost total devastation greeted us as we entered the FOB. The courage and strength of character displayed by the Strikers and their families shone like a beacon of hope on a scene of utter destruction. Of the 132 defenders, three were killed and 82 wounded, eight seriously. Injured by the initial enemy bombardment were 22 dependents caught by surprise in their makeshift dwellings outside the protective parapet, four were wounded seriously, including a small girl. How anyone survived that attack is yet a mystery, so complete was the destruction.

As the barge was unloaded, the 122 Chams from Phu Hoa were being returned by assault boat to their hamlet, largely unscathed by the battle that raged to the north and west of it.

Major Le and I walked around the perimeter with Lieutenant Thuan as Sergeant Hung organized medical evacuation by assault boat of the wounded CIDG and injured dependents. I was both saddened and heartened by what I saw when we broke through the enemy encirclement and reached the FOB parapet. Women, whose husbands had been killed or wounded, had taken their places alongside the remaining 47 Strikers to fend off the VC onslaught. The rifles and even the smaller carbines appeared large and cumbersome in the hands of these slight, small-boned women, yet they had stood their ground, as courageous as any man, fighting against tremendous odds to protect their children, their land, and their future.

The children, many too small to walk, were beside their mothers in the defensive positions. The older children busied themselves loading the shiny brass bullets we'd brought to Phu Hiep, into clips or magazines. It was a picture of unity of purpose, a special kind of courage that few will ever witness, much less possess. They smiled and shouted "hallo" as we passed each position along the pockmarked, bullet-riddled parapet, finally descending back into the inner area where the wounded were being treated and readied for evacuation to Camp Dan Nam.

The CIDG of the 445th Company quickly moved into position along the parapet to relieve the defenders who had held out against such odds and emerged victorious. It was reminiscent of a battle scene from a John Wayne movie, with the Hoa Haos triumphant over the Communist horde in this small, remote fortress located on freedom's frontier.

There was no wailing, moaning or outbursts of uncontrolled emotion among the many wounded men, women or children. It was instead a scene of quiet dignity with the acceptance and enduring of pain, and a comforting touch or calming word from a loved one or friend to soothe. Jim Taylor and Tony worked doggedly alongside the LLDB and CIDG medics tending the wounded, compressing and bandaging open wounds, applying temporary arm or leg slings, doing whatever they could to ease their pain and suffering.

By 1200 hours we had shuttled the original defending Strikers and their families to Camp Dan Nam, plus the seven captured VC, whom we turned over to Captain Tuoi after we'd completed our own tactical interrogation. The prisoners confirmed that approximately 300 of their comrades, all belonging to the 512th Heavy Weapons Battalion, had attacked the FOB. They also spoke of having felt safe from attack in the Bung Ven secret base, but that's all we were able to glean from them of significance.

After reviewing reports from sub-sector that told of six PF killed and 24 wounded in action during the attacks on PF outposts that had caused "significant damage" to outpost buildings and fortifications, Major Le and I decided to help where we could in the rebuilding of those outposts hit hard by mortar and rocket fire, at the same time giving a high priority to the repair of damage done to the FOB at Phu Hiep. "Lieutenant Kallunki and Sergeant Davis will go to Phu Hiep this afternoon to assess the damage and order necessary materials to do whatever has to be done," I told Major Le.

He would send his XO and an engineer sergeant to work with my men, advising that "We must make certain the barbed wire obstacles are intact as soon as possible." As we met, Major Le received a report from sub-sector that two RF platoons had searched the open area between the outposts at Phu Hoi and Vinh Loi and discovered a new antipersonnel minefield.

By late that afternoon we would receive a second report from sub-sector telling of the clearing of that minefield. A total of 443 mines were destroyed in place.

"We must destroy Bung Ven, Thieu-ta. We cannot allow our enemy to attack us from the safety of that place."

"Yes, Dai-uy, we will destroy their base soon and it will serve as a memorial to our brave people who have given their lives."

"Amen, Thieu-ta, that will be a fitting tribute."

Prior to leaving to return to my team house, I told Major Le that I would never forget the war-scarred embattlements of Phu Hiep. I reached out, shook his hand and told him, "I will never forget the courage of our Strikers, or seeing their wives with the big guns in their hands and the frightened but silent children at their sides, some loading ammunition. It was those people all together who won the victory!"

* * * * *

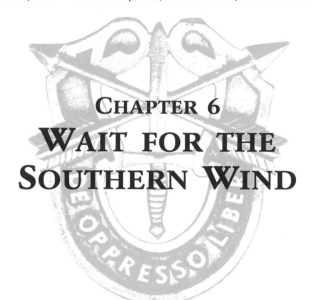

Chapter 6
WAIT FOR THE SOUTHERN WIND

Major Le grinned broadly as we headed back down river toward Camp Dan Nam from the FOB at Phu Hiep. It was 1630 hours on 15 March 1966. "Dai-uy," he boasted, "It is a much greater victory than I had hoped for. We have destroyed their secret base with no casualties among our own men." (Captured reports would confirm our forces had killed 238 VC, wounded another 411, and destroyed their ammunition factory and it's stockpiles along with a barracks and hospital complex.)

A powerful, thunderous roar, quickly followed by a sharp lightning-like percussion noise, swept down from the north, rushing through the command bunker like a runaway freight train on a downhill course. I glanced at my watch. It was 0120 hours on the 9th of February. When I pivoted to face the direction of the sound, I heard Major Le shout "There is bad trouble, Dai-uy," as he bounded up the steps of the command bunker to stand next to me. We both stared in the direction of Khanh An, thinking we would see the flash of enemy heavy artillery sending another projectile our way. We saw nothing. An eerie silence shrouded the area like a cloak of secrecy, adding to the alien feeling that affected our psyche. The shock wave of a tremendous explosion, reminiscent of a near miss by a 1000 pound projectile that had fallen far short of its target some 22 years earlier when I served in Korea, had passed. Differing from that experience of the past, there was no visible clue from our vantage point as to the nature of the blast.

We placed all of our forces on full alert, waiting and watching for the attack we expected. Minutes passed before the clattering ring of Major Le's telephone link to his communications bunker below broke the excruciating silence. "That was

Dai-uy Tuoi. He told me the loud explosion was from VC sappers blowing up the government building at Dong Co Ki," Major Le informed me, placing the handset back in place. "Only a number of reinforced concrete columns remain standing. All else is rubble, but there was nobody inside and no one was hurt." He paused for a moment as if to give me time to absorb what he'd said. "An old man in the village reported seeing nine or 10 men shortly after the explosion, wearing black uniforms and carrying rifles, go across the main road and down to the river. They boarded sampans that had been secured just a little ways north of where they blew the building. The last he saw of them, they had started across the Bassac River in the direction of Bac Nam Island."

"I'm glad no one was hurt," I told Major Le. "I would like to go inspect the rubble. Perhaps we can go after breakfast?"

"Yes, and we will pick up Dai-uy Tuoi at sub-sector and all go together to investigate." Our conversation was cut short by the loud, rumbling sound of enemy rocket and mortar rounds exploding all along our western border outposts from Vinh Hoi northward to Khanh Binh. Already on full alert, our mortars at Khanh Binh and Dan Nam responded with counter-fire in less than a minute, most likely surprising the enemy whom would have hoped to have caught us off guard.

All told, on the western front alone, elements of two VC battalions fired hundreds of rockets and mortar rounds into our FOB at Khanh Binh and the PF outposts at Khanh Binh, Tac Truc, Nhon Hoi, Phu Hoi and Vinh Hoi. After their aerial bombardment, they tested the perimeter defenses at each of those same locations using infantry armed with recoilless rifle and machine gun fire. Discouraged by the strength and ferocity of return fire our alert defenders sent their way, they quickly abandoned any attempt to continue what would likely have proven suicidal. The frontal assaults on all of their targets were called off.

None of our border outposts or FOBs facing the enemy safe-havens in Cambodia escaped the testing of defenses. Machine-gun and small arms harassing fire was also directed at the Phu Hiep FOB and PF outposts at Phu Loi, Khanh An and Dong Co Ki. Again, vigilant perimeter gunners, with recently added firepower of 60MM mortars and light machine-guns, gave the VC cause to break contact and withdraw back into Cambodia.

Taking into account that the enemy had launched a combined mortar and rocket attack, hitting all of our western outposts and the FOB simultaneously, we could have suffered severe casualties. In a strange twist of fate, the enemy's untimely sapper attack on the village office at Dong Co Ki caused us to place all of our forces on alert, thereby removing the element of surprise that would otherwise have caught us unawares, with many of our fighters in harm's way. All told we suffered three Strikers wounded and four PF wounded, none seriously. We had no estimate of VC casualties sustained during their early morning probes.

After a good breakfast of goose eggs and toast, Major Le, Captain Tuoi and I headed up the road at 0730 hours on 10 February to visit and assess damage done in the northern area. At the same time our XOs surveyed damage sustained in the western outposts of Phu Hoi and Vinh Hoi. The village office building at Dong Co Ki was totally demolished. Only four reinforced concrete posts remained, jutting up from one end of the stone foundation where a solid brick and masonry building had stood the day before. Bricks, stones, plaster and timbers were strewn in every direction with no pile higher than a man's knee. Fortunately the damage to nearby homes was slight due to a buffer stand of trees around the office building that had slowed or stopped the brunt of the flying debris. After inspection of the total devastation I estimated the charge used to have been at least 200 pounds of TNT or dynamite.

We then visited and surveyed damage at the nearby PF outpost at Dong Co Ki, continuing north to the Khanh An and Khanh Binh outposts. Damage was light except at Khanh Binh, where severe damage to overhead cover and outer walls was sustained. Repair work at all outposts was underway with sandbag-filling, concrete patching and structural wooden repairs moving along at a good pace. I was impressed with the many basic skills the citizen-soldiers demonstrated as they went about putting their outposts back in good order. I soon learned that the Hoa Haos, whether Regional Forces, Popular Forces or Strikers, were not just good fighters, but good workers, family men and citizens. Captain Tuoi then left our party and returned to sub-sector in his jeep, knowing he could communicate better from a vehicle with his own radio equipment. Major Le and I continued south about 2,000 meters from the Khanh Binh PF outpost to our FOB. It was where we found the most extensive damage of all. The FOB, situated in an old temple that stood within 10 feet of the border canal's east bank, was a prime target for enemy rocket and mortar fire from inside Cambodia.

Damage repair work was in progress, with the Strikers using hand-made forms, canal water and concrete mix to build new machine-gun bunkers, strengthen weakened bunkers and reinforce existing walls. Others were busy replacing broken and splintered wooden rafters and beams with new lumber being delivered by our barge as we stood watching the feverish activity.

With the level of enemy activity at its current peak, Major Le and I decided to declare our area a "purple" zone. Unarmed choppers would not be permitted to enter the area without armed chopper escort. We'd have to put a hold on daily mail runs until we could again declare it a clear "green" zone.

On return to camp in the early afternoon and finding that Specialist Menkins had been called to the B Team for reassignment while I was out with Major Le, I felt bad that I didn't get to see him off. We had first served together in the sixth group at Bragg and his good attitude and familiar face had made the transition from Fort Bragg to Camp Dan Nam painless. A late lunch and an hour of good sleep got my internal systems humming again. I checked with John Eleam in the commo bunker for the latest news from the B Team.

"We've got a new sergeant and an interpreter coming to join our team, Dai-uy," he reported, "They've held up Taylor and Davis at the B Team so they can bring the new man back up river with them later today. Sergeants Taylor and Davis had gone to the B Team to pick up mail, movies, and supplies because of our purple zone status. They would wait for the truck convoy from Can Tho which had our new man aboard. Major Le instructed the new interpreter to meet our men at the boat dock and come up river with them."

"Good, John. I want to welcome 'em aboard." A few hours later I went on down to our boat dock with Team Sergeant Valenzuela to meet and greet the men. On purpose we went a little early, wanting Map Map to teach me the tricks involved in properly riding a sampan. As I stepped in, Map Map grinned and then took me out just a little ways into the Bassac River where I proceeded to turn my upper body to wave to Val on shore and promptly went head over heels into the water. I was glad it was shallow water and even happier that I'd left my weapons on shore before my experiment with disaster. After three tries and three dunks, I knew I was not made to ride in that round-bottomed canoe the Orientals call a sampan. I did provide comic relief for everyone on shore who broke out into roars of laughter, particularly Sergeant Val. Gentleman that he was, he didn't say a word about the incident when we got back to camp.

Within 24 hours I had discussed my sampan balancing problem with Major Le and decided to order 50 sampans made special with flat bottoms. Ten would be placed in each of four strategic places out in the area and at our camp boat dock. No matter where I or any members of my team would go on a silent waterborne operation we would have the special sampans to ride in. Major Le, some 30 years later, would write and tell me, "Anytime you or your people went out on the sampans, I always told my troops to keep an eye on you and be ready to save you from drowning. It is very difficult for Americans or other western people to ride on a little sampan because they weigh too much and cannot keep balance, because they are not used to riding on such a boat."

Fortunately for my already shattered ego, the monsoon rains hit about that time and everyone was wet when the assault boats arrived from the B Team with our new Communications Supervisor, Sergeant First Class Raymond J. Johnson and interpreter Trung P. Nguyen, whom we would call Tony. Looking very much like drowned rats when they came out from under their ponchos, they told of their long and fearsome, nonstop, four hour trip from Can Tho to Chau Doc in an open 2 1/2 ton truck loaded with ammunition.

Ray Johnson, a slim, muscular, veteran Green Beret with receding blond hair, shook my hand as he came ashore from the assault boat, looked me in the eyes and said, "So you don't like sleep, Dai-uy?"

"Who told you that, Sarge?" I asked.

"Jim Taylor, Sir, and he said you ran a tight ship but had a good sense of humor, too."

"You know more about me than you'll probably let on after an hour or so on the river with Jim Taylor. No matter what he told you, I eat, drink and breathe like any other real human being."

With a slightly lower tone, Ray asked, "Is that why they call you the Purple Pimpernel at the B Team?"

"I'll fill him in on that one, Dai-uy," Sergeant Val said, as we all had a good laugh.

I welcomed Ray and Tony aboard. Tony was young, with black hair and an instant smile. He let me know the trip from Can Tho was a scary one for him. "No convoy, Dai-uy, just one truck full of ammunition and us sitting on top of that with a PRC-25 radio and nobody to talk to. Sergeant Johnson had an M-16 and there were two RF soldiers in the open cab of the truck with carbines, but that was it."

"You got here okay, Tony," I remarked. Gesturing to my jeep parked close-by, I spoke out "We're not doing any good standing out in the pouring rain. Hop in and we'll get you to camp. Sergeant Val will get you settled in and introduce you to the rest of the team." Taylor and Davis loaded the plastic bags full of mail, film and team supplies in the waiting 3/4 ton truck and followed us back into camp.

At 1430 hours on 12 February, after three days of quiet along the border, a brief fire fight took place. A platoon from the 444th company, out on daytime combat patrol five kilometers northwest of the Phu Hoi PF outpost, made contact with an estimated 40 VC who had crossed over into An Phu from their safe-haven along the Stoeng Takey River. After about five minutes, the VC broke contact and fled back into Cambodia, carrying two of their wounded comrades along. Our Strikers pursued the enemy to a distance of an estimated 150 meters inside Cambodia, stopping to survey what appeared to be a recently deserted trench system. They discovered a few of our Chieu-Hoi passes in the trench and captured a bloodied VC battle flag left behind by the fleeing enemy. There were no friendly casualties.

Early the next morning, we learned from an agent report that the 260th Heavy Weapons Company had moved from the Stoeng Takey River sanctuary area to another location inside Cambodia 1500 meters east of the Chau Doc River and 2500 meters northwest of our Nhon Hoi PF outpost. They would now be out of range of our mortars. A wise move on their part. I wondered if they knew we had no air or artillery support and had to rely on our own weapons and stratagems only? With the 260th's move deeper into Cambodia so went the threat of their anti-aircraft machine guns, signaling a return to green zone status in time for actor Hugh O'Brian to visit our camp. We were told by the B Team that he would arrive with the mail in the afternoon mail chopper.

That morning Lieutenant Kallunki and Sergeant Davis went up north to check on damage repair and rebuilding progress at the FOBs and PF outposts recently damaged by enemy actions and to witness progress being made on various civic action projects. Sergeant Tenorio and Sergeant Kuchen were out in the hamlets on routine medical patrol with Flash and nurse Co Lau along to lend knowing hands and a disciplined ear for hamlet sick call. Team Sergeant Val headed the 12 man CIDG security detail that led the way for our medical patrol in a 3/4 ton truck.

Another six pallet airdrop of much needed ammunition and demolition material came in at 1012 hours with all bundles hitting inside our small drop zone, a tribute to both pilot and navigator of the Army Caribou that made the drop. John Eleam manned the commo bunker while Bridgewater, Taylor, Johnson and I, along with Sergeant Hung Nguyen and half of his LLDB team recovered parachutes, de-rigged the bundles, and loaded the boxes on one of our $2^1/2$ ton trucks. Jim Taylor supervised the off-loading and storage of the ammunition and explosives in the two large bunkers, while Ray Johnson and I stored the parachutes and canvas bundles in our supply room and made certain the drop zone was cleared for the mail chopper to land. Hugh O'Brian would be aboard and we were all anxious to meet him personally, but the most welcome thing would be the mail from home.

Mail was a huge morale factor. Kate and I tried to write each other daily. Letters from wives and other family members or friends helped us to maintain a balanced perspective and allowed each of us to connect with our loved ones and with what was going on at home. Interestingly enough, we were all anxious to hear what the news media was telling the folks at home about the war. The mail chopper arrived 30 minutes early. John Eleam ran ahead of us and swapped mail bags as we approached the chopper. Hugh O'Brian threw his legs over the side of the chopper's deck, stepped out and started towards us, his military escort officer at his side. The beating noise of the rotors slowly faded as the chopper engine was shut down. Mr. O'Brian, unaware we could overhear, turned and asked his escort officer, a young Second Lieutenant, "How many more of these (expletive deleted) places do I have to go to?"

Before his aide could say or do anything, I shouted, "Mister, if you don't want to come to this (expletive deleted) place, just get back in your chopper and get your self out of here."

Mr. O'Brian apologized, but his words were empty and insincere and his attitude anything but humble. His arrogant manner and obvious hurry to do his thing and go on to the next camp permitted me to neither accept, reject or respond in any way to his meaningless rhetoric. Instead, I turned and walked away from him and towards our dining area. He followed, all decked out like the Hollywood cowboy character that he played, complete with low -slung six-gun.

In a vain attempt to erase bad first impressions, he showed off his fast draw routine, probably thought he'd dazzle us poor, uneducated, beady-eyed killers with his speed and agility.

Standing before us with legs spread apart, the open palm of his right hand resting against his black leather six-gun holster, a smirk on his face, he challenged John Eleam to face him. "Bring your hands up even with your waist, and when I start to draw, bring your hands together and clap before my pistol reaches your hands."

"Yes, Sir, Mr. O'Brian," John replied.

John stood toe-to-toe with him, watching his gun hand for the slightest movement. Ten times Hugh O'Brian drew his chrome-plated revolver and 10 times John

Eleam beat him to the draw! We all, to a man, cheered for John, shook his hand, patted him on the back and congratulated him on his victory.

Mr. O'Brian, sensing he was no longer welcome at Camp Dan Nam, slipped away quietly with his escort, boarded the already warming chopper, and flew out and away. "Good riddance!" I thought.

After dinner that evening, I disappeared into my office with four letters I had received that day from Kate and a cup of hot, black coffee. It was time for a visit with her and our girls. After I'd taken in her sweet way of sending me love, support and encouragement, I took pen in hand and wrote.

It was one of those times that reinforced my feeling that God was on our side. It was the dark of the moon on 14 February, a time to be especially alert for enemy activity. During the middle of the night, a VC Sapper Squad, most likely from the Bung Ven Secret Base north of Phu Hiep, came by way of Bac Nam Island, crossed the Bassac and somehow eluded our CIDG and PF night ambush patrols. They planted three pressure-actuated-type anti-tank mines in the road between Dong Co Ki and Ap An Thanh. That section of road is critical to our capability to quickly reinforce or send a reaction force to any point north of Lake Thien Lon. Early in the morning of the 15th, an alert PF squad, returning to their outpost at Khanh An, happened on that stretch of road and noticed the dirt surface had been disturbed in three different places. Leaving his squad to secure the area and to prevent any disturbance of the road surface, the Squad Leader hurried to his outpost and reported his suspicion that mines had been buried in the road to the outpost commander, who promptly passed it on to district headquarters.

Province was notified by district and the ordinance disposal unit, specially trained for mine removal was rushed to the scene. By 1000 hours they had disarmed and removed the mines. If that PF squad had taken a different path back to their outpost, or if the squad leader had not been sufficiently alert to notice the subtle difference in the appearance of the road surface, it would have proved disastrous. Our CIDG companies would be using that road during the next few days to rotate companies in our trucks, shuttling them back and forth over that very road. More than likely the first convoy crossing over that mined area would have had Major Le and I in the lead vehicle as was our custom.

Major Le wrote a citation commending the squad leader for his timely and effective action that saved many lives. The citation, along with a cash bonus, was presented at a brief ceremony by Captain Nguyen, with Major Le at his side, in the District Chief's office the very next day.

On the 18th day of February we completed our scheduled company rotation, sending the 444th by truck convoy to Khanh Binh and brought back the 443rd. At the same time we used our assault boats and the barge to carry the 445th to Phu Hiep in two trips up river, returning with elements of the 441st on each trip.

The VC were intent on demoralizing the local population and continued terrorizing the northern area of An Phu, hoping to change loyalties through fear tactics. At 0200 on 22 February, during the dark of the moon, a raiding party, comprised of 40 or more VC, again using Bac Nam Island as a clandestine stepping stone across the Bassac River, slipped into the village of An Thanh shortly after midnight. After surrounding the village chief's home, they entered surreptitiously and found him asleep next to his wife. They knocked his wife unconscious with a rifle butt, gagged him, tied his hands behind his back and forced him at knife-point out into his front yard. They then tied him to a tree and used his pajama-clad torso for bayonet practice, running their sharp blades into his body time and time again until his lifeless form hung limply from the now bloodstained ropes. The red liquid ran down his legs and dripped from his fingertips to form a grisly pool of blood at his feet.

The VC left a note pinned with a piece of wire through the skin of his cheek, warning the villagers not to help the "American Imperialists" or their soldier friends. The assassins entered the village chief's home once more to steal his South Viet-namese Flag. As they left the village, one of the VC accidentally knocked the prop out from under a bamboo window of a neighbor's home with his shoulder. The noise of the heavy window dropping and hitting its frame woke the occupants, who came out to investigate and ran into a hail of bullets, wounding them seriously. The VC then ran to their waiting boats and fled back across the Bassac the way they had come.

Later that same day, another 40 of the enemy were observed by a 10 man CIDG combat patrol as they departed the Cambodian outpost situated across the border from our PF outpost at Tac Truc, at the western end of Lake Thien Lon. They mas-queraded as Cambodian Militia, wearing khaki-colored uniforms and moving in a single file behind a guidon bearer with a Cambodian battle flag fluttering on his wooden staff. They literally strolled in a northerly direction along the west bank of the Binh Ghi River as if out on a routine border surveillance operation. The very size of the force gave it away. Our CIDG and PF were accustomed to seeing squad-size units of up to 12 men leaving the outpost and patrolling the border in that area. The full strength of their outpost was never more than 40 men, and that many only during hours of darkness. During daylight hours most of the men assigned to that outpost were working out in their fields or on fishing boats. Similar to our PF, they were part-time soldiers, so our patrol presumed it was a trick of the VC.

Believing their deception had worked, and unaware that a CIDG patrol out of the Khanh Binh FOB was watching their every move, they crossed the narrow border river on a bamboo monkey bridge and moved in the direction of AP III Hamlet. The Strikers, outnumbered four-to-one, were quickly ordered by their leader to set up at the edge of a grove of trees and on a slight rise of ground in ambush position. Once in place it was a matter of waiting until the enemy's lead element was within range. Then, on signal from the squad leader, they opened up with a heavy volume of fire, wanting the enemy to think their force to be larger then it was in reality. The enemy was fooled by that tactic, engaged in a brief fire fight, but quickly turned tail and fled back across the border, leaving one of their dead behind along with a Cambodian battle flag.

Once back at the Khanh Binh FOB, the squad leader reported to his platoon leader and they discussed the enemy's ploy. Why pose as Cambodians? Could it have been another terror and assassination mission in progress? His platoon leader agreed with the squad leader's assessment, believing they had stopped another terrorist attack, such as had recently taken place in An Thanh Village.

As we were cleaning up for lunch at 1130 hours on the 24th, the unmistakable beating sound of an incoming chopper filled the air. The mail chopper had come and gone earlier in the day and I wondered out loud, "Who could be coming here at this hour?"

Sergeant Johnson, who had just come up from the commo bunker, said "Beats me Dai-uy, I just talked to the B Team a few minutes ago and they didn't say anything about a chopper coming this way."

Curious, we all headed for the chopper pad, weapons at the ready, to see who or what was coming. We got there about the time the Huey set down and a Captain with a black bag, a cross on his collar and wearing a Special Forces shoulder patch, eased off the chopper floor and started towards us. Of course, that combination meant he was a welcome guest anywhere in SF. Sergeant Davis took the chaplain's traveling bag from a door gunner, and the helicopter took off, heading back in an easterly direction toward the Bassac River.

I welcomed him to our camp, we shook hands all around and I invited him to join us for lunch. He asked the Lord to bless our meal. After eating we sat around the table drinking coffee and talking about what had gone down the past few days. Not seeming to care what had happened in our area, he told us he was a Roman Catholic Priest from the Midwest and that he had a degree in psychology. "I just left Camp Tan Chau," he told us, "They have some real problems there." He didn't go into any detail, just left it at that.

He asked if he could hold a nondenominational service while he was with us and I gave him permission, telling him he could use my office for a confessional and that he'd have to hold the service quickly in our dining area so we could get back to duty. After hearing the confessions of two of my men, he used a counter in the dining area as an altar, laid out those things a priest lays out, and held service, with all of us present except John Eleam, who was in the commo bunker. After what I would call a nonplus sermon that didn't even come near discussing the fact that we were part of a God-fearing nation at war, he asked if he could talk to each man on the team privately.

Thinking only good could come of that, I told him yes. He spoke first with Ray Johnson, a seasoned SF type with a good sense of humor. They laughed and carried on like they were having a grand old time. After about 30 minutes Ray headed on out to the commo bunker to relieve John Eleam so that John could meet with the chaplain. John passed my office on the way from the commo bunker to the dining area and joined the chaplain where he sat.

About an hour later I walked from my office toward the dining area with the thought of getting a fresh mug of coffee. Before I got within sight I heard the chaplain and John Eleam going at it hot and heavy. I stopped in the hallway and listened to the conversation.

The chaplain was badgering Eleam, trying to convince him that racial prejudice existed in our team. Eleam was arguing, trying to convince him that just the opposite was true. The chaplain began tossing out innuendoes at John, as if to give birth to a problem by selective insinuation.

I'd heard all I wanted to hear. I literally stomped into the dining area, stood next to their table, looked at John Eleam and told him, "Call the B Team. Tell them to send a chopper here to pick up the chaplain and make it as soon as possible. Got it, John?"

"Sure thing, Dai-uy. It's as good as done."

When John was out of hearing distance, I looked down at the chaplain and told him, "You listen, and you listen good. We've got a good team here and we don't have any problems among ourselves. So Eleam is black, so I'm a high school dropout, so our Team Sergeant is a Mexican, and my XO is a Mormon and there's probably something about each of us that another could call him down for, but we don't. We just don't. Maybe it's that we really care about each other and we care about being a good team and doing good for these people. I don't know the psychology of things like you profess to, but I do know for a certainty that I'm not letting you stay here and mess up a good team. Don't say another word. I don't want to hear your voice again. Just pack up and be out there when the chopper comes in and don't bother looking back. I don't know where you'll go from here, Chaplain, but I hope you take what I said and think it over hard and long before you go and do the wrong thing in another camp."

He quietly got his things together and waited behind the aid station for the chopper. About a half hour passed. The chopper came and took him away. At that moment I felt like closing the entire area to everyone except Hoa Haos.

On 2 March, Sergeant Val and I sat down in my office, reviewed our previous month's combat statistics, SITREPs, SPOTREPs and entries in my daily action log. We then compiled the Monthly Operational Summary Report for February. Once in draft form, I met with Major Le, compared figures and made necessary adjustments based on the latest agent reports and captured documents.

The statistics pointed to increased enemy activity and a need to carefully analyze the latest intelligence. We proceeded to review our capability to deny the enemy any further encroachment into the district, and considered what additional forces we would need, if any, to hold back the enemy threat while continuing to maintain security in An Phu for its 64,000 residents.

Enemy losses in February included 23 KIA and 34 WIA. We were careful not to inflate the enemy casualty figures. The KIAs were physically counted and the WIA included only those we had seen, had blood evidence of or had been observed being carried or helped off the field of battle, with some of those figures taken from seized enemy documents. We captured seven VC, 19 individual weapons and disarmed or destroyed 443 mines. We lost nine Strikers killed in action and 113 wounded.

Civilians got hit hard by the enemy, with one assassinated and 24 wounded. At least 120 were now refugees due to the heavy fighting and destruction of their homes by enemy action. There were a total of 16 enemy initiated contacts compared to two for the previous month. Friendly initiated contacts increased by two over the previous month to a total of seven. The VC attack on the FOB at Phu Hiep was the most significant action in February, accounting for the majority of friendly casualties.

Captain Tuoi Nguyen honored our team for helping his people fight the terrible fire of 4 February in the district village, inviting us to his home for dinner and to a special recognition ceremony held after dinner. At 1300 hours on 4 March, Captain Nguyen praised our efforts, saying "The people of An Phu know that your hearts are good and they know that you risked injury to help them. We believe you are good friends of the Hoa Hao people." He then presented each of us with a Certificate of Appreciation signed by Province Chief Major Re Thoi Nguyen and dated that very day.

In part, my certificate read, "He and his assistants worked with all their hearts to stop the fire, and even helped the people to get the furniture out of the burning houses." We all felt honored and more than a few tears swelled up in the eyes of the assembled Green Berets.

The dinner was excellent, with courses of soup, meat, fish, rice, mixed vegetables, cola, tea and a fruit bowl for dessert.

Shortly after breakfast on the 10 March, Val and I went down to the boat dock to meet two new men who were reporting for duty with our team. They'd arrived before we got there and were laughing almost hysterically. Map Map, who had taken the assault boats to Chau Doc to bring them to camp, met us as we got out of our jeep and told us, "One of your new sergeants brings much steel with him, Dai-uy. I am happy he did not sink one of our boats." Map Map laughed again and Val, after taking a look-see into the boats, told me, "Sergeant Didion has a bunch of weights with him, Dai-uy. He's our new medic. Now we'll have to send Tenorio in to the B Team this afternoon since Didion is here, because he is needed at his new assignment as soon as possible."

"Yes, I remember. Please see to it and make sure everyone gets in camp for lunch so we can see T off." I reached out, shook Didion's hand and welcomed him aboard. He was tall, fairly slim, had hairy arms and wore glasses. He thanked me and said he was glad to be in An Phu, that he'd heard good things about the Hoa Haos.

Val then introduced Master Sergeant Barnes, who had been waiting in the background, laughing along with the Strikers about Didion's hardware. "Sergeant Barnes is our new operations and intelligence NCO, Dai-uy."

"Welcome aboard, Barnes," I said as I reached out and shook hands with him. About six foot tall, barrel-chested, big-boned with coal-black, curly hair, Barnes looked well fit physically.

"Good to be here," he responded. I don't know what it was that bothered me about him, but my gut reaction advised caution and demanded a time of testing. I decided to give him the benefit of the doubt and judge him by how he performed in the field. We had our little get-together in the team dining area to say good-bye to T. Johnson and Eleam spelled each other so they could both take part. We'd miss him for sure, but it was the local people who would miss him most, at least until they got to know the new medics who'd be seeing to their medical needs. When Sergeant Kuchen and Didion rode down to the dock with him, the true measure of the people's love for their "Bac-si" Tenorio was evidenced by the hundreds of local people, mostly women, children and elderly men, who thronged around him to bid him farewell. They would long remember this American medic who had proven his love for them through endless hours of selfless work out amongst the people. After seeing T off, I called a team meeting to discuss our sending two Americans to Phu Hiep, making it a full-blown FOB. "We'll need cot space for two, an interpreter and a house boy. Sergeant Barnes and Sergeant Eleam, you will be the first crew at Phu Hiep. Sergeant Davis will go up with you to draw plans, work up a bill of materials, arrange for whatever is needed and supervise the construction. I want you to move in at Phu Hiep on the 14th, no matter how much has been finished. That's just four days from now and ties in with the rotation of companies. It will be less obvious that way. Tony will be your interpreter and I'll ask Major Le to hire a house-boy ASAP. Any questions or comments so far?"

Lieutenant Kallunki asked if we would put in a shower and a latrine for the Americans.

I looked at Davis and told him to plan a water tower, shower and toilet where everyone could have access. "You'll need a pump and a power source, too."

Sergeant Johnson said he'd scrounge up a couple of 5KW generators, a water purification and treatment set with pump, a pedestal fan, hot plate, table and chairs, and a radio. "I'll put John Eleam in charge of setting up good communications between Phu Hiep, Khanh Binh and camp."

"Sounds good, Johnny," Val spoke up. "Menkins, try to get them a small kerosene refrigerator when you pick one up for us." Turning next to Sergeant Taylor, Val said, "Jim, you make sure they get all the ammo they'll need up there. And, George, you work it out with Sergeant Chet, and tell him we'd like a couple of LLDB medics to go up for a couple of days and look after the Cham people in Phu Hoa Village. I want you and Didion to spend a few days in and around the hamlets up in the area north of Lake Thien Lon. Everyone understand their mission?"

"Sure do, Team Sergeant," echoed Bill Menkins, Jim Taylor and George Kuchen.

Sergeant Barnes glanced at me, "Dai-uy, it sounds like you guys have got your act together."

"We do our best, Sarge, and I'm really counting on you to steer a good course up at Phu Hiep. It's key in the defense of An Phu. You'll be going up, lock, stock and barrel, with Lieutenant Luong Le and the 442nd CIDG Company in four days. Find out who of the LLDB are going and coordinate the move with them. All assault boats and the barge will be available."

After the team meeting I went to Major Le's office and brought him up to date on our plans. He liked what he heard and said that his men would be available to do whatever had to be done to make it work.

"If I were to ask Group for approval of a sixth CIDG company, how long would it take you to recruit 132 men to bring it to full strength?"

"Give me two to three weeks, Dai-uy, and we'll have them in camp and ready to train."

"How about housing and a Lieutenant to command?"

"When you get approval for a company, I will have approval to promote from within our existing companies and also promote the sergeants we will need for first sergeant, platoon sergeants and squad leaders. We have good men available, Dai-uy. I will talk to you later about housing."

"Okay, Thieu-ta. I'll work up justification for a sixth company and submit it through channels for approval. I'll give you a copy so you can begin to plan."

"Good, Dai-uy. I will have my engineer sergeant meet with your Sergeant Davis when he has completed his work at Phu Hiep. They can put together a plan for us to consider."

I told Major Le that sounded good and I went back to my office to began work on the request for a sixth CIDG company, taking a break only long enough to eat supper and brief the men on our plans. "Sergeant Johnson, I want you to work up a request for all that we will need to clothe and equip a sixth company, including bedding and other non-combat items. Jim, you work up weapon and ammunition requirements and make sure you include an 81MM mortar.

"Kuchen, you and Sergeant Chet get together and develop a list of medical equipment and supplies we'll need. Eleam, you can help Ray by getting with LLDB commo and developing radio and battery requirements. When you have it all put together, go over it with Sergeant Val, then bring it to me and we'll have a team meeting to go over all the details. It's best we each have an opportunity to help think this out and make recommendations so we get it done right the first time. If we goof, we may not get a second chance.

"I expect approval in four to six weeks for our sixth company. I want to be ready to order everything we'll need by the first week of April. Backing up a few days so we'll have time to massage the needs list, I expect you to have your part to the Team Sergeant no later than the 30th. "Just so you know, Major Le says he can recruit the entire company in two or three weeks and get approval to commission one of his sergeants as a 2nd lieutenant. The NCO platoon leaders and squad leaders will come from the ranks of our other five companies. It's an opportunity for Major Le to recognize and promote those who have proven themselves in battle."

Sergeant Val remarked, "Good way to handle it, Dai-uy."

"I agree" Lieutenant Kallunki added and the others echoed his sentiments. Lieutenant Kallunki then volunteered to meet with LLDB Lieutenant Ba Minh and work up all the housekeeping needs, such as bedding, cookware, utensils and whatever else came to mind as a potential need. "Thanks, John. There are many details to take care of and I appreciate the fact that each of you want to share the load. Now, unless you have a question or there's something you want to discuss further, let's get to work."

I grabbed a mug of coffee, returned to my office and took up the task of justifying a sixth company. Perhaps 30 minutes had passed when Major Le stopped by my office, stood in my doorway for a moment, and spoke in a troubled tone, a slight frown evidenced a concern, "You look puzzled, Dai-uy, is something the matter?"

"No, Thieu-ta, just trying to put the pieces together to justify a sixth company. You and I know we need the men and the firepower, but to convince headquarters is the real challenge."

He moved to stand in front of my desk, his expression now one of subdued joy with a faint smile and a pleasing tone of voice. He had a tactical map in his left hand and a notepad in his right.

"Please sit down, Thieu-ta. Let's talk about the sixth company. My gut feeling is that we need it now. When I consider the reports of enemy buildup across the border and add what we know of their recent probing actions, I have no doubt in my mind that we need more men to defend An Phu. And, Thieu-ta, you know better than I do that we'll have an even greater need for an additional company come 19 May when the VC celebrate Ho Chi Minh's birthday."

"You are wise to remember that, Dai-uy. We must be prepared for much action on that day. That is the reason for their buildup and for the Bung Ven base. They will try to take our area as a prize."

"The Bung Ven secret base is a thorn in our side, Thieu-ta. We must devise a plan to destroy it. If we don't, we may just contribute to our own demise. It's a real tragedy that our governments allow the VC their safe-havens. We should attack the enemy wherever they are with all the resources at our disposal."

"I agree, Dai-uy, instead they give us the job to do and they refuse us air, artillery or med-evac combat support. They even tell us they will deny knowledge of our mission if we are caught inside Cambodia even accusing us of heading up a rogue operation. I don't understand politicians or politics."

"Nor do I, Thieu-ta. But at least we are together and can lead our men against the VC, even into Cambodia. And we're ready to pursue the enemy until we reach a point where we feel it best to bring our men back to avoid suffering many casualties."

"I'm glad we are a team, Dai-uy. Let's talk about our immediate situation." With that remark, he spread the map out on my desk, pointed to a spot on the west bank of the Chau Doc River in Vinh Hoi Dong, 5000 meters northwest of Camp Dan Nam. "We should build an FOB in Phu My Hamlet. The VC would like to control the Chau Doc River. If they secure the river near Phu My, they would be in a position to attack and destroy the 155 howitzers and place our camp under siege. It would then be possible for them to have dominion over the Bassac River and most all of An Phu. Do you agree?"

"Yes. I've noticed increased probing activity west and northwest of Dan Nam and your agents report the VC now have two battalions west of Khanh Binh. I'll request a sixth company immediately and ask for funds to establish an FOB in Vinh Hoi Dong to protect our flank and the Howitzer Platoon. It makes good tactical and strategic sense."

"The area for an FOB is very easily arranged." Major Le advised. "There is a PF outpost in Phu My that is no longer used by sub-sector due to their own shortage of people. The outpost is made from brick and has very strong defenses. It is something I have wanted to do for a long time. When will you ask your headquarters?"

"My letter of justification will go out on the next chopper out of here, Thieu-ta."

The mail chopper came on 12 March, brought Specialist Five Richard Sirois, our new senior medic and took my request for the added company with the outgoing mail. It also took Sergeants Kuchen and Bridgewater back to the B Team for reassignment. It wouldn't take long for us all to realize that Specialist Sirois would be a very special addition to our team, a real "medic's medic." He would quickly win the respect of the people of An Phu as well as the LLDB and every man on our team. A good student of the Vietnamese language, he was especially fond of the local children and able to converse with them in bits and pieces. His ready smile and quick wit endeared him to young and old alike. Sirois came to An Phu from an assignment with the 8th Special Forces Group in Panama.

Richard Sirois, whom we all called Bac-si, was 25 years old, blond — and in his words, "very small but wiry" — always wore a Commando knife. Born in Lawrence, Massachusetts, he spoke with a very pronounced New England accent. His family was poor, as was mine, and he had 12 brothers and sisters. He remembered getting into many fist-fights before joining the Army, and recalls losing most of them due to his small size. Some 22 years later he would tell me that his greatest influences while yet at home were his Mom and Dad and "some teachers." He was an ideal Green Beret medic because he not only knew his stuff, he cared about the people he served and had a "can do" attitude.

He called himself a cutter. "You see, Dai-uy," he told me, "medics are either cutters or soakers." Speaking of the treatment of Cellulitis, he said that most medics preferred soaking or using a hot water bottle to bring it to a head. He was one of those who "went directly to the source" and cut it out, stuffed it with iodoform gauze and treated the patient with antibiotics.

That evening after dinner, Master Sergeant Val briefed us on the daily activities report. "Quite a few contacts were reported by the LLDB but nothing spectacular, except that the level of enemy movement in two areas was on the increase and taking place more and more during daylight hours. As you all know, this is unusual, and it concerns Major Le."

I asked Val for locations of the contacts.

"Four of the contacts were in the area North of Phu Hiep where we recently destroyed thousands of mines and took back the ground they had held for a time. The VC broke contact in each action and fled north into Cambodia toward the Bung Ven secret base. There were no known casualties on either side. "The other three contacts were made by squad-size patrols out of our main camp. Two of the patrols were operating about 1000 meters apart, checking the border between Phu Thanh, 2000 meters northwest of camp and Phu My, 4000 meters further up the border."

He told of the northernmost patrol spotting about 40 VC, with two of them carrying machine-guns on their shoulders, coming across the border from Cambodia and heading in the direction of Phu My where there is no PF outpost. Our patrol leader radioed the other two combat patrol leaders, telling them to meet at a point on the west bank of the Chau Doc River. From there they would go to set an ambush to deal with the VC.

Bac-si spoke up, saying, "It was scary and exciting at the same time, Dai-uy. I was out for my first time with Didion, Tony and a squad of Strikers to provide us security and help lug the medical supplies we carried for hamlet sick call. We were on our way to Vinh Hoi # 4 on the east side of the Chau Doc River when our CIDG squad leader got the call to converge in Phu My at the former PF outpost and help to ambush a bunch of VC.

"Tony was with me and I asked him, 'How are we going to get across the river to Phu My?' He told me that we would just borrow boats from the local people and make sure they get them back when we're done. Simple as that, he told me."

"So what did you do, Bac-si?," I asked.

"It was easy, Dai-uy. We borrowed four boats, stacked the medical supplies in a heap next to the river where we could return for them and kept enough supplies in our back packs that we figured we might need where we were headed."

Sergeant Didion interrupted, saying, "You should have seen Bac-si up there, Dai-uy. You'd have been proud of him. Cool as a cucumber under fire, he was, yes Sir!"

Bac-si blushed. I doubt he blushed very often. He continued, "Didion gave me half of his extra ammunition so we'd both have about the same. When we got on the other side of the river we joined the other two squads in the old brick PF outpost. We stood to the side while the squad leaders squatted on their haunches in a circle around a tactical map and planned the ambush.

"Didn't take long, Dai-uy, and couldn't, because they knew the VC were continuing to march toward them where they met in the hamlet of Phu My. Civilians would have gotten in the line of fire if they didn't move soon to engage the VC at a place of their choosing.

"We almost ran through the village, moving along the side of the river until we came to the cross-canal that ran from the Chau Doc River west to the Cambodian Stoeng Takey River. The VC had been spotted moving east, just below the canal. The canal ditch was plenty deep and without too much water. It provided excellent cover and concealment. We turned into the canal and moved along the south bank until our ambush party was halted. We then all spread out along the berm, faced south and made certain our weapons were ready to fire with safety off and a round in each chamber. We waited in total silence and darkness. Didion and I were the only ones with M-16s so we were told to direct our fire at the VC machine-guns. Just the thought of firing my M-16 at a real person about made me puke. I'm a medic, I thought to myself. What am I doing here? Then came my baptism of fire.

"We didn't have to wait but two or three minutes and here they came. About 40 VC walking single file toward the river and within range of our weapons. Would I be able to fire my weapon? When our ambush force leader opened fire, we were to join in, but I couldn't quite get myself to shoot. The enemy began returning our fire with a vengeance. Didion, as soon as he heard the rat-a-tat-tat of the enemy machine-guns, hollered out, 'There they are, Sirois!' and pointed to what I would soon recognize as automatic weapon muzzle-flashes.

"The VC machine-guns were aimed right at Didion and me, throwing up chunks of dirt and grass all around us. I spit out dirt that had sprayed into my mouth as Didion kept hollering, 'fire, fire, fire!' It was only then that I got the courage to stick my head up over the berm and see the muzzle flashes of the machine-guns. The thought of survival took control of my senses. I began shooting and I kept shooting at those muzzle flashes, pausing only long enough to shove one magazine after another into my M-16, shooting until the enemy machine-guns were silent."

Didion chimed in, "And the Strikers kept shooting until the VC were routed and broke contact, running as fast as they could back into Cambodia. Thanks to our excellent position in defilade and superior tactics directed by our ambush leader, we suffered no casualties. We found two dead VC and estimated, after the ambush leader discussed the action with all of us back in the Phu My outpost, that we'd wounded another six for sure."

Bac-si then told us, "We went back across the Chau Doc River in our 'borrowed' boats, left them where we had found them, recovered our medical supplies and then ran a sick call for the 200+ people of Vinh Hoi # 4.

"I got through it okay," he continued, "but I don't ever want to do it again. When I was shooting at them, I got excited and exhilarated and I don't like thinking I could be like that. Just telling you guys about it makes my adrenaline flow again, and that's not good. I like being a medic and healing people, not killing them. Now, I can understand why they didn't let medics carry weapons in World War II and the Korean War. A medic has to stay on the healing track."

After learning of the combat action and the medical patrol, Major Le made it a point to be at the main gate to our camp when Sirois, Didion and the others arrived back in camp, congratulating them on their bravery under fire and thanking them for the compassionate work they had done in Phu My after their first taste of combat.

The following day the VC engaged every border outpost with harassing fire, from Vinh Hoi north to Tac Truc, around the northern 'thumb' hitting Khanh Binh and Khanh An, then south to hit Phu Loi on the east bank of the Bassac River, and then continuing to the east where they harassed our FOB at Phu Hiep. Our men were alert and ready for their long-distance machine-gun attack and there were no friendly casualties. Major Le commented the next morning, "It was only a test, Dai-uy. They want to know what we've got and how vigilant we are."

That evening we waited until the new moon's darkness set in, then doubled the number of mortar rounds fired from camp and the FOBs into the former safe-havens of the enemy. We wanted them to know we could reach out and hit 'em if they were to get too close to the border. We hoped they were trying to take advantage of the moonless night to sneak up to and even across the border. In addition to our increased mortar bombardment, our CIDG night ambush patrols were out in record numbers and ready, willing and able to deny the enemy even a hint of victory in An Phu.

Shortly after breakfast on the 14th all available team members helped load the barge and assault boats for the big move to Phu Hiep. Sergeant Barnes and John Eleam, along with two LLDB sergeants, Flash and Tony's cousin whom we called "E," loaded their personal belongings, along with 1000 empty sand bags, two boxes of claymore mines, shovels, and other miscellaneous items in four assault boats. The barge was already fully loaded with a 5KW generator, lumber, poles, pipe, fittings, a dozen boxes of 81MM mortar ammunition, two empty 55 gallon drums for the shower tower, two drums full of gas for the generator, six five gallon cans of good water, a pedestal fan, hot plate, roll of screen wire, and some canvas tarps. It looked messy, like a gypsy caravan, but it was a necessary mess.

I was pleased to wave them off, along with part of the 442nd CIDG company in the 10 assault boats. It was 0900 hours, They had instructions to off-load the barge and boats quickly, then send them back with the first segment of the 445th company to return to camp to shuttle the remaining troops, completing the rotation cycle.

As we approached our camp's front gate, we were motioned to the side of the narrow road to permit the first convoy to pass by on its way to Khanh Binh. The 441st would replace the 444th, whom I can well imagine were anxious to get back to Dan Nam.

While we waited, Val told me how Sergeant Barnes had asked him if it was safe to take his camera to the FOB. "How do you keep these guys from stealing you blind?" he asked Val. "What did you tell him? I asked.

"Well, Dai-uy, I laughed out loud and he gave me a funny look when I did like I was crazy or something. I told him he could leave his wallet anywhere up there he wanted to and go take a shower, go on patrol, do anything he wanted to and when he got back to where he put it, his wallet would be there just like he left it."

"Do you think he believed you, Val?"

"I told him that he'd better believe me. I explained the kind of mutual respect we have here, and I told him that he'd find out why you were called Dangerous Dan if he did anything to mess it up!" He grinned and we both laughed and went on into camp as the last truck cleared the gate headed for Khanh Binh.

Meanwhile, the 50 flat-bottom sampans I'd ordered arrived at the B team boat dock. We would send assault boats to bring them to camp once the FOB rotation was complete.

Late that afternoon, when those same sampans reached An Phu and were unloaded at our boat dock, Strikers and local villagers alike stood by and laughed as they were brought ashore and marked by Map Map's men. Once tethered and floating in the river they looked just like their traditional cousins, the round-bottom sampans. When Lieutenant Kallunki and I arrived at the boat dock and got into the new sampans, we knew and appreciated the difference. There would be no more dunking of Americans or compromised ambush operations. I told Map Map to deploy them at various locations in the district as we had discussed previously.

Shortly after dinner Major Le and I met at Sub-Sector headquarters with Captain Tuoi Nguyen and presented a rather bizarre-sounding plan we had devised to accomplish the destruction of the Viet Cong's so-called "secret base" at Bung Ven. Located 1,200 meters inside Cambodia and only 3,600 meters from our FOB at Phu Hiep, it had to be dealt with.

A North Vietnamese ammunition factory, located in the Bung Ven base, and currently supplying the Southward Regiment with mines, booby-trap devices and small arms ammunition, was gearing up to full production. Stockpiles of other types of ammunition and gasoline were growing at an alarming rate, no doubt to support an all-out offensive against An Phu.

Combat training facilities, housing for a battalion and a 60 bed field hospital were all in the final stages of completion and readiness for their Spring offensive. All these factors posed a real danger to our forces and the local people who depended on us for security.

After pinning his tactical maps on a large easel and taping his prepared overlays, Major Le grabbed a wooden pointer hanging from the easel and began his presentation, first asking support from Captain Nguyen. "We have a plan to destroy the Bung Ven secret base, but we will need your assistance."

Captain Nguyen appeared apprehensive, knowing the limitations of Sub-Sector's forces and weapons, and understanding the political ramifications of any invasive activity by his Regional Forces or attached ARVN artillery. Firing across the border inside Cambodia was not an option.

Major Le, sensing Nguyen's uneasiness, continued, "We need your artillery support on this side of the border just north of our FOB at Phu Hiep. As you know, Dai-uy, the VC heavy weapons company is dug in along the border north of Phu Hiep." Using the pointer to relate his remarks to the map, he resumed, "Their anti-aircraft guns are in position around the Bung Ven base and a trench line has been dug in along the southern edge of their base to defend against a ground attack. Our agents report that the 407th VC battalion has been put in place at Bung Ven to protect the base.

"We have decided against a ground attack into Cambodia. It would be suicide without air or artillery support." At that point Captain Nguyen breathed an audible sigh of relief. Major Le went on, saying "We have devised a very unique strategy. It is a secret plan that we believe will succeed.

"The area east of the Co Lau River, from our FOB north to the border, is covered with dense, high grass that is now very dry. The grassed area extends to a thick stand of bamboo that continues to the Bung Ven perimeter trenches and beyond. We are told that southern winds will continue for two more days, peaking at 20 to 25 knots at 1200 hours each day."

Captain Nguyen now looked perplexed. Why the geography lesson and weather forecast?

Major Le continued to stretch the scenario out before him, revealing the strategy and bringing all the pieces of the puzzle together. "As you also are aware, there are no civilians within the area I have described on either side of the border.

"We plan to ignite a very large brush fire that will spread to the Bung Ven base and help us to destroy it. This is our plan." Pointing to the village of Phuoc My, about five kilometers north of camp, he said, "I would like you to move one of your big howitzers to Phuoc My with 20 rounds of white phosphorous and 20 rounds of variable time fuse high explosive for this mission.

"We will move one company and our four-deuce mortar from camp to the FOB. The company will be deployed 300 meters south of the border and east of the Co Lau River, as if preparing to attack the VC base with a frontal assault. The mortar will be positioned in the FOB for fire support.

"At exactly noon your howitzer will begin to fire 20 rounds of WP within 50 meters of the border. The first round will impact 15 yards east of the Co Lau River, then each successive round 100 meters east of the previous round. This will set the tinder-dry field grass on fire.

"At the same time our Strikers will fire their machine-guns and small arms at the VC defenses along the border. One minute after your howitzer fires its first round, our 81MM mortar in the FOB will rapid-fire 20 rounds of HE air-burst 200 meters north of the VC trenches in a fan shape, pretending to cut off the retreat of the VC in the trenches and denying them easy reinforcement from Bung Ven.

"When we believe the ground fire flames have advanced to the base, I will ask your howitzer to fire 20 rounds of HE air-burst directly over the border, using the same fire pattern as before. The VC will think it is preparation fire for a ground assault against their entrenched forces.

"You see, Dai-uy, we want them to believe it is an attack on their border positions. We hope the 407th VC Battalion will move from Bung Ven to reinforce their comrades. There will be many fires to combat also and that will bring many VC out in the open.

"Our mortar bombardment of Bung Ven will then begin. We will use our four-deuce to rapid-fire 20 rounds of a mixture of WP and HE into the enemy ammunition and fuel storage dumps first." Pointing to the locations of the dumps we'd obtained from aerial SLR photos, he continued, "This should bring the remaining enemy forces out in the open to fight the many fires. Then our men will fire another four-deuce mission of 20 rounds of HE air-burst, targeting the enemy barracks and the empty hospital facility. Their final target will be the arms factory, using a 20 round mix of WP and HE to destroy that capability."

Major Le paused long enough to let what he'd presented to be absorbed by Captain Nguyen and then asked, "What do you think of our plan?"

"It is very unusual strategy, Thieu-ta, and I think a good one, except that the second support mission target area for 155 howitzers must be 50 meters this side of the border. Province has given orders to the platoon leader of the howitzers to target no closer than that to Cambodia or he will order them removed from An Phu. We don't want to lose our only heavy artillery."

"I understand. It is best we do nothing that will risk our having the 155s in An Phu," Major Le agreed. Captain Nguyen asked, "When do you plan the operation?" "Tomorrow, Dai-uy. Will you have the howitzer in position?"

Captain Nguyen didn't flinch. He was familiar now with the way we operated and the importance of secrecy. "It will be in Phuoc My with the ammunition needed to fire their mission. I will tell no one of your secret mission and I wish you success." His high regard for the leadership and courage of Major Le was evident by the tone of his voice and the look on his face.

On return to camp I briefed my XO and Team Sergeant and asked Val to tell Jim Taylor that he'd be taking the four-deuce up with Don Davis as assistant gunner. "Okay, Dai-uy, and I'll brief him on the mission so he takes along everything he needs plus enough to cover the 81's mission."

"Good thinking, Val. And, I'll expect Jim to brief Barnes on his mission with the 81 after he gets in the FOB in the morning. And, ask Ray Johnson to check out and send whatever radio gear we'll need up there."

"Sure thing, Dai-uy."

Just before midnight on the 14th a VC squad harassed the Phu Hoi outpost with small arms fire for a minute or two and then withdrew into Cambodia. Overnight there were four contacts in the Khanh Binh area where an estimated 40 VC, attempting to infiltrate the FOB area, were spotted and fired on by Strikers in four different ambush positions southwest of the FOB. The first contact was at midnight near Binh Tien, and each succeeding contact was a little further south and about 30 minutes apart. We speculated it was the same platoon trying unsuccessfully to penetrate our defenses and terrorize citizens of local hamlets. There were no known casualties from any of the actions that night.

At 1130 hours on 15 March all units were in place at Phu Hiep, mortars were in position with missions pre-plotted and charges set, and the 155MM howitzer was standing ready at Phuoc My to launch our historic attack on Bung Ven with its introductory salvo of white phosphorous. Major Le and I had accompanied Lieutenant Triet Tran and his 443rd CIDG company as it quietly navigated the Bassac and Co Lau Rivers to arrive at Phu Hiep and deploy what the enemy would believe was our attacking element. After a short meeting with Jim Taylor and Sergeant Barnes to finalize supporting fire plans, I joined Major Le and Lieutenant Luong Le in the northernmost corner machine-gun bunker that served as the command bunker. We could readily observe the entire border area above Phu Hiep from this vantage point.

Major Le, wanting a better observation place from which to witness and control the rather unique strategy as it played out, hoisted himself up to an unprotected position on top of the bunker. Binoculars in hand, his steadfast radio operator at his side, Major Le stood, unafraid of enemy fire. I would like to have had a photograph taken of the two of them, standing like a defiant and fearless leader of old with his loyal armor-bearer, challenging a giant of an enemy, looking confident of victory, much as David facing Goliath.

Winds were gusting to 25 knots and coming from the south as noon approached. The grass was tinder-dry and the stage was set for action. At high noon we heard the flutter of the first 155MM projectile arcing over our heads on its way to the target area. The explosion on impact with the ground sent shock waves across the flat terrain to buffet the walls of our triangular fort. Through binoculars I could see the white hot fury spray out, covering a large oval expanse of high grass, setting it ablaze.

Almost instantly we saw tracers pierce the air and disappear into the bamboo thickets to our front where the entrenched VC defenders lay in wait for an expected assault. Lieutenant Triet and his men were playing their part well, keeping low to avoid casualties as the enemy returned their fire with a vengeance.

The flames were spreading like wildfire, fueled by high wind, feeding on the parched expanse of tall grass, building into a wall of flame 2,000 meters wide, finally cascading toward the border, consuming all in it's path.

The noise and shock waves of our 81MM mortar firing its mission over our heads and into an area between the enemy trenches and Bung Ven base let me know all was going as planned like clockwork.

Major Le, from his position atop the command bunker, watched as the flames engulfed the leading edge of the bamboo stand. Using a hand-held anemometer to measure wind speed, he calculated the flames would reach the wooden and bamboo buildings of Bung Ven in five minutes time.

At that moment, when the flames began to kindle exterior walls, Major Le called for the second and final mission of the big ARVN howitzers. In another 20 minutes, when we expected most of the 407th VC battalion to be busy trying to keep the flames from destroying everything the Communists had built in Bung Ven, Jim Taylor was called on to execute the first-ever bombardment of the Bung Ven base.

He and Don Davis were ready. Pre-set powder increments and high explosive warheads were laid out neatly next to the four-deuce tube. The first 20 rounds were on their way in a high parabolic path to the ammunition and gasoline dumps in just over a minute's time. The third round found its mark, scoring a direct hit on the ammunition stockpiles. Each successive round found its target, filling the air with the crackling and rumbling sounds of secondary blasts and bursting gasoline drums. Flames from the now raging inferno leaped skyward, fed by the bursting and rupturing gasoline containers. Dense columns of smoke now billowed above the trees, darkening the sky above Bung Ven.

Sergeant Taylor traversed the tube of his four-deuce and set the elevation for the next mission. Sergeant Davis fed the tube with one round after another of high explosive heads and variable time fuses that would cause them to burst in the air above the barracks buildings and just-completed hospital. Countless steel shards were propelled earthward to inflict casualties among the now terror-stricken VC, no longer shielded by the political umbrella of a former sanctuary.

The third and final mission of the four-deuce, directed at the ammunition factory, sent HE and WP rounds screaming through the air toward their target as Lieutenant Triet led his Strikers into the FOB, having successfully misled the enemy into believing there would be a ground attack. I joined Major Le on top of the bunker just as percussion waves from a tremendous explosion rocked our concrete structure. Major Le, grinning from ear to ear, cheered and pointed to a single column of black smoke that rose hundreds of feet above the surrounding layers of billowing, pitch-like clouds of smoke. "Your gunners have destroyed the factory, Dai-uy. They have scored a direct hit on the powder room, and whoooosh, there is no more factory!" So excited was Major Le that he almost fell off the bunker roof, unable to suppress his emotions.

Secondary explosions persisted for more than two hours as the many fires spawned by the initial WP bombardment fed on scattered mounds of boxed rockets, shells and mines. The flames were still visible as we boarded our boats and barge and headed down river for camp, basking in the glory of our triumph. "It is a much greater victory than I had hoped for, Dai-uy. We have destroyed their secret base with no casualties among our people."

I reached out, shook his hand, and told him, "I will never forget this time, this place, or what we have achieved together with the Hoa Haos of An Phu."

We would later receive confirmed intelligence attributing 238 Viet Cong KIAs and 411 WIAs to our attack on Bung Ven. The reports, some in writing, confirmed that we had destroyed their factory, field hospital, barracks and a large stockpile of ammunition and gasoline. Intelligence experts estimated the ammunition stocks to have been sufficient to support the Southward Regiment for 60 days.

There was a very sad note that day. We returned to camp to learn that Val had been referred by Bac-si Sirois to a field hospital near Can Tho after experiencing terrible pains in his chest. After arriving by chopper he was quickly diagnosed as having a collapsed lung, and was evacuated to Saigon for treatment.

I would miss Val. More than once I went to him, seeking advice and counsel on dealing with the men of our team, and received what I sought, straight from the shoulder. Always candid and forthright, Val once told me, in response to a request for his experience-based judgment, "Just remember back to when you were one of us and ask yourself how you would like to take what you are dishing out. You're a Mustang, Dai-uy, and that is a Mustang's recipe for success." I have thought so many times since those days with Val, Jim Taylor, Ray Johnson and Bac-si Sirois, how much better off I was as a leader when seeking the advice and even counsel of those who would be bearing the burden of my dictates.

Before the night passed, I brought Jim Taylor into my office and told him he would now be Team Sergeant. "But, Barnes is the ranking man, Dai-uy."

"I'm well aware of that, Sarge," I told him, "and I'm also well aware that you can get the job done. You are a man the men look up to and someone I can trust to get the job done - any job. Rest assured that I will go to Phu Hiep first thing in the morning and tell Barnes."

Shortly after breakfast, Don Davis, Flash and I, with a squad of Strikers for security, headed north to Phu Hiep in three assault boats. Sergeant Barnes and John Eleam greeted us at the FOB boat dock and gave us a tour of the FOB. I got Sergeant Barnes aside and explained my decision, and my confidence in Jim Taylor. I told Barnes he would stay at Phu Hiep and head up our side of all that happened in the FOB. "Sounds good to me, Dai-uy," Barnes returned, "I like it here."

* * * * *

CHAPTER 7
THE SHOTGUN

25 March 1966: "After my last visit with you here in Camp Dan Nam, I asked General Westmoreland to re-think his strategy. 'Double the number of Green Berets and don't use conventional forces in combat roles,' was my advice. Major Le and Captain Marvin, all I can say is that it fell on deaf ears." These were the words of Lieutenant General John A. Heintges, Deputy Commander under General William C. Westmoreland in South Vietnam during his visit to Camp Dan Nam.

As General Heintges' helicopter approached our landing zone, I thought back to his first visit to Camp Dan Nam on the 14th of January, when he told me that he would do what he could to see that I remained with Major Le through the camp's conversion to Regional Forces. It was then scheduled to happen "before summer was over." General Heintges was an unconventional warrior of the old school with experience few, if any, of us would ever match. When he was last here he also said that he'd like to see the SF presence doubled.

I whisked him right into the briefing area where Major Le and I brought him up to date on the tactical situation and told him of our recent activity above Phu Hiep. Nothing in writing, of course, but we both knew he'd appreciate how unconventional tactics were employed to destroy the enemy base at Bung Ven. He seemed particularly impressed that our CIDG company in the FOB at Phu Hiep had survived the 6 February attack by the VC's 512th Heavy Weapons Battalion. He commented, "Your people were outnumbered three-to-one and out-gunned and yet they won the victory. You must be very proud of them."

"Yes, Sir, they are good fighters, and their families stick by them in the battle. We want our land to remain free, General."

"I understand Major Le." After congratulating us on our victories, General Heintges looked both of us in the eye and said, "After my last visit with you here in Camp Dan Nam, I asked General Westmoreland to re-think his strategy. 'Double the number of Green Berets and don't use conventional forces in combat roles,' was my advice. Major Le and Captain Marvin, all I can say is that it fell on deaf ears."

On the way back out to his helicopter, General Heintges stopped for a moment, turned, smiled and said, "Almost forgot, Captain, you will be staying with Major Le until you've got the job done and MACV has taken over. Okay?"

I shook his outstretched hand and answered, "Yes, Sir. Thank you, General. I couldn't be happier."

We exchanged salutes as his helicopter lifted off to take him on to Chau Doc to discuss his visit here with the B-42 commander, Lieutenant Colonel Brewer.

Later that same day, as a few of us were playing horseshoes next to the team house, Second Lieutenant John E. Strait reported for duty, taking over as XO from Lieutenant Kallunki, who would leave us and report to Chau Doc in the morning for reassignment.

After introductions all around, I asked him if he played horseshoes. He replied, "Well, a little bit."

"Good," I said, let's have a game while we wait for supper."

"Can't be too bad here, Dai-uy, if you have time to play horseshoes and stuff." That was his first impression of Camp Dan Nam and life in An Phu.

After trimming him good one time, I learned it had been a long time since Lieutenant Strait played the game, and being we still had 30 minutes before chow would be ready, I took John on a tour of the outer perimeter defenses.

In May, 1988, then retired Major John E. Strait, taped his recollections of the time he was at An Phu. Of this first day, he said, "I thought this can't be too bad an area if they got time to play horseshoes and stuff. Then, not too long and [Captain Marvin] took me around the perimeter, showed me the positions and so forth and I was quite impressed with the way it was laid out and the claymores, firing sectors and so forth. Then we came back and there was this first realization that we were in a world of danger there. [He] took me in the command bunker and started showing me where all the demolition switches are and how this one destroys the right corner machine-gun bunker and this one the left one and this destroys the command bunker and this one destroys everything. I took it right then and there that we was in a pretty rough and tough spot and that maybe my first impression was kind of wrong."

As we walked, we talked. Mostly I listened as John told me a little about himself. "I came here from Company C of the 3rd Special Forces, Dai-uy. I finished jump school at Fort Campbell, Kentucky with the 101st Airborne Division in June 1954 and earned my Green Beret as an NCO in June 1962. I remember seeing you at

Fort Bragg when I was an intelligence sergeant in the 6th Group. You were the S-4 if I remember right."

"You're right, John. How did you get your commission?"

"Infantry OCS at Benning. Graduated in February 1965. Then I got into a short Special Forces Officer Course and earned my green beanie the second time. I have to ask you, Sir, how did a Quartermaster Captain get command of an SF camp?"

Lieutenant Strait, a tall, muscular, big-boned and awkward man, was above all a proud Infantryman and accustomed to thinking of Quartermaster officers as "bean counters" not equipped physically or mentally to lead men in combat. It was surely an intelligible question, considering even the normal attitude of combat branch officers to those who "were born to serve them."

"John," I answered, "As a Second Lieutenant I was in the Combat Engineers and served in Korea during the final days of that war. I was an Infantry Sergeant before that and I volunteered for SF the day after President Kennedy was assassinated. It just so happened that they were then only accepting applications from officers who had previously served in combat. The next month we moved to Fort Bragg. I passed all the training the same as any other SF officer and qualified for my prefix 3 and a Green Beret in April 1964."

I would later learn that John was born in Jonesville, Michigan, in April 1935 and had one brother and two sisters. Was "lower middle class" he wrote, lived in the country and enjoyed fishing, hunting, baseball and football. Said he'd "never got in a fist fight before [he] was in the Army." His greatest influence during his youth was his High School Agriculture Teacher, Mr. Spotts.

"Why do the guys in the B Team call you the Purple Pimpernel?" He asked me that just as we got into the team dining area where supper was waiting. Sergeant Ray Johnson was already enjoying the fried chicken and rice along with other team members.

"I heard the Lieutenant, Dai-uy. Remember me asking you the same thing when I got here?"

"I sure do, Ray. And Val said he'd fill you in on it."

"But he never did, Dai-uy, so I'll ask again, "What does the Purple Pimpernel mean? Does it have something to do with your purple scarf?"

"I'm not really sure where that name came from. I did talk to Val about it when he came back from meeting with the Sergeant Major of the B Team and told me they called me the Purple Pimpernel in B-42. That was the first time I knew of it. I figured it might have something to do with my purple Hoa Hao scarf because I wear it everywhere and am the only American I know of who was made an honorary Hoa Hao and who wears one. Purple is the color of royalty, especially kings, and I know that Colonel Brewer calls me the King of the Hoa

Haos — but not in a respectful tone — since I first went against one of his orders. I told him I was just an advisor to Major Le and had to get things done the way the Hoa Haos wanted them done. I couldn't tell him the truth, that my orders were to command an independent operation, that I'd answer to no one. So I've got to put up with his mean spirit. I don't know what would happen if he decided to put me up on charges for disobeying a lawful order and I hope I don't have to find out. The people who sent me probably wouldn't bail me out. I can't really blame him for being mad as a hornet at me, I'll just let that be and put up with it as best I can. You can be sure I'll stay away from B-42 and hope the old man stays away from An Phu.

"Back to Purple Pimpernel. Look in the dictionary and you'll see that Webster has many definitions for purple. I've mentioned royalty and another is 'vigorous and direct, often offensively so: strong.' I can understand why Colonel Brewer would tie that one onto me, but the word Pimpernel has me puzzled. It's a red, white or blue, starlike flower that has fruit similar to peppercorns. Figure that one out. I like peppercorns, but doubt anyone in the B Team knows that. From what Val told me, the B Team Sergeant Major said they'd had a movie titled, 'The Scarlet Pimpernel' and it was about some swashbuckling sword-wielding, lone avenger or something like that. It was shortly afterwards when I became known as the Purple Pimpernel.

"If any of you men learn any different, let me know."

Later that evening, Lieutenant Kallunki acquainted his replacement with the payroll and petty cash fund systems and explained how the self help program worked in An Phu. "Self help is very important to our mission," Kallunki told Strait, "Just about everything that gets done here in An Phu, whether it be building schools, maternity houses, boat docks, bridges or even roads is done by the people of An Phu. We help however we can. Sometimes we draw up the plans or pay to have them done, help financially and volunteer our own sweat to be a part of it with them. There are a very few things, like the bulletin boards you'll see when I take you around, that we help the local officials with and the VIS design, but they are made by an outside company and the local people install them." Most of his last day in An Phu John Kallunki spent with Lieutenant Strait visiting locations in the district to acquaint him with civic action projects in all stages of progress. He then introduced John Strait to the District Chief, Agriculture Chief, VIS Chief and other district officials he would be working with on military government, civic action and psychological operations activities. Kallunki also took time to bring together the LLDB he worked with on a regular basis for their first meeting with John Strait to help them get to know each other quickly. He wanted to be available to answer any questions about or to clarify their various roles in district activities and the interaction accomplished in the past between the two teams.

Late in the afternoon that same day Lieutenant Kallunki said good-bye to An Phu and the Hoa Hao people he had come to know and respect. John had an excellent relationship with the local people, having the same sensitivities about loving and caring for one another as the Hoa Haos, and they showed their love for him by coming to bid him farewell. There were hundreds gathered at the boat dock and thousands along the side of the road and on the river banks waiting to catch a last glimpse of the tall Lieutenant who was so kind to them, especially the children. John was the American Green Beret officer who had shown them by his actions that he cared about the people of An Phu. Except for our two men at Phu Hiep and Ray Johnson in the commo bunker, A-424 was there to wave Lieutenant Kallunki off at the boat dock.

Just before sunset on the 27th of March, we received word from Sub Sector that a VIS specialist had encountered a VC in the act of destroying a bulletin board in the village of Vinh Loc on the east side of the Bassac River, only 1,000 meters or so north of our boat dock. I took Lieutenant Strait and Flash with me and went by assault boat with a small security force to Vinh Loc to meet the brave VIS man and see the VC he had killed. On the way I told John Strait how much we all admired the VIS people and how they carried carbines and showed no fear of the enemy. "They will go into an area where the VC are terrorizing local people and help the people to escape to a safer place in the district where other Hoa Haos will care for them until they can return home. I never met such a courageous bunch of civilians, John. You'll enjoy working with them on their programs and especially enjoy helping them when the time comes for refugee assistance and morale-boosting interaction with civilians when the battles reach into and hurt people in the local hamlets."

When we arrived at the scene, the proud VIS employee welcomed us to Vinh Loc and led us to his victim. Flash interpreted as the VIS man told of being on special patrol to catch and punish the enemy who were destroying, even blowing up hamlet bulletin boards. The boards were important because of their capacity, if posted on a timely basis, to keep the people informed. The VIS man came upon the Viet Cong just as he was about to smash the bulletin board with an ax. When the VIS approached him to arrest him and take him to the police station, he reached for his Russian Carbine and the VIS man shot and killed him in self defense. Flash introduced Lieutenant Strait as the new XO who would be working with the VIS. They shook hands and exchanged pleasantries with Flash's able assistance.

John, after looking at the dead VC, turned to me and said, "He sure doesn't look very dangerous to me."

It would not be long before Lieutenant Strait would face the VC in actual combat. When the action was over and John was back in camp and reflecting on the effect actual combat had on his psyche, he told me: "Remember that night in Vinh Loc when you took me with you to see the VC that VIS man had killed and how I told you that the VC didn't look very dangerous to me?"

"Couldn't forget that night, John, Why?"

"After today, Dai-uy, I can tell you that a live VC sure is dangerous." With that we both laughed and grew just a little closer together. It is what happens to those who share the unknowns, the danger and the excitement of live combat.

The very next day, it was the other half of that dynamic CA/PO duo of Kallunki and Davis, that followed down the Bassac River to B-42 for reassignment to Project Delta. Ed wasn't with us long, but he had made a real impact by what we did to help the people: the Hoa Haos of An Phu. Arriving the day before the terrible fire of 4 February, it was Ed Davis who personally spearheaded the rebuilding project. I doubt that any other man alive could have done a better or more responsive job or endeared himself more to the people while doing it than Sergeant Davis. In concert with district officials and LLDB personnel, Ed drew up plans, developed funding, and expedited requests for materiel needed to construct the 97 homes destroyed by the fire and to repair the hundreds of homes and shop buildings damaged by that same conflagration. Davis, who loved the Hoa Haos and who admired their simple, but wonderfully satisfying way of life, worked and sweated happily alongside them to help bring their village back to life.

Most of those villagers who had been touched by Davis and were aware of his leaving the district for good, were at the boat dock or along the river's edge, waving farewell to a friend that was there and did all he could for them when they needed him most.

I'd completed the draft of our March combat statistics report, had set it aside and was preparing to write Kate as I tried to do every day in that time I'd set aside before my early morning bath and my 0330 hours snooze time. A loud blast, sounding like that of a shotgun, ripped through the air at 0025 hours on April fool's day. It came from the direction of our other team house. I ran out of my office and across the narrow hallway into my cubicle, grabbed my M-16, dashed down the hall, out across the yard and through the screen door of the other team house. Jim Taylor and Sergeant Didion were close behind and catching up. I'd no sooner entered the hallway when Lieutenant John Strait hollered out at the top of his lungs, "What did I do? What did I do? What am I going to do now?"

I saw John standing at the other end of the hall in front of the aid station door, his shoulders slumped, not moving a muscle. Seeing that John was white as a sheet, with no weapon in either hand, and assuming there had been some kind of accident, I told Sergeant Taylor that I'd handle it. He and Didion went on back to the dining room where they waited to learn what had happened.

Walking up to my XO, I asked, "What happened John?" Before he could respond, I glanced over his shoulder through the door of the aid station and caught a glimpse of what could best be called a disaster area. On the right side, where Ray Johnson's cubicle butts up against the bamboo partition that separates his quarters from the aid station, a jagged hole appeared that was big enough to stick one's head through. Inside the aid station, most of the medicine bottles and jars that had been so neatly arranged on a shelf near the operating table had been blown to bits. Shards of glass and contents of the many containers were scattered throughout the area. I turned and smiled at John, not wanting to make him feel any worse than he already did, and waited his response.

He stood still for a moment with his mouth wide open, for the moment incapable of speaking intelligibly. He slowly regained his composure, and said, "Dai-uy, do you remember telling me that I had to pull night watch like you do, right along with the rest of the guys on our team? This was my first time on night watch."

"What does that have to do with what just happened here, John?" I asked.

"Well, Dai-uy, I hadn't gotten over to the supply room to get my own shotgun from Ray Johnson. I had seen you carry your Ithaca shotgun when you made your rounds, so I thought I'd follow suit and grabbed Johnson's gun off the wall here and found Lieutenant Ba. We went around the perimeter together and I got to know him better."

"Was all well out there, John?"

"Yes, Sir, except for one Striker who'd gone asleep in a machine-gun bunker on the west side of camp. He was replaced right away and then marched off by a CIDG Sergeant to get his punishment."

"Then what happened? How did that hole get blown in the wall?

"Well, Dai-uy, I got back to Sergeant Johnson's cubicle, saw that he wasn't there, and put his shotgun back up there on the wall right where he had it. I did check the safety because I know it's a must to leave a round in the chamber of all our weapons just in case we need to grab one and use it to defend against a surprise attack, day or night."

"That's right, John. Go on."

"Well, Dai-uy, I no sooner put it back on the same nails where I'd gotten it from when it went off and fired its double-aught buckshot into the dispensary. I was really shook up at first, wondering if I'd killed someone. Man, was I relieved when I opened the aid station door and saw that the operating table and cot were both empty."

John reached up, removed his floppy black hat, wiped the sweat from his brow with a farmer's handkerchief, gave me a forlorn look, and added, "I don't know how many thousands of dollars worth of medicine I just blew to smithereens, but it sure is a mess in there, a real mess."

I picked the shotgun up off of the floor as it lay halfway under Ray's cot where the recoil had taken it. After I inspected the safety mechanism and let him know that it was defective, John Strait breathed a little easier. "Tried it three times and it failed three times, John."

About that time, the rest of our team showed up to help clean up the mess. When I left, Bac-si, Didion, and Ray Johnson were all doing inventory and putting together a list of what all was needed to put the aid station back in business.

Back in my office, I glanced at the figures in the combat statistics report for March, and reflected on action that had taken place during the month. We had confirmed figures of 240 Viet Cong KIAs and 417 WIAs plus one VC captured while we lost only one Striker KIA and four WIA. The numbers looked especially good and yet were misleading because most enemy casualties came out of our destruction of Bung Ven, particularly those who were killed in the arms factory,

POL storage and ammunition dump explosions. Forty of their 10 man huts were also destroyed along with a sampan and 43 mines.

I shared Major Le's delight with the statistics. We both recognized that the unique scheme we used to destroy Bung Ven didn't place our men in harm's way, thus our friendly casualties for the month were minimal. It had been a rare and incredible opportunity that would not likely present itself again in the future.

"Another factor," he told me, "is that they no longer have the security of safe havens so close to the border as before and their morale suffers. Now they lay awake and wonder where and when we will attack them with our mortars. It keeps them on edge, Dai-uy."

"But my friend, they will discover before too many weeks have passed," explained Major Le, "how deep our reach is into their territory and they will begin to realize that we may have lost our support from ARVN or our military air or other heavy artillery when we venture into Cambodia. The VC will then simply move back a little farther out of our reach and prepare for the time when they believe they can destroy us. It is then, and only then, that they will again attack our people.

"I believe, Dai-uy, that we must be ready for a big attack close to or on Ho Chi Minh's birthday - the 19th of May."

"Yes, Thieu-ta," I told Major Le as I was leaving his office, "and I know we must have the sixth company if we are to survive such an attack."

On 2 April, after finishing a letter to Kate, I took a short stroll with shotgun in hand out to the vicinity of the main gate, and noticed a Striker had been locked in one of the two barbed-wire "disciplinary" cages. I thought of them as quick and effective punishment chambers. Only three feet square and four feet high, they were placed in full view of anyone entering or leaving the camp, serving as reminders of the importance of obedience and the certainty of punishment should one decide to rebel against authority. The Striker — who now squatted in silence in that small and portable prison cell — would think hard and long before going to sleep when on duty in the future. After 24 hours without food or water in a barbed enclosure too short to stand in and too cramped to stretch out in, you don't soon forget the intended lesson.

If a unit is to be effective, as I learned in Korea some 22+ years earlier, discipline must be demanded and justice swift when one fails to follow orders. Perhaps the most tenacious fighting unit the North Vietnamese had to face in South Vietnam was the all volunteer Korean Tiger Division. Trained in tae-kwon-do, the Korean version of karate in which all limbs and the head serve as weapons, they were accustomed to a tough regimen of exercise and discipline. Their commander, General Chae Myung Shin, was also an advocate of regular consumption of Ginseng Tea which reputedly promoted stamina and general good health. I once witnessed the physical beating of a noncommissioned officer by his peers after having disobeyed a consequential order from his superior, who told me, "If I had not acted swiftly and with tough measures that were meted out by his fellow soldiers, he would have been apt to repeat his error and cost someone his life or even cause our unit to suffer defeat."

When I first got to Camp Dan Nam, I met with Major Le to jointly decide on a code of conduct with behavior standards and effective, timely, appropriate punishment designed to help deter future breaches in discipline. What I had learned in Special Warfare training and military chapel, coupled with what I had experienced both as an NCO and as an officer in a variety of assignments, including service in Korea as a combat engineer supporting American and Korean forces, guided me in my part of the discussions. The tough discipline within the Korean units which I had observed had left an indelible impression and contributed greatly to my thought process.

Major Le, in a few words, summed it up in a profound way: "We have much to learn from and about the past that could help to better shape our future decisions if we have the wisdom to use that knowledge which is our heritage."

The man we called "Tony" was Trung P. Nguyen. He didn't mince words recalling those days in the FOB at Phu Hiep when he served as our interpreter. Phu Hiep was our northernmost defensive bastion. Tony, some 34 years later, wrote[1] these words about his life at Phu Hiep: "The outpost was too far from town, obsolete and gloomy. It was surrounded by many barbed wire barriers, communication trenches and claymore mines, and was situated on the higher ground next to the Co Lau River that branched off of the Bassac. The local Cham people told me how the water would rise five meters, up to the outer perimeter mound of the outpost. They had built their homes on bamboo stilts with the floors above the expected flood level. They also told of having watched the Strikers float everything, even machine-guns and mortars, when the water was at its highest point. 'We know they will protect us' one villager told me.

"The radio call sign for the FOB was 'Outcast' and, believe me, I felt like an outcast at times in that remote place. They hung tin cans on the barbed wires in the perimeter defenses. The cans, together with the geese raised by the CIDG, were used to give warning to the guards at night if the VC went up against the barbed wire. "Even in daytime our movement was limited," he wrote, "We could not go far from the outpost or we risked getting zapped by sniper fire. I didn't want to take this kind of risk either. Confined in a small area of the bunker, I felt uncomfortable. We could get irritated or mad at each other very easily. All normal activities ceased at dusk. Even reading was hard because the candles and kerosene lights did not give off enough light.

"I felt bored and scared at night," he recalled, knowing there were more than 400 VC only 2,000 meters north of the FOB waiting for the right time to attack. The enemy had a three to one advantage so Tony was happy when, at odd hours during the night, Sergeant Barnes or John Eleam would call for him to help crew the 81mm mortar and send those high explosive projectiles in a soaring arc over the border and into VC territory. "We let them know we do not honor their safe-havens.

"If they fired at us with rockets or mortars, we would pound their positions using their gun flashes as our targets. We even sent more HE at them in different places and at different times throughout the night. When we didn't hear the cans jingling or the geese honking, we knew it was safe, that we'd had another good night."

Outcast was alive and well on the frontier of freedom!

* * * * *

CHAPTER 8
WE ALMOST BOUGHT THE FARM

I saw something out of the corner of my eye as we neared touch-down on the C Team chopper pad in Can Tho. There it loomed, larger than life, coming straight at us and not 20 feet away! It began a violent turn - Too late! In that instant, I thought we'd all bought the farm.

It was 0700 hours on 3 April. I stood ready near our camp chopper pad waiting for my ride to Can Tho. Three Hueys had been dispatched by the C Team to fan out over the IV Corps Tactical Zone, pick up and carry all the A Team leaders to a commanders' meeting in Can Tho. John Strait would command A-424 in my absence. Earlier, I had told him to rotate the commo men between Phu Hiep and camp, bringing John Eleam back and sending Ray Johnson up. I knew John would hold down the fort well and I trusted his judgment should a need arise for decisions of importance in my absence.

The meeting would bring A Team Commanders together to meet with Lieutenant Colonel Tuttle, his staff and the B Team Commanders. The B Team leaders had arrived a day earlier to confer with Colonel Tuttle separately. Their agenda would include command, control and logistical support operations of the CIDG program and various special camp requests, including my request to add a sixth 132 man Company to my CIDG at Camp Dan Nam. They would then be ready to meet with and brief their A Team leaders, shortly after our arrival today. After an hour lunch break lunch in the C Team mess we would then all participate in the commanders' meeting.

Get-togethers of this sort were rare. It wasn't wise to risk bringing together in one place the entire special warfare command structure for the IV Corps area on a regular basis. Conversely, the time and the logistics needed for the C Team Commander and his staff to venture out to the dozen or more CIDG camps for individual, on-site inspection visits, would constitute an unnecessary burden. Thus, this type of gathering was ordered only to satisfy major concerns in the overall IV Tactical Zone unconventional operations.

The meeting we would be going to on this day would be held in the small, relatively vulnerable compound near the Mekong River that Colonel Tuttle's Special Forces Command and Control Team C-4 called home. All messages relating to the meeting, transportation, pick-up times and names of attendees were coded and classified SECRET to avoid compromise and potentially disastrous consequences. The chopper that I boarded had flown from Can Tho to a camp called Cai Cai, west of Saigon, and on to three other CIDG camps before setting down to pick me up at Dan Nam. The pilot didn't stop the engine, wanting to keep on schedule. En route to Can Tho we flew at a cruising altitude of 2,000 feet, following the Bassac River to Chau Doc and continuing along the gently winding southeasterly course of the river as it took us in the direction of the South China Sea.

We flew over mostly friendly areas controlled by ARVN. The constant beating of the rotors produced a comforting sound, and we enjoyed the breathtaking vista of sunlit rice paddies, canals, and fishing hamlets in the patchwork quilt-like, lush, green Mekong River delta area.

As we approached the military airfield at Can Tho, I spotted another helicopter coming up from the south and heading in our direction. It was another chopper with more A Team Leaders being carried to the same meeting from other SF camps. The thought of seeing friends from previous assignments made me more anxious than ever to get on the ground. What none of us in either helicopter realized was that our two pilots would decide to fly a reckless race to the big white X that marked our destination on the landing strip below. We were all strapped in the canvas bucket seats behind the crew compartment and all that we could see was what the open sides of the chopper offered.

Without warning, our pilot suddenly banked the ship, nosed down sharply, gave her full throttle and took it in a full power approach and, unbeknown to us, was on a collision course with the other incoming chopper. I breathed a sigh of relief as we slowed, leveled off about 12 feet above the pierced-steel-planking deck that comprised the runway, and headed for what should have been a normal landing. The other ship was nowhere in sight, so I assumed the airborne hi-jinx of these two immature pilots were behind us. I was never before so wrong in my judgment.

As I twisted my upper body to reach the release for my restraining strap, I saw something out of the corner of my eye, a vision that spurred a surge of adrenaline through my veins, while momentarily freezing any physical response. The other chopper - larger than life - was coming straight at us and not more than 20 feet away! Both pilots strained their choppers in a turning maneuver, trying to avoid a collision. Too late! In that instant, I thought we'd all bought the farm.

Our chopper shuddered violently as its main rotor sliced into the tail boom of the other. The full force of the rotating blade tore through the aluminum skin, slicing it in two before imbedding itself further up the fuselage in the main frame. Their tail rotor ripped into and sliced off the nose of our cockpit, discarding what had been the protective glass and aluminum skin shell, while miraculously leaving the crew unscathed. The force of the initial impact of our main rotor with the other ship's main frame wrested the entire power train up and out of our chopper's fuselage. Hot fluid from the ruptured housing spurted and sprayed the troop compartment, quickly penetrating our light, cotton jungle fatigues and scorching our skin wherever it was deposited.

My first thought was how we would escape the fireball normally associated with mid-air helicopter collisions. We A Team Commanders would not have survived this long had we not been strapped in our seats. Gripping my M-16 in one hand, I placed my other hand on the quick release, anxious for the moment I could jump out of this bird and run from the anticipated explosion. I glanced toward the front of our ship and saw no windshield, no "bubble," just the pilot and copilot silhouetted against a jagged, halo-like outline of what had once been the nose.

Our two mortally coupled choppers plunged straight down the short distance to the pieced steel planking surface of the runway, slammed into it with a resounding crash that swirled through my head and momentarily disarranged my worldly focus. I was still alive! What remained of the chopper settled upright and stable. I activated my quick release, slid out and turned quickly to see if anyone needed assistance. The crew had already escaped the cockpit, jumping straight forward and out through where the nose had been. My fellow A Team Leaders had cleared out on the other side and were hi-tailing it away from the chopper as I now was, trying to put sufficient distance between myself and the twisted hulks that were due, in my mind, to explode any second.

We all stood at a distance, staring at the mangled wreckage. Ten of us Green Berets and the crews of the two choppers all found it difficult to comprehend why we had not perished. There would be no fire, no explosion, no loss of life and no serious injury. I had always been skeptical of what people labeled as miracles. Sure, I believed what I had learned in church about New Testament miracles, but this was Vietnam, this was 1966. Standing there, beginning to feel the prickling, burning sensation on my shoulders and back brought on by the hot transmission fluid being sprayed on my body, I realized that I had been a most fortunate participant in what should have been a total disaster and witness to one huge miracle that left none of us critically injured. There seemed no other logical explanation.

We were all ushered into the C Team aid station where Colonel Tuttle's medical staff checked us out thoroughly, treating the minor cuts and the many first and second degree burns, wrapping the affected, Vaseline coated parts with gauze bandages. Our green berets, which had protected our heads from most of the oil burns, would have to be replaced when we got back to camp, but the C Team supply sergeant broke out all new jungle fatigues for us to change into. I'd concern myself with sewing on patches, name tags, etc., after I was back home in my camp. After a much appreciated and very satisfying lunch, we were to a man ready to meet.

I would never see the chopper crews again. I wondered if anyone had written them up and reported them for reckless flying. I could have, and perhaps should have, but I figured they'd already been through the fringes of death along with the rest of us, had learned a hard lesson and had survived. If even one of us had been crippled or killed, it would have been different in my judgment. Today God had smiled on us and we had all walked away!

> *As unconventional warriors and commanders of operational A Teams we shared a certain appreciation for having lived through numerous combat actions, even surviving many encounters, day or night, against unbelievable odds. Yet, the irresponsible, cowboy maneuvers of two pilots on a non-combat milk run had brought us within one spark of eternity. It is a fact that those two helicopters had become powder kegs, ready to blow. If just one spark had reached the jet fuel... just one little spark, we would have all been the victims of reckless abandon. Sad, but true.*

Each of us had an opportunity to take to the floor to present our operational statistics for the month of March and answer questions from our peers, the B Team Commanders, Colonel Tuttle and his staff. Although Major Le and both our teams were aware of how we destroyed the Bung Ven base above Phu Hiep, I couldn't report those figures due to the highly classified and independent nature of any of our operations inside Cambodia. I was surprised and perplexed by the lack of any private and secret discussion arrangements whereby I could have briefed him on the status of our special mission, one he'd personally given me to head.

In a situation such as that, excluding only Colonel Tuttle himself, not a one of us at that meeting knew for a certainty what secret or even top secret mission any of the others might be involved in. What we did know is that we were all doing our individual and team best to help the South Vietnamese win their war and drive the Communists out.

Colonel Tuttle announced several decisions that affected one or more of our camps. I was pleased to receive approval to set up an FOB at Vinh Hoi Dong on our western border and preliminary approval for a sixth company of CIDG. All that it needed for final approval was concurrence of the South Vietnamese Special Forces headquarters. "A mere formality," according to Tuttle.

I came away with what I'd went for as far as the FOB and troop increases, and couldn't have been happier about that. Also I had the opportunity, while the floor was mine, to ask that all the commanders present, including and especially Colonel Tuttle, make it known to higher headquarters that we were doing it right in IV Corps: that the CIDG program should be doubled and close air, artillery and med-evac support should be beefed up to fill the needs of those of us in the field. It had been good to spend a few hours with fellow Green Berets. The trip to Camp Dan Nam was uneventful though physically uncomfortable. Whenever pressure was placed on any of the newly sensitive parts of my body, I was made keenly aware that I'd been hurt some. Yet I was confident that in time my skin would heal without a trace of surface scarring. Bac-si would see to that!

Upon return to camp, I shared the good news about the FOB and the sixth company with Major Le and every man on my team. At a team meeting held shortly after I'd arrived in camp, Sergeant Taylor briefed on the latest intelligence, Lieutenant Strait reported that all missions given him to command had been accomplished in my absence, including the rotation of personnel between Phu Hiep and camp.

John Strait mentioned how he'd handed our house boy, a 72 year old Cambodian named Win, a Chicom carbine and asked if he could take a picture of him holding it. "Dai-uy," John told me, "Win got right down on the floor in a good firing position and held that carbine like he knew exactly what to do with it." John, always amazed at how much work Win did for a man his age, even translating messages written in Cambodian that we'd intercepted or captured, said more than once about him, "I don't know how he does it. He's older than dirt." I'll never forget that or John Strait.

Tony Trung, up at Phu Hiep that day with Barnes and Johnson, would write me many years hence, to tell me about an incident that was kept secret from me and which had come close to terminating both him and Ray Johnson, including anyone else within a radius of 15 meters. In March, 2000, he wrote me,[1] "We had a routine counterattack plan, in addition to our mission to harass the sanctuary areas with our 81MM mortar during the hours of darkness. This one rainy night, after we radioed the base to report the current enemy situation, we set about to fire on a reported enemy position. After firing three rounds, I dropped one down the tube and it stayed there in the bottom of the tube. I got scared, upset and I hollered to Johnson, telling him it was still in the tube. Johnson calmed me down, saying 'Don't worry, Tony, we'll get it out.'

"He warned me that we had to be very careful because it was armed and dangerous. It had to be removed from the tube without any pressure being placed on the tip of the projectile. Johnson slowly tipped the tube up two or three times, but the round didn't budge. 'Let's take it down to the river and submerge it in the water and see if we can get it out there.'

"Johnson carried the tube on his shoulder, being careful to keep it tipped with the open end up. I led the way with a flashlight, telling the guards where we were going and what we were doing, and removed the concertina wire that had been pulled across the entrance to the FOB for added protection during hours of darkness. For 200 meters, Johnson toted that tube, walking behind me and my flashlight, all the while hoping he wouldn't trip. It was drizzling when we got to the Co Lau River, which was narrow and shallow at that point and, looking back, I could barely see the FOB.

"Johnson carefully lowered the tube into the water, and when I was in position to place my hands around the open end, he raised the base end. I placed my ear against the tube where it broke the water and listened for movement in the tube. Within seconds I was able to tell Johnson that I could hear it moving. I caught the round safely as it slipped from the tube, and while being careful not to touch the tip, laid it on the wet ground on the river bank. We marked its location for safety with a piece of white cloth on the concertina nearby. In the morning it was disarmed and recovered. "Then we just hoped the VC wouldn't spot us and shoot at us because we'd get caught in a cross fire. It didn't happen! We walked slowly up the slippery path to the FOB. I signaled with my flashlight and shouted the passwords and we were let in to complete our fire mission before settling down to sleep."

After reading and rereading Tony's letter, I was able to appreciate what he and Johnson had gone through. It caused me to again reflect on the helicopter collision and to recall that all it would have taken to finish us all was one little spark!

* * * * *

Exodus 21:23-25
And if any mischief follow, then thou shalt give life for life, eye for eye, tooth for tooth,
Hand for hand, foot for foot, burning for burning, wound for wound, stripe for stripe.

CHAPTER 9
BUT THEY'RE WOMEN, SIR!

13 May 1966: Four bullet-riddled female bodies, their tongues cut out as was the custom in the case of spies, were found floating in the border canal south of the Khanh Binh FOB. A penciled note was found pinned to one of the bodies. It read: "Death comes quickly to traitors of the Liberty Armed Forces." Our plan of deception had worked. The Viet Cong were convinced that the four terrorists had returned as double agents and deserved to die. They had unwittingly executed their own... for us.

Early in the morning on the 4th of April, as we were eating breakfast, Lieutenant Strait came hobbling in, one foot wrapped in a huge mass of white bandages. I might not have noticed John's condition, except that Bac-si Sirois, Didion and Taylor looked like they were about to bust out laughing when the screen door opened and John walked in.

"What happened, John?" I asked, "Look's like you got a club foot." It was the sheepish smile on his face that allowed me to treat the matter lightly. Otherwise I would have been genuinely concerned.

"Well, Dai-uy," John offered, "I had watch last night and somehow I lost track of the time until the phone rang. It was Lieutenant Ba. He'd been waiting to check the outer perimeter with me. I got in a small panic and didn't take the time to put my boots on. I just slipped my feet into my 'Goodyears' (rubber flip-flops) grabbed my shotgun and flashlight and met Lieutenant Ba at the guard shack near the main gate.

"We started around the perimeter with me following behind Ba and all was going good until I lost my footing on the berm and slipped down the slope right into one of our punji traps. Let me tell you, Dai-uy, one of those sharp bamboo punji stakes went right through my flip-flops and pierced my foot. It hurt like nothing I'd ever felt before.

"Lieutenant Ba helped me over to the team house right away and I woke Bac-si. He took one look at it, gave me a tetanus booster shot in my buttocks, cleaned up the hole in my foot and put this bandage on.

"That's why I skipped breakfast this morning," John continued. "I was hoping I could hide it but I couldn't get my boot on over it. Let's face it, Dai-uy, I was afraid you'd be real mad at me because just two days ago you warned me not to leave the inner compound without boots on."

I couldn't help but break out laughing and I turned to Bac-si once I'd gotten control of myself, and asked "How long does he have to wear that huge bandage?"

Bac-si grinned and answered, "Just a few days, Dai-uy. The punji went through the soft part and didn't hit any bones. He'll be all right so long as he keeps it clean."

Big John, wanting to steer the conversation away from his major goof, looked at me and asked, "What did you find out about us getting more men?"

"Might as well make this an update meeting because I should have covered this with you guys when I got back yesterday. Every team in IV Corps is short. We do have something going for us, though. We've had more action since January than all the other camps. I did get to brief them all about the big battle at Phu Hiep and how we'd cleared the area north of Phu Hiep and took it back under our control. I told them what I could about the fire destroying a lot of things at Bung Ven, but kept my mouth shut about anything we did inside Cambodia. I did learn that the people pipeline is dry of Green Berets. The S-1 didn't have a clue as to why we weren't getting enough volunteers off Smoke Bomb Hill to bring 5th Group up to strength.

"I personally think it's because of General Harold K. Johnson. President Johnson appointed him as Army Chief of Staff as soon as he took over the White House. You guys all know that General Johnson hates Special Forces. We'll just have to keep humping to get the job done as good as we can. I can tell you honestly that we've got the smallest team in IV Corps, but we've had more combat action and more civic action projects going and done than any of the others. I'm mighty proud of you guys for making that possible.

"Any questions, comments or suggestions?"

Lieutenant Strait spoke up. "Barnes is complaining about the lack of privacy in the FOB, Dai-uy. What really bugs him is that every time he takes a shower, the women and children and even some of the Strikers stand around and gawk at him. We all know they're just curious about Americans and Barnes is really different because his whole body above the waist, except for his neck, is hairy as all get out. I know what its like, Dai-uy. I'm almost as hairy as Barnes. All the Hoa Haos can see is from the waist up. You know how we built that shower up there. It's not bad as far as I'm concerned.

"What should I tell Sergeant Barnes, Dai-uy?"

"Tell him to grin and bear it, John. It would be different if they stood around laughing at him or taunting him. They are good people and just curious, as you said. Anything else, John?"

"I wanted you to know they're running some good medical patrols from the FOB down to the village of Phu Hoa where the Chams live and doing it with their CIDG medic. Bac-si is doing a good job training those Striker medics."

Sirois spoke out, "They learn fast, Dai-uy, and we make sure the FOBs have lots of candy and comic books to give to the children. It makes them happy and these kids are really great. I don't know how they do it, but they don't let the war bother 'em. The Hoa Hao families are very loving and close to their children. They know by what we do and say that we care about them too and that's real important in my book.

"Before I forget to tell you, Dai-uy, you'll be happy to know we hired a new nurse to help out in the aid station and take turns with Co Lau going out on medical patrols."

"That's great, Bac-si, we need all that kind of help we can get. How did the medical patrol go today?"

"Real good, Dai-uy. We went to Vinh Hoi hamlet, a little more than half way between here and the PF outpost at Nhon Hoi. We must have treated 100 villagers. It was pretty much routine. I checked teeth too as I looked into their ailments and decided we'd take another patrol up there in a couple of weeks and do some pulling. Co Lau is going back up with our new nurse later this week to teach the children how to brush and take care of their teeth. Of course their mothers are there with them so they learn from watching and listening as our nurses teach the children. There are no hurt feelings or embarrassment that way. Sergeant Hung will arrange for a security escort. They'll take lots of toothpaste, toothbrushes and special comic books that tell all about having strong teeth and give it all to the people, especially the children. It's a good thing!"

"Anything else, Bac-si?"

"Yes, sir. We had to react real fast to an incident that came up after we got back to camp. We'd just taken our stuff out of the jeep when a village health worker came running into the aid station, wanting help at the health center located just outside our front gate about a 100 meters on the right."

"I know where you're talking about. What happened?"

"She came in all out of breath and told us one of the local women was having trouble giving birth. Well, we didn't hesitate, Dai-uy. Co Lau, Tony and I went right away with her to the health center. When I saw the lady was in a lot of pain, I checked her out real quick and found she had a breech baby.

"I didn't want to take a chance of killing her baby or hurting her either, so we put her on a stretcher and took her right to the boat dock on the bed of our 3/4 ton truck. Co Lau, Tony and I stayed right with her. I had Map Map crank up the barge and take her to the Chau Doc hospital. I figured that way she could stay on the stretcher and get there fast because our barge is the fastest thing on the river.

171

Co Lau went with her to comfort her and to make certain she'd be seen right away at the hospital.

"They've got some good doctors there at the Chau Doc hospital, Dai-uy. I felt good knowing that the lady and her baby would have the best care available in this area." He smiled one of those real warm smiles of his and added, "You'll be happy to know that mother and little baby boy are doing just fine."

I reached across the table, shook his hand, and told him, "You did real good, Bac-si. That kind of work is important here. Taking care of the people like you and your crew do, when put together with all the other civic action and psy-ops projects that Big John is directing, are what let the people know we really do care about them.

"Anyone can be taught to kill and to destroy. We've all mastered the ugly parts of fighting a war. What's needed here in South Vietnam are compassion and love for the people and doing whatever it takes to help them win this war and not live in constant fear. That's something you men have already proven yourselves ready, willing and able to do. The Hoa Haos know that and nobody can take that away from you. It comes from your hearts, each and every one of you. I'm proud to be your commander and to be a part of it."

Our team meetings were very informal and when no one had anything else to say, we just got up from our chairs and went about our business. I normally went on up to the command bunker. I liked it there. It was solid, powerful in its **own way** and commanded a view at night of any enemy mortar, rocket, or tracer fire that took place the length of our western border with Cambodia. When the area was quiet, it was a place of peace and hope for the future, a place to reflect on one's own merits and shortcomings.

This particular evening, I invited Sergeant Taylor to join me, wanting to confide in him and seek his advice and counsel. We'd been together just a short time but I respected his judgment and trusted him.

As soon as we were up in the bunker, Jim turned toward me, looked me in the eyes, and asked, "What's up, Dai-uy?"

"Jim, I did a lot of soul-searching on the way back from the commander's meeting in Can Tho. The chopper crash was on my mind as I was thinking about our team and how you guys stacked up against the guys on other teams. What I told you all was true. We've done an awful lot with just a few men here in An Phu. At the same time, I know we might do even more and better for the Hoa Haos and I need to know what I can do to make that possible.

"Jim, we both know that I'm stubborn and like to have things go my way. My main concern is that I don't let my way get in the way of doing right for the Hoa Haos.

"One question keeps nagging at me since I walked away from that crash site intact, except for some burns. What if I'd been killed in that crash? Had I done a good enough job here in An Phu that you guys could keep moving forward, keep the momentum up? The more that question came to mind, the more I needed to know the answer."

"Just what are you getting at, Dai-uy?" Taylor asked.

"Sarge, I need you to talk to me like a brother. Tell me where you think I'm goofing up, what I'm doing wrong. I know it's not right for me to ask you, but I trust you and respect your judgment. Just let it all hang out, Jim. No holds barred and don't worry about my feelings. I very seldom ask for advice, but when I do I want it straight from the shoulder. Okay?"

Jim smiled and said, "Okay, Dai-uy. As a matter of fact, while you were gone, I asked the Lieutenant if we could have an old fashioned gripe session. I told him I thought it would be good for the team. He agreed, and after lunch that day we got together and got down to the nitty-gritty of what makes our team tick. Oh, there were a few gripes, but not anything like I've heard in teams I'd been in before An Phu.

"It was unanimous that you were too neat and tidy, kind of like a 'Mister Clean.' At the same time we all liked it because you did more than your share of any dirty work while you demanded high standards from all of us. The other guys that were here before you came aboard remembered what it was like then and I remembered what it was like in so many other teams and we agreed yours is the better way. We probably have the best looking and most secure camp in all of Vietnam and everything works too. You should know that the LLDB NCOs like the way you pitch right in and help no matter what's being done.

"They remember how you led the men to help the people of An Phu during the big fire. They know how little sleep you get and that you don't play around or abuse your power. They haven't said it exactly, but I think they feel a lot about you like they feel about Major Le, and that's one huge compliment.

"Oh, yes. We all agreed you are rather standoffish. You don't get involved much with the team. You spend a lot of time alone behind your desk or here in the command bunker. You don't even buddy around with big John. I figure you're just a loner and it's nothing you've got against any of us. Am I right, Dai-uy?"

"Right as rain, Jim, and I doubt I'll ever change. I enjoy working, no matter what the job is, and I wrap myself up in whatever I'm doing. I don't mean to offend anyone. There is one other thing you should know because I don't think I've discussed this with you yet. I don't get close to anyone because I don't want closeness to ever have any influence on decisions I make, especially when it comes to who I send out to where the killing is going on. I've always been that way."

"I'll tell you one thing we all appreciate, Dai-uy. You look out for our welfare. We'd much rather have a team leader who's a loner and takes care of us than one who is buddy-buddy but not willing to stick his neck out for us.

"The most critical point brought out during our gripe session and one that we all talked about is something that Lieutenant Strait was going to discuss with you. But, seeing as how you asked for my advice and comment, I may as well let it out right now. Okay, Dai-uy?"

"Sure thing, Jim. Shoot."

"We all think you go overboard on secrecy. You don't share a lot of what you know or are involved in, not even with Big John. The Lieutenant reminded us that you'd told us right up front how you'd handle the covert matters, that you'd keep them close to your chest. We all agreed we'd just have to trust your judgment, but we felt you should know that we are concerned and that we talked about it."

"I'm glad you men feel that way, Jim, but I doubt I'll change anything along that line. I honestly feel now, as I did from the beginning, that the less you know about certain things, the better off you'll be, especially if they go sour. You know from your training and what you've heard via the grapevine, that the CIA can react in many ways when something doesn't go their way. Basically, they don't like any loose tongues laying around that could finger the Company as the bad guy."

"You're right, Dai-uy, and I'll explain that to the men one more time. Now, before we get sidetracked, let me tell you the good stuff we talked about while I'm at it. Big John hit the nail on the head when he told us that he liked the fact that you listened to us. You're real good about letting us express our ideas on most decisions you've got to make, and once in a while you even let what we say influence you.

"To a man we like the fact that you'll admit when you're wrong, and that you'll flat out tell us when you don't know the answer to something instead of trying to fake it. And, I'll tell you something else, Dai-uy, I've been in this man's Army for 11 years now and you're the first officer that I've ever heard apologize openly to his men when he goofed. Big John Strait said that was good, especially for a Quartermaster officer!

"Let's face it, when you got here things were in pretty bad shape. None of us know exactly how you turned it around, but we know you sure didn't sleep much. Ray Johnson and I have been in a lot of SF camps, but we've never been in one where the Vietnamese and the Americans get along so well and have so much confidence in each other. We all know we've got a good fighting force here and that we try to do more for the people than any other camp we've been at. Really, Dai-uy, we've done more than I thought was possible."

"Thanks, Jim. I appreciate all that you've shared. I've got to tell you, Sarge, that it's easy for me to look good when I've got a good team behind me. When I was a young Sergeant First Class working for Captain Harry Corkill in the 82nd Airborne Division, I thought he was the greatest thing since sliced bread and so did all the other NCOs. Captain Corkill was a Mustang, an ex-Marine who'd fought in the Pacific Islands as a young Corporal in World War II and who, when I met him, filled a Lieutenant Colonel's position. He did the job better than any Lieutenant Colonel before him.

"One day when I was in his office, he told me, 'The secret to my success is real simple, Marv.' Jim, he's the only man who ever called me Marv, and from him it sounded good, but I don't want anyone else to call me Marv. Got it?"

"Clear as a bell, Dai-uy."

"Well, Captain Corkill went on to tell me, 'I pick the right people to work for me and then I take care of them.'

"I've got the right people here to get the job done, and if I don't do my best to take care of you all, then I deserve to fail. But, if I fail the mission fails and that is totally unacceptable. Simple as that, Sarge."

Jim glanced at his watch and told me he had to get down to the mortar pit to prepare for the next fire mission. I shook his hand and told him, "You're a good sergeant and I appreciate your honesty, Jim. Thanks."

He smiled and headed for the four-deuce pit. Within a few minutes Major Le joined me and we watched as our H&I mortar fire from Phu Hiep, Khanh Binh and camp began pounding the VC's sanctuaries. Major Le was first to notice a bright glow in the target area west of our Khanh Binh FOB. "I think our men have hit an ammo dump, Dai-uy." His suspicions were confirmed as we witnessed flashes of various magnitudes radiating from the impact area, and continuing for a number of minutes. Major Le smiled and remarked, "The fireworks of war, Dai-uy."

The profound quiet of a moonlit delta night followed. A time for men to lay in silent ambush along the border. A time for the villagers to sleep, feeling relatively secure in their bamboo and thatch homes, knowing other Hoa Haos were on duty, watching and guarding, eager to protect their own.

I asked Major Le to add my congratulations to his for a job well done by his FOB mortar crew at Khanh Binh. Major Le nodded his head, smiled, and then turned serious.

"Dai-uy," he said, "I think it is time for a photo reconnaissance of the border area. From southwest of Khanh Binh to northeast of Phu Hiep is the critical area. We are both pleased we hit an ammunition stockpile with our mortar attack, but I now wonder why they have put so much ammunition so close to the border. The only reason that would make sense is that they plan a big attack. It's time for us to take another good, long look inside Cambodia from the air so we can prepare for the worst that they have in mind for us. I don't like surprises such as this."

"I agree, Thieu-ta." I told him, "I'll ask Sergeant Taylor to request an SLR photo recon on an urgent priority."

Except for the excellent reports Major Le received from his agents who risked their lives daily inside Cambodia to keep us informed on enemy movements, the SLR (side-looking-radar) photographs were the only other way we had to learn what was going on inside their sanctuaries. All the pilots had been warned not to fly over Cambodian territory. The SLR photos would include an area approximately one thousand meters deep into Cambodia, but the SLR missions were time consuming: time to order, time to process, approve and fly the mission and time to process and get the photos to us for our evaluation via courier. It was a system not sufficiently responsive to answer our needs, but it was the only outside help we could get. General Westmoreland should have provided aircraft for our routine border and cross-border reconnaissance, but instead, he prohibited any flight over Cambodian territory. Criminal, I thought, when he knew for a certainty that our enemy was there in those safe havens and was able to re-

group, retrain, re-equip, rearm and prepare to attack our forces with impunity. In the book[1] **In the Jaws of History**, former South Vietnam Ambassador to the United States Bui Diem accurately delineates the problems associated with the self- defeating American strategy that precipitated Communist victory and the betrayal of South Vietnam by its once powerful friend, the United States of America: "Westmoreland's troops were prohibited from pursuing [the enemy] into their sanctuaries in Laos and Cambodia where the enemy would rest, regroup and fill in their ranks with reinforcements from North Vietnam ...As long as the enemy could escape detection or melt into the jungle, as long as they had inviolable sanctuaries along the borders, it was they, not the Americans, who would dictate the tempo and level of confrontation. For the Communists, the whole Indochinese peninsula was a battlefield, while the American ground forces restricted themselves to South Vietnam."

I blame President Johnson, his secretary of Defense and every military leader in the chain of command down to and including General William C. Westmoreland for sacrificing South Vietnamese and allied fighting men for political gain or any other insipid, ill-conceived and unverifiable rationale that caused them to give the enemy sanctuaries to operate from while tying the hands of our military leaders on the ground in South Vietnam. They should rather have demanded and then stood firm on the right to pursue and engage an enemy, any enemy, no matter where that enemy retreated to or attacked from and to engage any force that was being developed to wage war against South Vietnam no matter where or what that force happened to be.

On the 10th of April the mail chopper brought us the SLR photos we'd requested some five days prior. Shortly after lunch, Jim Taylor, who had gone over the photos with a fine tooth comb and compared them with the previous SLR photos taken some months ago, was ready to brief me on what he'd gleaned.

I met Jim in the joint operations center where he had the photos laid out side by side with previous photos. I was armed with my large magnifying glass. "Any surprises, Jim?" I asked.

Using a short pointer to direct my attention to specific areas, he began. "Well, Dai-uy, you can see along this area north of Phu Hiep they've rebuilt their trench line that we'd hit pretty hard a while back. It appears they've also added six fortified automatic weapons positions and cleared a field of fire in what was left of that bamboo stand after the big fire. Other than that, everything within mortar range in that area shows no signs of the enemy's presence.

"West of Khanh Binh there's just nothing, Dai-uy. You can see here, " as he pointed to where the ammunition dump was that our FOB gunners had hit dead on last week, "Only the tremendous mess where the ammo dump was. Other than that, no sign of VC activity anyplace along the border."

"Those photos just cover about a thousand meters into Cambodia. Am I right, Jim"?

"That's about it, and there's no sign of storage sites, encampments, new trenches, nothing. Those two battalions have moved out of range and we won't know where they are until we get the new agent reports from Major Le."

"That means our H&I fire has driven them back deeper into Cambodia. And that's good news. Lacking long range artillery or tactical fighter close air support, that's the best we can hope for."

"That's right, Dai-uy. But that at least gives us an earlier warning of an impending attack and we can be ready when they get close enough to do damage."

Major Le and Lieutenant Strait joined us and Sergeant Taylor went over the details of his analysis with them as he'd done with me. Major Le told us, "This ties in with a report I received from Lieutenant Thuan Nguyen at Khanh Binh. Two days ago the Cambodian flag was again seen flying over their PF outpost across from the FOB. Before that the outpost, as you know, was used by the VC as a command post. I will inform you of the latest enemy order of battle as soon as I get new agent reports."

"I'll be anxious as I know you are, Thieu-ta. We'll be getting some new men later this month. As soon as possible I'll get two Americans up to the FOB at Khanh Binh. " I thanked Sergeant Taylor for a good analysis and briefing and joined alongside a smiling Major Le as he walked toward his office, stopped and stood in front of the window overlooking our formation area and flagpole where the South Vietnamese Colors fluttered proudly in a slight breeze.

"I am happy to hear you are getting more men, Dai-uy. Your team has been very short of manpower and yet does so much. Do you have any word on approval for our sixth company? We will need those men when we open our new FOB at Vinh Hoi Dong. It should be ready in one month for the new company.

"No, I haven't, Thieu-ta, but I feel confidant we will have approval soon because they are allowing us to order all of the weapons, clothing and equipment for the new company as if it were here in camp. And, Thieu-ta, I don't think they would have approved the new FOB and disapprove the company we must have to man it."

Smiling even more broadly, he asked, "Should I begin to recruit in advance also, Dai-uy?"

"I think you already have, Thieu-ta. You don't let the grass grow under your feet."

Puzzled at what I said, he asked, "What about grass growing, Dai-uy?"

"Just an old saying, Thieu-ta. It means you don't stand around waiting for someone to tell you what to do once you know it has to be done."

"And you too don't let the grass get too high, Dai-uy." Major Le added. "We are very much like brothers."

A week passed with no word from our agents. We pressed forward with enthusiasm to help make progress on all of our civic action projects. We also touched base with all of our contacts to scrounge anything we could get our hands on to meet the needs of our new FOB. For some unknown reason the Saigon Army Depot was not responding to our requests for material. Sand bags, generators, standard radio equipment, barbed wire, concertina wire, steel posts, and all other conventional item needs were denied us. We had no choice but to go to the B-42, C-4 and our friends in other camps in the IV Corps area to get what we needed.

Shortly after breakfast on 15 April, Major Le and I headed up river to Phu Hiep FOB to witness the progress on rebuilding of defenses damaged or destroyed during the VC's vicious attack of 6 February. The immediate defensive needs were met within a few days, but the more permanent fortifications took a great deal more time and effort to accomplish. The last time I was up to Phu Hiep, it was with Major Le as we led the relief force that broke the VC's stranglehold on the FOB. We then entered an FOB literally devastated by their 82MM mortar fire which had sustained 65% casualties among the defending Strikers.

Though not a thing of beauty, the end result of a massive rebuilding program reshaped their defenses against indirect fire to resemble one big bomb shelter. Sergeant Barnes, whom we found to have gained a solid rapport with Lieutenant Luong and his Strikers, had done a magnificent job designing and coordinating the rebuilding and strengthening of Phu Hiep. I told Sergeant Barnes that Major Le and I were both extremely pleased at what they had accomplished under his able supervision. "I'll think of you as our sandbag architect from now on, Barnes. I'm mighty proud of not only what you've been able to help accomplish, but how you've managed to develop such a strong and viable rapport with the Hoa Haos."

Barnes then told me, "The Hoa Haos are brave and honest people, Dai-uy. When you first sent me here to the FOB, I felt like I was being sent into exile. But since I've been here, I've come to realize how important Phu Hiep is to our mission and, personally, I've come to know them as some of the finest people I've ever met."

"They are good people, Barnes, and I'm glad you're working well with them as a team. By the way, Sarge, I saw that double row of shoulder-high sand bags around your famous shower tower. Must be that you now enjoy your showers too."

He laughed and said, "That too, Dai-uy. That too."

From there Major Le and I went by boat back down the Co Lau River, turned north on the Bassac and followed it as far as Phuoc Thanh on the west bank, where Sergeant Hung waited with Major Le's jeep, a squad of Strikers, and a 3/4 ton truck. Map Map took the boats back to An Phu and we took the road up around the thumb. We stopped at a small eating place in Khanh Binh Hamlet where Major Le invited me to join him for tea and pastries. After a few minutes Lieutenant Thuan Hieu Nguyen, the 441st Company Commander joined us. There were just four tables and a young girl who served the tea and delicacies with a smile.

It was a brief and refreshing time, drinking tea, watching the villagers go about their daily routines and observing boats of many descriptions plying the Bassac River. It was a solid reminder of what life was all about, what freedom brought to those who were willing to fight for it and why we were there. All good people deserve peace and the opportunity to live a decent life.

We finished our tea and drove to the Khanh Binh FOB, a distance of about two kilometers from where we'd stopped. While there, we inspected the defenses, met and congratulated the mortar crew that had destroyed the enemy's ammunition dump inside Cambodia, and noticed the Cambodian flag flying over the Prek Thom Cambodian Militia Outpost. We thought of the agents, wondering if they were back home and safe.

We returned to Camp Dan Nam with Sergeant Hung and his security force close behind. On the return trip, Major Le told me he had finalized a program for the second anniversary celebration of the building of our camp. "Your Navy Seabees built Dan Nam," he said. "It is up to us to keep it strong and use it to protect our people from the Communists."

He reached into his shirt pocket, pulled out a sample program for the celebration, and handed it to me. "Have a look, Dai-uy, and let me know what you think. It will be on the 28th of April. We will have many visitors in our camp."

"Thank you, Thieu-ta." He had hand-written the English translation opposite the printed Vietnamese wording for my benefit. There would be a joint parachute jump at 0800 hours to kick off the festivities. Then the CIDG companies and American and South Vietnamese SF Teams would assemble in the open area in front of the raised platform where the guests would be seated. A prayer for the brave Strikers who had died defending An Phu, introduction of guests and a speech by Major Le would follow. I would address the guests next. Major Chuan, the LLDB C-4 Commander, would then present individual awards and speak to the assembled troops and guests.

I like your invitation, Thieu-ta. Thanks for translating it for me. I notice the camp is named An Phu in the invitation. Will that be changed to Dan Nam?" "No, I am sad to say that the headquarters wants all camps named after the district where they are located. I understand they want to avoid confusion and make it possible to improve the response time for air support, medical evacuation, and those kinds of things, but I will miss the old name also." Major Le offered.

"When I first came here and wrote my mother, she wrote back telling me how nice it was that you folks named the camp after me. I never told her any different."

Smiling, he said, "I will send your mother an invitation to our celebration."

"That will make her very happy, Thieu-ta. I really appreciate that. I'll give you her address."

As we passed through Dong Co Ki, the sound of multiple explosions and machine-gun fire erupted from the direction of Phu Hiep. Major Le turned and shouted to his radio operator who made immediate contact with our base station. A few minutes passed and we heard the crackly voice of the LLDB radio operator in camp coming over the small, hand-held HT-1 radio. Major Le, who had stopped the jeep and shut off the engine, listened intently then turned to me to translate what he'd heard. "No problem, Dai-uy. The VC fired their mortars at the FOB, but their aim was poor and all their rounds exploded in the outer defensive wire.

There will be some repair work, but there were no casualties and the machine-gun fire was directed at the PF outpost at Phu Loi as a harassing action only.

"Good, Thieu-ta. It is unusual to get daytime probes. What do you make of it?"

"Very unusual, Dai-uy. We must think about that."

From there back to camp the trip was uneventful. I'd missed seeing Sergeant Didion when he left camp for rotation back to the States. I'd miss him, barbells and all. He'd done a lot of good work out on medical patrol and the villagers liked the tall, lanky medic. They'd miss him too.

Later that evening, as we sat enjoying dinner in the team house, Sergeant Hung came rushing in, wearing a wide grin and sporting a new white tee shirt with the words, "DAN NAM" in blue letters superimposed on a red parachute symbol on the front. He rendered a cocky hand-salute and stood silently at attention, catching his breath. Hung always saluted and more likely than not had a smile on his face no matter what the circumstance. At the moment he appeared overcome with joy, ready to bust with what he had to say. Needless to say, we were on the edge of our seats waiting for him to open his mouth and say something. And say something he did. "Thieu-ta is waiting to see you in the briefing area, Dai-uy. He has much news." Without hesitation, Jim Taylor and I followed Hung as he strode down the hall to the operations center. We found Major Le waiting in front of the map boards, grease pencil in hand, a smile on his face.

"He greeted us with the words, "Our agents are all safe, Dai-uy, and they have brought much news from Cambodia."

I shook his hand and said, "That's good news, Thieu-ta. I know you worry about them and that you're relieved when they are back on this side of the border safe and sound. They are brave women, your agents."

"Thank you, Dai-uy." Major Le placed the grease pencil back on the map tray, picked up the long, tapered, brass-tipped rod and began, pointing to where each bit of intelligence was related to as he briefed us. "I will tell you what we have learned about the Southward Regiment. The 261st Battalion and the 267th Battalion west of Khanh Binh moved deeper into Cambodia after their ammunition dump was blown up by our men in Khanh Binh. They are now 4,000 meters from the border."

"As we suspected." I interjected.

"That is right, Dai-uy. Our destruction of their Bung Ven Base has made them aware of our capabilities inside Cambodia and they moved the 260th Heavy Weapons Company, from their close proximity to Phu Hiep, to a new location over six thousand meters distant from our FOB.

"The two battalions on the other side of the Bassac, north of Khanh An, and the Heavy Weapons Platoon west of Tac Truc have remained in place, perhaps because we have not threatened them with our heavy mortars.

Continuing in a very serious tone, he said, "Our big surprise is here near Phu Hoi where we now work on our next FOB. A new VC battalion is there with over

500 men and many rocket launchers and mortars. It is bad news, Dai-uy. We must get approval for the sixth company quickly."

"It is as we thought, Thieu-ta, they are now within striking distance of our camp and the Howitzer Platoon base. I'll send an urgent message requesting immediate approval. If I could give them a date we think the Southward Regiment will attack, it might help to expedite their decision."

"I can tell you this, Dai-uy, it will not be before the 17th of May."

"You sound very certain, how can you know this?"

"One of our agents speaks fluent Cambodian and her skin color is more brown like them, making it possible for her to pretend to be a Cambodian. She traveled to a casket factory more than 25 kilometers up-river from Khanh Binh to learn what she could. She told me it was her idea, 'something told me to do it.'"

"Anyway, Dai-uy, she went into the factory and told them she needed a job to make some extra money to buy a gift for her parents' wedding anniversary. They were not suspicious and hired her. She was put to work helping fill an order for 500 caskets for the Vietminh military. Her supervisor, thinking it would help to inspire the workers through patriotic zeal, showed them the order which required them to be in place in Prek Chrey by the 17th of May. He told her they would all get a bonus if the caskets were completed and shipped by the 15th and that it was important to the 'People's cause.'

"Wanting to get that important information to me," Major Le told us, "she waited a few days and pretended to be very sick and told them it was too hard on her and that she had to quit. When she got back to Prek Thom, where they normally cross the bridge into Khanh Binh, she met her sister agents who were waiting for the VC to remove roadblocks that sealed the bridge. It seems as though, from what the villagers said, the VC were looking for deserters from their ranks. So, our ladies hid out in the bamboo thickets until the roadblock was taken away. We now know why they were so long in coming back."

Jim Taylor spoke out, saying "I think there is going to be one big terrible battle if that whole regiment attacks us at one time. They didn't order those caskets for us and we now know they're prepared to lose a lot of men. It's as simple as that."

Suddenly Major Le slammed his fist down on the lectern and almost shouted out, "It is very clear to me now. Very clear."

"What's clear to you, Thieu-ta?" Jim Taylor asked.

"They will attack on the 19th of May. I am very certain of that because it is Ho Chi Minh's Birthday. That is why they must have the caskets by the 17th. They will have at least a day to move them to different places where they anticipate the greatest need because of expected casualties. I will send a high priority message to Major Chuan at C-4 asking him to speak with your Colonel Tuttle about the urgency of our need for a sixth company."

"It all makes sense now, Thieu-ta." I said, turning then to Jim Taylor and telling him to "bring Barnes and Johnson in from Phu Hiep tomorrow. I want the whole team, except for Eleam in the commo bunker, in the dining area at 1400 hours.

We'll discuss this whole situation and have a full blown team meeting. Tell Eleam he'll be going back up tomorrow with Barnes after the meeting. Barnes can bring him up to snuff on the way to Phu Hiep. I want Ray here to help on the logistics end, especially with Didion gone. And tell Eleam I'll be bringing him a very hot message shortly." Jim headed out with note pad in hand to get things rolling for the meeting. I thanked Major Le for the briefing and for his coming up with what I too thought was a logical date. "Please tell your ladies how proud we are of all of them, Thieu-ta. We owe them a big bonus. If you see Lieutenant Strait when you are down to sub-sector, please tell him I need him here."

"Certainly, Dai-uy. I am going now to see Captain Tuoi and tell him what we have discovered. When I return I will arrange for the bonuses as you suggested." Within a few minutes I was handing Eleam the urgent message for him to send to C-4. It read, "SECRET - TO CO C4- REQUEST URGENT APPROVAL OF SIXTH CIDG COMPANY. 2,000, REPEAT 2,000 VC OF SOUTHWARD REGIMENT PREPARING TO ATTACK AN PHU ON 19 MAY. NEW VC BN THREATENS CAMP FROM WEST. I ALSO NEED TWO WPNS MEN FOR NEW FOB. URGENT FM CO A-424 - SECRET. "Looks like we got our job cut out for us, Dai-uy." Eleam remarked after reading the message.

John Strait strode in, saying, "Thieu-ta said you wanted me."

I briefed John on the latest intelligence, informed him about the 1400 hour meeting and asked that he prepare a briefing on CA and Psy-Ops for the team. With a big battle coming up we both knew it was important that we be prepared to help the people in any way that we could and, perhaps more importantly, that we not drop the ball on any of our ongoing projects. The people of An Phu must always believe they would be first and foremost in our plans and our work. Only by doing that could we convince them we are loyal to them.

Jim Taylor led off the team meeting at 1400 hours on the 16th with an enemy situation briefing, highlighting the fact that the Southward VC Regiment was now around 2,000 strong with a lot of heavy weapons, including recoilless rifles and 82MM mortars. "Thieu-ta believes they'll attack on 19 May - Ho Chi Minh's birthday. Makes sense and that's why they're up inside Cambodia far enough so we can't touch them. They could hit Khanh An, Khanh Binh, and Phu Hiep in a coordinated assault with only a short march to cross the border. That's what we've got to be prepared to deal with.

"We got word yesterday from Major Le," Jim continued, "that a new VC battalion has moved into the area northwest of our camp and bivouacked on the north bank of the Stoeng Takey River, 7,000 meters away and out of our mortar range. It is a bad situation. Right, Dai-uy?"

"Sure is, Jim. I've asked Colonel Tuttle to approve the sixth company on an urgent basis. Major Le says he'll have no problem recruiting the infantrymen. He'll pull what sergeants he needs for the new company from our other companies and, as he recruits new men, promote combat-experienced men to sergeant within the old companies to reach combat effectiveness. That will give us enough manpower to go into that area and establish an FOB a short distance southeast of the hamlet of Phu My and on the west bank of the Chau Doc River." Pointing to its exact location on the tactical map, I went on, "Major Le and his men are putting that FOB together as we meet. We'll call it Vinh Hoi Dong."

Lieutenant Strait chimed in, "It's going to be darker then pitch the night of the 19th with no moon at all. We'd better get that FOB in and going before mid-May for a certainty. There's nothing between us and that new VC battalion but rice paddies and the Chau Doc River. Phu My and Phu Thanh PF outposts can't hold off anything like a battalion and we can't protect them as things stand right now. We have too much border to cover and too few Strikers to get the job done.

"I know, after having just met with the district staff that Captain Tuoi is prepared to reinforce Phu My and Phu Thanh outposts with RF troops if necessary. But we know, Dai-uy, that his primary concern will be to protect that ARVN 155MM Howitzer Platoon. I'm not arguing the point, just stating what I believe to be fact. District headquarters and the 155s are as vulnerable as we are until we get that FOB in place. We don't dare let anything happen to our only long range artillery support capability."

I spoke up, saying "True enough, John, and we need an extra company here in camp so we have our own reaction force capability to meet whatever need surfaces, especially in the northern area around Khanh Binh and Phu Hiep. There's just no doubt we have to get a sixth company in place and combat ready in a month's time. We'll send an experienced company to open the FOB and man it until we can, with confidence in their combat readiness, send the new company in ready for what they'll be facing.

"Lieutenant Strait, I want you to work with Sergeant Johnson and make sure we've got enough ammunition on hand and in the right places to hold off that regiment. Check out all the commo gear and make certain it works well," and, turning to Sirois, I directed, "Bac-si, you go along to the FOBs and check out medical supplies. Make sure we've got what you'll think we'll need and then add 25%. I want to be prepared for a lot of casualties. Also get whatever the nurses need in the health center outside the front gate to cover treatment of wounded refugees from the battle areas."

"Sure thing, Dai-uy," Bac-si responded. "John," I told Lieutenant Strait, "Give us a good look at our civic action program."

Pointing to locations on the mapboard behind him, John began, "Right there are many of our local volunteers and some contractors for the tough jobs, in the process of building nine schoolhouses. They are varying sizes and in one stage or another of construction. Most are two room schools with outside johns. Working together, we've also finished six bridges in these areas," pausing to point out where and what they crossed, "and expect to complete the large market house in Khanh Binh in May or June. The VC will most likely do some damage to everything in the thumb area around Khanh An and Khanh Binh. If they do, we'll help them to rebuild them, won't we, Dai-uy?"

"Sure thing, John. How is the boat dock at Da Phuoc coming along?"

"Should be done this coming week, and it's pretty much out of harm's way on the Bassac River and a long ways from the border."

"True enough, John. Bring us all up to snuff on corn and rice and other Agriculture matters."

"Well, Dai-uy, I've really gotten to know Mr. Duc, the District Agricultural Chief. He is a hard working individual and outstanding in his field." That perhaps unintentionally humorous remark caused the whole team to break out in laughter.

John continued, "Guess I said the wrong thing to you wise guys. Anyway, we've been able to really help Mr. Duc and local farmers with a soil test kit. My old 'Ag' teacher from Jonesville, Michigan, Mr. Spotts, sent it to me. Thanks to Flash, who translated the instructions, and Mr. Duc's positive attitude, there is now a real good program in place that has the capability to do what's necessary to bring the land up to snuff and to keep it fertile. You know, Dai-uy, within days of his being introduced to the kit, Mr. Duc went out amongst the local farmers, tested their soil, and began getting orders for fertilizer which he gave to me. I sent them to USAID and the stuff is already flowing into An Phu.

"That's not all, either. We finally got some of that IR-8 strain of rice from the Philippines, thanks to a USAID contact. The old strains they were using here were what I'd call 'sorry' strains. Let me tell you, they've really got some good rice going now."

"How about the corn, John?" I asked.

"Another good thing, Dai-uy. They'll be harvesting that first ever acre of field corn early in May and there's already two pig farmers signed up to buy corn for hog feed. Within a couple of weeks they'll see how it begins to fatten up their hogs and we'll see a line of farmers wanting to get that seed. Just wait and see, you guys, it'll be a happy time in the ole pig pen!" I thanked John for helping me put together a good Psychological Operations Estimate.[2] I told every member of the team just how important it was that they be familiar with every word in the report. "I really believe in what we're doing, Dai-uy," John said. "New leaflets will be dropped on the other side of the border shortly, along with lots of Chieu-Hoi passes. Captain Tuoi said he knows of an old pilot with an aged civilian airplane who will fly just over the border and spread leaflets over the area real good from west of Phu My up to the Bassac River where it enters Cambodia. Seems as though he's kind of neutral, so they don't bother him and we don't either when he's flying for them. It's a strange way to fight a war, isn't it?"

"Sure is," Jim Taylor spoke out. Lieutenant Strait continued, "VIS has been running a good psy-ops class for villagers and local officials over in the sub sector training facility. They'll be graduating within the week. Mr. Minh, our VIS Chief, introduced me to his instructors and the students. They're also learning the basics of how to use the mobile loudspeaker system, even the maintenance of the three-wheeled Lambretta motor scooter-like vehicle that carries it around, during this last week of instruction. I've been to a few sessions, even a group rally where they learn ways to effectively reach all the people living in their hamlets. Lots of things on their agenda, Dai-uy: bulletin board use and organization, leaflet design and distribution, people-to-people activities with emphasis on the many civic action programs we've got going that help the people to help themselves."

"That's good, John." I interrupted, "I had the privilege of attending the graduation ceremony for the previous class two days after I arrived in camp. I was impressed with what all they'd been through in the program. I'm especially glad that it is the Hoa Haos who now supervise the various aspects of the program. We were taught to do what we can to help the local people without having them become dependent on us and you and the others have done it here. That's a fact that's hard for some people to understand and appreciate. Most don't think of a Green Beret being humble enough to do as much as he can with and for others and do it in such a way as to work himself out of a job and then not want to take credit for bringing it about."

"True enough, Dai-uy," John added, "something else that really helped me was to learn their customs and discover from them what was real important from a purely human standpoint. I've been able to pass that on to the team, as you know Dai-uy, and I believe it's helped us to be just that much closer to the people."

Bac-si spoke up. "You're right, Lieutenant. One of the first things I recall Sergeant Chet telling me was how they respected you and Dai-uy because you take your hats off when you enter a pagoda. Hey, they don't have any weird hang-ups like some people do. They just like to lead a good, clean life and take care of their families, their animals and their land."

John Strait, agreeing with Bac-si, added, "I remember when I first saw Strikers holding hands as they were coming back from an operation. I wondered if they were effeminate. I soon learned that was the farthest from the truth, that these guys are tough suckers and not anyone to mess with. Among the Hoa Haos it's a sign of friendship, camaraderie among soldiers, and I've even done it myself. Believe it, Dai-uy. Not long after I got here, I was out on a combat patrol along the border with a platoon of Strikers west of here, just above Phu Hoi. We'd been slogging through miles of rice paddies and were all beat to our socks by the time we headed back towards camp. One of the Strikers, the one who carried a .30 caliber machine-gun and a couple of belts of ammunition across his shoulders, and who didn't look much bigger than a young American boy, moved next to me, looked up, smiled and grabbed my hand. And there we was, the two of us holding hands and walking across those rice paddies, coming back from fighting a battle together. At the time I thought, boy, if the people back home could see me now! I learned it was just a good thing between real men. And you don't have to be with them very long to know the Hoa Haos are real men."

"I'll sure echo that. Anything else, Lieutenant?"

"Yes, Sir," and he went on to tell, "I think it helps to always carry a camera and to take pictures of the people you come in touch with, especially the children, whether you're on medical patrol, a civic action project, psy-ops stuff or just getting a haircut or when out shopping in the local marketplace. Soon as you can, get the film developed and give the pictures to the person who's in 'em. If I'm getting a haircut and I take pictures of someone in the barbershop, I give the photo to the barber. He knows the people and he'll get the picture to the right one. They'll share when there's more than one family involved; there's nothing selfish about these people. Anyway, Dai-uy, I think it's something each of us can do that's very special to them. Hardly any of the villagers have a camera and they really appreciate the pictures."

Speaking to the team as a whole, I supported the good sense of what John had said. "Whenever it's possible to do some little thing like that to bring a smile on a face, to let them know we really care about them as people, especially the kids, like the XO said, let's do it."

Finally, Sergeant Taylor told us that Major Le would be rotating the 442nd company out of Phu Hiep on the 21st and replacing it with the 444th company from camp.

The meeting over, we began to leave the operations center when the sound of an engine backfiring was heard coming from the direction of the flagpole area, interrupting the relative quiet of the camp. I threw open the door and stuck my head out just as a $2^{1}/_{2}$ ton truck came to a stop directly in front of our headquarters building and backfired once more; its engine coughed, sputtered and died. By now most of the team was standing in front of the vehicle, waiting to find out what was in a very big crate roped to the corner of the truck's cargo bed. It would measure about three feet square and six feet high.

A young American soldier in starched green fatigues jumped down from the cab of the truck as Major Le approached from the vicinity of the front gate, no doubt as curious as we were. The driver recognized me, saluted and said, "I'm looking for a medic named Sirois, Sir. Is he here?"

About that time, Major Le came and stood next to me. The soldier ignored him. Looking up toward the huge box on the truck, Major Le asked, "What is in the box, Dai-uy?"

"Don't know, Thieu-ta, but we'll find out shortly. First let me take care of a matter with the driver." I walked over, stood nose to nose with him and asked, "Didn't you forget something, soldier?"

He looked around at the truck and answered, "I don't think so sir."

"Why didn't you salute Major Le when you saw him?"

Visibly shaken by my getting in his face, his lips quivered as he replied, "I've never saluted a gook yet, Sir. I'm an American soldier." Suddenly, an uneasy quiet hung like a shroud over us. Only the muffled drone of a small generator on the other side of camp could be heard by me over the sound of the driver's now heavy breathing. My men knew how I felt about military courtesy, especially how it disturbed me to have one of the Vietnamese called a "gook", and they stood by, unmoving and silent, waiting for the ax to fall on the young soldier.

186

I called out, "Bac-si," and Sirois came quickly up to stand in front of me. "This undisciplined excuse for a soldier says he's looking for you. What's in that big box, Bac-si?"

He grinned from ear-to-ear. "A kerosene refrigerator. I can't believe it. I asked for a small one to store perishable drugs and it looks like we got a real big one by the size of that box. There'll be lot's of room for chow in this one, Dai-uy."

Major Le laughed and said, "Your men are full of surprises, Dai-uy. What will it be next time? Maybe a tennis court like your General Westmoreland has?"

I grinned at Thieu-ta as he spoke and the driver began to move toward his vehicle. I reached out, grabbed him by the arm, jerked him back around to where we faced each other again. "You get in your truck, soldier," I hollered, "and you move it to wherever Bac-si tells you to so my men can unload that icebox. And then you ask Bac-si where my office is and you get there as fast as you can and report to me. I'll be waiting. Got that, soldier?"

A very weak "Yes, Sir" was his reply. He almost tripped over his own feet getting back into his truck. As he fumbled around getting it started, I apologized to Major Le for his lack of military courtesy.

"I accept your apology, Dai-uy, but I must tell you there are more like him, even of higher rank, then there are like you and your men. I do not blame them personally, I blame the officers who do not teach them better."

"Yes, Thieu-ta, and who do not set an example."

A few minutes later I confronted the driver in my office and told him, "If you ever come into this area again, and I'd just as soon you didn't, you'd better salute any Vietnamese you see who remotely resembles an officer. Where do you come from and who told you not to salute the Vietnamese?"

"Saigon, Sir. I'm just on loan at Chau Doc for a couple of weeks. In Saigon, my sergeants told me not to worry about the gooks. I'm not alone, Captain. Nobody salutes gooks where I come from."

Hearing him say that word over and over again got to me. I shot up from my chair, grabbed him by his fatigue jacket collar with both hands and came very close to losing my temper. "Soldier," I told him through gritting teeth, "Don't you ever use that word again. You are talking about South Vietnamese officers and you'll call them 'Sir' and you'll salute them because they deserve it. This is their country and we are here to help them. Got it?"

With a look of uncontrolled fear in his eyes, he responded, "Yes, Sir."

"And you keep your warm body out of this district and you tell whoever it was that sent you just exactly what I told you, understand?"

"Ye-ye-ye-yes, Sir-r," he stammered.

"Now, get out of here and drive your rig slow and careful all the way to the ferry landing where you'll cross over to Chau Doc."

As he was headed out and on his way, I overheard Bac-si, who was standing with Team Sergeant Taylor just outside the window of my office, ask Taylor, "Did you see the look in Dai-uy's eyes when that guy called Major Le a gook?"

"Sure did, Bac-si," answered Taylor, "That kid is lucky our Dai-uy didn't lose his cool."

Bac-si added, "That's for sure. He'd have found out why he's called Dangerous!"

Six days later, on the 22nd of April, Staff Sergeants Hilgartner and Brown, both heavy weapons men and both cross-trained as medics, reported for duty. Hilgartner forewarned us that he'd only be with us about two weeks and Brown would be going down-river by 1 June, on his way back Stateside to attend Artillery OCS. I met with Jim Taylor and decided to let Bac-si use Hilgartner on medical patrols as long as he was available. Jim asked for and got Brown to help him crew the four-deuce.

Just before noon on the 23rd, Sergeant Eleam came running into my office, nearly out of breath with excitement, and handed me a message from C-4. "We got it, Dai-uy, we got it!" he shouted.

The priority message said "NEW CIDG CO APPROVED. ESTABLISH FOB. FUNDS TO ARRIVE YOUR LOCATION 25 APR. GOOD LUCK."

"Thanks Eleam," I said and got right up from my chair to tell Major Le the good news.

"I can tell by the smile on your face that you have good news, Dai-uy," Major Le said as he looked up to see me approach him as he stood behind his desk, sorting through the many parts of his plans to build and man the Vinh Hoi Dong FOB. After reading the message, he told me, "I will send word to the Hoa Hao Council of our need for good men with fighting experience. I promise you we will quickly have a company ready and able to fight the VC."

"I can't ask any more than that, Thieu-ta. Lieutenant Strait will get with Lieutenant Ba and make sure you have the money you need to put the FOB together. Sergeant Ray Johnson has the field fortification material on order. Anything else you need that's not on hand or on order already will be requested from Group S-4 before tomorrow is over.

"Thieu-ta, we're having a team meeting after lunch. My plan is to get rolling on civic action projects, work with your team to help put together the FOB and make certain we have everything on order that we need to make this all come together quickly and in good order. As soon as we've worked up a tentative list, I'll get it to you for your review. We sure don't want to miss anything important. I'll be relying on you to help us think of every detail. You've been down this road before and I trust your judgment."

"Good, Dai-uy. I'll meet with my team after I receive your list then I'll get it back to you with any additional needs all checked out and written down." We shook hands and I left to wash up for lunch.

We all hurried through lunch, anxious to meet about our new company and the FOB. I told Bac-si to concentrate medical patrol activity in the Phu My area. We all went over the growing list of items needed to be ready for the expected attacks on Ho Chi Minh's birthday. What we required for the new company was spelled out in a table of organization and equipment (TO&E) so all we had to do was order by the TO&E listing. Conversely, requirements to build an FOB took a lot of thought and it was a case of many heads being better than one to put together a good list, one that would get the job done.

"Ray," I said, "I'll type this up and give a copy to Major Le. He'll have it back to me within a day, even sooner. Then, you, I and Lieutenant Strait will meet, go back over the list with a fine tooth comb and get it on the way to C-4." That was the last word, the meeting was over, and we all went about our business.

I'd walked up to the command bunker shortly after midnight and found Major Le quietly surveying the border area west of camp, binoculars to his eyes. I propped my M-16 against the wall, lifted my binoculars off the post-hook and searched the border area further north and towards Khanh Binh. Neither of us spoke. The command bunker was a special place where we both could come to enjoy a time of quiet and collect our thoughts, undisturbed. Many a time we'd been there, together, without a word spoken between us, like silent kindred spirits, often for but a few minutes, while at other times, as much as an hour might pass before one of us would sense the other wanting to break the silence. We respected each other's need for solitude, yet enjoyed each other's spirited company. It was a special camaraderie we had between us.

Perhaps 40 minutes after I'd joined Major Le, he broke the silence, saying, "I have a feeling the enemy will attack before dawn."

"I have the same idea, Thieu-ta." It was eerie, I reflected, knowing that our shared sense of foreboding had inevitably preceded every significant combat action in the months we had been together in An Phu. I hung my binoculars back on their hook, looked at Major Le, and asked, "How many ambushes are in place, Thieu-ta?"

"We have 20 along the border, Dai-uy, but it is not enough." We were both aware of the impossibility of sealing 50 kilometers of border with the number of men we had. I figured it out one time: if we lined up every one of our 692 Strikers along the border, side-by-side, setting aside all other missions we had, there would be 80 meters between them. Kind of like trying to stop the flow of water with a sieve.

Suddenly, at 0020 hours on the 24th, we saw flashes of light to the west, followed by sounds of multiple explosions as enemy mortar and rocket rounds hit in the area around the PF outposts at Vinh Hoi and Phu Hoi. "The new VC battalion is making its presence known, Dai-uy," shouted Major Le.

We continued to scan the entire border area through our binoculars and were quick to note many flashes all along the border to the north, accentuated by the moonless night. The muffled sounds of exploding rounds reached our ears, sounding much like a rumbling, muted thunderstorm. Our 81MM Mortars at Phu Hiep and Khanh Binh would soon answer the VC's aerial attack on the FOBs and neighboring PF outposts. From our vantage point in the command bunker, it appeared to Major Le and myself that all PF outposts and FOBs over the entire length of our border area were under mortar or rocket attack.

Our men swung into action as Lieutenant Strait set up his fire direction control center in the command bunker. From there he could see the enemy tube flashes to the west of camp, plot their location on his board and give the azimuth and distance to Sergeant Taylor, who was already set up and waiting target acquisition data in the four-deuce pit, a crew ready to perform and punish the enemy before they moved back out of range of our mortars.

A very unsophisticated system it was. The mortar crew would fire by direction of Lieutenant John Strait. John stood with binoculars in one hand, lensatic compass in the other and a field telephone dangling from a post nearby in the command bunker. He'd pick up the handset and shout azimuth and distance through it to Jim Taylor after he'd plotted the location of an enemy weapon's firing flash on the fire control board map. Chief interpreter Flash would then come into play in the scenario that would allow success in counter-fire action. He stood by, a field phone in his hand, listening intently for word from the outpost's spotter, telling distance and direction from target that our round exploded. That would be relayed by the LLDB commo man in the bunker below. Flash stood by Big John to translate and repeat the correction from the spotter. John would then plot the corrections, right or left and range by meters and call Jim Taylor with the new azimuth and range. Cumbersome as it was, the system worked if everyone hustled and the commo link didn't break down. We were able to occasionally score a direct hit during counter-fire missions due to the ever-increasing efficiency and smooth interaction of the different components of the system that we lived by.

This time, however, the VC were testing our reaction time and attempting to find out what we had to throw back at them. They must have made their judgments early, ceased fire, and slithered back deeper into Cambodian territory before we could get a lock on their positions and destroy them.

All was once again quiet. Major Le and I remained in the command bunker awaiting casualty reports from our FOBs and from sub-sector. Via the latter, we would learn how the outposts fared. It was a time for prayer and hope.

Within 30 minutes we were made aware of our combat losses, both dead and wounded. The light casualty figures were testimony to our people's ability to maintain a constant state of high alert and combat readiness. One Striker was wounded in the Khanh Binh FOB and two children were killed at Phu Hiep. It hurt more than I could ever have imagined, to lose children in an enemy attack, young innocents who depended on us for protection. It was a real tragedy and it served to strengthen my resolve to never purposely allow civilians to be placed in harm's way or to knowingly precipitate an action that would endanger civilians, particularly women and children whether enemy or friendly.

The 444th Company had just rotated to the FOB three days prior to the attack. As was normal, their families went with them. They always did, wanting to be together no matter what, and we did our best to protect them. Sometimes they paid an awful price for that love and that family closeness. This was one of those times.

John Strait, 22 years later, would record on audio tape³ his recollections of that fateful night of VC probing actions. One of the two children killed at Phu Hiep was a victim of concussion. She was a young girl, at the most six years old, who had, along with most of the children whom John was around for very long, developed an attachment to him. The powerful shock-force of an 82MM high explosive mortar round bursting close by literally shook her brain loose from her cranium, killing her instantly without leaving a mark on her body. "Another incident I remember," John tells, "was about a small girl up at the Phu Hiep FOB. You always favor a child, particularly there, who is kind of partial to you. You know." And this little girl was partial to John. "She was the one, that every time I'd come up there, she'd be the first one on the boat to greet me and the last one to wave good-bye. She was probably 4, 5, 6 years old. Hard to tell the age of some of those little kids up there, but anyway, one day, back at the main camp, after they'd been mortared up there, they brought this girl into camp dead. There wasn't a mark on her because she'd been killed by a concussion, which to me was worse, seeing that little girl there, with not a mark on her, than it'd been if I'd seen her tore up real badly. I took that kinda personal but nobody ever knew that."

So very true, John never mentioned that time of intense personal trauma until we met at Fort Bragg, North Carolina in 1988, some 22 years after the fact.

The round that killed those innocent, brave children in the Phu Hiep FOB was fired out of a VC mortar located 2,000 meters inside Cambodia on 24 April 1966. The enemy had their safe-havens but the families of our friends whose country we were there to assist, had none. Recoilless rifles were used by the VC to penetrate the defenses of PF outposts at Khanh An, Tac Truc and Vinh Hoi and 82MM Mortars lobbed the missiles that did the damage at the Phu Hoi, Nhon Hoi, Phu Loi and Da Phuoc PF outposts. All told five PF were killed and another 16 were wounded in action, most of them the victims of the recoilless rifles.

Major Le and I had a lunch meeting with Captain Tuoi at sub-sector head-quarters and discussed the morning's probes of our FOBs and PF outposts. "They must have moved into position near the border during daylight hours." Major Le began, "Knowing we had fired our previous H&I mission just before midnight the night before, and based on recent experience, they felt relatively safe moving within mortar and recoilless rifle range of our locations shortly after midnight. Once in place they then launched lightning-quick probes, immediately withdrawing out of our mortar range when they'd fired their final pre-planned round."

Captain Tuoi thought that very plausible and suggested that he too felt the VC may have assumed that we would fire our next H&I mission closer to daybreak, and he told us, "they know you do not fire into Cambodia during the daylight."

"It is then time we change our strategy." Major Le said with conviction. "Do you agree, Dai-uy?"

"Yes, Thieu-ta, I agree. And you Captain Tuoi?" I asked.

191

Captain Tuoi, hamstrung by political constraints, did not respond, but nodded his head in agreement. Prohibited from conducting any kind of military activity inside Cambodia, he relied on our independent mission actions to keep the enemy off balance and back a distance from the border. At the same time, we could count on Captain Tuoi to do anything within his power to help us and to do so without hesitation.

After about 30 minutes of discussion, Major Le and I decided on a strategy very pleasing to Captain Tuoi. We would begin firing two additional H&I missions from camp and both FOBs on the 26th of April. "Our plan is to fire the first round after the activation ceremony," Major Le said with a happy smile, evidencing his joy at the thought.

"You must be very pleased about your new company, Thieu-ta," Captain Tuoi suggested.

"Yes, I am," Major Le responded. "Now we have another important matter to take care of. We must have leaflets printed that will warn the Cambodian people of our need to fire into the VC safe-havens during daylight hours. We must not purposely endanger our Cambodian friends, Dai-uy. The leaflets will let them know it could be very dangerous for any who would enter those places. We have tried hard in the past to avoid civilian casualties and we have done well."

I asked Major Le, "Is it true that we haven't killed or wounded even one Cambodian since the day we began firing into the sanctuaries?"

"Yes, Dai-uy, apparently that is true. I have had no reports that would deny that fact." Reaching out to each of us with a piece of paper, he told us, "this is a copy of the leaflet I propose we drop inside Cambodia. Please take the time to read it and let me know what you think of it." The leaflet read: "To our Cambodian friends in the border area: Request you stay away from the military areas occupied by the invaders from the north at all times. Your friends across the border in An Phu do not wish to hurt you when we strike out day and night against our enemy who stations himself in your peaceful country."

We all agreed it was what was needed. Major Le had it hand-carried to the VIS Chief by Lieutenant Ba, who told Mr. Minh to print ten thousand leaflets as soon as possible in the Khmer language. "Let me know when they are ready," he told Mr. Minh as he left the VIS office to return to camp.

Early the next day at the breakfast table, I briefed my team on the latest H&I strategy and asked Ray Johnson to make certain additional mortar ammunition was requested to support the increased H&I activity." Sure thing, Dai-uy," he said and went about his work.

The mail chopper arrived a short time after lunch with a pouch containing the money needed to activate our new CIDG company. As soon as I told Major Le, he scheduled a small ceremony for the next day, inviting the Province Chief, the Vietnamese press, and at my request: Colonel Brewer. Mr. Minh was asked to coordinate press coverage, making maximum use of the propaganda value of our increase in fighting strength.

I left Major Le's office after learning that he had selected Lieutenant Sang Dan Ngo as the 446th Company Commander. "Good choice," I'd told Major Le. I remembered Sang well as the young XO of the 441st Company. I'd seen him in action and he was without a doubt a strong leader of men.

Entering the team dining area to get a cup of coffee, I found Team Sergeant Jim Taylor virtually seething with anger. Seeing me, he vented his frustration, saying "What are they trying to pull on us Dai-uy?" He pointed to a letter that lay open on my desk.

I picked it up, read it, and threw it back down and let Jim know I was just as angry. "How could they possibly disapprove this?" I yanked open my file cabinet drawer and pulled out a file marked *Soldier's Medal*. I threw it on the desk, on top of the letter we'd just gotten. I'd recommended each of my men, who had so bravely fought the February fire in the district village, be awarded the Soldier's Medal. "You guys earned that medal and it should have been awarded to each one of you. I was there and I saw you guys pour water on each other so you wouldn't go up in flames. You almost died from heat exhaustion. Bac-si was there. He would swear to it. And someone up there in higher headquarters cuts it down without so much as asking one question of anyone who was there, not even the local people, I guess."

Sergeant Taylor had calmed down some while I was ranting and raving. He told me, "I should have known we'd get short shafted on this Dai-uy. The other day when I was down to the B Team to meet with the Sergeant Major, I got to talking with one of the guys at lunch. I won't mention his name because I don't want to accidentally get him into trouble. Anyway, he told me Colonel Brewer hates your guts! He calls you King of the Hoa Haos all the time and storms around the Chau Doc compound saying that he'll get you some day. He is really mad that you ignore what he tells you to do, and that you do your own thing. "And," Jim went on, "I don't think the situation is helped much by the attitude in the C Team. From what I heard, Colonel Tuttle blames you personally for all the border violations, but he won't let Colonel Brewer relieve you or put you up for courts-martial. At least we can be thankful for that."

"Jim, I thank you for confiding in me, telling me what you'd learned at the B Team. I appreciate your attitude and I'm glad too that you understand the strange methods of operation and the conflicting actions that are a part of these independent operations. Not simple and not the best way to survive when the enemy may reside in our own higher headquarters. A pure and simple chain of command functioning up and down would be like a piece of cake, but I want to finish what I was sent here to do."

I knew this was bound to happen, but hoped it wouldn't. I asked Jim not to blame Colonel Tuttle, who was forced to play the 'game' according to the rules the CIA had set down. I was sure glad that Tuttle was strong enough to keep Brewer from destroying me.

"This is one risky business we're involved in." I told Jim. "The covert nature of what we do provides a breeding ground for enemies of our own kind and more."

I went on to explain that I had taken action[4] to protect us against the CIA's or even SF headquarters' wrath should they decide to take us out of here for some reason unknown to us and set about to make us the fall guys. Some day he would know what it was that I was talking about. I let him know that I hoped it would be me telling him.

"But, disapproving the Soldier's Medals for you guys was a low-down, contemptible act. I never figured Colonel Brewer would stoop that low. I'm real sorry about that."

"No sweat, Dai-uy," Taylor comforted me, "We can all live without the medal. Oh, we would have felt honored to get it because it's real special, but I figure I know why they were disapproved. You see, Dai-uy, we all put you in for one too. You were in the hot and heavy of the fire too. Let's face it, you led us into the battle to help those people rescue their belongings and save the village from total destruction. The way I see it, if Colonel Brewer recommended approval for ours he would have had to do the same for yours. "Tell you the truth, Dai-uy, I don't think he'd throw you a life jacket if you were drowning, much less see you get a Soldier's Medal."

"I sure goofed earlier, Jim."

"What did you do?"

"I asked Major Le to invite Colonel Brewer to the activation ceremony."

"Listen, Dai-uy, you have to keep your cool. Colonel Brewer doesn't matter to any of us. We've got to think of the Hoa Haos first and we've all got to stick together. Let Major Le handle Colonel Brewer. He'll know just what to do."

"Good advice, Jim. I'll do just that. By the way, Jim, I really appreciate what you said and I won't forget it."

"I know, Dai-uy, and I believe you. By the way, you'll be happy to hear that Tony's cousin Jean Pham arrived earlier today. We sure needed another good interpreter. Jean was cleared by Major Le and Lieutenant Strait hired him on the spot."

"Thanks Jim, that's good news."

I went over to Major Le's office and explained the situation to him. He smiled and let me know that Major Re had told him that there was bad blood between Colonel Brewer and me. "Don't worry, Dai-uy," Major Le said, "I will take care of him tomorrow."

I wasn't sure I wanted to know what he meant by that, so I didn't ask. I thanked him and started to leave his office when he said, "I have good news, Dai-uy."

I stopped, turned around and asked what it was. He told me, "We have 50 recruits for our new company. They will arrive in camp in the morning and be here in time for the activation ceremony. And, Dai-uy, I am told we will have 30 more in time for our anniversary celebration."

I told him that was "outstanding" and that we could issue them uniforms to wear at the ceremony if they were in camp by 0800 hours. What did he think of that?

"I think we will have a good day tomorrow, Dai-uy. I will make certain they are here in time." We shook hands and I left his office, went to our commo bunker, and told Ray Johnson to make certain he was available in the morning to issue uniforms and other initial issue items to the new men.

Ray told me there'd be "no sweat", that Sergeant Brown would cover for him in the commo bunker. He would take care of the new Strikers with help from the LLDB. Ray looked up from the radio he was working on and let me know that Jim had told him about the Soldiers' Medal. "I just want you to know we all appreciate what you tried to do for us, Dai-uy. Thanks."

I thanked him and told him that just knowing the team had asked that I be awarded the same medal meant the world to me.

Lieutenant Colonel Brewer arrived in camp at 0900 on the 26th of April, having flown in from Chau Doc by helicopter. Major Le met him at the chopper pad and escorted him to the reviewing stand that was being prepared for the anniversary celebration. Major Re, Captain Tuoi and Lieutenant Strait arrived a short time later, having met first at district headquarters with Mr. Minh, the district VIS Chief to discuss a matter related to psychological warfare operations and to decide what would be permitted as far as coverage of the activation by the South Vietnamese press. The press corps, led into camp by Mr. Minh, arrived shortly after the B Team CO. They were restricted to taking photos in the drill and ceremony area only. Interviews were limited to officials and officers present in the reviewing stands. They were very cooperative, understanding the importance of denying the enemy information about our camp, its defenses, weapons or personnel strength, knowing that unintended disclosure of such matters could be harmful, even deadly, to our men and the people of An Phu.

Major Le conducted a brief activation ceremony that included the presentation of a new staff and company flag to Lieutenant Sang Dan Ngo, who stood tall and looked proud as he accepted the flag on behalf of the 50 uniformed men of the 446th CIDG Company. The thunderous roar of the four-deuce firing into Cambodia at maximum range, climaxed the ceremony. Guests were not told where the rounds were headed, but we knew it would be within the sanctuary areas. Once the H&I fire mission, which Colonel Brewer assumed was a local tactical action, was concluded, he told Major Le that he'd like to visit the new FOB site. Major Le quickly accepted the invitation to show Colonel Brewer how things were progressing on the ground at Vinh Hoi Dong. "You will go with me, Colonel," Major Le told the B Team CO and then led him to a waiting assault boat by the moat dock in camp. I joined them, along with Sergeant Hung, Map Map and a radio operator. Lieutenant Strait and Lieutenant Ba followed us in a second assault boat with a security detail while Bac-si Sirois, Sergeant Chet and five Strikers brought up the rear. We pulled out of camp, went under a low bridge and turned north onto the Bassac River. We then turned west on the Kinh Thau Ban Canal where it entered the Bassac just north of the District Village and navigated that channel to reach the Chau Doc River.

As we entered it, Major Le told Colonel Brewer that the old PF outpost and its brick building had been taken over for use as the site of our new Vinh Hoi Dong

FOB. Suddenly, 3,000 meters short of the FOB site, our boat pulled up on the west bank of the river and Major Le told the operator to secure it to a nearby tree. "Something fishy here," I thought. The other assault boats continued up-river towards Phu My Hamlet.

Major Le looked back at me and winked as he followed Colonel Brewer out of the boat and onto shore, where we climbed a muddy bank, strode over the dike and down into a rice paddy where the stagnant water was knee deep. I stayed well behind Colonel Brewer, not wanting to get into a conversation with him. I'd happily allow Major Le all the time he needed to do whatever he had in mind with Brewer. Major Le expertly led us through rice paddies, up over berms and across bamboo pole bridges, called "monkey" bridges that spanned the many cross canals. I'm not certain, but I think the name of the type bridge was derived from the fact that a monkey could easily traverse them. For a human it was different, but for a human with jungle boots it was downright impossible, at least until you got the hang of it. Single bamboo poles were tied to the crotch of bamboo uprights that formed an X with the legs embedded in the canal bottom and often with lighter bamboo poles on one side attached as a rail to the upper portion of one of the bamboo uprights.

We learned to master crossing the monkey bridge, but only after a number of dunkings into the water below, when we'd end up wading or swimming the rest of the way across depending on the depth of water. There was no choice but to learn to navigate these engineering marvels, as there was no other way to cross the many canals without getting immersed. The local people had no problem. They went barefoot and were brought up crossing monkey bridges. The Strikers were pretty well off because their boots were more like hi-topped gym shoes with soft rubber soles and heels. The jungle boots made crossing a challenge as the hard rubber soles and heels slipped off the round poles with ease. There were times when I knew we'd be going a long ways on patrol over that kind of terrain when I would wear my black sneakers with armor insoles made for my jungle boots to protect against the ever present danger of punji traps.

Colonel Brewer had more than his share of dunkings that day. An awkward person by birth, big-boned and heavy by build and diet, he flailed his arms like a crippled crow time after time in five futile attempts to regain or maintain his balance, each time slipping and falling into the water below with the grace of a 55 gallon drum.

Arriving at the FOB site, Major Le pointed out the excellent fields of fire fanning out in three directions, making advance across the open fields from Cambodia suicide with the FOB manned. Looking to the east, the only direction not having a good field of fire, and seeing trees and even homes of Phu My Village in the path of gunfire from the FOB, Colonel Brewer pointed and asked, "What is beyond those trees, Major Le?"

"The Chau Doc River, Colonel. Come, let me show you."

Colonel Brewer, walking alongside Major Le, asked, "Why did you put the river between your FOB and the base camp? You force yourselves to fight with your backs to the river."

"For many reasons, Colonel," Le answered, "It is easy to send out patrols to the border without having to cross the river and the villagers will be better protected. You see, if we put the FOB on the east side of the river, the VC would use the village as a shield during their attacks. This way we protect our people and they are happy we do not put them in harms way."

As soon as our party broke through the tree line, Colonel Brewer saw the three assault boats tied up at water's edge and knew he had been tricked, subjected to humiliation and made to look like a fool. He turned and glared at me. He didn't say a word to Major Le, nor me and began walking toward the boats, looking meaner than sin, most likely wishing he was back on his own turf where he would call the shots.

Lieutenant Strait walked up from the river's edge to where I stood. He smiled and said, "You sure like to live dangerously, don't you?"

I didn't answer, but instead asked him, "Did you and Ba get what you came here for?"

"We're all set," John replied, "Lieutenant Ba brought Major Le's plans with him and we're ready to roll. We'll start on barbed-wire and other outer perimeter obstacles tomorrow."

The boat ride back to camp was uneventful. I sat next to Major Le and Colonel Brewer sat alone in the bow, silent and angry.

I heard the sound typical of a light, single engine aircraft as we turned off the Chau Doc River and headed northeast up the Kinh Thau Ban Canal. I twisted around and looked skyward in time to see it flying low and just inside Cambodian air space along the border north of Vinh Hoi. A steady stream of leaflets began flowing from its fuselage, fanning out to form a narrow, lengthening cloud of fluttering papers riding a "friendly" breeze, and then slowly drifting down into the Cambodian villages all along the border canal, with some carried even deeper into the safe havens of our enemy.

Major Le nudged me and said, "We are very lucky, Dai-uy. The wind is again carrying our message to the people of Cambodia. Captain Tuoi, Mr. Minh and I thought it best to fly a second mission to reach as many people as we can." "Good idea, Thieu-ta. We can't do any more than that." We pulled in at our Bassac River dock long enough for Colonel Brewer to disembark, get into his waiting jeep, and then speed off down the dirt road toward Chau Doc. We continued on into camp to get cleaned up for lunch. As we approached the team house, I reached over, put my hand on Major Le's shoulder and said, "Thanks, Thieu-ta." He smiled, nodded his head, and went on into the building.

By noon on the 27th a total of 80 Strikers were present for duty in the new company, excellent progress was being made at the Vinh Hoi Dong FOB and preparations were well under way for the big celebration, just one day away.

Later that day, as I sat behind my desk writing a short speech, I heard the wailing of a siren. The high pitched sound grew louder with each passing moment. We had no ambulance or fire engine in the whole district, so what could it be? I joined a gathering crowd of inquisitive people, including Major Le, who asked, "What is your surprise this time, Dai-uy?"

I told him that I had no idea what the noise was or where it was coming from. We all tracked the noise as it seemed to come nearer to the village, approaching from Chau Doc on the river road, maybe? As the sound neared our boat dock south of the village it suddenly became quiet and an uneasy stillness clouded our reasoning and heightened our apprehension. Suddenly Major Le shouted, "There it is, Dai-uy," pointing to a cloud of dust seemingly charging the front gate to our compound. We all watched as the massive steel and interlaced barbed wire covered outer gates began to swing into place to block the entrance to camp. The siren faded and a chorus of laughter and cheers of joy swelled up and spread throughout the camp. The CIDG guards pushed the gates back open and my jeep came into view sporting a shiny siren mounted on the left front fender. Sergeants Taylor and Hung beamed with pride as they pulled the jeep to a stop in front of Major Le and me with our chief mechanic and his son grinning from ear to ear at us from the back seat.

Jim Taylor was the first to speak, "What do you think of it, Thieu-ta?" and then hesitating a few seconds before asking me, "Dai-uy?" I waited for Major Le to answer. With a big grin he said, "It is fine, Sergeant. My people will be happy when they hear your siren."

I then spoke up, saying, "I'll tell you what I think about it when I find out where and how you got it."

"Well, Dai-uy, you sent Ray and me to Chau Doc with the requisitions for the stuff to do the work on the FOB and suggested we do some scrounging while we were there. I decided to take our mechanic along to see what he could find to fix our broken-down ¾ ton truck. Of course his son came along, Dai-uy. You know how they stick together."

"I know, Jim. So do you and Sergeant Hung, like glue. Tell me what happened."

"Well, Dai-uy," Jim answered, "As we approached the B Team boat dock I saw this make-shift fire engine. Don't know who it belonged to but it had a siren on the fender and I told Hung that I'd sure like to have one like that for our jeep. Honestly, Dai-uy, I didn't think they'd steal it right off the fire engine."

"Jim, you knew better than that. Your buddy Hung would probably go to Saigon and steal Premier Ky's purple flight suit if you asked him to. Look, what's done is done, but I want you to put the word out at the C Team and with any contacts you have in Saigon, and see if you can get a new siren to take to whoever owns that fire engine. Okay?"

"Yes, Sir, I'll do what I can."

I agreed that it might be a morale booster around the district because it was different, like a loud scream of victory. "But, I don't want to disrupt any religious activities or offend the people in any way, so before you blow that siren again, Jim," I went on, "Ask Captain Tuoi if its okay with him."

"Sure thing, Dai-uy. I'll go there right away. If I come back into camp with the siren screaming, you'll know its okay." When he returned there was no doubt Captain Tuoi had given the green light, but I did tell Jim Taylor to exercise restraint when going through the villages.

We fired our second mission of the day just after dinner, hoping to surprise VC patrols in our fire zone. I finished my speech and gave it to Tony to translate as he would be echoing me in Vietnamese at tomorrow's celebration.

I met briefly with Major Le after breakfast on 28 April to go over the schedule of events planned for the 2nd Anniversary celebration. We walked around camp, taking in the festive atmosphere with the many flags, banners and streamers fluttering in the light breeze. A feast was being prepared in the camp kitchen and the aroma of barbecued pork and other delicacies drifted through camp, causing my mouth to water with anticipation.

"Come, Dai-uy, let me show you the two hogs we prepare for the feast," Major Le told me, starting across the drill and ceremony field to the large barbecue pit where one pig was turning on a long spit as the other fully cooked hog lay on a checkerboard pattern oil cloth with rose motif that covered a large table in the serving area. One of the cooks was busy brushing the entire hog with a final coating of special sauce. It made my mouth water just watching him. "All around the hog there will be many bowls of rice and vegetable dishes to choose from." He had that look of a happy host. He asked, "What do you think, Dai-uy, is there enough pork for all of us?"

"Sure looks like it to me, Thieu-ta. I can hardly wait."

Men from both teams were out around the helicopter that had arrived a few minutes earlier to support our parachute jumping activity. I joined them as Major Le went on over to discuss details of the day's festivities with his team and the CIDG company commanders.

The jump went off without a hitch with everyone landing within the confines of our miniature drop zone. To miss it would mean landing in the concertina, tanglefoot or other barbed wire obstacles that made up our outer defensive belt. Not a place where you could land without suffering injury. The VIPs arrived on schedule and the formal celebration began promptly at 0940 hours with three companies of Strikers and the US and South Vietnamese Special Forces Teams in their best uniforms, standing tall in the field to the front of the reviewing stand from which the VIPs would observe the ceremonies.

After the colors were presented, Mr. Chau, Chairman of the Hoa Hao District Council, led in prayer. Major Le then welcomed the guests, spoke of the many accomplishments of the camp and praised the Hoa Hao fighters for their courage and honor in battle. He also spoke of the many accomplishments in civic action projects, psychological operations and joint activities with sub sector organizations, the RF companies and the ARVN 155MM artillery platoon. He then praised the men of both Special Forces teams for their past work and courage in battle. Major Le was a dynamic speaker, holding his audience spellbound, a fact evidenced by the expressions of those who sat in the VIP area. Even through a translator I was impressed with what he said and stirred emotionally by his obvious feeling of pride, patriotism and a fierce loyalty to the people he led and those he was pledged to protect.

I followed Major Le, speaking from my handwritten text[5] as Tony translated. Within the emotional speech I'd put together for the occasion, I mentioned how "especially proud" I was to have served for the past four months at Camp An Phu with all of those brave and honorable men. I told them of my hoping to stay to serve with them until it was time for me to return to my family in America. After telling how I had been with them on many patrols, both day and night, and had seen their courage and discipline, I mentioned that those of their camp who were no longer with us were "brave and honorable men" who had fought and died for what they believed to be right.

Tears flowed from my eyes as I stepped away from the podium and took my place back on the field in front of my team.

An awards and decorations ceremony followed with Major Chuan, commander of Vietnamese Special Forces Detachment C-4, presenting Major Le with the Viet-namese Cross of Gallantry for valor and then awarding me the Vietnamese Honor Medal for valor. He then gave heroic action bonuses to twelve of the assembled Strikers and told of the bravery and dedication of the men of An Phu. He spoke of Major Le as "a courageous and intelligent leader," congratulated us on our past victories and wished our camp continued success.

The ceremony concluded at 1100 hours and we all joined in a real feast in the camp mess hall. Guests were gone by 1230 hours and the camp began settling back to its routine.

In the morning of the next day Lieutenant Strait brought word to me from Mr. Minh that my speech would be published in the Saigon Post. I must admit I felt for a moment like a celebrity.

My speech[5] in the Saigon Post was well received by its Vietnamese readers. There was a general in MACV, however, and I assume it was Westmoreland, who was "displeased" with my speech. And, according to Colonel William R. Desobry, senior U.S. Advisor to Lieutenant General Quang Van Dang, the IV Corps Commanding General, the "MACV General" accused me of "Trying to usurp the power of the State Department." He cited the part of my speech that read, "If my country should become at war and should need help, I would like for the Hoa Haos of An Phu to fight alongside me because I know we would win." Colonel Desobry directed me to clear all future speeches through him. I wrote a two word message through C-4 to Colonel Desobry and gave it to Ray Johnson to send out ASAP. It referred to his message and read, simply, "Horse Manure."

Early that same afternoon one of our 12 man combat patrols made contact with an estimated 12 VC southwest of Khanh Binh, engaged the VC in a short fire fight and chased them back across the border. Our CIDG patrol leader spotted blood on their escape trail and reported at least one VC WIA.

There were no friendly casualties.

In another daylight incident 1,000 meters west of our new FOB site, a 12 man combat patrol from camp engaged an estimated 40 VC in a brief fire fight. The patrol leader wisely withdrew to the FOB location where the remainder of the company was at work installing the barbed-wire outer perimeter defenses. The VC did not pursue our men, choosing instead to withdraw across the border into Cambodia. No casualties were reported.

It was May Day, an important Communist holiday, and we expected a great deal more enemy activity than we experienced. Shortly after midnight on 1 May a 12 man ambush patrol out of Phu Hiep FOB, in position northwest of the FOB, 500 meters from the border, spotted ten VC in black uniforms moving in their direction. Their leader called the VC's position in to the FOB, asked for indirect fire support and engaged the enemy at close range with small arms fire. Two of the unsuspecting VC were hit with the initial burst of fire from the ambush squad and dropped to the ground. The others turned tail and began to run through the waist high grass toward the border. Their location and direction of movement were radioed to the FOB. Within a minute Barnes and Eleam dropped an 81mm white phosphorus marker round in their midst.

They then lobbed three rounds of HE on the enemy's route of escape, following it with an illuminating round. The squad leader reported a direct hit on the VC squad and described seeing only four VC making it back across the canal into Cambodia. At dawn the ambush squad searched the area and found three dead VC. The wounded had either crawled to safety or their comrades had returned to carry them away, using the high grass to shield a low-profile rescue. There were no friendly casualties, due in part to the excellent fire support provided by Sergeants Barnes and Eleam.

Major Le and I met in his office after breakfast and discussed the unusually low level of enemy activity that we'd experienced during the month of April. We decided the VC probing actions were most likely a prelude to an all-out invasion of An Phu. "I believe we are wise to expect their attack on Ho Chi Minh's birthday, Dai-uy," was Major Le's final comment before I left his office.

Major Le's words rang true. The entire month, except for the 24 April probing of FOBs and outposts, was relatively quiet. There were no confirmed enemy KIA, WIA or captured, and we had not yet received agent reports that would give us some idea of the level of casualties that the VC had suffered inside Cambodia from our H&I fire. We had one Striker wounded and four civilians killed during the month. A total of 22 VC mines were captured or destroyed in place and we tripled our mortar fire bombardment of VC unit locations inside Cambodia. Our agents continued to provide sound intelligence on enemy units, strengths, locations and weaponry. From what we'd received in the way of agent reports, May should be a real testing ground for Strikers, Regional Forces, Popular Forces and civilians alike in An Phu. Increases in enemy strength appeared to be bringing them to a troop level in excess of four times the strength of our defending forces. I was confidant of the Hoa Haos' ability to turn back the enemy onslaught, no matter what their strength in numbers and superiority in weaponry.

We received word from the B Team that Lieutenant General Heintges would be arriving by chopper at 1100 hours on the 2nd of May. When he learned of the general's upcoming visit to An Phu, Major Le asked if he could brief the general. Major Le had developed a good rapport with General Heintges during his two other visits and was a far better briefer than me, so I readily approved, knowing in my heart it was the right thing to do for the people of An Phu.

Our team would be very busy that day, with Lieutenant Strait and Sergeant Brown heading up to the new FOB in the morning to observe progress and returning to camp around 1300 hours. After a late lunch, they'd go out into the district with Mr. Duc, checking farm project status. Bac-si Sirois and Sergeant Hilgartner were scheduled to spend most of that day on medical patrol near the Vinh Hoi Dong FOB project. Sergeants Barnes and Eleam would be actively engaged with the 444th Company at Phu Hiep just as Team Sergeant Taylor would be heavily involved in weapons training for the new CIDG company here in camp. Sergeant Johnson would man the commo bunker and I would be standing by to meet General Heintges as he got off the chopper.

Major Le and I met in the command bunker at 0200 hours on the 2nd to discuss the agenda for General Heintges' visit later that day. I anticipated that he would bring with him final approval for my remaining in An Phu until the CIDG were converted to Regional Forces and a MACV advisory team was in place. Major Le would have a paper prepared and brief General Heintges on enemy strength and capability, along with a detailed report on the status of our forces. Should the general have sufficient time, we would take him on a tour of the Khanh An and Khanh Binh areas.

After writing a short note to Kate, I went to bed on schedule at 0330 hours, pleased at how things were taking shape as we prepared for the big attacks we knew would come. I woke easily at 0600 hours, took a cold shower, shaved and ate a good breakfast of goose eggs and bread. I took time to observe the early morning training of new recruits in the care and cleaning of rifles and carbines. Jim Taylor, with Flash translating, worked with LLDB and CIDG sergeants to take the new Strikers through their paces in this important phase of their training. I was impressed with Flash's expertise in nomenclature and field-stripping techniques of the various weapons. I would expect such talent and know-how in our Sergeants, but in a South Vietnamese interpreter? I watched as Flash and Sergeant Taylor, side-by-side flawlessly demonstrated blindfolded disassembly and reassembly of the M-2 carbine. It brought back memories of basic training and the hundreds of push-ups demanded of me as I fumbled my way through weapons instruction, finally mastering it after building a good set of biceps. I left the training area convinced our new men were on the receiving end of the best possible instruction.

The Huey bringing General Heintges to An Phu settled down on the landing zone pad at exactly 1100 hours. As the general deplaned and approached, I saluted him, told him it was good to see him again, and asked him if he had some good news for me personally. Returning my salute and then reaching out to shake my hand, he smiled and answered, "Yes I do, Captain. It's been cleared with your Group headquarters. You'll stay until the camp is converted."

I thanked him and told him that's what I was hoping for. As we walked together toward the Operations Center, I asked if he'd heard anything about the elimination of the VC safe-havens or if his suggested doubling or tripling of SF strength levels in country had been seriously considered by General Westmoreland.

He stopped, turned toward me, looked me in the eyes and told me that he could not comment on the sanctuary situation. "I can tell you that the timetable to remove Special Forces from Vietnam is locked in concrete." As he told me that his hands were tied and that there was nothing he could do about it, his face was grim, his tone heavy-hearted.

"I think that's a big mistake, General. I still feel the same as I did the last time you were here. There is some kind of conspiracy against the Green Berets." He ignored that remark, turned and began walking toward the Operations Center. I told him that Major Le would be his briefer.

"That's fine with me, Captain, I have a great deal of respect for Major Le and his people." Major Le met us outside the entrance, looking the sharpest I'd ever seen him.

"Welcome to An Phu, Sir," he said with a snappy salute. How much time do you have with us today, General?"

"I must be airborne at 1130 hours, Major Le."

Gesturing to a chair pulled out from a small table set with tea, sugar wafers, and fresh flowers, Major Le said, "Please have a seat, General. The young lady will serve you." A pretty Vietnamese girl in traditional dress went about her duties as soon as we were seated. Major Le moved to the lectern, picked up his pointer and proceeded. He covered the enemy situation in great detail, emphasizing their use of Cambodia as a sanctuary, telling of the numerically superior odds we faced in each area of probable confrontation. He spoke with pride of our recent victories, pointed out the location of our new FOB on the briefing map and discussed the training status of the new CIDG company.

He then spoke slowly and firmly about our need for medical evacuation support, close air support and artillery support when the enemy launched its great offensive, telling General Heintges, "We are certain it will be on the 19th of May."

Without answering Major Le's concerns, General Heintges instead asked, "How is the morale among your men, Major Le? Are they prepared to accept conversion to Regional Forces?"

"The morale is very high," Major Le answered, "What concerns all of us about the conversion is why the Green Beret Team must go and why we must accept others who are not trained to fight this kind of war. Can you explain this to me, Sir?"

"It has been decided and we must accept it." General Heintges replied. "There is a timetable and we are committed to that end."

Major Le bravely expressed his dissatisfaction with the General's answer. "It is foolish not to learn from experience," he said. "Our leaders give the enemy his sanctuaries and soon they will also take away the Americans who are best suited to help us fight the Communists. Do you agree this is best, General?"

Not wanting to answer, General Heintges looked at his watch, got up from his chair, and said, "I'm sorry but I have no more time. Thank you for an excellent briefing, Major Le, and thank you for your hospitality, Captain Marvin. I wish you all success, and I will be watching for news of the battles."

As we escorted General Heintges to his waiting chopper, I felt sadness and anger in my heart. He understood the situation very well. I thought that he should resign rather than allow Americans or South Vietnamese to suffer the consequences of simple-minded, inequitable decisions that permitted the enemy safe-havens from which to kill or maim our people while denying us the ability to protect or defend on a level battlefield.

General Heintges returned our salutes as his chopper lifted off, along with its escort gun ships. I shared my good news with Major Le about staying at An Phu through conversion. He smiled, slapped me on the back, and said, "That is good news, Dai-uy, we are a good team." Major Le and I were of like disposition, and could count on the fact that we would do as much as we could while together in An Phu to make it better for those who would remain.

The rigid and ill-suited conventional force attitude of the US military hierarchy was borne out by General Heintges' refusal to discuss the safe-haven issue and was confirmed by the ill-advised decision to phase out the American Army's Special Forces by a specific date, regardless of the situation or the historically proven need for same. In my judgment, the latter was precipitated by the well publicized hatred of unconventional forces by senior US officers, particularly Army Chief of Staff Harold K. Johnson, a man of tremendous influence who openly embraced anti-Special Forces teaching. The loss of the only effective organization whose proven performance, based on a strategy that had secured victory over insurgent movements of the past, would surely be cause for celebration in Hanoi, the power behind the anti-democratic and pro-Communist war of insurgence.

The attitude of high American officials, civilian or military, toward the South Vietnamese whom they were charged to help or even serve, was for the most part condescending at best. A good example: Major Le invited me to join him for dinner and some big USAID/USOM doings in a huge banquet hall in the province capitol of Chau Doc the evening of the 4th of May. After an excellent five course meal, we all sat back to listen to USAID and USOM high-level officials boast of their many so-called "glorious" achievements. Not once during their pompous and lengthy dissertations did any one of them say how pleased they were to have the opportunity to help the people during these trying times. The one speech which angered Major Le and me most was that of a USAID official.

He spoke of a newly designed hog pen complex that had recently been completed and dedicated by his agency. This puffed-up fool stood there in front of a mostly Vietnamese audience, and expounded on how much the project cost and how great it was that USAID would do such a wonderful thing for pig farmers. He then went on to say in what I thought to be a malicious tone of voice, "My only concern is that the hog pens are so nice that the farmers may move into them instead of using them for their pigs."

It was utterly disgusting, that anyone, much less a high ranking official of an agency that existed solely to help others, would articulate something so demeaning about the local people. Major Le and I got up and walked out of the hall as did many others. Just outside the banquet hall door we saw and heard Lieutenant Colonel Brewer speaking with his XO. "When that sorry, good-for-nothing speaker comes out this door I'm going to tell him to get out of this province as fast as his feet will take him and stay out!"

Major Le and I decided to stay and watch the fireworks. And watch and hear we did as Colonel Brewer confronted the USAID official, blocked his path and told him exactly what he'd told his XO. When Colonel Brewer blocks a man's path, there are few men who, weighing the situation wisely, would attempt to push this huge man aside. We who knew Colonel Brewer up close called him the "terrorist."

The ugly American official didn't say a word. He instead waited until Colonel Brewer turned and strode out of the building. He then left without comment, not looking back. I doubted that USAID bigwig would ever return to Chau Doc for fear of again crossing the path of Colonel Brewer. Lieutenant Strait, earlier in the day, as he told it to me, had joined Mr. Duc, the district Agricultural Chief. They experienced a happy day, visiting the local farm where the first corn crop was harvested, after meeting the farmer and his family he took photos of them with the harvest. It was the kind of project, with the positive results it brought to the people, that helped different cultures respect each other's ways while working together to reach common goals. A Guatemalan priest, a Jonesville, Michigan agriculture teacher and a team of Green Berets had made a difference here in An Phu and in the entire Delta region through the introduction of field corn. We were pleased to be a part of it.

With the enemy situation growing more ominous each day above Phu Hiep I had Lieutenant Strait, Sergeant Brown and Jean Pham go to Phu Hiep to replace Sergeant Barnes, Sergeant Eleam and Tony Trung who then returned from the FOB to camp. John Eleam would help Sergeant Johnson put the communications setup together for the Vinh Hoi Dong FOB. Our numbers would dwindle again, with Sergeant Barnes and Sergeant Hilgartner ordered to report to the B Team for reassignment on the following day.

When Lieutenant Strait went out to where the action was he went prepared. He was big enough and strong enough to carry a combat load that would bring most men to their knees. I watched on this day as John put his gear on for the trip up-river to Phu Hiep. He carried his M-16 rifle, a holstered .45 caliber pistol, two hand grenades, a claymore shoulder bag full of M-16 magazines, two pounds of plastic explosive, two smoke grenades, a canteen, Bowie knife, IV kit, and three syrettes of morphine plus a special forces survival kit in the side pocket of his rucksack that was loaded with changes of clothes, personal hygiene items, shaving gear, poncho liner and poncho. I handed him my short billed, camouflage cap which he called his "good luck hat" and that he liked to borrow whenever he was going to see combat. John Strait was a man of action and a fine Infantry officer. It would be important to me to have him leading the Phu Hiep operation for the next few weeks. John would take the war to the enemy and not concern himself about stepping across the border in the process. He had a pet peeve against a Cambodian Pagoda that stood almost due north of the FOB on the east bank of the Bac Nam River. "I figure the VC are using it as a base to launch raids into our area," he told Ray Johnson before he left, asking him to send up as much mortar ammo as he could get his hands on.

Sergeant Johnson told me about John's request, "His favorite is the 81mm HE with VT fuses, Dai-uy."

I gave Ray the green light to scrounge whatever he could and send it up to Phu Hiep. "Big John and will keep the VC wondering where the next round will hit and they'll begin to fear moving anywhere close to that FOB." There would be no peace in the Bung Ven area as long as the enemy occupied it so we were here to do something about it.

Major Le chose the 443rd CIDG Company, commanded by Lieutenant Triet Van Tran, to open the Vinh Hoi Dong FOB. Their lead elements departed An Phu at first light, using all 14 assault boats and barge. The shuttling of men, weapons, materiel and ammunition was accomplished before nightfall in just three trips.

The same day, using all available trucks, we managed to rotate companies between the FOB at Khanh Binh and camp, sending the 442nd under the leadership of Lieutenant Luong Hoang Le to the FOB and bringing Thuan Hieu Nguyen and his 441st company back to camp.

Early in the morning of 6 May, as I sat writing to Kate, Major Le walked into my office looking very troubled. He sat down in the chair next to my desk. "Dai-uy," he began, "before I tell you of a serious new problem we have at Khanh Binh, I have other news. I have received a report from one of our agent handlers, telling of a report he received telling of 500 new wooden caskets being unloaded at Prek Chrey, Cambodia. They are now stacked near the Bassac River for the Southward Regiment. I feel certain this confirms our previous report of a major attack we received from other agents."

I agreed and asked "What is the problem at Khanh Binh? You look very worried, Thieu-ta." "I am very worried and I will tell you why. Lieutenant Thuan came to my office after he saw that his men were all settled down here in camp. He tells me the VC are trying a new tactic in Khanh Binh. It is an evil thing they are doing and we must stop them before they kill someone and destroy the morale of our Strikers."

"What is this new tactic, Thieu-ta?" I asked. Major Le answered, "They are now using women terrorists to put fear in the hearts of our men by threatening their families. Because they are women they can cross the border bridge without suspicion just as our agents do. After pretending to shop they walk through the village of Khanh Binh and then disappear into a secret hiding place they have located in the extensive bamboo thickets south of the FOB. It is where they can safely cache weapons and booby-trap devices.

Thuan had told him that it was early evening when the women did their evil deeds. They did not move when his men could spot them, staying close to their cache until the CIDG had left their homes to go to the FOB. "I may not have told you, Dai-uy, but when a company is on duty at the Khanh Binh FOB, the Strikers whose homes are nearby are allowed certain times during daylight hours when they can be with their families. When the men are in the FOB and before the night ambush patrols leave the FOB in the early nighttime is a good time for the terrorists to make their move.

"They sneak into the village from behind and go to the houses of our Strikers. They threaten the wives by talking to them through the thin walls. They do not go near doors to betray their identity. They tell the wife that she must convince her husband to desert the American aggressors and to join the People's Army. She is told that she will be killed if she cannot convince her husband to do these things."

"That's tough to live with, Thieu-ta."

"Yes it is, Dai-uy. I have instructed Lieutenant Luong to organize daylight ambush operations in the area south of the FOB and catch the terrorists. They will begin later today."

I told Major Le that his plan was good and that maybe it would be a good idea if a few of his agents were to cover the marketplace. "They may be able to spot the terrorists before they get out of the village or as they leave the village to go to their cache site," I suggested.

"Good idea, Dai-uy I will also devise a way to get the news of suspected terrorists to the FOB command post quickly.

After breakfast I will go to Khanh Binh. Will you go with me?" he asked.

"When do we leave?"

"From the flagpole at 0700 hours." We shook hands and he left my office. Sergeant Taylor came in as Major Le left, and asked, "What's up, Dai-uy,? Thieu-ta looked as if he'd had a rough day."

I briefed Jim on what Major Le and I had discussed and told him I'd be going to Khanh Binh with Major Le at 0700 hours. Sensing he had forgotten, I asked Jim, "Did you have something to tell me when you came in my office?"

"Sure did, Dai-uy. Wanted to remind you that Barnes and Hilgartner will be leaving tomorrow morning. That's going to make us real short and the Sergeant Major has no idea when we'll get new blood."

"We'll be back down to eight men doing the job of 24, but I won't pull our men out of Phu Hiep. We owe it to these people to man that FOB. We'll just have to spread ourselves a little thinner."

"If we get any thinner we'll have to cancel sleep, Dai-uy. We can't spare anyone for a commissary run and we've already canceled even the thought of going on R&R. Maybe you should publish an order against getting sick or dying while you're at it?" he added, a grin on his face.

"Good idea, Jim. I'll take care of it in the morning." I was wakened by the shouting of John Eleam. "Dai-uy, Dai-uy. Major Le wants to see you right away!"

I swung my legs out from under the mosquito net, lifted the net and eased out of my cot. It was still dark and all I could see was Eleam's silhouette, framed by the doorway to my cubicle. "What day is this, Sarge?"

"It's the sixth of May, Dai-uy."

"What time is it?" I was stalling. I sleep less than four hours a day, and when I do sleep, I get fairly cold and clammy and my body kind of shuts down for the most part.

"0530, Dai-uy, Major Le wants to see you in his office. He just got bad news from Khanh Binh. Sergeant Trang's wife and child were killed by a booby trap."

That tragic news jolted me to full awareness. I always slept in my black pajama uniform and wool cushion sole socks and all I had to do was slip my feet into jungle boots, grab my rifle and head on out. I thanked Eleam and then almost knocked him down getting through the doorway on my way to Le's office. He was sitting behind his desk. I shook his hand and told him how sorry I was to learn of Sergeant Trang's loss. "How did it happen?" I asked.

He motioned for me to sit down. "It is a very sad thing, Dai-uy. Trang had just come back from an all night ambush and was on his way home from the FOB. Maybe 20 feet away from his house, he stepped on a tripwire and blew up his own home with his wife and baby trapped inside." Tears formed in Major Le's eyes and rolled down his cheek as he continued, "They were killed instantly. Because of the way this tragedy took place, I think we should go to Khanh Binh and talk to Lieutenant Luong as soon as possible."

I told him I'd be ready to go in 30 minutes, washed my face and upper torso, shaved, donned jungle fatigues and boots, grabbed a hunk of bread and a slab of cheese and gulped that down. Back to my cubicle, I gathered my combat gear, and rushed out to meet Major Le at his jeep at exactly 0600 hours.

The sun's pre-dawn reflection off the scattered cumulus clouds lent a pinkish tint to the morning sky as we drove north along the river in Major Le's jeep. The beauty of it all did little to soften the hard reality of Trang's family tragedy or sweeten the bitter feeling in our hearts against the killers of an innocent baby and her mother. Would there be any comfort to Sergeant Trang, who would not forget that it was he, whose innocent stepping on the trigger wire, had unknowingly brought about the death of his own wife and baby?

The trip to Khanh Binh was void of conversation as we both grappled inwardly with the need to be swift and brutal in response to this tragedy or suffer a significant lowering of morale and perhaps precipitate a rash of desertions.

The Striker who became discontent with his role as an irregular warrior and left did not "desert" in the traditional sense. All Strikers were, in reality, paid mercenaries. The CIDG program had, for the most part, developed into a loyal group of paid irregulars who did not consider themselves mercenaries. They did, however, enjoy the flexibility of "quitting" whenever they so desired, so long as they left their weapons, ammunition and other issued military items — except for clothing — with their unit.

Lieutenant Luong met us at the gate to the FOB and ushered us on into his command post. The air was hot and humid inside the former Buddhist temple and it smelled of sweaty bodies. We sat around a table as tea was poured and we expressed our grief to Luong for Sergeant Trang's loss. Major Le asked Luong how Trang was holding up under the strain.

Lieutenant Luong told us that Trang did not blame himself, but was anxious to avenge the death of his wife and child. Luong was concerned that others, whose families were threatened as his was, might leave the CIDG so they could protect their families from the terrorists.

Major Le promised Lieutenant Luong quick action to capture and deal with the terrorists. He outlined his plan and told Luong that the families of the Strikers must remain in their homes, acting very normal, until the terrorists were captured. He explained how their presence in and around the village was essential to bait the trap. "Your men must be told to take them alive if at all possible," Major Le told Luong "and bring them to us for interrogation."

Luong told Major Le that they would not rest until they were captured or dead and they would try to bring them back still walking. We all shook hands then Major Le and I rode back to camp, satisfied that we had set the stage for proper action during our visit with Lieutenant Luong.

I felt bad that we didn't make it back to camp in time to shake hands with Master Sergeant Barnes and Staff Sergeant Hilgartner and wish them well before they left for Chau Doc and reassignment. The next 24 hours were fairly quiet, except for enemy harassment of the Phu Hiep FOB and PF outpost at Nhon Hoi with small arms fire. There were no casualties reported for either place.

Our agents and agent handlers maintained continuous daylight surveillance of the local Khanh Binh marketplace while the CIDG conducted ambush operations on a 24 hour schedule in the border canal area and the areas south and east of the FOB. There would be no slack time until the terrorists were prisoners in our camp's barbed-wire cages waiting interrogation. Major Le and I figured the VC would lay low for a couple of days before setting another booby-trap.

At 1000 hours on the 7th we received a detailed and significant intelligence report from sub-sector. It told of an enemy strategy meeting held in or near the Cambodian hamlet of Bak Dai, 2,000 meters west of our PF outpost at Bac Day. VC Commissioners from Chau Doc, An Phu and Tan Chau had met with battalion commanders, Major Xuong of the 510th (AKA 364th) and Major Khoanh of the

267th on 24 April. They decided on a two-pronged strategy for their invasion of our northern areas and reorganized the Southward Regiment to suit the two front plan. The 510th (AKA 364th) Battalion, held in reserve above Prek Chrey, would control all forces attacking in the Khanh An and Phu Hiep areas. That attack force would include the 512th Battalion (AKA 264th), the 407th Battalion and the 260th Heavy Weapons Company. The 267th Battalion would attack the FOB and PF outpost at Khanh Binh.

Shortly after lunch we received an airdrop of 81MM mortar ammunition that included a welcomed surprise. On top of one of the boxes was a special "package" made from honeycomb shock absorbing material. The parachute riggers had painstakingly made recesses within the layers that brought three dozen eggs safely to us and had wrapped two pounds of bacon in a plastic bag with dry ice to go with the eggs. I figured it had to have been the idea of Lieutenant "Tiger" Teasdale to put our "care" package together. Tiger commanded the parachute riggers at 5th Group headquarters in Nha Trang and had once served as my assistant S-4 in the 6th Group at Fort Bragg. With the awesome and time demanding responsibility of air-resupply of all 85 Special Forces camps in Vietnam a 24 hour a day challenge, it was a wonder that Tiger's people would sap their time and energy even further to package and drop such a luxury as bacon and eggs to our team in An Phu. After we'd cleared the drop zone and stored the ammunition, I wrote the Tiger and thanked him for his "air mail special" breakfast treats.

Major Le and I arrived at Captain Tuoi's office as his wall clock struck 0800 hours on the 8th of May. We reviewed FOB and PF outpost strengths and weakness, with particular attention to those located north of east-west grid line 06. We agreed on the need for aggressive patrols and ambush operations coming out of the Vinh Hoi Dong FOB to protect our western flank. Captain Tuoi was pleased to report that he had spoken with Major Re the previous night and had arranged for Province to supply two BARs with a good stock of ammunition to each of the six PF outposts north of Phuoc My. "They will be in place by mid-morning tomorrow," Captain Tuoi advised.

We agreed to meet again on the 18th of May to review the latest intelligence and make necessary changes in our plan of defense. I agreed to request a high priority SLR photo recon in time to have a fresh analysis of enemy activity inside Cambodia along our border area available for that meeting.

On return to camp I met with Taylor, Johnson, Brown and Sirois while Eleam held down the commo bunker. After bringing them up to date on our meeting at sub-sector I asked Jim to request an SLR mission at the latest date they could make the run and get the photos to us by the morning of the 17th. "Shoot for that, Jim," I emphasized. "You'll have the afternoon to go over the photos with a fine tooth comb and then brief Major Le and me that evening. We'll get together with Captain Tuoi early on the 18th to decide what realignment is needed to defend against the Southward Regiment."

Jim said he'd take care of it. "Anything else, Dai-uy?"

"Yes, you and Ray go over to Vinh Hoi Dong after lunch and see how things are going at the new FOB. Do what needs doing to make certain that mortar crew is ready with their 81. In fact, I'll give you a target to throw some out into so you can gauge their capability as a crew."

"Whip it on me, Dai-uy."

I told him there was a patch of high ground in grid square 0498, west of the FOB. The last meeting of the VC 267th Battalion commander and his company commanders was in that area. "Make it ten rounds of whatever 81 ammo they have at the FOB.

"Ray, you check out their communications and do anything that needs doing to give them double back-up on radio equipment, generator and antennas. We don't want problems in their making contact with the LLDB here in camp."

"Okay, Dai-uy, I'll get with Ray and Sergeant Hung so he can help me. Their commo man can work with Ray. It'll be better if we do it together."

"Go to it. I'm counting on you guys."

It was early that same afternoon at the Khanh Binh FOB that three squads of CIDG were sent out to their pre-selected[6] ambush sites. Wearing leopard suits and armed with rifles and carbines, they moved in a southeasterly direction for about 500 meters and then circled around to the west. Stopping for a moment in the waist-high grass south of the village, they waited instructions from Platoon Sergeant Troch to move into position.

One squad leader was Sergeant Trang, the Striker who had lost his wife and child to the terrorists' booby-trap. More than eager to capture the vicious females who had set the deadly trap, he moved his squad into position on the east side of what would be a "V" shaped trap, wanting to be in on the capture. Sergeant Troch directed the second squad into position to form the western side of the "V", leaving a gap of approximately 60 meters at the open end while joining Trang's squad at the base of the "V." The prey would enter the trap from the north after passing through the village of Khanh Binh. The third squad, led by Sergeant Phuong would take position between the second squad and the border canal. They would wait for the signal to close the open end of the "V" on orders from Sergeant Troch. That maneuver, assisted by fourth squad action, would block the terrorists escape back across the border canal into Cambodia.

Each squad had an HT-1 radio but radio silence would be maintained until Troch received the message **MIDNIGHT RACER,** a code word signaling that our agents had spotted the VC moving through the village towards our trap. Once the agents reached the tree line south of the village, the fourth squad, having received the code word **RACER BY** from Troch, would move silently out of the FOB, through the village and assist the third squad in closing the open end of the V trap. After the third and fourth squad were in place, the fourth squad leader would radio the signal **GATE CLOSED.**

Continuous surveillance would then be maintained on the VC. The plan was to wait until the VC had reached their cache site (revealing its location) and had settled down and were thought to be asleep. Then Troch would radio the message **TIGHTEN NOOSE**, signaling all squads to converge on the unsuspecting terrorists.

Hours passed slowly as they maintained a silent vigil. Sergeant Trang continued to reflect on that terrible event of only two days past. He was nearing his home, anxious to see his wife and hold his small child in his arms, when he felt a tug at his foot, glanced down to see the trip wire, only to be stunned by the explosion of the booby-trap that killed those he loved. He again felt himself running to the ruins of his home and seeing the bloodied, lifeless bodies of his wife and six month old child laying there before him. He asked himself over and over again, "will these terrible memories haunt me forever?"

The click, click of the radio receiver, signaling a low-volume transmission, brought him back to reality. The words **MIDNIGHT RACER** came through low, but clear. These words were passed from man to man in a whisper. Soon each man in the ambush force was aware that the VC were walking into their trap. The long hours of anxious waiting were over. Adrenaline was now surging through their veins as they pondered the capture of those who had killed Trang's wife and daughter.

The fourth squad now moved stealthily from the FOB and south along the canal road through the village. The intertwined branches from trees on either side of the road formed a natural canopy, excluding the light of the bright overhead moon. A southerly breeze carried the shuffling sound of their feet to the north and away from the earshot of the VC. They were in place at 2130 hours, with half the men facing into the V and the other half facing the opposite direction, acting as a rear guard. The message **GATE CLOSED** was sent.

The four female figures strode through the high grass unaware their every move was being watched. Confidence in their plan had clouded their judgment. Three of them wore long-sleeved tops that buttoned down the front (one gray, two white), while the fourth wore a white shawl over her black pajama outfit. They carried no weapons at the time.

The Strikers, on one knee with weapons at the ready, were almost indistinguishable in the tall grass. Minutes dragged as the intruders moved closer to the bamboo thicket and their hidden cache. Sergeant Trang lifted his binoculars to his eyes and trained on the VC with the white shawl, whom he took to be the leader by her actions. She motioned to one of her women who got down on her knees, pushed a small amount of earth aside and, when she stood, held a large plastic bag in both hands. The cache location was now known. Within a few minutes they were asleep on the soft ground. Trang sent the message **VC IN TRAP TWENTY METERS FROM V BOTTOM. ALL IS QUIET.**

Sergeant Troch waited five minutes after receiving Trang's message and then gave the order **TIGHTEN NOOSE.** The first three squads moved slowly and cautiously to converge on the slumbering females. The fourth squad moved closer to the V but remained in a position to block any escape back into Cambodia. Sergeant

Trang's squad was first to reach the thicket. They would have stood their ground until the others had closed the gap, had not one of Trang's men stepped on a dry twig, making a loud cracking sound and awaking the VC.

Reacting instantly, Trang ordered his men to attack. The startled VC jumped up and dove towards the large cache bag but Trang grabbed the bag and tossed it out of their reach. The squad moved in and ordered them to lie face-down on the ground. Instead the women fought in an attempt to escape their captors. Showing no fear, they attacked, pounding with their fists, scratching, biting, clawing and trying to take the men's rifles to use against them.

Their actions forced the CIDG to knock them unconscious, using rifle butts. Trang ordered them bound, gagged and shackled. Sergeant Troch and the other Strikers arrived as Sergeant Trang opened the plastic bag and dumped its contents on the ground. It yielded five hand grenades, trip wire, cutting pliers, two knives and two .38 caliber pistols with extra loaded magazines.

The captives were led back to the FOB and placed in barbed wire cages, their shackles and gags removed. Their wrists remained tightly bound and secured behind their backs to prevent escape.

I was in the command bunker when Major Le received the message from Lieutenant Luong telling of the successful capture and of Sergeant Trang's part in the victory. It was as if a weight had been lifted off Major Le's shoulders. He turned, smiled at me, and said, "It is a small but great victory, Dai-uy."

I offered my congratulations and asked when they would be brought to camp for interrogation.

"In the morning, Dai-uy. Luong tells me that two of the VC are maybe 18 or 19 years old, one in her 20s and their leader is maybe 30 years old."

The four VC arrived at the moat boat dock in camp early on the 9th of May, shackled with hands bound. From there they were taken to an area next to the interrogation building and placed in nearby individual barbed-wire cages, their shackles removed. They were given water to drink and then gags applied to keep them from talking to each other.

I had just walked out of my office, wanting to see the prisoners, when I saw Lieutenant Strait coming from the direction of the boat dock. I asked, "John, did you come all the way back to camp to interrogate our new prisoners?"

"No, Dai-uy. I wasn't even aware you had any prisoners. I came back to see Mr. Minh about some new leaflets. When did you take the prisoners and how many?" he asked.

"Strikers from Khanh Binh captured the four of them last night. Get Tony and meet me in the interrogation room."

"Sure thing, Dai-uy."

It was a small room, about ten by ten, in the corner of the metal-sided building near the gate. I was waiting outside the room when John and Tony came my way, stopping to look at the females in the cages just outside. John walked up to me, a pained expression on his face that mirrored the deep sense of anguish he felt, and said, "But, they're women, Sir! I can't handle this, Dai-uy. I know I just can't do this to a woman."

I looked at him, put my arm on his shoulder and told him, "That's all right John, I'll take care of it. Have a safe trip back to Phu Hiep."

He looked at me and thanked me for understanding, saying, "You know I'd do anything for you, Major Le, or the Strikers. It's just that they're women."

"John," I said, "you know how I've relied on you in the past to keep me straight on infantry matters and that I appreciate your indulgence of a bean counter for your commanding officer. I understand this is just not your bag. I'll take care of it like you've taken care of me on other matters in the past. Okay, John?"

"Yes, Sir. I think I'll grab my good luck cap and get my self back to Phu Hiep where I belong. Thanks again."

The interrogation went well and, with Flash's help, we gleaned a lot of useful information from the four terrorists. Their words corroborated our agent's report that the 267th Battalion, with a strength of an estimated 500, was located west of Chrey Thom, Cambodia. All four had been schooled in terrorism, including the use of booby-traps, in Phnom Penh Cambodia by Chinese instructors. In their words, the teachers "had come a long way." The one named Na Bang told of how her unit was forced to move farther back into Cambodia because of our mortar shelling.

I asked Na Bang if she knew about our raid on Bung Ven and she told us, "It was in Bung Ven where we were taught how to move secretly at night and how to use a compass. I remember hearing the officers speak of having more than 600 of our comrades killed or wounded at that time."

After the interrogation was finished Flash and Sergeant Hung went to brief Major Le about what we had learned. Major Le came into my office and told me that he had been briefed on the results of my interrogation and was very pleased. "It will be written up and you will get a copy, Dai-uy."

"I'm glad, Thieu-ta. What will you do with them now?"

"I have a plan, Dai-uy. As you know these are the worst kind of killers who will trap wives and babies and then fix a booby trap that will have a man trip a bomb that kills his own family. It is my idea to revenge our dead and have the blood of the terrorists on the hands of their own leaders, their comrades."

"Good idea, but how do you expect to do that?" I asked.

He went on to outline how we would pretend to bring the prisoners into the Cheiu-Hoi program. We must make believe that they had voluntarily surrendered. They would attend sessions in our camp for political indoctrination as if we were repatriating them. In two days time they would be taken to Khanh Binh and it would be made to appear that they were then friendly to our people.

"That's a big order, Thieu-ta?" I asked.

"Not so difficult, Dai-uy. It will be made to appear that they have complete freedom in the FOB. They will be in plain view of the Cambodian outpost, and we will keep them there for two days. Of course they will always be in sight of our guns. Lieutenant Luong will make certain they do not escape.

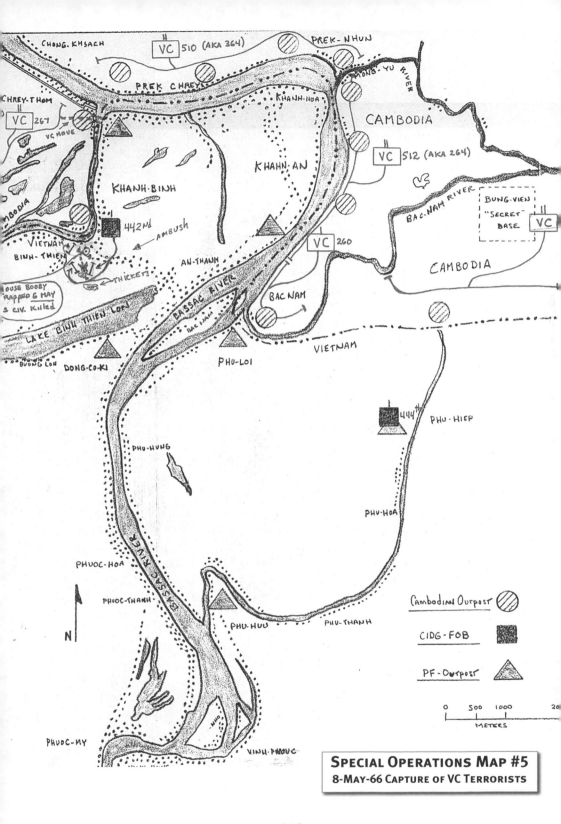

CHONG. KHSACH

VC 510 (AKA 364)

PREK-NHUN

PREK CHREY

MONG-YU RIVER

CHREY-THOM

VC 267

VC HOUE

KHANH-HOA

CAMBODIA

KHAHN-AN

VC 512 (AKA 264)

KHANH-BINH

442nd

AMBUSH

BAC-NAM RIVER

BUNG-VIEN "SECRET" BASE

VC

CAMBODIA

VIETNAM

BINH-THIEN

AN-THANH

THICKETS

BASSAC RIVER

VC 260

HOUSE BOOBY TRAPPED 6 MAY 3 CIV. Killed

LAKE BINH THIEN LON

BAC NAM

BAC NAM

VIETNAM

BUONG LON

DONG-CO-KI

PHU-LOI

444th

PHU-HIEP

PHU-HUNG

PHU-HOA

BASSAC RIVER

PHUOC-HOA

PHUOC-THANH

PHU-HUU

PHU-THANH

Cambodian Outpost ⊘

CIDG-FOB ◼

PF-Outpost ▲

N

PHUOC-MY

VINH-PHUOC

0   500   1000   20
METERS

SPECIAL OPERATIONS MAP #5
8-MAY-66 CAPTURE OF VC TERRORISTS

215

"They will be given new clothes the day they are set free. Our tailor in Khanh Binh will make the clothes and sew a secret pocket in the pants that must be reached from the inside only, and our tailor will hide a note in the pocket that will give phony locations for our intelligence drops. I am certain the VC will search them when they return across the border bridge and have not been harmed. When the note is discovered they will be executed as spies."

Major Le stopped me as I was heading towards the team house from the command bunker later that day. "Our sixth CIDG company is now at full strength, Dai-uy. We now have a total of 792 Strikers and we can face the Southward Regiment with greater strength now, Dai-uy. Our new company is doing very well in their weapons, ambush and combat patrol training."

"Good to hear, Thieu-ta. We'll need every man."

As if someone was listening to me, we got a new man that day. His name was Marvin E. Woolley, a specialist four who was trained in weapons and communications also cross-trained as a medic. He would be a real asset to our mission.

On the 10th of May Lieutenant Strait came into my office after a boat ride down from Phu Hiep to suggest that we send the reconnaissance platoon with four assault boats and as many .30 caliber machine guns as we could spare up to Bac Nam Island and use it to set up floating ambushes to guard the Bassac River entry into our area. Their home base would be Khanh An PF outpost if the Bassac rose over the island plain.

Major Le and I both liked the idea and put it in motion, sending them up on the 11th after coordinating with Captain Tuoi, not wanting the PF outposts in that area to get the wrong idea when they started seeing men with guns on the island where it had been relatively free of human habitation for some time.

On the 13th of May, we would learn that our plan for retribution against the female terrorists had been carried out. Four bullet-riddled female bodies, their tongues cut out as was the custom in the case of spies, were found floating in the border canal south of the Khanh Binh FOB. A penciled note was found pinned to one of the bodies. It read: "Death comes quickly to the traitors of the Liberty Armed Forces." Our plan of deception had worked. The Viet Cong were convinced that the four terrorists had returned as double agents and deserved to die. They had unwittingly executed their own… for us.

* * * * *

II Timothy 1:7 — *For God hath not given us the spirit of fear;*
but of power, and of love, and of a sound mind.

CHAPTER 10
HELL'S FURY UNLEASHED
AT KHANH BINH

19 May 1966, Khanh Binh FOB: Where our Strikers had been killed or
seriously wounded in the trenches by an overwhelming VC onslaught, coura-
geous widows now stood as defenders, armed with rifle or carbine, engaged in
mortal combat with the enemy, some straddling their husband's lifeless bodies,
helping to defend the FOB against the withering fire of a numerically superior
aggressor. Children huddled next to them, tears rolling down their cheeks,
many busy loading ammunition into empty magazines for their mothers to
use against the enemy invaders. Hope was mirrored on the faces of young and
old as we entered the trench area to help them fend off the ensuing attack. We
found that courage was everywhere among the Hoa Haos.

Our unique and first-of-a-kind flat bottomed sampans caused quite a stir
when all 50 of them arrived at the B Team boat dock in Chau Doc on
the 14th of May. They were like nothing any of the local people had ever
seen. Each and every person, from the day they first traveled the rivers, knew only
of the traditional round bottom boats used throughout the delta area. I honestly
didn't care what anyone thought at the moment of their introduction. In my judgment, once they were tried by local paramilitary and irregular forces there would
be little doubt of their value for water-borne patrols and night ambush operations.
This was particularly true when foreigners such as me and others on my team, who
lacked the balance the South Vietnamese possessed, compared the round-bottomed
sampans with our new models. Our Hoa Hao boat platoon members admitted
quite readily that a flat bottom improved sampan handling and stability.

SLR photos of the border area were received early in the morning on 15 May via the mail chopper. They'd been taken three days earlier than I'd requested due to scheduling priority conflicts within the airborne reconnaissance unit. Sergeant Taylor completed his review early that afternoon and presented his analysis to me at 1500 hours in the operations center. Jim picked up his red-tipped pointer and directed my attention to a location on the border canal almost due west of the Khanh Binh FOB. Before he could utter a complete sentence the monsoon wind and rain hit our camp. The furious downpour pounding on our tin roof drowned out his words. The monsoon must be experienced to truly appreciate the awesome nature of what I will attempt to describe in mere words.

You could actually see it coming! The advancing cloud cover and wall of rain blotted out the sun, creating a dark, dank, night-like atmosphere. The accompanying high, gusty winds buffeted the bamboo walls of the building, sending sheets of rain dancing around the compound, searching for ways to intrude on our humid refuge. Major Le had warned us of the approaching monsoon season and the effect it would have on us if we didn't prepare for it. That was some weeks ago and we had begun stockpiling empty 55 gallon drums and five gallon cans to use with rafts we would make to float everything essential to the camp's operation. Generators, commo equipment, mortars, gun positions, living quarters and command and control space would require a great number of rafts of varying sizes if we were to continue to function when no part of the camp is above water. The overflow from Tonle Sap Lake in Cambodia would put the Mekong and Bassac Rivers over their banks, flooding all of the delta area.

This, my first experience, was a preliminary bout as Major Le pointed out to me. The real daily downpours, when it would come out of Cambodia like a wall of water, would be coming in July. By mid-August the water would reach its maximum height, an average of 15 feet above the February low extreme.

Sergeant Taylor laid aside his pointer and ran out of the building, braving the elements to shut down our generators, not wanting a storm-induced shorting to damage communications equipment. Radios were our lifeline to the outside world and we didn't want anything to happen that would further isolate us. As Jim went about his task I inspected the interior of the operations center and the US half of the headquarters building, making certain all the hinged, bamboo storm covers were closed and secured on all sides. They were taken care of before I got to them. Later I would learn that our 72 year old house boy, Win, had gone around and secured the storms as the wind and rain descended. It was easy to respect a man like Win. We were so fortunate to have good and loyal civilian help in every aspect of camp operation and maintenance.

Sergeant Taylor came back in through the team dining area door looking much like the proverbial drowned rat. I kept from laughing out loud, knowing that the next time it would be my turn to go out in the monsoon as Jim had done. In A Team operations, all shared in good and bad situations and duties. There was never a doubt who the team leader was and who made the decisions, but we were a team and gladly took our turns in all that we did, officer and NCO alike.

Jim and I were enjoying a second cup of coffee when the rain stopped abruptly, as if someone up there in the clouds had turned off a faucet. Jim got Ray Johnson on the field phone to ask him to start the generators, knowing that Ray would then make a communications check with the B Team to let them know we were okay and to receive any messages that had been held back by the storm.

On return to the briefing area, Sergeant Taylor updated me on the current enemy situation and the results of the latest SLR photo mission. "Not too much change, Dai-uy," Jim began, "You can see here," pointing with his finger to a picture on the table before me, and then to the map with his pointer, "the so-called secret bridge across the border canal west of the FOB is now complete. Sergeant Hung told me earlier today that Major Le has everything geared up to blow the bridge when the first VC attempts to cross. Charges have been laid and covered and will be blown from inside the FOB on order from a spotter." Moving his pointer to the north shore of the Bassac River across from Khanh An, he went on, "The 500 caskets we were told about earlier are being stockpiled here in the village of Prek Chrey.

"Leaving one company in the area west of Vinh Hoi Dong, just north of the Stoeng Takey River, the VC battalion has moved to a location above our FOB at Phu Hiep." Pausing for a moment, Jim continued, "Those are all the changes we've gotten from the SLR photos and our agents, Dai-uy."

"Thanks, Jim," I said. "I think it's time to rotate our people at Phu Hiep. They've got a good LLDB 81mm mortar crew up there so we can send Sergeant Eleam and Bac-si Sirois up to Phu Hiep very early on the 18th. They can increase the medical support around the FOB and keep the communications gear humming. Later that same day Lieutenant Strait and Sergeant Brown will return to camp. Don't want them ambushed coming back down and this rotation timing should help. Unless you've got some other recommendation, have Ray send a message to Lieutenant Strait telling him of our plans."

"Will do, Dai-uy," Taylor answered. "We'll send a platoon of Strikers up for security and have them tow the ten flat-bottom sampans that you've assigned to the FOB while they're at it. I'll get with Sergeant Hung and make the arrangements."

"Good plan, Sarge. That will complete the distribution of the flat bottoms, won't it?"

"Yes, Sir."

On schedule, Sergeant Eleam and Bac-si Sirois settled in at the Phu Hiep FOB on the 18th. My XO and Sergeant Brown returned without incident to camp later that day, their sweat-soaked camouflage fatigues filthy from an all-night ambush mission in the low, wet grasslands north of the FOB and along the Cambodian border. On arrival I told them both to get some rest.

At 1330 hours that same afternoon one of our CIDG squads on combat patrol out of Khanh Binh FOB made contact with a VC squad 50 meters from the border canal. The VC had obviously waded across the border canal a short distance from where they were detected as their black pajama uniforms were still soaked up to their armpits. After a ten minute firefight, with our Strikers in hot pursuit, the VC fled to and across the new bridge, located 2,000 meters west of the FOB. Our Strikers stopped 50 meters short of the bridge, knowing it would be blown on orders from the FOB once the VC were observed crossing it. Sure enough, the spotter, alert to the situation, radioed the FOB and the bridge was blown before the last VC was out of harm's way. The injuries required two of his comrades to carry him bodily into the relative safety of the bamboo thicket beyond the canal road inside Cambodia. One of our Strikers was seriously wounded by a booby-trapped hand-grenade placed by the VC in the path approaching the bridge.

At 1600 hours Major Le's intelligence sergeant and Jim Taylor completed an intelligence summary[1] telling of the current status of enemy units. Major Le brought my copy over and asked that I join him in a meeting with Captain Tuoi in his district office at 1640 hours to discuss our defensive alignment. We assumed that the VC's 510th (AKA 367th), 512th and 267th Battalions would attack Khanh An, Khanh Binh, Nhon Hoi, Phu Huu and Dong Co Ki early the next day: Ho Chi Minh's birthday. Their 261st Battalion would likely be held in reserve west of Chrey Thom, Cambodia. It was thought that the 260th VC Heavy Weapons Company located west of Vinh Hoi Dong would move further south to bombard our camp and the 155mm howitzer position with their 82mm mortars.

On the way to sub-sector Major Le told me that an old man had come to see him earlier that day with information that corroborated certain intelligence we'd received. "He told me there was a large number of VC in Cambodia and they were very close to the border. He also said the VC had bought a large number of first aid kits from a store in Chrey Thom just two days earlier. He thinks they plan to attack some of our outposts tonight. We must be very careful to prepare for their attacks."

"I agree, Thieu-ta. Do you have any specific concern that I should be thinking about?"

"Yes, Dai-uy. We must make certain that we have a way to reinforce our northern area if they are overwhelmed and need help. The hamlet of Phuoc Hoa and its vital MSR bridge are important to us, therefore I believe the enemy will attempt to capture it. If they hold the bridge, they'll control the road north from there and the Bassac River where it is narrow by the hamlet of Phuoc Khanh. We would then have no road or river to use for taking reaction forces to the northern area. We must protect those things." "Yes, I agree, Thieu-ta. Let's discuss it with Captain Tuoi."

Major Le, Captain Tuoi and I met at sub-sector headquarters at 1640 hours, analyzed the agent reports, discussed the meeting Major Le had with the old man and placed all units, FOBs and outposts on 100% alert. Major Le discussed the Phuoc Hoa situation as being ripe for a VC ambush of CIDG, RF or PF reaction forces going to the aid of our forces in the areas of Khanh An and Khanh Binh. It was decided that we would move very quickly to dispatch a combined force with two of my men, two LLDB and a CIDG Platoon who would be reinforced by a PF Platoon in Phuoc Hoa, secure the bridge site and counter any attempt by the VC to deny our use of the road or river.

"We now believe the mission of the 512th VC Battalion will be to make certain no reaction force can get through from here to the northern area," Captain Tuoi remarked, "so we have decided to send one RF company to secure the west bank of the Bassac River from Phouc Khanh north past Dong Co Ki and up to our Khanh An PF Outpost. A second RF Company will reinforce our Phu Huu PF Outpost and be prepared to clear Bac Nam Island if the VC try to move across the Bassac in that manner."

Major Le and I agreed with Captain Tuoi and together we felt confident in what we'd devised in our defensive plan.

As testimony to the state of preparedness and the spirit of cooperation between our various forces, Lieutenant John Strait would organize and lead that force, departing from camp within an hour of receiving the mission. It had been a rude awakening for John when I jarred him out of a deep sleep to tell him he'd be heading the counter-ambush force. Not one to complain about duty, John just grunted a couple of times and went about the business of getting himself and his force together. John Strait, Marvin Woolley, two LLDB sergeants, the 2nd platoon of the 441st CIDG Company and a PF platoon that would join them in Phouc Hoa, made up the force. The Strikers would take a 60mm mortar and two light machine-guns; John would carry an M-79 grenade launcher and wear my good luck "Dangerous Dan" hat. Before they left camp, John Strait let me know that his only gripe was that he and Woolley would miss a John Wayne movie that we'd be showing later that evening. Ray Johnson and Jim Taylor were setting the bed sheet screen on the fence-line between inner and outer compound as Strait led his men onto trucks that would carry them to Phuoc Hoa within minutes.

As big John got into the cab of the lead truck, I reached up, shook his hand, and promised, "I'll make sure we keep that flick for you and Woolley to watch when you get back here." John smiled, pulled his hat down tighter on his head, and replied, "That's a deal, Dai-uy, that's a deal."

John's force was in place at 1830 hours, with the bridge secured and the ambush set along the west bank of the Bassac River, tying in with the RF company just below Phuoc Khanh. They would remain in place until daybreak or until relieved by additional Regional Forces. Once their mission was accomplished they would assemble at the Phuoc Hoa bridge site and join any reaction force that would be sent north as it moved along the MSR from camp to relieve any situation requiring reinforcement from camp assets. Major Le and I stood anxiously in the command bunker, continually scanning the border with our binoculars, watching for the first sign of the expected attack. It would come tonight and we knew it. We'd done what we could to prepare for it. The night air was still and the humidity oppressive. It was as if you could wring water out of the air. The black, moonless sky was in and of itself foreboding, yet we were thankful for the lack of clouds, a vital factor if we were to call on Spooky, the AC-47 gunship, for close support.

Major Le put down his binoculars for a moment and told me a little of the history of the Southward VC Regiment. "They were organized from parts of the 'Plain of Reeds' Regiment that had been moved from an area west of the upper Mekong Tactical Zone on order of the VC Western Committee into Kandal and Takeo Provinces in Cambodia for training and re-equipping to attack our area. They now have four combat infantry battalions, an artillery section, a signal company and a large medical unit.

"We made it more difficult for them to prepare their men and train them on new weapons and tactics when we destroyed the Bung Ven Secret Base. It was initially their primary area designated to bring together, train and equip the Regiment for their invasion of An Phu.

"They have the 76mm mountain guns in their artillery section, but as you know, Dai-uy, we are ready for them. Captain Tuoi has ordered his big howitzers on full alert and they are pointed toward the northern area outposts which have been assigned 'Priority of Firepower.'"

"I think we have done all we can do, except wait, Thieu-ta. With the RF Companies and our ambush force in place to protect the MSR," I told Major Le, "we now stand ready for their attack."

"Yes, Dai-uy, and we are also ready to mount reaction forces to help when and where help is needed. I do wish you had more men on your team. You are already spread very thin."

He was right as rain. If we must send a reaction force to help our men at Khanh Binh or Phu Hiep, I would have to go alone with Major Le, ignoring a cardinal rule of SF in battle: there must always be two SF when going into battle with indigenous forces.

Jim Taylor and an LLDB sergeant were standing by in the four-deuce pit, ready to respond to enemy fire from the west. Ray Johnson was manning the communications bunker while Sergeant Brown laid out surgical instruments and wound dressing material in the aid station, assisted by nurses Co Lau and Tran Thi. Brown hoped his cross training as a medic would prove adequate when the casualties started coming in for treatment.

At 0325 hours on the 19th, just as I was beginning to wonder if we'd been lured into thinking an invasion was imminent, when it was a ruse, two bright blue flares lit up the sky above Khanh Binh, the signal for a coordinated attack by the Viet Cong on all of our northern outposts.

The 261st VC battalion[2] reinforced by the 267th with an estimated strength of 700 men, armed with 81mm mortars, 60mm mortars, 57mm recoilless rifles, 3.5 rocket launchers, light machine-guns and assorted small arms, attacked and then surrounded our FOB at Khanh Binh. Bombarded with hundreds of rockets, mortar rounds and artillery shells, the 132 lightly armed defenders, commanded by

Lieutenant Luong Le, though outnumbered five to one held their ground against human-wave assaults launched every 15 to 20 minutes. The enemy soon learned how courageous and ferocious the Hoa Haos could be as they tried in vain to penetrate their defenses and seize the FOB.

The mortar barrage of most of the Khanh Binh and Khanh An areas continued for 25 minutes. Though not able to take the FOB at Khanh Binh, they continued to surround it as they moved to occupy all the hamlets located above the Khanh An PF Outpost. The frightened villagers fled south in front of the Communist invaders, but many were cut off from their escape route and forced to flee into the central marsh area west of Khanh An and south of our FOB where they hid from the VC.

Units of the 510th Battalion swept across the Bassac River from the north and the border canal from the west to surround and capture the PF Outpost at Khanh Binh and to control the bridge that linked Khanh Binh with Prey Thom, Cambodia. Villagers evacuated the war zone as their homes were being destroyed by VC artillery and mortar fire and joined other refugees in the marshy area and the few nearby hamlets not yet taken by the enemy.

At the same time the PF Outpost at Khanh An, reinforced by Sergeant Dung and his CIDG Reconnaissance Platoon, was attacked by an estimated 200 VC of the 512th Battalion using 81mm mortars, 57mm recoilless rifles, light machine-guns and small arms. They also had two trailer-mounted .50 caliber, anti-aircraft machine guns to defend against aircraft brought in to support outpost defense.

VC gunners from the 512th Heavy Weapons Battalion placed recoilless rifle, rocket and machine gun fire on the Nhon Hoi PF outpost. They also hammered the PF river outposts at Phu Huu and Dong Co Ki, fortified positions vital to our defense of river and land routes needed by reaction or relief forces answering calls for help in our northern area.

The Southward Regiment's general attack on the forces of An Phu had begun. Captured documents would tell how the Southward Regiment Commander believed their superior numbers and extensive array of powerful weapons would permit rapid destruction of our "weaker and smaller" forces. He bragged of certain victory within the first two hours and of making An Phu his base for future operations.

"But," as Major Le told me, "their tactics were known in advance by our forces prior to the attack and our artillery immediately countered their fire, thus denying them the advantage of surprise. "The prompt reaction of sub-sector's 155mm howitzers caused disorder and panic among the enemy's ranks. So expert was the communication between the forward observer in the battle area and the gunners at Phuoc My, the high explosive shells of our 155 artillery destroyed many of the forward strength of the enemy in the first moments of the battle."

Earlier, a reinforced VC company from the 512th Heavy Weapons Battalion with a sapper squad had slipped quietly into the Bassac River from its east bank at Phu Hung, less than 2,000 meters north of the Phuoc Hoa bridge. Their mission was to destroy the bridge and set up a deadly ambush along the MSR, cutting off our only route for reaction forces to proceed north to reinforce the Khanh Binh and Khanh An area. The noise of heavy combat in surrounding areas would make it impossible for listening posts down-river to detect any sound of their movement. In their 40 or more commandeered sampans, they drifted silently southward, riding the slow moving current, not knowing they would soon be detected by an alert Lieutenant Strait using high-powered binoculars. The luminous dial on John's wrist-watch let him know it was 0330 hours.

He nudged Marvin Woolley, who lay next to him searching the river for enemy over the sights of his M-16 rifle, and said in a low voice, "VC at ten o'clock." Woolley passed it on. John watched the sampans slowly and quietly swing in towards the bank at the bend in the river just north of his position. Quickly assessing the situation, John decided to attack the VC while they were still in the water. If permitted to reach dry ground, he reasoned to himself, his men would give up the tactical advantage. Outnumbered and out gunned, their best hope was to startle and rout their foe in the water. Return fire from moving sampans would have limited accuracy and little effect on the ambush force whose low profile was yet hidden in the underbrush.

Lieutenant Strait fired his M-79 grenade launcher as the signal for his men to lay down a hail of bullets aimed at the approaching enemy force. The first 40mm fragmentation grenade exploded in the midst of the VC flotilla, causing confusion among the ranks of the sampan-borne VC. For 18 minutes Woolley, the CIDG and PF together poured a deadly stream of machine-gun and small arms fire into the midst of the enemy as Lieutenant Strait fired 40mm grenades into sampans nearest the west bank. The enemy panicked and fled to the opposite shore, leaving one BAR behind.

Most of the dead VC were taken downstream by the strong current of the Bassac River. One of their dead remained on the western river bank while others were carried along with their wounded to the opposite shore in sampans. A surprise attack was our ally, causing panic among the VC, who hadn't expected an ambush but got hit and hit hard in the middle of the Bassac River. It had been their mission to furtively take the bridge and wait in ambush for our forces. They would regret not sending out men to scout the area. After receiving Lieutenant Strait's report, I met with Major Le and passed on details of the action at Phuoc Hoa. He smiled and told me, "We were right to set the ambush at Phuoc Hoa. We were in a very high spirit and we studied which place was the most serious and we got it right! We will reinforce Khanh Binh as soon as possible, going by truck to Dong Co Ki and from there we will go on foot. We must make contact and drive those VC who now try to take the FOB far back inside Cambodia.

"We must move quickly," he added, "because we know very clear the enemy situation and what they will try to do. Also," he added, "if we do not get there in time we will lose all of our people in Khanh Binh. And it would not be because the VC were strong and tenacious, it would be instead that we lacked the courage to do what was right."

Elements of the Southward Regiment harassed PF outposts at Khanh Binh, Phu Huu, Nhon Hoi and Dong Co Ki with small arms fire for 90 minutes. After posting all known enemy units and actions on our battle map[2] which included the order of battle of friendly and enemy forces, we decided on two specific courses of action: flareship support and reinforcement of the FOB.

At 0340 hours we requested a flareship in the Khanh Binh and Khanh An areas. It was disapproved due to the close proximity of the Cambodian border. "It is a curse of the devil that your government gives the enemy their safe-havens," Major Le retorted when I told him of the refusal.

I agreed and told him, "We must defeat the enemy even with no support from my government." Inside I felt ill at the thought of our president giving the enemy a hand in the battle we now fought.

At 0515 hours, Major Le and I led the reaction force consisting of two LLDB and three platoons of CIDG, departing by truck from camp, linking up with Lieutenant Strait's ambush force at the Phuoc Hoa Bridge site at 0615 hours. We then organized for a two-pronged assault against the VC positions south and east of the FOB. We left Phuoc Hoa by truck and proceeded along the MSR through Dong Co Ki to a point southwest of An Thanh at the northeast tip of Lake Binh Thien where we de-trucked and proceeded on foot along the road connecting Khanh Binh to the lake, wanting to surprise the enemy who had surrounded the Khanh Binh FOB and now held it under siege. One RF company was in position north and south of An Thanh along the west bank of the Bassac River and the other was located in and around the Phu Huu PF outpost to prevent enemy action against our rear as we moved through that area to reinforce our FOB. At 0615 hours Major Le and I led our two platoon force along a dirt road through the western part of An Thanh for about 1,000 meters, turned north and positioned ourselves for an assault on the enemy's rear. The din of battle covered the sound of our movement. We would launch our counter-offensive, attacking the enemy's eastern positions at 0645 hours.

Lieutenant Thuan Nguyen led the second element with Lieutenant Strait, Specialist Woolley and two platoons of Strikers. They moved steadily through the high grass south of An Thanh Village in a westerly direction for about 1,500 meters. This brought them to a point due south of the FOB and 400 meters from the outer perimeter defenses. At 0640 hours, Lieutenant Thuan would move his men across the dirt road and position them in a grove of trees 300 meters from the FOB. They would begin their assault at 0650 hours, the objective being to trap the VC in a crossfire as they fled from our attack element toward the safety of the border. The VC had launched their third assault at 0600 hours behind a fierce mortar and rocket barrage. The enemy advanced against a steady outpouring of machine-gun and rifle fire from the defending Strikers to break through and occupy ten meters of the eastern trench line, including a machine-gun bunker. Lieutenant Luong Le, the FOB commander, immediately directed his men to use their hand-grenades to neutralize the entrenched VC and the machine-gun bunker, which they did with great success.

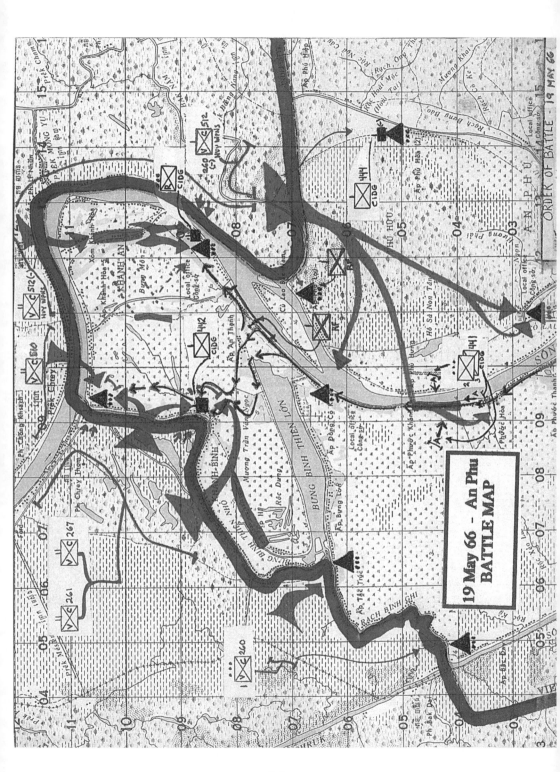

19 May 66 – An Phu
BATTLE MAP

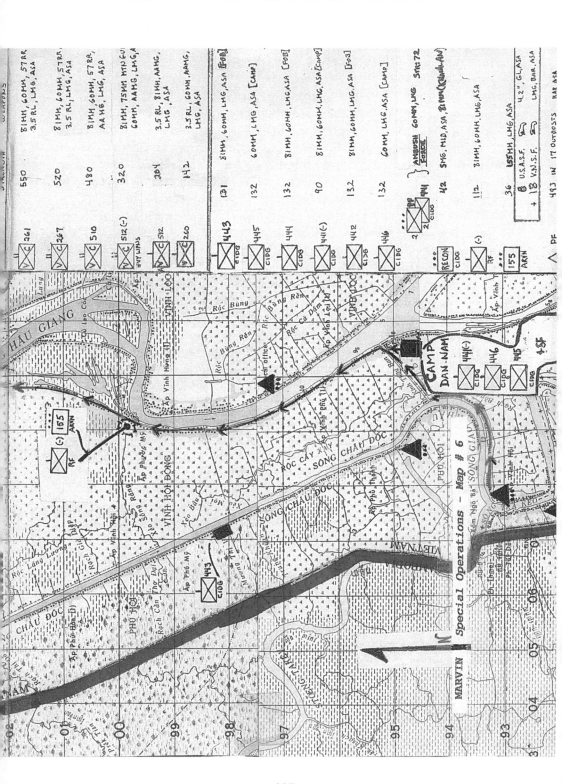

MARVIN *Special Operations – Map # 6*

The first gray light of dawn appeared as we launched our attack against the rear of the VC assault force, catching them by surprise in a withering crossfire between our men and the FOB defenders, causing them to panic and flee toward what they imagined would be the safety of the border. Instead they ran into a second, more intense crossfire, this time from Lieutenant Thuan's fresh two platoon CIDG force. Two VC bravely turned and rushed directly at Thuan's men, guns blazing, wanting to give their comrades time to flee back into the safety of Cambodia. The first was hit before he'd taken three steps but his forward momentum carried him another two or three meters, as his finger continued closed with a death grip on the trigger of his AK-47. The automatic rifle continued to spew its bullets in an upward arc toward the sky until the magazine was empty and his bullet-riddled, lifeless body fell face down to the ground. The second ran the gauntlet of intense fire from Lieutenant Strait and Strikers on either side of him. Reloading his SKS Carbine as he ran, he got within ten feet of my XO before John almost cut him in two with a long burst from his M-16 rifle. The momentum of his charge carried him another six feet, and as he fell the carbine flew out of his outstretched arms and landed across the toes of John's steel-toed jungle boots. He picked it up, slung it over his left shoulder, and continued on the offensive.

Lieutenant Thuan led his men up to the outer perimeter of the FOB and then did a flanking movement, leading his men in hot pursuit of the VC all the way to the border canal. Major Le continued to lead our force, mopping up scattered resistance. Somehow Major Le recognized their leader among the fleeing VC. He gestured to me and shouted, "There is their commander, Dai-uy," but before I could get him in my sights, Major Le shot him in the chest, killing him instantly. As we continued forward, Major Le ordered the battalion commander be searched for possible intelligence.

The last VC I hit with a burst from my M-16 fell like a ton of bricks and then turned over on the ground and leveled his AK-47 at me. After I put two more rounds in his chest, his arms went limp, the AK-47 dropped to his chest, blood oozed from his mouth and his eyes rolled back in their sockets. I grabbed his rifle, slung it across my back, took a deep breath and searched the battleground for movement. It was still.

The VC had retreated back across the border into Cambodia when our reaction force placed heavy fire on their lines after regaining the trenches. It was a scene I would never forget as we fought to break through the encircling 700 man enemy force that had laid siege to the FOB: a wide gap had been cleared in the outer defensive perimeter wire obstacles by well placed VC "bungalow" mines (their peculiar version of the bangalore torpedo). It was that gap, so neatly cut through the triple concertina, tanglefoot and claymore mines that had allowed them to access and gain a foothold in the outer defensive trenches. Where our Strikers had been killed or seriously wounded by that VC onslaught, brave widows now stood with rifles or carbines at the ready, some straddling their husband's lifeless bodies, helping defend the FOB. It was their courageous stand, coupled with our reaction force attack, that dislodged the enemy and sent them packing. Children were huddled in the trench, some loading ammunition into the empty magazines at their feet, wanting to help as they stayed close to their mothers. Courage was everywhere among the Hoa Haos. Relief showed on their faces as we entered their trench area to reinforce against the next attack.

The last thing I took account of before joining Major Le when he spoke to the waiting Strikers in FOB trenches was how many dead the enemy had left behind. Our quick reaction, the fierceness of the Hoa Hao fighters and the accuracy of the 155 supporting fire had allowed fear to detract from the taking back of their dead from a battle.

Than Van Bui, one of our FOB machine-gunners facing the enemy's assault in the outer perimeter defenses at Khanh Binh, tells of his experience: "I saw them approaching too close to us. I had no time to react, their rocket launcher was only ten meters away from me when it fired at our bunker. The rocket exploded with terrific strength. After a minute, being shaken by the explosion, I pointed my machine-gun in the direction of the enemy's rocket launcher and emptied the belt on that crew.

"I loaded a second belt, at the same time I see they did not move. I immediately ran out to the rocket launcher position, covering myself with fire from my carbine and saw five bodies surrounding the rocket launcher. At the same time, the nearby VC opened fire on me and I am surprised I was not injured by their bullets, only the butt of my carbine was broken, saving my life."

Another Striker combatant, Thanh Van Nguyen, showed off a Chicom machine-gun he'd captured and said, "I cannot understand why the VC are crazy like that, they know they will die under our fire, but they continue to move ahead."

The truth of the matter is that soldiers of all armies follow orders and go when, where and how they are told to go. During the battle of Gettysburg in the American Civil War, thousands of Southern soldiers died when they followed orders and crossed a wide open wheat field where they were as rifle and cannon fodder to the Northern Forces. Leaders make good and bad judgments and give the orders in battle and it is seldom that they pay the extreme price of death for their own errors in wisdom. Rather, it is the man on the ground with the weapon in his hands, who follows those orders without question, that gives his all, spills his blood. I recall the words of my best friend and fellow Green Beret, Gerard V. Parmentier, who was killed in action on 17 May 1967 near Dak To, South Vietnam: "Remember, Dan, the ones who give the orders to kill are seldom close enough to the battle to hear the sound of our guns being fired, the clamor of incoming rockets and artillery or the whoosh of the enemy's bullets rushing by."

By 0700 hours the VC battle group had been forced to pull back from all sides of the FOB. Our reaction force had regained the trenches taken earlier by the VC and had joined the 442nd Company in their compound. The enemy continued to bombard the FOB with mortar fire while directing machine-gun and recoilless rifle fire at pointblank range into the western FOB defenses from across the border canal. We answered with counter-fire from our 81mm mortars and machine-guns, wanting to silence those weapons within range of our FOB. We immediately requested close air support to go after enemy gun positions out of range of our weapons.

Major Le and I sat down on the ground inside the FOB with our backs against a tree for a much needed break. Lieutenant Strait, a PRC-25 radio slung on his back, hand set in one hand and M-16 in the other, walked over and stood next to me. He was trying the air-to-ground frequency, hoping to hear someone on the other end, wanting to direct them as they would bomb and strafe enemy weapon positions.

With big John towering above Major Le and me, I got this feeling that one only experiences in combat. Something bad was headed our way and would be coming down near us. Without hesitation, I shouted "Incoming", reached up, grabbed John by both shoulders, and forced him down to the ground beside me. About the time we were stretched out flat, a high explosive mortar round impacted just a few feet from us on a slight rise, exploding and slinging its death dealing shrapnel in all directions. Our low profiles prevented our being hit by the hot fragments. As we lay there waiting for the dust to settle, John Strait turned his head toward me, spit out some dirt, and said, "You saved my life, Dai-uy. I appreciate it."

Strait and Woolley were soon back in the center of the FOB compound helping the LLDB medic treat wounded Strikers. Though exhausted from the action and lack of sleep, they did what they could to help. Major Le noticed them toiling to aide the LLDB medics and told me, "They are good men, Dai-uy. They have made many friends in An Phu."

The close air support failed to appear and the med-evac chopper we had requested to carry wounded CIDG to our camp's aid station didn't show. I came to believe that the message from med-evac to us was: "If you've got Americans hurt, call us and we'll come. If not, don't bother us."

So we took care of our own, evacuating the wounded by foot or litter 500 meters to the road west of An Thanh, where they were then taken by VIS personnel on their three-wheeled Lambrettas two and a half kilometers to the Bassac River near An Thanh. From there the wounded traveled by assault boat twelve kilometers to Camp An Phu. After treatment and trauma stabilization by Sergeant Brown and our two nurses, seriously wounded men would then be evacuated by assault boat or barge the remaining ten kilometers to the Province Hospital in Chau Doc.

Later that morning Lieutenant Strait and I took a short break and talked about the things we'd learned in medical cross-training from Specialist Sirois. What he'd taught us allowed us to help save lives during the many battles fought in and around Khanh Binh and other hot spots in An Phu. John Strait tells it this way, "I spent quite a bit of time with Sirois in the dispensary and on a few medical patrols learning as much as I could about emergency medical treatment. The training he gave us was extra good and helped make it possible for a lot of Strikers to live to fight another day. I've given a few IVs of blood expander to guys hit here at Khanh Binh, Dai-uy. I didn't know if any would have died for lack of blood but I knew as weak and pale as they were I'd better try to help them. I did it the way Bac-si taught me and the fact is they all survived."

The 261/267 VC battle group broke off their rocket and mortar attack at 1030 hours and ceased harassing the Khanh Binh FOB with small arms fire but retained control of most of the northern portion of the district above grid line 09 and the Khanh An PF Outpost. During the first battle at Khanh Binh we lost eight CIDG killed and 29 wounded. The VC captured an M-2 carbine and one M-1 rifle. The enemy lost 116 killed and 130 were wounded and carried away. Of those killed, one was a battalion commander and another was a female company commander. Solid ivory chopsticks found on her body were given to me by Major Le. We captured one Chicom machine-gun, ten AK-47 assault rifles, a B-40 anti-tank rocket launcher, a Russian rifle with grenade launcher, one flare pistol, four claymore mines, five large bungalow mines, 89 small anti-personnel mines, one field telephone (used as a detonating device), an extra barrel for the Chicom machine-gun, one VC flag and three camouflage hats. We would learn from 5th Group S-3 that we were the first in IV Corps to capture the AK-47 and B-40 weapons.

At 1100 hours, the 512th VC Heavy Weapons Battalion broke off their attack on the Khanh An PF Outpost and withdrew north into the Khanh Hoa area. Enemy losses at Khanh An were 34 killed and 54 wounded and carried away. We captured a 57mm recoilless rifle, one light machine-gun, a BAR, Thompson submachine-gun, three other weapons and miscellaneous equipment including a tripod and barrel for a .50 caliber anti-aircraft machine-gun.

As we left through the breach blown by the VC in the outer defenses of our FOB, we took note of the obvious effectiveness of the VC's Chinese made 'bungalow' mines in completely destroying the deep belt of barbed-wire obstacles that had stood between the defenders and the enemy.

Hardly a blade of grass stood higher than a foot for some two hundred meters out from the FOB defenses. The combination of artillery, mortar, machine-gun and small arms fire had literally mowed down the area's vegetation. Dead VC littered the open killing zone and I counted another ten bodies in the bamboo thicket we passed through to reach the dirt road leading to Khanh An. Some wore the black uniforms of the VC guerrilla fighter while others wore the khaki shirt and shorts of the NVA. Most were barefoot and carried but a few personal possessions in pockets or small back packs, such as rice, chopsticks, incense, family photos and little else.

Refugees fleeing from the enemy occupied areas began moving south toward An Phu Village nearby our camp. Much of the northern area was uninhabitable at the time due to destruction caused by the fierce fighting. As much as we were distressed after a battle to see the tragic effect war had on the hamlets, we tried to think positively once any lost ground was regained, knowing we could be a part of the rebuilding and revitalization efforts.

On the way to Khanh An, Major Le and I would observe the results of intense combat action on our FOB and in the surrounding areas, particularly in the hamlets. The thatched-roof bamboo homes located at the edge of the battle zone had been totally destroyed by artillery and mortar fire, friendly and enemy alike. Little remained that could be salvaged.

When we reached the river road two kilometers south of the Khanh An PF Outpost we met Colonel Brewer, Major Re and Captain Tuoi. Two RF companies stood by on the road, waiting their orders to clear the occupied village areas to our north. The leaders were planning an artillery barrage to prepare the area for their advance over it. Major Le and I told them that many thousands of our people were still in the area who would suffer death or injury if they were to go through with their plan.

VIS Chief Minh Van Tran and his personnel were standing nearby, as were JUSPAO and Province Social Welfare staff. Mister Tran suggested that we allow his VIS people time to infiltrate the occupied area after dark and warn the people to move out of the area so we could then bombard the VC invaders without risking their lives. "The social welfare men have volunteered to help in this," Tran told us, "and Dat Van Vo (National Police Chief for An Phu) will have his men available for refugee traffic control and assistance, even in the movement of the wounded."

I told those gathered, "These are brave and selfless people, willing to risk their lives to help others in a very dangerous situation. We must give them a chance." Major Le and Province Chief Re agreed and Major Re ordered that the artillery barrage be delayed until the next day when we would reassess the situation.

With that resolved, Major Le and I boarded the waiting assault boats and headed back to camp. En route, knowing the battle would be continuing and realizing that many wounded Strikers were either in camp or on the way who were in need of medical treatment, I ordered Bac-si back to camp and Brown to Phu Hiep. Lieutenant Strait radioed instructions to Ray Johnson back in camp and Ray was able to convince the pilot of the mail chopper, with a small gift of a VC flag as inducement, to fly the rotation run for us. Ray didn't tell him we had the flag made by a local seamstress.

Upon arrival in camp, and after a hurried lunch, John Strait and Marvin Woolley again joined in to help treat the wounded, this time working alongside Bac-si Sirois, LLDB Sergeant Chet and our two nurses in the camp aid station. Somehow, though beat to their socks from a long night and day of combat and physical exertion, they dug deep into their reserve of strength to help well into the night to aid the injured. All told, 31 Strikers and 20 civilians were treated in our aid station before it was closed down at 2300 hours. Only four Strikers required evacuation to the Chau Doc Province Hospital for treatment.

Early in the afternoon of the 19th Major Le and I met with Captain Tuoi and discussed the overall tactical situation. With only two companies remaining in camp we considered pulling some men out of Phu Hiep, but agreed the risks of such a move outweighed the advantages. Captain Tuoi was pleased to advise us that

Major Re had committed the two RF companies to help defend An Phu under Tuoi's command for at least another full day. "They will continue to reinforce the PF outpost at Khanh An and remain in ambush position along the west bank of the Bassac River from Phuoc Hoa to Phuoc Khanh."

At 0005 hours on the 20th, an estimated 120 VC armed with BARs and small arms attacked and seized a portion of the western outer perimeter defenses at our new Vinh Hoi Dong FOB. With Lieutenant Triet Tran providing enemy locations by radio to our commo bunker, Johnson relaying to Jim Taylor in the four-deuce pit, Jim and Marvin Woolley were able to provide excellent fire support from Camp An Phu. A 20 minute firefight forced the VC to break contact and withdraw into Cambodia north of the Stoeng Takey River to a point beyond the reach of our four-deuce. Four CIDG were wounded and the VC lost three killed and eight wounded.

At 0030 hours, a 180 man heavy weapons company from the 512th VC battalion launched a second attack on the Khanh An PF Outpost whose numbers had been increased by our decision to have our Recon Platoon in place for reinforcement. The RF Company that Captain Tuoi had sent to help defend the outpost had moved during the night but had gotten only as far as Dong Co Ki. Once the attack was in motion, it was moved quickly by truck to just south of the Khanh An PF Outpost. From there the company moved on foot to attack the exposed southern flank of the VC assault force. Their lightning attack surprised the VC, forcing them to break off their assault and move north into the Khanh Hoa Village area. The almost three hour long battle accounted for two men killed and 14 wounded in the RF Company. Three PF defenders were wounded, while the VC lost 13 killed and 42 wounded as counted on the field and seen being carried away. At 0130 hours the 261st and 267th VC Battalions, with a combined strength of approximately 990 men, launched a second attack on the Khanh Binh FOB defended by 250 CIDG of the reinforced 442d CIDG Company. Using the extra "muscle" of their 76mm 'mountain gun' for the first time along the Cambodian border, they fired at PF outposts in Phu Loi, Tac Truc, Nhon Hoi and Dong Co Ki in a failed strategy to draw the fire of our 155mm howitzers away from defense of the Khanh Binh FOB.

Lieutenant Luong Le radioed camp from Khanh Binh, asking for resupply of much needed ammunition and reinforcement. Major Le and I met quickly and organized a reaction force, using the 446th Company from camp and taking an LLDB crew to set up an 81mm mortar to support Khanh Binh from the An Thanh area.

I then briefed Lieutenant Strait and Sergeant Taylor and we discussed our options. "Only six of us here in camp and Sirois stays to treat the wounded while Ray Johnson keeps the communications humming and ammunition coming to fill our needs. We're doing good but we can't fight off a whole regiment without ammunition.

"John," I said, looking Lieutenant Strait in the eyes, "if we have to go north again to break through to help Khanh Binh, I'll need you to run the show here.

I'll take Taylor, Woolley and Tony with me. Keep in touch with Captain Tuoi to make certain the refugee situation is under control. If you get attacked while we're gone, you'll have to man the four-deuce. Get a good LLDB sergeant lined up right away to help on the mortar and use Flash in the command bunker to keep things straight between me, you and Lieutenant Hanh, who'll be standing in for Major Le up there with you. Co will help Bac-si in the aid station and interpret for him."

"We'll do our best, Dai-uy. That you can count on."

About that time Ray Johnson walked in to let us know he'd just heard from Sergeant Eleam at Phu Hiep. "Their new interpreter and houseboy are both working out just fine and the morale among the Strikers is good. He seems to be enjoying being away from camp, Dai-uy."

"He's probably taking time to study for the warrant he'd like to get when he goes back to the States," Jim added.

I remarked that Eleam would make one real good warrant officer in the communications field. "He's got what it takes," I told them, "and he's cool under pressure, too!"

Major Le and I met for a few minutes to iron out the details of reaction force deployment to Khanh Binh, give me a penciled list of ammunition requirements for his FOBs and to discuss the refugee situation. "We now have more than 3,000 refugees from the north passing through Dong Co Ki and Captain Tuoi has made arrangements for temporary shelter and food for them. We must clear that area of the enemy as soon as possible. We have maybe 6,000 more of our people left in that area to take care of at this end." Major Le emphasized.

The 155mm howitzers had been moved to Phuoc My, within range of all direct support missions for the Khanh Binh area where we had the most urgent and greatest need. Within minutes of their arrival they began hammering the VC assault forces which outnumbered our defenders at Khanh Binh four-to-one.

At 0450 hours a med-evac chopper was requested to land at Camp An Phu at 0700 hours to pick up casualties for transport to the Chau Doc hospital. It never arrived. Wounded fighters from Khanh An and Khanh Binh were evacuated and treated as before.

Our Khanh Binh reaction force was moved by truck to An Thanh hamlet, leaving camp at 0500 hours in a single convoy, thanks to sub-sector's loaning us four of their 2¹/₂ ton trucks. Major Le and I, along with Sergeant Taylor, Specialist Woolley, two LLDB, the 446th CIDG Company and four tons of ammunition were moved without incident.

When the VC first attacked the outnumbered defenders of Khanh Binh, a critical shortage of authorized vehicles seriously affected our ability to come to their relief on a timely basis. Though authorized six 2¹/₂ ton trucks we had but two and one of those was in the maintenance shop for major work at Chau Doc. There would have been fewer friendly casualties and less damage to our outer perimeter defenses had we been able to mount our reaction force in a more responsive manner. In this instance Captain Tuoi saved the day by loaning us trucks from the RF companies attached to sub-sector. Together with our meager resources we were able to transport all the men and desperately needed ammunition at one time. Once we fought our way through the encircling enemy forces and entered the FOB compound, the besieged Strikers, who were about to run out of ammunition, would jump with joy once that last truck, loaded high with all the bullets, mortar rounds, claymore mines and hand grenades they so desperately needed entered their FOB.

Armed choppers were requested at 0520 hours to provide close ground support to aid in our pushing back the enemy who surrounded the FOB. It was disapproved "due to the close proximity of an international border." I hated the politics of that war.

Our reaction force de-trucked and assembled southwest of An Thanh Village at 0540 hours. The two LLDB Sergeants, with the help of two CIDG ammo bearers, established an 81mm mortar fire base in an area secured by an RF company at nearby Khanh An and prepared to support the Khanh Binh FOB. Radio contact was made and they were preparing to fire their first support mission as we continued on in a two-pronged attack against the VC who now surrounded our FOB.

I was alongside Major Le as he led two platoons of the 446th Company in one prong of the attack while Jim Taylor, Marvin Woolley, and Tony Trung followed Lieutenant Sang Ngo as he led the other two platoons of that same unit in the second prong.

We would move along the tree line on the north side of the road leading to Khanh Binh and launch our attack in a northwesterly direction to penetrate the VC stranglehold on the south side of the FOB.

Lieutenant Sang would take his men north across the flats and to the east of An Thanh, using it as a screen between the enemy and them, wanting to move undetected for 800 meters. At that point Sang would flank his troops to the west and assault the enemy, using the tall grass to mask their movement until they got within range of where they now engaged the FOB defenders, having taken a portion of the outer defenses in the northeast corner of the FOB compound.

At 0550 hours we called in a pre-planned artillery barrage with the 155mm howitzers dropping in 20 rounds of HE into the ranks of the encircling VC. The artillery fire was lifted as we began our advance at 0600 hours with our LLDB gunners firing their 81mm mortars into the VC ranks in close support of our advance.

Major Le led us forward in stages. Machine-gun fire was laid down for cover as we lunged forward in short but rapid spurts, denying the VC good targets, with heavy fire being placed on them each time we were exposed.

At the same time, we were unaware of the movement of two companies of the 512th VC Heavy Weapons Battalion which had been attacking Khanh An PF Outpost to position themselves for an attack on the PF Outpost near the border bridge at Khanh Binh. Those VC spotted Lieutenant Sang's reaction force as it moved to within 700 meters of the FOB and engaged them in an intense firefight. It was a dangerous and fierce machine-gun and small arms duel between 380 Viet

Cong to their north and another 120 entrenched VC firing from the west, catching Sang's 72 man force in a withering crossfire.

Taylor, Woolley and Tony were with Sang when the surprise attack hit them. Outnumbered nine to one, with only bamboo thickets for cover, they would surely die from the murderous fire coming at them from two directions unless they came up with a plan.

Sergeant Taylor crouched next to Lieutenant Sang and suggested a plan to create a diversion and draw the VC fire coming from the north away from their location. Sang thought for a brief moment, approved the plan, and told Taylor, "We will all be grateful if your deception works, Sergeant. You are a brave friend of the Hoa Haos."

Taylor handed his M-16 and two bandoleers full of ammunition to Tony, grabbed a machine-gun and threw a long, linked belt of ammunition over his shoulder, picked out five Strikers who were armed with BARs or sub-machine guns and had Tony pick up a full box of machine-gun ammunition and then led his small group of courageous men directly into the face of the 380 VC who had attacked Sang's reaction force.

Firing bursts from all of their weapons into the ranks of the VC ahead of them, then dropping to the ground, moving low and speedily to a new location, firing many more bursts and on to more locations and more of the same, they meant to deceive the enemy into thinking that Sang's whole force was attacking them.

Jim Taylor and his small crew of fighting men seemed oblivious to danger as a steady stream of bullets from more than 300 enemy rifles and machine-guns buzzed by them like a swarm of lethal bees. It was a miracle that none of them had taken a bullet or faltered due to physical exhaustion. Under cover of the pitch black night they continued their perilous hoax. Fire a burst, move, crouch down, fire a burst, move, crouch down and on and on. The physical stress was enough to kill most men, but they continued until they were about to run out of ammunition. Just about that time they realized their deception had worked. The two confused VC companies, thinking it was a tactic to lure them into a crossfire, broke contact and withdrew in a northwesterly direction toward the Khanh Binh PF Outpost. Jim and his men chased the two companies for about 100 meters, firing longer bursts into their backs, stopping just shy of being without ammunition.

Lieutenant Sang and his reaction force, with Specialist Woolley were silent as they moved stealthily in the direction of the village road, taking advantage of the thickets to mask their secret withdrawal. Taylor's valiant deception had worked, allowing Sang to maneuver his force into a position where they would then launch a surprise attack against those VC entrenched on the east side of the besieged FOB.

Sergeant Taylor, Tony and the five Strikers paused to rest for a few minutes and then moved in a westerly direction for an hour before catching up to Sang's force 30 minutes after they had dislodged the VC from their siege of Khanh Binh.

Lieutenant Sang had led his men in a bold frontal assault with well coordinated mortar support from within and without the FOB. The previously confident VC who had maintained a stranglehold on our FOB by sheer strength of numbers, now found themselves caught between a two pronged attack from the south and east with withering fire from the defenders of the FOB. The constant raking of their positions by machine guns and small arms on two sides and the rain of high explosive mortar rounds in their midst caused a panic among their ranks. The now terror-stricken enemy searched for a way out of hell's fury and began to flee like a mob that had lost its leader, incapable of an organized defense, concerned only with putting this horror behind them.

Those VC who chose to go around the southern side of the FOB reached that area just as Major Le, with me at his side, led our attack with two platoons of Strikers abreast of us. Our supporting mortar barrage, initiated after Sang's force had proven victorious on the eastern side, left a pockmarked trail littered with dead and wounded VC to our front before it was lifted. The fear-crazed enemy were again caught in a savage death zone as our crossfire riddled their ranks. We continued across the field of fire and entered the FOB through breaches in the outer defense wire obstacles.

As Major Le and I took the time to relax for a few minutes, sitting back against trees inside the FOB compound, an enemy mortar round exploded about ten meters away, injuring three Strikers with its flying fragments. One piece of shrapnel, a little smaller than a Zippo lighter, sliced through the air and cut a path through my hair just above my right ear and embedded itself in the bark of the tree I was leaning back against. I turned around and pried the hot metal chunk out of the bark with my Bowie knife to keep as a souvenir. Major Le looked at me, smiled, and said, "You are very lucky, Dai-uy."

Lieutenant Sang reported to Major Le and told him of the brave exploits of Taylor's small crew. Major Le called for them to report to him, personally commended them for their actions which were clearly above and beyond the call of duty, and told them, "I will ask that you each receive a medal for bravery."

We lost six Strikers killed and 19 wounded in the Khanh Binh action while the enemy lost 84 killed and we estimated 150 VC were wounded and carried away. Many weapons were also found in the area where the VC had fallen, mostly Chinese made assault rifles and carbines.

It was 0700 on the 20th and a quick survey of ammunition reserves at the FOB showed them to be virtually nonexistent, even considering the truckload we'd brought in with our reaction force. That ammo was needed to resupply the Strikers' with their basic loads plus a back-up in their defensive positions. I asked Sergeant Taylor to call Ray Johnson and tell him to order a triple basic load of ammo for our camp. Jim got on the radio and told Ray in words Ray would understand, but some VC listening in wouldn't: "Tell Tiger that Dangerous Dan needs a triple issue of NRA stock. Must have today or he cashes in the chips. Got that, Ray?" Jim asked.

"Gotcha, Jim, I'll demand airborne express."

A group of Strikers and their wives worked alongside the LLDB medics and Specialist Woolley, treating the wounded and making field-expedient litters, using bamboo poles and mosquito netting to fashion them.

Everyone else not assigned to perimeter watch pitched in to help rebuild the battered defenses of the FOB. Priority was placed on installing barbed wire obstacles and replacing sandbags around the automatic weapons' positions, using wire and bags we had wisely stockpiled in the FOB, anticipating such a need. To help us prepare for future situations, Major Le and I would get together with some of our men that had experienced the last major action and develop a list of do's and don'ts to help us be better prepared for future battles. In this instance our previous analysis and our action to do some stockpiling of field fortification material in the FOBs paid off.

The last of the wounded Strikers, their dependents and villagers had been evacuated to the Bassac River pick up point at Dong Co Ki by 1030 that day. Assault boats took them to our aid station in camp as quickly as they could make the round trip.

We then started back down the road with our reaction force, having to shuttle again because the RF company at Khanh An had reclaimed their trucks to carry them back to their compound in Chau Doc. Thankfully, time was not of the essence for our return trip, so the three-round shuttle was not critical to us.

When Major Le and I arrived back in camp, we noticed a lot of activity in and around our postage-stamp size drop zone. Lieutenant John Strait ran to meet and welcome us back, sweating profusely from the waist up, looking well worn and tired but grinning from ear to ear. "The first bundles came in at 0930 hours, Thieu-ta and Dai-uy; you've got a surprise in that first batch, Dai-uy."

I asked, "What surprise, John?"

"You gotta see it. I'm not about to spoil it for you."

Major Le, as curious as I was about my surprise, walked with me out into the drop zone following big John Strait to a point where he turned and gestured to a big plywood sign propped up against the inner perimeter machine-gun bunker. "It was on the first bundle of ammo that hit the ground," John pointed out.

The three by four sign read, "GOOD LUCK DANGEROUS DAN, FROM TIGER TEASDALE." Tears came to my eyes as I thought out loud, "It's good to have a friend when you really need him!"

Ray Johnson brought word from the B Team that we would be getting two new men on the mail chopper today. They'd be attached for only six weeks. It would be an operations and intelligence Master Sergeant by the name of Edwards and Sergeant Cannon, a heavy weapons specialist. "That's the good news, Dai-uy, now comes the bad news. An estimated 200 VC attacked and surrounded the PF Outpost at Khanh Binh. There wasn't much left of it after the last big battle, and the VC are out to completely destroy it and everyone in it. Major Le took action as soon as he got word and ordered Lieutenant Hong Luong to use his company at Khanh Binh FOB to rescue the PF."

"Ray, I talked to Major Le a short time ago and we both believe the Viet Cong will do anything to take our northern area. With those two men coming in, I'm going to send Lieutenant Strait and Specialist Woolley up to make Khanh Binh a full FOB. Can you get their commo gear put together by 1700?" I asked.

"Sure thing, Dai-uy. I'll tell the XO and Woolley what you just told me so they can get their act together. They'll need a lot of gear to set up their quarters, the commo gear and to get settled in. The mail chopper will be here in a few minutes with our new men. I'll let Jim know right away."

I thanked Ray as he headed out to take care of those things. I wondered what we'd do without Ray and I hoped we wouldn't have to find out. Come to think of it, there wasn't a man on my team that didn't do the work of two, and I knew in my heart that I'd better not take them for granted. I'd try to think of some way to show I really appreciate what they've done and how I've come to rely on them. At 1730 hours, Lieutenant Hong Luong led two platoons of his 445th Company out of the Khanh Binh FOB and attacked the VC positions surrounding the PF Outpost located 2,000 meters north of them and near the border bridge. Preparatory fire from their 81mm mortar had softened the VC resolve to maintain their noose around the outpost. They fled across the border bridge into Cambodia as soon as they sighted the CIDG headed their way. The old outpost had been nearly leveled by the VC mortars and rockets. With the Strikers lending a hand the few PF remaining carried their dead and wounded, following Hong and his men back to the relative safety of the FOB. After emergency medical treatment, the PF not requiring evacuation were taken to the outpost at Khanh An where their added numbers were welcomed.

That same afternoon the sound of a woman's screams attracted the attention of two off-duty Strikers who happened to be walking by her house in Vinh Phu Hamlet just north of Camp on the west bank of the Bassac. They immediately ran into the house and caught a young man in the act of defiling the young woman. They lunged forward, grabbed the rapist and pulled him off the half-naked body of the still screaming girl. She quickly covered herself as the Strikers dragged the man out of her house and forced him to lie face down on the ground while they bound his hands tightly behind his back with a shoelace.

One of the Strikers recognized the pretty young girl as the wife of one of his friends who was on duty at the Vinh Hoi Dong FOB west of camp where dependents were not yet permitted due to lack of temporary quarters. He went back into the house, comforted her for a moment and told her, "We will take your attacker to camp to receive his punishment. Please come with us and see our Bac-si. He will examine you to see what you have suffered, then you must tell Major Le what happened."

Both Strikers waited outside as she got dressed. Then, with the prisoner between them and the woman walking close behind, the Strikers entered camp by the main gate. Sirois examined her, and with her at his side, reported his findings to Major Le. He left her with the Major to relate details of the attack and rape.

The death sentence was ordered according to our camp decree and carried out without hesitation. The rapist, who had been caught in the act, was beaten to death in front of many onlookers and his body was then removed from camp and taken to his family for burial. As I stood by Major Le and watched the now lifeless body being loaded onto a two wheel cart, I turned, looked at him and said, "Thieu-ta, this was justice: pure, simple, final and an example to would-be offenders."

"Yes, Dai-uy, that is true. He knew the law, and it is our duty to protect our people from such things. I hope, as you say, that it is a good example and that such a thing does not happen again in An Phu." As the shuttle trucks brought members of our reaction force back to camp, they would return to Khanh Binh with Strikers of the 441st Company going north to replace the 442nd at Khanh Binh. Once the 441st was in place the 442nd and their dependents would be trucked back to camp for a well deserved break.

Lieutenant Strait and Specialist Woolley took in stride the news they'd be going to the FOB. Coming from a meeting at sub-sector, John told me, "Mr. Minh said that 7,800 refugees have now passed through the checkpoint at Dong Co Ki. He says it is now all right to permit ARVN's big guns to go after the VC who have taken over that area. Captain Tuoi agreed and said he would inform Colonel Brewer and have the howitzers stand by to fire a mission."

"That's good news, John," I said, "those VIS guys are really a gutsy bunch, aren't they?"

"Sure are. " John echoed, "They not only got shot at when they went behind the VC lines to help the trapped villagers escape, they even fought like our Strikers to protect the people they were helping. They did a super job earlier too, when they evacuated the wounded from Khanh Binh to a place on the river where we could boat them to camp. They had a few casualties, but they killed quite a few VC too and let their number be counted. Just shows you the loyalty and brave support we get from all the people of An Phu."

I told Lieutenant Strait how much I appreciated his attitude about going back up where most of the fighting was going on. "You'll be controlling and directing artillery and air support, John, so make certain you've got all the right frequencies, especially for Spooky. Oh, almost forgot, you can take my hat if you want."

John smiled like only he could smile and reached out and shook my hand, saying, "Thanks, Dai-uy. I'd better get your Dangerous Dan hat and get ready to scat."

Within a few minutes the chopper came in with mail and our two new men. Jim Taylor went out to welcome them to camp and bring them in to meet with me in my office. Master Sergeant Edwards was a serious-minded master jumper with over ten years of heavy weapons duty, combat experience in operations and intelligence and looking to be in good physical condition. He seemed ideally suited to head up an isolated but important fire base. Sergeant Ralph Cannon, also a heavy weapons man and master parachutist, was heavier and shorter than Edwards and we would later learn that he had a good sense of humor.

"We're to get another new man on tomorrow's chopper. When his feet hit the ground, you two will take an 81mm mortar up north to Dong Co Ki and set up a fire base in the PF Outpost. That will be your home until we clear the VC out of our northern area or until your six weeks are up. No LLDB, CIDG or RF with you. Only PF and your radio to keep in touch." Pointing to locations on a tactical map on my desk, I told them, "You'll support the FOB here at Khanh Binh and the one at Khanh An on a first call, first mission basis. Captain Tuoi will provide an interpreter and he'll be here in the morning so you can get to know each other. If all goes as planned, you'll be on your way by truck at 1600 hours tomorrow. If you've got any questions, save them for Jim Taylor. Edwards, I know you understand that your being attached for such a short time means you'll be answering to Team Sergeant Taylor though you outrank him."

"No sweat, Dai-uy, I'm just here to help any way I can."

"Good attitude, Sarge. Taylor will take you both from here to the operations center and brief you in detail on the enemy situation and team policies. Okay, Jim?"

"Will do, Dai-uy."

Lieutenant Strait, Specialist Woolley and Tony Trung reported to Lieutenant Thuan Nguyen at the Khanh Binh FOB at 2030 hours on the 20th of May. No sooner had they set up their tent, familiarized themselves with the mortar pit and ammunition storage and checked out their air-to-ground communications when enemy flares lit the sky over their heads. Looking at Woolley, Big John said, "Looks like it's going to be gangbusters for us. Those aren't our flares!" And they weren't! Lieutenant Nguyen and his men didn't have to wait long to feel the brunt of a Viet Cong attack as an estimated 800 VC of the 261st, 267th and 510th VC Battalions attacked the FOB at 2045 hours their first night back at the FOB. Using recoilless rifles, rocket launchers and light machine-guns in an attempt to soften the FOB's defenses, they then assaulted and threatened to overrun the 441st CIDG Company defenders on the south side of their defensive perimeter. Within minutes Thuan asked Major Le for help to relieve the situation. ARVN 155mm howitzers were first brought into play as we requested Spooky, the AC-47 flare and gunship, known also as "Puff the Magic Dragon," for close ground support. In the interim, John's 81mm mortar and the ARVN howitzers proved effective in temporarily halting the enemy advance, their HE finding the target. All indirect fire was lifted as Spooky arrived on the scene only 20 minutes from the time we radioed for support to our C Team in Can Tho. The AC-47 was controlled by Lieutenant Strait, with target determination made by Lieutenant Thuan in an excellent joint operation using air to ground radio and smoke grenades to signal the location of targeted enemy locations and friendly forces. On its first run over the VC assault force, Spooky dropped flares to illuminate the battlefield.

Major Le and I, from our vantage point in the camp command bunker, aided by high powered binoculars, witnessed the flare and gun runs as they played out dramatically before us, though some 14 kilometers distant.

The VC would immediately drop to the ground and lay prone when the area was lit by flares or airborne flood-lights, knowing they would otherwise present a silhouette target easily hit by the FOB's defenders. What they didn't consider was, by laying prone, they presented an excellent target for Spooky's 7.62mm

Gatling guns as they spewed out 6,000 rounds a minute from above. The next run of the AC-47 was death-dealing to the attackers. Lawrence M. Greenberg, in his article *"Spooky": Dragon in the Sky"*[3] writes eloquently of the gun runs, telling the reader, "As the VC went to the ground, a roar, as if from some unseen dragon, filled the night as streams of fire and death licked the earth from above, directed at the guerrillas below. Faced by a devastating new weapon, the VC withdrew." Indeed, Major Le and I watched as the tongues of flame extended from Spooky to the enemy who lay in that target area where a red hot bullet hit in every square foot of ground.

Lieutenant Strait would recall communicating with the gunship, which he referred to as "Puff," on his PRC-25 radio. "Puff, this is Challenge. VC have anti-aircraft machine-guns on north side of Bassac River 3,000 meters north of our position. More of same on east side of Bassac another 3,000 toward the east from here. Over."

The pilot responded, "Roger, Challenge. I'm going to make a dry run with my floodlights and get the lay of the land. Over."

. "Roger, Puff. The VC are within 100 meters of our southern defenses. Look for red flare to locate our southeast corner. Over."

John picked up his HT-1 radio and called for Lieutenant Hong to fire a red flare from the southeast corner bunker. Within seconds it arced up, lit and then dropped down into the wire obstacles nearby the bunker. The drone of Puff's mighty, lumbering engines were soon heard approaching.

The pilot switched on his powerful floodlights, bathing the entire area in bright light for a half mile in all directions. "I roger your red flare, Challenge. Enemy in clear view. No need for flares. Next run is live so keep your heads down. This is a tough area to maneuver in. Over."

John responded, "Roger, Puff, and thanks. Standing by."

The pilot circled over Khanh An, staying clear of the river, but drawing heavy anti-aircraft fire from the 512th Heavy Weapons Battalion located due east of the FOB and inside Cambodia. He called again, "Challenge, this is Puff. We are receiving heavy fire. This is our only run but we'll do our best. Good luck to you guys. Over."

Puff made its run, cutting loose with its rapid-firing Gatling guns. Woolley, who could also mouth some eloquence when he wanted to, remembered it "as a tongue of flame spewing out of its belly, piercing the air with a dancing tip of death, licking the ground and laying waste to everything in its path."

Strait got on the radio, "Puff, this is Challenge. You saved our buns. Thanks a bunch. Over."

"Challenge, this is Puff. Glad we could help. Good luck, and by the way, you were right about the AA guns. Over."

"Puff, this is Challenge. Did you get hit? Over."

"Roger, Challenge. We took three .50 caliber slugs in the belly. No big deal. See you around. Out."

As the VC pulled back from the FOB, Big John and Woolley pounded their retreat route with the 81mm mortar, adding to the VC casualties, further demoralizing their ranks. Though forced to retreat from their southern approach, the VC continued a more limited attack from the west, firing almost point blank from the Cambodian Outpost facing our FOB. At 0300 hours on 21 May the VC broke off their attack on Khanh Binh FOB, fleeing back deep into Cambodia, leaving 14 of their dead behind. They were seen carrying or dragging another 36 of their wounded comrades as they retreated. We lost one Striker killed, two wounded and one .45 caliber pistol in that battle. "Thank God for Spooky," I can now reflect. What that pilot and crew did, in coming to our aid, was to not only set aside their fear of the enemy's anti- aircraft machine guns we'd warned them of but to venture into forbidden territory because of the close proximity of the border with Cambodia. Thank God they cared more about all of us on the ground than their own skin, politics and possible disciplinary action for breaking "the rules." The VC continued to occupy the area above Lake Bien Thien Lon except for our FOB at Khanh Binh, the Khanh An PF Outpost and their surrounding fields of fire. They doggedly probed our other FOBs and outposts to keep us occupied defensively. At the same time they were able to bring in replacements and more weapons to build up their fighting strength for an even more aggressive push to take control of our district and the Bassac River down to the Province Capital at Chau Doc. That was their goal as we would learn from documents we captured later.

Major Le and I discussed the need for some outside help to clear the enemy out of the northern area. Reports of 80 VC digging deep trenches and stockpiling ammunition in caches southwest of our Khanh Binh FOB, within 100 meters of Bien Thien Hamlet, concerned us. Casualties had taken their toll on our fighting strength, and with 30 Strikers in the hospital, we were 100 men short. We agreed that we had to retake the enemy occupied areas and begin immediately to rebuild housing and infrastructure. As Major Le put it, "We must allow our refugees, almost 8,000 now, to return to their villages. And it will help also to relieve the strain on our over-committed resources." Immediately following our meeting, I sent a priority message to Colonel Brewer asking for reinforcement. We would need two Mike Force companies to assist in clearing the occupied area in a joint ARVN/RF/PF/CIDG operation scheduled for the 24th, just three days away. Major Le requested the RF companies be returned to assist in the operation and asked for an immediate VNAF air strike to deal with the new threat near Bien Thien.

Within 20 minutes of Major Le's call, four VNAF fighters arrived above the VC trench area with a forward air controller. He took instructions from Major Le who directed multiple rocket and strafing runs against the entrenched VC and their ammunition caches. They received heavy ground fire during their mission, but completed it unscathed. The FAC reported four secondary explosions and estimated that 30 VC were killed by the low flying, prop-driven fighter aircraft.

Sergeant Clark, a heavy weapons man, came in by assault boat from Chau Doc. "I'm just here for two weeks," he told Sergeant Taylor, "but I'm yours every minute of it. I heard you guys have had a tough time up here."

We liked him right off. He was a barrel-chested, robust sort of man, with ears that lay close to his head, a short, thick neck and a good attitude. "We're sure glad to see you, Sarge," I told him. "You'll be going up to our FOB at Phu Hiep for as long as you're here. We need to get John Eleam back here to work with Ray Johnson in the communications bunker. Team Sergeant Jim Taylor will brief you and take you up to the FOB ASAP. Any questions?" I asked.

"No, Sir, I'll do whatever I can."

Taylor then took Clark to the operations center for a detailed briefing, and within an hour they and an armed CIDG security force were on their way to Phu Hiep in three assault boats.

At the same time, Master Sergeant Edwards and Sergeant Cannon headed up to Dong Co Ki on a $2^1/2$ ton truck with their personal gear, an 81mm mortar, 200 rounds of HE, 20 WP rounds and radio gear. A platoon of Strikers led the way in another borrowed $2^1/2$ ton truck as security. By 1800 hours they had established a temporary FOB with a mission to fire in support of the Khanh Binh and Khanh An areas. An interpreter from sub-sector joined them at the outpost.

A CIDG Company of 105 Cambodian KKK (Khmer Kampuchea Krom) fighters, all members of that Cambodian religious sect, from A-429's SF camp, with two Green Beret NCO advisors, arrived on B Team trucks and was attached for reinforcement. When Jim Taylor returned from Phu Hiep with John Eleam, I asked him to inspect the KKK company. Within 30 minutes he'd returned to my office and told me "These guys are no where near ready for a combat mission, Dai-uy."

"What's wrong, Jim?"

"No radios, not enough ammunition for their shoulder weapons, and they have no machine-guns or hand grenades. Not one in the whole company, Dai-uy, and the attitude of their two sergeants stinks. They're just not ready for combat, but I don't blame the Strikers. I chewed the two sergeants out, and if we had more men on our team I'd ask you to send these guys packing and let one of us take over."

"I understand, Jim. See what you can do to shape 'em up. Let 'em know how I'll deal with them if you have to send them to me. Restrict the whole shebang to camp tonight and then take them up to 100 meters or so south of the PF Outpost at Dong Co Ki to set up a bivouac site at first light. I'll get on the horn with Colonel Brewer and let him know the sad state of that company. Tell Ray to loan them two machine guns and a PRC-10 radio. Give 'em a triple basic load of ammunition and hand-grenades.

"If you can't get that outfit shaped up by noon tomorrow we'll send 'em packing and I'll arrange for a court-martial for those two route-step sergeants. Okay, Jim?"

"Sure thing, Dai-uy. I'll do my best. How they got to be Green Berets I just can't figure out. It's hard to believe that we're hurting that much for replacements."

That evening saw a repeat of the previous two nights with attacks by VC battalions against Khanh Binh. Spooky was again called into action after a pounding of the VC ranks by the ARVN artillery and the FOB mortar manned by Lieutenant Strait and Specialist Woolley. This time Puff winged its way through heavy anti-aircraft fire without a scratch, helping to drive the VC back across the border after a three and a half hour battle. The 81mm mortar at Dong Co Ki was also called into action to hit the border canal area about 100 meters north of Tac Truc PF Outpost, just out of range of the Khanh Binh 81mm mortar. It was directed by Lieutenant Strait via radio, with target acquisition data coming from a CIDG ambush patrol at the western tip of Lake Binh Thien Lon. That patrol sighted about 100 VC getting ready to cross the canal, most likely to reinforce the VC attacking Khanh Binh. Five heavy ropes were being secured in place across the 40 meter wide canal, a waterway too deep to ford. To obtain maximum casualties and cause considerable psychological trauma, they waited until all the ropes were in place and watched closely until they could see three or four VC hanging by their hands in mid-canal and treading water at each rope crossing, and then gave the order to fire. It was relayed through Big John to an anxious mortar crew that did their thing, lobbing ten rounds of HE into where the struggling VC were caught unawares, doing so accurately without a marker round!

After the dust of battle settled, we learned we had lost three Strikers killed and ten wounded. VC casualties were 12 killed and 24 wounded in the vicinity of the FOB and an estimated 65 killed or wounded at the rope crossing area.

A CIDG Squad on combat patrol from the Vinh Hoi Dong FOB engaged a VC Platoon in a 20 minute fire-fight near the village of Phu Hoa at 1320 hours. The VC were getting ready to board sampans they'd stolen from the villagers and cross the Chau Doc River, perhaps on a mission to attack the ARVN Howitzer location at Phuoc My. When they saw our Strikers coming toward them along the river's west bank they abandoned the sampans and struck out across the open fields toward the border with our men in hot pursuit. The CIDG patrol killed three of the enemy while sustaining no casualties. They captured an M1D sniper rifle in the death grip of a young VC killed in that action. The words "Best Sniper Award - Bac Dai" were engraved on a half-moon shape brass plate affixed to the stock of the rifle.

Lieutenant Triet Tran, the FOB commander, had a notice placed on the bulletin board of Bac Day, Vietnam's sister village to Cambodia's Bac Dai (1,000 meters up-river). The notice told of the young VC and the award winning plate on his sniper rifle. The mother claimed her son's body and Lieutenant Triet was compassionate enough to let her take his rifle too after he'd had the barrel plugged. I liked what Triet did and hoped that I would be as understanding of an enemy mother's need.

The KKK Company, now equipped properly for battle, was moved to its bivouac location, departing camp at 0700 hours by a combination of truck and assault boats with Team Sergeant Taylor along to monitor their combat readiness and brief their two SF Sergeants on call signs, radio frequencies and order of battle, both friendly and enemy. The assault boats returned with Jim Taylor aboard. Once in camp he found me in the operations center and signified the readiness of the KKK Company with a thumbs up, telling me, "It wasn't easy, Dai-uy, but I hammered some combat sense into those two noncoms. I think they'll do just fine. Right now they're more worried about you than they are the VC!"

A report received from Major Le's agent net at 1900 hours on 22 May told of the VC having sustained over 400 killed in action in the Khanh Binh area and verified that the 267th Battalion Commander, Vo Hoang Chien, and the Commander of the 2/267th Company, Hong Son were killed by our forces. The total strength of the 2nd VC Company had been whittled down to 30 men.

At 2030 hours an estimated 600 VC from the 261st, 267th, and 510th Battalions attacked the Khanh Binh FOB, using their 76mm mountain gun, mortars, machine-guns and small arms in an all-out attempt to breach the defenses of the FOB. Accurate support by ARVN 155mm Howitzers, the FOB's 81mm Mortar and Sergeant Edwards' mortar in Dong Co Ki turned the tide of battle, forcing the VC to retreat into Cambodia, to a deeply trenched area west of AP III hamlet at 2100 hours. In that half hour of furious fighting, we lost two Strikers killed and 13 wounded, four of them seriously. The heavy firepower of the FOB's reinforced company, together with the excellent artillery and mortar support caused the VC to lose 79 killed and 44 wounded in that same action.

I had Ray Johnson put in an urgent request for helicopter gunships to attack the VC who had settled in near AP III. "Have the lead ship pick me up to guide them to the target, Ray."

"I'll take care of it, Dai-uy."

A report received at 0500 hours on the 23rd from sub-sector agents told of the 260th VC Company digging in about 1,200 meters above the Khanh An PF Outpost, near the west bank of the Bassac River, armed with three light machine-guns, one anti-aircraft machine-gun, and at least two rocket launchers. Their mission: Stop Puff!

Mike Force Company A-430, with 65 Chinese Nungs and their three Green Beret leaders, arrived by chopper ready for combat at 0900 hours. I briefed the Lieutenant and his two sergeants on the tactical situation, order of battle and their role in the clearing operation that was scheduled to kick off in just 23 hours. I pointed out their bivouac location on the map and asked if there were any questions. The commander, a young Lieutenant of Puerto-Rican ancestry, asked that heavy artillery or air-strikes be brought in to level the villages that stood between his bivouac location and the enemy objective on the border canal. "I don't want to take any chances going through those villages, Captain," he told me.

"Lieutenant," I told him, "those are our villages, not the enemy's. There won't be any of that kind of thing going on in my district." I told him.

"Hey," he told me, "They're all gooks and how do I know who the enemy is?"

"Like Major Le told me when we had our first discussion on that subject, 'The enemy is the one shooting at you.' It's just that simple, Lieutenant."

"Listen, Captain, I'm not leading my men through that area unless I can level those huts first."

"You said it, Lieutenant. In fact, you're not leading them anyplace here in An Phu. As of this moment you are relieved of your command. You go get your stuff together and get on down the road to B-42 and report to Colonel Brewer. I'll let him know you're on the way and I'll put one of my men in command of your company. Now, get out of here before I get real mad."

"Yes, Sir, Captain, I'll go, but I'm going to tell Colonel Brewer what kind of an operation you're running out here."

I looked him narrowly in the eye, lowered my voice and told him, "Do it, Lieutenant. Do it."

After appointing Sergeant Taylor as acting commander of A-430 and briefing the two sergeants who had come with the Nungs of the changed command situation, I sent a message to Colonel Brewer explaining my actions and asking that the Lieutenant lose his SF status. Within the hour all of A-430 were in their choppers and en route to where they would set up a bivouac area 600 meters southeast of the Khanh Binh FOB with Jim Taylor in command.

I called Ray Johnson in and asked that he quickly alert Lieutenant Strait at the FOB to expect the Mike Force Company and to explain Taylor's role to him. I continued, "also get with Sergeant Hung and have him send two trucks with a CIDG Platoon for security to Dong Co Ki to pick up our mortar, ammo and crew and take them to the FOB at Khanh Binh where they'll remain overnight. Tell Edwards too. Sorry I have to load you up, Ray. I'll be glad when Jim is back here with us."

Ray nodded in agreement and headed back out to the commo bunker, writing on his note pad as he went.

At 1100 hours a platoon of gun-ships arrived over our camp and the lead ship swooped down, picked me up, and headed north towards Khanh Binh. The pilot took us up above small arms range and I pointed out the trench area near AP III as we flew parallel to and east of it. "There are at least 100 VC down there," I told the pilot, "but no anti-aircraft guns in that area that we are aware of." I went on to show him where the .50 caliber guns were that hit Spooky two days prior and the new anti-aircraft machine-gun location reported above Khanh An just six hours earlier.

We circled over the Mike Force bivouac area and started on the attack run. My adrenaline was surging as the flight leader took our ship down in a steep dive, leveled off just above the bamboo thickets, and bore down on the VC trenches. The other choppers followed in trail close behind. I watched as he pulled the trigger mechanism that launched many rockets into the trenches below, most of them hitting the target. We drew heavy small arms and light machine-gun fire from the VC below, but none hit their mark.

The next run was a strafing run, coming from the opposite direction not more than 40 feet above the enemy. He cut loose with his machine guns, firing directly into the trenches while seeming to ignore the intense ground fire directed against us. Like so many rag dolls, the enemy's bodies were slammed against the walls of the trenches or, for those who attempted to abandon the trench and leave for the safety of Cambodia, thrown backward into the knee high grass by the shower of machine-gun bullets.

I was able to get a fair handle on the number of VC in the trenches as we zipped along above them, with the other choppers following suit, unloading their machine-guns on the exposed enemy positions. I estimated that 200 VC occupied those trenches when we arrived on the scene. After the final strafing run, we flew above small arms range and I was able to count 16 bodies from that distance. I had no doubt they'd gotten many more than that during their rocket and strafing attacks. I would estimate 50 VC killed and another 40 wounded. When we sat back down in my camp I shook hands with the crew and thanked them for helping us out.

Team Sergeant Taylor, after getting the company of Nungs settled in near Khanh Binh, judged that the Mike Force Green Beret Sergeant was well qualified and capable of leading the Nungs in battle. Taylor asked me to give that Sergeant command of the Nungs.

"Done, Jim. Let him know and wish him well. Tell him I'll see him in the morning before we kick the operation off."

Everything was set in place, like the lull before the storm. We would now rest, with anticipation of the next day's battles. All we could do was hope that it was enough for "the winning edge."

* * * * *

CHAPTER 11
VICTORY AT KHANH BINH

It was the kind of letter[1] a soldier dreams of receiving, particularly when facing a tough and demanding situation. Kate wrote me on the 26th of May from our home in Ithaca, New York, "My Dearest Danny, Received your letter[2] dated 20 May today and my heart and prayers are with you as never before. I know you and your people are doing a brave and wonderful duty and you must be an inspiration to everyone in your camp. As always, I'm so very proud of you both as a soldier and as a person.

"I do appreciate your writing all that goes on there. If it were possible I'd be by your side so I'm happy to share (through your letters) your life there even when the news isn't too good. I know it doesn't sound practical for American wives to be in such places but you are my life and what happens to you happens to me anyway and I do long to be with you no matter where it may be. I do thank God our girls have never had to share what the children there do. They are indeed brave and it is so heart-rendering to realize how they must love and respect their Daddies. Our prayers are for them also and I promise I'll long remember this and so much else if ever we get dissatisfied ... "

B y early morning of 24 May we had brought together all forces available for the clearing operation and assembled it near Khanh Binh without undue risk to the security of the rest of An Phu District. The mission was to take back the area between Lake Binh Thien Lon and an imaginary line drawn between the Khanh Binh FOB and the Khanh An PF Outpost. The larger enemy-held area north of that line would have to remain in their hands until the ARVN armored unit promised by Colonel Brewer was on the ground and ready to spearhead the attack.

The concept of Mike Force availability to reinforce camps threatened by overwhelming enemy strength was wise and we were going to learn just how valuable that concept was. The Mike Force companies of Cambodian KKK and Chinese Nungs were a perfect fit in our attack strategy. We felt confident that we would return most of the occupied area to our control. With Major Le at my side to afford me the benefit of the wisdom he had gained during almost two decades in combat, I would command the multi-lingual operation. Using interpreters whenever feasible, but relying on hand and arm signals and coded blast sequences from my "thunderer" whistle I would relate simple combat orders to direct desired actions that we'd met on and planned in detail in the marshaling area.

All units were in place at 0800 hours: A-430 with two USASF and 65 Chinese Nungs on the right flank near the Cambodian border canal 200 meters southwest of the FOB, where we expected the stiffest resistance; A-429 with two USASF and 105 Cambodian KKKs in position on the left flank, beginning 1,000 meters west of An Thanh Hamlet to clear the area north of and closest to Lake Binh Thien Lon; and our reinforced 446th CIDG Company with Lieutenant Strait, SFC Johnson, SP-5 Sirois, two LLDB and 200 Strikers. Their mission was to clear the center portion of the target zone and reinforce the other units if called. Our mobile Command Post, mounted on two jeeps and a ¾ ton truck, included Major Le, myself, SP-4 Woolley as commo man, a US Air Force FAC (Forward Air Controller) and 12 Strikers from the 442nd CIDG Company for security. The CP was initially located 200 meters behind the center of the attack elements where an 81mm mortar fire support base, manned by the CIDG Recon Platoon, would remain to provide indirect fire support of the clearing operation. East of the Command Post and covering the area between the northeast tip of Lake Bien Thien Lon and the Southeast corner of our Khanh Binh FOB, MSG Edwards and Sgt. Cannon with two LLDB Sergeants put in position a blocking force consisting of 70 Strikers from our 445th CIDG Company. Their mission was to protect against interference with our clearing operation from the VC units occupying the northern area.

At 0817 hours the ARVN 155mm howitzers began pounding the VC positions we would be attacking with a pre-planned 13 minute barrage to soften their resistance. At 0830 we began our assault with pre-planned support from the CP Fire Base and FOB lobbing high explosive rounds 500 meters in front of and parallel to our line of advance, continuing to soften the enemy's defenses even as we advanced. The Mike Force Nungs made first contact, coming under intense machine-gun and small arms fire from an estimated 200 well-entrenched VC dug in along the tree-lined border canal west of the FOB. Pinned down for a few minutes out in the open, the Nungs rallied under the courageous leadership of their American Green Beret Sergeant who led the way across that open area, charging into a hail of enemy bullets, firing an assault weapon into the enemy's ranks and reloading his weapon as he moved forward with his other Sergeant and their Nungs now alongside. Seemingly fearless to the enemy, they now rushed as a dedicated combat unit. Their hand-held weapons spewed out death and destruction among the enemy forces who had the advantage of cover but lacked the courage and fighting spirit of those highly motivated Mike Force Nungs. To those who weren't physically present on that field of battle, what I said might sound like so much poetic nonsense, but to those who were there and who took part or witnessed an impossible victory where freedom won out over Communism by the sheer strength of courage and faith in our cause it was more like an answer to prayer. It did happen. The VC, who had outnumbered an attacking force that lacked cover and concealment, were forced to cut and run, retreating into Cambodia where the politics of a compromising White House, unchallenged by the less than courageous US Troop Commander, General William Westmoreland, provided them the protection that those who had made it across the border would enjoy.

Major Le and I received word during the operation that an important radio message was intercepted by sub-sector. It was a plea from the Commander of the VC's Southward Regiment to the Cambodian Minister of Defense asking for help from the militia in their border outposts until reinforcements arrived from another area. It told of the casualties the regiment had suffered since the start of their campaign on 19 May. They claimed 532 killed in action and 312 wounded by the forces of An Phu. "Those are higher figures then ours because we do not know how many dead they carried back and how many wounded made it back across the border," Major Le told me, "and we do not know that they are true figures. Maybe he speaks bigger numbers to make the Cambodians feel sorry and want to help them more." Smiling, he looked at me and added, "But, you know, Dai-uy, I would like very much to believe what they say in this message is true."

"Me too, Thieu-ta. We will learn more before the day is over how strong the enemy is now since they have suffered so many losses."

The Sergeant commanding the Nungs, the same NCO who rallied them during the initial assault, was the first US casualty, wounded by a booby-trapped mine as he led his men to do their part in sending the VC packing into their safe havens inside Cambodia. By 0930 hours all of our attack elements were receiving machine-gun and rifle fire from an estimated 450 VC in shallow trenches they'd hurriedly dug roughly parallel to our line of advance. A great many barbed-steel punjis, embedded in fire-hardened bamboo had been set in shallow, camouflaged traps that saturated the area in front of us. The Green Beret Sergeant who was leading the KKK Company against the entrenched enemy, stepped into one of those traps. The tough steel punji penetrated the armor insole of his jungle boot, speared his foot with a buffalo dung coated tip, poisoned his blood and took him out of action.

Howitzer and mortar fire was directed at the newly discovered trench-line and an air strike was requested at 1015 hours. In less then 20 minutes, we lifted the howitzer and mortar fire and marked our forward positions with yellow smoke grenades to allow three American F-100 fighter-bombers to exact a deadly toll on the VC in those trenches. With the FAC guiding from an excellent position atop our $^3/_4$ ton truck, they laid down a scorching bath of napalm directly into the trenches on their first pass, circled and fired rockets into the bamboo thickets directly behind the trench line where the VC command element was situated and where their anti-aircraft guns were positioned. Finally, on the third and final pass, they expertly strafed the entire VC line and the thickets, totally disrupting the enemy and causing them to abandon their positions and bolt across the border. Our men in the KKK unit and our own CIDG company then laid down a withering stream of fire into their fleeing ranks while our mortars were again put into play, dropping HE into their escape area by the border canal. The Nungs were quickly moved to cover that same crossing area by the alert Sergeant who now commanded the Mike Force Company. As the mortar fire was lifted, they blocked the retreat of the enemy forces, resulting in the capture of 47 khaki-clad NVA troops.

All told, in a little under two hours of actual contact with the enemy, we counted 48 enemy bodies on the ground and in the trenches. We would have to wait on possible capture of enemy reports or interception of their messages to know how many were wounded and fled or were carried across the border to safety. Our casualties were so light that Major Le and I found it hard to believe. Two Americans were wounded and, as a result of having US casualties, we received a med-evac helicopter for the first time in An Phu. We lost none killed among any of the units, but did have seven Nungs, six KKK and three of our own Strikers wounded. The med-evac chopper carried all the wounded in two runs from the battle area to our camp aid station for treatment.

We learned that multi-lingual operations were feasible, in this case very effective, and an excellent example of a type of flexible response that would serve all of our camps up and down the border area. By noon the next day A-430 with all their Nungs and A-429 with their Cambodian KKK CIDG company intact, even the wounded men from each company, were taken by a fleet of helicopters back to their home bases.

Major Le rotated companies, sending the 442nd from camp to Khanh Binh and bringing back the 441st. Lieutenant Ba and I visited the Phu Hiep FOB in the afternoon of 25 May and I had a good talk with SSG Clark and SGT Brown who, by that time, were well grounded in FOB operations and very capable of providing excellent mortar support of their combat forays near and into Cambodian territory. Lieutenant Ang Nguyen told Lieutenant Ba that he was very pleased with both Sergeants.

Early in the morning of 26 May, Sergeant Eleam came into my office with a message in his hand. "You're not going to like this, Dai-uy," he said as he handed me the message.

He was dead right; I was not happy. It seemed some MACV Major whom I didn't know (and didn't want to know) was telling me that he wanted a complete investigation to account for the ammunition we claim to have expended in the recent battles. By that I assumed he meant that our emergency ammunition request exceeded his expectations. "MACV is not happy with the rounds expended to body count ratio," he wrote. Until that moment I'd never heard tell of such a ratio. I did know we were careful not to use B-52s, 155mm Howitzers or any other heavy ordinance unless it was absolutely necessary. We never did use B-52s in An Phu and relied more on our fighters and their individual weapons to win the battles and to protect the citizens of An Phu. I looked up at Eleam, wrote a short reply on a piece of scrap paper and handed it to Eleam, telling him to make certain he referenced the MACV message and its sender. "I wouldn't want the wrong person to get it," I told Eleam.

He looked at my three word message which read simply, "GO TO HELL," then eyed me and said, "You're not usually a man of few words, Dai-uy, but when you are I'm sure glad I'm not on the receiving end."

Colonel Brewer made good on his word to provide armor and troops sufficient to clear the enemy-occupied northern area. Together with Province Chief Major Re, he brought a clearing force up the Bassac River on US Navy landing craft and debarked at Dong Co Ki at 0900 on 27 May, 1966. The force they had assembled was impressive with an ARVN full colonel commanding the task force, which consisted of an ARVN Infantry Battalion, an ARVN Recon Company mounted on armored personnel carriers and two RF Companies. Major Le and I joined the command element, while providing the 446th CIDG Company with Lieutenant Sang Ngo commanding to join in as part of their assault force.

Sang would lead his Company through the area on the east and north sides of the Khanh Binh FOB and sweep the area from there up to the border crossing bridge where the border canal meets the Bassac River.

The reconnaissance company was selected to clear the area southwest of the Khanh Binh FOB where we last saw heavy action. They were the only attack forces to meet resistance, encountering heavy machine-gun and small arms fire from the tree line along the border canal and the trench area near AP III Hamlet. A 20 minute fire fight ensued in which the VC found themselves trounced by the more powerful firepower and armored mobility of the Recon Company, as Colonel Brewer witnessed in the lead APC. The VC withdrew into Cambodia, leaving 39 bodies in An Phu per a count by Colonel Brewer. He estimated another 64 were killed or wounded and carried off the field of battle. There were no friendly casualties.

After liberating the area in and around the villages of Khanh Binh and Khanh An, Major Le and I, along with the ARVN Colonel and Major Re, surveyed the devastation wrought by the enemy. We were shocked by the extent and degree of destruction and vowed we'd never forget the losses our people suffered during those eight days of enemy occupation. At the same time we felt a great sense of relief, finding not one dead villager among the ruins of hundreds of shops and homes that had been reduced to smoldering ashes, twisted metal and scorched earth. Not one body, not one animal carcass: testimony to the wisdom and strength of conviction that Major Le and I were somehow able to muster when we forbade Lieutenant Colonel Brewer and Province Chief Re from bombarding the area with heavy artillery while the people were yet there, hostage to the VC. Even more, it was testimony to the courage and resourcefulness of Mr. Minh and his VIS personnel who selflessly engineered the dark of the night clandestine exit of the villagers from what would have been certain death at the hands of the Viet Cong occupation or by the high explosive barrage of ARVN's 155mm Howitzers.

Once the entire area had been cleared and the RF Companies were firmly in control, the force brought up river by Colonel Brewer, Major Re and the ARVN Colonel assembled near the Khanh An PF Outpost where their landing craft waited to carry them back to Chau Doc. General Thi Quang Lam, Commanding General of the 9th ARVN Division, then flew in by ARVN helicopter, congratulated the commander of the clearing force and visited the outpost. He presented bravery medals and heroic action bonuses to the PF fighters and the CIDG Recon Platoon from our camp that had fought alongside the PF at Khanh An. This activity was reported in a Saigon newspaper[3].

I was impressed that a Commanding General would come to such a remote outpost and even more impressed that he would be prepared to recognize their bravery under fire with medals and bonuses. It was something the South Vietnamese did very well, knowing it was important for morale and esprit de corps. Time and time again I'd seen Major Le, Major Chuan and Captain Tuoi recognize their men for bravery, sometimes within hours of a battlefield victory. I couldn't but think that by the time one of our men was awarded a medal, the memory of what he'd done to earn it had all but faded away.

After the informal award ceremony concluded, General Lam flew off in his chopper; the clearing force boarded the LCUs and departed for Chau Doc.

Once again, it was just us against them. We knew too, that with help during difficult times, we could hold our own! We were strong because, as Major Le put it so aptly, "We had good successes because we had a very good relationship between us, our troops and the civilians in An Phu. I hope that young people in schools would understand what is Civic Action in the war before going into the Army."

Rebuilding began in earnest with all of us, Americans and South Vietnamese alike, pitching in to help in any way we could. Priority of effort went to medical assistance, then came the rebuilding of bridges, homes, maternity houses and schools. As soon as a home was put together for a family to move into, that same family would help others, even shopkeepers to rebuild all that had been destroyed.

The Catholic Relief Agency coordinated all church sponsored relief. They worked together with JUSPAO, USAID and Province Social Services, and were most helpful in taking care of the immediate needs of the people. Knowing that women and children suffered so much in this war, we did our best to keep the war at a distance from our villagers, but we didn't always succeed. When we failed, it was they who paid the horrible price: 34 of our civilians were killed and another 141 injured during the first two days of fighting in the northern area. Though refugees in the recent past, most having lost their homes and many their livelihood, they were nonetheless a proud and resilient people who now worked together to rebuild, holding their heads high while doing so.

On 29 May, the 260th VC Heavy Weapons Company placed harassing fire with their 82mm mortar on our PF Outpost at Vinh Hoi, southwest of our camp and about 3,000 meters distant. During counter-fire support, our camp's four-deuce accidentally dropped a short round into the hamlet of Phuoc Thanh, killing a young boy and slightly injuring his mother.

Lieutenant Strait, Bac-si Sirois and interpreter Jean Pham, along with Mr. Minh, the VIS chief and his assistant visited the boy's mother to express our regrets and to console her. John Strait explained that it was faulty ammunition that killed her son and wounded her. The outpost had called for our support, requesting we destroy the enemy mortar that was bombarding the outpost. That outpost protected her village. "The neighbors were all gathered around the home when we got there, and together with the VIS we gave the family food, clothing and blankets to replace some of what was lost when the explosion occurred," John told me on return to camp. "If there was one thing that was obvious to me it was that these people cared about each other. It's like you told me when I first got here, Dai uy, the Hoa Haos are like one big family that cares."

On the 30th we scattered thousands of leaflets, dropping from a civilian airplane along the length of our western border with Cambodia, allowing the east wind to carry them into the enemy's Cambodian sanctuaries. While others labored to help the people recapture a sense of normalcy, my attention was directed to preparing the Monthly Operational Summary[4] that seemed like an endless list of reports due shortly after the end of the month. A huge effort, but important if a record of unclassified information was to be available for statistics and future application as a resource of facts. Few would otherwise know of the tremendous effort that went into intelligence,[5] civic action,[6] psychological operations[7] and logistics.[8] In our civic action role we could boast about the first crop of field corn being harvested this month in An Phu and in having 250 farmers signed up for the next years seed corn. We saw the construction of a boat dock and three bridges completed and were involved in the construction in progress for eight schools and latrines in our area.

In psychological operations we were meeting ourselves coming and going trying to keep up with the demands that came with many battles and especially enemy take over of an area that encompassed two large villages. 8,000 newspapers were distributed throughout the district, 260,000 leaflets handed out, placed on bulletin boards all across the area and dropped from civilian aircraft. 1,250 posters were designed, printed and posted on bulletin boards, walls, and trees. 215 loudspeaker appeals were made to assembled groups totaling 20,200 people using the Lambretta mobile loudspeaker system. Another 141 group meetings were held with an attendance of over 10,900 and 27 movies were shown with some 15,000 looking on.

Only five scheduled medical patrols were conducted, treating 552 civilians. Most medical support and treatment effort was restricted to the battlefield and our aid station in camp.

Combat statistics were still being adjusted by numbers shown in captured documents, but the following figures represent a fairly accurate picture of what happened during the month of May in An Phu: 532 VC KIA, 684 VC WIA, 51 VC captured, 112 weapons and 337 mines seized. We lost 46 CIDG KIA, 122 WIA and two USSF WIA, and five of our weapons were captured. A total of 35 civilians were killed and 141 wounded. A total of 7,800 refugees were cared for during the eight day occupation of the northern area by the VC.

Sergeant John Eleam left on the 31st of May and we all wished him well, hoping he'd make warrant officer. We needed people like him as warrant officers, the truly expert people in their field.

On the 2nd of June, I received a letter Kate had mailed from home on the 26th of May.[1] It was the kind of letter a soldier dreams of getting, particularly when in a tough and demanding situation. She wrote, "My Dearest Danny, Received your letter dated 20 May[2] today and my heart and prayers are with you as never before. God be with you and may you feel all the love we have for you both now and always.

"I know you and your people are doing a brave and wonderful duty and you must be an inspiration to everyone in your camp. As always, I'm so very proud of you both as a soldier and as a person.

"I do appreciate your writing all that goes on there. If it were possible I'd be by your side so I'm happy to share (through your letters) your life there even when the news isn't too good. I know it doesn't sound practical for American wives to be in such places but you are my life and what happens to you happens to me anyway and I do long to be with you no matter where it may be. I do thank God our girls have never had to share what the children there do. They are indeed brave and it is so heart-rendering to realize how they must love and respect their Daddies. Our prayers are for them also and I promise I'll long remember this and so much else if ever we get dissatisfied as at Yuma.

"This is a short letter because it is so very full of feeling. Somehow a regular chat just doesn't come as I write and yet my love is bigger. My heart and soul are with you my sweet, wonderful Danny and more love then even you shall ever know. We love you - We love you - Yours Forever, Kate and Your 3 little ones."

Major Le and his men took the time to decorate the camp in preparation for a big victory celebration planned for 4 June. Morale was high in camp and in the district at large as we prepared to show off our exploits to visiting dignitaries and enjoy a real food feast.

Even the Lord contributed to the celebration with a glorious day of uninterrupted sunshine without the usual monsoon rains. The air was dry and there was a light breeze, like frosting on the cake for a day that would be special in all our hearts.

Shortly before we were due to begin, the air was full of helicopters bringing the many VIPs to camp for the celebration. One of the first to arrive was someone I was eager to meet, Lieutenant General Quang Van Dang, the Commanding General of the IV Tactical Zone. Major Le had spoken very highly of him as a leader of men and a man who respected the Hoa Haos. I met him as he stepped down out of the chopper, accompanied by Colonel William Desobry, his senior American advisor. General Dang had a pleasant manner and a firm handshake, and unlike most higher ups I'd known, he didn't scorn to talk to a lowly Captain such as myself.

A few minutes after some light conversation with General Dang, Colonel Desobry called me aside, wanting to discuss the ammunition investigation ordered by MACV. We were interrupted by Major Le's urgent request that everyone please take their seats. Colonel Desobry was clearly not happy with the message I'd sent back to MACV and the look in his eyes told me that he was not done with me yet.

There were speeches and ceremonies. General Dang presented bravery medals and heroic action bonuses to many of the Strikers and Major Re presented the Vietnamese Cross of Gallantry to a number of men cited by Major Le for their bravery under fire during the five day battle, including Lieutenant Strait, Specialist Woolley and myself. Major Chuan, the LLDB C Team Commander, announced the promotion of all the CIDG Company Commanders to First Lieutenant as he pinned their new insignia of rank on each of them.

After the ceremony, we took the VIPs by helicopter to Khanh Binh where they toured the scene of the many battles, visited the FOB, and walked through the devastated villages, even seeing where the Khan Binh PF Outpost had been leveled to the ground by intense attacks of the VC. The cruel scars of destruction were still painfully evident and many of our visitors wondered aloud how any had survived. Even Colonel Desobry was impressed. He turned to me as we were boarding choppers for the return trip, shook my hand and said, "Forget the ammunition investigation. I've seen enough."

On return to the camp I learned from Major Le that Tuoi was now to be called Major Tuoi. I called on the field phone and congratulated him on his well deserved promotion. "We have a good team now here in An Phu," he told me, "that is why we have so many victories."

"Yes, Thieu-ta, you are right and I am proud to be with you, Major Le and the Hoa Haos."

I was then treated to a glimpse of Communist propaganda when Major Le handed me a translated excerpt (Appendix 6) from the Cambodian neutral news-paper TRUNG-LAP,[9] published in Phnom Penh, Cambodia on 23 May. Reading that perverted report of our recent five day battle, you'd think we had lost the war, not the VC. "They try to win in the papers when they cannot win on the ground," Major Le told me with a broad grin, adding, "but we know who really won, Dai-uy!" The real story of the five day battle was published in a Saigon paper and translated[10] into English for us to read. After seeing the article, I was doubly glad that I'd already written[11] Kate on the 24th telling her the truth of what had gone on during the battles.

We moved the 441st CIDG Company into the Khanh An PF Outpost and established a special FOB there, while bringing the reconnaissance platoon back to Camp. The 442nd CIDG Company was withdrawn from Khanh Binh FOB to have available in camp to support our reaction force capability.

We had some changes in personnel with Bac-si being med-evaced for malaria and possibly blackwater swamp fever, Sergeants Clark and Brown left An Phu to rotate back to the States and Sergeant Olanda Gore came to beef up our team a little. Gore was a senior jumper and a much appreciated heavy weapons man.

We got what we thought was a gift from higher headquarters when two river patrol boats (PBRs) reported to me for duty on the Bassac River. Major Le and I were both excited at first because the PBRs had a tremendous amount of .50 caliber firepower, speed and maneuverability. We saw them as a good addition to our reaction force capability. But I soon learned that they were not permitted to go within six kilometers of the border and, within hours of their deployment on the Bassac we received numerous complaints from our local fishermen and others who needed the river for their everyday existence. They were being swamped by the fast moving heavy boats whose captains seemed to care less about the local people. During their first three days on the river they'd swamped more than 100 sampans without getting within firing range of the enemy.

Major Le and I got our heads together and decided they did us more harm than good. I called in the Navy Lieutenant who was in charge of the two PBRs and ordered him to take his boats out of our district, never to return.

Colonel Brewer fumed when he got word that I'd countered his orders for them to patrol the Bassac River. I sent a note to Colonel Brewer which probably did little to diffuse the situation, but it told him why I did what I did and also let him know that I compared the policy of restricting the PBRs from going near the border as being in the same class of ignorant thinking as was the case with whoever dreamt up the VC sanctuaries. It was not good company!

* * * * *

II Thessalonians 2:12 — *That they all might be damned who believed not the truth, but had pleasure in unrighteousness.*

CHAPTER 12
MISSION: ASSASSINATE A PRINCE

As I turned to exit the command bunker, with Major Le close behind me, I looked CIA agent Walter Mackem in the eyes and told him, "You can tell your 'highest authority' just what I told you. If President Johnson insists the enemy be permitted to have their sanctuaries inside Cambodia, I refuse to send my people to risk their lives to kill Prince Sihanouk." Major Le smiled.
Mackem glowered at me, turned and went down the stairs in front of us to join Lieutenant Strait who would escort the agent to his waiting helicopter. Before he'd gone two paces toward the chopper with John, he turned, glared and shouted out to me, "You can't fight the system, Captain, because you know you can't win."

It was early in the morning on the 10th of June, already 85° in the shade, and the humidity hung in the air like a wet blanket. Wiping the sweat from my brow I continued to analyze the latest agent reports Jim Taylor had laid on my desk earlier, just before breakfast. He'd noted on the cover sheet, "Looks like the Southward Regiment is recruiting well and should be back to full fighting strength soon. They're deeper inside Cambodia, but my guess is they're getting ready to hit us again."

The screen door that opened into the operations center and briefing area from our command and communications bunker slammed with a loud noise as Ray Johnson rushed through the building to my office, handed me a message, and blurted out, "From the B Team, Dai-uy, it's a hot one!" Short and to the point, it read, "Company man en route your location. ETA 0900." I glanced at my watch. It was 0820.

"Hot all right Ray, but not the kind of heat I expected. Wonder what they're up to?"

"Got me, Dai-uy. Didn't you expect a monumental chewing out by Colonel Brewer for telling the Navy to stay out of our area?"

"Sure did. I figured he'd bust a gasket, call me on the carpet, order me to let the PBRs run loose on the Bassac and try to Court Martial me. We'll know soon enough who the spook[1] is and what he wants in An Phu. Tell Lieutenant Strait to meet me at the chopper pad and ask Jim Taylor to clear the area around the command bunker. I'll meet the company man up there. Once you've done that, I'd like you to stay close to the communications bunker in case I need to call you on the field phone, at least until our visitor has come and gone. Okay?"

"Sure thing, Dai-uy, Woolley is holding down the fort while I'm gone, but I'll be there when you're upstairs with Mister CIA." The screen door slammed once more as Ray headed out to locate Strait and Taylor.

Colonel Brewer wasn't one to ignore junior officers countermanding his orders. He'd sent the two Navy patrol boats up the river into our area and I'd ordered them out of An Phu, even threatening to fire on them if they ignored my demands. Colonel Brewer made no pretense of his dislike of me in the past, so I was baffled by his silence at my actions against the PBRs thus far. I surmised that the "company" needed something from Brewer and they'd told him to stifle his anger until whatever they wanted done was accomplished.

John Strait joined me as I started across the inner compound toward the chopper pad. "What's up, Dai-uy?"

"I don't know, John."

The sound of the incoming Air America helicopter signaled the arrival of our visitor. The small white chopper set down on our landing pad without any fuss. A short, muscular man, whom I'd guess to be in his mid-thirties, wearing khaki slacks and a short-sleeve, gray shirt slid out of the chopper and walked toward me. A black leather shoulder holster with a .38 special was tucked under his armpit and a thin, black leather briefcase dangled from his left hand. A young, attractive, blonde woman followed out of the chopper close behind him. She wore tan colored slacks and blouse, carried a note pad in her right hand and had a purse slung over her left shoulder. She was a surprise visitor. I would keep her out of range of any conversation I had with the spook. He flashed his ID. It read: Walter Mackem, CIA, and had a photo of his likeness. Reaching out to shake my hand, he said, "We need a place we can talk, Captain." Turning to Lieutenant Strait, he introduced the woman, whose name I cannot recall, telling John, "You can talk to her. She's a radio reporter."

Looking more like a professional model, with lots of long, blond hair being tossed about by the wash from the slowing rotor blades, she smiled and reached out to shake John's huge outstretched hand. John, taking the hint from Mackem, motioned the woman to follow him and led her away from us and on into the team dining area. Jim Taylor and Marvin Woolley were already there, having a cup of coffee.

> *Years later, John would record for me on audio tape,[2] "About the CIA visit in June. I thought it was kind of a flimsy cover, because [Mackem] came in [with this woman] and left her with me and said, 'You can talk to her, she's a radio reporter.' But she never asked a damn thing. She just sat there and BS'd with us. I thought that was kind of crazy for a reporter.*
> *"I kinda figured something was up there, but just kinda let it go. If you need somebody to back your story, damn it, I guess I could do it."*

And the agent Mackem. I'd met him before but didn't recall right off when or where. Then, like a picture out of the past, the time and place suddenly came to mind. It was five months earlier that I'd refused Mackem's counter-terrorist (CT) team entry into An Phu District. It was somewhat confrontational. I'd even penned a note as part of my continuing effort to document a kind of "insurance policy for me" telling of my distrust of Mackem and the whole business of CT teams operating under the auspices of the Phoenix Program. We didn't need strangers in our midst who would make independent judgments without consulting local authority and who would imprison or assassinate whomever they determined to be VC sympathizers. I told Major Le at the time that "I'd rather anger them and their bosses in the Phoenix Program than adversely affect the almost perfect relationship my team enjoyed with the LLDB, the Hoa Haos of An Phu and their leaders."

> *A reliable source in the B Team at Chau Doc had told me of messages sent by Mackem directly to Washington about political activities of various religious sects. "Even the Hoa Haos," he told me. It was about that time that I closed the district to all Americans unless I personally cleared them.*
> *In his book,[3] "The Phoenix Program," Douglas Valentine writes, "Behind every province chief, of course, was a CIA paramilitary officer promoting and organizing the CIA's three-part covert action program. Walter Mackem, who arrived in Vietnam in early 1964, was one of the first. After spending two months observing the CIDG program in Ban Me Thout, Mackem was transferred to the Delta to institute similar programs in An Giang, Chau Doc, Sa Dec, and Vinh Long provinces. Mackem also reported directly to Washington on the political activities of the various sects and favorable ethnic minorities in his area of operations, the most important were the Hoa Hao (Theraveda Buddhists) and the closely related ethnic Cambodians, the Khmer."*

Mackem asked if we had a secure place to talk.

"Follow me," I said, leading him toward the command bunker and up the concrete steps to the deck area behind the .50 caliber machine-gun. "This is where

Major Le and I come when we are in camp and there is enemy activity anywhere along our border area." Standing there, one could view the entire camp and much of the Cambodian border area. "You can't get any more secure than this, Mister. What brings you here?" I asked.

He very matter-of-factly told me that the Agency had been asked to dispose of a very delicate situation. He looked around suspiciously before unlocking his briefcase and removing a folder stamped with the words "TOP SECRET" in bright red letters in both top and bottom margins. "We've been asked to terminate Prince Sihanouk. Yours is the closest Special Forces Camp to Phnom Penh; you've got all Hoa Haos in your CIDG and their record is good. We want you to take care of it, Dangerous, because we believe you can get the job done." With that he handed me the file folder.

"You want us to assassinate Crown Prince Sihanouk?" I asked, not really believing he'd come to ask us to kill Cambodia's head of State. "Don't get me wrong, I've got no love for Sihanouk, but don't you have some of your own people in Cambodia who could make the hit?"

I knew Sihanouk had severed diplomatic relations with the US early in May of 1965 and none of us liked the fact that he allowed his territory to be used by the VC as a safe-haven from which to attack us from. At the same time I'd been told by a reliable source in the 5th Special Forces Group chain of command that it was President Johnson himself who permitted the enemy their sanctuaries inside Cambodian "neutral" territory. My source told me it was even "against the wishes of South Vietnam's Premier: Ky Cao Nguyen." It appeared evident that those in the US Embassy who controlled the money going into Saigon's coffers, who decided how many American troops would be allowed in South Vietnam and how much of what kind of weaponry would be made available were who really called all the shots. Lack of confidence in their own people, forces and capabilities allowed the Saigon leadership to mistakenly think of their dependence on Americans as their only hope to win the war against Ho Chi Minh's Communist intruders.

"Yes, Captain, we want you to do the job." Mackem went on to tell me their analysts had determined that the Cambodians would take up arms against VC and NVA forces and push them back into Laos or North Vietnam if their Prince was thought to have been killed by the Viet Cong. "Your job," he went on to say, "will be to bring about his death and make it appear to have been done by the VC."

I opened the folder and began to study its contents, telling him, "I'm not certain about this and won't be until I've given it some study and discussed it with Major Le. It'll be his men we send in to do the job and the risk will be theirs, not ours." I briefly scanned CIA intelligence summaries that spoke of Sihanouk's comings and goings. It detailed the number of vehicles and strength of the security forces that accompanied him, and pinpointed possible ambush sites as well as the nearest Cambodian military garrison that might be expected to respond to an ambush. The key to the timing of this mission was a planned trip by Sihanouk to the port of Kompong Cham that would take him north on Route 6, through a narrow pass and over a timber trestle bridge south of Skoun, Cambodia, on the 23rd of June.

"It's a big job, Mackem. It means crossing the border undetected, moving over unfamiliar ground and water a distance of 160 kilometers, conducting the ambush and then returning that same distance through a gauntlet of Cambodian militia who would, by that time, be on a high state of alert. After threading their way through that mess, our men would be heading into and through areas controlled by Viet Cong forces if they were to reach and cross the border back into An Phu." I concluded in a not too friendly tone of voice, "What you've brought to us is a suicide mission with a short time fuse."

He looked rather angrily at me and told me that he was "well aware that these missions are inherently risky," demanding to know if I would accept the mission.

"I'll need topographical maps covering the area from our Khanh Binh PF Outpost north to Phnom Penh and then through Skoun to Kompong Cham. I will also need current strength and weapons data on every Cambodian garrison near the ambush sites and also all along the routes of ingress and egress. Once that information is in hand, I'll meet with Major Le and we will decide within 48 hours."

"Good," Mackem said. "I'll have it to you in two days. I need a decision within a week or I'll have to go to another camp to get the job done."

I looked him in the eyes, "If you had an alternate plan, you'd have it in the mill as we speak. You're not dealing with a novice, Mackem. I have to be convinced it's a workable plan before I'll ask Major Le for volunteers. It's as simple as that." By the time I'd finished we were nose to nose with little space between us.

The look on his face told me he didn't like hearing what I was saying and that he just wasn't used to confrontation of any kind. "Do you have some kind of a problem, Captain?" I didn't respond but I stayed right in his face.

He backed off a little, sucked in his gut and stuck out his chest as if wanting to appear bigger and fiercer than he really was. In the harshest tone he could muster, he told me, "This mission is from the 'highest authority.'" I could have laughed in his face and wouldn't soon forget his almost comical attempt at intimidation. Did he think I was stupid? Who else but President Johnson, our highest authority for sure, could order the assassination of Sihanouk?

"Listen to me, Mackem. I wasn't born yesterday. You know all that President Johnson has to do is declare the sanctuaries past history and let us all go after the enemy no matter what direction he goes. It has to be that way before I ask our Hoa Haos to risk their lives to kill the Prince. President Johnson must do it and tell the American people what he's done."

The folder went back into his briefcase which he locked in a single, practiced motion of his hand. "I'll be back in two days," he said "and then I'll want a decision fast."

"No problem," I responded.

Within a few minutes Mackem and the blonde woman were back on the white Air America helicopter, airborne and heading toward Chau Doc.

In less than an hour I met with Major Le and went over the details of my conversation with Mackem, including my demands of President Johnson. "What do you think, Thieu-ta?" I asked.

"We must think long and hard once we have what you asked for in our hands and have time to study it, Dai-uy. I do believe it is possible and I am certain we will have no problem getting many volunteers among our Strikers. You were wise to demand an end to the safe havens, Dai-uy. I wonder what your president will say?"

"I also wonder, Thieu-ta. When Mackem returns, we will meet with him together in the command bunker. You are a good judge of character and I'll be anxious to know what is your initial reaction to Mackem. Okay?"

"Sure, Dai-uy, and I think it will be a good time to discuss the matter of Communist ships taking war supplies like ammunition to the VC inside Cambodia. Just two days ago I received a report from two of our agents who had watched a large ship with a foreign flag off-loading thousands of wooden crates clearly marked with weapons or ammunition at an enemy-controlled dock inside Cambodia. Those things were quickly taken by canal and over land to the new Bung Ven Secret Base north of Phu Hiep to help rearm the Southward Regiment. The situation has not changed since early last January when you and I visited Tan Chau Camp. You remember how the SF, the LLDB and even the National Police were only permitted to inspect the cargo manifest and not the cargo itself on those ships that go into Cambodia on the Mekong River. This kind of wicked deception that helps the enemy must be stopped, Dai-uy."

I pulled 3x5 cards from my pocket and made notes as Major Le was talking. "I agree, Thieu-ta, and I'll lay that on Mackem when he comes back."

Major Le laughed and chided me about the index cards. "Is your memory in the cards, Dai-uy?"

His laugh was contagious. I finally blurted out, "It works for me, Thieu-ta."

On schedule, Mackem returned on 12 June, only this time he was alone. As soon as he was on the ground and the Air America engine silenced, Major Le and I walked to meet him. Mackem and I shook hands, but he chose to ignore Major Le's outstretched hand, exchanged greetings with me and acted as if Major Le wasn't there, though he had himself tendered a friendly welcome and offered his outstretched hand to Agent Mackem.

Mackem rambled on about the weather and other mundane matters of little consequence on the way to the command bunker, directing his conversation at me and ignoring Major Le. As I grew increasingly angry with Mackem's rude and obnoxious behavior, Major Le noticed the color in my face grow scarlet and my voice assume an angry tone. Reacting as the true friend and gentleman of honor that he was, he touched my arm and told me it was "no problem." Such grace, I thought. And Mackem? He was just a CIA puke.

Once inside the command bunker, I told Mackem, "Major Le has agreed that the sanctuaries must be officially terminated and the public informed of that fact by the President of the United States before we would accept such a dangerous mission." It was now Agent Mackem's composure that appeared shaken and even more so when I made him aware of our unshakable opposition to Communist ships or any other large ocean-going ships being permitted to deliver war goods on the Mekong River to our enemy in Cambodia. "Those weapons and ammunition are used to kill and wound our people," I told him, "and that too must be stopped if you want us to take out Sihanouk."

Mackem only glared at me and then, not wanting Major Le to hear, spoke close and directly into my ear, saying, "I want to discuss these matters with you, I don't deal with Vietnamese."

I told him point-blank and loud enough so there would be no doubt that Major Le would hear, "You'll either deal with both of us or not deal at all. It's as simple as that!" With obvious reluctance he pulled out a large folder and a number of topographical maps from his briefcase.

"These maps cover the area all the way from Khanh Binh to the port of Kompong Cham." Pushing them aside he laid out two tactical maps with overlays marked to show potential ambush sites inside Cambodia and the route that Prince Sihanouk would take on the 23rd as he traveled to visit the Mekong River port. Mackem pointed out what he considered to be the preferred ambush site, an ideal location in our judgment also, in a narrow pass southwest of Skoun Village. The nearest reaction force was in Skoun and that force would have to cross a timber trestle bridge on Route 6 between their outpost and the ambush site to come to Sihanouk's rescue.

"The bridge could be blown to block vehicular traffic," Mackem offered, "and with no likely place to ford on either side of the bridge, the reaction force would have to disembark and continue on foot, giving your men time to get out of there."

I turned to face Major Le and conferred openly but quietly, my back to Mackem. I then faced Mackem and told him, "We have what we need to accomplish the mission." I also let him know that we both thought he'd done an excellent job putting the plan together.

Smiling, he said he'd like to see our plan, including infiltration and exfiltration routes. "When will it be ready?"

After conferring once more with Major Le as I'd done before, I responded, "We'll be ready in a week but you won't be seeing our plan. I reminded him of our need to have proof that President Johnson had officially ended the sanctuaries and that it had been made public. "An article in the New York Times to that effect will get the job done. I won't take anyone's word for it, unless it is published for all the world to see." I added, "In case you wonder how I'll know it was published, I'll call a contact at Fort Bragg and ask him to read the article to me. I'm not about to accept some special company edition of the paper you had printed up just for me."

He snarled a response, asking just how would I get someone at Fort Bragg on the phone. "You know as well as I do, Mackem. I think it was CIA instructors at Bragg that taught us about the ionospheric bounce."

That really got his blood boiling. He'd figured I was bluffing and that he'd called my bluff, but my reference to the bounce shook him to the core. No bluff here. He now knew I wasn't guessing or pretending and that I meant what I said.

"Remember," Major Le said to Mackem, "we will accept the mission, train my people and be ready to get the job done on time, but you've got to come through with your end of what Dai-uy has asked from your White House before we step foot inside Cambodia."

I interjected, "That means the sanctuaries and the Mekong River traffic too."

Major Le continued, "As far as your seeing any part of our plan, that will not be possible. You must remember that we want to make sure our people don't get ambushed on this side of the border when they return. It is possible that your people may not want any witnesses, but we want our men back."

Mackem became livid with rage, too angry to respond for a long minute. He closed his briefcase, leaving what he'd brought for us to use, and stood glaring at me. In a quaking voice, he warned, "People like you don't make demands of the CIA. You know how the system works."

"Only too well, and that is why we must do everything in our power to protect our CIDG. You can be confident, Mister, if you make certain our demands are met, we will see that the job is done on this end."

Not happy, but his business finished for the moment, Mackem left. No cordial farewell, not even a handshake for me.

Major Le and I agreed to meet after lunch in the operations center and start putting the pieces together for our plan. We also agreed to keep this entire matter close to our chests, at least for the time being. The less exposure the easier the deniability if the mission were compromised. Those who knew little or nothing would be a lot safer if this thing were to blow up in our faces.

I carried the folder and the maps from the command bunker to my office. Sergeant Jim Taylor stopped by just as I had everything spread out on my desk. "What's going on, Dai-uy?"

"It's a special project, Jim. Eyes only for Major Le and myself for now. I need time without interruption from now until noon. I'll be meeting with Major Le after lunch in the briefing area. Make sure nobody disturbs us. And I mean nobody! Okay, Jim?"

"Must be something hot, Dai-uy."

I told him it was just in the planning stage. "Once we have a go, I'll tell you and the rest what you need to know."

"Want me to get the XO, Dai-uy? You got to tell someone what's going on. What'll happen if you get zapped or med-evaced?"

"No, I don't want the XO, I don't want anyone right now. The answer to your question is simple, Jim. Just make real certain that nothing happens to me."

Jim left my office muttering something under his breath.

I began putting things together for the mission that I'd dubbed *Operation Snuff Crown*. An interesting play on words, I thought. The ambush site Mackem suggested seemed best to me also. It was 17 kilometers to the nearest hamlet where troops were stationed and within a mile and a half of a decent exfiltration route with sufficient jungle cover to mask cross-country movement almost the entire distance to the Mekong River. We'd have to send our volunteers up the Bassac River to Phnom Penh, then into the Mekong and north to a point closest to the ambush site. Debarking at night in an area between hamlets, they'd then go by foot 16 kilometers to where they'd set up the ambush and prepare the timber trestle bridge for demolition.

My idea for their return would be to take a more-or-less parallel path back through the jungle to a pre-designated pick up point on the Mekong River. From there they could quickly ride the current and head south past Hoa Hao Village to the cross canal which they'd take over to the Bassac and back to camp.

Organization of the ambush party needed careful consideration and I was now anxious to meet with Major Le and take advantage of his almost two decades of combat experience. We would need a command element, demolition party, security force, boat crew and the ambush force itself.

I outlined training requirements, special equipment and supplies needed then estimated the number of men each party would call for in a planning paper.[4] Finally, I made a list of administrative tasks: securing volunteers, obtaining a boat and other matters relating to the mission. After I'd reviewed it a few times, I typed it up with a carbon copy for Major Le.

By then I'd missed lunch. I secured everything except the unclassified, unmarked topographic maps and went to the kitchen for a bite to eat. Finding everyone gone, even the cook, I heated a can of chicken-noodle soup, grabbed a box of saltine crackers and a big hunk of cheese and had my own version of a feast.

I met with Major Le at 1300 hours and laid out in front of him all that I'd put together. He liked the plan. As we discussed the mechanics of getting our men to the ambush site and back we began to realize how much would hinge on our ability to get the right boat. "It must be a boat the border police recognize, one that has crossed the border many times before without incident," Major Le suggested. "An unfamiliar boat would draw suspicion when our men would attempt to take it up river. I will meet with the Police Chief and obtain a list from his customs team of the owners of boats that have trafficked across the border many times in recent months." He said he'd tell the Police Chief a story about needing supplies to take to people he was recruiting in Cambodia for a special mission. "I will ask the Chief to go with me to speak to the boat owners of those boats large enough to do the job and we will hire one of them."

"Good thinking, Thieu-ta. Let me know how much you need and I'll have the cash available. What if nobody is willing to do what you ask?"

"We will commandeer the one we want. This is war!"

With a break for supper in the CIDG mess, we continued massaging the plan until after midnight. I mostly listened and learned as Major Le detailed how best to accomplish the ambush, bridge demolition and the roadblock that would be placed south of the ambush site. We left no detail to speculation, taking advantage of Major Le's 18 years of wartime experience, resulting in what we both felt to be a tight and workable plan.

"I will ask for volunteers after breakfast," Major Le told me. "They will be told only that it is a very dangerous ambush operation outside of our area that we train for. No mention will be made of place or target. After we select from the volunteers we will seclude those men in camp and begin to train them for the mission. When we have given the green light to Mackem we will then tell them the missing details of our mission. Sound okay?"

"Sounds good, Thieu-ta. I will tell my men our plan."

After breakfast on the 13th, as Major Le stood before his assembled Strikers asking for volunteers, I briefed my men on Operation Snuff Crown and gave copies of the planning paper to Lieutenant Strait, Sergeant Taylor and Sergeant Johnson. Telling them the training must begin on the 14th, I instructed John Strait to meet with Lieutenant Ba as soon as we broke up and get squared away on LLDB cadre support and scheduling. I asked Ray Johnson to get what was needed for a "sterile" operation. "It's okay to use our HT-1 radios," I told Ray, "because the Southward Regiment has many that they stole from supply rooms in other camps or captured in battle. Just use your head and make certain, between you and the LLDB cadre that these volunteers carry nothing that would point to this camp. No family photos, no money, nothing. Oh, don't forget to make certain we have sufficient unmarked black pajama uniforms to issue each man two complete sets. Beg, borrow or steal what is needed so we have it all in just five days. Okay, Ray?"

"Got it, Dai-uy. I'll do my best."

"With Bac-si in the hospital and four of our team in the FOBs, it's going to be tough sledding to get the training done in time and in good order. You know better than I do how fortunate we are to have good men available in the LLDB to team up with. I feel confident, with their help, you'll be able to get the Strikers ready for this mission. Lieutenant Strait will be meeting with Lieutenant Ba as soon as we're done here, and each of you will get together with your counterpart to develop a training plan for the area you're responsible for. Remember, we start training at 0700 in the morning and everything except boat drill must be completed in four day's time. If this mission is a go, our Strikers have got to be prepared. If they're not ready they won't be coming back; it's as simple as that. Major Le is out in front of the flagpole right now talking to his men and asking for volunteers for what most others would call a suicide mission. Whoever volunteers and is selected by Major Le to go deserves the best equipment for the job and the best training we're able to muster.

"For your own future protection, Major Le and I are keeping you in the dark about the specific mission you're training these guys for. Once we decide to accept the mission and after our men are in the boat and headed up the Bassac you will be told all that you need to know. It will be TOP SECRET. No answers to any of your questions until then, so don't ask any."

To a man, they accepted what I'd told them and asked no questions. I don't know for certain if I could have done the same. John Strait, in his 1988 recollections[2] on audio tape, remembered it this way to me: "I always figured something like that [the assassination mission] was coming down due to the fact that you kept some intelligence from me, there was a change in training and some of the other things that were going on. But I didn't get involved in it or question people too damn much because I didn't think it really involved me at the time. I'm not sure when you got the mission. But these people [the readers] can doubt you, but my experience with you, damn it, if you said you had a mission, you did. I don't doubt it, not for one minute, which I don't know if it's any consolation to you. But I'm sure if you'd decided to carry it out, it would have gone and it would have been a success."

Looking first at Lieutenant Strait, I began to give each man his specific role in what lay ahead. "John, you'll oversee land navigation and escape and evasion training. Jim, you and Sergeant Hung will work together to make certain the demolition party knows how to destroy a timber-trestle bridge using C-4 and those new electrical detonation systems. Make real certain they are familiar with how to use claymore mines to block a road, using a combination of trip wires and remote detonation. Ray, besides the load I've already put on your back, I want you to head up communications training. You don't have to instruct, but make certain the best of the LLDB commo people are doing the teaching with emphasis on the importance of maintaining radio silence when necessary. This is a very dangerous and highly classified operation. One slip-up and they're dead meat. Simple as that."

I told Woolley he'd supervise first aid instruction with emphasis on field IV injection using blood expander and practical work in putting together field compress, splint, IV and bandage kits they'd carry with them. "Don't worry about ID on any of that stuff. The VC, NVA and even the 'Cambodes' have a lot of what we have. Some they bought, others stolen and yet other stuff was taken in battle. So much has changed hands and a good share of what we have is unmarked, so don't worry about being ID sterile. Ray will get you whatever you need. We're short interpreters with our two FOBs, so use Nurse Co Lau to help in the training and as your interpreter. Okay?"

Woolley nodded.

I continued, "The LLDB is going to make up a phony paper that each Striker will carry with him that would, if he were captured or killed, make him appear to be a VC pretending to be a South Vietnamese irregular. Something different will be on each Striker: mundane, even personal, yet tying him to someplace or something under Communist control, even a Viet Cong unit or village."

Flash, excited and anxious with news he wanted to share with us, burst into our midst and shouted, "Major Le has gotten 102 volunteers for the mission and Lieutenant Luong Hoang Le has asked to be their leader. And, Dai-uy," he added, "they were told it would be a suicide mission."

We rose to our feet as one and cheered the courage of our Strikers.

With that, I dismissed everyone so they could get busy then I disappeared into my office to draw up the Snuff Crown[5] planning paper with situation, timetable, training, special equipment needs and major challenges all laid out, simple and hopefully complete. I personally delivered a carbon copy of the paper, along with a map[6] showing routes to and from the ambush site near Skoun to Major Le and congratulated him on his success at readily obtaining volunteers for the mission. I also gave copies without the map to Lieutenant Strait and Sergeant Johnson.

Major Le smiled, thanked me for the paper and said, "We will screen 50 men from our brave volunteers to begin their training in the morning. I am sure your men will be ready to do their part."

"Yes, Thieu-ta, they will be ready."

"One more matter, Dai-uy," he spoke now in a very serious tone, "we must have absolute proof that your President Johnson has taken away the enemy safe-havens before we send our men into danger. We will not sacrifice our men to a politician's whims." Tears welled up in Major Le's eyes as he spoke. He loved his men.

I reminded Major Le of what I had told agent Mackem in Le's presence about my having proof from someone I trusted at Fort Bragg. "We will not sacrifice our men, Thieu-ta. You have my word on that." I asked him to review the planning paper very thoroughly and let me know where any changes were needed before midnight. It was 1900 hours. He agreed.

As I prepared to leave his office, Major Le received a message telling him that a MACV Advisory Team — to arrive in camp on 27 June — would replace our team. "One day after our mission force is back if we go with the CIA's plan, Thieu-ta. Not much time to dispose of what must remain secret."

Our team would leave a week later, the day the CIDG were scheduled to be converted to Regional Forces. "This is bad news for An Phu," He said.

"General Harold K. Johnson wants us out of Vietnam. It's so stupid, Thieu-ta. They will send away the people who work best with the South Vietnamese against the enemy insurgents."

"Perhaps," Major Le suggested, "if we do this job they will let you stay?"

After shrugging my shoulders at what he'd said, I left Major Le's office feeling a sense of disgust at what senior US officers were doing by removing the Green Berets from the very kind of war we were trained and best suited for. All they had to do, I thought, was to look where the South Vietnamese were holding their own, ask why and discover the truth. Our record in An Phu would surely stand the test. Putting the notice of the MACV team coming to An Phu in the very back of my mind, I continued toward my office still awestruck by the fact that more than half of the

CAMBODIA

⑥

AMBUSH SITE

⑥ ㉒

● SKOUN

● KOMPONG CHAM

⑥

PHNOM PENH ★

MEKONG RIVER

BASSAC RIVER

SOUTH VIETNAM

Camp Dan Nam

CHAU-DOC

HATIEN

★ SAIGON

GULF OF SIAM

CAN THO ○

HAU GIANG RIVER

MOUTHS OF THE MEKONG

SOUTH CHINA SEA

SPECIAL OPERATIONS MAP #7

OVERVIEW OF OPERATION "SNUFF CROWN" · JUNE 1966

Strikers in the camp, when told of a need for men to go on a suicide mission, had volunteered to be a part of it! The Hoa Haos were a gutsy bunch.

As it now stood, assuming all went according to schedule, our ambush force would be back in camp the day before the MACV advisory team was scheduled to arrive. We were all aware of the special precautions each and every man had to adhere to if we were to deny that we had taken any action against the enemy inside Cambodian territory. Poorly defined borders on hard-to-read maps, coupled with a well-documented history of faulty Korean War vintage ammunition, especially 4.2" and 81mm mortar rounds that we were forced to use, comprised the foundation of our denial "cover" stories. We would continue to play a stupid game of subterfuge unless President Johnson came through and made it clear that the enemy could no longer use Cambodian territory as a safe-haven.

Later on the 13th of June, Jim Taylor completed an analysis of recent agent reports and sub-sector intelligence, prepared an updated Intelligence Summary[7] and brought it to me. "Doesn't look good, Dai-uy," Taylor said as he laid a copy on my desk along with a map and an overlay showing friendly and enemy orders of battle. Pointing to a location just inside Cambodia and north of the Stoeng Takey River, he advised, "They've moved the 364th VC Battalion to within easy striking distance of Vinh Hoi Dong FOB and also our camp." He told me that their 76mm Mountain Gun could reach our camp from its present location. "Smart move on their part, Dai-uy. They can hit us but they're just out of reach of our four deuce."

"Right, Jim, but Fox and Gore can take that out if they can find it with their 81mm mortar at Vinh Hoi Dong. Make certain they've got enough ammo up there. Okay, Jim? We've got to get that mountain gun."

"True enough, Dai-uy. True enough. You can also see up here above Phu Hiep where they've brought in a flame-thrower company, beefed up the total number of recoilless rifles, even have four 75mm, recoilless rifles in the northern area." Pointing to the bottom line on his report, he noted, "They've got about 2,400 men in the Southward Regiment now, and that doesn't count the bunch who run the Bung Ven Base."

"Jim, go get Lieutenant Strait. We'd better talk this whole thing over."

"Will do, Dai-uy."

Within moments my XO and Jim Taylor were standing in front of me, looking down at the maps, studying the situation. I asked them to hear me out. "They outnumber us six to one up around Khanh Binh and have nine times the heavy weapons we have up there. At Khanh An they've got us by four to one in numbers alone and eight times as many heavy weapons. We've got a slight edge at Phu Hiep. Phu Hiep is strategically less significant than the other of our FOBs and extremely isolated, yet it has borne the brunt of many attacks.

"That battalion to our west bothers me because it puts a whole new face on the VC's strategy. They can hit our 155mm Howitzer base from there and bombard our camp without our being able to answer their fire. They know as well as we do that we're not getting any support in our battles against them as long as they stay inside Cambodia. We could go after them but we're getting stretched mighty thin as it is.

"That flame-thrower company above Phu Hiep has me puzzled. Any ideas?"

Taylor suggested it could be a diversionary tactic, with the Flame-thrower Company and 260th Company hitting Dong Co Ki and then taking and holding that narrow strip of land between Lake Binh Thien Lon and the Bassac River. They would then effectively disrupt, even control, any access to the northern area. "We would have automatically sent a reaction force up to clear the road to Khanh An and Khanh Binh and gotten ourselves ambushed or in the least bogged down in that close corridor."

He went on to speculate, "The 364th could hit camp hard once our reaction force was well on the way to Dong Co Ki."

Lieutenant Strait agreed with Jim and asked, "What about the TOP SECRET plan we start training on in the morning, Dai-uy? How does it affect us?"

"It would mean 42 fewer CIDG defenders here in camp. I'll get with Major Le as soon as we've finished brainstorming. We may have to re-think the other mission or ask for reinforcement."

Sergeant Taylor wondered out loud, "What next?" On the edge of their chairs, they were both anxious, knowing the problem and mindful that we'd not yet worked out a solution.

"When is the last time we fired H&I missions into Cambodia?" I asked.

"Not since the big mop-up operation almost three weeks ago," Taylor answered. It was true. We'd gotten so busy celebrating victory, resettling and caring for refugees, rebuilding, getting our companies back up to snuff and putting together a new psychological warfare program to take advantage of recent victories, we had let down our guard.

"It's my fault," I admitted, "I've been focusing on recuperating from the last battles and haven't taken the necessary precautions to protect us from a big surprise and it is almost upon us. John, get with Ray right away and get word to all FOBs to start H&I fire immediately. Give 'em the latest intelligence and start hitting those areas where we believe the VC are now located, trying for the battalion command post if known. Have 'em go with 20 rounds HE to start with from each mortar. You too, Jim, get out as close to that mountain gun as you can with the four-deuce and make certain we've got ammunition at all locations for our mortars. If we need an emergency air drop let Tiger know. If there are no questions, I'll go tell Major Le what we're doing and discuss the other mission."

"Not a question, Dai-uy, just a suggestion."

"What's that John?"

"Pray a lot, Dai-uy, pray a lot."

I found Major Le behind his desk, staring out his office window in the direction of the flagpole. I then noticed a grieved expression on his face. "What happened, Thieu-ta?"

"I am sad, Dai-uy. Our best agent was captured, tortured and killed cruelly by the VC. We found her body floating in the border canal where it turns south, not far from the FOB. They had cut her tongue out."

I put my hand on his shoulder to comfort him. "I am very sad also, Thieu-ta. She was a brave woman who so often saved many lives by her accurate reports of enemy movements."

"Yes, Dai-uy, thank you. I trained her just one year ago. She came to me after losing her husband to a VC bullet, offering to help in any way she could to avenge his death. She has earned a place among the bravest of our heroes."

I then told Major Le of my decision to renew H&I fire and asked if we should, based on the latest intelligence, rethink the assassination mission.

"There are many sides to this puzzle, Dai-uy," Major Le began. "If the VC attack before our task force would get up the Bassac past Prek Chrey, they would be slaughtered in the boat then we would gain nothing and lose many good men. On the other hand, if we go ahead, and insist that our demands be met, the VC would lose their sanctuaries and we would gain artillery, air and medical evacuation support when inside Cambodia. The victory would be ours and the VC would not likely attack.

"When Mackem returns, we can test the truth of what he says by asking for American bombers to hit the battalion that is west of us!"

"Good idea, Thieu-ta, except that they may give us a token raid to trick us. We must wait until I have what he tells us verified by my friend at Fort Bragg."

"I agree. When will Mackem be coming next?"

I told Major Le that I would send a message asking him to meet with us in two days because of the change in the enemy situation. As we spoke, the first round of the four deuce H&I fire mission left the tube with a mighty roar, a comforting sound to my ears just knowing it was on its way to do harm to our enemy, if only to weaken their fighting spirit.

In less than five minutes the delta atmosphere had returned to normal and only the sound of muffled voices and the whining of our camp's generators could be heard. The fire mission eased my mind much like a welcomed rainstorm in the middle of an extended drought. Just as the rain eased the problems of a long, dry spell on the farm, our shelling of the so-called VC sanctuaries gave me comfort in the knowledge that our enemy might think twice before staging their attack forces too close in so dangerous an area and move even farther back from the border.

During daylight hours on the 14th the VC engaged in considerable light probing in the Phu Hiep, Khanh An, Khanh Binh and Tac Truc areas. Oddly enough, as if to trick us into letting our guard down in one area, there was no action initiated by the VC in the west, from Nhon Hoi south along the Chau Doc River, past Vinh Hoi Dong FOB, to the PF Outposts at Phu Hoi and Vinh Hoi.

The day was otherwise calm in and around camp as our men began training the 50 man force for the mission inside Cambodia. Darkness fell as Major Le and I stood in the Command Bunker, observing a quiet, but dark night with low-hanging clouds obscuring the stars and a gentle, westerly breeze rambling through our camp. The quiet was suddenly shattered by the explosive sounds of a horrendous barrage being placed by the enemy in and around Phu My Hamlet and the FOB at Vinh Hoi Dong.

The field phone rang and I quickly picked up the handset. Ray Johnson was on the line, telling of a message he'd just gotten from Sergeant Gore at the FOB under attack. VC were attacking from the northwest out of range of our four deuce and Gore was on his way to help Sergeant Fox on the 81mm mortar. Major Le was on his field phone, speaking with Major Tuoi in an effort to get support from ARVN's 155mm Howitzers. The VC were sticking too close to the border and using their long range weapons for the attack, so ARVN was not able to help. The mortar, recoilless rifle and machine-gun battle raged for four or five minutes longer and then the enemy's guns fell silent as abruptly as they had erupted.

Standing next to me, Major Le said, "The attack was from inside Cambodia. Their recoilless rifles were aimed like rocket tubes and the first salvo surprised our FOB but missed it and hit in the village of Phu My on the west bank of the Chau Doc River. The FOB was not hit directly and Lieutenant Triet Tran told me that your men on the mortar were doing a good job answering the guns of the VC. There is one serious concern, Dai-uy. One of the ambush patrols out of Vinh Hoi Dong has not answered its radio since the beginning of the battle."

"Perhaps," I said to him, "they haven't answered because of a bad radio and they are all okay." I told him I was saddened about the village being hit and that I hoped not many villagers were hurt."

"I always worry about the innocent people in wartime, Dai-uy. It is the older men, women and children that stay in the villages who get hurt in this war so often."

My telephone rang again. Ray again. Fox and Gore okay, six Strikers wounded and morale inside the FOB very high.

Major Le answered his phone before the first ring faded. His face reflected what must be grim news coming from Lieutenant Triet. The report complete, Major Le placed the handset back on the cradle and spoke of the news from the FOB. "The missing ambush patrol took a direct hit from a recoilless rifle. Seven Strikers were killed and three wounded. There were also six Strikers wounded, but not as seriously, in the FOB defenses answering the enemy machine-gun fire.

"The village of Phu My was hit very hard with mortar fire and their first salvo hit in the center of the village killing five and injuring six. The injured people were taken to the FOB for treatment.

"They also booby-trapped the Village Chief's house. He was injured very seriously when he went to go from his house to help his people. Lieutenant Triet thinks he will live."

I told Major Le that I would send Specialist Woolley and Co Lau to treat the people at the FOB and then arrange to transport more serious cases to Chau Doc Hospital. He agreed and said he'd send Sergeant Chet and tell Sergeant Hung to take charge of med-evac. "I know it will get done with Hung on the job," Major Le told me.

After breakfast Major Le and I visited Phu My Village and witnessed the good spirit of the people among the destroyed and partially damaged homes and shops. Villagers had organized into work parties and begun to clear the debris and rebuild. Major Le's physical presence boosted spirits as he consoled the bereaved and spoke of the valor of their revered Village Chief. From there we went to Vinh Hoi Dong FOB and awarded heroic action bonuses to deserving Strikers.

The sight of a familiar CIA helicopter, its rotors still, greeted us on our return to camp. Major Le and I went directly to the operations center where we found agent Mackem talking casually with Lieutenant Strait. I told John that Major Le and I would meet with Mackem in the command bunker and that I would rely on him to make certain we weren't disturbed.

"I'll stand guard myself, Dai-uy," John Strait said as we left.

This time I didn't offer my hand to Mackem. I told him he was a day early and asked if he was here because he had good news for us.

"What kind of good news did you expect?" he asked me.

Recent events had already strained my patience close to the breaking point. I moved to within an inch of Mackem's face and suggested that he not act like an ignoramus because I wasn't in the mood to play mental gymnastics. "I asked did you bring good news?"

He ignored my question, asking instead how the training was coming along.

I asked again, this time pressing him backwards until he was up against a post. He said he couldn't give me an answer yet. "Can't or won't?" I pressured him.

No response. Only silence this time.

I grabbed him by the shoulders, spun him around and faced him toward the west, looking directly at the Cambodian border. "Listen to me and listen good," I told him, "you are looking at one of those sanctuaries. There's a battalion right straight ahead of you with a mountain gun, two 81mm mortars, a half dozen 57mm recoilless rifles and 400 men wanting to kill all of us who are here in An Phu. Is President Johnson taking the action I demanded if we are to go after Sihanouk?"

Still no answer. Instead, a question: "What is the status of your training?"

I took a deep breath and told Mackem, "You get in your chopper and get out of here. There is no more mission and there is no need to waste time talking to someone who doesn't listen." As I turned to exit the command bunker, with Major Le close behind me, I told Walter Mackem, "You can tell your 'highest authority' just what I told you. If President Johnson insists the enemy be permitted to have their sanctuaries inside Cambodia, then I refuse to send my people to risk their lives to kill Prince Sihanouk." Major Le smiled.

Mackem glowered at me, then turned and went down the stairs in front of us to join Lieutenant Strait who would escort Mackem to his waiting chopper. Before he'd gone two paces toward the helicopter with John, he turned and shouted to me, "You can't fight the system, Captain, because you know you can't win."

* * * * *

Proverbs 3:33 — *The curse of the Lord is in the house of the wicked:*
but He blesseth the habitation of the just.

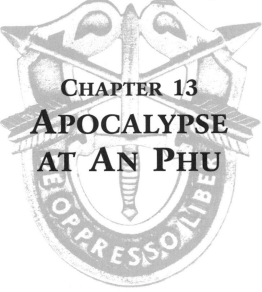

CHAPTER 13
APOCALYPSE
AT AN PHU

1300 Hours, 17 Jun 66: Marvin Woolley came running in from the com-
munications bunker and interrupted my meeting with John Strait and Jim
Taylor. He stopped in front of me, a message in his hand "This is a hot one,
Dai-uy. I knew you'd want it right away."I took it and read it out loud,
"SECRET. TO CO A424. URGENT, REPEAT, URGENT. A424 MUST
DEPART AN PHU AND REPORT TO B-42 NLT 2000 TODAY. CO,
B-42 ADVISED. FROM CO C4."
"In other words, we've been ordered to abandon ship, to desert the Hoa
Haos, to betray our pledge to help them against the Communists. I can't do
that. They'll have to come and take me out of here. How do you guys stand
on this?" I asked.
Lieutenant Strait, sitting across the table from me, was the first to speak up,
"I can't quit these good people, Dangerous. I'm staying with you."

With the special training for the aborted CIA mission no longer needed,
Major Le and I met on the 16th of June and decided to realign all of
our forces to best defend against the renewed, even greater VC threat.
We attached the 2nd Platoon of the 442nd CIDG Company to the 445th at the
Khanh Binh FOB, moving them up from camp by truck. Further, to strengthen
what we felt was a vulnerable area, we attached the 2nd Platoon of the 444th
CIDG Company to the 441st in the Khanh An PF Outpost, moving them from
the Phu Hiep FOB by river craft. Finally, to assure our control of the key bridge
and narrow land area near Dong Co Ki, we moved the 3rd Platoon of the 444th
CIDG Company out of Phu Hiep to establish security in that area. The boats and

277

barge sent to Phu Hiep to move the 2nd Platoon would also move the 3rd platoon to their new site. The end result of the moves was the following positioning of CIDG forces:

Camp: 446th + 442nd(-2nd Platoon) + Recon Platoon. Khanh Binh FOB: 445th + 2nd Platoon/442nd Khanh An Reinf: 441st + 2nd Platoon/444th Vinh Hoi Dong FOB: 443rd Phu Hiep FOB: 444th (-2nd & 3rd Platoons) Dong Co Ki Security: 3rd Platoon/444th

After meeting with Major Le I got together with my XO and brought him up to date on all the changes and asked if there was anything he was aware of that I may not have taken into consideration.

"Well, Dangerous, I'd say that our kitchen cupboard is almost bare and we need to send someone to Saigon to get PX and Commissary items for the team."

"John," I said, "with all that's been going on and with how short we've been of men on the team, I'd neglected that whole matter. Thanks for bringing it up. That is a valid concern because we sure don't have much of anything on the shelves. I enjoy the Vietnamese cooking and our cook has done well on what we've given him, but I'd sure like some good old American pizza, spaghetti mix and a lot of canned beans, peas and whatever. Get with Taylor, Johnson and Woolley and draw lots to decide who'll go, then get it set for the 17th with a squad of Strikers for security on the river. Whoever goes, let's give 'em an extra two days. We haven't let anyone take an R&R since I got here and this is a good time to give a little slack."

John grinned, reached out and we shook hands. "Hey, Dai-uy, I like to eat and I need some things the mail chopper never seems to have. I'll take care of it and let you know who's going."

Ray Johnson won the draw and the rest of us, including Sergeants Edwards and Cannon at Phu Hiep and Sergeants Fox and Gore at Vinh Hoi Dong, gave Ray buy lists and money to make the run. It would be a well deserved five days away for Ray, him having been cooped up in that concrete cage called a communications bunker for more hours than any man should have had to endure. Not quite an R&R, but as close to it as anyone would get from our camp. Ray, with a squad of CIDG for security, would take two assault boats and go by river to Can Tho, departing An Phu after breakfast on the 17th and staying overnight in Can Tho at the C-4 compound. Early on the 18th he would board an Army Caribou aircraft and fly out of the C-4 airstrip in Can Tho directly to Saigon. He would spend three days and two nights relaxing and visiting friends. The fourth day would be devoted to shopping at the commissary and PX, hoping to get everything on the lists we'd given him. Early in the evening of the 20th, with the help of Special Forces Support Detachment B-52 in Saigon, whose 2 ½ ton truck he'd borrowed to shop with, he would stack and secure everything on a four by four pallet with a container of dry ice to keep what perishables he'd bought in the commissary from spoiling, and load that pallet on the first Caribou aircraft that was headed for Can Tho. Another night at C-4 and our Strikers, who'd been enjoying their own little R&R in the Can Tho area, would meet him at the C-4 boat dock on the Mekong

River early on the 21st, transfer all the goods from the pallet to the two assault boats and head back upriver to An Phu.

It was almost 0930 on 17 June when I saw Ray and his squad of Strikers off. As he boarded the lead assault boat to head down-river toward Chau Doc, I told him we'd expect him back in camp before dark on the 21st.

Ray was happy and told me he was looking forward to seeing some of his buddies in Detachment B-52, adding, "I might even enjoy a little more sleep than I've been getting here, Dai-uy."

"Just don't forget to come back with the goodies," I chided.

I hurried on back to the dining area where I'd scheduled a meeting with Strait and Taylor to discuss all that had to be done when our camp was converted to Regional Forces and our two teams of Green Berets, both Vietnamese and American, would leave An Phu. Our six companies would then be advised by a MACV advisory team. The one point I stressed again and again was our need to turn over most of the spare parts, ammunition, field gear, medical supplies, aid station equipment and field fortification material to the Hoa Haos and not the MACV advisory team. I just didn't trust a bunch of "legs" to do right by our friends. Seemed to me like we were deserting them as it was. With Sirois in the hospital since the 9th, Woolley had been stretched pretty thin, taking care of the medical end of things as well as helping Ray Johnson out in the communications bunker. With Ray gone on the Saigon run, I told Jim Taylor he'd have to help out in the commo bunker. "It's not going to be easy on any of us and I just hope things stay fairly calm along the border," I cautioned.

Our meeting was interrupted at approximately 1000 hours on the 17th as Marvin Woolley rushed in and handed me a message, saying, "This looks real important, Dai-uy, so I brought it right to you."

I read it aloud, "SECRET. TO CO A424. URGENT. GROUP HQS RECEIVED PRIORITY MSG FROM LLDB. KY HAS WITHDRAWN AMNESTY FROM CIDG OF AN PHU. ALL WILL GO BEFORE MILITARY TRIBUNAL AFTER CONVERSION TO REGIONAL FORCES. DO NOTHING UNTIL ADVISED. CO C4."

"What's it mean, Dai-uy?" Lieutenant Strait asked.

"I don't know, John, I just don't know." Looking at Sergeant Taylor, I reminded him, "Just five days after you arrived, Jim, I went with Major Le to Saigon and we met with the Minister of Defense, General Nguyen Huu Co. What was said was said in Vietnamese, but I do know that what he did pleased Major Le. As we went to leave the Minister's office, the General bid me courage for the coming battles and handed Major Le a document with a gold seal and his signature that granted amnesty to all the CIDG of An Phu. Does that ring a bell with you, Jim?"

Jim Taylor, a look of excitement in his eyes, said, "Yes, Sir. I remember you telling us that when you got back with Thieu-ta. Me, Val, your old sidekick Menkins, Tenorio, Kuchen and that Mormon Lieutenant, we were all there and heard you tell it. John Eleam missed out because he was in the commo bunker. All those other guys have either rotated back to the States or moved on to another team, but I remember it like it was yesterday. Amnesty was a hot issue with the Hoa Haos. Major Le and you went right to the top man under the President of South Vietnam to get it squared away. Who could forget that?"

"Thanks Jim," I said, "So why is this coming down now? That's the question we need the answer to. I'm going on over and talk to Major Le and find out what's happening."

Lieutenant Strait sounded off, "You won't have to, Dai-uy, Thieu-ta is headed this way."

I glanced to my right and down the hall and saw Major Le walking briskly toward us, a look of anger in his eyes. "Not like Major Le," I thought to myself.

I stood, reached out to shake his hand and told him, "From the look in your eyes, I believe you came over to talk about amnesty. I was just coming to see you to ask you about the amnesty problem. What do you make of it, Thieu-ta?"

"It is the work of people who want to destroy the Hoa Haos. I received a message saying I must send a list of all my Strikers to Major Chuan at C-4 today. I cannot do this, Dai-uy. I cannot betray my people."

Excusing myself from our meeting, I asked Major Le to join me in my office where we could discuss strategy. Once inside, Major Le sat down and told me, "I do not trust this order, Dai-uy. Why do they do this now and not wait two weeks? Your team would be gone and all my men would then be Regional Forces soldiers under an oath of allegiance, under Saigon's complete control."

"Colonel Tuttle has told me nothing, Thieu-ta, just to wait for orders from him. Do you have any idea what's going on? None of this makes sense. Two weeks ago our many victories had won our camp all sorts of honors for the Hoa Haos and those honors were triumphantly bestowed upon our Strikers by the highest military brass in IV Corps. And, it was reported in all the major Saigon newspapers. Now a sudden shift from honors to a military tribunal action. Why?" I asked Major Le.

Major Le speculated, "They must surely realize that many of our men will desert when this is known. We will become very weak in An Phu while the VC grow stronger in Cambodia."

"Maybe they want us to become weak, Thieu-ta. It sounds bizarre, but it seems they want to sacrifice the Hoa Haos for some reason. Is that possible?"

Major Le thought for a moment before coming to the same conclusion I'd come to, which I realized was true once he spoke, saying, "Maybe your CIA is angry because you stopped the plot to assassinate Prince Sihanouk. Maybe they do this to punish us and to do it while your team is here with us, especially you, Dai-uy. You are the one who sent the agent away from An Phu. You are the one who aborted the mission.

"When we would become weak from our men deserting for fear of court action the CIA could leak reports of our weakness to the VC and set us up for a big defeat."

"That was my first thought, Thieu-ta. Remember what Mackem shouted at me just after I ordered him out of An Phu?"

"Yes," he said, "and, I won't soon forget. He hollered out 'You can't fight the system, Captain because you know you can't win.' It was a threat for certain, Dai-uy."

"The way I see it, Thieu-ta, we must stick together and fight for amnesty or we play into their hands. If we do nothing we will be easy prey for the Southward Regiment once our numbers have become very low because of desertions. I'll do anything I can to help. You know that I will not desert your people."

"Thank you, Dai-uy, I believe you are as one of us. Shall we both let our commands know of our common resolve?"

Of course I agreed, and within minutes we had put together and transmitted messages to our C Team commanders. Mine read: "SECRET. URGENT. TO CO C4. RE YOUR MSG OF THIS DATE ON AMNESTY. I STAND WITH MAJOR LE. WE DEMAND TOTAL AMNESTY FOR STRIKERS. SOUTHWARD REGIMENT POISED TO ATTACK WITHIN NEXT THREE DAYS. AN PHU IS CLOSED TO ALL US AND RVN OUTSIDERS UNTIL AMNESTY IS RESTORED. FROM CO A424."

English translation of Major Le's message to his C Team: "SECRET. TO CO C4. CAPT MARVIN AND I JOIN IN DEMANDING AMNESTY GRANTED 10 JAN 66 BE RESTORED TO ALL CIDG. VC WILL ATTACK SOON AND DESERTIONS CAUSED BY YOUR MESSAGE WEAKEN US. WE ARE FORCED TO CLOSE AREA UNTIL AMNESTY IS RESTORED. FROM CO A147."

Major Le then handed me a translation of a separate message he had written to his six CIDG Company Commanders: "I HAVE RECEIVED MSG FROM MAJOR CHUAN TELLING ME THAT PREMIER KY HAS WITHDRAWN AMNESTY FROM CIDG AT AN PHU. SITUATION IS VERY BAD. WE MUST CONTINUE TO SHOW STRENGTH AGAINST VC. CAPT MARVIN JOINED ME IN SENDING MESSAGES DEMANDING THAT AMNESTY BE RESTORED. WE HAVE CLOSED AN PHU TO ALL OUTSIDERS. WE WILL STAND BY OUR PEOPLE UNTIL WE HAVE WON. WE WILL DO OUR BEST. KEEP ME INFORMED OF DESERTIONS."

"Do you believe many Strikers will desert, Thieu-ta?" I asked.

"Yes, Dai-uy, I believe they will. I cannot blame them if they leave us, and remember, Dai-uy, it is okay for them to leave anytime they want. They must only turn in their weapons and ammunition to us. Many have families and are afraid for their families."

I nodded in understanding and told him of my concern that the VC would learn of our desertions. I asked if all of our units were now in place to defend against the expected big attack.

"All except the ARVN Howitzers. They will move up to Phuoc My tomorrow with an RF Company for their security. I must go now to meet with Major Tuoi and tell him what has happened about the amnesty. We will need his help to secure the river near Chau Phu. I will send our best two agents to Chau Doc to report back to me if they see any unusual activity."

"Good idea, Thieu-ta. I'll be briefing my men that are here in camp at noon. Maybe you and I should visit all the FOBs later today so we can talk to your people and mine directly. I can show my loyalty to your people by standing with you. I believe it will help to keep some of your men from leaving the CIDG."

He agreed and we decided to head north at 1500 hours. Major Le left to brief his team and I grabbed my papers and went on into the dining area. Lieutenant Strait and Sergeant Taylor were sitting, waiting.

Big John spoke up before I could sit down. "What's up, Dai-uy? There's a lot of strange activity in both commo bunkers and Woolley says you told him not to tell anyone what was going on."

"That's right, John." I grabbed a cup of coffee, sat down, and shared everything Major Le and I had discussed, even our concern that the CIA was behind what's going on, read the messages to them that we'd sent out, and told them, "Unless there's some sort of miracle, we're in a real hurting situation. All we can do is wait for responses to our demand for total amnesty and make certain that the Strikers know we're not selling them down the river. Major Le and I are going to make the rounds of all the FOBs to let them and our men know that we are together standing by the CIDG. We leave here at 1500.

"John, while I'm gone this afternoon, make certain that between you and the LLDB there is someone in the supply room to take in weapons and ammunition from any Striker who decides to call it quits."

"Sure thing, Dai-uy. You just mentioned that you and Thieu-ta believe this has something to do with the CIA. The Company is big time. What's going on?"

"All I want you to know is that there's a good chance that this whole business is tied in with what happened a couple of days ago. John, I'm sure you remember what Agent Mackem said after I ordered him out of camp."

"Yes, Sir. Couldn't ever forget that, but I don't know why he said it."

"Until that moment we were training Strikers who had volunteered for what they were told was a very dangerous mission, a suicide mission. That's all they were told and Major Le has kept his team in the dark the same as I have you men about the mission the CIA brought to us and what was behind the abrupt departure of Walter Mackem. I'd accepted a highly classified mission from the CIA while making a counter-demand that Major Le and I had agreed to. They didn't come through with what we demanded which had to do with the President and the end of enemy sanctuaries, so I aborted the mission. When I ordered the spook out of camp, I was more or less put on notice by Mackem that I had not heard the last from the Agency on that matter."

A quick glance at John and Jim left no doubt in my mind that they were apprehensive. Jim Taylor spoke up, suggesting that not many who mess with the company get away with it. He wondered what would happen next.

"Wish I knew, Jim. You men now know as much as I'm going to tell you. The less you know about some things dealing with the CIA, the better off you are. Too often, you do a job for them and then you are declared expendable, if you know what I mean."

"I know what you mean," John Strait answered, "and so does Jim."

"Now comes the heavy part," I advised, "Each man on this team has to make a decision. I aborted a CIA mission two days ago and then was warned by the agent that I had disobeyed orders by backing Major Le on the amnesty issue. Those were my decisions and I purposely kept you guys out of the process. As long as I'm commanding this independent operation, I don't have to answer to anyone. The time has come for each of you to decide if you want to go or stay. I want you to know that anyone who decides it's best to go and report to the B Team for reassignment will go with my blessing.

"I don't know how many Strikers will desert. I don't know if or when the VC will attack and I sure don't have the least idea what headquarters will do with our messages. Premier Ky is involved, the CIA is involved and we're smack dab in the middle. I believe it's up to us to stand by the Hoa Haos. I'm here to the end. Anyone who is leaving has got to get his stuff together and be in a boat on the way to Chau Doc in time for our boats to get back here before dark."

Again, Marvin Woolley rushed in from the communications bunker to our team dining room, interrupted our meeting, and handed me a message he'd just received at 1300 hours, saying, "This is another hot one, Dai-uy. I knew you'd want it right away."

It read: "SECRET. TO CO A424. URGENT. REPEAT. URGENT. A424 MUST DEPART AN PHU AND REPORT TO B-42 NLT 2000 TODAY. CO, B-42 ADVISED. FROM CO C4."

"In other words," I told John Strait and Jim Taylor, "we've been ordered to abandon ship, to desert the Hoa Haos, to betray our pledge to help them against the Communists. I can't do that. They'll have to come and take me out of here. How do you guys stand on this?"

Lieutenant Strait, sitting across the table from me, spoke first, "I can't quit these good people, Dangerous. I'm staying with you."

I shook his outstretched hand. "Thanks, John. I appreciate it. But, look, you men know what the message said. So far none of you have gone against orders. I can't or won't ask you to stay. If you decide to stay, I'll cover you by ordering you to stay and I'll send a message to B-42 telling them so. You'll have that on file for your protection later, if there is a 'later.' Just think about it for now then let me know your answer when we get back from the FOBs."

"We will, Dai-uy. But, you know it's possible that they have another reason for ordering us all out at once and having us on that open river this afternoon?"

"John, the possibility of our being ambushed on orders of the company and then reported as casualties of a VC action crossed my mind. We could by-pass Chau Doc, going cross-country over to Tan Chau and bum a ride down the Mekong River past Hoa Hao Village to Can Tho, but who's to say how friendly the rest of our guys would be if they were told we'd gone against the CIA? Anyway, John, none of us want to desert the Hoa Haos, so go and talk to Lieutenant Ba and find out what we can do to help the families of any who choose to leave the CIDG. I say 'leave' because I like that word better than 'desert.' It just doesn't fit.

"Jim, I want you to get with Sergeant Hung and his demolition people, and make certain there's enough plastic explosive wired in the two big ammo bunkers and each of our commo bunkers to blow this whole camp to the moon if I have to pull the switch. We're not going to leave this to the VC, the company or anyone else."

"Sure thing Dai-uy. And, I'm staying with you too."

"Thanks, Jim. Woolley, I know you've got to get back to the commo bunker pretty quick. Take this message and send it to C4 and copy B-42." I handed him a short message that read, "SECRET. TO CO C4. AMNESTY MUST BE GRANTED STRIKERS OF AN PHU. WILL ADVISE LATER TODAY IF I WILL SEND TEAM MEMBERS TO B-42. I AM STAYING. FROM CO A-424."

"Will do, Dai-uy. And you can also count on me to ride this thing out with you. We smiled at each other and shook hands.

On the way to Khanh An, Major Le told me about his meeting with Major Tuoi. "He supports us in our stand for amnesty, Dai-uy, but he is very nervous about putting his men near Chau Doc, where they might be forced to fight against other RF soldiers."

"But, did he agree to do it?"

"Once I saw he was nervous about that, I devised another plan which he is pleased with. Let me know what you think of this, Dai-uy. We will use his RF Company to secure the reaction force route from Dong Co Ki south to An Phu Village and use our Strikers for any action on the river between our camp and Chau Doc."

"Fast thinking, Thieu-ta. We'll have better control if we have to set up an ambush on the Bassac."

It was a whirlwind trip, visiting four FOBs in a matter of hours, but well worth it. The Striker's morale was visibly improved, just seeing Major Le. Edwards, Cannon, Fox and Gore, after my briefing them on the situation, decided to stick it out with the CIDG. On the return trip, Major Le told me how pleased he was that my men had each made a decision to stay with his people. Noticing how quiet I had become after talking to my men in the FOBs, he touched my shoulder and remarked, "You have been very quiet, Dai-uy, it is not like you."

"I was just thinking about my men, Thieu-ta. As you know I was ordered to take my team to Chau Doc. Each of my men has said he wants to stay with you and your people. If I allow them to stay, they could all end up in prison. If they were to leave by a safe route, they'd be deserting your people. It boils down to a question of honor, and I'll tell you, Thieu-ta, I'm mighty proud of each and every one of them for their courageous decisions."

We were both silent until we were back in camp and walking together toward the Operations Center. Major Le stopped short and I followed suit. He looked me right in the eyes and said, "Each man must decide what is right in his own heart,

Dai-uy. You first made the decision to stay and I am very happy you stay. Could you now order your men to go, knowing they want to stay and would have to live with their shame forever if they left their Hoa Hao friends?" Without my answering, we went our separate ways once inside the headquarters building.

Coming into the team dining area, Lieutenant Strait, with Taylor and Woolley standing nearby, reported with a smile and a firm handshake, saying, "It was good news that we heard from the FOBs, Dai-uy. So, we're all together on this now. What's our next move?"

"Mostly waiting and sweating, John. By the way, who's holding down the commo bunker?"

"Flash is, Dai-uy. He's got it down pat. I figured we'd need some back up as short as we are, so I trained Flash," Woolley proudly reported.

"Good thinking, Woolley. Jim, how'd you do on the demolition preparation?"

"Done, Dai-uy. Pull those two switches and this place is going to look like one huge litterbox. There won't be anything left," Taylor answered.

During dinner we talked a lot about what was happening at home. The distance between us and our loved ones seemed so much greater than it had been just a few days ago. We'd cut ourselves off so completely that no one dared think, let alone mention, how uncertain our future had become.

After breakfast on the 18th, I went into Major Le's office to find him sitting behind his desk, shoulders slumped, eyes fixed on a note that lay on his desk in front of him. Always the gentleman, he reached out as a common courtesy and shook my hand in greeting.

"Dai-uy," he began, "I have been in many battles, and I have faced many dangers before this day, but never before have I been afraid." He paused a moment, stood and looked past the flagpole and out across the drill field. I am afraid for the first time now. Almost two hundred of our men have turned their weapons in. It is a bad situation already, but what I learned this morning concerns me more. I am truly afraid for my people."

I wondered what had happened. Had his family been taken hostage? I'd never seen him grim, intimidated, until now. I asked, "What has happened, Thieu-ta?"

He gestured at the note on his desk. "I have just received word from a trusted friend in Can Tho. He tells me that an ARVN Regiment is being sent to Chau Doc to enforce the edict that Premier Ky has directed at An Phu. He tells me they are coming here with armored personnel carriers and many big weapons."

It took a minute for the full impact of what he'd said to hit me. When it did, a cold sensation of impending doom took control of my mind and spirit momentarily. Quickly, I pushed that feeling out of my mind, knowing it was exactly the reaction 'they' would want. I stood tall and erect, letting Major Le know I was with him, was there to help and not hinder.

Major Le continued, "Our agents in Chau Doc report that the police are ordering people to move their boats away from the entire docking area in front of your B Team and beyond. The cleared area is to be 1,000 meters long. They are told that government boats will be using the docks."

"That makes sense, Thieu-ta. They know the road from the Chau Doc Ferry landing in An Phu to our camp is muddy and that it would be impossible for their heavy vehicles to make it that way. They can put their armored personnel carriers, even their truck-drawn howitzers, on LCUs, which we know they have available to them."

Major Le added, "And then they will come up the Bassac River to attack our camp. It is very logical."

I asked Major Le how long he thought it would take to assemble the Navy boats, load the APCs, other vehicles, weapons and 1,500 men and be ready to move upriver to attack our camp.

He thought for a short time, did some figuring on a note pad and told me it would be the morning after the boats and the regiment were assembled in Chau Doc. "They will not try to come up the river after dark, Dai-uy, so I believe they will not be prepared to attack us before the morning of the 20th. So, my friend, in case I am wrong, we must be ready the day before!"

"You know better than I do, Thieu-ta, that we must be prepared to fight the Southward Regiment and the ARVN Regiment at the same time."

"Yes, Dai-uy, and with 200 fewer Strikers than we had just yesterday."

As if on signal, Sergeant Taylor and Sergeant Hung, who had been standing in Major Le's office doorway, cleared their throats to get our attention. They each had a proud look on their face and a map in hand.

"Got something for us, Jim?"

"Yes, Sir. Hung and I have put together a map[1] showing both friendly and enemy order of battle. We thought you and Major Le would like one for your meeting."

"Sure would. Thanks to both of you. It's uncanny, we were just talking about the tactical situation." Major Le echoed my thanks as I took the map and laid it on the desk in front of Major Le where we could both review the situation. In the margins they had noted the strength of opposing forces. In the Phu Hiep area we were outnumbered almost four to one. Over around Khanh Binh was the worst scenario with the VC outnumbering our forces five to one. Down around our main camp area, the 364th VC Battalion had been relocated to threaten our FOB at Vinh Hoi Dong, Camp An Phu and the three PF Outposts at Phu Hoi, Vinh Hoi and Vinh Lon with a two to one strength ratio in the enemy's favor.

It showed that the Southward Regiment had been brought up to 2,400 man strength with one 75mm Mountain Gun, four 75mm Recoilless Rifles, 14 of the 57mm Recoilless Rifles and six 81mm Mortars against our two 155mm Howitzers, five 81mm Mortars and one four deuce.

"We are outnumbered and out gunned yet we have not counted the ARVN Regiment's men and guns," Thieu-ta added, "it is not good." Smiling and standing to shake hands with Taylor and Hung, he told them, "You have done a good job to

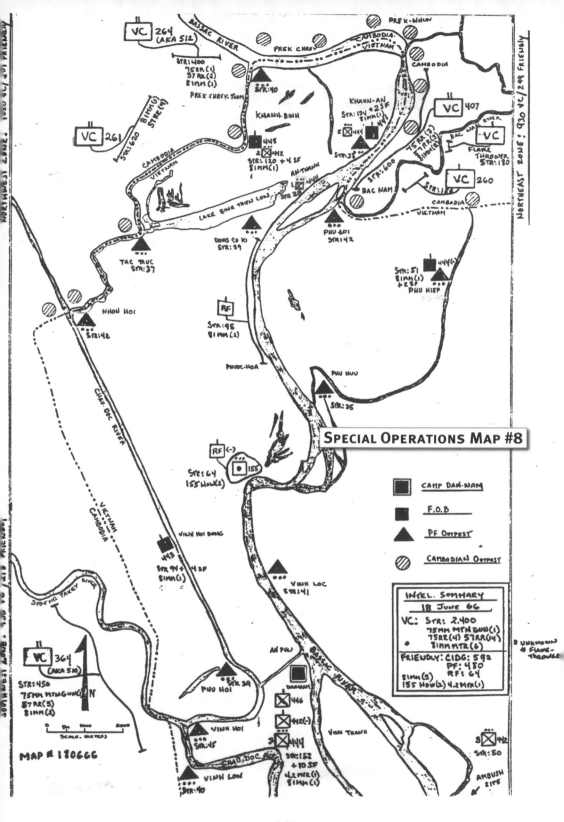

SPECIAL OPERATIONS MAP #8

put all this information down in one very important document for our planning. Thank you very much. You are a good team!"

After the two sergeants left I suggested that we let our higher headquarters know that we are aware of their plan and that they do not intimidate us.

"They will think we are bluffing, Dai-uy."

"We will be to a certain extent, but I believe in the old Indian adage, 'If we make the enemy believe that we do not fear him, then he will fear us, if only a little.' As you know, Major Le, the heat of actual battle intensifies whatever level of courage or fear you possess at the time."

"That is true Dai-uy. I feel as you do. I will send a message to Major Chuan"

"And I will send one to Colonel Brewer, Thieu-ta."

Within a half hour I took my message to Woolley in the commo bunker and told him to send it to B-42: "SECRET. TO CO B-42. OUR AGENTS REPORT NINTH ARVN DIV UNITS MARSHALING YOUR LOC TO ATTACK THIS CAMP. I REMIND YOU THAT AN PHU IS CLOSED TO ALL OUTSIDERS. WE DEMAND AMNESTY FOR ALL STRIKERS. WE WILL ENGAGE ANY FORCE ENTERING OUR AREA. FROM CO A-424."

At lunch on the 18th of June I discussed the message flow and the threat now posed by friend and enemy alike. I asked Jim Taylor how we stood on ammunition. "We would be in good shape on everything if it was just the Cong we were fighting," Jim answered, "but I'm not sure we've got enough to hold off the Cong and ARVN. Are you sure about the ARVN Regiment, Dai-uy?"

"Dead serious, Jim. Unless they back off, we have no choice." Turning to Lieutenant Strait, I asked about the families of those Strikers who chose to leave the CIDG, "Can we possibly help them in any way, John?"

"Apparently there is no problem, Dai-uy. Lieutenant Ba simply reminded me that the Hoa Haos take care of their own."

Woolley was back again, this time with Colonel Brewer's response to my earlier message. I asked him to read it out loud. "SECRET. URGENT. TO CO A-424. YOU MUST COMPLY WITH ORDERS FROM C4. I WILL SEND ESCORT TO BRING YOUR TEAM TO THIS LOCATION. NO KNOWLEDGE OF MISSION OF 9TH ARVN DIV UNITS ARRIVING VIC THIS LOC. FROM CO B-42."

Grabbing a pen I wrote a quick answer and read it aloud before handing it to Woolley to send: "SECRET. URGENT. TO CO B-42. I HAVE ORDERED MY MEN TO REMAIN IN AN PHU. DO NOT SEND ESCORT. THIS AREA IS CLOSED. ALL MILITARY TRAFFIC WILL BE FIRED ON. WE DEMAND IMMEDIATE AMNESTY FOR ALL STRIKERS. FROM CO A-424."

Woolley was concerned with Colonel Brewer's possible reaction. He advised, "I'll send this, Dai-uy, but I don't think Colonel Brewer is going to like it. Are you bluffing about shooting at our own people if they come up river?"

"No bluff, Woolley, we can't afford to bluff. If we let them in it will serve no useful purpose. If we leave, who knows what will happen to Major Le and his people?

And, who knows what will happen to us once we are under Colonel Brewer's control? The CIA, Premier Ky and our Embassy all knew a lot of the Strikers would desert if they withdrew amnesty. If we hadn't stood by them, how many more would have left? I don't know, but I believe we'd of been sitting ducks for the Southward Regiment. And then what? I'll get with Major Le and let him know about the escort party. We have an ambush in place on the Bassac River three kilometers from Chau Doc. They have orders to fire warning shots at all intruders. If their warning goes unheeded, they are to do whatever is necessary to stop them."

"Even kill them?" asked Woolley?

"Yes," I answered.

Sergeant Taylor lifted up his voice in support, saying, "I agree with Dai-uy. This is serious business. Our Hoa Haos could be slaughtered if we don't stand tough."

I found Major Le in the Command Bunker and asked him to read Colonel Brewer's message regarding the escort party.

"Thank you, Dai-uy," Major Le said. "Lieutenant Luong Le has a reinforced platoon of 48 CIDG laying in ambush on the west side of the river just south of Vinh Thanh Island. They have two 60mm Mortars, two Light Machine-guns and four BARs. I have also asked Mr. Minh to send a Lambretta loudspeaker vehicle to the ambush site for Captain Luong's use in warning those on the river who are not welcome in our area to turn back or risk death and injury."

"Sounds good to me, Thieu-ta. Nothing much else we can do right now." After a few minutes looking out across a quiet expanse that lay between our camp and the Cambodian border, I walked down out of the Command Bunker and around camp to see what was going on. Two men were cleaning the four-deuce mortar tube, three black-pajama clad laborers, their eyes shaded by conical rice-straw hats, were cutting grass in the inner compound. They moved along slowly but surely in a squatting position, swinging hand-held sickles in front of them, trimming the lawn areas to a fairly consistent three inch length. All around the outer defensive perimeter Strikers were busy filling new sandbags and placing them where needed on the parapet to provide additional protection against enemy direct fire during a ground assault.

Having missed my normal afternoon sleep, I went to my cubicle for a short rest at 1600 hours and was fast asleep within a few seconds of my head hitting the pillow. My rest was short-lived as I was wakened by Lieutenant Strait shaking my shoulder.

"What's up, John," I asked, half asleep.

"I hate to bother you, Dai-uy, but Major Le just brought a report from the ambush site."

That woke me with a start. "What happened, John? Any casualties?"

"None, Dai-uy. Lieutenant Luong Le's spotters sighted three assault boats coming up the river with two Americans and about 15 RF soldiers. They ignored a loudspeaker warning to turn back broadcast by Minh's man on the Lambretta. Luong then ordered his men to fire warning shots with two light machine-guns and then threw two rounds of 60mm HE in the path of their boats but far enough to their front to be a warning only."

"Did they turn back?" I asked.

Big John laughed. "The way Major Le tells it, they almost lost control of the lead boat, trying to turn back too fast. The last our Strikers saw of them, they were roaring at full throttle straight down the river towards Chau Doc."

"It goes to show they thought we were bluffing and they learned different. We'll be hearing from Colonel Brewer soon. You can bet on that. I'm going to get a little more shut-eye. Wake me in an hour, Okay?" I was snoring before he left my cubicle.

The aroma of fresh coffee woke me. Jim Taylor stood in the doorway of my cubicle with a mug in each hand. "Thought you could use this, Dai-uy." He handed me my mug and then told me, "It's almost time for dinner and I figured you wouldn't want to miss that." He paused to take a sip. "It's been real quiet all along the border. No probes, no nothing. I wonder what's going on? Think they'll hit us tonight?"

"So many weird things going on now, Sarge, nothing would surprise me. But I'd sure like to know what's going on down in Chau Doc with that ARVN Regiment. Have Woolley get with the LLDB communications people and ask them to monitor the ARVN air-to-ground frequency. We can't rule out a helicopter assault on our camp. They may believe we have moved most of our men and weapons to ambush positions on the Bassac River. Believing it best to hit the camp with choppers before their force reaches the ambush point, they may try to draw our people back to defend the camp and make it easier for their boats to get up the river."

"Will do. Anything else, Dai-uy?"

"No, Jim, thanks for the coffee."

After dinner, I got my M-16 rifle and went on up to the Command Bunker and stood and scanned the border area for action. The sun disappeared over the horizon and the dark, moonless night accentuated a feeling of foreboding. The air was still, hot and humid. Sweat trickled down my face and back. I heard footsteps behind me.

It was Major Le. "Hello, Dai-uy, do you remember General Quang Van Dang?"

"Yes, Thieu-ta. The IV Corps Commander and a real gentleman as I recall. I met the General at our victory celebration two weeks ago and I felt good because he spoke with me as if I mattered to him."

"Good, Dai-uy. General Dang is a friend of the Hoa Hao people. I am very certain in my mind that he is not aware of the present situation." I asked, "Do you think they are using one of his regiments without his knowledge?"

Major Le laughed, "Did your B Team know anything about your secret mission when the C Team sent you to An Phu?"

"No, Thieu-ta, and if what you say is true, then my theory about the CIA is dead on. And, in that case, can General Dang help us?"

"I have just sent a message to the Chairman of the Hoa Hao Central Council, Tuong Trong Luong. He is a trusted friend. I have asked him to meet with General Dang as soon as he can get to Can Tho and tell the General about our predicament. And, yes, I believe General Dang will help."

I then told Major Le, "Your friend is a brave man. If General Dang is in this with the CIA, Mr. Luong Tuong will be a dead man."

"I think not, Dai-uy. I trust General Dang and I am certain he will not allow anything like this to happen if we can get to him in time."

I hoped Major Le was right. "But," I told him, "if you are right and General Dang comes to our rescue he may get himself in hot water."

"What is it you mean by 'hot water', Dai-uy?"

"Serious trouble, Thieu-ta, real serious trouble."

Major Le reflected on what I said and then went on to tell me that "General Dang is a very powerful man. He has led the IV Corps in battles against the enemy and has kept the whole IV Corps the most secure in all Vietnam. Who would trouble him, Dai-uy?"

"The CIA. They are like a beast with many claws. They have many secret operations and many ways to destroy a man." If General Dang spoils their plans, you can count on the fact that they will somehow try to make him regret it. Of that I am certain, Thieu-ta."

Major Le and I stayed in the Command Bunker until 0300 hours on the 19th of June. It was a strangely quiet night, without incident. Only the pounding of the sanctuaries by our mortars disturbed the peace. No enemy action of any kind was heard, not even counter-fire to our mortar barrages.

At breakfast we puzzled over the situation, wondering why the lack of enemy activity when all signs had pointed to an all-out invasion? All we could do, we decided, was wait for agent reports that would explain the calm. It was my hope that Major Le's friend had gotten through to General Dang in time.

Woolley came running in again, with a "burning message" from C4. I read it aloud. We all had to know what was going on. The message was, "SECRET. TO CO A-424. SITUATION VERY DANGEROUS. SF HAS NO CONTROL. YOUR TEAM MUST LEAVE AN PHU ASAP. REPORT TO COL BREWER. NO AMNESTY. ARVN UNDER ORDERS TO TAKE CONTROL OF AN PHU NLT 201500 JUN. NO DANGER FOR YOUR MOVEMENT TO B-42 LOC THIS DATE. URGENT REPLY REQUESTED. FROM CO C4."

Looks like we've got a whole day before the stuff hits the fan," I said, "and I think I know who is in control. It's Premier Ky and the CIA together wanting to destroy the Hoa Haos and, at the same time, revenge my aborting of the Sihanouk assassination mission."

I quickly wrote a reply to Tuttle's message and gave it to Woolley to send after reading it aloud for the others to hear, "SECRET. TO CO C4. RE YOUR MSG TO ABANDON STRIKERS. SUGGEST SF GAIN CONTROL OF SITUATION. WE WAIT WITH MAJOR LE FOR AMNESTY. FROM CO A-424."

Major Le was given a copy of my message and he quickly wrote a note and had it hand carried to me. It read, "Your men are very brave to stay with us in this very dangerous situation. Thank you."

Lieutenant Hanh came in shortly and handed Jim Taylor new agent reports from our people in Chau Doc, telling us, "They saw maybe 1,500 ARVN soldiers and many armored vehicles. They have begun to load the big boats. One of our agents spoke with a Chau Doc nightclub owner who told her of a big party tonight with many soldiers coming to his club."

Hanh's report left no doubt in our minds that we would be attacked by that ARVN Regiment in the morning.

Major Le stopped by to say, "Our fate is now in the hands of General Dang. I only worry that my friend reaches him in time. Dai-uy, will you join me for dinner? It may be our last opportunity to share a meal."

"I'd be proud and pleasured to, Thieu-ta."

Later, as Major Le and I walked to the camp mess, he told me that the VC had secured the border bridge at Khanh Binh and were checking papers on every person who crosses into our area. Lieutenant Hong Luong says the VC are patrolling the border canal south of that bridge and all the way to Lake Binh Thien Lon. That is why we have not received reports from our agents in that area. I think they will sneak across the border canal after dark tonight. Lieutenant Hong will create some diversions to mask the sound of their crossing the canal."

"I sure hope they get across okay, not just for their safety but also because we have so many questions and no answers. I know you are as anxious as I am to hear their reports."

I enjoyed a long, leisurely meal with Major Le. We had fried catfish, sour soup with chicken bits, bean sprouts and coriander, together with a fresh salad, small cakes and bananas for desert. We enjoyed reminiscing about our six months together. I told him that I agreed wholeheartedly with his final after-dinner words.

"We have been through many trials and have shared many victories together, my friend. We now face a struggle against enormous odds and against a force that none of us could have imagined, but we face it together!"

Yes, Thieu-ta, and at this moment I feel confident of victory, yet not having the least idea how we will achieve it, but certain because we are doing what is right for our people on both sides of the ocean."

We then went our separate ways. I went on out and up into the Command Bunker, my place of sometimes solitary refuge where I could be quiet and think. The darkened sky seemed to seal us off from the rest of the world. My thoughts went home to Ithaca to Kate and our three girls. I hoped that Kate was getting help in the way of caring and compassionate companionship. Would her sister Beverly or her folks be there to share her burden of caring for the girls while concerned about my well being? I knew, from what Kate had written, that the only reports in the news about Green Berets had been of camps being overrun.

I never worried about the girls. Kate had always taken good care of them and loved them to pieces. I did hope that Kate would be all right, no matter what happened here in the next few days. Major Le's earlier words came back to weigh heavy on my thoughts, "It may be our last opportunity to share a meal," with that possibility lingering in my mind the evening faded into night.

Major Le joined me a little after 2230 hours. "I have news from Chau Doc, Dai-uy. All of the boats have been loaded. There are ten LCUs with six armored vehicles and at least four 2¹/₂ ton trucks pulling 105mm howitzers on the boats. The ARVN troops have left the dock area, going toward the center of town."

The phone from Major Le's commo bunker rang. He picked it up, listened for a moment and broke out in laughter. He was laughing almost hysterically as he hung up the handset.

"What's so funny, Thieu-ta?" I asked.

"Fate has smiled on us, Dai-uy. An enemy agent, or perhaps a VC covert reconnaissance patrol, saw the ARVN soldiers, the armored vehicles and the big boats at Chau Doc. They naturally thought the ARVN was there to help us!" We both laughed as Major Le continued, "The commander of the Southward Regiment has pulled his battalions a long ways back from the border and now awaits orders from his superior. If the reports are true, we are very lucky Dai-uy. But we must keep our strength up all along the border just in case it is not true and is just a ruse to throw us off guard."

"I agree, Thieu-ta. I just hope it is true. Then our only real immediate threat is from our friends!"

Major Le left to meet with his team and discuss the change in enemy activity as Lieutenant Strait came up the stairs to join me in the Command Bunker. "What were you guys laughing about, Dai-uy?"

"The VC saw the ARVN Regiment in Chau Doc, thought it was sent here to help us to have victory over them and the whole regiment scurried back deep inside Cambodia. So, John, it is only the CIA and their ARVN Regiment that threatens our camp and poses a danger to our Strikers."

"And us too, Dai-uy," John added.

"You're right, John. Very right."

The rest of the night passed slowly and without incident. Major Le and I met again in the Command Bunker after breakfast on the 20th, and within a few minutes received word that the big boats had departed the dock area and were forming on the Bassac River for their approach to attack An Phu. We both broke out in a cold sweat.

I wondered if the US Advisors with the ARVN Regiment were aware of what was happening. At 0940 hours the lead LCU was within ten minutes of our ambush site. Major Le radioed Lieutenant Luong at the ambush site to advise that the ARVN 155mm Howitzers had been repositioned and would be available for support. Everyone was at his battle station, sweating, wondering, hoping.

I looked at Major Le. "Thieu-ta, I am sorry it must end this way." I reached into my pocket, took out my key ring and unlocked the demolition control box. "If I have to pull those final switches..." was the thought that went through my mind.

Major Le reached out and shook my hand. "From the start we have been a good team, Dai-uy. It seems like much time has passed since we first tested you at Phu Hiep, and yet the time has gone by so fast. We have been so busy and I now realize how good it would have been to know each other even better."

Major Chuan, Commander of LLDB Detachment C4 in Can Tho had reported to Lieutenant General Quang Van Dang, the IV Corps CG, that he had heard rumors of a Hoa Hao coup. He told General Dang that the Hoa Haos of An Phu were thought to be joining the Buddhist movement against the Central Government in Saigon. General Dang had heard rumors about a Hoa Hao coup, but gave it little credence because he knew it was not the intention of the Hoa Hao religious leaders to foster an armed rebellion against Saigon.

In a hand-written statement[2] prepared for my use in corroborating certain events discussed in this book, General Dang recalls that early morning visit on 20 June 1966 by the Hoa Hao Chairman, who had traveled there at the request of Major Phoi Van Le to advise General Dang of the serious situation that existed in An Phu: "I was working in my office when Mr. Tuong Trong Luong came and asked me to receive him. It was in a small house converted into rooms for offices. My office was opposite that of Colonel Desobry, my senior US advisor. I saw Colonel Desobry almost every day and I used his command and control helicopter when I needed to move someplace quickly because we had not yet received ARVN helicopters."

General Dang respected Mr. Luong and knew him to be an honest patriot, staunch anti-Communist, and a man of honor with a constructive mind who was willing to cooperate with the government. When Mr. Luong told General Dang about the danger of South Vietnamese killing South Vietnamese, Dang immediately met with Colonel Desobry, made him abreast of the situation and, Dang said, "I let him know that I will talk to Ky and the Minister of Defense and ask them to let me handle the whole situation.

"When I told Ky and the Minister of Defense that I trusted the Hoa Haos, and wanted to take charge and handle the situation fully, Ky agreed and seemed to me to be relieved." General Dang immediately told Colonel Desobry and Mr. Luong, leaving Can Tho with Desobry in the Colonel's helicopter to reach the ARVN Regiment while there was yet time to stop the killing.

"At the moment I did not know the real scope of the problem at An Phu because I did not have all the detailed information." He would later learn that "the problem was real big and heavy of consequences."

Four armed helicopters flew as escort for General Dang and Colonel Desobry while their helicopter raced to reach the ARVN Regiment in their LCU Boats before any shots were fired.

General Dang recalled arriving and then hovering over the Regiment's command and control element with its US Advisors and establishing radio contact with the ARVN Colonel in Command. Colonel Desobry, who in flight had received directives from MACV headquarters to advise the MACV Advisors with the Regiment that it would be turned back, asked the senior US Advisor on the ground why they were going to attack An Phu Camp and was told "There is a renegade Green Beret Captain named Marvin leading the Hoa Haos against Saigon."

General Dang ordered the Regimental Commander to turn his men back and to return to Can Tho. Then General Dang and Colonel Desobry continued on toward Camp An Phu where General Dang would personally[3] tell the Strikers that their amnesty had been restored.

At 0945 hours Major Le received word that the boats were turning around and heading back down river towards Chau Doc! "Why?" we asked each other and were puzzled until we heard the sound of the five helicopters approaching our camp, their rotors beating the air and getting louder and louder by the second. Major Le alerted the perimeter gunners in case this was the air assault we had feared. Within seconds every machine-gun and rifle in camp was pointed skyward toward the fast approaching choppers.

Major Le's telephone rang and he snatched it up. The radio operator was picking up air-to-air communications between the approaching helicopters. He had gotten Woolley into their commo room and on the radio set because it was US pilots who were talking back and forth. Woolley asked them to identify themselves. Major Le hung onto the handset white-knuckled as he waited further word.

Sergeant Taylor, whose view to the east from the mortar pit was unobstructed, called me on the phone and reported five Hueys crossing the Bassac River. "Four of 'em are gunships, Dai-uy."

I passed this news to Major Le, who hollered into his handset, "Haven't they identified themselves yet?" I knew the answer was good news by the way his face lit up even before he'd put the phone back. He turned to me just as the four armed choppers came into full view and said, "It is General Dang! He is coming here, Dai-uy."

I jumped and shouted "Airborne" at the top of my lungs and gave Major Le a big bear hug, shook his hand and congratulated him. Our perimeter gunners were ordered to turn their guns away from the helicopters. I'd never known that a helicopter could look so beautiful. Like angels of mercy the gunships hovered over us as the unarmed Huey brought General Dang and Colonel Desobry gently down on our landing zone. Major Le and I sprinted out there as fast as we could to greet them while the four gunships set down in each corner of the landing zone and shut down their engines.

We stood at attention, our hearts in our mouths, as the door was slid back along the fuselage and General Dang, with brass-tipped swagger stick in hand, stepped down with Colonel Desobry close behind.

After exchanging salutes, General Dang looked at Major Le and said, "I have come to tell your brave men that they have my personal guaranty of amnesty. They will not go before a tribunal." Tears came to my eyes as the ominous threat that we had all endured suddenly vanished.

General Dang, swagger stick in his left hand, shook Major Le's hand, then mine. We walked on either side of the General as he strode along, the stick accentuating

295

the brisk swinging of his arms. He looked proud and powerful as he approached the now assembled Strikers.

He stood tall, directly in front of the formation, waiting for Major Le to present his command. Lieutenant Strait had assembled our team next to the LLDB. I took my place with my team as Major Le called us all to attention and ordered us to present arms, pivoted sharply to face General Dang, and presented his command to the General with a hand salute.

General Dang returned the salute, gave the commands to bring us to order arms and then parade rest. He spoke to the Hoa Haos of their tremendous courage. He reminded them of his recent pleasure in sharing their great victory celebration after the five day battle they'd won against such tremendous odds. He finished his short but dramatic speech with a promise, "I came here to tell you that your amnesty has been restored, and that I personally guaranty it will no longer be questioned. I am proud to know the Hoa Hao fighters of An Phu."

To a man, we all cheered. General Dang called us to attention, saluted the gathered warriors of An Phu, and dismissed the formation. That small, final act, that salute, was a measure of his respect for the Hoa Haos. None there would forget that day or the courage of General Quang Van Dang.

Major Le offered General Dang and Colonel Desobry refreshments but these were declined. The General had to leave immediately. He wished us luck in future battles and we both thanked him again for coming to our rescue. After another round of handshakes, he climbed back aboard his chopper. Colonel Desobry, not wanting to take anything from the moment that rightfully belonged to General Dang, was already inside, waiting.

As the chopper lifted off and disappeared from view, its armed escorts in their places, Major Le looked at me and said, "Well, Dai-uy, my friend, these three days past we will never forget."

In 1989, some 23 years later and after he had been told the full story, the whole truth about the top secret mission, John Strait, a retired Major, told[4] of that time and that day, "My definition of the politicians and the CIA versus the Green Berets is that they use us and when they get through using us and have no further use for us, they just discard us like they would a condom. Kind of like when they brought you that secret mission and you balked and I know you were right in why you balked, they not only discarded you and the rest of us who were with you, they decided it's best to wipe out the whole bunch of us so we couldn't tell what had almost gone down with Sihanouk. Even now you'd have one heck of a time trying to prove it.

"I remembered about that 9th Division Regiment from ARVN that was going to come and take our camp by force and how I told you that, if we were captured, I would take command of us as prisoners because I would be the senior combat arms officer seeing as how you were Quartermaster. I got a big chuckle out of it just telling you about that and that it was the only way I could ever get [one]

over on you." John added, regarding the ARVN Regiment, "I doubted at the time that they could take the camp. Those six companies we had - I think they'd be a match for that Vietnamese Regiment. Our people were so well organized and trained and everything. So I had my doubts at the time whether that regiment or even a division could have taken us. They'd had a heck of a time anyway. I'm just glad we never had to find out.

"General Dang - I remember he came down, he and Colonel Desobry, and they turned the regiment back and came right into camp and gave 'em [our CIDG] amnesty. It took the situation (which was getting kinda hairy all over - you could feel it in the troops there) and kinda eased things up a bit."

That, to me, was the understatement of the year, maybe the war.

It was that very moment, the time we were rescued by a South Vietnamese General from the wrath of our own government, that I knew what it meant to be a part of "the expendable elite." It is no wonder that we lost the war!

* * * * *

Lieutenant Colonel Brewer

Song of Solomon 8:6
Set me as a seal upon thine heart, as a seal upon thine arm:
For love is strong as death; jealousy is cruel as the grave:
The coals thereof are coals of fire, which hath a most vehement flame.

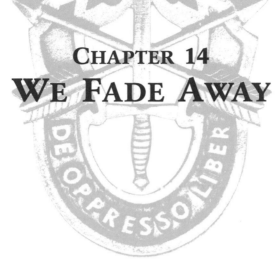

CHAPTER 14
WE FADE AWAY

2 August 1966. I found Lieutenant Colonel Brewer right where the Sergeant said I would: in the B Team bar. Seeing me come through the front door, Colonel Brewer slipped off his bar stool and strode toward me with a look of vengeance on his face. He stopped so close to me that our noses touched for a split second. His huge right fist was poised as if to strike me, but he controlled himself, and instead opened his fist and poked me hard in the chest with a forefinger the size of a Polish sausage.
"Your butt belongs to me now, Dangerous Dan," he snarled, you're no longer King of the Hoa Haos." And, after poking me one more time even harder than the first, he threatened, "I'm going to break you!"

On 21 June, Major Le and I, through our separate channels, requested that the conversion of our six CIDG companies be delayed a month with an effective date of 1 August 1966. As the higher headquarters were aware, during the five days of major battles in May, we had suffered many casualties. It was a fact that we needed time to rebuild the units, recruit Strikers to replace combat losses, refurbish equipment and reconstitute stock levels of ammunition and other combat essential items drawn down by the action. And, perhaps even more significant was the need for time to rebuild morale and attempt to instill loyalty to the central government after each had been reduced so drastically during the recent three day confrontation with our own government forces. The psychological wounds suffered by our men and even their families, when that ARVN Regiment was about to attack our camp could not be accurately calculated in human terms. The very fact that the ARVN Regiment was only minutes away from engaging our forces in combat, and had been ordered to do so by Premier Ky (even setting aside the CIA influence on Ky's actions), had a devastating effect on the matter of trust in the central government's integrity, resulting in a significant decrease in the combat readiness of our six companies. Those traumatic few days had cut very deep and adversely into the spirit of our people.

Major Le initiated a personal and intensive program of encouraging those who had left in the face of what had been an ominous threat of military tribunal action, to return. Concurrently, he launched an aggressive recruiting effort to replace combat losses and fill the ranks of all companies. Reflective of the impact of his direct action and evidence of the loyalty that Hoa Haos had to him as their spiritual and military leader, was the fact that all but 10 of those Strikers who had turned in their weapons and ammunition had returned within a week. By the end of the month all units were back to full strength with only 15 men remaining in the Chau Doc hospital recuperating from combat wounds.

We brought the reinforcing platoons (2/442 & 2/444) back from the FOBs at Khanh Binh and Khanh An and into camp to join their parent companies.

On schedule and just before dark Sergeant Johnson, his CIDG security squad and their two assault boats which were loaded to the limit with commissary and PX purchases for our team, pulled in and tied up at our boat dock. Sergeant Taylor was waiting there to welcome them back. He had brought along a ³/₄ ton truck to bring the goods Ray had bought for us back into camp.

Ray's first question of Jim was, "Any excitement while I was gone?" Johnson, unknowing, just stood there as Taylor roared with laughter for a couple of moments and then grabbed Ray by the shoulder and told him, "Sure was, Ray. Soon as we get into camp I'll tell you all about it."

Our two teams worked together to do everything we could to complete civic action projects, refurbish our CIDG companies, and help the people of An Phu in any way possible to recover from the trauma of a near confrontation between South Vietnamese forces that would have had brother killing brother before heading down river to Chau Doc the last time.

We deactivated the Reconnaissance Platoon on 30 June, as it did not fit into the organization scheme for Regional Forces. Sergeants Fox and Gore were brought back to camp from Vinh Hoi Dong to help out in camp as they awaited reassignment orders.

Just before lunch on 2 July, the six men of MACV Advisory Team # 64, who would replace our team, drove into camp. Their commander, an optometrist Captain of short stature, speaking to me, made no bones of the fact that he was not a combat officer and that civic action would be his primary emphasis. We were encouraged when we learned that their team included two very enthusiastic medics. Not the kind of dog-lab trained all-around combat medics we were fortunate to have in the Green Berets, but nonetheless men who were committed and anxious to help in the medical prevention and treatment program of An Phu. Specialist Woolley would have little time to do anything but acquaint them with facilities in camp and out in the district as he would depart for reassignment the very next afternoon, along with Sergeant Fox.

Major Le introduced the MACV Team Leader to Major Tuoi early in the morning of 4 July at District Headquarters with Lieutenant Strait at his side. Our team handed over the sub-sector advisory role to the MACV team at that meeting.

On 8 July Bac-si Sirois returned to camp after 30 days in the Third Field Hospital in Saigon, where he'd come close to dying from a combination of blackwater fever and falciparum malaria. Though he'd lost a lot of weight, was now a gaunt 116 pounds and had suffered the ravages of a severe, often deadly type of malaria, Sirois hadn't lost his sense of humor. "If I was going to get something I figured I'd get something bad enough to give me some rest time in Saigon," he said with a sheepish grin.

All kidding aside, he told us little about his own treatment due to his concern that he'd forgotten to relate some weird questioning he'd gone through. "They had a special team of doctors from Walter Reed Hospital who asked me a million questions about what I'd done, where I'd been and they wanted it more or less put to them on a day-to-day basis because I was from An Phu. They told me they were concerned about moving an American Infantry Division into the area. Did you hear anything about that, Jim?" he asked Sergeant Taylor.

"No, but I'll tell you all about an ARVN Regiment that almost paid us a visit," Jim quipped, a big grin on his face.

"Almost?" Bac-si asked. "Why, almost?"

We all laughed and Jim set about bringing Sirois current on what had been going on since he was med-evaced on 9 June.

Sergeants Edwards and Cannon were brought in to camp from the Phu Hiep FOB on 9 July and departed the next day for reassignment. At the same time, the CIDG companies began their rotation through camp to facilitate the inspection and repair or replacement of weapons and equipment and to ready them for conversion. Sergeant Gore departed for reassignment on 20 July.

There were two minor skirmishes up around the Khanh Binh FOB on 21 July. One was a daylight CIDG-initiated contact that resulted in one VC KIA and no friendly casualties. The other was an after dark enemy-initiated contact with unknown enemy casualties and no friendly losses.

During the month of July, as much time as possible was devoted to making the CIDG units as combat ready as possible before conversion. Ray Johnson worked day and night on communications gear while assisting me in the paperwork involved in the transfer of our team equipment to the MACV Team. Jim Taylor headed up the effort to repair or replace weapons and other combat equipment, while Bac-si devoted every waking hour until the very last day doing what he could to steer the MACV medics in the way that would best help the soon-to-be RF Companies and the Hoa Hao people. Lieutenant Strait, with the same frame of reference, wanted to pave the way for continued efforts in civic action geared to help the people where they needed and wanted help and not where the MACV planners decided it would help them whether they wanted it or not. The importance of maintaining good relations between the troops and the people was emphasized in all my dealings with the MACV team leader.

I hoped too that they would have the funds available to them to keep the South Vietnamese father and son mechanic team on board who had done such a fine job for us maintaining the water purification equipment, trucks, outboard motors, generators, and other items that a remote operation such as ours must depend on.

On 28 July the final CIDG unit moves to facilitate inspection and refurbishing the companies were accomplished. While this process was ongoing, 28 Strikers, not wanting to be a part of the Regional Forces, turned in their weapons and left the CIDG ranks. Replacements were recruited and in place by the 31st of July for conversion to RF.

Two NCOs whom we all depended on for so much and did even more than was ever asked of them, Sergeants Taylor and Johnson, said good-bye on 28 July and 31 July, respectively. The only Green Beret enlisted man remaining in camp was Specialist Sirois.

As time passed, I found myself getting more and more sentimental about leaving An Phu.

In conversations some 22 years later with John Strait I asked that he tell me how he remembered the men in our team. In the audio tapes[1] used to record his recollections he told me, "I have a lot of fond memories of An Phu, especially the enlisted people there. I figured we had the best in the whole Army, the cream of the crop!" John was right. Although we never had more than 50% of our authorized strength, I believe we had one of the best, if not the best team in all of South Vietnam and our combat and civic action record, if read, would show that to be fact.

I kept hoping for a miraculous change of military strategy that would allow my team to remain here with Major Le and his people for the duration. I naively figured that at some point in time the higher command would wake up and discover that what we were doing here worked and should be copied throughout South Vietnam, not erased. I wanted so much for my low regard for CIA covert operations to be wrong and I yearned to learn that the CIA had nothing to do with that ARVN Regiment breathing death down our necks. But, I knew in my heart that what we'd lived through right here in An Phu was an example of the terrible reality of high level CIA, Embassy and White House skullduggery. It was not, as the 'company' would want to pass it off, a crazed CIA renegade's one time foray into international assassinations and subterfuge that could send a 1,500 man ARVN Regiment with orders to attack and take a US Army Special Forces Camp as an act of retribution.

My former counterpart in An Phu, ARVN Major Phoi Van Le, now a US Citizen, wrote[2] me on 29 May 1995 from his home in the United States. He stated unequivocally that I was "absolutely right, if the US Embassy, the CIA, all of the District and Province Chiefs and Saigon politicians were very honest and worked together to clean up the government - there would have been no reason for the people to go Communist."

He went on in that same letter to respond further, saying , "You are right." When you wrote me: "I believe the entire IV Tactical Zone was fairly secure in 1966 compared to the other Corps, and with no American conventional forces in IV Corps! I was impressed, even wrote my wife from An Phu about the fighters and the people of An Phu and how brave they were and how hard they fought, and that it was their homes, their crops, their fishing boats and nets, their families and their villages that they fought for."

"Today as I write you," he went on, "I believe the war was winnable and that the only way it could have been won was to work together as we did in An Phu and to have the weapons, ammunition and back up support (by other South Vietnamese units) needed and all work very hard at keeping the government representative of all the people and keep it fair and just. I still believe it was the Americans trying to run the war while not really being committed to winning it, the bringing into South Vietnam of all the conventional American forces and the failed strategy of General Westmoreland that lost the war.

"If it had been American Green Berets working with Vietnamese Green Berets and the various irregular, paramilitary and regular military units waging the war — while taking care of the people — we would have made it very possible to win out over the Communists."

The head of the Buddhist Institute, Hoa Thien Thich , on 28 July 1966, stated, "The Buddhists have much sympathy for the Americans but oppose their mistaken policy here. They have not helped the Vietnamese people as such, but only individuals or cliques, who did nothing but oppress the people." In their book "The United States in Vietnam — An analysis in depth of the history of America's involvement in Vietnam,[3] " George McTurnan Kahin and John W. Lewis saw the so-called "Democratic elections" as politically irrelevant gestures that were, in effect, controlled by officials acting for Saigon. "The political polarization imposed upon the population," they wrote, "was being maintained, leaving little opening that might permit access to a third course — some other road that may lead to a peaceful resolution of the conflict they have suffered under for more than two decades." While this writer does not agree with even the remote possibility that there may have been a peaceful solution to the war, I do agree with their concluding statement in chapter X of their book, "So long as the United States planted itself so firmly behind the army leadership, this polarization was likely to endure. But if this could be considered stability, it was an artificial one and in all probability would collapse as soon as American power had withdrawn. For that power was being applied in a way that obstructed internal evolution toward a government capable of winning popular support." In their last sentence of this final paragraph of chapter X, they accurately predicted the tragic end of that nation that was South Vietnam some eight years later, writing, "If thereby *the United States was buying time, in the end it would be the Vietcong that would be most likely to benefit."*

That very same "army leadership" mentioned by Kahin and Lewis was influenced by the American military, who after all provided the funds needed for their daily functioning, and who for the most part despised the very forces who could get the job done — the Green Berets (South Vietnamese and American). It was Army Chief of Staff General Harold K. Johnson, a strong foe of Special Forces, who convinced other senior officers and anti-elitist civilians in the Defense Department hierarchy to move to rid South Vietnam of the Army's Green Berets, accomplishing that act of strategic stupidity in March of 1972.

The first day of August brought conversion of all CIDG forces in An Phu to Regional Forces. Their advisors would be the MACV Team, which left John Strait, Bac-si Sirois and me there as visitors in Camp An Phu.

We spent most of that last day saying our good-byes. Lieutenant Strait was treated to a farewell lunch by Major Tuoi and Mister Duc, the Agricultural Chief. LLDB Sergeant Chet and the nurses threw a party for Bac-si Sirois in the dispensary with all the former CIDG and LLDB medics there to say good-bye to a man they all loved.

I was already close to being overwhelmed by emotion before I stepped foot into Major Le's office for the last time. I knew I'd see him again in the morning, but that would be a hectic time with no opportunity to let him know how I felt about my seven months with him in An Phu. He was expecting me and had set out a special tea on his desk. I reached out and shook his right hand, unaware of the surprise he held in his left hand and out of sight behind the desk.

Major Le smiled and handed me a gaily wrapped package, saying, "This is a small reminder of my feelings towards you, Dai-uy. You have become like a brother." Unwrapping revealed a CIDG machete in a newly painted wooden sheath. The blade had been chrome-plated and engraved with the message:

Captain Dangerous Dan Marvin
Commander, USASF Det A-424
Special Forces Camp An Phu
26 December 1965 - 1 August 1966

Tears filled my eyes and I choked up with emotion. Only after a moment or two to gain control of my tongue and composure was I able to thank my hero and comrade-in-arms for that precious memento of our time together. "I will treasure it forever, Thieu-ta, as I will my Hoa Hao scarf." He smiled again and we did something we'd never before done: we hugged each other. Neither of us seemed capable of finding the right words to say, and we were just too overcome to speak. Instead, we just sat down in his office and quietly enjoyed the last cup of tea we would have together.

Back in my cubicle packing my gear, I decided to wear my new machete and my silk Hoa Hao scarf when we left in the morning for Chau Doc. I went on into the operations center briefing area, removed the A-424 Detachment Flag from its flag staff, folded it and put it with my gear. A-424 was no more! I finished putting my stuff together and sat down on the edge of my cot to take a short break.

Suddenly I heard familiar voices speaking Vietnamese. Getting up and going down the hall and into the team dining area, I found Sergeant Hung, Map-Map, our three interpreters, the father and son mechanic team, our nurses, cook, and even the 72 year old Cambodian house boy waiting for me. I shook hands with each of them, recalling so many good things we had done together. Flash was at my side, bridging the language gap once more as he'd done so often in the past.

It was Flash who told me that they'd brought me a gift to remember them by. Sergeant Hung reached behind Flash to pull out a shallow cardboard box. Inside I found a framed oil painting depicting "War and Peace in An Phu." The artist had skillfully interwoven everyday scenes in An Phu with the terrible drama of combat in a montage representation of familiar things and places. Tears again streamed down my face and my emotions got the better of me as I attempted to thank them for their friendship, their service and their gift. Only when I was again alone did I find a small blue card in the box that read, "We sincerely represent this little handicraft included with our heartiness gratitude to you to thank you for your kindness and your noble sentiments to us and also the people in An Phu District."

I completed the 31 July MOPSUM[4], the last one I'd sign, and which, as was the rule in the past, contained no narrative or statistics relating to cross border operations or to Operation Snuff Crown, including the events of 18-21 June. I did make certain that some day the full story of what had taken place during the period 1 January through 31 July 1966 would some day be made available to the public: See Appendix 14.[5]

That night I was in my cot and fast asleep before midnight. Never before since setting foot in An Phu!

It was with sadness in our hearts that Big John, Bac-si and I threw our gear into the 3/4 ton truck Sergeant Hung had brought around to the back of the team house to take us and our stuff to the boat dock. It was 0800 on the second day of August.

"You must see Major Le before you go," Hung told us, gesturing in the direction of the flagpole. We walked slowly to the end of the headquarters building, around the corner, and turned toward where their national banner flew proudly and glanced out across at the parade field, we were awestruck and moved to tears. All of our former Strikers along with the LLDB in their Special Forces' berets stood at parade-rest in formation as if formed for a victory celebration. As we approached Major Le, he called the gathered troops to attention and ordered them to present arms. It was a salute to our team, a final tribute, a gesture of friendship and camaraderie. We passed in review, saluting the Hoa Haos of An Phu as we walked toward the waiting truck which Sergeant Hung had moved to the front gate area.

We jumped in the truck, waved good-bye and set off for the boat dock. It was a slow and personally rewarding journey: villagers lined the street waving and cheering as we passed through a throng of well-wishers. Many of the children waved small American flags and all were smiling and shouting "Good-bye" as we passed. It had always been "Hallo" that we heard before. Tears streamed down my face as I waved back and shouted good-bye to them.

Major Le was at dockside to shake hands one more time. Sergeant Hung and Map Map insisted on conducting us to Chau Doc, and when we arrived at the B Team dock they carried our gear out of the boat, placing it on the dock in neat stacks. On the dock we shook hands all around, hugged each other and wished each other good health and victory in every battle.

A Sergeant from the B Team walked out to meet us, with instructions for Lieutenant Strait and Bac-si Sirois to follow him to their quarters. Then, turning to look at me, he said, "You, Sir, are to meet Colonel Brewer in the bar," and he pointed to the sandbagged front entrance which I remembered led into the former hotel lounge and bar.

I found the CO right where the Sergeant said I would: in the B Team bar. Seeing me come through the front door, Colonel Brewer slipped off his bar stool and strode toward me with a look of vengeance on his face. He stopped so close to me that our noses touched for a split second. His huge right fist was poised as if to strike me, but he controlled himself, and instead opened his fist and poked me hard in the chest with a forefinger the size of a Polish sausage.

"Your butt belongs to me now, Dangerous Dan," he snarled, "you're no longer King of the Hoa Haos," and after poking me one more time even harder than the first, he threatened, "I'm going to break you!"

* * * * *

CHAPTER 15
A PRESIDENT'S FANTASY IS A SOLDIER'S CURSE

I couldn't believe what I heard asked by US Army Chief of Staff General Harold K. Johnson as he interrupted Colonel Brewer's briefing: "Why are large areas of Cambodia near the South Vietnam border colored in yellow?" He was pointing to the tactical map in front of him. "The yellow represents known VC sanctuaries," Colonel Brewer responded, pointing out where the enemy was located within each one, while beginning to give him the enemy's strength and their weapons capabilities.

General Johnson, in an angry tone, interrupted again, "Remove them from the map Colonel. The President of the United States has told the American People that Cambodia does not permit its territory to be used by the enemy."

An uneasy stillness filled the room. I had written the General's words down, wanting a record of what was an all-consuming lie of extraordinary impact. Surely we could erase the color but that wouldn't take away the safe havens nor the enemy who could continue to plague our side with death and destruction. They needn't fear our taking the war to them with our men, guns and bombs.

I stood my ground, taking the blunt jabs Colonel Brewer was inflicting with his powerful right hand. I looked him dead-on and told him, "Colonel, you may bend me a little, but nobody breaks me."

He dropped his hand to his side but continued his mean-spirited attempt to intimidate me. He pressed close, eyeing me with a contemptuous stare. With a heavy rucksack on my back, M-16 slung and my left hand gripping the handle of my dufflebag I continued unyielding in my stand against the force of his body.

He backed off slightly as I continued. "I did what I had to do in An Phu, Colonel, and I offer no apologies. If I had capitulated to the demands of the system I would have betrayed the very people my team was there to help. I love and respect the Hoa Hao people. If it weren't for those brave folks standing tall against more enemy than we could count, that same enemy would've swept through Chau Doc and cleaned your clock and you'd have become just another number in the body count!"

Colonel Brewer seemed to be paying attention as I added, "I knew all along that one day we'd have this confrontation. It was inevitable because I had a job to do and I couldn't tell you about it. You now know it was merely the circumstances my secret mission created and that neither you nor I had any control over. Don't blame me, Colonel, blame the system that can't stand up and be counted, that can't be honest with the American people, the soldiers it sends out to do a job or the people they're committed to help. Ask Colonel Tuttle about what he'd sent me to do in An Phu now that we're out of there. Maybe he'll tell you the truth, maybe he won't.

"Now that's all behind me, Colonel. My loyalty goes with the truth and with the territory. This is your turf, and I'm your man. If you want us to be enemies, we'll be enemies. If it's friends, we'll be friends. I don't fear any man, including you, and if you give me a job to do and let me do it, before two weeks is out I'll guaranty you'll think I'm one of the best damn officers who's ever served in your command."

He backed off a foot or two, smiled, grabbed my hand with an iron grip, shook it, and said, "Okay, Dangerous, we've got a lot of work to do. I'll give you that two weeks and we'll take it from there. You'll be S-4 when Captain Bryant leaves. Spend the next two weeks getting to know that job backwards and forwards. Right now, get settled in to your room and I'll show you around the compound in about an hour. The Sergeant Major will show you to your quarters."

"Fair enough, Colonel."

Colonel Brewer and I would learn each other's strengths and weaknesses and we would both work together as a team dedicated to doing the best we could to support the many A Teams depending on our team for command, control and support. He learned that I would not heed his terrorist type demands of his subordinate officers and he grew to respect me for that. I was the first of his staff officers to refuse to put my watch in a beer mug and let it stay in the freezer overnight - to see if it was an acceptable watch for one of his Green Berets. Silly, you bet, but that's the way he was. He would also learn that when I played "no-rules" volleyball I would just as soon punch him in the belly when he got up to spike one across the net as let him do the same to me. The day I did that and caused him to puke on the court, he canceled the games for a few days. After some thought he set the play back in motion, picking me every time to be on his team.

I would learn that his way of testing officers was what he did to be known as the "Terrorist." Thinking back, I'm glad the Lord gave me the guts to stand up to a man who would come to be an officer whom I admired for his combat sense and fortitude.

Years later, with Kate by my side, I would meet Colonel Brewer in the parking lot of the Officer's Mess at Fort Bragg, North Carolina. He still appeared tough as nails, and when introduced to Kate, he let her know what he and I had been through together, to the extent of admitting he had threatened to "destroy me" and to tell her how he'd come to appreciate having "Dangerous Dan" on his staff.

The Sergeant Major led me to my room overlooking the front gate and I put my gear in order. After a hot shower, my first since going to An Phu seven months earlier, I put on fresh fatigues and was shown around the compound by Colonel Brewer, who introduced me to Captain Bryant in the S-4 office. Bryant was understandably anxious for me to sign for all accountable property just in case he could arrange to get out of country early.

At breakfast the next morning, Captain Bryant told me that the Army Chief of Staff was coming to visit the B Team near lunch time. "If there's any one General in the United States Army that I'd hoped never to meet personally," I told Bryant, "it's General Harold K. Johnson because he hates our guts. As a matter of fact, I think he'll get rid of all Green Berets if he has his way."

"That bad, huh?" Bryant posed.

"Better believe it, friend. Why is he coming here?" I asked.

"No special reason that I know of. Just a routine briefing." Bryant offered.

Later that day Colonel Brewer and the B Team Sergeant Major met General Johnson at the chopper pad and escorted him back to the B Team Compound where we waited at parade rest in one rank in front of the headquarters building. General Johnson was introduced to us by Colonel Brewer and he then trooped the line and shook the hand of each of us before going on into the briefing area.

The room had been scrubbed down and squared away with everything in its proper place and there were sufficient chairs to seat all the B Team staff and all of the A Team Commanders who'd been flown in by chopper for this meeting.

Immediately after General Johnson was served fresh coffee, Colonel Brewer began the briefing, using a long pointer and freshly posted maps to acquaint the General with the combat situation in all the A Team areas under B-42. He introduced each A Team CO as he briefed on the tactical situation in their Team area, telling General Johnson we were available to answer any specific questions he may have.

I couldn't believe what I heard questioned by General Johnson as he interrupted Colonel Brewer's briefing: "Why, he asked, are large areas of Cambodia near the South Vietnam border colored in yellow?" He was pointing to the tactical map in front of him.

"The yellow represents known VC sanctuaries," Colonel Brewer responded, pointing out where the enemy was located within each one, while beginning to give him the enemy's strength and their weapons capabilities.

General Johnson, in an angry tone, interrupted again, "Remove them from the map Colonel. The President of the United States has told the American People that Cambodia does not permit its territory to be used by the enemy."

An uneasy stillness filled the room. I had written the General's words down, wanting a record of what was an all-consuming lie of extraordinary impact. Surely we could erase the color but that wouldn't take away the safe havens nor the enemy who could continue to plague our side with death and destruction. They needn't fear our taking the war to them with our men, guns and bombs.

Colonel Brewer was stunned. Facing the highest ranking officer in the US Army, he held his ground for the moment, saying, "The sanctuaries are real, General, and what you see here is based on good intelligence. There are officers sitting behind you who will verify what is on that map, if you so desire."

General Johnson, ignoring the available sources of truth as if not wanting to hear anything further that might sear his conscience, responded, "Take it off the map right now, Colonel. The President of the United States has told the American People that Cambodia has not allowed its territory to be used by the enemy."

When Colonel Brewer hesitated to do as directed, General Johnson got up out of his chair, walked over to Colonel Brewer and whispered something in his ear. There was no doubt in the minds of us listening and watching in that briefing room that he had threatened our commander with some drastic action should he continue to insist on the truth because Colonel Brewer immediately ordered the Operations Sergeant to remove the yellow hi-light from the map and delayed the remainder of the briefing until it was gone.

The briefing was cut short and those of us who were available to address the General about combat operations within those areas we had served as advisors or commanders were not permitted to do so. A good move perhaps, because I had it in my mind to first ask the General if he'd like to visit An Phu District and accompany me on an operation into those areas that he had just informed us did not function as safe havens for the enemy.

When General Johnson departed, not a one of us offered to shake his hand or so much as said a word of farewell to him. In my mind, General Johnson was a living example of a lack of integrity and courage within the military hierarchy from General Westmoreland all the way to the White House. The extent to which subterfuge was and would yet be used to satisfy immoral political purpose was an obvious evil perpetrated by those in power at the pleasure of our President. American Embassy and CIA leadership would steer that course with full knowledge it would lead to the killing and maiming of South Vietnamese combatants and innocent civilians alike. Americans and other allies too would be sacrificed in this, a global farce and a tragedy.

In his book[1], "*A Soldier Reports*" General Westmoreland wrote, "The enemy's obvious use of Cambodia as a sanctuary and refusal of Washington authorities to allow me to do anything about it was frustrating." Why then, knowing the facts, didn't General Westmoreland resign and tell the American people the truth rather than be a part of the power structure that knowingly aided and abetted the enemy? Pure and simple: No honor, no guts!

The President's fantasy was indeed the soldier's curse!

— THE END —

The South Vietnamese children are who mattered most to us in the U.S. Army Special Forces: the Green Berets. Our goal was to bring about a lasting peace and a strong central government that could protect its people from the Communist Insurgency, or with the help of Allies, defend itself against a Communist Invasion. To win the hearts and minds of the People was as important to *lasting* victory as the mightiest military machine.

We had the opportunity to help provide these children with lasting peace and security. Instead, we as a nation, abandoned and betrayed them.

My prayer is that we some day are bold and courageous enough to honor our original commitment and again be an honorable and trustworthy democracy, the home of the brave.

4 August 1966 — US Army Chief of Staff General Harold K. Johnson visits Special Forces Detachment B42 at Camp Amn in Chau Doc Province's capital of Chau Phu. General Johnson, an anti-elitist foe of all "Special Forces" was one who also lacked the courage to stand up to Congress and the President and demand an end to the policy of our nation permitting enemy sanctuaries in Cambodia. During his briefing by LTC Brewer, General Johnson demonstrated his lack of concern for US and allied military personnel who were being killed and wounded by VC units based inside Cambodia who would attack and then disappear back into their safe-havens with total impunity. General Johnson is shaking the hand of B42 XO, Major Williford as LTC Brewer observes from behind the General. To Major Williford's left are Capt Bryant, the author, an Air Force Intelligence Officer and other members of Det. B42.

EPILOGUE — PART ONE
OFFICIAL DENIAL AND SUBTERFUGE

"Egregious nonsense," a U.S. government official told Upstate New York's <u>Syracuse Herald American</u> *reporter Frances Dinkelspiel in March of 1988, when questioned regarding my claim that the CIA had asked me to orchestrate the ambush assassination inside Cambodia of Crown Prince Norodom Sihanouk in June 1966. It was to be a "sterile" operation using Hou Hao irregulars and developed so as to make it appear to have been perpetrated by the Viet Cong. This same official, who did not want his name or title used, told Dinkelspiel that "By 1966, the CIA had agents in Cambodia, and it would have been far easier for them to kill Sihanouk than for untrained Vietnamese, who had to penetrate the border."*

I first met reporter Frances Dinkelspiel in March 1988, four years after my daughter Danilee, reading from her 1611 King James Bible in the cab of a U-Haul Truck, led me to confess my sins to almighty God through his Son, Jesus Christ, and ask Him to save me. Coming to know the Lord Jesus Christ as my personal Saviour, in and of itself, gave me the courage to launch a personal crusade to make public the truth of what I had experienced in covert operations as a US Army Green Beret.

Prior to that day I feared no man, but feared what our government could do and was capable of doing to me or members of my family should I decide to reveal what I had been a part of, knew was morally wrong, demonstrably evil and in violation of US or International Laws.

At the time I was an officer with First National Bank in Ithaca, New York, and Frances had her office in our bank building. My boss, Senior Vice President Tony

DiGiacomo, knew Frances and told me she had courage and journalistic integrity. "She writes straight from the shoulder," he told me.

With that sterling recommendation I went straight to her office, wanting to meet her and convince her of the continuing significance of what I had experienced as commander of U.S. Army Special Forces Team A-424 in An Phu, South Vietnam, some 22 years earlier. Her interest seemed piqued once I suggested what went wrong in South Vietnam should serve as a basis for rethinking policy and strategy at a national level. "The truth should be used as a vehicle to forewarn the White House, the Congress and the military establishment of the absolute need to establish, maintain and enforce safeguards deemed adequate to prevent the repeat of such a disaster," I told her.

I suggested that I would prove to her through the truth in my manuscript[1] that our nation was engaged in political subterfuge, dishonorable negotiation, aiding and abetting the enemy, and the outright betrayal and abandonment of the South Vietnamese people and their nation. Within the political and military command and management structure, I suggested to her, we needed to recognize the awesome potential that exists for the wanton abuse of power by those in government who commanded or controlled covert operations using CIA, Special Forces, or other unique highly motivated units anywhere in the world. Secrecy was too often used as a cover for illegal, immoral, unprincipled, even personally lucrative activities conducted within the framework of a legally constituted national or international mission force activity. I wanted to convince Frances, using my first draft manuscript for this book as evidence, that there was an absolute need for extreme caution when putting a covert operation of any kind in place.

After a short discussion, I gave Frances a copy of my draft manuscript to read. She would then get back to me for an interview if she decided to write an article. When she had finished reviewing the manuscript, Frances came to my shop office and interviewed me. Even after being told of the deniability factor that had been built into my covert operation under the "compartmentalization" process, and being warned that forces existed within our government who would rather my revelations be denied the public, Frances went on to glean facts and opinions from others whom she presumed had some knowledge of clandestine activities. Her goal was to corroborate, disavow or challenge the charges I had leveled against the Central Intelligence Agency, General William Westmoreland and the White House within the pages of my manuscript.

The 3 April 1988 edition of the Syracuse *Herald American* newspaper included the article,[2] *Ex-Green Beret rebuts stated U.S. Policy in Vietnam*, the result of her probe. She wrote that a "U.S. government official, who worked in the Special Forces in Vietnam, but who did not want his name or title used", when questioned by her, claimed that, "By 1966, the CIA had agents in Cambodia, and it would have been easier for them to kill Sihanouk than for untrained Vietnamese, who had to penetrate the border. Additionally," he asserted, "an assassination attempt did not make political sense, for the U.S. government needed Sihanouk."

It was a patently false assertion made by a nameless U.S. official who lacked the courage to lend his true identity to a bogus claim. In reality, had the ambush and murder been carried out as outlined in the CIA's TOP SECRET action plan conveyed to me in my camp by CIA agent Walter MacKem, and made to appear to have been perpetrated by the Viet Cong, it would have made political sense. Had my quid pro quo been honorably acted on by President Johnson, the military situation would have been vastly improved. The waffling Prince would have been dead, the North Vietnamese alienated from the Cambodians, sanctuaries would have been a thing of the past and all allied forces would then be permitted to engage the enemy wherever that enemy led them in offensive operations.

Factually, Prince Sihanouk had severed diplomatic ties with the United States in May of 1965, 13 months prior to my being asked to terminate him. Why, then, was the government official certain of a U.S. "need" for Sihanouk? I suspect President Johnson had something up his sleeve "needing Sihanouk", permitting sanctuaries for our enemies while limiting our air strikes against North Vietnam, denying our forces full engagement when in hot pursuit of the enemy, and all the while telling the American people he was "confident of victory."

I spoke to Frances years later, on 27 September 2001, and asked her if she realized that the "unnamed government official," whom she had quoted in her 3 April 1988 article had, perhaps unwittingly, boasted of the CIA having "had agents in Cambodia" by 1966 who could have been used to assassinate Sihanouk? She agreed with my understanding after I read her the quote in that 3 April 1988 article, and though she'd like to let me know now who it was she quoted, a fire in her home some years ago had destroyed all of her files. Once he'd rescued my men, American and South Vietnamese alike, from certain death by turning back the heavily armed ARVN Regiment sent by the CIA to attack my camp, the fate of Lieutenant General Quang Van Dang was sealed and he would, over time, become a desperate man. As provided me in his hand written notes[3] in February 1990, "The first article appeared in the magazine *Newsweek*: the same allegations that people keep repeating time after time: corruption, selling weapons & rice to the VC. Narcotics..."

That initial collection of lies precipitated a CIA/media based 23 year-long character assassination campaign that effectively destroyed his name and reputation throughout the reading world. It is interesting to note that at the time of that first article (two weeks from the day General Dang rescued us, he would later recall) the Newsweek staff were co-located with CIA staff in a billeting complex in Saigon. The character assassinations of General Dang and his wife, Nam, were orchestrated in great detail and carried out with the help of William Colby, General Westmoreland and others, many of whom were also unhappy with Dang for his insistence on the IV Corps Tactical Zone being defended and secured by ARVN and regional forces, aided by the Special Forces CIDG program. Conventional US forces were refused entry into the area. Only those Americans who wore a Green Beret and a few MACV advisory teams were stationed in the Delta area, at that time the most secure tactical corps zone in South Vietnam.

This author engaged in an 11 month crusade to free General Dang from the postwar 14 year character assassination campaign that had forced him to remain a virtual hostage in Montreal, Quebec, working as a janitor, dishwasher and re-cords-keeper under an assumed name while he was listed officially by the Canadian Government as an "undesirable alien." Dang was under threat of certain deportation to Vietnam where he faced a promised execution at the hands of the Communists. General Dang was cleared by an interdepartmental and interagency investigation of all accusations that had kept him prisoner in Canada and issued a permanent entry visa by the US on 7 September 1989. I personally escorted Dang into the United States 17 days later, yet the State Department consistently refuses to publicly acknowledge Dang's having been cleared of any and all of those heinous charges of wrongdoing. Books written by American and foreign authors alike have been published since Dang was cleared that contain the same vicious lies and innuendos against Dang that had plagued him before he was officially exonerated. I have led a campaign to clear Dang publicly since I escorted him into this country. I hope and pray that President George W. Bush, Secretary of State Colin Powell, Senator Hillary Rodham-Clinton and Congresswoman Cynthia McKinney, all of whom have been provided evidence of Dang's innocence, force the State Department to issue a press release that tells of Dang having been cleared in no uncertain terms. A book is in progress, titled *Dang - Victim of Subterfuge* that will tell Dang's life story with great detail on what he has faced in life and how he has been subjected to unfair, unwarranted, libelous and heinous attacks by individuals, organizations and political entities alike. To date they have all turned a deaf ear to the truth and the need for it to be published.

Now an American citizen, a former ARVN Lieutenant Colonel who worked with the US Army's Special Forces in irregular operations and who has asked to remain unnamed as he yet has relatives living in Vietnam, wrote of his recollections of 13 years in what the Communists called their "reeducation camp" system.

"For a time we were in Can Tho military prison. In those days we had enough food and our families could come to see us now and then. In July, 1976 they car-ried us to North Vietnam by boats as if we were cattle. We landed at Vinh, a town destroyed by bombing, and went northward by train. They put us so crowded in each car that some died because they could not get enough air. Later we went to Sonla Province by trucks where there were the old prisons built by the French, but only the four walls were left. They covered the roof with nylon, and we slept on the ground shoulder by shoulder!

"They ordered us to chop down bamboo and other trees to build fences and beds. The first month we had enough rice, and then they begin to cut down the amount; first by 25%, then 50%, then 75% until there was no more rice to eat.

They replaced rice with cattle corn and then tapioca from the cassava plant roots. We tried to grow corn, cassava and other vegetables but were short of water to grow good crops for ourselves.

"When we ran short of water we would be ordered to carry the framework to build a new camp maybe 10 or 15 miles away. They took all of our medications. When somebody got sick, regardless of what kind of sickness, they gave him only one kind of pill made in the north from some kind of leaves. One out of every 10 men in my camp died of sickness mainly due to shortage of food, mostly dying by dysentery.

"Every day we are forced to work very hard, going up and down many hills six or seven miles from prison camp to cut down trees and bring wood back to camp or to chop down trees and clear the forest to grow cassava plants for tapioca. It was a terrible time for us. Those are a few things I tell you."

I am hopeful the reader will question American and Communist Vietnamese honor, integrity, and human compassion in relationship to those negotiations and policies of subterfuge that permitted the Kissinger-negotiations with the enemy to bring about our betrayal and abandonment of the South Vietnamese and the treatment of South Vietnamese ex-military and civilians alike by the Communists whom we allowed to take over and swallow up their nation. When I arrived in An Phu, South Vietnam, a Green Beret Captain a long ways from home, I entered a land and joined together with a people I would come to know, respect and love.

Perhaps South Vietnam in total, a home to 18 million people, was much like those 64,000 Hoa Hao residents of An Phu District who I know welcomed our help as they strove for peace, a secure family life and freedom from oppression.

I found Vietnam to be a beautiful land with good people. People, who had put their trust in American friends to stand by their side when the Communist North tried by way of insurgency and outright invasion to replace their freedom with the tyranny of Communist rule.

We did well in the beginning to help the people to help themselves, but soon our government's ways took over, using the very things we had promised (weapons, ammunition, funds and air support) as a bargaining chip to gain the leadership role, effectively turning the Vietnamese struggle against Communism into what a courageous Vietnamese told me was "a war of body count, bombs, and safe-havens for the enemy." Sad, but true.

A well decorated combat veteran and Green Beret officer, who was known for his courage and his candid qualities, waxed somewhat poetic when he described how he felt about the men who wore the Army's Green Beret: the Special Forces troopers:

"Green Berets and SEALs were sent home, men who best worked and fought side-by-side with the South Vietnamese to safeguard their homes, their lands and their living, whether it be farming, fishing or some small business enterprise. Suffice it to say we commandeered their ship of state and sailed it under a flag of "Americanization" against the winds of Communist Insurgency. We then ran it aground in a sea of public dissent and government apathy, abandoning it in Communist-infested waters. Manned by a new crew under the banner of 'Vietnamization,' we watched as the tide of hope and trust lifted the ship off the sand bar of despair, only to sail into a sea of subterfuge. There it ran aground on broken American promises, its keel of renewed faith ripped and torn by the coral of a Kissinger-negotiated cease-fire conspiracy of subterfuge and surrender.

"Courageous efforts by the valiant crew of desperate South Vietnamese patriots who now stood alone to defend their ship against the rising red tide of encroaching Communism, but their valiant efforts were frustrated by the callous indifference of an American Congress ill equipped morally, mentally and politically to fend off radical demonstrators' demands, instead caving in to the selfish and cowardly attitudes of those Americans who let their voices be heard. The immoral blockade of betrayal that halted the flow of fuel, funds and ammunition torpedoed any chance the crew may have had to continue its course against the invaders from Hanoi. Lacking the means to chart a new course, the ship listed and sank in a sea of despair and the nation of South Vietnam died - yes, that nation of real people who had looked to America for their very survival ceased to exist on the last day of April in 1975."

What happened to South Vietnam is a tragedy and a black mark on this nation's honor, integrity and world stature. We cannot go back in time and correct the mistakes we as a nation made in the past, but we should assist the people of Vietnam by diplomatic means to achieve the desired result of a protected democracy that we failed to help them achieve during years of conflict.

Sadly, the pervasive influence of drugs, moral depravity and lack of integrity, all brought about by a series of actions sponsored by those with a liberal bias, have effectively taken God out of schools, government, other public and many private institutions, giving ground to devil-pleasing degradation and sin. This has resulted in the crippling of our will as a nation, thereby undermining our resolve, and compromising our credibility as the global defender of freedom. I pray that this once great United States of America is blessed with the revival of a national spirit that clings to the principals of duty, honor and country, one that respects the Christian heritage we were founded upon.

Our national will is so weak at this point in time we cannot resolve internal problems much less muster the courage needed to help stem the tide of evil and reverse the continuing spread of human rights abuses throughout the world. We must be careful to choose our national friends well, never compromising, instead demanding that to be a friend of these United States is to stand by the God-given rights of individuals as our constitution provides.

I am hoping and praying that the mental, moral and nationalistic fervor that has risen from the smoldering ruins of the Pentagon and World Trade Center is the kind of patriotic cohesion that will lead to committing our vast resources in an honorable crusade to rid the world of tyranny, rid it of undemocratic governments that prey on their people and other, weaker nations, and cause any government-sponsored terrorists to tremble in their boots.

We should not support nor defend dictatorial regimes in their quest to exercise power or to enrich their personal coffers at the expense of their own people. The name given the government's ideological slant should be of no significance in this regard. Neither the strategic relevance to our national security, the availability of natural or man-produced resources, nor the abundance of sophisticated technology should be considered as factors in determining our compassion for a nation's people. It is the people themselves, that vast majority who hold no political office, and who exert little or no direct influence on governmental affairs, who comprise the foundation of a country and it is they who must matter to other civilized societies.

* * * * *

EPILOGUE — PART TWO
SPEAKING WITH FORKED TONGUES

On 7 April 1965 President Lyndon B. Johnson, in a major speech[4] given at John Hopkins University, made a promise. "Why are we in South Vietnam?" he asked rhetorically. "We are there because we have a promise to keep. Since 1954 every American President has offered support to the people of South Vietnam. We have helped to build and we have helped to defend. Thus, over many years, we have made a national pledge to help South Vietnam defend its independence.

"And I intend to keep that promise. To dishonor that pledge, to abandon this small and brave nation to its enemies, and to the terror that must follow, would be an unforgivable wrong. We will not be defeated. We will not grow tired. We will not withdraw, either openly or under the cloak of a meaningless agreement."

For those who doubt that the South Vietnamese were lied to, coerced, manipulated and forced to accept as fact the fiction that was cleverly woven into the framework of subterfuge known as the "Paris Peace Accords," you need only read the following brief selection of lies and truths attributed to Presidents, statesmen and other high level dignitaries and agencies. A common thread of deception, purposeful manipulation of people and events and a failure to honor national resolve are factually portrayed herein.

HIGH LEVEL SUBTERFUGE AND BETRAYAL

THE LIE: On 2 September 1963 President John F. Kennedy[5] said, "In the final analysis, it is their war. They are the ones who have to win or lose it.

321

We can help them, we can give them equipment, we can send our men out there as advisors, but they have to win it - the people of South Vietnam - against the Communists. All we can do is help, and we are making it very clear. But I don't agree with those who say we should withdraw. That would be a great mistake."

THE TRUTH: In the Spring of that same year, President Kennedy had confided[6] to Senator Mansfield that he agreed on the need for a total military withdrawal from Vietnam but was firm in telling Mansfield that any public statement to that effect would have to wait until after the 1964 election. Later, he told[7] Kenneth O'Donnell, "In 1965, I'll be damned everywhere as a Communist appeaser. But I don't care. If I tried to pull out [of Vietnam] completely now, we would have another Joe McCarthy red scare on our hands, but I can do it after I'm reelected. So we had better make damned sure that I'm reelected."

THE FACT: The day[8] President Kennedy was assassinated in Dallas, a total of 43 Americans had been killed in action in South Vietnam.

THE LIE: On 7 April 1965, President Lyndon B. Johnson, in a major speech[4] given at John Hopkins University, made a promise. He said, "Why are we in South Vietnam? We are there because we have a promise to keep. Since 1954 every American President has offered support to the people of South Vietnam. We have helped to build and we have helped to defend. Thus, over many years, we have made a national pledge to help South Vietnam defend its independence.
"And I intend to keep that promise. To dishonor that pledge, to abandon this small and brave nation to its enemies, and to the terror that must follow, would be an unforgivable wrong. We will not be defeated. We will not grow tired. We will not withdraw, either openly or under the cloak of a meaningless agreement."

THE TRUTH: Less than three years later, on 31 March 1968, President Johnson went back on his promise to the people of South Vietnam, announced[9] he would not run for a second term, ordered that American forces be brought out of South Vietnam using "Vietnamization" as a cover to obscure what would be the beginning of the abandonment process. This decision was made after Secretary of Defense Clark Clifford, his wartime senior advisor, shared with Ambassador Bui Diem what he'd learned from secret meetings with the Joint Chiefs of Staff: that they had no solution for winning the war.

THE LIE: On 14 May 1969, more than two years prior to his giving North Vietnam just the opposite assurance, President Richard M. Nixon said, "We have ruled out either a one-sided withdrawal from Vietnam or the acceptance in Paris of terms that would amount to a disguised defeat. To abandon them now would risk a massacre that would shock and dismay everyone in the world who values human life."[10]

THE TRUTH: On 16 August 1971, at President Nixon's direction Henry Kissinger, during secret talks with North Vietnam's chief negotiator, Le Duc Tho, promised that the U.S. would withdraw American troops within nine months of an agreement.

THE LIE: In early January 1972, prior to President Nixon's trips to Peking and Moscow, Ambassador Ellsworth Bunker hand-delivered a letter[11] from President Nixon to President Thieu which outlined the objectives of his trips, saying in part, "Should the question of the Vietnam war arise in Peking, I want to assure you that I will set forth clearly and forcibly the position of the United States and the Republic of Vietnam that the war in Vietnam must be ended through direct negotiations with Hanoi, or failing that, by the growing inability of the Republic of Vietnam to defend itself against Hanoi's aggression," going on to assure Thieu, "You can continue to rely on the assistance of the United States in your efforts to bring peace to Vietnam and to build a new prosperity for the Vietnamese people."

THE TRUTH: On 20 April 1972, during a secrecy-shrouded trip to Moscow, Kissinger told[12] party boss Leonid Brezhnev that the United States would not insist on a total NVA withdrawal from the south as a prelude to settlement, providing the North Vietnamese drop their demand for Thieu's removal. The CIA and the majority of Washington's policy makers were not informed nor was Thieu. Kissinger did not, and would not, keep Thieu apprised of the many secret exchanges he had with Communist leaders destined to decide the fate of Thieu's country.

THE LIE: On 16 October 1972 President Nixon wrote President Thieu, ..."In the period following the cessation of hostilities you can be completely assured that we will continue to provide your government with the fullest support, including continued economic aid and whatever military assistance is consistent with the cease-fire provisions of this agreement [Paris Peace Accords]."[13]

ANOTHER LIE: On 14 November 1972 President Nixon wrote President Thieu, warning that he would sign the draft accord, with or without Thieu's support, but added a sweetener. "You have my absolute assurance," he wrote, "that if Hanoi fails to abide by the terms of the agreement, it is my intention to take swift and retaliatory action."[14]

THE LIE: On 5 January 1973, President Nixon wrote President Thieu, "Should you decide, as I trust you will, to go with us, you have my assurance of continued assistance in the post-settlement period and that we will respond with full force should the settlement be violated by North Vietnam."[15]

MORE LIES: On 17 January 1973 President Nixon wrote President Thieu, "Let me state these assurances once again in this letter: First, we recognize your government as the sole legitimate Government of South Vietnam. Secondly, we do not recognize the right of foreign troops to remain on South Vietnamese soil. Thirdly, the U.S. will react vigorously to violations of the Agreement ..."[16]

THE TRUTH: On 20 January 1973 President Nixon, in a blunt message to President Thieu, made the point, "As I have told you, we will initial the agreement on 23 January. I must know whether you are prepared to go along with us in this cause and I must have your answer by 1200 Washington time 21 January 1973."[17] Staring total isolation in the face, President Thieu capitulated.

MORE TRUTH: In February 1973, as President Nixon publicly reaffirmed our support for President Thieu, Kissinger, who was in Hanoi, assured our enemy that the U.S. was indeed ready to help with North Vietnamese reconstruction, promising $4.25 billion in economic aid to Hanoi with only a cursory mention of the need for Congressional approval.

THE FACTS: On 25 March 1973 the exchange of military prisoners was completed and on 29 March 1973 the last U.S. combat troops left South Vietnam.

MORE LIES: In April 1973, during a meeting with President Thieu in San Clemente, California, President Nixon and Kissinger outlined the need for President Thieu to make preparations to establish the National Council, the tripartite commission called for in the Paris Agreement. To sweeten the pill, they also made new commitments to him. Nixon assured Thieu unequivocally that Saigon could count on continued military aid at the "one billion dollar level" and "economic aide in the eight-hundred million dollar range" for several years. Kissinger promised that if "Hanoi's lack of good faith in the agreement could be demonstrated," American retaliation would be "massive and brutal."

President Thieu, quite understandably, was delighted by these reassurances. The United States was giving him an explicit pledge of economic and military aid at precise levels and a very nearly explicit promise to bomb Hanoi into submission if necessary. That Nixon and Kissinger were essentially talking out of turn, offering far more than they could deliver without Congressional approval, did not trouble him. Being an accomplished manipulator himself, he assumed they would find a way.

THE HARD TRUTH: A 31 July 1973 amendment[18] to the Cooper-Church Amendment prohibited American combat support in Cambodia, Laos, North Vietnam and South Vietnam effective 15 August 1973. That meant that the Seventh US Air Force based in Thailand and the Seventh Fleet in the Philippines were legally no longer available to the South Vietnamese. On 4 April 1974 Congress voted not to increase the Vietnam aid budget.

THE LIE THAT SET THE STAGE FOR ABANDONMENT AND BETRAYAL: On 10 August 1974, one day after being sworn in as President, Gerald Ford wrote President Thieu, "I do not think that I need to inform you that American foreign policy has always been marked by its essential continuity and its essential bipartisan nature. This is even more true today, and the existing commitments this nation has made in the past are still valid and will be fully honored in my administration."[19]

THE TRUTH: On 11 August 1974 the House cut the actual amount of dollars available to support aid to South Vietnam from the requested $1.45 billion to less than $450 million.[20]

DESPERATION PLEAS - THE TRUTH: On 19 March 1975 CIA Station Chief Thomas Polgar cabled CIA headquarters in Virginia that the situation in Military Region I was unraveling with dramatic speed. After a detailed account of the North Vietnamese situation, he ended his message with a very blunt appeal for American action, advising that the survival of independent South Vietnam depends in large measure on U.S. actions, stating unequivocally that there was no doubt in his mind that a lack of U.S. determination in the Vietnam context would kill the nation which earlier U.S. efforts had helped to create.

Instead of the message of unilateral military support he had hoped for, he was advised by CIA headquarters to mount some sort of propaganda campaign. Polgar, enraged by such insipid advice at such a time of crisis, wired back to CIA Headquarters on 21 March 1975 advising in strong terms that propaganda in favor of South Vietnam would not make any difference. North Vietnamese could not be stopped with words, only with antitank weapons and aircraft, he warned, telling his bosses that the failure of the U.S. to hinder an all-out North Vietnamese effort would inevitably terminate existence of an independent South Vietnam and that no amount of words will change that."

FINAL PLEA: On 25 March 1975, President Thieu wrote President Ford, "... As I am writing to you, the military situation in South Vietnam is very grave and growing worse by the hour. The serious dis-equilibrium of forces in favor of the North Vietnamese as well as the strategic advantage accumulated over the past two years have led to the present critical situation, especially in MR II, as you already know.

...."Hanoi's intention to use the Paris Agreement for a military takeover was well known to us at the very time of negotiating the Paris Agreement. You may recall that we signed it, not because we naively believed in the enemy's good will, but because we trusted in America's solemn commitment to safeguard the peace in Vietnam.

...."Firm pledge was then given to us that the United States would retaliate swiftly and vigorously to any violation of the Agreement by the enemy. We consider those pledges the most important guarantee of the Paris Agreement. We know that the pledge is most crucial to our survival.

...."At this crucial hour when the fate of South Vietnam is at stake and when peace is severely threatened, I hereby solemnly request that the government of the United States of America live up to its pledge. Specifically, I earnestly request hat you take the two following actions: To order a brief but intensive B-52 air strike against the enemy's concentrations of forces and logistic bases within South Vietnam, and to urgently provide us with necessary means to contain and repel the offensive. ...."Once again, I wish to appeal to you, to the credibility of American foreign policy, and especially to the conscience of America ... "[21]

This was the last letter President Thieu wrote to an American President. It was never answered.

ON 30 APRIL 1975 SOUTH VIETNAM CEASED TO EXIST AS A NATION.

EPILOGUE — PART THREE
WORDS OF PAIN, ANGUISH AND WISDOM

"For the first time, I am ashamed to be an American, because we failed Vietnam and its people," Yung Krall cried out on 30 April 1975.

"I owe them my life in the war ..." one of my courageous interpreters, Trung P. Nguyen, wrote from his new home in America, recalling his time with me in An Phu. "Many Hoa Hao friends of ours died for the right cause and their belief. Many were imprisoned for a long time after the country collapsed. Many lost their families, wives and children at sea during their perilous journey to freedom. Our heroes sacrificed their lives for their now living friends. I owe them my life in the war. My family owes them the comfort we now enjoy. We owe them a lot of things... and we shall remember them as long as we live."[22]

"We lost Vietnam forever." Yung Krall, a woman of integrity and courage, wrote in her heart-wrenching book *A Thousand Tears Falling - The True Story of a Vietnamese Family Torn Apart by War, Communism, and the CIA.*[23] It is the truth about South Vietnam from a different perspective. She writes of a telephone call she received at her home in Hawaii on 23 April 1975, just seven days before South Vietnam would cease to exist. "We are out of Saigon," her sister Hoa Binh said in a tired voice that buried her sadness. She had just arrived in Guam.

"Are you all right?" Yung asked. "We left everything behind," her sister sobbed. "We have each other, Hoa Binh," Yung told her, yet knowing she couldn't do much to comfort her over the telephone.
"We lost Vietnam forever," Hoa Binh cried.

The day that Saigon fell, Yung, who had been in the United States since 20 June 1968, cried out, "For the first time, I am ashamed to be an American, because we failed Vietnam and its people."

"We turned our backs on them and just left them there all alone ... "[24] recounted retired Major John Strait, my former XO in An Phu, when discussing the tragic end of the war in South Vietnam. Voicing his recollections on audio tape some 22 years after we'd worked and fought side by side with the Hoa Haos of An Phu, he told how "The whole situation kind of saddened me the way that the Americans tried so long to develop loyalty with the people in Vietnam, and then we turned our backs on them and just left them there all alone and we don't even know how many of them got slaughtered.

"I just can't hardly have too much respect for the politicians and the statisticians who planned and conducted the withdrawal of the whole American part of the war. It was terrible, like you said, Dangerous Dan, the way they, President Johnson and some of the other politicians — that had never cocked a cannon — called all the shots over there."

Evidence of our lack of moral values: As if to echo the truth of our abandonment and then betrayal of the South Vietnamese people and their military, when a number of ARVN General officers arrived in May 1975 at an old metal barracks building on the Island of Guam, including former III Corps Commanding General Toan Van Nguyen and General Truong Quang Ngo (the defender of Da Nang) an American Naval officer marched into the building and ordered them to remove their uniforms. When asked if they could keep their "shoulder stars" the American replied callously, "No, you have no army, no country any more."

"The truth of this war lies buried with its victims ... " in the final paragraph of his book *In the Jaws of History*[25] former South Vietnamese Ambassador Bui Diem wrote, "The truth is in the millions of Vietnamese families that have suffered the most horrible tragedies, people who understood what was happening only in the vaguest way. The truth of this war lies buried with its victims, with those who died, and with those who are consigned to live in an oppressed silence, for now and for the coming generations - a silence the world calls peace."

"I can say the Hoa Hao troopers were the heroes, brave fighters; the untouchables. They are the Vietnamese Communist's enemies." So wrote another of my former interpreters from An Phu in a 11 March 1999 letter,[27] also recalling the surrender to North Vietnam, "Properties were confiscated, land lords, business owners evicted by the new government — the Communists. While we were arrested for re-education (no trial or sentence at all) I met some Hoa Hao members, we ate together and helped each other so as to keep our morale and survive."

"... South Vietnam lost the war in Washington ..." On 25 August 1989, in a telephone conversation with this author, the CIA's last Station Chief in Saigon, Thomas Polgar, expressed his continuing concern for the people of South Vietnam and indicated his willingness to testify before Congress that he had been ordered to destroy all records, even logs and notes pertaining to his activities and those of his office as CIA Station Chief in Saigon during the period January 1972 through 30 April 1975. "It was to be as if we did not exist," he painfully told me. Then, on 9 October 1989, in a letter[27] to former ARVN Lieutenant General Quang Van Dang, Polgar wrote, "I, for one, am convinced that South Vietnam lost the war in Washington and that Saigon was a casualty of Watergate."

Be Ye Vigilant - Lest We Forget and Sacrifice Others through our Lack of National Integrity

Crown Prince Norodom Sihanouk, pictured here in the mid 1950s, survives today as the King and Head of State for life of Cambodia, now a democratic constitutional monarchy.

AFTERWORD

Books sometimes create their own story. *Expendable Elite* is a book that was looking for a publisher for almost twenty years. It wasn't searching because its tale of the Vietnam Conflict lacked drama, intrigue or excitement but because of the political truths the book told.

I first heard about Lieutenant Colonel "Dangerous" Dan Marvin and his book when I happened to speak with author Jim Marrs about supplying a "blurb" for TrineDay's first book, *America's Secret Establishment — An Introduction to the Order of Skull & Bones* by Antony Sutton. Jim, finding-out that TrineDay's calling was to bring suppressed views and works to a wider audience, told me that he had just that day received a call from an author who couldn't find a publisher. Jim gave me "Dangerous" Dan's phone number and we spoke later that day. Needless to say, Dan had quite the story to tell. He had been "hunting" for a publisher for almost twenty years. The story was being rejected not for literary reasons but because he dared to tell some of what goes on behind the veil of secrecy surrounding Special Forces Operations — a world of political assassinations, psychological warfare and the gritty, true reality of the tactics of war.

Coming from the family of a repented CIA officer, whose publicly declared reason for leaving the agency was the CIA's predilection for using the ends to justify the means, I could relate to Dan's desire for telling his story. *Expendable Elite* affords us all the opportunity to learn from a clearer historical record, garner some understandings into the use of Special Forces in conflicts and hopefully spread the balm of daylight that may help heal some souls of their secret burdens. Truth, as has been said, is the first casualty of war, and with variance from truth our humanity and our republic suffers.

Robert A "Kris" Millegan
Publisher
TrineDay
3/26/03

Phum Poste Chass

Phum Prêk Khtô

Phum Prêk Da

m Phum
kê Borei
60'

Krau

Kâmpóng Youl

VT WT

Phum Kâmpóng Âmpil

WS

ôch

Phum Rômênh

Daeum Chan WS
Cham

Chhuk

ng

ik CAMBODIA

VIETNAM

Phum Khpôp
11

5

Phum Kôpal Kŏăng

Phum Chrey Thom

KHET KANDAL

Ấp An Thanh

Ấp Phú Lợi

Ấp Tắc Trúc

Ấp Phước Khánh

Phum Bak Dai

Ấp Phước Hòa

Ấp Phước Thạnh
(3)

Ấp Phú Hòa
(1)

Sông Châu Đốc

2

Phum Nêm Vang

Ấp Vĩnh Phú
(1)

Ấp Phú Thạnh
(2)

Ấp Vĩnh Thạnh
(2)

Ấp Vĩnh Hội (2)

137

CU LAO BA

Phum Kdol Chŭmrun

3

Phum Dăngkum
Méan Chey

Phum Bantéay Thleay

Detail of the Vietnam - Cambodia
border area near An Phu

Ấp Vĩnh Phú

NÚI SAM

Ấp Vĩnh Đông
2.3

LTL
10

Ấp Đông
Hòa

Ấp Tây Hưng
16

3

Vĩnh Tế

Ấp Vĩnh Tây
(2)

Phum Chŏng Kaôh
Phum Kăăm
Sâmmã Léu

Phum Prêk Tŭnléa
Phum

Kăăm Sâmpa Kraom
Indefinite

Chua Minh Dinh

Ấp Phú Hiệp

10

Ấp Phú Hưng

Ấp Vĩnh H
(2)

Ấp Phú Thạnh (1)

Ấp Tân Thạnh

Ấp Tân Vĩnh

Ấp Vĩnh Phước

Ấp Tân

SÔNG HẬU

Ấp Vĩnh Thanh (1)

Vĩnh Hậu

Kinh Châu Đốc

Ấp 2

Ấp Vĩnh Trinh

Ấp Vĩnh Trường

Ấp Hà Bao

Ấp Phước Quản

138

Châu Phong

Kinh Vĩnh An

Ấp Vĩ

Châu Giảng

Ấp Trung

CHÂU PHÚ
(CHÂU ĐỐC)

Ấp Phố

140

CHÂU ĐỨC

Khánh Hòa

Ấp Khánh An
(2) Ấp Chánh
(2)

Ấp Khánh
(1)

Ấp Khánh

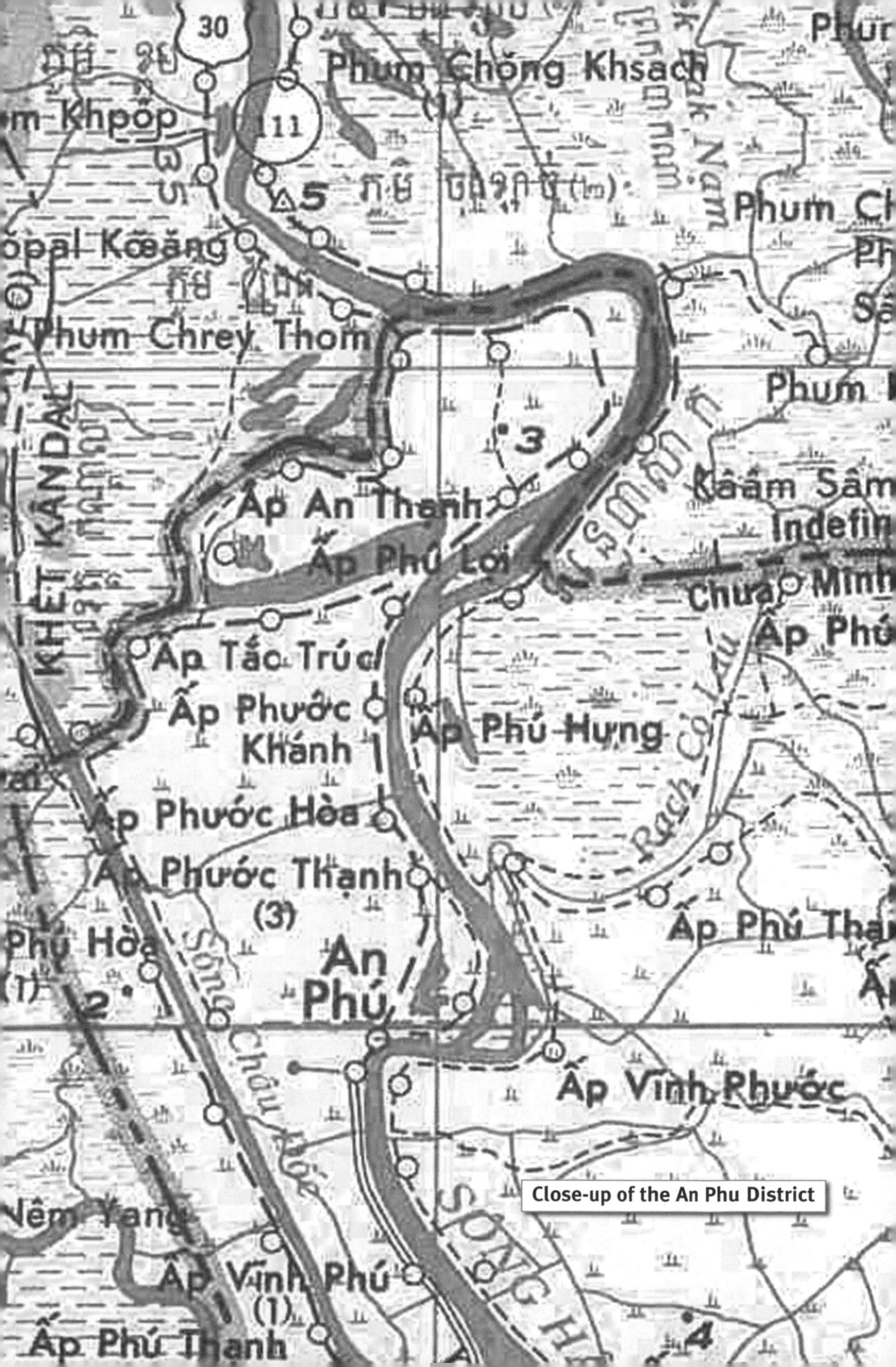

Close-up of the An Phu District

6 May 66 — Home of CIDG Sergeant Trang located in Binh Thien Hamlet near Khanh Binh FOB. Sergeant Trang's wife and daughter killed here by VC booby-trap.

8 May 66 — Four female C terrorists who rigged the booby-trap that killed Mrs. Trang and her baby. Captured by men of the 442nd CIDG Company. Interrogation area.

APPENDIX 1

<u>An Phu District, Chau Doc Province</u>

<u>Republic of South Vietnam</u>

<u>INTELLIGENCE SUMMARY - December 27, 1965</u>

261st Bn: Strength 500
            1,500 meters due west of Khanh Binh FOB
            1 ea 81mm Mtr, 5 ea 60mm Mtr, 4 ea 57mm RR,
                Unk 3.5 RL, Unk LMG, ASA

267th Bn: Strength 450
            2,000 meters northwest of Khanh Binh FOB
            2 ea 81mm Mtr, 3 ea 57mm RR, Unk 3.5 RL,
                Unk 60mm Mtr, Unk LMG, ASA

367th Bn: Strength 400
            In Bung Ven Secret Base NNW of Phu Hiep FOB
            2 ea 81mm Mtr, 6 ea 60mm Mtr, 5 ea 57mm RR,
                2 ea .50 cal AA MG, Unk 3.5 RL, Unk LMG, ASA

512th Hvy Wpns Bn(-): (AKA 264th) Strength 320
            Across Bassac River and north of Khanh An
            1 ea 81mm Mtr, 2 ea .50 cal AA MG, unk 60mm Mtr,
                Unk LMG, ASA

260th Hvy Wpns Co (p/o 512th) Strength 150
            1,200 meters north of Phu Hiep FOB
            1 ea 81mm Mtr, 1 ea .50 cal AA MG, 1 ea 60mm Mtr,
                Unk 3.5 RL, Unk LMG, ASA

All above units belong to the newly formed SOUTHWARD REGIMENT
They are being re-equipped, trained, and supplied for attack
against the northern areas of An Phu District.

Total strength .... <u>1,820</u>

30 day projected strength... **<u>2,200</u>**

Intelligence summary: 27 Dec 65

APPENDIX 2

USASF DETACHMENT A-424
An Phu District, Chau Doc Province, Republic of South Vietnam

FACILITY, WEAPONS & EQUIPMENT STATISTICS - DECEMBER 28, 1965

<u>Dimensions</u>:   Main camp: 180 meters square
                    Inner Compound: 50 x 70 meters
                    Drop/Landing Zone: 60 x 180 meters

<u>Outer Defensive Obstacles - Camp Dan Nam (60 meters deep)</u>
        5 belts/triple concertina wire
        4 belts/double apron barbed wire
        1 belt/tanglefoot barbed wire
        1 belt/Claymore mines
        Moat - 8 meters wide

<u>Crew Served & Individual Weapons</u>

Type of Weapon	Camp Dan Nam	Phu Hiep FOB	Khanh Binh FOB
4.2" mortar	1		
81MM mortar	4	1	
60MM mortar	6	3	3
.50 cal. MG	1		
.30 cal. MG	17	4	4
M79 grenade launcher	2	1	1
BAR	27	8	8
M1D sniper rifle	6		
M1 rifle	60	20	20
Carbine (M1/M2)	276	90	90
Sub machine gun	52	14	14
12 gauge shotgun	8	4	4
.45 cal. pistol	15	2	2

<u>Ammunition stock</u> 15 day sustained rate level in two large ammo bunkers in Dan Nam & FOB bunkers. 3 day sustained rate level in small bunkers & all mortar pits and automatic weapons positions.

<u>Power Generation Equipment (Dan Nam only)</u>
2 ea: 10KW, 5KW, 2½KW AC gas powered + 2 ea DC battery chargers

<u>Communications Equipment</u>
1 ea AN/FRC-93 SSB, 1 ea AN/GRC-87, 1 ea AN/GRC-109
5 ea PRC-10, 2 ea PRC25, 38 ea HT-1, 8 ea TR-20 & internal camp telephone system.

<u>Water Purification Equipment</u> Diatomite (charcoal filter) #2

<u>Vehicles</u> 1 ea 2½ ton, 2 ea ¾ ton, 2 ea ¼ ton

<u>Boats</u> 14 Assault boats (7w/25HP motors & 7w/40HP motors)
       50 Sampans w/7½HP long stem motors (10 per company)
       200 Sampans w/o motors (40 per company)
       1 Barge w/2½ ton truck motor & 6 speed transmission

Facility, weapons and equipment status: 28 Dec 65

APPENDIX 3

USASF DETACHMENT A-424
An Phu District, Chau Doc Province, Republic of South Vietnam

MISSIONS AND FORCES - DECEMBER 28,1965

MISSIONS:

1. Security and surveillance of 50 kilometers of border with
    Cambodia and control of Bassac River entry into Cambodia.
2. Clear & hold operations to secure all areas within An Phu
    District (220 square kilometers).
3. Unconventional warfare operations against Viet Cong infra-
    structure, secret bases and sanctuaries in Cambodia.
4. Civic action in support of the local government and the
    64,000 people indigenous to An Phu District.
5. Advise & assist sub-sector in military government, civil
    affairs, psychological operations, and combat operations.
6. Logistical and administrative support of all forces assigned
    within the CIDG program.
7. Other covert missions as deemed necessary.

FORCES:

CIDG Program:

USASF Det A-424:	2 Off, 5 NCOs
VNSF Det A-147:	9 Off, 1 WO, 10 NCOs
Bodyguards:	10 men
CIDG Companies:	5 companies of 132 men each
Recon Platoon:	42 men
TOTAL FORCES:	11 Off, 1 WO, 727 men

Sub-Sector:

*RF Companies:	2 companies of 2 off & 120 men each
** PF Forces:	12 Plat & 5 Squads (Total:12 Off/500 men
TOTAL FORCES:	16 Off & 740 men

Deployment of CIDG Forces:

Main Camp Dan Nam	Khanh Binh FOB	Phu Hiep FOB
7 USASF & 12 VNSF	4 VNSF	4 VNSF
10 Bodyguards	442nd Company	444th Company
3 Companies (441st, 443rd, 445th)		
Recon Platoon		

* The two paramilitary RF companies have a primary mission of securing district
(sub-sector) headquarters and the 155MM Howitzer section site. They are also
available to Province for operations outside the district.

** The paramilitary PF platoons and squads are made up of nighttime fighters
that man the PF outposts in or near their native hamlet and engage in night
ambush operations within a 2,000 meter radius of their hamlet. They are very
lightly armed, having no machine guns, mortars or fully automatic weapons.

NOTE: A 155MM Howitzer Section (2 guns) is located in the
district & controlled by sub-sector. Can be pulled by Province.

Mission and forces report: 28 Dec 65

APPENDIX 4

PSYCHOLOGICAL OPERATIONS ESTIMATE

CAMP: AN PHU

DATE: APRIL 1966

1. Target Audiences:

  a. Civilians:

    (1) Ethnic Groups: The majority of the population within the operational area of the camp is Vietnamese (95%), with the remainder composed of Cambodians, Chinese, and Indians.

    (2) Religious Groups:

      (a) The predominant religion of the area is Hoa Hao. The Hoa Hao sect has been characterized by militant spirit even though it practices a form of the passive Buddist religion. The history of the sect reveals that it has, at times, resorted to acts of banditry, has attained considerable political influence, and has frequently aligned themselves with the government in power, only later to oppose the same government. The loyalty of the sect is very difficult to evaluate when its rather erratic past is considered; however, this behavior is somewhat understandable in light of historical events affecting the sect. The Hoa Hao have at times been troubled by internal struggles for power, but generally seem to demonstrate a fairly consistent loyalty to the sect itself. At present they appear to be completly united with their leadership.

      (b) The Hoa Hao Sect has four principal precepts: to honor their parents, to love their country, to respect Buddhism and its teachings, and to love their fellow men. They say in order to be a good Hoa Hao you must first be a good citizen of your country. Although Buddhism is normally a passive religion, they believe that it is good that a man try to improve himself, that it is not enough just to accept one's fate and sit back praying. They believe that a person must do good actions to help himself, his country and fellow men. This allows them to be more aggressive than other Buddhists.

      (c) One very desirable characteristic of the HOA HAO is their great hatred of the Viet Cong. The loyalty of the HOA HAO to the government in power has varied since 1947 when the Viet-Minh killed Huyen-Phu-So, the founder of the HOA HAO sect, but their hatred of the VC appears constant and deeply rooted.

    (3) Attitudes toward:

      (a) GVN: At present the HOA HAO leaders are actively supporting the GVN in its attempt to rid the country of VC; however, the duration of this support cannot be determined.

      (b) Military/Paramilitary forces: The intense hatred of the VC has made the Hoa Hao a militant sect. As long as the military is seeking to defeat the VC, the HOA HAO will support it.

Psychological Operations Estimate: Apr 66

APPENDIX 4 *(CONT.)*

PSYCHOLOGICAL OPERATIONS ESTIMATE (CONT'D)
Detachment A-424 (Camp AN PHU)

(c) Local Government: The Province Chief and the District Chief are both members of the HOA HAO sect and are supported by the people of the area. It is difficult to estimate the degree of loyalty to the local government if either were replaced by a non-HOA HAO.

(4) Key Communicators:

(a) The key communicator within the district appears to be the Camp Commander (Maj Le-Van-Phoi). He is definately pro-American and supports RVN government programs though he is cautious about accepting government promises due to past disappointments. He has the complete loyalty of the CIDG and his influence is felt throughout the district. If programs have his support they have every chance of succeeding. Without his support programs have a great deal of difficulty getting off the ground, and particularly if he opposes them.

(b) Another primary communicator within the area is the Chairman of the Hoa Hao District Council, Doan-Ngoc-Chau. He is also very favorably disposed towards the US advisors and supports the government. His voice is highly regarded in the central committee Hoa Hao sect and his influence within the predominantly HOA HAO district is great.

(c) Captain Nguyen-Van-Tuoi, the District Chief, rates approximately third in influence among the leadership of the district. He is a career army officer in ARVN and is a Hoa Hao. His status within the sect does not place him in as high a position as Maj Phoi or Mr Chau. He is also pro-American and pro-RVN government.

(d) Tran-Quang-Minh, the VIS Chief, has a following of his own throughout the district. His influence is felt through the propaganda program in the district and being editor of the district newspaper places him in a rather important position as a communicator. He is pro-American and pro-RVN government.

(e) The National Police Chief, Vo-Van-Dat, is well liked throughout the district and travels a great deal visiting all the villages and hamlets. His personal influence is extensive. He is pro-American.

(f) Tran-Van-Duc, the District Agricultural Chief is another well liked and well known individual. He works daily with the farmers of the area and he is well known. He conducts classes and cooperative meetings for adult and youth in Agriculture and thus has the ear of one of the major industries of the district. He is pro-American and RVN. Another interesting side-light is that Mr Duc rarely asks for material support from the American Advisors but very much appreciates ideas and moral support.

(5) Degree of literacy: Education is an important goal of the HOA HAO sect. Their literacy is high at approximately 55%.

(6) Local superstitions, customs, taboos, etc: The HOA HAO possess no particular taboos or superstitions. The use of common courtesy is sufficent to establish good rapport.

Psychological Operations Estimate: Apr 66 *(cont.)*

PSYCHOLOGICAL OPERATIONS ESTIMATE (CONT'D)
Detachment A-424 (Camp AN PHU)

    (7) Percentage committed to the VC, Against the VC, Uncommitted:

        Pro-VC: 2-5% (relatively inactive); Anti-VC: 95-98%.

    (8) Aspirations of the people: The HOA HAO people want to defeat the VC. In addition they want to practice their religion without excessive controls or restrictions placed upon them by the government.

    (9) VC Propaganda: The Viet-Cong tried various forms of propaganda but it is found to be ineffective with a least 95% of the population.

    (10) Themes most used by the VC: Discredit the RVN and point out their poor treatment of the HOA HAO under the Diem government. Discredit Americans as imperialistic adventurers and war-mongers.

    (11) Effects of RVN propaganda: Programs in the field of education have had the greatest propaganda effect upon the people and the younger generation tends to be pro-government.

  b. Friendly Forces (Military/Paramilitary)

    (1) Ethnic groups: Same as for civilians.

    (2) Religious groups: CIDG is 100% HOA HAO.

    (3) Attitudes Toward:

        (a) GVN: Same as civilians.

        (b) Military Service: The militant, aggressive nature of the sect provides for ease of assimilation into military service.

        (c) Leaders: Providing their leaders are of the same sect, the HOA HAO have no problems with leadership. At present all civilian and military leaders are of the sect.

        (d) Civilians: Since the majority of the people are of the same sect the military enjoys good rapport with the civilians. The CIDG is recruited easily from within the district.

    (4) Morale: At present the morale of the local military is high because the VC have yet to defeat local troops in battle and have been badly beaten themselves on several occasions.

    (5) Discipline: Extremely well disciplined. The soldiers respect and obey their appointed leaders.

    (6) Informal leaders: (See par 1a(4))

    (7) Effect of VC Propaganda: Negative

Psychological Operations Estimate: Apr 66 *(cont.)*

APPENDIX 4 *(CONT.)*

PSYCHOLOGICAL OPERATIONS ESTIMATE (CONT'D)
Detachment A-424 (Camp AN PHU)

(8) Themes used by VC: Same as for civilians.

(9) Effect of GVN Propaganda: Intangible. Propaganda that has greatest application in this district is localy developed, area oriented, with tie-in to Saigon government.

c. There are no enemy units in our area.

2. Exploitable Psychological Opportunities:

a. Civilians

(1) One of the basic precepts of the religion is that a good HOA HAO is one who is a good citizen. In this instance, the HOA HAO pride should be called upon to strengthen relationships between them and the government.

(2) Hatred of the VC should be exploited.

(3) The HOA HAO desire for education and improvement could be exploited by sound programs of education and reconstruction, thereby providing them with a moral obligation to repay good programs with loyalty.

b. Friendly Forces:

(1) Victories over the VC should be exploited.

(2) The part the paramilitary and military forces play in the overall rural reconstruction program should be exploited.

(3) Benifits of RVN soldiers should be compared with life of average Viet-Cong guerrilla.

c. Enemy Forces: Continual aggressive day and night patrol actions beared toward continued fear of the HOA HAO's by the VC.

3. Suggested Themes:

a. For Civilians:

(1) HOA HAO

(a) GVN support and respect of HOA HAO.

(b) Progress will be found in support of the GVN.

(c) Programs of public welfare are supported by the GVN.

(d) US assistance in the war is due to the work of GVN.

Psychological Operations Estimate: Apr 66 *(cont.)*

APPENDIX 4 *(CONT.)*

(2) Non-HOA HAO: The HOA HAO are fighting with the Non-Hoa Hao to rid the country of a common enemy, the VC.

b. Friendly Forces:

(1) Superior training, equipment and leadership enables them to defeat the VC.

(2) The civilians are with them in their fight for the VC.

(3) There is great honor in defending their country.

(4) The Vietnamese are winning the victories.

c. Enemy Forces:

(1) All returnees are welcomed by GVN.

(2) GVN offers them a new life.

(3) VC promises are false ones.

(4) GVN training and equipment is superior to those of the VC.

(5) Prices for VC weapons.

(6) Pay is much better.

(7) Living conditions and food is much better.

4. Miscellaneous:

a. Conduct toward the HOA HAO:

(1) The HOA HAO like Americans and are not easily offended by them. They have a good sense of humor and enjoy joking. They readily overlook a breach of their customs by an American that they probably would not overlook if committed by another Vietnamese.

(2) They very much appreciate attempts at speaking the Vietnamese language and eating of their native food.

(3) Some HOA HAO do not desire to discuss the death of Huynh-Phu-So; however, they will answer questions concerning this subject. Many do not believe he is actually dead, according to the teachings of their religion.

b. Current US policy:

(1) In dealing with the people in the operational area stress the US commitment to GVN and that any actions against GVN are against the US position. The US is here through the invitation of the government.

DANIEL MARVIN
Captain   QMC
Commanding

Psychological Operations Estimate: Apr 66 *(cont.)*

APPENDIX 5

USASF DETACHMENT A-424
An-Phu District, Chau-Doc Province, Republic of South Vietnam

INTELLIGENCE SUMMARY - 18 MAY 1966

261st Bn: Strength 550
2,500 meters due west of Khanh-Binh FOB
1 ea 81MM Mtr, 5 ea 60MM Mtr, 4 ea 57MM RR, Unk 3.5 RL,
Unk LMG, ASA

267th Bn: (AKA 407) Strength 520
3,000 meters northwest of Khanh-Binh FOB
3 ea 57MM RR, 2 ea 81MM Mtr, Unk 3.5 RL, Unk 60MM Mtr,
Unk LMG, ASA

367th Bn: (AKA 510/364) Strength 480
Across Bassac River from Khanh-Binh PF OP
2 ea 81MM Mtr, 5 ea 57RR, 6 ea 60MM Mtr, 2 ea .50Cal AA MG,
Unk 3.5 RL, Unk LMG, ASA

512th Hvy Wpns Bn (-): (AKA 264) Strength 320
Across Bassac River from Khanh-An PF OP
1 ea 75MM Mtn Gun, 1 ea 81MM Mtr, 3 ea .50 Cal AA MG,
Unk 60MM Mtr, Unk LMG, ASA

260th Hvy Wpns Co (-): Strength 104
2,500 meters NW of Phu-Hiep FOB.
1 ea 81MM Mtr, 1 ea .50Cal AA MG, 1 ea 60MM Mtr, Unk 3.5 RL,
Unk LMG, ASA

1st Plat, 260th Hvy Wpns Co: Strength 42
Across Binh-Ghi River 2,000 meters NW of Tac-Truc PF OP
2 ea 3.5 RL, 1 ea .50Cal AA MG, 1 ea 60MM Mtr, Unk LMG, ASA

Total Strength of Southward Regiment Units: 2,016

Potential Battle Odds:

In Khanh-Binh area.. 1,550 VC against 182 Friendly [132 CIDG & 50 PF]

In Khanh-An area.... 320 VC against 179 Friendly [131 CIDG & 48 PF]

In Phu-Hiep area.... 104 VC against 90 Friendly - all CIDG

In Tac-Truc area....   42 VC against 45 Friendly - all PF

Overall Odds........ 2,016 VC against 496 Friendly

Heavy Weapons Odds:

	VC	CIDG
81MM Mortar	6 ea	3 ea
75MM Mtn Gun	1 ea	0
57MM RR.............	12 ea	0
.50Cal AA MG	4 ea	0

Intelligence summary: 18 May 66

APPENDIX 6

Translated excerpt from the Cambodian neutral newspaper <u>TRUNG-LAP</u>
published in Phnom-Penh, Cambodia on 23 May 1966

* * * * * * * * * *

The continued information of VC attacks against enemy positions which were located along Bassac River of An-Phu District, Chau-Doc Province, started on 18 May 1966.

Press information: It is saying that at 0200 hrs on 18-19 May 1966, The VC Liberty Armed Forces of An-Giang Province attacked together on same time enemy's positions which were located along Bassac River of An-Phu District, Chau-Doc Province; included Khanh-Binh, Khanh-An, Dong-Duc, Cai-Coi, Dung-Thang posts and two companies which located at the field with the command of US American. The fighting is continuing.

The first information was said that the VC Liberty Armed Forces have destroyed two of the companies above and Khanh-An post, especially the Khanh-Binh outpost, there were only 6 men left (20 May 1966).

The VC Liberty Armed Forces killed 250 men in the fighting and captured 38 others, besides the Recon platoon has been surrendered.

The VC Liberty Armed Forces and local people also captured more and more troops of enemy who always been harassing the Viet & Khmer border. Particularly the VC Liberty Armed Forces seized a lot of weapons and equipment.

The victory news had made the people to be happy.

* * * * * * * * * *

Note: During the first three days (the period covered by the article) of the five day battle, the VC had killed 25 of our people (not 250), had wounded 83, and had captured none. They only captured 2 of our weapons (1 carbine & 1 M-1 Rifle) and the Recon platoon did not surrender. In fact they had been given heroic action bonuses for their bravery at Khanh-An.

Cambodian newspaper article: 23 May 66

APPENDIX 7

USASF DETACHMENT A-424
An-Phu District, Chau-Doc Province, Republic of South Vietnam

INTELLIGENCE REPORT: 1-31 MAY 1966

1. Intelligence Net (Managed by Major Phoi)

   a. Number of Agent Handlers: 6

   b. Number of Agents: 15 (All female)

   c. Area covered by net: All of An-Phu District and VC Sanctuary areas in Cambodia.

   d. Net operational expense for month: 6,000$ VN ($200 US)

   e. Agencies in District that provided intelligence: Sub-Sector and National Police.

   f. Intelligence received from outside District: None

2. Viet Cong propaganda: The VC used loudspeaker appeals from across the border in their sanctuaries and spread leaflets near the border. Their efforts were relatively ineffective and all were oriented toward an anti-American Imperialist rule in Vietnam.

3. Foreign nationals in area: None

4. Ethnic and Religious composition of the Strike Force (CIDG): All companies are comprised solely of Hoa-Haos. RF and PF forces are also Hoa-Haos.

Intelligence report: 31 May 66

APPENDIX 8

USASF DETACHMENT A-424
An-Phu District, Chau-Doc Province, Republic of South Vietnam

CIVIC ACTION REPORT - 1-31 MAY 1966

1.   General Evaluation: Efforts were centered around the estimated 8,000 refugees from Khanh-Binh and Khanh-An villages, forced southward by VC attacks in those areas. With the help of District and Province social welfare and civic actions teams, and the Catholic Relief Agency, over 6,000 refugees were given food, clothing, and temporary shelter.

Local people, living outside the battle areas, sheltered and fed an estimated 1,800 refugees in addition to the above.

2.   Civilian casualties and other losses:

35 Civilians were killed and 141 injured by VC actions.
46 houses were destroyed and another 220 damaged by the VC actions.
The loss of livestock, boats, and personal goods have not been determined.

3.   Items distributed included:

164 Bags of rice	247 Gallons of fish sauce
100 Bamboo sleeping mats	5 Cases canned evaporated milk
10 Bales of clothing	67 Mosquito nets
47 Blankets	70 Bags of gifts for children
20 ponchos	10,700$ VN ($354 US)

4.   Self-Help Projects:

Completed: Boat Dock at Da-Phuoc & 3 bridges (Da-Phuoc, Vinh-Loc, and Phu-Huu)

In Progress: Market House at Khanh-Binh and 8 schoolhouses with latrines (3 room: Vinh-Hoi-Dong / 2 room: Phu-Hau, Nhon-Hoi, Phu-Hoi, Vinh-Loc, Khanh-An, & Vinh-Truong / 1 room: Vinh-Hau)

Initiated: Major rebuilding effort being developed in the area devastated by the five day battle.

5.   Agricultural Activities: Planting of several new crops to enhance the economic growth in the area and harvesting of the first crop of field corn, which yielded an estimated 2,000 kilos. Fertilizer for field crops received and distributed.

6.   Problem Area: No civic action personnel assigned.

Civic Action report: 31 May 66

APPENDIX 9

<u>USASF DETACHMENT A-424</u>
An-Phu District, Chau-Doc Province, Republic of South Vietnam

<u>PSYCHOLOGICAL OPERATIONS REPORT: 1-31 MAY 1966</u>

1. <u>General Evaluation</u>: Psy Ops efforts reached a peak during this month due to the VC attacks in our northern area with short periods of VC occupation of Khanh-An and Khanh-Binh. The Vietnamese Information Service (VIS) immediately dispatched teams into the areas of heavy fighting where they performed above and beyond the call of duty. They assisted in the evacuation of wounded civilians and then turned their attention to organizing the refugees. The VIS teams surreptitiously infiltrated the VC encirclement during hours of darkness and appealed to the people to move south and out of danger. It was a courageous effort on their part and it cleared the area, allowing our forces to use the weapons at our disposal to push the VC back into Cambodia without endangering the villagers.

Other VIS teams successfully appealed to villagers in safe areas to take displaced families into their homes or to provide food, clothing, or money to help the refugees. Concurrently with these efforts the VIS somehow managed to counter VC propaganda thru continuous loudspeaker appeals and leaflet distribution in the affected areas.

The scheduled presentation of new bulletin boards throughout the district was delayed, but should be completed in June.

2. <u>Printed Material Disseminated</u>:
   8,000 newspapers were distributed throughout the entire district.
   260,000 leaflets were distributed throughout the entire district.
   1,250 posters were placed on bulletin boards, walls, & trees.
   125 personal messages were delivered to bereaved families.

3. <u>Loudspeaker Operations</u>:
   215 appeals made using the mobile Lambretta loudspeaker system.
       Over 20,200 attended.

4. <u>Face-to-Face Media</u>:
   141 group meetings (10,900 attended)
   27 Movies (15,000 attended)
   14 personal meetings (bereaved families)

5. <u>CA/PO & Medical Patrols</u>:
   5 medical patrols treated 552 villagers.
   3 CA/PO patrols gathered information for future projects.

6. <u>Problem</u>: No assigned CA/PO personnel.

Psychological operations report: 31 May 66

APPENDIX 10

<u>USASF DETACHMENT A-424</u>
An-Phu District, Chau-Doc Province, Republic of South Vietnam

<u>WEAPONS, AMMUNITION & EQUIPMENT STATUS - 31 MAY 1966</u>

I: Weapons & Ammunition:

Type Weapon	Total	Bunker Ammunition
Pistol, Cal. .45	19	41,339
Carbine, Cal. .30, M1/M2	540	123,300
Rifle, Cal. .30, M1	100	32,095
Rifle, Cal. .30, sniper	6	(see M1 rifle)
Rifle, Cal. 223, M16	8	2,680
Rifle, Browning Automatic	51	23,580
Sub-Machine-Gun, Cal. .45, M1/M3	87	(see pistol)
Shotgun, 12 ga.	2	240
Light Machine-Gun, Cal. .30	29	144,500
Mortar, 60MM	12	1,066 HE
		456 WP
		0 ILLUM
Mortar, 81MM	5	410 HE
		119 WP
		416 ILLUM
Mortar, 4.2"	1	114 HE
		210 WP
		286 ILLUM
Launcher, grenade, M79	4	224

II: Vehicles:

2 each 1/4 ton trucks
2 each 3/4 ton trucks   (1 inoperative)
2 each 2-1/2 ton trucks   (1 inoperative at B Det since Jul.65)

III: Signal Equipment:

5 each AN/PRC-10   (1 inoperative at C Det)
1 each AN/GRC-87
2 each AN/GRC-109   (1 inoperative at C Det)
38 each HT-1   (12 inoperative at C Det)
8 each TR-20   (8 inoperative at C Det)
4 each AN/PRC-25   (1 inoperative/handset)
1 each AN/FRC-93
15 each TA-312 telephones (3 inoperative at C Det)
2 each AN/GRA-4 antennas

Weapons, ammunition and equipment status: 31 May 66

APPENDIX 11

 Planning   120700

<u>Target & Enemy Situation</u>: Target travels over ambush site on a regular basis monthly. Convoy of 4 or 5 vehicles. Security force of 30 lightly armed personnel.

<u>Force, Equipment & Training Needs</u>:

Party	Special Needs	Training	Force
Command	HT-1 Radio Binoculars Flare pistol	Special operations	2
Demolition	C-4 explosive Elec. detonating system HT-1 radio	Timber trestle bridge demolition	4
Security	HT-1 radio (2) Binoculars (2) Claymore mines	Radio/claymores	8
Ambush	M79 launcher (2) HT-1 radio (2) BAR (2) Binoculars (2)	Coordinated ambush	20
Boat	HT-1 radio (2) Lght Mach-Gun (2) Binoculars (2)	Boat handling and night running	8
ALL ......>	Rations, water Weapon & ammo Grenades Compasses Rucksacks (- boat party)	Escape & evasion Sterile mission needs Land navigation	42

<u>Major Tasks</u>:

1. Securing volunteers of proper mix.

2. Obtaining a boat large enough to do the job that has routinely navigated the designated route and won't draw suspicion.

3. Maintaining secrecy and sterile nature of operation.

4. Specialized training in minimal time.

Operation Snuff Crown planning paper: 12 Jun 66

APPENDIX 12

███████ Planning   131800   ░ ?/ ░

<u>Ambush Situation</u>: Site located on two lane improved road in narrow
pass. Nearest troop reaction force is 17 kilometers beyond timber
trestle bridge. Convoy of 4 or 5 vehicles usually travel closed-up.
The 30 man security force is most likely a typical ███████ guard, not
proficient at counter- ambush techniques, and lightly armed.
Exfiltration route appears to be heavily forested with no troop
garrisons between ambush site and Mekong River.

<u>Timetable</u>: (June 1966)

13	Task Force personnel selected
14 - 17	Specialized training - Task Force restricted to camp
18	Task Force training including boat drill
19	Depart An-Phu at first light
21	Debark - west bank site after dark
22	Arrive ambush site
23	Conduct mission - exfiltrate to west bank site
24	Embark before dawn for return to camp
26	Arrive back in An-Phu

<u>Special Training Assignments</u>:

Lieutenant Strait	Land navigation
	Escape & evasion techniques
Sergeant Taylor	Demolition techniques - timber trestle bridge
	Use of claymore mines
Sergeant Johnson	Radio communications
Specialist Woolley	First aid
Vietnamese SF	Boat operation, navigation, emergency drill
	Sterile mission needs
	Site security
	Ambush operations

<u>Special Requirements</u>:

HT-1 Radios	9 ea	Binoculars	7 pr
Rucksacks	34 ea	M79 launcher	2 ea
Flare pistol	1 ea	Browning auto. rifle	2 ea
Lght machine-gun	2 ea	First aid kits	2 ea
C-4 & elec. detonator	*	Claymore mines	*
Rations	9 days	Ammunition, grenades	triple load
Flares	*		

　　　　* = Determined by training staff

<u>Major challenges</u>:

1. Securing the boat in time.
2. Securing the needed special equipment.

Operation Snuff Crown planning paper: 13 Jun 66

APPENDIX 13

<u>USASF DETACHMENT A-424</u>
An-Phu District, Chau-Doc Province, Republic of South Vietnam

<u>INTELLIGENCE SUMMARY - 13 JUNE 1966</u>

261st Bn: Strength 620
        5500 meters due west of Khanh-Binh FOB
        1x81MM Mtr, 5x60MM Mtr, 4x57RR

364th Bn: (AKA 510/367) Strength 450
        6000 meters west of Camp & 2000 meters from Vinh-Hoi PF OP
        1x75MM Mtn Gun, 2x81MM Mtr, 5x57RR, 6x60MM Mtr

407th Bn: Strength 600
        Directly across Bassac from Khanh-An FOB
        3x75RR, 3x57RR, 2x81MM Mtr

264th Bn: (AKA 512) Strength 400
        Due west of Khanh-Binh PF OP & 2000 meters NW of FOB
        1x75RR, 2x57RR, 1x81MM Mtr

Flamethrower Co: Strength 180
        6000 meters NNE of Phu-Hiep FOB
        Unknown # flamethrowers

260th Co: (Inter-district) Strength 150
        2000 meters NNW of Phu-Hiep FOB
        1x60MM Mtr

Total Strength of Southward Regiment Units: <u>2,400</u>

Intelligence summary: 13 Jun 66

APPENDIX 14

COMBAT STATISTICS - CAMP DAN-NAM
An-Phu District, Chau-Doc Province
South Vietnam - 1 January thru 31 July 1966

DESCRIPTION	JAN	FEB	MAR	APR	MAY	JUN	JUL	TOTAL
VIET CONG KIA	11	23	240		532	5	5	816
" " WIA	41	34	417		684	4	5	1185
" Captured		7	1		51		1	60
VC Weapons	4	19	1		112			136
VC Mines	2700	443	43	22	337			3545
Sampans			1			6		7
Hospital			1					1
Huts [10 man]			40			8		48
Arms Factory			1					1
POL Dump			1					1
Ammo Dump	1		1					2
FRIENDLY KIA	4	9	1		46	7	1	68
" WIA	4	113	4	1	122 +2 USSF	9		263 +2 USSF
" Weapons					5			5
CIVILIANS Killed		1		4	35	8 +1 Agt		48 +1 Agt
" Wounded		24			141	6		171
" Refugees		120			7800			7920

		ACTIONS INVOLVING CONTACT						
DESCRIPTION	JAN	FEB	MAR	APR	MAY	JUN	JUL	TOTAL
VC INITIATED								
Attacks		1			10	1		12
Probes		13	13	11	7	10	1	55
Ambushes					3	2		5
Mine/Booby Trap	1	1	1	1	3	1		8
Assassination		1						1
Sabotage	1							1
Total VC Initiated Contacts								82

FRIENDLY INITIATED								
Day contacts	3	3	10	2	5	3	2	28
Nite contacts	2	4	4	1	4	8	1	24
Total Friendly Initiated Contacts								52

+Irregularly scheduled mortar H&I fire into Sanctuaries - entire period

Significant Actions:

January	Clearing VC area north of Phu-Hiep
February	VC Attack on Phu-Hiep FOB
March	Destruction of Bung-Vien Secret Base in Cambodia
May	VC Southward Regiment attacks on our northern area

Above statistics derived from MOPSUMS, SITREPS & Captured Documents

Combat statistics: 1 Jan through 31 Jul 66

Notes

CHAPTER 1: *SECRET ORDERS*

1. Department of the Army Field Manual FM 31-21, September 1962 *Guerrilla Warfare and Special Forces Operations.* See Appendix II *Catalogue Supply System.*
2. US Department of State Country Study – Southeast Asia, South Vietnam as provided this author and all other students attending the Counterinsurgency and Special Warfare Staff Officer Course (33-G-F7) at the US Army Special Warfare School, Fort Bragg, North Carolina during the period 17 January through 15 February 1964.

CHAPTER 3: *A TIGER NAMED LE*
1. SOI – FOB COMMO NET

CALL SIGNS:	CO A-424	24 THUNDERBOLT
	Camp Dan Nam	24 WILLOW PILOT
	Khanh An	24 BADBOY
	Khanh Binh	24 CHALLENGE
	Phu Hiep	24 OUTCAST

Frequencies:	Normal	43.1 (Alternate air/ground)
	Alternate	48.1 (Locally assigned)
	Primary Air/Ground	39.5

*Contact times: **2130– 2230-2330-0030-0130-0230-0330-0430 & 1200
  * Time check each contact ** Ammo report from FOBs at 2130
  Make Commo Check with 02 WILLOW PILOT after FOB Checks

2. Acronyms, Terms & Abbreviations.
3. Book, *A Soldier Reports*, by General William C. Westmoreland (Doubleday & Company ©1976).
4. Appendix 1, *Intelligence Summary.* 27 December 1965.

CHAPTER 4: *TAKING THE WAR TO CAMBODIA*

1. Appendix 2, *Facility, Weapons & Equipment Status – 28 December 1965.*
2. *Mustang* is a common term used to identify an officer who had begun his service career as an enlisted man.
3. Appendix 3, *Missions and Forces* - 28 December 1965.
4. Book, *Killing Hope – US Military and CIA Interventions since World War II*, by William Blum, (Common Courage Press, ©1995) and source document: *Congressional Record – House* PP9977 & 9978
5. Map # 2, *Target Patterns* – 1 January 1966.
6. Book, *A Soldier Reports*, by General William C. Westmoreland (Doubleday & Company ©1976).
7. *World Almanac & Book of Facts* (Pharos Books, Sempts-Howard Co, NY, ©1987) P482.
8. Book, *In Retrospect-The Tragedy and Lessons of Vietnam*, by Secretary of Defense Robert McNamara (Vintage Books, NY ©1966).

CHAPTER 5: *A TEST OF COURAGE*

1. Book, *The Phoenix Program,* by Douglas Valentine (William Morrow and Company, NY ©1990). P155.
2. Article, *An Phu Village Burns – 2,000 homeless* (12 February 1966 edition of *The Observer,* an English language newspaper published in Saigon, South Vietnam). Two pages.
3. Map # 3, *Enemy Situation & Clearance Operation,* 17 January 1966.
4. Map # 4, *Enemy Attacks & Friendly Relief Force Strategy,* 6 February 1966

CHAPTER 7: *THE SHOTGUN*

1. Six page letter dated 12 March 2000 from Trung P. Nguyen to this author.

CHAPTER 8: *WE ALMOST BOUGHT THE FARM*

1. Six page letter dated 12 March 2000 from Trung P. Nguyen to this author.

CHAPTER 9: *BUT THEY'RE WOMEN, SIR!*

1. Book, *In the Jaws of History,* by Ambassador Bui Diem & David Chanoff (Houghton Mifflin Co ©1987).
2. Appendix 4, *Psychological Operations Estimate,* April 1966. Six pages.
3. Set of three audio tapes prepared in May/June, 1988 by retired Major John E. Strait.
4. Notes, maps, SITREPS, SPOTREPS and MOPSUMS sent via international mail to secret repository in America during author's independent operations assignment in An Phu where they would be held in sealed envelopes waiting his return or, should he not return, be accessed by a trusted attorney for release to the US Congress as evidence of foul play.
5. Original text of 28 April 1966 An Phu Victory Celebration speech given by author.
6. Map # 5, *Capture of VC Terrorist,* 8 May 1966.

CHAPTER 10: *HELL'S FURY UNLEASHED AT KHANH BINH*

1. Appendix 5, *Intelligence Summary,* 18 May 1966.
2. Map # 6, *An Phu Battle Map with friendly & enemy Order of Battle,* 19 May 1966.
3. Article, *Spooky, Dragon in the Sky, by Lawrence M. Greenberg* (Vietnam Magazine). PP22-28.

CHAPTER 11: *VICTORY AT KHANH BINH*

1. Letter from Katherine A. Marvin (author's wife) to author, 26 May 1966.
2. Three page letter to Katherine A. Marvin from her author husband, 20 May 1966.
3. Article, *IV Corps Combatants get cash reward,* (English Language Daily News, Saigon, Vietnam) 7 June 1966.
4. USASF Detachment A-424 *Monthly Operational Summary,* May 1966. 24 pages.
5. Appendix 7, *Intelligence Report,* 1-31 May 1966.
6. Appendix 8, *Civic Action Report,* 1-31 May 1966.
7. Appendix 9, *Psychological Operations Report,* 1-31 May 1966.
8. Appendix 10, *Weapons, Ammunition & Equipment Status,* 31 May 1966.
9. Appendix 6, Translated excerpt from Cambodian neutral newspaper, *Trung-Lap,* 23 May 1966.

10. Translated seven page article, *5 Days of Fierce Fighting with the VC at A FOB*, Saigon, Vietnam newspaper.
11. Four page letter to Katherine A. Marvin from her author husband, 24 May 1966.

CHAPTER 12: *MISSION: ASSASSINATE A PRINCE*

1. Acronyms, Terms & Abbreviations.
2. Set of three audio tapes prepared in May/June, 1988 by retired Major John E. Strait.
3. Book, *The Phoenix Program*, by Douglas Valentine (William Morrow & Company ©1990).
4. Appendix 11, *Snuff Crown Planning*, 12 June 1966.
5. Appendix 12, *Snuff Crown Planning*, 13 June 1966.
6. Map # 7, *Overview – Operation Snuff Crown*, June 1966.
7. Appendix 13, *Intelligence Summary*, 13 Jun 1966.

CHAPTER 13: *APOCALYPSE AT AN PHU*

1. Map # 8, *Intelligence Summary*, 18 June 1966.
2. Hand-written notes prepared by former ARVN Lieutenant General Quang Van Dang in February 1990 while °visiting author's home on the Trumansburg Road outside of Ithaca, New York. These notes corroborate certain facts in this book and were prepared by Quang Van Dang prior to the CIA obtaining a signed document from him that effectively silenced him beginning that day.
3. Letter from Quang Van Dang to this author, written on 10 November 1988, after reading an earlier manuscript (then titled *The Bassac Bastards)* and corroborating certain pertinent facts relating to the events of this chapter.
4. Set of three audio tapes prepared in May/June, 1988 by retired Major John E. Strait.

CHAPTER 14: *WE FADE AWAY*

1. Set of three audio tapes prepared in May/June, 1988 by retired Major John E. Strait.
2. Letter from former ARVN Lieutenant Colonel Phoi Van Le to this author in which he recalls our successes as counterparts in An Phu and relates his view on the political tragedy of his nation's demise.
3. Book, *The United States in Vietnam – An Analysis in Depth of the History of America's Involvement in Vietnam*, by George McTurnan Kahin and John W. Lewis (Dell Publishing Co. Inc. ©1967, 1969).
4. USASF Detachment A-424 *Monthly Operational Summary*, July 1966. Three pages.
5. Appendix 14, *Combat Statistics*, 1 January through 31 July 1966.

CHAPTER 15: *A PRESIDENT'S FANTASY IS A SOLDIER'S CURSE*

1. Book, *A Soldier Reports*, by General William C. Westmoreland (Doubleday & Company ©1976).

EPILOGUE

1. Original 1988 draft manuscript titled *The Bassac Bastards* and now titled *Expendable Elite*.
2. Article, *Ex-Green Beret rebuts stated U.S. Policy in Vietnam*, by Frances Dinkelspiel (3 April 1988 Syracuse Herald-American newspaper, Syracuse, NY).

3. Hand-written notes prepared by former ARVN Lieutenant General Quang Van Dang in February 1990 while visiting author's home on the Trumansburg Road outside of Ithaca, New York. These notes corroborate certain facts in this book and were prepared by Quang Van Dang prior to the CIA obtaining a signed document from him that effectively silenced him beginning that day.

4. Book, *In Retrospect,* by Robert S. McNamara with Brian VanDeMark (Vintage Books, NY ©1995, 1996). P181, referring to major speech given by President Lyndon Johnson at John Hopkins University on 7 April 1965.

5. Book, *JFK and Vietnam,* by John M. Newman (Warner Books, NY ©1992). P365.

6. Ibid. P322.

7. Ibid. PP322 & 323.

8. Military Assistance Command Vietnam Operational Summary as of 2400 hours, 23 November 1963.

9. Book, *In the Jaws of History,* by Ambassador Bui Diem & David Chanoff (Houghton Mifflin Co ©1987). PP225, 227 & 237.

10. Book, *The Palace File,* by Nguyen Tien Hung & Jerald L. Schecter (Harper & Row, NY ©1986). P35.

11. Ibid. Appendix A, Letter # 1.

12. Ibid. P58.

13. Ibid. Appendix A, Letter # 9.

14. Ibid. Appendix A, Letter #13.

15. Ibid. Appendix A, Letter #18.

16. Ibid. Appendix A, Letter #19.

17. Ibid. Appendix A, Letter # 20.

18. Book, *The Fall of Saigon,* by David Butler (Simon & Schuster, NY ©1985). P89n.

19. Book, *The Palace File,* by Nguyen Tien Hung & Jerald L. Schecter (Harper & Row, NY ©1986). Appendix A, Letter # 32.

20. Book, *Decent Interval,* by Frank Snepp (Random House NY ©1977). PP108 & 113.

21. Book, *The Palace File,* by Nguyen Tien Hung & Jerald L. Schecter (Harper & Row, NY ©1986). PP286 & 287.

22. Six page letter dated 12 March 2000 from Trung P. Nguyen to this author.

23. Book, *A Thousand Tears Falling,* by Yung Krall (Longstreet Press Inc. Marietta, Georgia ©1995).

24. Set of three audio tapes prepared in May/June, 1988 by retired Major John E. Strait.

25. Book, *In the Jaws of History,* by Ambassador Bui Diem & David Chanoff (Houghton Mifflin Co ©1987). P343.

26. Letter from Jean Pham to this author, 11 March 1999.

27. Letter from former CIA Station Chief Thomas Polgar to Quang Van Dang, 9 October 1989.

Index

WITH PRONUNCIATION AIDE

N

Camp Dan Nam, 28 Dec 65 – View toward the south
An Phu Village and Bassac River in background

Camp Dan Nam Operations & Intelligence Briefing Area
Note USSF and KKDB Crests

My bunk area in Team House part of HQ Building in Camp Dan Nam. Note folding cot w/ mosquito net, 12 Gauge riot gun in canvas case, M-16 Rifle with full magazine, patrol hat, bayonet, flashlight & rucksack. Bamboo mat partition & floor.

Three Tiered Tower houses the water purification equipment and water tank. Tin roofed building with crescent moon houses the US & VN SF latrine & showers.

A view of 4.2" Mortar with CIDG Quarters and CIDG Mess Hall behind pit. Team Mascot relaxes.

81mm Mortar, machine guns, outer perimeter guns

Lawn cutting detail

SFC Taylor

Maj. Phoi going to shower

December 1965 – Village Scenes, An Phu, Vietnam

Road north of An Phu along Bassac River

Market vendor

Popular market stall

December 1965 – Village Scenes, An Phu, Vietnam

RF fighters and children of Vinh Hoi Dong.

National Police interact with villagers

Local boats on Bassac River at marketplace

Market boat, house boat and fishing boat on Bassac River

December 1965 – Bassac River Scenes, An Phu, Vietnam

Fishermen setting nets in Bassac River

Houseboats & sampan

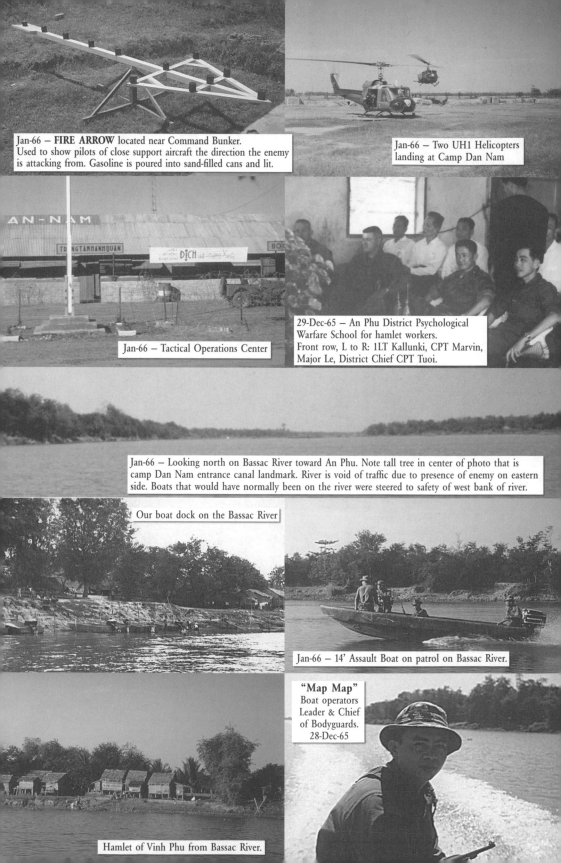

Jan-66 – **FIRE ARROW** located near Command Bunker. Used to show pilots of close support aircraft the direction the enemy is attacking from. Gasoline is poured into sand-filled cans and lit.

Jan-66 – Two UH1 Helicopters landing at Camp Dan Nam

Jan-66 – Tactical Operations Center

29-Dec-65 – An Phu District Psychological Warfare School for hamlet workers. Front row, L to R: 1LT Kallunki, CPT Marvin, Major Le, District Chief CPT Tuoi.

Jan-66 – Looking north on Bassac River toward An Phu. Note tall tree in center of photo that is camp Dan Nam entrance canal landmark. River is void of traffic due to presence of enemy on eastern side. Boats that would have normally been on the river were steered to safety of west bank of river.

Our boat dock on the Bassac River

Jan-66 – 14' Assault Boat on patrol on Bassac River.

"Map Map" Boat operators Leader & Chief of Bodyguards. 28-Dec-65

Hamlet of Vinh Phu from Bassac River.

Civic Action Projects, An-Phu District

Covered boat dock on the Bassac River at Vinh-Phu.

Foot and bicycle bridge with bulletin board.

Vehicular bridge on road north of District village.

One of eight Maternity Houses built and stocked by A-424 SF Team Medics during 1965/1966. Staffed by trained mid-wives.

Four room school in progress. Self-help with USAID material.

A proud teacher poses in front of newly opened school in the Khanh-An area. Note the happy children waiting class to begin.

Bulletin Board being installed outside Village Chief's office.

Lieut. Colonel Martha Raye coming in with black bag to help our medics treat wounded Strikers.

L-R: SSG Tenorio, 1LT Kallunki, LTC Martha Raye, CPT Marvin, SSG Eleam, SSG Kuchen, and SP6 Menkins near command bunker.

CPT Marvin

Lieut. General John Heintges

5-Feb-66 – Lt. Tran, Knanh Binh FOB Commander, Major Le and Captain Marvin outside the FOB, backs to the border canal. Note Cambodian Popular Force outpost entry gate, a stones's throw away and inside Cambodian territory used by the Viet Cong for sanctuary.

Captain Marvin helps Strikers run up new South Vietnamese flag in An Phu. Old flag was scarred by the fire on 4-Feb-66.

Captain Daniel Marvin (wearing Green Beret) meets with Madame Bo Huynh, is presented a Hoa Hao purple scarf and named an honorary Hoa Hao.

Major Phoi Van Le

Madame Huyhn

Scenes of fire that consumed two-thirds of An Phu village on 4-Feb-66

District Chief consoles fire victim, gives him some cash and asks that he takes what he needs to help him care for his family. Captain Marvin and Lieutenant Kallunki sit at table.

Everyone digs in to help the victims of the fire that destroyed so many homes and businesses in An Phu Village

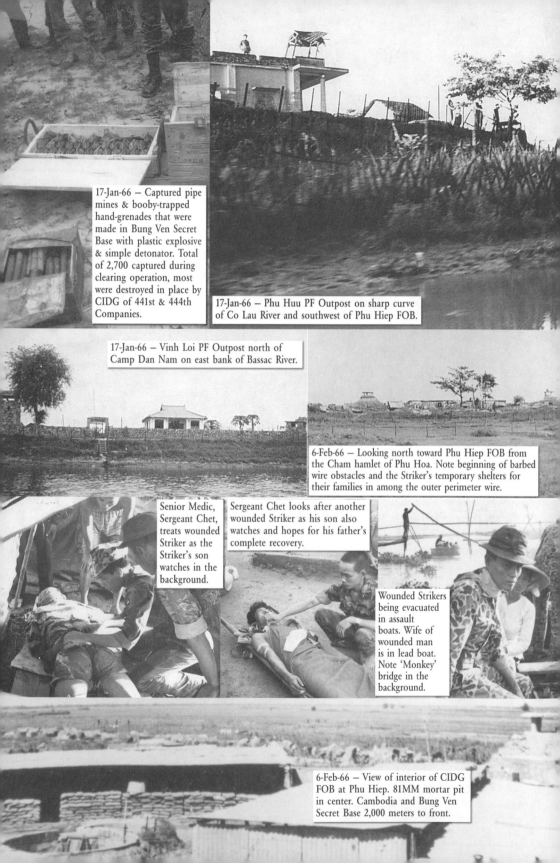

17-Jan-66 — Captured pipe mines & booby-trapped hand-grenades that were made in Bung Ven Secret Base with plastic explosive & simple detonator. Total of 2,700 captured during clearing operation, most were destroyed in place by CIDG of 441st & 444th Companies.

17-Jan-66 — Phu Huu PF Outpost on sharp curve of Co Lau River and southwest of Phu Hiep FOB.

17-Jan-66 — Vinh Loi PF Outpost north of Camp Dan Nam on east bank of Bassac River.

6-Feb-66 — Looking north toward Phu Hiep FOB from the Cham hamlet of Phu Hoa. Note beginning of barbed wire obstacles and the Striker's temporary shelters for their families in among the outer perimeter wire.

Senior Medic, Sergeant Chet, treats wounded Striker as the Striker's son watches in the background.

Sergeant Chet looks after another wounded Striker as his son also watches and hopes for his father's complete recovery.

Wounded Strikers being evacuated in assault boats. Wife of wounded man is in lead boat. Note 'Monkey' bridge in the background.

6-Feb-66 — View of interior of CIDG FOB at Phu Hiep. 81MM mortar pit in center. Cambodia and Bung Ven Secret Base 2,000 meters to front.

28-Dec-65 — The beginning.

10-Jan-66 — Framed!

16-Jan-66 — CIDG Showers & toilet completed and in use.

SSG Kuchen - Fun on the river

SP5 Sirois filling sand bags

SGT Didion sucks on an egg

SP5 Sirois & Interpreter Tony

Bat House: The production of Guano (bat droppings) for fertilizer is an important enterprise around Khanh Binh.

Command Bunker in Camp Dan Nam, An Phu, looking NNE

INTERPRETERS – Quang and Chief Interpreter Lo Lap Co "Flash" 28-Dec-65, Camp Dan Nam.

5-Feb-66 — Medical patrol leaves camp for Khanh An. Front: Flash, Co Lau, Sgt. Kuchen. Rear: two CIDG & Sgt. Chet.

5-Feb-66 — MSG Valenzuela & CIDG Security Force watch traffic in the vicinity of Khanh Binh FOB.

Looking south toward Cham Hamlet of Phu Hoa

Note large hole nearby Striker's wife and two children and also their "quarters." Hole is for protection if an attack comes too quick to move back and into FOB shelter area.

Close-up of corner machine-gun bunker. Striker's family quarters in foreground.

USSF quarters on left Striker's children playing

15 March 1966 SFC Davis out in An Phu district with our senior interpreter "Flash" checking on progress of numerous civic action projects.

22 Feb 1966 Our Senior Interpreter Co Lap Lo "Flash". A very brave man, well respected by everyone.

Our barge on dry dock for inspection work on the engine and to rig for 81MM mortar use in March 1966

Barge used to take MSG Barnes, SGT. Eleam and supplies to open full FOB at Phu Hiep. SGT. Eleam and mascot dog at front of the barge and Strikers at rear cabin area. 14 Mar 66

Nhon Hoi PF Outpost where Binh Ghi River joins Chau Doc River

9 Feb 1966 SVN Government Building at Dong Co Ki destroyed by VC Sapper Squad

April 1966 — The Vinh Loc PF outpost. Located on east bank of Bassac River 3km north of Camp An Phu.

28 April 1966 "Monkey" bridge (bamboo poles) on cross canal south of Vinh Hoi Dong FOB. LTC Brewer, B-42 Team Commander was led across this bridge by Maj. Le and fell off Mid-way across.

Aerial view of VC bridge built across border canal 300 meters west of Khanh Binh FOB — Early May 1966

L-R Front row: LTC Tuttle, Major Chuan, LTC Neller

LTC Brewer

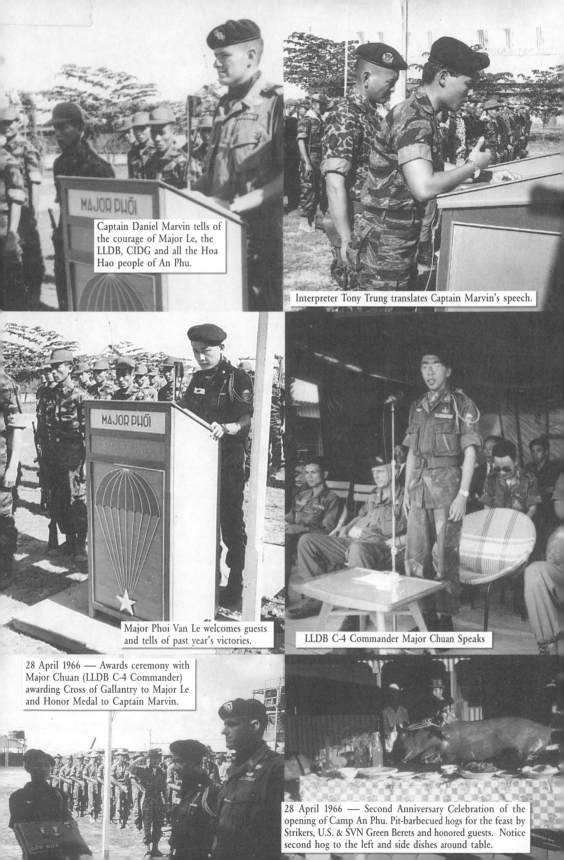

Captain Daniel Marvin tells of the courage of Major Le, the LLDB, CIDG and all the Hoa Hao people of An Phu.

Interpreter Tony Trung translates Captain Marvin's speech.

Major Phoi Van Le welcomes guests and tells of past year's victories.

LLDB C-4 Commander Major Chuan Speaks

28 April 1966 — Awards ceremony with Major Chuan (LLDB C-4 Commander) awarding Cross of Gallantry to Major Le and Honor Medal to Captain Marvin.

28 April 1966 — Second Anniversary Celebration of the opening of Camp An Phu. Pit-barbecued hogs for the feast by Strikers, U.S. & SVN Green Berets and honored guests. Notice second hog to the left and side dishes around table.

Bac-si Sirois eats special treat!

Jean Pham – 2dLt.John Strait – Tony Trung A-424
Team XO and Interpreters. 24 April 1966

April 1966 — Villagers assemble for treatment.

Cook "Bon" and SFC James a Taylor with five of Patches' puppies in front of ammunition bunker. — 18 April 1966

Some of the people who made it run smooth.
L to R: LLDB 2dLt, 3 Civilian employees, and father and son maintenance team. — May 1966

30-Jan-66 — Lieutenant Kallunki smiles at Team Sergeant Valenzuela (not pictured) as a CIA Air America helicopter comes into camp to take Captain Marvin on a border reconnaissance mission — 2,000 meters inside Cambodia.

Partial look at a Lambretta mobile loudspeaker. Flag with Red Cross on bulletin board in front of a building where medical patrol was treating villagers. April 1966

Graduation Ceremony for village workers. April 1966

Group Rally in District village of An Phu. April, 1966

Marvin and Mr. Minh, An Phu District VIS Chief Minh, May 1966

Vinh Hoi PF outpost 3km west of Camp An Phu and only 700 meters from Cambodian border.

Security is established to protect medical patrol

Lieutenant John Strait and Bac-si Richard Sirois with interpreter Tony Trung visit the outpost after VC attack on 24 April 1966 to observe battle damage and to access medical needs.

SP5 Richard Sirois Treats boy's hand injured by VC booby trap. Tony Trung assists.

Dead Viet Cong near Khanh Binh FOB – 19 May 1966

Front of damaged four room school with dead VC

19 May 1966 Relief force reaches An Thanh. From here the men will go by foot to the FOB and attack the encircling VC forces.

Striker hit five times by VC bullets or shrapnel during early morning attack by two battalions of the VC Southward Regiment on 19 May 1966. Med-evac was requested and refused due to proximity of border.

Lt Luong Le, Cpt Dan Marvin, Lt Minh Ba inside Khanh Binh FOB after our relief force breaks through 19 May VC siege.

19 May 1966 Major Phoi Van Le in An Thanh village organizing reaction force. He holds an HT1 radio. Note calm of villagers in background. Also note that Major Le wears a Hoa Hao scarf.

Khanh An village smolders from attack

Khanh Binh village destruction evident

Part of 7,800 refugees that fled south

Edge of battleground shows up in Khanh Binh village.

19 May 1966 – Cpt Dan Marvin with AK-47 Chinese Assault Rifle he captured.

Lt John Strait looking to VIS & JUSPAO personnel to help rescue trapped people of Khanh An & Khanh Binh areas who are victims of NVA and VC invasion.

21 May 1966 Bac-si Dick Sirois with cap on backwards and 2Lt. John Strait on ground in front of truck.

John Strait and Bac-si shared this lovely home away from home at the Khanh Binh FOB.

Five Strikers relaxing in Lieutenant Strait's 81mm Mortar Pit at Khanh Binh.

Chinese machine-gun, ammo magazines

American, Chinese & Russian hand grenades

Hand grenades rigged for booby-traps

3.5" white phosphorous shell

Chinese Bungalow mines, Anti-tank rockets, NVA Claymores

VC Co. Cmdr.killed near FOB on 19 May 1966

28 May 1966 First field corn crop harvest in the Delta Region, South Vietnam. Mr. Duc has arm on shoulder of the farmer who holds three good-size ears of corn in his hands. Very quickly 250 hog farmers in An Phu District signed up for seed corn for the 1967 crop.

On the far right as you look at photo is Mr. Duc, Agricultural Chief of An Phu District. Next to him, with his family, is the farmer who volunteered to plant and harvest the first crop of field corn grown in the Delta area.

CAMP AN PHU

A.424

1Lt Kallunki, SP6 Menkins, Sgt Elsam, SSG Kuchen
SSG Tenorio, Cpt Marvin, MSG Valenzuela

JANUARY 1966

A.147

CAPT MARVIN   USSF   LLDB   MAJ PHOI

Close-up of photo from Camp An Phu poster

CAMBODIA / S. VIETNAM

BAC NAM ISLAND

Looking out the door of an HU1 Helicopter on the way to our FOB at Phu Hiep on 25 May 1966.

4-June-1966 Tour of Khanh Binh Battle Area by VIPs

CPT Marvin briefs LTC Tuttle on way to Khanh Binh

Choppers land just outside FOB barbed wire defenses

CPT Marvin • COL Desobry • 1LT Hong Luong • LTG Dang

CPT Marvin briefs COL Desobry and LTC Neller

Corner machine-gun bunker that accounted for 12 VC KIA

CPT Marvin • LTC Brewer • LTC Tuttle • LTC Neller
Looking at captured .45 pistol

5 June 1966 US Navy Patrol Boat River out with District PF, RF and CIDG aboard to get acquainted with the boat. Total of three 50 caliber Machine-guns on board! Were instructed to depart An Phu when they sped and swamped local villager's sampans.

SGT Brown, SGT Clark, CPT Ang Nguyen, CPT Marvin, Lt Ba
25 May 1966 inside Phu Hiep FOB

LT John Strait and interpreter Jean Pham console mother of boy who was killed by a short round of 4.2" mortar High Explosive.

25 May 1966
CPT Marvin
by Operations
Center door

VIS Lady and 2LT John Strait help replace items that were destroyed when the HE round hit the home of the lady whose son was killed and who herself was injured.

TRUNG TAM

27 May 1966 BG Thi Quang Lam visits Khanh An PF Outpost

General Thi looking at captured VC weapons.

ARVN Lieutenant General Quang Van Dang, IV Corps CG, congratulates the fighters of Camp Dan Nam

MAJ Re

MAJ Chuan

LTG Dang

MAJ Le welcomes

• MAJ Le   • LTG Dang   • BG Thi   • MAJ Chuan   • CPT Tuoi

Looking at captured weapons and photo display of 5-day battle scenes

4 June 1966 Victory Celebration

•CPT Tuoi   • CPT Marvin   • MAJ Chuan

• MAJ Le   • LTG Dang
present heroic action bonuses.

MAJ Le briefs VIPs with USSF/LLDB/CIDG behind

VIP stand w/LTG Dang behind table as Major Le briefs.

OLD SOLDIERS NEVER DIE, THEY JUST ... GO TO COURT?

Retired Green Berets Dan Marvin and John Strait in July 1988 at the entrance to the Special Forces Association's Team House in Fayetteville, NC.

Top: Jim Taylor and Dan Marvin enjoying the fine weather.
Middle: Jim Taylor, Dan Marvin and John Strait celebrating the manuscript *The Bassac Bastards* that contains input from all.
Bottom: John Strait, Martha Raye, "Bac-Si" Sirois and Dan Marvin celebrating "Colonel Maggie's" Foreword to Dan's book.

All photos from the July 1988 SFA Convention in Fayetteville, NC.

EPILOGUE FOUR
SHOCKED!
... BUT NOT FORSAKEN

*I was momentarily incapable of accepting the fact that my own men had
turned on me and had denied the truth of what they themselves had shared
with me in An Phu. How could they collaborate with the Special Forces
Association in a legal action meant to bankrupt me and take everything
from my family?*

In the preceding, which is exactly as the book appeared in its original edition
except for the correction of errata, I have written the truth about the war and
about civic actions in the district of An Phu when I was independent warfare
commander. I did my best to give proper credit to all those who served with me in
An Phu, including John Strait, Jim Taylor, Ray Johnson, George Kuchen, "BacSi"
Sirois, and William Menkins. These were brave and honorable men who excelled
in every role they performed while under my command, and it was my duty to
portray them as such. They were highly regarded by our CIDG fighters and the
64,000 Buddhist Hoa Haos who called An Phu their home, and who relied on
our joint effort for their protection.

Therefore, imagine my surprise when, on 31 March 2004, a staff writer for the
Star-News of Wilmington, North Carolina, called me to ask about a lawsuit filed
against me and my publisher, TrineDay, and that the suit—for libel, no less—had
been filed by my own men! Reporter Ken Little told me that a Wilmington attorney
named Deaver had told him that a lawsuit had been filed in the Federal Court in
Charleston, South Carolina. The filing had been signed by Strait, Taylor, Johnson,
Kuchen, Sirois, Menkins, and the former CO of the C Team, Colonel William
Tuttle, the very man who had asked me if I would volunteer to command the
TOP SECRET independent operation that this book is all about. After speaking

391

with both me and my publisher, in the person of Kris Millegan, Little wrote an article, "Vietnam Vets Resist Renegade Tag In Lawsuit," which was published in the *Star-News* on 4 April 2004. He mailed each of us a copy.

Of course, from the beginning I had understood the risk of revealing TOP SECRET information relating to a CIA covert operation that I had personally participated in, or even merely had personal knowledge of. To me it was important to get the truth out, even to the extent of naming CIA operative Walter MacKem within the text, and also revealing his specific role in an assassination mission that would have seen Cambodian Crown Prince Norodom Sihanouk murdered in cold blood. The warnings expressed to me by Colonel Tuttle, recorded on page 11, clearly delineated the dangerous nature of the assignment, which began once I set foot in An Phu and took command.

The plaintiffs' counsel himself brought this home to me when he called me as the first witness to testify, on 31 October 2005, in the Charleston, South Carolina Federal Court, with Judge David C. Norton presiding. Amidst the several hours of my testimony, Mr. Deaver asked me, "Releasing TOP SECRET information is a serious offense isn't it?" After some banter I responded: "I would have welcomed going to court about the situation in Vietnam, because every bit of TOP SECRET information in the book is based on illegal operations…." This same Bobby Deaver also just happens to be an attorney for the Special Forces Association (SFA), and this is quite relevant, as you will see.

I had joined the Special Forces Association (SFA) in January 1988, and I used their quarterly publication. *The Drop,* to help me locate former team members, telling SFA Secretary James Dean that I would be at the July 1988 convention. While at the convention, John Strait, Jim Taylor and Richard Sirois joined with me to celebrate with, and to thank, Martha Raye for the Foreword she wrote for this book, then entitled *The Bassac Bastards.* The manuscript had been updated with much of what Strait and Sirois had provided earlier that same year.

Years later, on 20 April 1994, I wrote Don Koch, Secretary of SFA Chapter #61, explaining how I had been ignoring their communications because of my many crusades, which had pitted me against the CIA, DOD, DEA, State Department and the White House, to help South Vietnamese who had been with me in my CIDG Camp in An Phu, South Vietnam into this country. I enclosed with that letter a total of ten articles which together detailed my battles with the CIA, including their sending of "a borrowed Regiment in June of 1966" to wipe out my camp and how a South Vietnamese General rescued us.

On 10 July 1995, I wrote James Dean, Administrator of the Special Forces Association, after having spoken with him on the phone, and enclosed a photo of "Colonel Maggie and Dangerous Dan" taken in my camp during her visit, a newspaper article, "The CIA in need of a watchdog of its own," and another article about my Flag Day commemoration speech.

Mr. Dean then wrote me back on 29 July 1995: "Dear Dan, Thanks for your patience, I enjoyed chapter 7 very much, written like a man who was on the ground and knows of what he speaks. Maggie's foreword was a piece of art, her language is ours, as she was. I wish you luck with the book." He went on in that same letter to write, "We have a great display of Col. Maggie artifacts in the SFA Memorial Building and that is where your photo [from page xii of this book] will go." What was it—or who was it—that caused him to do a complete turnabout, and to lead the effort to bring together an ill-founded, but well organized, effort to destroy me and my publisher?

I have often wondered about the SFA reversing its earlier stand on my book. Clearly, there had been much outright support. Why had they changed their tune? Why the attempt to keep my book off the market, and then the campaign to bankrupt TrineDay and me after it was finally published. Why was it so important to the Special Forces Association? The SFA, through Jimmy Dean, had attempted to intimidate the man holding movie and television rights into halting his project, saying that "there would be serious repercussions" should the work be completed.

Yet despite all of this and my long experience of covert operations, I had still been expecting a more direct assault. I was temporarily incapable of accepting the fact that my own men had turned on me, and had denied the truth of what they themselves had shared with me in An Phu. How could they collaborate with the SFA in a legal action meant to silence me, to bankrupt me and take everything from my family? What had we fought for in Vietnam? Hadn't all this happened almost forty years ago? What was happening to freedom of expression in America? What had happened to my men?

THE PLAINTIFFS
RAYMOND JOHNSON

The fact that Ray Johnson was a part of the lawsuit troubled me the most, as we had maintained contact since we became reacquainted in the 1990s, and were, I thought, good friends. Shortly after hearing from Ken Little, I called Ray, and told him I was "hurt" upon hearing that he had signed the lawsuit. He replied, "I'm hurt too, Dai-Uy," (Vietnamese for "captain").

I asked Ray why he had done this. I reminded him that we had, only weeks before, planned to meet up in Worcester, Massachusetts that coming April or May. We, and our wives, were going to celebrate our long friendship. "They called me down there," he answered, "and told me to sign it, and I did," adding that he was "told not to say anything about it." Reflecting back on my prior communications with Ray has reinforced my belief that he was coerced into joining in the lawsuit.

Earlier, on 3 August 1997, Ray and I had had a good chat on the telephone, which was recorded and can be found in full at www.ExpendableElite.com, along with many other audiotape transcripts and other documents concerning our case. As we spoke, Ray praised me as his commander, recalled the wiring of the ammunition bunkers, and talked about patrolling "far into Cambodia" with Major Phoi. He said he would send me some pictures, and he asked me to send him pictures of the considerable weaponry and ammunition we had captured. We each sent the photos, and then maintained contact until the lawsuit forced our friendship into a different track. Ray had been one of the last members of my team that I had made contact with, he had been hard to find, we had resumed a warm friendship, and I was hurt.

In fact, just a few days before Christmas 1999, when Bob Logan touched base with Ray regarding a documentary film about my book, he agreed to help with the project, saying he'd forgotten a lot about An Phu, but that he "would be glad to answer questions." He said that he did recall his time in the Phu Hiep FOB with Tony, the interpreter.

Later, on 13 July 2001, after the SFA had expelled me for my speaking and writing, I called Ray. He kept saying, "I'm not involved in that," adding that he was upset that the SFA had blackballed me. At the same time he "didn't want any part of" what I was doing to get my manuscript published, but agreed to read it and let me know what he thought of it via phone. He seemed afraid of possible consequences if he were to put anything in writing. I mailed Ray a spiral-bound *Operation Snuff Crown* manuscript, as this book was then known, on 14 July 2001, and on 10 December of that same year, I received a special Christmas Card from Ray and Marlene.

We kept in touch, and in February 2002 Ray sent me some new pictures of him and some special cards from the SFA gift shop. We spoke on the phone frequently.

I called Ray on 8 October 2002 to thank him for sending me the Fall 2002 issue of *THE DROP,* with a photo of Strait, Sirois and Taylor on page 35. Ray told me that they had not been nice to him in recent years. Could it have been due to the fact that he had been communicating with me?

It was late in May of 2003 that I mailed Ray a copy of *Expendable Elite*, and on 2 June 2003 he wrote,

Hi Dan,

Just a few lines to let you know I rec'd your book. I just finished it yesterday. Now I'm sending it off to my brother in Fayetteville. He wants to know what the "Sneaky Pete" were up too. After he finish reading I will get it back.

I hear Jimmy Dean got his copy.

As for your book it's good and good reading. But I can't remember a lot of what I did. First off I was not there when the fire hit An Phu. I got there after the fire. I don't remember no CIA Agent or the blond lady. There is more but I'll give you a call. To much writing to go thru the whole book.

I sending $35.00 for the book. If you have another copy send it too me. My daughter wants one. Please send it the cheapest way

Give my best to your family & hope all is fine with them. As for me & Marlene we are doing alright.

Please take care and be well

/s/ Ray

I no good at writing any more. I make to many mistakes as you can see.

This did not seem to be a letter from someone thinking my book to be a fabrication, as alleged in the lawsuit. It was a letter from a friend named Ray who had enjoyed reading my book. What he said about his not being there when the fire hit and also not recalling anything about the CIA Agent or the blond lady's visit to our camp was no surprise, because, as the book clearly shows, he wasn't in camp when those things happened

Later, Ray sent me a copy of the September 2003 issue of the Special Forces Association Chapter I-XVIII newsletter, wherein he had circled on page 3 a short note stating that "Jimmy [Dean] also briefed Chapter 1-18 on LTC(R) Dan Marvin and his book 'Expendable Elite', which has been proven to be 100% lies."

To this day I feel bad about Ray being caught up in this attempt to break me.

John Strait

In 1984, after I was saved and started to write this book, I attempted to locate each of my former team members. Finally, early in 1988 and shortly after I finished a first draft, I was able to locate John Strait, James Taylor and Richard Sirois. I mailed each of them a copy of what was then titled *The Bassac Bastards*, along with a questionnaire titled "Background Information and Personal Data" (BIPD), and I asked them to help make the book more complete by providing me their own recollections.

Retired Major John Strait, my former Executive Officer in An Phu, was the first to respond, calling me on the telephone, and then later, in May and June of 1988, recording and mailing me audiotapes of what he recalled from his time with me in An Phu. Again, these audiotapes can be listened to in their entirety at www.ExpendableElite.com. What John provided in those audiotapes that was not already in the first draft was carefully integrated into a new 1988 manuscript, copies of which I took to the July 1988 Special Forces Association Convention and gave one to him and his two former comrades.

Prior to the trial, I had received nothing from John that would negate or contradict any of what he had said on the audiotapes he provided me in 1988.

Richard "Bac-Si" Sirois

Richard Sirois, whom we called "Bac-Si" (Vietnamese for "doctor") also recorded audiotapes for me of his recollections, and mailed them to me, along with his completed BIPD form, in May 1988. Included was a tape that told of the "Dog Lab" component of Special Forces Medical training.

Bac-Si was my senior medic in the final months of A-424 in An Phu, and his input was very helpful in my piecing together the accounts of the many good civic actions and medical support activities we engaged in.

These accounts help the reader understand the great value of Special Forces personnel acting in roles usually unheard of, and surely not experienced by most who have gone to war with conventional "force on force" military units. These tapes are also available for you to hear on the book's Web site. Some of Bac-Si's

BIPD comments relating to me, and listed as my worst traits, were, "Too tidy, wanted to be 'too' neat. Was too 'conventional' on our unconventional minds. Did not keep us posted, kept by [himself]. Not too involved with EM [enlisted men] - officer oriented. Had office away from rest of team. Spent too much time behind desk."

Under "Best Traits" he stated, "Demanding standards were met, not allowing drunks on [our] team. Making sure we portrayed the best of the best (i.e.) appearance, maintenance, etc. Looking out for our welfare."

There was nothing in what Sirois sent to me for inclusion in the book, or as comments on what he'd read in the manuscript, that would cause me to believe that he thought himself to have been defamed or libeled in any way whatsoever. Further, almost all of his proposed additions or changes were included in the drafts that followed.

JAMES A. TAYLOR

Retired Sergeant Jim Taylor, though provided the same 1988 manuscript as Strait and Sirois, returned only the BIPD form to me. Interestingly enough, he commented on my worst traits as being "Headstrong at times, impatient at times," and "Bad Cigars." Under "Best Traits" he wrote, "Willing to learn, ability to listen, and realized we had to work as a team. Good sense of humor in good and bad times." I never received any other comment, criticism or complaint from Taylor prior to the trial. He had a copy of the manuscript, clearly labeled non-fiction, and there was no communication whatsoever that would indicate to me that he felt defamed or libeled by the content of this book.

GEORGE KUCHEN

Never having located George Kuchen prior to my receipt of the lawsuit, I had had no communication with him since our time together in Vietnam, and therefore of course had received nothing from him that would indicate to me that he felt defamed or libeled by the content of this book.

WILLIAM MENKINS

William Menkins, though a plaintiff in the lawsuit, did not take part in the actual court proceedings, and I have had no communication whatsoever with him since the events of 1966. In court, when the Judge asked about Mr. Menkins, the plaintiffs' attorney said something to the effect that "he didn't know … that he may be dead."

I pray not, as I would like to talk to him some day.

WILLIAM TUTTLE, JR.

Colonel William Tuttle, LTC Marvin's commanding officer in Vietnam, was in ill health and was not able to appear at the trial. A deposition taken over two dates in early 2005 was read into the trial record. Tuttle declared the book to be "fantasy," and claimed Martha Raye "never carried a black bag," implying that Dan's pictures of her at An Phu in 1966 were somehow fraudulent. He knew this, he said, because a friend of his, a retired LTC Carr, had said so. That hearsay was their only "evidence" discrediting Colonel Maggie's abilities. Tuttle also claimed in his deposition that part of the fantasy was that Marvin had "stated" that he, Tuttle had given the "secret order" to assassinate Prince Sihanouk, which of course Dan never claimed, the order having come from a CIA agent. The complete deposition is available at www. ExpendableElite.com, separately and as part of the full trial transcript.

Colonel Tuttle honorably served in WWII, the Korean and Vietnam Wars. He taught at the Citadel in Charleston, SC for four years. Tuttle's residency in South Carolina was the basis used to file the lawsuit in Charleston. Colonel Tuttle passed away in June 2006.

A Brigadier General Fears the "System's" Wrath

In attempting to determine what had happened to my men, the inaction of a retired US Army General may well provide a pertinent example. Apparently, the General's nephew had heard me speak in Worcester, Massachusetts, on 11 September 2004 about being told that one of my men had been threatened with the loss of retirement pay should he so much as talk to me, and the nephew had reported this to his uncle. According to the nephew, the General assured him that he would write a letter to me, one that would state unequivocally that "no service-man or woman can be legally threatened with the loss of their retirement pay." It would be a letter that I could scan, and then send a copy of to each of my men whom I believed had been threatened by our own government.

I was told that the General had promised his nephew to write this letter in February 2005, and, after waiting two months, I called the nephew and told him I'd not received his uncle's letter. He was taken aback, having trusted his uncle to follow through on what he'd promised. When speaking to his uncle later, the General mentioned the presence of "two really mean CIA agents" in his area, causing him to fear the prospects and renege on his promise. The nephew was told to tell me that there would be no future contact. He told me that the General said he would have nothing to do with me. I had prayed and hoped that he would come through, wanting his letter to possibly dissuade my former team members from persisting in the lawsuit.

Isn't it a sad state of affairs when so many walk in fear of the CIA?

My primary goal in revealing all of what we did in An Phu under the umbrella of an "Independent Operation" was to motivate people within the Special Warfare Center, the CIA and DOD to develop and establish a control system that would preclude other Special Forces personnel from being placed in the same precarious operational circumstance that came close to bringing about the massacre of my team and those South Vietnamese under my control.

I firmly believed that when I wrote of TOP SECRET documents and missions, and revealed the name of CIA operative Walter MacKem, along with details of his asking me to arrange for the assassination of the Crown Prince of Cambodia, that I had effectively placed my head on the Justice Department's chopping block. It would have been worth a few years in a federal penitentiary to have our government try to fight in open court the truth of what was revealed in my book. It would force a cleaner role for Special Forces—or so I thought.

What impact would it have on the conduct of future covert operations, the revelation that a twelve-hundred-man, heavily armed force had been sent to en-gage—to wipe out—a Special Forces A-Team and the South Vietnamese allies who were with them in Camp An Phu? What about the impact of what I wrote in the Epilogue regarding the lies and the political machinations that affected American involvement in, and support of, the conduct of the war, and the hard truth that our nation betrayed and abandoned the South Vietnamese?

As a specific and powerful example, Thomas Polgar, the CIA's last Chief of Station in South Vietnam, after reading this book, emailed me to let me know that he was present at one of the April 1973 meetings between President Nixon and President Thieu in San Clemente, California. "I remember distinctly the promises President Nixon gave, in the presence of Secretary of State William Rogers, the incoming American Ambassador Graham Martin and others," he wrote. "The betrayal of South Vietnam was the bitterest and most traumatic experience of my life." Regarding this book, Tom Polgar elsewhere wrote, "It is very noble of Colonel Marvin that he took up the crusade to publish the truth about ARVN LTG Quang Van Dang."

ARVN Lieutenant General Quang Van Dang

I was blessed to have had the opportunity, even enlisting the services of then-President George H.W. Bush, to be the driving force behind the 1989 effort to demand an investigation to clear former ARVN Lieutenant General Quang Van Dang from a long list of false and heinous charges against him that the United States government had put on file in Ottawa, Canada. It was General Dang, former Special Assistant to South Vietnam's President Nguyen Van Thieu, serving as IV Tactical Zone Commander, with US Army Colonel William O. Desobry at his side, who had rescued me, my men and our Vietnamese forces from the planned retribution of June 1966, as outlined in chapter 13.

Later, after the fall of South Vietnam, General Dang had been in the US, but while he visited relatives in Canada, our government officially listed him as an "undesirable alien." We would later learn that it was through CIA influence at the State Department, in collaboration with the US Consul General's office in Montreal, Quebec, that he had been refused so much as an interview in the US Consulate for some fifteen years.

After eleven months of frustrated demands for an investigation by the State Department, in coordination with the Justice Department, to clear General Dang,

I went directly to the White House. President George H.W. Bush, in response to my letter of 17 July 1989, apparently caused a government-wide probe to be initiated. Soon after my entreaty things happened, and I received a response from the State Department referring to my appeal to the President. This cleared the way for General Dang receiving a permanent-entry visa on 7 September 1989. Seventeen days later, I personally escorted him into this country from Montreal, Quebec. He and his wife Nam now reside in this country as United States citizens.

Not a single man of Team A-424 that I was able to reach and tell of General Dang's whereabouts bothered to call or write the man who had saved our lives. I could not help but wonder ... why? Once in the 1990s, when I attempted to contact one of my former team members by telephone, wanting to know if he was ever going to touch base with General Dang to thank him, his wife answered, and she told me that her husband couldn't so much as talk to me, or they would "lose their retirement pay." When at last I asked General Dang if any of my men had written or called to thank him and to inquire into his circumstances, he replied with a sad tone indeed that not one of my men had contacted him, and that only two of the surviving Vietnamese interpreters, whom I had also told of the General's whereabouts, had extended their most grateful thanks for doing what he did to rescue us all from certain death at the hands of forces sent against us for our refusal to abandon our Hoa Hao friends.

General Dang, after reviewing my initial manuscript, had written me a letter on 10 November 1988, in which he corroborated the account of events involving him given in the chapters titled *Mission to Assassinate a Prince* and *Apocalypse at An Phu*. When it appeared that ill health would preclude him from attending the trial, as indeed it did, General Dang, in April 2005, signed a notarized affidavit verifying the truth and completeness of his earlier letter. The SFA-hired lawyers fought hard to keep these documents away from the jury, but we were able to introduce the 1988 letter as Defendants' Exhibit 35, after Judge Norton overruled strenuous objections from the plaintiffs' attorneys. Interestingly there were many documents that the plaintiffs' counsels didn't want the jury to see. Imagine that.

It seems that the CIA, DOD, State Department, and perhaps even the White House itself, dared not directly challenge this book, lest they reveal the truth of their own past, and perhaps present, actions. It seems that a way had to be devised to shut down TrineDay and bankrupt this author without compromising their positions and past illegal activities. Was it the influence that the CIA has in Special Operations, and those who serve in Special Forces, that enabled it to bring pressure on the Special Forces Association to instigate legal action against me and my publisher? I do not know, nor were there any exhibits presented at trial to show evidence of the SFA's contention that my former team went to them with complaints and asked for the SFA's assistance ... but I can wonder, and also share with you some events that may well have turned the SFA and some of its membership from friends to foes.

On 2 October 1997, I contacted retired Major General William Yarborough, the first Commanding General of Special Forces. I telephoned the General about William Pepper's first book on the Martin Luther King assassination, *Orders to Kill*, thinking that my Vietnam and other Special Forces experiences might help to unravel the truth. The General was friendly, informing me that the portrayal of him in *Orders to Kill* was incorrect, suggesting that I give his longtime aide, Rudi Gresham, a call. Gresham was leading the campaign against Pepper's book.

As I then spoke of an assassination assignment that I had been proffered by a CIA officer, the General became both more inquisitive and somewhat guarded. He said that my information "ought to be investigated, because that was certainly never within the charter of Special Forces, at all." I then asked, "Weren't there CIA people there [at SF training schools] that trained in counter-assassination techniques?" The General confirmed that some Special Forces personnel went through counter-assassination, counter-sabotage and counter-terror training, that "guerrilla warfare came close to the line [of illegality]," and that Special Forces personnel may have been used overseas for assassination, but "certainly, not inside the United States." (Again this conversation may be heard in its entirety at www.ExpendableElite.com).

When I then informed the General that I had spoken to my Congressman about my experiences, the tone of the conversation became still more serious and guarded. The General was concerned that the Congressman would use the "shock value … for their own advantage. And we certainly don't want the Army to look bad…." In short order the General wanted to know, "Who is this Congressman?… What Committee is he on?… Well, what exactly did you report to him?"

I told him about the assassination plot against Prince Sihanouk. The General was amazed at the story, and after a while he said, "I think … I think the fact that you got an order is of interest historically, and I think, perhaps, it ought to be run down to find out where the hell it came from. But if you put it to the Congress, and find it then in the *National Review*, and the shock newspapers and all of that, you do the country a disservice, you see." I then offered to send him "a write-up of the whole situation." The General suggested that I send it to Rudi Gresham, and gave me his address.

The General asked what else I had reported to my Congressman. I then related more information about my other experiences. He said, "Well, I'll tell you, if these things occurred, they were because individuals were outside their sphere of authority…. It certainly wasn't because of any kind of official posture."

I informed the General that I had written a book about the assassination plot, in which I had also included much about the Vietnamese people and the various civic actions that we Green Berets had undertaken. The General said, "Well, that positive side is seldom mentioned. You know it is always the other. Well, anything you can do to ease the impact of what you told me." We chatted for a while. I told the General I would have something to Rudi within a week. We discussed some more events, some touching upon *Orders to Kill*. Towards the end General Yarborough asked me to "do whatever damage control you can," and we soon said our good-byes.

Within the hour I received a phone call from Rudi Gresham. Mr. Gresham informed me that he was on the SFA's National Advisory Board, and also was the senior investigator in the SFA investigation into *Orders to Kill.* He also said, "I can speak on behalf of the US Army, and the US Army Special Forces, and the Special Forces Association. And I'm also the national spokesperson for all network affiliates and all newspapers." He also said that he "would appreciate it if you don't discuss anything, since you are a member of the Association, with any other person than Jimmy Dean or myself, because we're—you know, this is extremely sensitive, and it's been ..."

He wanted to know what I had sent to the Congressman. I told Rudi I would send him that information, and soon the conversation ended. Inexplicably, Rudi called back a short time later, focused on the King assassination, and told me my "loyalty has to be to SF and the Association."

Within the week, on 10 October 1997, I sent Rudi the information that I had sent to my Congressman and Senators, regarding my participation in a documentary concerning the JFK assassination, and some more information I had personally become aware of about other CIA-associated assassination plots directed against Prince Sihanouk.

I ended with the following:

People are naïve to think that government-sponsored assassinations or other deadly covert actions can be corroborated, but even more naïve to believe they never happened. There was to be no "trail" of any kind. Even in the instances of botched, failed or aborted assassinations, there are few indeed who are willing to stick their neck out from under the umbrella-shell of secrecy and thus incur the wrath of the intelligence community.

On the other hand—it is far better for this great nation of ours, and for unconventional forces that now exist, that we clean our own closets, admit our bad judgments and dirty deeds, and help to build a stronger and morally-directed force to protect and defend our vital interests.

On 13 October 1997, three days after my letter to Rudi Gresham and eleven days after my phone conversation with General Yarborough, I wrote Jimmy Dean and enclosed a number of photographs, a 19 May 1966 battle map, a copy of the 31 May 1966 *Weapons, Ammunition and Equipment Status* and a copy of the May 1989 *Grapevine* article "No Laughing Matter" along with two follow-up articles.

Immediately on receipt of my 10 October 1997 letter to Gresham, the SFA initiated an investigation, as they so notified me via Secretary James Dean's letter of 27 May 1998, in which he mentioned "over 50 interviews, the collection of documents and statements/affidavits," and a continuing investigation.

Not wanting to deny the truth of any activity or assignment of my past life, I wrote James Dean on 3 June 1998, advising the SFA that I had written the truth of what I had experienced, and that it included: "No allegations, fiction, or subterfuge, just information of what I recall to the best of my knowledge and belief." I included an AUTHORIZATION AND PRIVACY WAIVER for their use "in obtaining any documentation on file in any agency of the United States government that may be of help in developing factual answers" to their questions or queries.

The Special Forces Association announced on page 57 of its Fall 1998 issue of *THE DROP* that it had "revoked" my membership. I was also notified of this on 19 August 1998 in a letter from James Dean.

A series of communications ensued between Dean and me, culminating in blatant actions to attempt to deny my right to publish or otherwise take the truth to the American people of what was contained in this book.

In July of 2000, James Dean apparently found it necessary to call Arthur H. Weed, attorney for Robert Logan, the owner of screenplay rights for this book, and to tell him, "There would be repercussions" if Logan were to go "ahead with the [movie] project." Told of what had taken place between James Dean and Bob Logan's attorney, I wrote James Dean on 4 September 2000 regarding his "false Statements made to Arthur H. Weed, Esq. in July 2000." These interactions with James Dean of the SFA resulted in more letters and emails back and forth.

Upon publication, I sent a signed copy of *Expendable Elite* to the President of the SFA (received by him on 16 May 2003), and asked SFA President Fred Wayne Lawley to read my book and advise me of his conclusions. I also told him of my having sent a copy of an earlier draft of this book four years previously to ex-President George H.W. Bush.

On 13 August 2003, the SFA threatened Kris Millegan with legal action if he did not change the catalog description of this book to "fiction by a dreamer" or remove it from "all avenues and sources of sales" by 13 September 2003. A copy of this letter was published in the Fall 2003 issue of *THE DROP*. Kris posted the letter on his Web site, and I replied to Jimmy Dean both by letter and emails.

On 22 September 2003, the SFA again wrote Mr. Millegan, this time noting the fact that he had ignored their 13 August 2003 letter, and advising him that "SFA will assist those libeled soldiers obtain counsel, obtaining true statements (already we have more than 20) of the duty and activities that contradict the fantasies of Marvin, and will do whatever we legally are permitted to do in defending the honor of Special Forces, the CIA, and the memories of those of our brethren who have made the ultimate sacrifice in upholding the honor and traditions of our proud individual units and our nation. The next communication will be from the attorney for those men in the Secret Life of Dan Marvin." This letter was signed by SFA President Wayne Lawley and Secretary/Administrator James C. Dean. Again, Kris posted the letter on the book's Web site, and I replied in writing. Kris told me that the SFA had supplied him with no proof of their charges, and that his mother had told him to ignore bullies.

Duly recorded in the September 2003 SFA Chapter I-XVIII Newsletter under "Report from National Headquarters" was the statement "Jimmy [Dean] also briefed Chapter 1-18 on LTC (R) Dan Marvin and his book 'Expendable Elite,' which has been proven to be 100% lies." That so-called "proof" has never been provided, simply because it is non-existent.

The Winter 2003 issue of *THE DROP* contained word of a court action having been initiated, and that "attorneys were obtained by the Association and full support will be given the prosecution of the case."

SERVED WITH LAWSUIT

On 14 April 2004, a Madison County, New York deputy sheriff came to my door and served me with the lawsuit dated 25 March 2004. Just as Ken Little had written, the plaintiffs claimed I had defamed and libeled them in this book. These were some of the men who had served with me in combat some 38 years prior in An Phu, South Vietnam. My men who were plaintiffs were indeed the heroes I portray in this book. I was shocked by their demonstrated lack of integrity that targeted me and my publisher. I was, at first, incapable of accepting the fact that my own men had turned on me and had denied the truth of the experiences they themselves had lived and shared as a team with me in An Phu. I wondered, how could they collaborate with James Dean and the SFA in a legal action meant to bankrupt my publisher and me and take everything from my family?

After much prayer and reflection on what I knew of the processes of mind control, coercion and intimidation, I realized that I must instead sympathize with those who folded under these circumstances. After all, we were all taught that the Special Forces was our first loyalty.

I thereafter took on the task of revisiting the past to find what I truly believe to have been the force behind this lawsuit: the Special Forces Association and the lies that have been told to the American people about our history—about how wars are really fought. I am not anti-military. I am proud of my service and my families' continued service. One of my daughters was a nuclear weapons technician in the U.S. Navy. A grandson has been in Iraq as an Air Force cop, and will go back again soon. Another grandson is in the 82nd Airborne Division, and anxious to go to Iraq with his brigade.

And the fact that three of the plaintiffs (Strait, Sirois and Johnson) had, after reading the original draft, provided me with freely-given written and taped commentary that was used to more fully develop the text proved to be ... providential.

ON TO CHARLESTON!

It is important to me to understand that I was expecting more of my men than I would have expected prior to my getting saved. The reality of the circumstance came to me only after a former Green Beret and friend became a catalyst in my awakening to reality in the days following the jury's verdict. May God bless him for helping me to respect my men anew.

L to R Christopher Ogiba, Barry Bachrach, LTC Dan Marvin, Kris Millegan in front of the Federal Courthouse in Charleston, SC.

The military life has a long history in Charleston. Here is a view of the Citadel from the Roof of the Orphan Asylum in 1865.

Luke 12:2 – *For there is nothing covered, that shall not be revealed neither hid, that shall not be known.*

EPILOGUE FIVE
TRIALS AND ...

The trial had an unreality about it that was over the top, and as I watched the plaintiffs' lawyers trying to pull the patriotic wool over jurors' eyes, the paucity of their case became more apparent. Why was I there?
—Robert A. "Kris" Millegan

WHY CHARLESTON?

The Plaintiffs attorney's were quite open about the fact that it had been a calculated decision to file the lawsuit in Charleston, South Carolina. They felt it would be to their advantage because the average citizen of Charleston has a pro-military stance, given the area's long military ties. With the over-160-year-old military college, The Citadel, as well as major US Navy port facilities, Charleston would supply the plaintiffs with a pro-military jury. Further, one well-loved native son is General William C. Westmoreland, not exactly one of the heroes in my narrative. It was hoped by the plaintiffs that my image before that jury would be that of an anti-military renegade trying to pull down their heroes, and the system that keeps us all free. Our job would be to prove to each and every jury member that my book is factual. In truth there can be no libel.

Kris and I found the city to be warm and friendly, with polite, charming people, elegant buildings and churches everywhere. We chatted with the ladies selling basketry at the courthouse, and visited some of the many historical places. Kris introduced me to Mexican food there, which I now relish, and we both, I know, enjoyed Charleston. What would the days ahead bring?

WHY GO TO TRIAL?

Shortly after I was served with the lawsuit, I was asked by my good friend Donald Krueger, "Why don't you settle out of court, Colonel Dan?"

He continued before I could answer, as well as I can paraphrase, "You've told me about your four years of dedicated writing and the cost in dollars and cents that it took to put together a readable manuscript that you began in the 1980s. You then sweated out thirteen years of costly and continual rejection from 120 publishers, most of whom did not want to tangle with the CIA. You spent all you had, and went into debt in excess of $40,000, while family and close friends were receiving threats of one kind or another. Yet you did not give up your quest to publish the truth.

"Kris Millegan of TrineDay Press, who was introduced to your work by Jim Marrs, found you and published your book, and soon the potential of its impact became known to our clandestine agencies. Then your debt and your troubles increased, and the powerful Special Forces Association with its thousands of Green Beret members threatened your publisher, and also the man who had purchased film rights, with *serious repercussions*. Now you face a $700,000 lawsuit rather than cave in to what you know they would accept with no money changing hands—a simple letter signed by you stating unequivocally that your book was fantasy … fiction.

"Why do you insist on continuing to march against the powerful force of an organization that you believe is backed by the *Company*?"

I explained how important I believe it to be that this nation institute systems and controls established to guaranty, yes *guaranty*, that what had happened in An Phu to my team in 1966 would not happen down the road to another group of unconventional warriors. If, by circumstance evolving when engaged in covert or independent missions, most of which are within a "compartmentalized" frame of reference (i.e., sealed-off, and therefore deniable), our warriors find themselves in the crosshairs of the CIA because they refused to obey illegal demands upon them, they must then be assured proper legal representation, even the right to demand that related TOP SECRET documents be made available to their attorneys.

WHY *EXPENDABLE ELITE*?

When Kris and I first discussed his publishing my book, I submitted three or four possible titles for his consideration, having been told previously that it was the publisher who decided on the title, the cover, etc. It was Kris who chose *Expendable Elite — One Soldier's Journey Into Covert Warfare*. I had explained the title in a telephone conversation initially. It meant that though I and other Green Berets feared no enemy, inasmuch as we were trained and motivated to such an extent that they should fear us, what we did fear was that our own government might decide, for reasons privy only to those in power, that we were "expendable," as happened to me and my men in An Phu. A bizarre and well-coordinated action reportedly approved by Premier Nguyen Cao Ky, a Catholic, and instigated by our own CIA, came near to wiping out my team and the Buddhist Hoa Haos with whom we served. Without the courage and integrity of General Dang, we would be but a memory: over 400 fighters for freedom in a mass grave, labeled as rebels who had to be destroyed.

LEGAL COUNSEL AND THE TRIAL

We were blessed with attorneys who possessed the legal acumen needed to represent the truth in a case fraught with unconventional challenges and involving the highly classified information inherent with independent and covert operations. They were also endowed with the courage and stick-to-it-iveness needed to represent us against the plaintiffs in this case and, more importantly, to take on the Special Forces Association, which had committed to provide attorneys and pay plaintiffs' expenses. The SFA is a non-profit veterans' fraternal organization formed in 1964 at Fort Bragg, North Carolina, and chartered in that State. As stated on its Web site (sfahq.org), "The purpose for which the Association was formed was to unite, fraternally, all men who are now or ever have been assigned to the United States Army Special Forces, to perpetuate Special Forces traditions. No person is barred from joining the association because of race, color, religion, sex, or political affiliation."

The SFA is an organization comprised of thousands of tough, battle-hardened active and retired unconventional warriors who had, for the most part, been taught to do "whatever is necessary for victory." I was once a part of that elite force, and can recall vividly the teaching that intended to cause all of us to believe in our hearts that what we did in each and every overt or covert mission, even assassination, terrorism and industrial sabotage, was for the good of this nation, and that we who wore the Green Beret owed our loyalty first and foremost to Special Forces. We were taught that we were expected to automatically follow orders from our superiors, without question or hesitation. Should any truth represent a threat to who we are, what we now do, have done in the past, or may be asked to do in the future, that truth may be obliterated, or surrounded by the constructed walls of secrecy that create plausible deniability for the official channels, while leaving the men out in the cold.

I never felt for a moment that we would be found guilty of defaming or libeling the plaintiffs. I knew it would be our duty to make certain the whole truth was presented to the jury, and I prayed that they would make their final decision based on the truth.

Barry Bachrach, our lead counsel from the Boston area, spent the time needed to understand the intricacies of the case, and never wavered in his support. His great find, our Charleston counsel Christopher Ogiba, did a yeoman's job, bringing out numerous points of our case, many times from the plaintiffs' own witnesses. Both of these attorneys persevered, though knowing it would be at great personal, professional, and financial risk. I thank them sincerely for leading us fearlessly and for all their lawyerly skill.

There were actually two trials. The first began on Halloween 2005, when they surprisingly put me on the stand first. I put my hand on the Bible, pledged to tell the truth, sat down, and the trial's testimony began. I was on the stand for over half the day. After lunch, they played some of General Yarborough's taped phone conversation with me and questioned me about that. It appeared from the questioning by plaintiffs' attorney, Mr. Bobby Deaver, that their basic tactic was to try to make me out as delusional, to assassinate my character, and to insinuate that I had made the whole story up.

Then the deposition of Colonel Tuttle was introduced to the jury, by having the plaintiffs' lawyers read the document aloud. After Colonel Tuttle's deposition, Jim Taylor took the stand. He was likely to be their best witness, in that he had not supplied me with materials for my book, as three of the other plaintiffs had. All of this testimony, along with transcripts of this incomplete trial, is also available at www.ExpendableElite.com.

The next day, November 1, was a very strange day in court. Attorney Bobby Deaver left the courtroom shortly before the 9 A.M. beginning of the day's session. When he didn't return, the court waited while Bobby Deaver's son and co-counsel went to look for his father, to no avail, and then court began with the plaintiffs' two remaining counsels unable to explain their lead counsel's absence.

They soon called publisher Kris Millegan to be their first witness, just as I had been the surprise first witness the day before. The basic tactic appeared to be to make Kris out to be a crazy "conspiracy nut." This tactic worked no better that day with Kris than with myself the day before. We were both relying on the truth, and our testimonies were based on firm foundations. We both knew the book and the history surrounding the book's actions, official and unofficial. It didn't help their cause any when Kris revealed himself to be the son of a career OSS-G2-CIA officer who had been involved in covert operations in Vietnam in the 1950s.

John Strait took the stand next, and the drama began building, as the playing of the audiotapes in open court came near, but … that was not to be.

Just at the moment when attorney Ben Deaver had his finger on the button, saying, "OK, I am going to play these tapes," the court took its morning break.

And then Bobby Deaver never returned, and a mistrial was declared.

We would have to do it all again. According to comments made by the Deavers at the next trial, the health problem was acute indigestion—a "Tums" moment that cost us over $40,000.

By the time we came back in January 2006, there was more interest in the proceedings, and there were two reporters, several spectators, and supporters for both sides. To relate to you the whole trial would take a book in itself. There are accounts of the trial online at our Web site, one by our good friend Tim Bates, who sat in the courtroom observing and taking notes all week long.

This time the moment of drama did come, the tapes were played, and we got feedback almost immediately, from both courtroom observers and personnel, that the plaintiffs' contention that the tapes were made by drunks, or were made-up war stories or whatever, was nonsense. But a trial is a trial, and you never know until it is over.

Here is an excerpt from an unpublished piece about the trial written by Kris Millegan that was submitted to a local paper:

The faces of the jury went aghast, then cycled through disbelief, wonderment, betrayal, and sadness as they listened to the plaintiffs' voices from the tapes being played through a small boom box into the courts' PA system. I had heard the voices many times. Several times before I made the decision to publish LTC Marvin's Vietnam War memoir, *Expendable Elite — One Soldier's Journey into Covert Warfare, a*nd then again several times after a lawsuit for libel was filed against Col. Marvin and my publishing company, TrineDay by these same men. The very same men I had heard on these tapes made decades before, when Col. Marvin was gathering material for his book, encouraging, confirming and congratulating Lt. Col. Marvin's writings of their time together in Vietnam in 1966.

Interestingly, this moment of high drama, the playing of the tapes in open court, had been stopped in an earlier trial. Precisely as an anxious court was about to hear their first tape, a mistrial was declared because the plaintiffs' main attorney had left the courtroom and checked himself into a hospital for heartburn.

As the faces of this new jury showed, the audiotapes completely shattered the plaintiffs' case. Their lawyers tried at least four excuses to explain away these tapes.

1) The tapes were given for a fiction book, or
2) They were barroom war stories, or
3) They were regurgitating what Col. Marvin had told them, and
4) One had been drinking before and while making his tape.

None of those excuses flew with the jury, because as I had myself heard, these were genuine conversations. These recorded voices talking to an old colleague were believable, not the shallow courtroom mantras of: "No, we never fired into Cambodia.... We never shot our weapons.... The camp was a resort.... The book is all lies...."

The most ludicrous accusation was the charge that TrineDay had defamed two individuals because we published a book describing them as members of a team that had fired into Cambodia in 1966. Even though nowhere in our book was it stated that these particular individuals had ever shot into Cambodia. (They were medics.)

They still petitioned to the court that they were damaged to the tune of $100,000 each, plus any extra punitive damages that the jury would care to assess. It was absurd that we had libeled and caused harm to individuals because we had asserted in a memoir of a covert command in Vietnam the fact of " firing into Cambodia in 1966." Covert incursions into Cambodia have been addressed in many different news-articles, books, television and movie presentations. *The World Almanac and Book of Facts*, for example, states that US forces began firing into Cambodia in 1966. General Westmoreland in his memoirs, *A Soldier Reports*, details that he was given permission for cross-border firing into Cambodia in 1966.

The whole charade of accusing us of libeling the plaintiffs, subjecting them to hate, ridicule and contempt came only through a very tortuous legalistic reading of *Expendable Elite*. Even the plaintiffs' own witness, a retired Major General and former top JAG officer of the Army, couldn't produce the standing general orders against firing into Cambodia that the plaintiffs claimed the book accused them of having violated.

All that the plaintiffs presented were their stilted statements of denial, testimony from people who weren't there and days of fishing for a mistake.

Hours were spent on the question of comedienne Martha Raye's appearance in the book. The questions ranged from declaring to LTC Marvin that he never even knew her, to asking the Colonel if the picture with Martha Raye carrying a black bag was a "set-up" (You see the plaintiffs had a statement from the individual that put her on every chopper when she visited a camp that she never had a black bag. And since LTC Marvin and TrineDay had shown a picture of Martha Raye visiting LTC Marvin in Vietnam in 1966 carrying a black bag, it must be a fake. Ergo the whole book is a fantasy created by LTC Marvin and abetted by me, gets published, gets read by thousands of people nationwide, harms the plaintiffs).

BETRAYAL?

Prior to entering the courthouse I had prayed for justice. The most difficult part for me was realizing that the finest men I'd ever served with—men that were heroes and friends to the Buddhist Hoa Haos in An Phu, South Vietnam, men who cared about why we were there and did their utmost to meet the test—were now sided against me.

Positioned on the other side of the courtroom as I entered were John Strait, Raymond Johnson, George Kuchen, Richard Sirois and Jim Taylor. Were they now my enemies? I think not.

I felt pity, remorse, anger and even bitterness, and yet I would have loved to have been able to give each one a big hug and to talk about the time we served together in An Phu. I controlled my natural desire to just reach out and shake hands with my men. I ignored their legal counsel, whom I assumed to be merely tools of an evil within the SFA. We who had served so honorably and bravely together some forty years prior were now adversaries in a lawsuit. How sad.

A very special catalyst in my thinking about this has been my friend and former Green Beret, Brent Selleck. Before I would write critical comments on what I had thought of as my men betraying me, Brent took the time to help me again recognize the true "nature of the beast" that is the Special Operations environment. That environment began with having to three times volunteer for the undertaking, followed by the most difficult and most trying training a man could possibly endure, physically and psychologically—and only a small percentage would "complete the course" and be permitted to wear the Green Beret. All through the different segments of the training, the absolute need for continuing loyalty and secrecy would be emphasized, sometimes subtly, and more often in tough language. If those who wore the Green Beret were to openly reveal to the public what they knew to be illegal but had nonetheless been given the mission to accomplish (always having the "flag" held up as justification), there would soon be but a limited role for Special Operations types. This fear seemed the rationale for the round-the-clock secrecy laid down by the dictate of higher authority.

Brent made me think back to the many and varied covert operations, and less critical subterfuge activities, that I had been proudly involved in, and which, when I knew the action to be illegal, I would justify as being important to this nation—to our flag! And, those in the Special Forces "community" took what we were trained to do for granted, most times not considering the deadly, awful reality of its outcome.

It was most unusual for any of us or any of our family members to mention any of what we did or were trained to do to anyone outside the "circle of SF friends," especially the media. Simply put, we didn't talk to the press, and they didn't talk to us. During the seven months that I commanded at An Phu, I did not permit any American news media in my district. It was as simple as that. I would learn to regret it, but this was what I felt to be right based on my indoctrination into special-warfare covert operations.

I had kept silent about "questionable" activities I was involved in, and, in particular, the facts surrounding the time in early June of 1966 when the CIA decided to kill me and my men, as well as the time Master Sergeant J. H. and I met with the Mafia don in the vicinity of Boston, and were offered a job to work for him as a "hit team." "You won't have to kill any cop," he told us. Sadly, thinking back to that day in 1964, I know now that if I had not been married, I would have seriously considered his job offer. After all, I rationalized, it's all right to do it for Uncle Sam, why not the Mafia, which, to my understanding, Uncle uses for jobs here in the States? My mentality at the time was geared toward doing what was necessary to achieve victory—right or wrong, legal or illegal. Thank God I no longer feel that way.

It was on the 29th day of January 1984 that my daughter Danilee led me to the Lord Jesus Christ, and I asked Him into my heart. That very day I no longer feared "them" sending anyone—anyone like me—to kill me for not holding my silence. I would fear only the Lord from that day to this.

Thanks to Brent Selleck, I can now understand why my men could so readily seem to turn against me ... to betray me. They were merely following the dictates of their unconventional master—believing it more important to be loyal to the "system," or, having lived within the unconventional warfare mindset for so long, they were utterly convinced that the threats made against them and their families to make them participate in the lawsuit would be carried out as a matter of course.

Perhaps now, in the aftermath of the trial, readers will understand just a little more of the truth of unconventional, covert warfare, and the dangers it can pose to a civilized nation.

Would each of these once-brave souls be sworn in and then sit in the witness chair and perjure themselves? Would they deny the truth of what they had written or recorded on audiotapes at a time when their honor was still in good stead, when they wanted, in 1988 or in 1997, not only to support the need for this book, but also to provide their own personal recollections to bolster the content.

WHY DID THEY ATTACK COLONEL MAGGIE?

Why did the plaintiffs and their attorneys attack Martha Raye? Bobby Deaver seemed determined to destroy Martha Raye's credibility, to assassinate her character. He did his best to classify the lady that nearly all Green Berets knew as "Colonel Maggie" as an illiterate who did nothing but entertain the troops. He tried to portray her as if she was never even capable of helping the medics in the camps she visited, much less had actually done so. Bobby Deaver even accused me of faking the photo in the book that showed Colonel Maggie coming off the helicopter with her black nurse's bag. Oh, I would dare the Deavers to say what they did to demean Martha Raye at an SFA Convention. They'd be fortunate to make it out with their skins intact!

The Deavers' apparent rationale for attacking Martha Raye was to argue that I must have fabricated the Foreword, and that therefore I had likely fabricated the whole book. Another motive was surely the truthfulness and relevance of what she had written contrary to the official lies. That one-page testament of truth written by Martha Raye amply illustrated the very nature of our unconventional operations in An Phu, and they wanted that discredited.

Perhaps it was her description of our being in "a place of high enemy activity," even recalling her visit to my camp when, "Just before landing, our Huey was hit twice with ground fire from a .50 cal. machine gun." Moreover, Col. Maggie's clear statement, based on her long experience, directly contradicted the SFA's published assertions, which they were now attempting to substantiate in Court. "The men and events recorded … in the following pages," she wrote, "give the reader a true overall picture of both conventional and unconventional warfare in overt as well as covert situations carried out by U.S. Special Forces Teams." She would have to be discredited.

Shame on them. Shame on anyone who attempts to slander Martha Raye, *the* Martha Raye, who had, in fact, been awarded the Presidential Medal of Freedom by President Clinton, as well as many special recognitions by other leaders and organizations. One may read in Noonie Fortin's excellent book, *Memories of Maggie*, about her nurse's aide training and her many awards, and also learn of the incredible positive impact that Martha Raye had in three wars: World War II, Korea and Vietnam. Nonetheless, Bobby Deaver was purposely ripping at the very heart of Martha Raye's reputation of rewarding service to this nation.

Furthermore, as I had firmly expected this book to be published long before her death in 1994, this unfounded slander against Martha Raye by the SFA—to attack me by saying I had made-up her foreword—rings hollow. For shame!

I believe I can honestly say that all us who were Green Berets anywhere in the world, and particularly in South Vietnam, loved the lady we knew as "Colonel Maggie."

Every A-Team sergeant or officer that I have talked with—particularly during the July 1988 SFA Convention—spoke highly of Colonel Maggie and talked of how they appreciated her help with the wounded. I was truly shocked when the plaintiffs' attorneys—in Federal Court in Oct '05 and Jan '06—attacked the good name of Martha Raye in their attempt to discredit my book and bankrupt me and my publisher. They accused her of being "illiterate"—of not helping treat wounded in any camp in Vietnam, of not being capable of writing the Foreword to this book. It seemed to me that attorney Bobby Deaver was particularly mean-spirited about Colonel Maggie.

I hope and pray any of you out there who knew this fine woman will take the time to write the Special Forces Association and tell them that they should apologize in the *The Drop* for besmirching the memory of Colonel Maggie. As a tribute to her devotion to the men who wore the Green Beret, she is buried *in uniform* with her Green Beret at Fort Bragg, NC. So, please do what you can to let the world and the SFA know that Colonel Maggie, our Martha Raye, was a patriotic American, who went above and beyond her call to be with us in times of danger and who helped us to treat the wounded.

How could the SFA disparage her memory to attack me as they did about events now forty years old? What else might they do?

It has been a long haul for me to carry the torchlight of truth about our operations, And I'm proud of the vindication we received from that second jury in Charleston. I thank them for their verdict.

Our attorneys did a wonderful job and represented us honorably. We had filed counterclaims, as we were told early in the process that we needed to do that, for simply defending ourselves and winning … does not pay any bills. We had all discussed the matter and decided before the trial that we would not attack my men, nor did we want any money from them. They were just doing what they were told. Our attorneys could have savaged the men on the stand—confronting them without mercy about the obvious misstatements in their testimony. But our attorneys did not, for the absurdity of the case, the plausible deniability aspects and the … tapes were quite clear in court. We did not pursue these counter claims aggressively, hoping someday to hold to account the real culprit in the lawsuit, the SFA.

I looked around in court at the dramatic point, when during the second trial the audiotapes of John Strait were first played and noticed that neither the AP reporter nor the local reporter was there. The local reporter was there during some of the subsequent tapes, but no mentions of the damning audiotape evidence were made in his or the AP news reports. And as Kris had said during the nervous weekend before the verdict, "Our case is good, based on the truth. They have a slim maybe, but it won't matter, for when they lose, they will just *spin* it away." And spin, they did, heralding the jury's decision as a "draw" rather than the victory that it was—for me, for Kris, for our lawyers and hopefully for our country.

After the trial, Judge Norton told the bailiff that the jurors could keep the books they had used during the trial. Soon, to everybody's amazement, the bailiff came back in the courtroom, carrying the stack of books as though the jurors didn't want them and were returning them to us.

No … they actually wanted the books autographed.

As a fitting ending I'd like to allow the rest of the story to be told by my publisher, Kris Millegan, adapted from an opinion piece published in the Eugene *Register-Guard* in February 2006.

Kris had an opportunity to bail-out of the trial, but choose to stay in the fight with me and did stick with me through these last trying years. His observations about the current management of information in this country should be of concern to every American.

The trial had an over-the-top unreality about it, and as I watched the plaintiffs' lawyers trying to pull the patriotic wool over jurors' eyes, the paucity of their case became more apparent. Why was I in a federal courtroom in South Carolina?

I was just a small fry from up the McKenzie River near Walterville, Oregon. My company, TrineDay, had published a book, which I took to be a highly credible memoir of a CIA-directed operation in Vietnam, written by a retired lieutenant colonel who had served with the U.S. Special Forces. The author and my company had been sued for libel, and the whole lawsuit was ludicrous.

The jury agreed. It took jurors only about two hours on Jan. 30, 2006—just long enough to eat lunch and fill out multiple forms—to come back with the verdict denying all the plaintiffs' claims.

We had libeled no one. We had presented evidence of the truth of the matter, and with these facts in evidence there could be no libel.

We had called the plaintiffs heroes. If anything, the book castigated American political leadership for putting America's fighting forces in the militarily-untenable situation of being exposed to harassment and attack from inviolate "enemy sanctuaries."

Yet win or lose, the lawsuit was chilling—and ruinously expensive. That was its intent.

The lawsuit was a "steamroller" operation—which is spook slang for an attempt to cover up history, deny questionable activities, and flatten opposition to the official story. The Special Forces Association, a fraternal organization of retired and active Special Forces personnel, obtained the lawyers, financed the lawsuit, and even paid the plaintiffs' out-of-pocket expenses.

The association has carried the ball on similar steamroller operations, operations in which our true history is covered up by official denials, obfuscations, and political lies. Let's review a few of them.

"Special Forces don't talk to reporters, and reporters don't talk to Special Forces." That was the direct message delivered to a member of a CNN news crew that reported a covert U.S. military operation in Laos during the Vietnam "police action." The story was part of a broadcast on the secret warfare activities of the Studies and Observations Group, an elite commando unit of the Army's Special Forces.

CNN Producers April Oliver, Jack Smith and their news crew had spent eight months on the story, lining up interviews ranging from the grunts on the ground all the way up to Adm. Thomas Moorer, chairman of the Joint Chiefs of Staff at the time. Interference to suppress the news story included pressure on CNN board members by Henry Kissinger, a threatened boycott of CNN by veteran groups, and an alleged threat to freeze out CNN from Department of Defense background briefings.

After being fired from CNN, members of that news team have won judgments arising out of the litigation surrounding the affair … and stand by their story today.

Another steamroller operation: Last year in New York, I had lunch with international attorney and author William Pepper, an associate of Martin Luther King, Jr. Pepper prevailed in a 1999 court case that showed that there was a conspiracy—including "governmental agencies"—involved in the King assassination, discrediting the official "lone assassin" theory.

I had to chuckle when Pepper urbanely told me, "You know, I can get on the *Today* show any time I want, as long as I do not talk about my books about the King case." Almost seven years after the jury's verdict, few have heard of Pepper's works.

How free is our national discourse when authors aren't allowed to speak, and when publishers can face bankrupting and ludicrous (though hardly frivolous) lawsuits for printing our history?

Many of us think (as I did, before my recent episode) that if you defend yourself in a civil case and win, the other side must pay your attorneys. Sadly, that is not the reality. But this isn't about court reform. This is about our ability to understand and discuss our own history.

The Bush administration is currently removing thousands of historical National Archives documents from the public—some of which have been on college library shelves for years—and reclassifying them. Listen to historian Matthew Aid, who blew the whistle last December on the seven-year-long secret program, when he discovered documents from the Korean War and others missing:

"The stuff they pulled should never have been removed. Some of it is mundane, and some of it is outright ridiculous."

Why all the secrecy and subterfuge, even to the extent of trying to suppress books? During the infamous Inquisition, books themselves were put on trial—show trials before the actual burning of the books (and sometimes their authors and publishers).

If we were ignorant of our history, would it, perhaps, be easier to lead us deceptively along to a future of paying for, and fighting in, an unreasoned continual war?

Well, *perhaps.*

It has been said that, "Those who cannot remember the past are condemned to repeat it."

I do not know about you, but I'd rather ... not.

—K. M.

It is now history. – Let us learn from it for a better future.
—Lt. Col. D. M. (Ret.)

LTC Daniel Marvin (ret.)
A Soldier and his Country

The Documents

Official Speaker's Bureau Photo of Major Daniel Marvin
in September 1968. Taken by Ralph Ashburn.

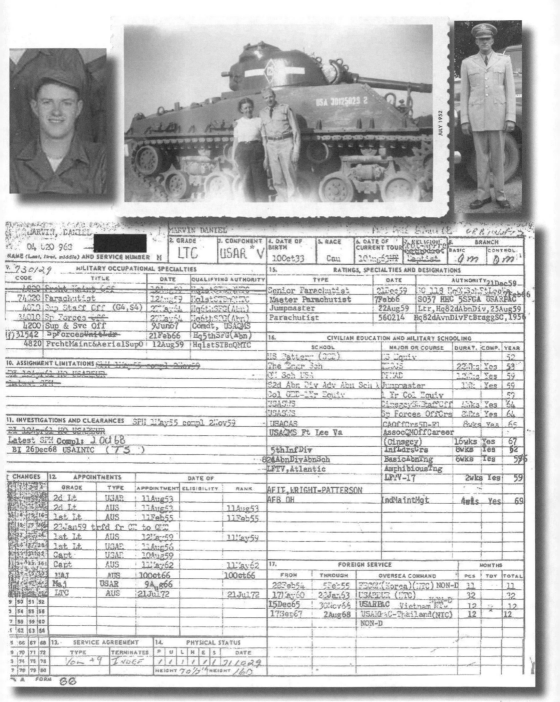

Top: Recruit Dan Marvin June 1952, Private Dan Marvin with his mother in front of a tank at Indiantop Gap Military Reservation in July 1952, Brand new Combat Engineer 2nd Lt. Dan Marvin in August 1953.
Bottom: LTC Marvin's service records – DA Form 66

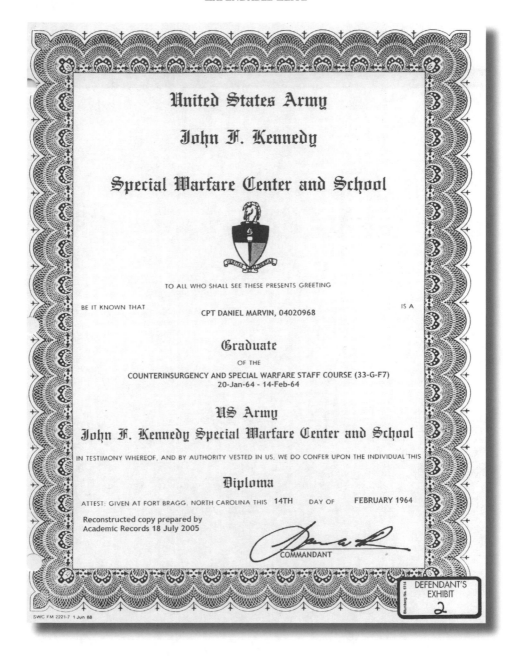

Official Graduation Diploma showing that then-Captain Daniel Marvin graduated from the Counterinsurgency and Special Warfare Staff Course (33-G-F7) on the 14th Day of February 1964

Middletown Rotarians Hear of Special Forces Operations

—Patriot Photo

Maj. Daniel Marvin of the Defense Depot Mechanicsburg, shows scrapbook to officers of Middletown Rotary Club at meeting which he addressed last night. With Major Marvin, whose topic was "U.S. Army Special Forces Operations in Vietnam," are Paul Daily, center, program chairman, and George Fuoti, club president.

Top Left: Major Marvin giving talk to Middletown, PA, Rotarians – 1969
Top Right: A newly qualified Green Beret – February 1964
Bottom: MSG Joseph Hill and Captain Dan Marvin ready to jump test Special Forces gear in January 1965 for US Army Natick Laboratory.

DEPARTMENT OF THE ARMY
HEADQUARTERS, UNITED STATES ARMY VIETNAM
APO SAN FRANCISCO 96307

IN REPLY REFER TO

AVHAG-PD

16 JUL 1967

SUBJECT: Foreign Awards

THRU: ~~Commanding Officer~~
5th Special Forces Group (Airborne)
~~1st Special Forces, APO 96240~~

TO: Captain Daniel Marvin, 04020968
Detachment B-42, 5th Special Forces Group (Airborne)
1st Special Forces, APO 96240

1. The Gallantry Cross with Bronze Star, presented to you by the Republic of South Vietnam for your heroic actions from 18 May 1966 to 19 May 1966, has been accepted and approved by the Commanding General, United States Army Vietnam under the provisions of DOD Directives 1005.3 and 1348.16 dated 22 January 1966.

2. This award is authorized for wear as prescribed by paragraphs 155, 160, and 162, AR 672-5-1.

FOR THE COMMANDER:

DONALD G. MOFFAT
CPT, AGC
Asst Adjutant General

2 Incl
1. Vietnamese Orders
2. English Translation

Maj. Daniel Marvin, son of Mr. and Mrs. John F. Ewald, formerly of Ithaca, has been promoted from captain to major while stationed at Camp Arnn, a U.S. Army Special Forces camp on the Cambodian border.

For actions during engagements he led against the Viet Cong, Major Marvin was awarded the Viet Nam Honor Medal and the Vietnamese Cross of Gallantry with Bronze Star. He also has been nominated for the U.S. Bronze Star with "V" for valor.

He has been serving with the U.S. Army in Viet Nam since Dec. 20, 1965. A veteran of the Korean War, Major Marvin enlisted in the Army in 1952.

During his first seven months in Viet Nam, he and his nine-man detachment of Green Berets advised and directed six companies of Hoa-Hao religious sect civilian irregulars who were responsible for securing 30 miles of Cambodian border area in the delta area west of Saigon, according to the Army.

Marvin's wife is the former Katherin Henderson, daughter of Mr. and Mrs. David Henderson of 60 Halseyville Rd. She is living with their three daughters at 434-B Winthrop Drive.

ITHACA JOURNAL
OCT 1966

Top: DA approval of Vietnamese Cross of Gallantry for heroic action during the battle at Khanh Binh, which is the subject of chapters ten and eleven of this book.
Bottom: Newspaper announcement of awards and promotion to Major.

HEADQUARTERS
UNITED STATES ARMY VIETNAM
APO San Francisco   96307

GENERAL ORDERS   27 December 1966
NUMBER   7058

AWARD OF THE BRONZE STAR MEDAL FOR HEROISM

1. TC 320. The following AWARD is announced:

MARVIN, DANIEL 04020968 CAPTAIN QUARTERMASTER CORPS United States Army
Detachment A-426, 5th Special Forces Group (Airborne), 1st Special Forces,
APO 96240
   Awarded: Bronze Star Medal with "V" Device
   Date action: 7 August 1966
   Theater: Republic of Vietnam
   Reason: For heroism, not involving participation in aerial flight, in
            connection with military operations against an armed hostile force
            in the Republic of Vietnam: Captain Marvin distinguished himself
            by valorous actions on 7 August 1966 while serving as senior advisor
            to a friendly Vietnamese convoy near Tri Ton. Enroute to a training
            center, the convoy was attacked by an estimated Viet Cong platoon.
            While arranging the tactical distribution of his troops, he received
            word that a truck preceding his convoy had been mined and ambushed.
            Captain Marvin immediately reorganized his troops and started an as-
            sault toward the mined area. He exposed himself to intense hostile
            fire to drag two of his wounded men to safety, and then continued
            to drive through the Viet Cong positions. At the explosion site,
            Captain Marvin, with complete disregard for his personal safety,
            ran to the side of two wounded men in an exposed location. Since the
            two casualties could not be moved, he administered intravenous
            treatment while directing his troops to prevent their position from
            being overrun. With the arrival of reinforcements, he led the as-
            sault which completely dispersed the Viet Cong force. Captain Marvin's
            personal bravery and devotion to duty were in keeping with the highest
            traditions of the military service and reflect great credit upon
            himself, his unit, and the United States Army.
   Authority: By direction of the President under the provisions of Executive
               Order 11046, 24 August 1962

         FOR THE COMMANDER:

                                          RICHARD J. SEITZ
                                          Brigadier General, US Army
                                          Chief of Staff

S. A. MacKENZIE
Colonel, AGC
Adjutant General

In their closing address to the jury, the plaintiffs lawyers continued their character assassination and obfuscation, remarking that LTC Dan Marvin was just
a quartermaster not a combat warrior and that he didn't serve in any command
capacity in any other A-team after his duty at An-Phu. As can be seen by this
award, those remarks were … untrue.

Opinion

The Ithaca Journal
Thursday, April 9, 1987 | 10A

Editorial Page Editor
Jane Marcham
272-2321, Ext. 13

Why 'Platoon' is a must-see for Americans

By DANIEL MARVIN

Every American should see the movie "Platoon." I believe it is an important film which serves to illustrate for concerned Americans the true dilemma of the unpopular Vietnam War.

It certainly is meant to represent some of the extremes of the war on the ground, not shying away from the truth about atrocities, 'inept leadership and low morale — all infected by a drug culture that was another truth of the war.

All of us who were there understand, after watching "Platoon," that not all our fighting men were involved in or subjected to the same situations, and yet we know it happened — and happened to a greater extent than the politicians and military hierarchy would like to admit.

The members of the platoon in the movie, and for that matter the members of any platoon that served "on the ground" and met the enemy on the field of battle, were not at fault.

The "System," starting at the top, made the ludicrous decisions, ignored history, flaunted what were felt to be the ultimate warfare tactics and transformed a Peoples' War against communist insurgency into a White Man's War, propelling this country into the depths of a self-destructive mode which, in my judgment, was the ultimate in political and military absurdity.

LOCAL OPINION

The big mistake: Transforming a People's War into a White Man's War.

This nation had no logical or historically proven theory that would support the bombing of Hanoi, which served only to solidify further the people of North Vietnam against the American "imperialists," or the introduction of American conventional forces, which served to destroy the practical movement for countering the Viet Cong insurgency through the people of South Vietnam fighting for their freedom, fighting for their ground, fighting for their causes.

I was fortunate, and indeed honored, to command a U.S. Army Special Forces "A" Team in the delta area along the Cambodian border. Our small team of seven Green Berets worked, lived, ate and fought with the people in our area, and we were successful in pushing the Viet Cong out of our area, securing 30 miles of Cambodian border and winning victory after victory against numerically superior Viet Cong forces.

The strategy was rather simple, and President John F. Kennedy understood it: Use Special Forces trained and psychologically motivated to help the people win out against the invaders from the north. It was their land and they fought valiantly, with their wives in the trenches alongside them, loading their weapons and taking their places when they were killed.

President Johnson changed all that. Soon it became an American war, and Viet Cong propagandists had a field day. Gen. Maxwell Taylor, as chairman of the joint chiefs, and Gen. Harold K. Johnson, the Army chief of staff, joined in a conspiracy to rid Vietnam of the "elite" Green Berets they hated and turn the conflict into their kind of conventional war. William Bundy warned against it, advising them we would be going the way of the French.

So this great nation of ours was propelled into an unpopular war with our brave fighting men being ordered to fight in an alien land against an unknown enemy, with ineffective leadership and no mandate from the people.

Our leaders did a great disservice to the men and women of our armed forces by trying to refight the Korean War in Vietnam. Our leaders misled the people at home, caused an unknown number of atrocities through their almost fanatical demand for body count —

no matter who — and led more than 47,000 to their deaths in a war they had no business being in.

No doubt the American presence, specifically presence of the U.S. Army Special Forces (the Green Berets), was an absolute necessity. They were all volunteers, they all knew what they were getting into and they wanted to be a part of it, as was certainly true in my case.

"Platoon" is important because it may well educate the people to assure we don't make the same mistake twice. It would be even more disastrous than the first time.

At the same time, we should remember other movies that serve yet another purpose — to remind us that our military, if properly led and trained, can cut the mustard. The "Green Berets" and "Top Gun" are movies we should also remember. But we should never forget "Platoon."

Marvin, who served in Vietnam in 1965-66 and retired from the Army with the rank of lieutenant colonel, now operates an antiques repair and restoration business on Trumansburg Road.

Exercising one of the freedoms that he had fought to protect, LTC Marvin began to raise his voice questioning the wisdom of our political leaders "sending troops to fight in an alien land, against an unknown enemy, with ineffective leadership and no mandate from the people."

The Bassac Bastards
and
The People of An Phu

Nonfiction manuscript *The Bassac Bastards and the People of An Phu* provided to John Strait, Richard Sirois and James Taylor prior to the 1988 SFA Convention.

LEADS
The Bassac Bastards & The People of An Phu
A True Account of Independent WarfareDecember 1965 - August 1966
Military Region IV, South Vietnam
Lieutenant Colonel Daniel Marvin AUS (ret)
    More than two decades have passed since I lived the experiences candidly expressed in this book. My notes, documents and photos of what had been a highly classified unconventional mission gathered dust over the first twelve years. In 1978 I began putting together a "military diary," a chronological record of events structured as a teaching vehicle - hardly exciting reading, but important in my mind. I queried Department of the Army to determine their
interest in my book as a reference for Special Forces soldiers and was told to clear my manuscript with the Central Intelligence Agency and the Special Operations Office of the U.S. Army. In my judgement, that would have resulted in a watered-down version, a distortion of the facts with few revelations of high-level subterfuge, the majority of the real truth of covert operations relegated to the editing room floor. No longer a book of "hard" truth but at best a pro-bureaucracy manual pretending to depict the unconventional warfare aspects of that far-off conflict. ⅃⅃Thus, in 1981 I began re-writing it as fiction based on fact, a novel
called "THE BASSAC BASTARDS." Three years of rejections helped me to realize that presenting the truth as a novel betrayed the trust
of the people we had abandoned in South Vietnam. I temporarily set the project aside, troubled that important revelations of the Vietnam war would be considered by many readers as anti-establishment fiction.
    Nonfiction? I knew, from personal experience, that assets within the US Government could be called on to silence my efforts to get the truth published. On 29 January 1984 my daughter, Danilee, led me to the Lord Jesus Christ and I knew that I no longer had to fear anyone on this earth. I would fear and follow my Lord Jesus. I began to assemble and organize all that I had in my possession relating to An Phu. In 1986, inspired by the enthusiasm Professor Robert Doherty radiated for my project and his empathy for the people of South
Vietnam, I launched into the task with renewed vigor, finishing in a little over two years time. Multiple rejections followed multiple submissions, but my spirits were buoyed by two publishers who read the manuscript and felt that it was an important story that should be told. THE Bassac Bastards and the People of An Phu was born!
           Lt Col
Daniel Marvin AUS (ret) Ithaca, New York ⅃⅃

This book is dedicated to: ⅃⅃The memory of U.S. Army Special Forces Master Sergeant Gerard V.
Parmentier. My best friend, best man and a courageous Green Beret;
Jerry was killed in action in Dak-To, South Vietnam on 16 May 1967.⅃⅃U.S. Army Special Forces Major John E. Strait, U.S. Army Special Forces
Sergeant Major James A. Taylor, ARVN Special Forces Lieutenant Colonel
Le Van Phoi, all the men assigned to U.S. Army Special Forces Detachment A-424 and ARVN Special Forces Detachment A-147 during the period of 27 December 1965 thru 2 August 1966, the Hoa Hao irregular warriors and the people of An-Phu, South Vietnam. None braver have I met.⅃⅃ARVN Lieutenant General Quang Van Dang, who risked his all to save my
life and the lives of more than five-hundred others, American and South Vietnamese, in June, 1966.⅃⅃My wife, Kate, whose strength, trust and courage girded me with a shield
of love.⅃⅃⅃⅃⅃⅃   Lieutenant Colonel Daniel Marvin AUS (ret)⅃
⅃   Ithaca, New York
      ⅃⅃⅃

This was a "Leads" paper meant to outline how the idea for a book progressed from thought to a possible novel, and how a personal salvation encouraged LTC Dan Marvin to proceed with the endeavour as a book of truth, a work of nonfiction.

THE BASSAC BASTARDS & The People of An Phu
CHAPTER SUMMARY

1.   SECRET ORDERS
        It was Christmas Day, 1965 when Captain Dan Marvin
volunteered to take the war to the enemy in their Cambodian sanctuaries.
The historic first incursion would involve American and Vietnamese Green
Berets and their irregular fighters striking out across thirty miles of
border in a place called An-Phu. As a passenger enroute to his camp in
an Army helicopter, Marvin witnesses the massacre of unarmed peasants by
the American helicopter crew. Threatening to destroy the aircraft, he
forces the pilot to cease the cowardly attack against the men, women,
and children below - the innocent victims of "body count" mentality.

2.   ALMOST LIKE SUMMER CAMP
        Marvin meets the men of his "A Team"
and is introduced to life in a remote Special Forces camp complete with
counterparts, mercenaries, bodyguards, and interpreters. After deciding
he and his men would be known as the "Bassac Bastards", Marvin takes on
the challenge of gaining rapport with his counterpart and the irregular
warriors of An-Phu. Marvin learns why Americans don't drink the water.
He and his tough counterpart, Major Le Van Phoi, agree on imposing the
death penalty for any woman-molester in An-Phu.

3.   THE INNER SANCTUM
        Defining the inner compound - where access is
restricted to American and Vietnamese Green Berets, their bodyguards,
and selected civilian employees. Marvin inspects border outposts, gets
acquainted with the area and its people, and learns the role bats play
in the local economy. Major Phoi explains the rationale behind the all-□female
agent net and border-crossing shoppers. Viet Cong mine a bridge
and destroy a boat dock. Marvin directs the historic first cross-border
fire mission into Cambodian sanctuaries and then joins Major Phoi in a
successful effort to obtain amnesty from Saigon for the irregulars of
An-Phu. Visits a neighboring Special Forces camp located on the Mekong
River and learns that merchant ships routinely carry enemy war goods up
the Mekong into Cambodia. Handcuffed by political constraints and
silenced by secrecy the Green Berets are helpless to stem the tide of
death-dealing weapons and ammunition flowing past their noses and into
the sanctuaries of their foe - to be used against them in days to come!

4.   A TEST OF COURAGE
        Hoa Hao leaders test Marvin's mettle and then
honor him with a purple scarf in a brief ceremony at their village.
Enemy forces attack the forward operations base at Phu-Hiep, inflicting
65 percent casualties. Marvin and Phoi lead the reaction force and push
the Viet Cong back into Cambodia. Special Forces, irregulars, and other
volunteers build ninety homes and shops in just seven days to replace
those destroyed by a disastrous fire in the district village.

5.   WAIT FOR THE SOUTHERN WIND
        Martha Raye's helicopter hit twice by
anti-aircraft machine gun fire as it approaches Marvin's camp to visit.
A unique strategy results in destruction of a Communist secret base in
Cambodia using wind as a weapon. Enemy combat activities increase as
Westmoreland's deputy, Major General Heintges, brings good news to
Marvin. Marvin orders a trouble-making Chaplain out of his camp.

6.   WE ALMOST BOUGHT THE FARM
        Ten Green Beret combat commanders
miraculously survive a mid-air collision of two helicopters.

7.   BUT THEY'RE WOMEN, SIR!

A two page Chapter Summary for the manuscript *The Bassac Bastards and the People of An Phu* used as a tool to test the market for publishers' interest. Notice that many of the chapter headings are the same as when the book was published as *Expendable Elite* in 2003, and the synopsis of the chapters tells the same consistent narrative that LTC Marvin has been relating throughout the years.

Visiting Lieutenant Colonel fails the monkey bridge
test. Marvin rebuked for speech given at camp celebration. Irregular
strength is increased to 792 men and arrival of a kerosene refrigerator
is heralded. Marvin initiates daytime cross-border fire missions as the
enemy buildup continues. Four female Viet Cong terrorists are captured
and interrogated. Enemy increase their probing activity all along the
border.

8.   ALL HELL BREAKS LOOSE AT KHANH-BINH
        Monsoon rains begin as agent
reports verify enemy stockpiling of five-hundred caskets just across the
border in Cambodia. Two-thousand plus VC attack An-Phu outposts on
Ho-Chi-Minh's birthday. A detailed account of the bloody five day
battle includes the use of Mike Force mercenaries and "Puff the Magic
Dragon" gatling-gunship to help the irregulars of An-Phu. An airdrop of
ammunition arrives in the nick of time to avoid a disaster as over 8,000
refugees flood the district and are cared for in an awesome display of
cooperation and compassion.

9.   THE SWEET TASTE OF VICTORY
        An ARVN Infantry Battalion and a Recon
Company help in mop-up operation. Viet Cong settle into their Cambodian
safe-havens and prepare for their next human-wave attack against An-Phu.
A victory celebration is held in camp to honor the irregular fighters.
Refugees begin moving back and rebuilding their lives and their homes.

10.   TO ASSASSINATE A PRINCE
        A Central Intelligence Agency
mission to assassinate Cambodian Crown Prince Sihanouk is initially
accepted by Marvin. One hundred Hoa Hao irregulars volunteer for the mission.
Lack of a response to Marvin's demand for an end to the sanctuaries in
trade for "terminating" Prince Sihanouk angers him and he unilaterally
aborts the mission. CIA agent threatens Marvin when ordered to leave.

11.   APOCALYPSE AT AN-PHU
        Phoi and Marvin are convinced it is a CIA
revenge tactic when are told that Premier Ky has rescinded the
amnesty for all the Hoa Haos and ordered all of their irregulars be sent
before a military tribunal. Marvin, ordered to bring his men out of
An-Phu, honors his commitment to the Hoa Haos and ignores the order. An
ARVN Regiment is sent to attack Marvin's camp if necessary to enforce
the edict from Premier Ky. His men prepare the camp for demolition.
Two hundred irregular fighters turn in their weapons as the area is
closed to outsiders. The three day drama lasted until General Quang Van
Dang courageously put his own life on the line - and decided the outcome
of what had been a truly bizarre stand-off between friendly forces.

12.   THE "BASSAC BASTARDS" FADE AWAY
        The final days in An-Phu. ☐

13.   THE PRESIDENT'S FANTASY - THE SOLDIER'S CURSE
        US Army Chief of Staff General Harold K. Johnson visits Detachment B-42 and
gives us first hand knowledge of the fantasy that our President, General Johnson and
General Westmoreland propogate on the American people regarding their aiding and
abetting of the enemy.

Feb 20, 1988

Throughout American History patriotism has always been an honorable estate. In times of peril, deserters were vilified as cowards, and the cream of our youth were willing to lay down their lives for their country.

The Viet Nam era ended that tradition. It was the only time in American history when patrotism was unpopular. Draft dodgers were exonerated, cowards were applauded as they deserted, and the underprivileged were called to arms while the cream of our youth was deferred from service.

It was the first and only time in American history our flag was bloodied on the field of defeat and almost drowned in the sea of shame.

Time will sort out the right and wrong of it all . . . as it always does. But just as history soon forgets cowards, it also honors the valiant who stood up and were counted. Those who fell will be remembered along with the founders of our country who taught us that liberty is not an abstract term, and America's willingness to insure freedom in the world is something of which we must be manifestly proud.

Bless you Dan + Hope you like it. Martha Raye A.K.A. col. Maggi

Here is the signed first page of a draft foreword as originally received by LTC Marvin from Martha Raye. A foreword that Special Forces attorneys implied Marvin had fabricated.

Herald American

Rosemary Robinson, Regional Editor (315) 470-2200   Sunday, April 3, 1988

Ex-Green Beret rebuts stated U.S. policy in Vietnam

By Frances Dinkelspiel
Staff Writer

JACKSONVILLE — Lt. Col. Dan Marvin is a man who never learned how to give up a fight.

He may have retired from the U.S. Special Forces in 1973 and traded covert military actions for a furniture refurbishing shop in his Trumansburg home, but the impulse to challenge, to think strategically, to charge — that has never left him.

"Dangerous Dan," is the military nickname Marvin still uses to refer to himself, and he recently began a new battle. This one is a manuscript Marvin wrote concerning the seven months he spent in Vietnam in 1965-1966. His story challenges the United States government's official version of that war.

"They're not going to be happy when I publish this book," said Marvin from his Jacksonville shop, which also serves as a kind of shrine to his 21 years in the Army. Medals and photos line the walls, which are draped with velvet.

Marvin, then a captain in the Green Berets, was sent to the An-Phu district to help guard 30 miles of the South Vietnamese border across from Cambodia. During that period, groups of Viet Cong used Cambodia as a sanctuary from which to shell South Vietnam.

President Lyndon Johnson's official policy was that Cambodia was a neutral country. No U.S. Army personnel would violate that neutrality.

"The official policy line was not to shoot across the border," said Marvin.

But that official policy was false, writes Marvin, whose manuscript is not yet published. As captain of a team of 12 Special Forces men, his group was ordered to secretly shell and attack the Viet Cong

The team worked with a squad of Vietnamese Special Forces, composed of Hao Haos, a Buddhist sect. Together they launched a number of offensives on the Viet Cong hiding in Cambodia, and killed hundreds of enemy soldiers, said Marvin.

"Our mission was surveillance of 30 miles of border, and the clearing of any of the enemy in the territory," said Marvin.

Another of Marvin's assertions in the manuscript is even more intriguing. The CIA enlisted him to organize an assassination attack against Prince Sihanouk, the leader of Cambodia and an American ally, he said.

Marvin and his Vietnamese counterpart, Maj. Le-Van-Phoi, planned the mission, which would have sent 42 Vietnamese into Cambodia to kill Sihanouk. The murder would appear to have been carried out by the North Vietnamese, and in retaliation, the Cambodian government would have ousted the Viet Cong from their sanctuaries, said Marvin.

But Marvin, against the wishes of the CIA, said he aborted the mission. Marvin had tried to make a deal: If President Johnson stated publicly that the U.S. would no longer tolerate the Viet Cong taking sanctuary, his men would go on the assassination mission. The CIA did not hold up its end of the bargain, so Marvin called off the trip, he said.

Verifying Marvin's accounts is difficult, but a number of Vietnam experts said the cross-border shelling claims were entirely plausible.

Leo Crawley, a veteran, Vietnam scholar, and radio talk show host for

WBAI in New York City, said there were frequent incursions into "neutral" countries such as Cambodia and Laos. The border was not well defined.

As for the Sihanouk assassination attempt, Crawley is skeptical. The political situation in Cambodia was volatile, and it would have been easy for the CIA. to recruit a disgruntled politician, he said.

A U.S. government official, who worked in the Special Forces in Vietnam but who did not want his name or title used, said the Sihanouk claim was "egregious nonsense."

By 1966, the CIA had agents in Cambodia, and it would have been far easier for them to kill Sihanouk than for untrained Vietnamese, who had to penetrate the border. Additionally, an assassination attempt did not make political sense, for the U.S. government needed Sihanouk, he said.

Marvin stands by his story. The manuscript, tells the "hard truth," he wrote.

Marvin is not telling this story because he wants to get back at the Army, he said. If anything, he is a company man. The most exciting times of his life were in the Army, he said, and he has recreated its regimen since his retirement, rising at 5:30 a.m., sleeping only four hours a night. If Marvin was called on a mission, he would go in an instant, he said.

"War is . . . the most challenging job you could ever have," said Marvin. "I used to hunt before I went into the Army. After hunting people I find hunting defenseless game something I'm not interested in."

Like many former Vietnam veterans, Marvin feels let down by the U.S. government, and that is one motive for writing the manuscript, he said. The U.S. government fought the war in the wrong way — a way it could not win. Marvin wants to show what went wrong.

The United States government betrayed the people of South Vietnam and dishonored our nation as a defender of freedom," writes Marvin in his manuscript.

The real problem came when Johnson replaced President John Kennedy as commander-in-chief, said Marvin. Kennedy's strategy relied on the Special Forces — the Green Berets — to play the same game as the enemy: guerrilla warfare.

But Johnson fought the war in a conventional way, by bombing the major cities and sending masses of troops into the field, he said. And Johnson's policy of letting the Viet Cong take refuge in Cambodia and strike Vietnam defenses from there still frustrates Marvin, he said.

The war is long over, but Marvin is still plotting and planning how to bring some good out of it. For hours each day, he sits behind his IBM computer, where he once sculpted his manuscript. Now the words are letters in search of a publisher, or pleas to find his co-commander, Phoi, who probably is still jailed in a Vietnamese prison camp.

This article in the 1988 Syracuse *Herald-American* is the first news article about this book, and again LTC Marvin consistently tells the same story.

SGM Richard Sirois (USA ret'd)   BAC-51   May 88   (3)
   WIFE: Ellie

BACKGROUND INFORMATION & PERSONAL DATA

Where were you born? Lawrence, MA — LAWRENCE, MA.

When were you born? 21 Sep 40

How many sisters and brothers do you have? 12

Was your family wealthy _____ middle class _____ Poor X _____

Were you raised in the city or country? City

Did you ever get in a fist fight before you joined the Army?
Yes, plenty but lost most of them because of my size (very small but wiry)

Who was the greatest influence on you before you joined the Army?
Some teachers, Mom & Dad

When did you join the Army? 1958 (Dec)

Where did you go to Basic training? Ft. Dix

When did you go to jump school? 1963   Where? Ft. Benning

What caused you to volunteer for Special Forces? After a nine month break in service the recruiter said I had all the requisites for passing SF.

When did you go thru SF training? Feb 1963 – June 1964

When did you go to Medical training? Feb 1963 – Dec 1963

What were your assignments before you came to An-Phu?
Panama (8th) June 1964 – Mar 66

> DEFENDANT'S
> EXHIBIT
> 31

What did you do at Muc-Hoa? "B" team not assigned – assigned to a place called AP BAC – was FOB for Kieng –

Was there much action there? Quan II – none directly on my camp but nearby yes. (plain of reeds).

What comments (Very candid please) do you have about my performance as the A Team CO? I'd like to use your comments .5 give the reader some do's & don'ts:

   a.   Worst traits: Too tidy, wanted to be "too" neat was too "conventional" on our unconventional minds. Did not keep us posted, kept by yourself. Not too involved with EM – officer oriented, Had your office away from rest of team. Spent too much time behind

   b.   Best traits: Demanding standards were met, not allowing drunks on your team, Making sure we portrayed the best of best (i.e.) appearance, maintenance etc – Looking out for our welfare.

LTC Dan Marvin sent a manuscript to Richard Sirois, John Strait and Jim Taylor in May of 1988 along with a form for personal information and a request for recollections and corroboration for his manuscript. Dan soon received this handwritten response from Richard Sirois. Richard and John also sent Dan audiotapes of their recollections of An Phu; some excerpts are on the page 432.

BACKGROUND INFORMATION & PERSONAL DATA

James A. Taylor

Where were you born? _BeARdsTowN, ILL_

When? _6/16/38_

How many sisters and brothers do you have? _15_

Were your folks: Wealthy ____ Middle class____ Poor _✓_ (like mine)

Were you raised in the city or country? _CiTY_

Did you ever get in a fist fight before you joined the Army? _yes_

Who was the greatest influence on you before you joined the Army?
MY BROThERS

What were your favorite sports? _FootbAll_

When did you join? _17 JUN 55_ Did you enlist? _yes_

When did you graduate from Jump School? _Feb 56_ Where? _FT BRAGG, N.C_

When did you earn the Green Beret? _FT BRAGG_
How many started in your group?_____ How many Graduated?_____
What were your Special Forces assignments before you came to An-Phu?
FT BRAGG, KOREA, ~~FT BRAGG~~, BAd TOLZ, ~~FT~~ VIETNAM, ITALY, GReeSe

Evaluation of Dangerous Dan at An-Phu

What comments (VERY <u>candid</u> please) do you have about my performance as
the Team Leader? [as it helped or hindered our ability to get the job
done & as it affected a solid A Team concept best suited to meet the
actual situation at An-Phu] I'd like this kind of honest response so I
can attempt to cover some of the "dos and don'ts" of A Team leadership,
mostly to help others from making the same mistakes that I did. Also -
to allow them to take advantage of whatever I did that worked well.

    a. Worst traits: _HeadSTRONg AT TIMES; IMPATIENT AT TIMES_
      BAd CIgARS

    b. Best traits: _williNg To leARN, ABiliTY To listeN, ANd
    ReAlize we hAd To woRkAs A TeAM. good seNce OF HumoR
    iN good ANd BAd TiMes_

DEFENDANT'S
EXHIBIT
9

A handwritten response from James Taylor to LTC Marvin. While, we, the defendants
submitted many historical documents to the court, plus the many pictures and documents in the book to substantiate its account of events, the plaintiffs simply repeated
over and over again that An Phu was a "resort camp," there was "no action," etc. They
presented *no* documentary evidence of any value. Instead, they brought in the "Big
Guns," a Major General, who had served as the top JAG officer in the nation, and
then a Medal of Honor winner, all to impress and wow the jury. The tactic backfired,
though, as attorney Chris Ogiba brought out the issue of "plausible deniability," and
in the end chalked-up these witnesses testimony on our side of the ledger.

EXCERPTS FROM:
<u>JOHN STRAIT'S AUDIOTAPES SENT TO DAN MARVIN MAY & JUNE 1988:</u>
"First realization that we were in the world of shit there was when you took me in the command bunker there and started showing me where all the demolitions switches are. You tell me this one destroys the right one [machine gun bunker], this one destroys the left one [machine gun bunker], this destroys the command bunker and this one destroys every damn thing. I figured right then that we was in a rough spot."

"Getting back to Phu Hiep again, at the Cambodian border there. There were several operations that we run from the FOB to and across the border here. We were constantly firing at the Pagoda over there [inside Cambodia] and we had intelligence reports that we got quite a few casualties from up in there. Most of the incidents that we went over across the border there, it was never reported, even back to the main base there so anything official we were on operation there, but never give 'em the directions or anything like that. I believe the border violations that time was called the code word *Nantucket* there and I don't know how damn many we had on us there, but we were always in and out of the border and firing across the border."

"We sure as hell did a lot with very few people here. I never realized that we never did have a full team over there all the time I was there and I can see now why we were always turning around and meeting ourselves coming and going over there. Either you was going out to the FOB or you was coming back and then it was twice as bad, we manned two of 'em [FOBs]."

"I'm aware that 9th Division Regiment was going to come in and take the camp there which I doubted at the time that they could. Because those six companies we have I don't think there would be any match for that Vietnamese Regiment there that didn't have any incentive to do anything where our people did and they were well organized and trained and everything. So, I had my doubts at the time that that regiment or a division would have had a heck of a time taking that [our camp]. I'm just glad that we never had to find out. General Quang, I remember when he came down [after turning the regiment back] ... and give 'em amnesty."

"Getting back to the politics and stuff, my definition of the CIA and the politicians versus the Special Forces missions and people - they're just like a damn cundum [condom]. They [CIA] use 'em and when they get through using 'em they throw the damn things away there. That's just about like they did on your operation. When they seen they couldn't use you or you balked and they discarded you and you'd play one heck of a time trying to prove it."

"You could hear all hell breaking loose [19 May 66] up at Khanh Binh. And there was green tracers and red tracers all over the place and first light we were on our way up there with the ambush platoon, I think it was a platoon, maybe a little better than a platoon, but we were up there on foot and then I remember you coming with the relief column there and I don't know how close you come up on truck there—I believe a little bit beyond the bridge there —so we accomplished our mission and held the bridge for you. And then you came in on the right side and I came in with the company that had joined us [the ambush platoon] on the left side there into Khanh Binh there as relief force. I know by the time we hit [the VC encirclement of the FOB] that all hell was breaking loose again up there. They were getting recoilless rifle fire and mortar fire from the Cambodian outpost that was just across the river [border canal] from 'em. And I remember I had the radio and I was talking to the air support and you came up there and all of a sudden you grabbed me and pulled my ass down and just about that time a mortar round hit just a few feet away from us there so I credit you with saving my ass right then."

"I don't have the figures right now. I know they killed an awful lot of the VC out there"'"

"When we had the victory celebration [on 4 June 1966] which I have several pictures of that was in a book I sent you that Wooley and myself of An Phu Camp history I believe we were of the only two or three of the Vietnamese Crosses of Gallantry that was issued out which I considered that probably one of the higher honors of getting any medal that I'd got in Vietnam, because one out of three for I don't know how many years the camp was there I figured that was quite an honor for anybody."

"That was an excellent Foreword that Colonel Maggie wrote for you and I can see why and justifiable that you be damn proud of that because it was real choice words. It reflects I think what I believe a lot of people have been thinking for a long time. Whether it does any good or not—I don't know."

"You mentioned the other day about using fictitious names and like that. You sure got my permission to use my name and any incidents that you want. One thing I think about using real names there it offers a little more authenticity to the story here."

RICHARD SIROIS' AUDIOTAPES HE SENT TO DAN MARVIN. MAY 1988:
"Right after I got there [An Phu] I kind of remember a lot of the things that were going on. There was a lot of action up around where we used to go for our, I can't remember the outpost [Phu Hiep], but we used to have to travel and go up there. It took about an hour by boat and I was always really, really scared going up there.

"There was a lot of action up there [Khanh Binh] and I remember you guys had a big victory party. You had sent your soldiers out there from An Phu and you kinda caught them in a pincer. They [VC] attacked at night but the end result was that you kicked their damn asses and you captured a lot of weapons. There was a lot of dead bodies. The Hoa Haos did suffer some casualties."

"Also I remember about the operations that we used to go on. Holy Mackerel. I remember we used to go on the pincers, the hammer and pincers operations up all around the Cambodian border and everything."

"I just wanted to tell you that I hope you can understand all of this goobely gock. I can't talk to a damn tape recorder. Hopefully what I told you just now will bring back some memories and maybe you can insert some of them into your book. By the way I really do hope that you have success with your book and I'm really looking forward reading it and I'm also looking forward to see you in July [at the SFA 1988 convention]."

RAYMOND JOHNSON SPEAKING TO DAN MARVIN 3 AUGUST 1997:
"I remember going on a mission, Sir. I remember going. I went with myself, Major Phoi, oh hell, we went into Cambodia and then all of a sudden we walked back. I don't know who went with me. I was the commo man and another guy."

"We were in Cambodia and then we came back."

"You never talked down to us. You were strict, you were good. We called you Dangerous Dan.

Audiotapes may heard in full at www.ExpendableElite.com

10 November 1988

Lt Col Daniel Marvin AUS (ret)
1604 Trumansburg Road
Ithaca, New York 14850

Dear Friend,

I have fully enjoyed the reading of the two chapters from your coming
book The Bassac Bastards (Chapter Ten, Mission to Assassinate a Prince
and Chapter Eleven, Apocalypse at An-Phu).

Though many years have passed since the events of June, 1966 I assure
you that I recall Major Le-Van-Phoi's emissary coming to me in my
headquarters in Can-Tho and explaining the situation in An-Phu with the
Hoa-Hao Irregulars. It was a very dramatic and crucial event that would
hardly escape my memory. At the time I commanded all Vietnamese Forces
in the IV Corps area as a Lieutenant General.

I would like to say that it was my duty to go to your green beret camp
in An-Phu with my U.S. Army advisor, Colonel William Desobry and
personally assure the brave irregular fighters that they were safe from
military tribunal action and that their amnesty was restored to them. I
wanted to avoid any bloodshed between two friendly anti-communist forces
and to work toward national unity and reconciliation.

The Hoa-Hao people were a very strong asset for my country and I worked
very closely with Colonel Desobry to have a happy ending to the very
troubled situation in An-Phu. It was our joint success.

Though I do not have knowledge of all the details included in your
chapters ten and eleven of "The Bassac Bastards" I do believe you are
honest in what you say and I do not know of anything that would
truthfully contradict your revelations.

May the Lord bless you and your family.

Sincerely yours,

Dangvanquang
Quang Van Dang
Your comrade in arms

Having his story questioned, LTC Marvin seeks to find people who can verify his
story. In searching for former ARVN Lieutenant General Quang Van Dang, Dan
finds that the General has been stranded in Canada for years, and is working as
a dishwasher. Marvin leads a 11-month-long battle to get former ally, General
Dang admitted to the U.S.

Here is letter from General Dang corroborating significant portions of Dan's
book. Over the plaintiff's strenuous objections, the jury was finally allowed to
view this letter. Later, among these pages you will see historical documents that
the plaintiffs attorneys made sure the jury did not view.

GRAPEVINE

Tompkins County's Weekly   May 11-17, 1989

COVER STORY

Laughing

continued from cover

I t began as a courtesy call. Retired Green Beret Colonel Dan Marvin of Jacksonville wanted to thank South Vietnamese General Dang Van Quang for risking his life to save Marvin's and 700 of his men, 22 years earlier in Vietnam. After years of searching, including a campaign of letters to friends and former associates, Marvin finally located Quang in Montreal. The man he found was a shadow of the man he had known.

Stateless, struggling for survival on the edge of poverty, Quang has nearly lost hope that he may live to realize his dream of emigrating to the United States. Fearful, alternately persecuted and ignored by a government that once exploited his talents, Quang's sad circumstances came as a complete surprise to Marvin.

"It is like being in a prison without walls," Quang told Marvin last fall. How he got there is closely related to the last days of the United States' involvement in Vietnam.

BEFORE THE FALL. General Quang visited the An Phu troops when the — and he — were still winning. PHOTO COURTESY COL. DAN MARVIN

6   The Grapevine May 18-24, 1989

No Laughing Matter

> "Quang, a fat man who giggled so often that the Americans called him 'Laughing Boy,' was thought by his fellow countrymen to be the most corrupt man in South Vietnam. No one ever proved that Quang was the country's major drug smuggler, or the front man for Thieu in all the other varieties of corruption that permeated the government. But both charges were assumed to be true."
>
> — The Fall of Saigon, by David Butler (Dell Publishing Co., Inc., 1985)

The Past

As President Thieu's assistant for security and intelligence during the final years of U.S. support for South Vietnam's war against the North Vietnamese communists, Quang was the second most powerful man in that nation. He was also a CIA confidant and a staunch ally of the United States.

Quang first met Marvin on June 4, 1966, at a victory celebration in Marvin's Special Forces camp near the Cambodian border. As Commanding General of Tactical Zone IV, Quang had come to the party to honor and reward the irregular fighters of An-Phu (South Vietnamese civilian soldiers recruited and paid by the U.S.) for their victories over the Viet Cong. This force of 792 South Vietnamese was under the joint command of then-Captain Marvin's nine-man Green Beret "Independent Warfare" unit and his South Vietnamese counterpart, Major Le Van Phoi.

Sihanouk Assassination Plot

According to Marvin, six days later, an Air America helicopter brought a CIA agent and his female companion to Camp An-Phu. (Marvin doesn't remember their names, only the CIA ID's that were swiftly flashed and re-pocketed.) The agent had an assignment for Marvin's group: a covert mission to assassinate Cambodian Crown Prince Sihanouk. CIA plans called for the use of irregulars from Marvin's camp, intending that the North Vietnamese would be blamed as perpetrators. The CIA apparently hoped that the Cambodians would then accomplish what the US government had so far refused to do: evict North Vietnamese guerrillas from their sanctuaries in Cambodia. These safe-havens across the Cambodian border were used by the Viet Cong for cross-border shelling. Since Cambodia was officially a neutral nation, U.S.-directed soldiers were not allowed to fire back.

The cost in human lives was staggering. In five months, Marvin saw nearly 200 deaths in his small area directly attributable to enemy attacks from those safe havens. The U.S. government, in tolerating the Cambodian sanctuaries, had acquiesced in the continuation of a no-win situation: U.S. and South Vietnamese soldiers were unable to secure the South Vietnamese border and were unsafe, even in their own territory.

Knowing that it would be suicidal to move through heavily defended and equipped enemy lines, Marvin counterproposed to the agent an end to the toleration of these sanctuaries as a precondition for his involvement in the CIA scheme. Had President Johnson announced such a move, the risks of engagement would have immediately changed. Political pressure on the Cambodians, bombing of the safe havens — or at least, permission for the South Vietnamese soldiers to shoot back when fired upon — would have made a covert incursion into Cambodia a safer proposition.

No-Win Strategy

On June 15, just two days before volunteers from Marvin's detachment were to begin their 100-mile trek into Cambodian territory, Marvin learned that his demands had not been met. This must not have been a great surprise, since one of the predictable outcomes of such a policy shift could have been overt Cambodian involvement in the war. However, after consulting with Major Phoi, Marvin aborted the mission and ordered the CIA agent to leave his camp. The final angry words of the agent to Marvin were, "You can't fight the system, Captain. You know you can't win."

But Marvin tried. Two days later, South Vietnam's Premier Ky (head of the military; President Thieu's bailiwick was the civilian power structure) ordered the irregular fighters of Camp An-Phu to stand before a military tribunal (court-martial). Believing this to be CIA-instigated revenge for the cancelled Prince Sihanouk assassination mission, Marvin and Phoi refused to accept the edict. Within hours, Marvin was ordered by the C-team commander to bring his Green Beret A-Team out of An-Phu to Chau Doc, where they would join another detachment. Aware that to do so would be abandoning the irregulars to the possibility of wholesale slaughter by both friendly and enemy troops, Marvin instead closed his area to all outsiders.

The following day, the besieged special forces group learned that a 1500-man regiment of ARVN [*South Vietnamese regular army*] infantry was preparing to converge on its camp with orders to attack if Marvin and Phoi continued to defy Ky's edict. Phoi sent an emissary to General Quang's headquarters to inform him of the situation and to request Quang's intervention on their behalf. Because Quang hadn't known of the ARVN deployment, Marvin was convinced that this

> *Unwilling to face capture, the men wired two large ammunition bunkers and the command bunker for simultaneous detonation, using large quantities of plastic explosives. If the ARVN regiment overran their defenses, a simple pull of one switch would destroy the entire camp — and them with it.*

was a CIA-directed scenario.

Marvin received a second order to bring his unit out of An-Phu but again, after consultation with his men, he refused. Unwilling to face capture, the men wired two large ammunition bunkers and the command bunker for simultaneous detonation, using large quantities of plastic explosive. If the ARVN regiment overran their defenses, a simple pull of one switch would destroy the entire camp — and them with it.

But on June 20th, 72 hours after the nightmare had begun, General Quang flew in by helicopter to rescue the beleaguered unit. Enroute to their camp he

---

LTC Marvin soon began a campaign to get General Dang, a man who had saved his life, admittance into this country. This complete multi-page article and more documentation are accessible online at www.ExpendableElite.com

435

17 June 89

Jim Taylor

You are a big part of the story! and I'm sure proud to know you!

Your Comrade-in-arms

Dangerous Dan

THE BASSAC BASTARDS

THE TRUE STORY

ABOUT U.S. ARMY SPECIAL FORCES DETACHMENT A-424

AND

INDEPENDENT WARFARE

IN AN-PHU, SOUTH VIETNAM

December 1965 - August 1966

© Copyright by Lieutenant Colonel Daniel Marvin AUS (ret) 1989

Keeping Jim Taylor in the loop, LTC Marvin sent him a second manuscript in 1989, hoping for some feedback and comments. The manuscript is clearly labeled "The True Story."

1604 Trumansburg Road • Ithaca NY 14850 • 607 273 1496

17 July 1989

President George Bush
THE WHITE HOUSE
Washington, D.C. 20500

RE: General Dang Van Quang
Case File # 84173048

Dear President Bush,

I first wrote you on 31 March 1989 about the situation involving General Quang (the man who saved my life in June, 1966) asking that you order Secretary of State James Baker to aggressively pursue the matter.

I again wrote you on 3 May 1989, enclosing a copy of a letter that I had mailed out that same day to Senators Moynihan, D'Amato, and Levin and Congressmen McHugh and Pursell, wherein I asked that they do what they could to get to the truth in the case of General Quang. I also mailed you a copy of my 2 June letter to those same Senators and Congressmen, wherein I pleaded for each of them to press vigorously for final action in the matter of General Quang's visa application of May 1984.

I understand that very few letters ever reach your desk in the oval office - but certainly someone who works for you has read my letters. It bothers me that I have yet to receive the courtesy of a reply to indicate that my letters reached your staff. Nor have I received any written or oral communication advising me of what action is being taken to look into the matter of human rights abuse that I brought to your attention. Why is this so? It is as though nobody in the White House nor the State Department wants to answer any questions relating to their treatment of General Quang. Why is this the case, Mr. President?

Senator Moynihan's and Senator D'Amato's staff have both informed me as recently as the 26th of June - that they haven't been able to get any answers out of James Baker or his people regarding General Quang. Just today, Congressman McHugh's Ithaca office staffer (Jean McPheeters) informed me that State Department representative Cindy Gardner told her that this [General Quang's visa application] was "clearly an unusual case", that it would probably go all the way to the seventh floor (I assume she meant that James Baker would be in on the action) for a decision and said that the case was "being treated very special".

What must I do to resolve this matter, Mr. President?

Sincerely,

Lt Col Daniel Marvin AUS (ret)

Enclosure: Karey Solomon article: "No Laughing Matter"

Copy furnished: General Quang   Maj. John Strait
               Jack Anderson   Magdalene Jourdan
               Karey Solomon

Continuing in his effort to get General Quang Van Dang into this country, LTC Marvin went so far as to write a strong letter to President George H.W. Bush, demanding answers with regard to getting to the truth about General Dang. This letter inspired immediate action, which led to General Dang being issued a Permanent Entry Visa on 7 September 1989.

GRAPEVINE

Tompkins County's Weekly | September 7-13, 1989

THE VIEW FROM ALBANY STREET

Quang Update

Former South Vietnamese General Dang Van Quang, a stateless refugee in Montreal since the fall of Saigon, was informed last Monday by officials of the U.S. Consul that he may now apply for a United States Visa, an application that is expected to be approved within a few days.

Grapevine readers may recall Quang's story "No Laughing Matter," which appeared in our May 11, 1989 issue. Asserting that he was the victim of unsubstantiated allegations, Quang has spent the years since the end of the Vietnam War living with his wife in a basement apartment in Montreal, working as a dishwasher and attempting to clear his name. [Retired Green Beret] Colonel Dan Marvin of Jacksonville, who credits Quang with saving his own life as well as those of other friendly forces, first learned of Quang's plight last winter while researching his forthcoming account of wartime experiences in Vietnam, The Bassac Bastards.

Convinced that an injustice had been done, Marvin relentlessly petitioned state and national officials for speedy resolution of this case and located additional support. It seemed likely that a congressional inquiry would be needed. Those Americans who knew and had worked with Quang in South Vietnam agree that accusations of drug trafficking and influence peddling were without foundation. But establishing the truth in the face of controversy is a long, disheartening process. Undaunted, Marvin pressed on, even writing to President Bush who was head of the CIA when the U.S. borders where closed to Quang. Until Monday, few of his letters had met with response.

On Mon., Aug. 28, Quang was called to the consulate for a meeting and informed that he may now apply for a visa. He later told Dan Marvin in a phone call that "he was very happy to be treated like a human being for a change," and he is anxious to talk to his children [some of whom live in the U.S. and are U.S. citizens].

Jean McPheeters, district representative for Congressman McHugh, was delighted to confirm that there are now "no problems with the security check," and the entire process should be completed by mid-September. (This was the stumbling block which allegedly held up Quang's visa application over the previous 14 years.) In a brief telephone interview, Quang said that these developments "are like a dream come true." He's not ready to talk about future plans, though he expects to be settled in this country by Christmas.

— K. Solomon

General Quang

NOTE: LTC Dan Marvin personally escorted General Dang Van Quang (AKA Quang Van Dang) into the United States from Canada on the 24 of September 1989. General Dang became a U.S. Citizen in 1998!

Courtesy of Daniel Marvin

WARTIME BUDDIES shown in a recent snapshot are Quang van Dang, right, a former general in the Army of the Republic of South Vietnam, and Daniel Marvin of Trumansburg, who as an American lieutenant colonel was rescued by Dang during the war.

I KEPT GEN. DESOBRY ABREAST OF THE SITUATION AND LET HIM KNOW THAT I WILL TALK TO KY AND THE MINISTER OF DEFENSE. EFFECTIVELY I TALK TO KY AND TO VY (THE MINISTER OF DEFENSE) AND ASK THEM TO LET ME HANDLE THE WHOLE SITUATION PEACE FULLY. KY AGREES AND SEEMS TO BE RELIEVED OF THE PROBLEM. IN FACT HE HAS QUITE A FEW BIG POLITICAL PROBLEMS IN SAIGON. HE EXPLAINED ROUGHLY TO ME HIS STRONG STAND BECAUSE HE LIKES TO CONSOLIDATE THE POWER AND PRESTIGE OF THE CENTRAL GOVERMENT WITH THE CONSENT OF "THE U.S. SIDE" I DIDN'T ASK HIM WHAT, WHO, WAS IN THE U.S. SIDE. I TRUSTED HIM IN HIS RELATIONSHIPS AND DEALINGS WITH THE OFFICIALS REPRESENTATIVES OF THE US. GOVERNMENT.

AFTER HAVING KY AUTHORISATION TO SOLVE THE PROBLEM AS I HAVE SUGGESTED, I LET GEN. DESOBRY KNOW RIGHT AWAY AND ALSO MR. LUONG TRONG TUONG . . . .

AFTER RETURNING FROM ANPHU I DID REPORT TO KY AND VY AND THE J.G.S.

AT THAT MOMENT I DID NOT KNOW THE REAL "SCOPE" OF THE PROBLEM BECAUSE I DIDN'T HAVE ALL THE DETAILED INFOR- MATIONS WITH ALL THE FACTORS CONTRIBUTING TO RAISE IT. RIGHT NOW WITH YOUR DISCLOSURE I CAN SEE THE PROBLEM WAS REAL BIG AND HEAVY OF CONSEQUENCES.

: TO THE 9th INF DIV. I TOLD THEM TO STOP ALL OPERATIONS AGAINST THE CIDG CAMP, BECAUSE I HAVE JUST RECEIVED ORDERS FROM SAIGON. EVERYTHING MUST GO BACK TO NORMAL. FURTHER DIRECTIVES WILL COME LATER.

TO THE PEOPLE IN THE CAMP, I DISPEL ANY FEAR, I LET THEM KNOW THAT THE GOVERNMENT THRU ME UNDERSTAND THEIR SI- TUATION AND WISHES, THEY WILL HAVE A DELAY TO STRAIGHTEN THE RECORDS, AND THEY'LL HAVE A STABLE AND SAFE STATUS WITHIN THE A.R.V.N. THEY'LL WILL NOT BE A SECOND CLASS SOLDIER. THERE IS NO USE TO FIGHT BETWEEN FRIEND. OUR ONLY AND COMMON ENEMY IS THE V.C.

: COL. DESOBRY GAVE ORDERS TO THE U.S. ADVISORS IN THE SAME TIME I COMMUNICATE WITH MY SUBORDINATES. SAME EXPLANATION _ SAME COOL TONE, TO AVOID ANY SUREXCI- TEMENT.

A vitally important hand-written summary, by General Dang, explaining some of the background of the actions taking place in *Expendable Elite*, including personal contact with Premier Nguyen Cao Ky and Minister of Defense Vy that led to Dang's turning back an ARVN Regiment (1200 men) that was en route to destroy Camp An Phu in early June of 1966. General Dang wrote this for LTC Marvin during their visit after Dan helped get the General into this country in 1989.

UNCLASSIFIED

P890113-1127 RELEASED IN FULL

United States Senate
WASHINGTON, D.C. 20510

September 8, 1989

Mr. J. Edward Fox
Assistant Secretary for
   Legislative Affairs
Department of State
Washington, DC 20520

Dear Mr. Fox:

I am writing to express my interest in the State Department's investigation and advisory opinion on General Dang Van Quang.

General Quang was the assistant for security and intelligence for President Thieu during the later stages of the Vietnam war. Apparently, the General was air-lifted out of the U.S. Embassy during the fall of Saigon and upon his arrival in the United States, was settled for a brief period in an Arkansas camp. While in Arkansas, General Quang obtained permission from Canada to visit his children in Montreal. He left the United States for Montreal in 1975 and has not been allowed to re-enter. In 1984, General Quang's son who settled in Virginia filed an immigrant visa petition in behalf of his father; however, to this date, a decision on whether General Quang can immigrate to the United States has not been made.

From what I have been informed by retired Lt. Colonel Dan Marvin of 1604 Trumansburg Road, Ithaca, NY 14850, the decision on General Quang's immigration to the United States is pending on the completion of an advisory opinion.

It would be most appreciated if you would inform me on the status of any progress made in determining if General Quang will be permitted to immigrate to the United States. Please direct all correspondence to my Detroit office at the address listed below.*

Thank you for your attention to this matter.

Sincerely,

Carl Levin

CL/ts

-1-

*1860 McNamara Federal Bldg.
Detroit, MI 48226
(313) 226-6020

OUT

1989 SEP 19 PM 2:15

UNCLASSIFIED

89CONST009688

LTC Marvin enlisted many in his campaign for General Dang's repatriation into the U.S. Here is a letter from Senator Carl Levin.

United States Department of State

Visa Services

Washington, D.C. 20520

September 14, 1989

Colonel Daniel Marvin Aus
1604 Trumansburg Road
Ithaca, NY 14850

Dear Colonel Aus:

Thank you for your letter of July 17 to the President concerning the visa case of General Dang Van Quang.

I am pleased to advise that General Dang was issued an immigrant visa on September 7, 1989.

Sincerely,

James L. Halmo
Director,
Office of Public
and Diplomatic Liaison

E. O. 12356: N/A
TAGS: CVIS (DANG, QUANG VAN)
SUBJECT: ADMISSION OF DANG, QUANG VAN

REF: MONTREAL 2928 AND PREVIOUS

WE HAVE BEEN ADVISED THAT FORMER SOUTH VIETNAMESE
GENERAL QUANG VAN DANG CROSSED THE BORDER AT
CHAMPLAIN POE ON SUNDAY SEPT. 24, 1989. NO PROBLEMS
WERE REPORTED AND HE IS CURRENTLY RESIDING WITH HIS
SON IN VIRGINIA. HIS BUDDY, COL. MARVIN, DROVE THE
GETAWAY VAN. CASE CLOSED (WE HOPE).   ANTIPPAS

UNCLASSIFIED

NNNN

Current Class: UNCLASSIFIED

**UNITED STATES DEPARTMENT OF STATE
REVIEW AUTHORITY: ROBERT R. STRAND
DATE/CASE ID: 23 JAN 2002 199902347**

UNCLASSIFIED

Letter from Department of State to LTC Marvin that ties in Marvin's earlier letter to then-President GHW Bush with the issuance of a visa. Also a cablegram from Consular General Antippas to State Department, with an interesting comment.

Lt Col Dan Marvin · AUS (Ret)

1604 Trumansburg Road · Ithaca N Y 14850 · 607 273 1496

Congressman Matthew F. McHugh   28 November 1990
Carriage House - Terrace Hill
Ithaca, New York 14850   VIII-A-MMH-1190

Subject: Colonel Le Van Phoi

Dear Matt,

Reference is made to my letters dated 9 June 1990 and 10 July 1990 regarding former South Vietnamese Colonel Le Van Phoi, the latter including a copy of the Camp Release Certificate dated 4 February 1988 which verifies Le Van Phoi's incarceration as a political prisoner from May 10, 1975 to that date (almost 13 years).

I asked that Colonel Phoi be allowed to immigrate as a person having had close association with the United States and suggested the CIA discreetly inform the State Department of that fact and offer Phoi resettlement monies. I also asked if you would "Please check into this matter and see what can be done to help Colonel Phoi and his family get to the United States."

You wrote to the Orderly Departure Program on 18 June 1990 on my behalf regarding Le Van Phoi. I have received no indication of any action other than that, nor of any response provided you by CIA or ODP.

I called Jean McPheeters on 21 June 1990 and told her to please remind you that protection be provided Colonel Phoi - his being the only non-CIA person alive [other than myself] who witnessed the CIA bringing the mission to assassinate Prince Sihanouk to me at An-Phu in June 1966.

In my letter of 1 August 1990 to William Fleming, Director of the ODP program [which was copied to you] I included documents needed to put Colonel Phoi on the list for interview. His response was to tell me that Le Van Phoi was not yet on a list!

Matt, after what [allegedly] happened to former CIA Erbe and Grey, I am **VERY** concerned for Colonel Phoi's safety. What have you done or what are you doing to accomplish the following?

1) Expedite the processing of Colonel Phoi and his wife and four children to the United States.

2) Provide that Colonel Phoi and his family is protected from harm [at the hands of people within <u>our</u> government] due to his being witness to the White House plot to assassinate Sihanouk in June 1966.

3) Assure that the people in the ODP program are aware of the potentially dangerous nature of Le Van Phoi's immigration to the U.S.

Please let me know immediately if you are taking action on this matter - particularly those aspects relating to the safeguarding of the life of Colonel Phoi. Someone is keeping my mail from getting to Col Phoi - perhaps the same someone that sandbagged your mail to me for six months earlier this year? I am praying for the Lord God to watch over Le Van Phoi and his family.

Sincerely,

[signature]

Copies furnished: Lan Le   ODP, Bangkok Thailand
Lightning Bolt   David MacMichael   Goodyear
Kathy Hovis, Gannett   Karey Solonon   Thunderbolt II

[handwritten in left margin:] 12 Mar 91 No Response yet on any matter or question (Dan)

> Proverb 3:27 Withhold not good from them to whom it is due, when
> **it is within the power of thine hand to do it.**

LTC Marvin continued to help his Vietnamese Hoa Hao friends get into America. Here are two letters written advocating help for the courageous Colonel Le Van Phoi, Dan's Vietnamese counterpart commander during the events depicted in *Expendable Elite.*

TRUE COPY

_____ 27 Mar 91
Lieutenant Colonel Daniel Marvin AUS (ret)   Date

Lt Col Dan Marvin · AUS (Ret)

_____

1604 Trumansburg Road · Ithaca N Y 14850 · 607 273 1496

12 March 1991   VIII-A-AHCFILE1

Alicia H. Cooper, Director
International Rescue Committee, Inc.
1801 West 17th Street
Santa Ana, CA 92706-2392

                              RE: Le Van Phoi OC# 14366
                              ODP # IV-48420, HO-20
Dear Alicia,
     Thank you for your prompt reply of 6 Mar 91 and a copy of your
letter of the same date to Lan Thanh Le. I spoke to Lan Le last night.
He will mail the "Apocalypse at An-Phu" manuscript to you today.
     With my letter to you of 15 Dec 90, I enclosed a copy of my 14 Dec
90 letter to David C. Pierce in which I quoted Vietnamese Department of
Interior information notice dated Oct 15, 90 which advised Le Van Phoi:
"We listed the names of your family in the roster of <u>HO20</u> and it was
sent to the State Department for forwarding to the U.S. government for
scheduling the interview and considering their entry into the U.S.A.."
     Reading "Apocalypse at An-Phu" will further convince you of the
seriousness of my concern for the safety of Col. Le Van Phoi. Since I
learned this past May 30th that Col. Phoi was alive in Vietnam, I've
been concerned that people within our system of government may decide
it's best that Col. Phoi never leave Vietnam. He may tell about the
events of June, 1966 when a CIA operative came to me and Col. Phoi with
a secret plot to assassinate Cambodian Crown Prince Norodom Sihanouk.
It was that mission that I first accepted and later aborted, that led to
the apocalyptic situation that General Quang Van Dang rescued us from.
     It is vital to the safety of Col. Phoi, his wife and children that
responsible people within our government openly recognize the danger
that exists and take action to expedite their safe entry into the U.S..
     I enclose a sampling of letters that convey the seriousness of the
situation and which point, in my judgement, to the existence of a well
orchestrated stonewalling campaign. I believe that Congressman McHugh,
ODP Director William Fleming and Embassy Counselor David C. Pierce have
failed to candidly recognize the truth of the situation. The CIA's past
involvement concerns me. I believe that Col. Phoi and his family are in
imminent danger. <u>Please advise your Executive Committee of this matter</u>.
I am extremely proud that your organization has sponsored Col. Phoi and
I feel in my heart that he needs your help and that he'll get it!
     Thank you for your continued support of the truth.
     Cordially,

_____

<u>Copies with enclosures to:</u>   President George Bush   Lan Thanh Le
Congressman McHugh   William Fleming, ODP   David Pierce, ODP
Senator Moynihan   Senator D'Amato   Karey Solomon
FBI Director Sessions   Kathy Hovis, Gannett   Lightning Bolt
Frances Dinkelspiel   Pearce Williams

Copy without enclosures to: John Camp, CNN ——> ┌─────────────────────┐
          Thunderbolt II & Thunderbolt III——> │ See note on reverse │
                            Goodyear ——————> ┐ │ regarding   │
Note: List of enclosures on reverse   ┘ │ enclosures   │
                                                 └─────────────────────┘
                                          └——> See note 2 on reverse

443

Lt Col Dan Marvin · AUS (Ret)

1604 Trumansburg Road · Ithaca NY 14850 · 607 273 1496

29 June 1991   VIII-D-PRES

President George Bush
THE WHITE HOUSE
Washington, D.C. 20500

                                    RE: Colonel Le Van Phoi

Dear President Bush,
    I truly don't like to bother you in another matter involving a
former ARVN military officer - but it's an absolute fact that it wasn't
until I wrote you personally on 17 July 1989 regarding the plight of
General Quang Van Dang that a concerted investigative effort was made,
resulting in his being issued a permanent entry visa on 7 Sep 89.
    I ask again, Mr. President, that you direct the State Department to
look into situations involving former ARVN Colonel Le Van Phoi's past
and present predicaments which relate directly to the same incident in
June of 1966 that has affected General Dang, the undersigned and <u>many</u>
others for the past quarter of a century.
    <u>Please</u> help Colonel Phoi and his family, Mr. President. Though I
feel certain your staff has a complete file on this matter, to have
certain matters at your fingertips, I enclose the following:

DATE	FROM	TO
17 Jun 91	Lan Thanh Le	LTC Dan Marvin
21 Jun 91	LTC Dan Marvin	Congressman McHugh
23 Apr 91	**Ithaca Journal** article "Ex-Green Beret seeks truth in 'crusade'" by Kathy Hovis	
11 Apr 91	LTC Dan Marvin	Alicia Cooper, IRC
4 Apr 91	Alicia Cooper, IRC	Bob DeVecchi, Exec Dir, IRC
4 Apr 91	Alicia Cooper, IRC	LTC Dan Marvin
12 Mar 91	LTC Dan Marvin	Alicia Cooper, IRC
6 Mar 91	Alicia Cooper, IRC	Lan Thanh Le
6 Mar 91	Alicia Cooper, IRC	LTC Dan Marvin
24 Jan 91	Paul L. Boyd, ODP	LTC Dan Marvin
28 Dec 90	David Pierce, Embassy	LTC Dan Marvin
14 Dec 90	LTC Dan Marvin	David C. Pierce, Embassy
6 Dec 90	Alicia Cooper, IRC	LTC Dan Marvin
29 Nov 90	LTC Dan Marvin	Congressman McHugh
28 Nov 90	LTC Dan Marvin	Alicia Cooper, IRC
28 Nov 90	LTC Dan Marvin	Congressman McHugh
28 Nov 90	LTC Dan Marvin	William Fleming, ODP
16 Aug 90	William Fleming, ODP	LTC Dan Marvin
1 Aug 90	LTC Dan Marvin	William Fleming, ODP
12 Jul 90	LTC Le Van Phoi	LTC Dan Marvin
10 Jul 90	LTC Dan Marvin	Congressman McHugh
21 Jun 90	LTC Dan Marvin	William Fleming, ODP
18 Jun 90	Congressman McHugh	Orderly Departure Program

Flyer - America at War - about "Apocalypse at An-Phu"
    I will most anxiously await your action, Mr. President.
    Cordially,

<u>Copies furnished:</u>
Lan Thanh Le   Casey Stevens   Kathy Hovis   BC - Alicia Cooper

Again, LTC Marvin writes a letter to President George H.W. Bush seeking help,
this time for Colonel Le Van Phoi. This letter also shows the persistence, thor-
oughness and organization that Dan brings to bear in his activities..

The Ithaca Journal Monday, March 21, 1994

DAN MARVIN/Guest columnist

The CIA in need of a watchdog of its own

The psychological indoctrination of intelligence agents who would be used as intelligence agents —spies— is little different from when I first volunteered to engage in the world of covert information gathering. That was during Special Forces-Green Beret training in 1964 at Fort Bragg, N.C.

I doubt that 30 years has changed the psyche of aspy, no matter what nation or other entity that spy is employed by. A spy by any other name is still a spy.

Marvin in 1968

Spying is inherently both exciting and dangerous. The challenge is to ferret out, by whatever means necessary, the truth about anything a foreign nation has or does that may affect our "national security."

The nation being spied on need not be our enemy. When I was stationed in Europe, we were spying on our allies and potential adversaries. Strategic military intelligence gathering and pure industrial espionage is big business conducted in secrecy and subterfuge against governments and other power bases with little regard to current diplomatic standing.

We spy on friends and enemies alike and they do the same when they can afford to.

The greatest danger in this episode involving the Ames husband and wife spy team — turned double-agents — is the lack of overt focus on what, within the Central Intelligence Agency, allowed this to happen.

The government seems bent on exploiting the fact that several —perhaps a dozen or more — Russian citizens who were spying for the United States were comprised by Ames and subsequently executed by the Russians. Why should we care? If a person is a traitor to his or her nation there should be a quick and

deadly end to their activities once discovered. It matters not how much a person is paid for secrets sold to another country.

If any one single military secret is given or sold to a foreign nation by an American citizen, whether or not he or she is a double agent — that citizen should fear from the start that death by public execution would be the reward of disclosure. There should be no room for plea bargaining or waiving or even pardon.

If you sell your country out — you forfeit your right to live and it should be as simple as that.

Spies aren't drafted — they are all volunteers who enjoy the mere thought of being involved in such dangerous work. A person must want to be a spy. To assume the role of a mole — a double-agent — is to sign your own potential death warrant.

Sooner or later a careless act or an equally evil-minded mole's misdeed will see the two-faced agent compromised.

He or she should be executed. Yes — a double agent should die. There is no good reason for such a traitor to be permitted another free breath on earth.

I commanded an independent warfare operation in South Vietnam in 1965-66.

We had an active combat intelligence net comprised wholly of 12 courageous South Vietnamese women trained by my counterpart South Vietnamese Green Beret Major. Each knew only too well the danger they would face every day they infiltrated the enemy sanctuaries in neighboring Cambodia. If caught by the Communists they would be tortured and executed in some gruesome fashion.

They knew what they faced and they served valiantly, providing our forces with the intelligence we needed to maintain military superiority.

They also knew what they would face if they attempted to work both sides of the bor-

der. It would be instant death by our hands. That was my order.

The most glaring hole in our intelligence armor is the inability of the CIA to police itself.

Ames was a mole for almost a decade before he was stopped, perhaps even longer! Our intelligence community is a loose cannon.

The CIA needs oversight and needs it bad. That oversight must be by a Congress properly equipped and chartered to do the job right. All activities and all funds used to operate all intelligence activities within our government must be brought under scrutiny and control. The CIA, ASA, DIA and other organizations cannot be expected to police themselves. Perhaps more typical then I would like to imagine of the twisted pschye of managers and operatives within our intelligence organizations is the image that any decent and Intelligent person would glean from this quote: "I toiled wholeheartedly in the vineyards because it was fun, fun, fun. Where else could a red-blooded American boy lie, kill, cheat, rape and pillage with the blessings of all the highest?" That statement is attributed to former OSS officer Colonel George White, one of the founders of the CIA.

This brazen assertion by Colonel White was broadcast nationally in an ABC television show produced by John Marks in 1979. I have personally dealt with and been threatened by equally deranged characters in positions of power within the CIA or its "oversight" committees.

Perhaps we need spies but certainly we don't need an intelligence system unconcerned with moral rights and self-discipline and dedicated more to their own survival than to doing their share to maintain our nation's security.

———

Lt. Col. Daniel Marvin, U.S. Special Forces (Retired) is a resident of Ithaca.

A March 1994 article by LTC Dan Marvin refers to his personal experience in an effort to acquaint citizens with the dangers of a CIA gone awry

A similar case in point: Among the biggest reasons that the lawsuit against Marvin and TrineDay went forward were the persistent hints from the plaintiffs' attorneys that they were going to call former CIA agent Walter MacKem to the stand to refute Dan. They kept the suspense till the end, Judge Norton remarking at the conclusion of the Plaintiff's rebuttal witnesses, "So, ya'll are *not* going to be calling Mr. MacKem?"

It was a "ploy." A lie. Just like the lies told that allow a few to spend secretly our tax dollars, while telling us citizens untruths in the pursuit of specious goals, and our military gets abused … creating troubles abroad and at home.

20 April 1994   I-F-NY-SFA.61

Don Koch, Secretary
SFA - New York State Chapter # 61

Dear Don,
    I must apologize for ignoring the correspondence I've received from the
New York State Chapter. I've been up to my eyeballs and have just about gone
bankrupt working on a number of crusades that pitted me against our own CIA,
DOD, DEA, State Department and the White House to help some South Vietnamese
who I worked and fought with along the Cambodian Border. One saved my life,
another was my counterpart, others were in my CIDG at Camp An-Phu. Thus far,
with the Lord's help, I've been victorious in bringing General Dang into this
country and in seeing my counterpart, Lt Col Phoi Van Le and his wife and four
children come to the USA this past December. Others our Lord is leading me to
gain victory for of one sort or another choose to remain anonymous.
    I am still fighting for other Hoa Hao fighters and have been trying now
since September 1989 to gain a public exoneration by our State Department of
General Dang.
    I am member number M4835 - a member in good standing. I have been
sending my annual dues to Jimmy Dean - but, starting next December - I'll send
them to you. Please include me in your chapter. I did want you to know that
I bought $20.00 worth of raffle tickets for the Memorial Building Fund and I
noted the NY State Chapter so as to give you credit toward a chapter prize.
    I enclose some articles you may or may not want to keep for the Chapter
archives - if there is an archives.. The articles relating to General Quang
Van Dang (AKA Dang Van Quang) are a few of the many I have in file that tell
of just how far and wide the CIA's disinformation and defamation campaign went
against General Dang after he rescued me and my team and the Hoa Haos from the
CIA's "borrowed Regiment" in June of 1966.
1. 17 May 89 GRAPEVINE "No Laughing Matter"
2. 21 Jun 89 GRAPEVINE "Follow-up: Quang's Case"
3. 24 May 75 LOS ANGELES TIMES "CIA Role Seen in Viet Officer Exit"
4. 24 May 75 MONTREAL STAR "General Seeks Life in City"
5. 17 Jun 76 MONTREAL STAR "Trudeau, Ford discuss fate of undesirable general"
6. 25 May 78 MONTREAL STAR "Kitchen dishwasher was once the second most
                    powerful man in Vietnam"
7. 7 Sep 89 GRAPEVINE "Quang Update"
8. 23 Apr 91 ITHACA JOURNAL "Ex-Green Beret seeks truth in 'crusade'
9. 4 Mar 92 ITHACA JOURNAL "On a Mission"
    I've also included an article I wrote recently' The CIA in need of a
watchdog of its own"
    Please keep me posted on Chapter events. I'm not certain when I'll be
able to come up for one - but I surely wish you all the greatest success.
    I have written a book "CODE NAME: THUNDERBOLT" about my experiences in
An-Phu and now wait for my Literary Agent to find a publisher and producer.
    If you or any other Chapter member comes to Ithaca - please call me and
I'll put on the coffee pot.

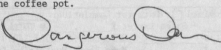

Typical action by LTC Marvin to inform. The many attached newspaper articles
told the full story of the ARVN Regiment sent by the CIA to attack Camp An Phu
and how they were rescued from certain death by ARVN General Quang Van Dang
and his senior American advisor Colonel William O. Desobry.

446

10 July 1995   I-F-JIM-DEAN.SFA

Jimmy Dean, Administrator
Special Forces Association
Post Office Box 41436
Fayetteville, NC 28309-1436   *12 Jan 66*

Dear Jimmy,
        It was good to hear your voice and I anxiously await your letter
explaining what you plan to do with the stuff I sent you about Colonel Maggie.
        I trust your judgement in this matter - so please forge ahead without
concern for what I may think. I think you are a great administrator!
        I enclose a small color photo of Colonel Maggie and Dangerous Dan taken
in my camp on 10 Feb 68 during her visit. Use and keep as you see fit.
        Surely, I understand how you missed the last issue with regard to comment
on my mother's passing. She was a proud supporter of Green Berets and I know
she'll be pleased (from Heaven of course!) to note something in your next
issue of THE DROP.
        I also enclose a copy of a local newspaper article that consists of
excerpts from my Flag Day Commemoration Speech in Ithaca. Do with it as you
feel right to do.
        I do anxiously await a copy of the National Park Service Report on the
move of our statue. Also - a photo showing my friend (Gerard V. Parmentier)
now has his name spelled right on the SF Memorial.
        Your comrade-in-arms,

                Dangerous Dan

A letter from LTC Marvin to SFA administrator James Dean. Dan is writing to
inquire about the SFA's reaction to materials he sent to them earlier, especially
the Foreword to this book by Martha Raye (Colonel Maggie).

Notice that Dan is never shy about telling his story publicly. His story is consistent. He is the subject of contemporary news accounts, writes opinion pieces
and letters. Dan tracks down old comrades and talks with others closely involved
to gather their remembrances, etc. His Vietnam "police action" brothers-in-arms
and the SFA supported Dan and his story for many years, as these documents and
the audiotapes show. Then, for some reason, came a lawsuit to squelch a citizen's
free speech rights and a publisher's right to print the story, and *to deny all of us the
ability to be able to read, to study and … to learn from our historical actions.*

SPECIAL FORCES ASSOCIATION
Post Office Box 41436
Fayetteville, North Carolina 28309-1436
29 July 1995

LTC (Ret) Dan Marvin
715 Hector St.
Ithaca, NY 14850

Dear Dan,

Thanks for your patience, I enjoyed chapter 7 very much, written like a man who was on the ground and knows of what he speaks. Maggie's foreward was a piece of art, her language is ours, as she was. I wish you luck with the book.

I will keep your articles on the Agency and preserving the flag for possible future inclusion in the Drop. We have a great display of Col. Maggie artifacts in the SFA Memorial Building and that is where your photo will go.

I am sorry but we have not heard from Ray Johnson since 1971 and have no idea of what happened to him. Here is his last known address. ██████████ ██████████████████████ I am enclosing the page from the SFA KIA's listed on the plaza wall to show you that Parmentier's first name is still incorrectly spelled, however, I will bring this to the immediately attention of Col. John McMullen and it will be corrected. Good Luck and take care.

Fraternally,

James C. Dean
Secretary

A 1995 letter from SFA secretary James Dean wishing Dan luck with this book, ironically the same James Dean who helped to bring the men together, that then participated in the SFA financed lawsuit against author LTC Marvin and publisher TrineDay for the same book.

The address Secretary Dean supplied for Ray Johnson was out-of-date, but Dan kept on looking.

25 July 1997
K-JOHNSON.97B[K-1H]

MSG Raymond Johnson
US Army Special Forces (Retired)
████████████████

Dear Ray,
    It was so good to hear your voice - to be back in touch -
and to know you are alive and well. I enjoyed our chat on
the phone today - you sound the same as I remember from 1966
in An-Phu.
    I'm awful sorry you lost your photos from Vietnam -
especially from An-Phu. I have put together about 300 photos
from our old camp amongst the Hoa Haos. I'll make sure you
get copies of some of them before too long.
    I enclose the article "NO LAUGHING MATTER" and another
one titled "ON A MISSION."   My files show you came to An-Phu
in Feb 66 and left in July 66.
Any comments you have on the articles will be appreciated.
    I've enclosed some copies of photos taken last month of
Kate and I and two old and dear friends of ours. They just
moved to Arizona.
    I also enclose a two page paper titled "BACKGROUND
INFORMATION AND PERSONAL DATA". I've gotten these from Jim
Taylor, John Strait, and Bac-si Richard Sirois. John Eleam
is filling one out to send to me. I really would like you to
fill one out and return both pages to me.
    Must close for now. I will be anxious to hear from you.
I will always remember you, Ray, and I pray that some day we
can meet one more time.
    God bless and keep you and yours,

This was my first ltr to Ray after Vietnam

Dan finally gets back in touch with his old service buddy Ray Johnson and sends
him an information sheet to fill out. They continue as friends until 2003, when
the lawsuit gets in the way. Getting reacquainted with his old army buddy encouraged Dan to work on his manuscript and to increase his contacts with the
SFA. Which lead to some interesting consequences …

10 October 1997   A\SFA-RG.97A[H]

From: Daniel Marvin
          715 Hector Street
          Ithaca, New York 14850

TO: Rudi Gresham
          ████████████████████████

Dear Rudi,
    My primary interest is in the truth, and assuming that is what you are
striving to bring forth on behalf of General Yarborough and the Special Forces
Association - I am with you in mind, spirit, and prayer.
    You asked that I advise you regarding what I have sent to Congress. What
I have provided Senators Moynihan and D'Amato, Congressmen McHugh (I believe
McHugh is now Counsel for the President of the World Bank), Congressman
Hinchey, and others has related directly to my thus far successful efforts to
bring South Vietnamese into this country whose presence was not desired by our
CIA due to their intimate knowledge of USASF Team A-424 covert operations
during the period 1 Jan thru 3 Aug 66 in An-Phu District, South Vietnam.
These missions were first given me by then LTC William Tuttle, CO, C-4, at
Can-Tho, South Vietnam.
    I told them all about the mission brought to my camp by CIA Agent McKem
in June 1966 which involved the ambush and assassination of then Cambodian
Crown Prince Norodum Sihanouk. It was the truth of what I told to Congress -
especially Congressman McHugh who at the time was a member of the House Select
Committee on Intelligence - that brought about a government-wide investigation
into what the CIA had done to ARVN General Quang Van Dang (Dang Van Quang) as
a result of their anger at his coming to the rescue of my A Team and our South
Vietnamese counterparts and Hoa-Hao Irregulars when we were about to be
attacked by a "friendly" ARVN Regiment at the direction of the CIA.
    I enclose two of many articles articles that relate to my past and
present involvements in covert operations that may be of interest:
    a.   22 Aug 96 ITHACA TIMES Jay Wrolstad article "SMOKING GUN." I do
hope that you have seen British producer Nigel Turner's documentary "THE MEN
WHO KILLED KENNEDY - THE TRUTH SHALL MAKE YOU FREE," aired repeatedly on the
HISTORY Channel. The documentary and Wrolstad's article tell about the
killing of US Navy LCDR William Bruce Pitzer, I believe at the direction of
the CIA and with possible SF involvement.

Page 1 of 2 - 10 Oct 97 letter from Dan Marvin to Rudi Gresham.

This is the two-page letter that LTC Marvin wrote to Rudi Gresham at the behest
of Major General William Yarborough, after speaking with the General on the
telephone (discussed on pages 397-398). After the phone conversations with
General Yarborough and Rudi (which stressed that Dan's loyalty should be to
Special Forces), and this letter to Rudi, Dan's relationship with the SFA and his
men's support for this book changed.

    b.   11-17 May 89 GRAPEVINE Karey Solomon article "No Laughing Matter"
with 15 Jun 89 GRAPEVINE "Follow-up: Quang's Case," and 7 Sep 89 GRAPEVINE
"Quang Update." This article and its follow-ups tell the story of An-Phu, the
plot to assassinate Prince Sihanouk, my unilateral aborting of the mission,

the attempt to destroy An-Phu and those of us who were there, the rescue of
our team and the Hoa-Hao Irregulars by General Dang, the CIA's 22 years
campaign of character assassination and forced exile against General Dang, and
the 11 month-long investigation that cleared Dang's name.
    Perhaps you have information from former US Army Special Forces Captain
John McCarthy. John MCArthy and I were introduced by David MacMichael, a
former CIA operative and now a member of The Association of National Security
Alumni (ANSA). David, who cannot (due to his oath of secrecy) divulge actual
details of Operation "Cherry," was nonetheless the CIA clandestine operative
in Bangkok, Thailand in 1967, responsible for the Thailand "prong" of that
1967 three-pronged failed plot to assassinate then Prince Norodom Sihanouk.
David MacMichael called one day to tell me that I should meet John McCarthy
because John and I shared a rather unusual role in our pasts. We both, as US
Army Special Forces Captains were trained as assassins at Fort Bragg, North
Carolina in 1964. I was asked to assassinate Prince Sihanouk in June 1966
and John McCarthy participated in a much more sophisticated attempt to kill
Sihanouk in 1967.
    People are naive to think that government-sponsored assassinations or
other deadly covert actions can be corroborated, but even more naive to
believe they never happened. There was to be no "trail" of any kind. Even in
the instances of botched, failed, or aborted assassinations, there are few
indeed who are willing to stick their neck out from under the umbrella-shell
of secrecy and thus incur the possible wrath of the intelligence community.
    On the other hand - it is far better for this great nation of ours and
for the unconventional forces that now exist that we clean our own closets,
admit our own bad judgements and dirty deeds and help to build a stronger and
morally (based on the Bible) directed force to protect and defend our vital
interests.
    Sincerely,

Enclosures: as stated

Copies less enclosures: Covert back-ups Eagle I and Thunderbird

Colonel Daniel Marvin
U.S. Army Special Forces *(Retired)*
A Born-Again Christian

715 Hector Street
Ithaca, NY 14850-2031

By Appointment only
Call (607) 272-0473

13 October 1997

Writer and Antique Restorer K\TEAM-ROOM.SFA[K1C]

Jimmy Dean
Secretary & Administrator
SPECIAL FORCES ASSOCIATION
P.O. Box 41436
Fayetteville, NC 28309-1436

Dear Jimmy,

My former A-424 Communications Sergeant - RAYMOND J. JOHNSON - visited the SFA Team House this past April and then wrote and asked me if I would send some pictures for possible display for our old team.

I have enclosed the following that relate to USASF Team A-424 which I commanded from 27 December 1965 to 3 August 1966:

1.   Good aerial view of Camp Dan-Nam in An-Phu District looking towards the border of South Vietnam with Cambodia taken in March 1966.

2.   Photo of myself and my counterpart - ARVN Major Phoi Van Le. Taken in Camp Dan-Nam in Early January 1966.

3.   Photo of eight of the men of USASF Team A-424 taken in Camp Dan-Nam on 4 June 1966.

4.   A Battle Map showing friendly and enemy positions in An-Phu District, South Vietnam on 19 May 1966.

5.   Weapons, Ammunition, and Equipment Status on 31 May 1966.

6.   Combat Statistics - Camp Dan-Nam, An-Phu South Vietnam for the period 1 January 1966 through 31 July 1966.

7.   GRAPEVINE Article "No Laughing Matter" May 89 with follow-up articles.

If other material is desired - such as photos, manuscripts, articles, etc., please advise.

Sincerely,

Copy (less enclosures) furnished John Eleam, Ray Johnson, John Strait, and Jim
     Taylor.

LTC Marvin sends photos and some of the historical documents presented in this book along with this letter to the SFA. Later, although the SFA had been given the documents almost ten years ago, the plaintiffs' lawyers, without offering any proof, simply implied during the recent trial that some of these documents were fraudulent.

SPECIAL FORCES ASSOCIATION
Post Office Box 41436
Fayetteville, North Carolina 28309-1436
Telephone: 910-485-5433
Fax: 910-485-1041
E-mail: sfahq@aol.com
27 May 1998

Daniel Marvin
715 Hector St.
Ithaca, NY. 14850

Dear Mr. Marvin,

The Special Forces Association, reacting to your letter dated 10 October 1997 to Rudi Gresham and a subsequent letter to the SFA Secretary, initiated an investigation of your stated allegations. In addition, the investigation team has reviewed tapes of interviews you have made on Channel Five in Syracuse, NY. and from the History Channel, part 5, "The Men Who Killed Kennedy-The Truth Shall Make You Free".

During these past months, the investigation has included over 50 interviews, the collection of documents and statements/affidavits, and the investigation is continuing. If the allegations are determined to be false, you are in violation of Article IV, Section IV and Article IV, Section VII (C) of the SFA Constitution.

Because of the seriousness of your allegations, the Association Board of Officers has taken action under the provisions of Article IV, Section VII (C) to temporarily suspend your SF Association membership until 12 August 1998. At 1600 hours on 12 August 1998 at the SFA National Headquarters in Fayetteville, North Carolina a hearing will be conducted to determine your status as a member of the SFA.

You are here-by cited to appear before the Board of Officers at the appointed time and place. Failure to appear is a cause for summary expulsion. All written reports, documents, tapes, affidavits, and any other information or witnesses must be made available in their entirety to the National Board of Officers prior to 5 August 1998. This hearing is not a court of law, however, you may have an attorney present to give you advise only, he may not participate in the process.

Sincerely,

James C. Dean
Secretary
Special Forces Association

In May of 1989 the SFA informs LTC Marvin that he has been the subject of an eight-month-long investigation and is summoned to a Board of Officers "hearing," to answer charges. No documentation of the "allegations" are provided, nor is any opportunity offered to Dan to view any of the SFA's alleged contrary documentary evidence. Yet, Dan "must" provide "all written reports, documents, tapes, affidavits, and any other information or witnesses" to this Board a week before the SFA hearing.

3 June 1998   K\SFA-JCD.98A[K1A]

From: Daniel Marvin, 715 Hector Street, Ithaca, New York 14850-2031

To: James C. Dean, Secretary; Special Forces Association, P.O. Box 41436
          Fayetteville, NC 28309-1436

Dear Mr. Dean,
          Reference: Your letter dated 27 May 1998 in which you stated that the
Special Forces Association, reacting to my letter of 10 Oct 97 to Rudi Gresham
and a subsequent letter to the SFA Secretary, "initiated an investigation of
[my] stated allegations." I wrote Rudi Gresham at his request, after I'd spoken
with General Yarborough, so as to provide information he desired to study that
may or may not relate to his efforts to respond to what William F. Pepper wrote
about the use of Special Forces personnel in his book "Orders to Kill." Also,
please correct your reference to the Nigel Turner documentary I took part in.
It is Part VI of the "Men Who Killed Kennedy" series and its title was "The
Truth Shall Make You Free.
          I assume that the "subsequent letter to the SFA Secretary" you refer to is
my 13 Oct 97 letter in which I, at the request of Raymond J. Johnson, sent you
pictures, a map, and an article for your "possible" display in the "Team Room."
          You indicate, in your second paragraph of referenced letter, "If the
allegations are determined to be false, [I am] in violation of Article IV,
Section IV and Article IV, Section VII (C) of the SFA Constitution." I have
made no allegations of any kind against the Special Forces Association or the
U.S. Army Special Forces. I have spoken and written of the truth and I have
recalled my own personal experience as a U.S. Army Special Forces Officer for
the purpose of supporting efforts to reveal acts or actions that were not in
keeping with the high standards of Special Forces operations. In each and every
instance, I assume that such actions were predicated on the belief that higher
authority had approved same and that the Special Forces personnel involved, with
few exceptions, assumed what they were doing or had done was in the interests of
national security. No allegations, fiction, or subterfuge, just information of
what I recall to the best of my knowledge and belief.
          I enclose an AUTHORIZATION AND PRIVACY WAIVER for your use in obtaining any
documentation on file in any agency of the United States government that may be
of help in developing factual answers to your questions or queries. Perhaps the
most valuable information you could request under the FOIA would be the State
Department Case File (# 841-730-48) relating to the inter-agency investigation
of allegations against former ARVN Lieutenant General Quang Van Dang (subject of
the article NO LAUGHING MATTER which you possess) that was completed in early
September 1989, exonerating General Dang and authorizing issue of a Permanent
Entry Visa to Dang on 7 September 1989. The exhaustive investigation included
CIA review of how General Dang had saved nine US Army Green Berets and approximately 500 South Vietnamese who served in my command from almost certain death
in June 1966, when under imminent attack by an ARVN Regiment sent to destroy my
camp because I had refused to send my Hoa Hao Irregulars into Cambodia to Kill
Prince Norodom Sihanouk. Senator Alfonse D'Amato, Senator Patrick Moynihan, and
former Congressman Matthew McHugh are familiar with that investigation inasmuch
as they, especially Senator D'Amato, assisted in bringing the investigation to a
just conclusion in a timely manner. CIA General Counsel's Mary Shiraishi was my
contact to obtain $20,000 from the CIA for Dang's resettlement to the West coast
and former US Consul General Andrew F. Antippas was involved in the Montreal
Consulate's part in this investigation in the Summer of 1989.
          I enclose a self-addressed and stamped envelope for your convenience in
responding with copies I have requested of SFA Constitution parts.
          Sincerely,

JOHN 8:32 AND YE SHALL KNOW THE TRUTH, AND THE TRUTH SHALL MAKE YOU FREE

Copy furnished: Jerry Willsey, President, Chapter LXI, SFA; and Eagle II.

LTC Marvin's reply to the SFA, upon being informed of their investigation.

2 June 1998 · K\PRVCY-WV.SFA[A]

AUTHORIZATION AND PRIVACY WAIVER

I, Daniel Marvin, declare and say as follows:

1. I was born on the 10th day of October 1933, at Detroit, Michigan, United States of America.

2. I currently reside at 715 Hector Street, Ithaca, New York, 14850-2031, in the county of Tompkins, U.S.A..

3. My Social Security Number is 320-26-5983

4. I hereby authorize the following federal agencies to release any and all materials concerning me to James C. Dean, Secretary of the Special Forces Association, Post Office Box 41436, Fayetteville, North Carolina, 28309-1436: United States Army, United States Navy, including but not limited to the United States Marine Corps; Central Intelligence Agency; Department of Defense; National Security Agency; United States Department of Justice, including but not limited to the Federal Bureau of Investigation; Department of State; and Drug Enforcement Administration. Insofar as release of such materials to James C. Dean as Secretary, the Special Forces Association, is concerned, I hereby waive any and all right of privacy which I may have.

5. I hereby certify that I am the person who has signed this declaration and that the signature which appears below is my signature.

I declare under penalty of perjury of the laws of the United States of America that the foregoing is true and correct. Executed this 2d day of June, 1998.

DANIEL MARVIN
SSAN: ▮▮▮▮▮▮

Copy of United States Uniformed Services Identification Card Attached for comparison of signature.

LTC Marvin's unlimited authorization for the SFA to obtain any and all information about his past by waiving his rights of privacy.

15 July 1998   K\SFA-JCD.98B[K1A]

From: Daniel Marvin, 715 Hector Street, Ithaca, New York 14850-2031

To: James C. Dean, Secretary; Special Forces Association, P.O. Box 41436
         Fayetteville, NC 28309-1436

Dear Mr. Dean,

Reference: Your 27 May 1998 letter in which you stated that the Special Forces Association, reacting to my letter of 10 Oct 97 to Rudi Gresham and a subsequent letter to the SFA Secretary, "initiated an investigation of [my] stated allegations."

Reference is also made to your 15 Jun 1998 letter in which you stated that you (SFA) had "requested information from various agencies under the Freedom of Information Act."

Perhaps you will then receive from Military Intelligence a complete set of documents relating to a 1967/1968 investigation of the involvement of Lieutenant Colonel Robert H. Bartelt and Captain Ernest Buttler, of the 46th Special Forces, Thailand in illegal activities, or the cover-up thereof, which included, but were not limited to, illegal weapons shipment to CONUS.

I believe it is the duty of <u>any</u> true and loyal Special Forces Officer or Non-Commissioned Officer to report any and all illegal activities to their commanders, or should it be the commander who is involved in any way, manner, shape, or form in illegal activity; that person should report it to the appropriate CID or MI authorities. This is what I have done during the entire time I was on active duty in the United States Army. In SF the line between legal and illegal in covert activities is not <u>always</u> readily discernible.

Libel is a written form of defamation. I suggest Libel in those instances wherein a statement would be published in THE DROP which told of my being summarily expelled because I failed to attend a hearing on 12 August 1998 and which told of the hearing having been ordered to discover the truth about my allegedly having made serious allegations about SF. According to the Writer's Encyclopedia, "three prerequisites to a libel suit are defamation, identification, and publication." The best defense against libel is TRUTH. What I have written, what I have said, what I have communicated with regard to any aspect of SF is based on the TRUTH. Pure and simple, I have told the truth and the truth is what is important. I pray that you, as editor of THE DROP, stand by the truth and distance yourself from libellous allegations or rhetoric.

I will not be present at the 12 August 1998 hearing, nor any SFA hearing. The record will show that I have told the truth.

Perhaps you should have a very private and confidential conversation with General Yarborough and ask him "off the record" about any of the areas of concern to you that I have brought out in the past. Colonel C. W. Patten, when I spoke to him some time ago, suggested I contact General Yarborough for the truth of what part the CIA had in training or using our people in covert activities. I did call General Yarborough and I have all of what we both said on audio tape for archival accuracy. I want no "he said" or "I said" in areas of such tremendous significance.

You have informed me of my being temporarily suspended from SFA and I believe you have acted prematurely in doing so. I do insist that I continue to receive THE DROP so long as my dues are current.

Sincerely,

Just a reminder: Do not call me.

> Galatians 4:16 Am I therefore become your
> enemy because I tell you the truth?

Copy furnished: Jerry Willsey, President, Chapter LXI, SFA; and Eagle II.

Another response by LTC Marvin to the SFA investigation, where Dan informs the SFA that he will not be appearing at the hearing. "The record will show that I have told the truth," says Dan.

SPECIAL FORCES ASSOCIATION
Post Office Box 41436
Fayetteville, North Carolina 28309-1436
Telephone: 910-485-5433
Fax: 910-485-1041
E-mail: sfahq@aol.com

19 August 1998

Daniel Marvin
715 Hector St.
Ithaca, NY. 14850

Dear Mr. Marvin,

The National Board of Officers met in session on 12 August 1998. At a hearing for the purpose of determining your status as a member of the Special Forces Association, the following determination was made:

In accordance with Article IV, SectionIV and Article IV, Section VII, paragraph C, the Board of Officers revokes the membership of Mr. Daniel Marvin, effective 12 August 1998. A member expelled forfeits all dues and fees paid prior to expulsion.

Sincerely,

For the National Board of Officers:

James C. Dean
James C. Dean
Secretary
Special Forces Association

cc: Mr. Gerald Willsey
     President, C-LXI
     Special Forces Association

The SFA informs LTC Marvin that he has been expelled from the organization.

Isaac Comancho Awarded DSC
Advocacy and Intelligence Index for Prisoners of War/Missing In Action, Inc.
Notice:
On August 27th, 1998, the Distinguished Service Cross will be awarded to **Isaac Comancho**, first POW to successfully escape, in a ceremony to be held in Meredith, New Hampshire at 7 PM.

Attendees include the **Donald Cook** family, **Sharon Roraback**, sister of **Kenneth Roraback**, and **Charles Crafts**, a returned POW who was held in the same camp as Isaac Comancho.

SFA Members from Chapter 54, Chapter 72 and a contingent from Isaac's Chapter 9 in El Paso, Texas, will also attend the ceremony. ✄

SFA Educational Grants

Matthew W. Taylor	Kentucky (C-31)	Col. Aaron Bank Award
Amy Jordan	South Carolina	Martha (Col. Maggie) Award
Heidi Erdmann	Massachusetts	Frenchy Amundson Award
Sheri Stickney	Tennessee (C-33)	Larry Thorne Award
Stacy Archer	Tennessee (C-33)	Larry Thorne Award
Virginia Sorenson	California (C-38)	SFA Award
William Schwartz	Connecticut	SFA Award
Bridget McLamara	Ohio	SFA Award
Howard Ennaco	Kentucky	SFA Award
James Colvin	Oklahoma	SFA Award
Brian Fisher	Massachusetts	SFA Award
Tara Lyman	Ohio	SFA Award

SFA Raffle Winners

1st Prize	Ronald Robben	KS	$1,000.00
2nd Prize	Doris Price	NC	700.00
3rd Prize	James Gritz	ID	500.00
4th Prize	L.W. Phillips	NV	300.00
5th Prize	Jim Wipf	NV	200.00
6th Prize	Eugene Gutierrez	TX	100.00
7th Prize	J.D. Willberg	MD	100.00
8th Prize	D. Price	NC	100.00

Announcement
In accordance with Article IV, Sections IV and VIIc, of the Special Forces Association Constitution, the Special Forces Association Board of Officers has revoked the membership of **Dan Marvin.**

Association Budget for 1998
Income

Dues	127,500
Sales	6,000
Ads	4,500
Miscellaneous	3,000
L/M Transfer	5,000
	146,000

Expenses

Drop	43,000
Printing	4,000
Postage	17,000
Drop Contract	3,000
Salaries	30,000
Taxes	3,500
Utilities	7,000
Purchases	8,000
Admin	3,500
Travel	7,000
L/M Fund	14,000
Operating Costs	6,000
	146,000

/s/ Jack L. Bonner
JACK L. BONNER
TREASURER

The SFA informs its members that LTC Dan Marvin has been expelled from the organization in its Fall 1999 publication, *The Drop*. On the same page is printed the SFA yearly budget. LTC Marvin and TrineDay rang up bills of over $150,000 to defend themselves. How much did it cost the SFA to mount the losing lawsuit, and what have the members been told?

7 September 1998   K\SFA-JCD.98C[K1A]

From: Daniel Marvin, 715 Hector Street, Ithaca, New York 14850-2031

To: James C. Dean, Secretary; Special Forces Association, P.O. Box 41436
         Fayetteville, NC 28309-1436

Dear Mr. Dean,
         Reference: Your 19 Aug 98 letter stating that the National Board of
Officers had met on 12 Aug 98 and revoked my membership in the Special Forces
Association (SFA) effective 12 Aug 98.
         If the SFA's resolve is to sweep under a rug of secrecy and subterfuge
those acts or deeds perpetrated by or ordered by SF personnel that were in
violation of U.S. or international law, or were immoral or repugnant to human
decency, then the SFA is not an organization that I want to be a member of.
         I hope and pray the SFA would want to support the revelation of truth of
any misdeeds of special forces personnel so as to assist in bringing justice
to bear on those who are indeed guilty of having performed a nefarious act or
of having covered up same.
         In your letter of 19 August 1998, you stated that my membership was
revoked in accordance with Article IV, Section IV, and Article IV, Section
VII, Paragraph C of the SFA Constitution.
         Specifically, the SFA Constitution, Article IV, Section IV spells out the
obligation of each member "to abide by its governing documents, work toward
achievement of its purposes, and act in accordance with its precepts. A
member who fails to do so may have his or her membership suspended or
revoked." Mr. Dean, I would like to know what I did <u>specifically</u>
that warranted the revocation of my membership under Art. IV, Sect. IV.
         Secondly, SFA Constitution Article IV, Section VII (Termination of Mem-
bership), Paragraph C, grounds for expulsion are "Falsification or misrepre-
sentation in an application; violation of Section IV of Article IV; or any
arbitrary actions, deeds, or behaviour, by a member which brings discredit,
humiliation, or embarrassment upon the Association or any chapter." Mr. Dean,
which of the aforementioned applies in my case and what specifically am I
accused of having done to deserve expulsion?
         Do you believe that it is the duty of any Special Forces Officer or
Non-Commissioned Officer to report illegal activities to their commanders?
And, should it be the commander who is involved in any way, manner, shape, or
form in the illegal activity, should that person report it to the appropriate
CID or MI authorities?
         I ask that a copy of THE DROP that contained any reference to my being
expelled from SFA be provided me.
         Did you, as I suggested, have a private and confidential conversation
with General Yarborough and ask him "off the record" about any of the areas of
concern that I have brought out in the past?   Would the SFA support bringing
the entire investigation of the 46th SF, Colonel Bartelt and Captain Buttler
into use in the JFKCSW as a tool to help future SF officers understand the
need to maintain ethical (moral and legal) standards so as to avoid being
corrupted by the enormous power vested in them when involved in covert or MTT
missions?
         I specifically request that you review the action taken by SFA and
re-instate me as a full and regular member of SFA.
         Sincerely,

> Galatians 4:16 Am I therefore become your
> enemy because I tell you the truth?

Copy furnished: Jerry Willsey, President, Chapter LXI, SFA
               Kathy Hovis, Editor THE ITHACA JOURNAL
               Peter J. DeMott and Dave Emory   BC: William F. Pepper

LTC Dan Marvin's response to the SFA after being expelled from the organization. In it Dan raises many ethical questions and asks for some specificity in the
charges against him.

March 11th, 1999

Dear Col Marvin,

Last letter I sent to you, I have already corrected person names in pictures:

Number 1 picture: (From Left to Right) is QUANG - FLASH (Lo Lap Co/Killed on the line of duty in Can Tho - C.4 Heaquaters during 1968/1969

Number 2 picture: FLASH alone on a boat

Number 3 picture: JEAN (me) and Lt Strait

And the rest pictures are O.K.

I'll enclose herein my $ 20.00 check for a book (when the books are ready just send me one).

What you have indicated in the book of "The Bassac Bastards..." about the C.I.D.G (or Hoa Hao forces in Chau Doc province was true. After you guys left for America, Home sweet home I remained in Chau Doc until mid-1967. During this time I used to fly commanding chopper with Col Brewer (PSA) and his counter-part Col Nguyen Dinh Phuong (Province Chief) to visit remote outposts; participated those Hoa Hao units to combat operation in That Son (Seven Mountains). I can say these Hoa Hao troopers were the heroes, brave fighters; the untouchables. They are the Vietnamese Communist's enemies.

After we were forcebly surrendered, put down guns and waited for the so-called national liberation front comrades (Big Minh, the last RVN President had broadcasted on National Radio) to give them our side-command. The Vietnam war was ended. North and South united, the America was defeated. Million people of us were put in the so damn-called Re-education camps for fucking re-educating. Many brave men killed themselves with their own weapons, executed, died, passed away.... Properties were confiscated, land lords, business owners evicted by the new government - the communists. While we were arrested for re-education (no trial or sentence at all) I met some Hoa Hao members; we eat together and help each other so as to keep up our moral and survise. We assisted some to escape; one who could not make it, returned dead after the guards seized him. In the nights we wept for a fallen friend

I stop here and will write you again. You take care. Tell me about Major Phoi and General Quang to see I can help them, or do they need help ?

Jean Pham

LTC Marvin continued to gather information for his book, looking for different viewpoints and experiences. This March 1999 letter from Jean Pham, one of the Vietnamese interpreters in An Phu, corroborates certain details in this book, then known as *The Bassac Bastards*.

March 12, 2000

Ltc. Daniel Marvin

Dear Col. Marvin:

I owe you a lot of apologies for my procrastination. I hope you understand my situation, raising four college kids and having a busy career, and forgive me. I could not believe the time has passed really fast, especially in America, where I never thought one day I would live. It has been 33 years since you left Vietnam.

After the closing of Camp Dan Nam when the area was considered pacified (that's right!), I went to work for the "company" in Can Tho province, where the C Team located. My last post was in Tay Ninh province, the west part of which was the headquarters of the COSVN (Central Office for South Vietnam). The government collapsed April 1975. I arrived in San Diego in May 1975 and settled down with my family: a wife, a son and three daughters. The oldest daughter was then six years old and the youngest daughter was 6 months, all born in Vietnam. We were hit hard by the culture shock. Though being bewildered and confused with an unforeseen future, we continued to live and grow in the new environment. I was too busy struggling to make a living: going to school while working to support my family. It was extremely hard. I started to forget the past; I could not afford to think of it, even if I wanted.

Until I met Lan, he told me about his contacts with you. Then I received your letters. The pictures of the Team, the camp, the bunker, the 4.2 mortar, the military operation map, and your story about the skirmish at Khanh Binh...that really brought me back to those days. I showed the pictures to my children. They were astonished and started asking me about the war, which they were too young to remember.

I was assigned to Team A424. Coincidently, I met Sgt JOHNSON at the C Team. He told me he was also assigned to Team A424. We rode on a 2-½ ton truck that carried ammunition to re-supply the B Team. It was a single truck convoy without escort. We left early in the morning. We had a PRC-25 radio for communication. You know how its range was. Only JOHNSON carried an M-16. The CIDG driver and another member carried Carbine M1. I did not have my weapon yet. We drove on single lane road, paved but eroded by weather and time, left behind by the French. I was terribly concerned. "I am with Special Forces. No wonder!" I thought. "If we run into an ambush, what's the heck can we deal with it?"

A six page March 2000 letter from Tony Trung, another of the Vietnamese interpreters in An Phu, corroborating and providing added detail for incorporation into this book. Tony has recently retired from the San Diego Police Department as a Captain, after serving with the department for over twenty years.

Somehow my fear diminished with the presence of the local buses coming and passing by and the farmers working on their rice paddies alongside.

On the way, at one point, JOHNSON needed to release his bladder. There was no town nearby, nor could we stop because our truck was loaded with ammunition. JOHSON pissed in a coke can and dumped it on the roadside as the truck continued its route. We all laughed. We arrived in Chau Doc Province late in the afternoon after approximately 4 hours. It was my first time to Chau Doc Province. The majority of the population was Hoa Hao followers, who were extremely anti-communists for the killing of their founder in French time.

Before the sunset, it started raining. We met two team members from Camp Dan Nam A424. They came to pick us up, new movies, and supplies for the camp. It poured harder. It was in monsoon season. We covered ourselves in ponchos. We got on an outboard boat. Four of us on a small boat traveled on the large Bassac River. The man knew the route well, I believed, because I noticed he steered boat the on the friendly side of the river and beyond the range of small-arm fires of the enemy. I was soaking wet and cold. We arrived at the destination safely in 2 hours, I guessed. You picked us up at the dock in a Jeep. The muddy dirt road led us into the camp. Dirt and mud were everywhere. I saw little sign of civilization.

Colonel, what's the heck we were doing then? The sitrep meeting took place in the morning. Our daily activities included day and night foot patrols joint by the CIDG's. Lt. Strait, "Bac si" Sirois, and I conducted our regular missions to the remote areas to dispense medicines to the sick villagers. They loved Sirois for his generosity in giving them antibiotics that, they misconceived, could cure all ailments. Lt. Strait and I talked to the villagers in attempt to do our "psychological warfare" jobs, to win people's heart, and to get their relatives in the enemy rank to "chieu hoi" or to return to the government. At night, we set the 4.2 mortar to fire on the enemy positions, or to cover our patrols in the village. The 4.2 round was bigger than the size of my thigh and heavy. Sgt Taylor read the map, measured the distance, adjusted the bipods, and called out the charges. I attached the charges to the round and dropped it into the tube, muffling my ears with fingers. After dropping about 20 rounds, my arms got tired, especially when we fired a short range and the tube was raised high and the top reached over my head. It bounced on the concrete base so hard that we had to repair it frequently.

Our team members took turn to man the FOB at Khanh Binh with a CIDG platoon every two weeks (am i right?). The FBO was built on the south side of the river. The other side belonged to Cambodia. We could see Cambodian soldiers carrying French rifles, riding bike, whistling happily, and showing no concern for the war. They were the host of the VC. The outpost was too far from town, desolate, and gloomy. Enclosed within several layers of barbed wires, communication trenches, and claymore mines, it was situated relatively on a high ground near a creek branching off the Bassac River. The thatched houses of the local people hanging really high on the supporting posts, about 5 meters above the ground, amazed me. The people told me the water level of the Bassac River would rise to the floor of the house in the rainy season. The water would reach the outer perimeter of the outpost. The team at this outpost had the radio call sign "Outcast." Do you remember it? I really respected the one who gave us this call sign, for we were truly outcast when we came here. We sit on our butts all day doing nothing. We just waited for the enemy's attack. The days here were very long and dull. To kill time, I joined the CIDG guys in the shooting match for money. I preferred the Colt 45 pistol. We shot at the aluminum cans hung on the barbered wires. The cans, together with the geese raised by the CIDG, were used to give warning to the guards at night when the Charlie struck the barbered wire on the perimeter. I wished we had had electronic motion detectors in that era. I won most of the shooting matches. I did not know that this practice had helped sharpen my skill to win the sharp shooter trophy in the San Diego Police Academy in 1985. Even in daytime, our movement was limited. We could not go far from the outpost or we risked for sniper fires. I did not want to take this kind of risk either. Confined in a small area of the bunker, I felt uncomfortable. We could be irritated or got mad at each other very easily. All activities ceased at dusk. Even reading was hard because candles or kerosene lights did not give enough light. Boring and scared at night I felt. Johnson and I prepared a routine counter attack plan, set up the 81 mm mortar at the nightfall, after we radioed the base to report the enemy situation. It was raining off and on. We fired 81mm mortar on the reported enemy position. After firing a few rounds, we had a dud. "My God! It did not go out," I said and got really upset. Johnson calmed me down, "Don't worry. We will get it out." I started to lower the tube. Johnson raised its bottom slowly and carefully. He warned me, "It is an "HE". We got to be extremely cautious, or else it will go off and we'll be dead!" I wrapped my hand around the mouth of the tube, trying to catch the dud round without touching its tip. Johnson kept raising, but the round got stuck. Johnson lowered and raised the tube or shook it several times without success. Johnson said, "Fuck, I can not raise any higher because it becomes very dangerous when the round comes out too fast." "But we can not leave it in the tube overnight because the Charlie can attack us any time," I said. Johnson suggested, "Let take it down to the creek and submerge it in the water to see if we can get it out." Johnson carried the tube on his shoulder. I led the way with a flashlight. I removed the concertina wires, opened the gate, and made sure that the guards knew what we were doing. The way to the creek, about 200 yards away, was muddy, greasy, and slippery. We walked downhill very slowly and made sure we would not slip or fall. When we reached the creek it started drizzling. Looking back at the outpost, we could hardly see it. In the creek, Johnson laid the tube in the water. When the water filled up the tube, Johnson raised the base-end. With my hand ready to catch the round, I placed my ear against the tube to listen to any sound of the round moving. "Yes, I hear it. It's moving," I told Johnson. I caught the round safely without touching its tip, and laid it down on ground. I marked its location for safety and for recovery the next day. At this moment, if the enemy shot at us from the other side of the creek, we would be caught in the crossfire, big time! It did not happen! We walked back to the outpost. I signaled the guard with the flashlight and shouted the passwords. He let us in. We cleaned the tube and resumed our choir. We pounded the enemy position with more rounds throughout the night... We did not hear the aluminum cans jiggling or the geese honking. We had another safe night.

The next morning, the intelligence reported our 81mm rounds fell short of the enemy position and caused no damage. But the enemy had to disperse the strength. Intelligence, my ass! It became very boring and unreliable with the routine information like "About 3 VC companies, about 250 men, clad in black pyjamas, seen in the village so and so, fully armed, gathering food from people to prepare an attack on the outpost, etc. " It never took place. Intelligence was bullshit. We idled all the morning after transmitting the sitrep to the camp. At noon, our relief showed up in three outboards with supplies. "Flash" (La Lap co) came to relieve me. We returned to the A camp by sunset without incidents.

I felt I had more freedom at the camp. We watched John Wayne's movie "Green Beret." The CIDG guys loved it. But I did not like the movie. The villagers and the Vietnamese soldiers in the movie did not look like the Vietnamese and could not speak the language. The story was spiced with Hollywood features. It frustrated me. We went to bed about midnight. Not for long, I was awakened to the footsteps running about in the hallway. The radioman shouted, "Khanh Binh was under attack!" "Shit!" I said, "It was quiet last night when I was there." The ARVN Artillery Battery started firing their 155mm and 105mm flares and HE rounds on the outpost perimeter, where its coordinate had been preplanned. I heard "Flash" screaming over the radio, "Charlie on the outer perimeter. Heavy on the north." The CIDG's requested the artillery fire for effect. I ran outside and looked in the direction of Khanh Binh. A corner of the horizon and a large portion of the dark sky were illuminated by flares. The sound of small arms fire could hardly be heard. It was too far away. Thirty minutes passed by. It seemed too long to me. Radio from Khanh Binh reported the enemy was being held off but it still received incoming B40 rockets and mortar rounds. The CIDG had KIA's and WIA's in the initial report. Enemy casualty was unknown.

A meeting was immediately held in the camp to plan for a counter attack. Major Phoi and you discussed the plan. We could move faster by boats, but the risk for B40 rocket fires at the bottleneck of the river was extremely high. The final plan: We went on foot in two elements. I felt a lot better to go on foot. We might run into an ambush and stepped on mines or booby traps, but at least we had the ground or something for cover. Traveling by boats in this situation, we became a sitting duck for the enemy firepower.

Lt. Sang and Sgt. Taylor took two platoons. I was assigned to them. We started out early before dawn. Actually, we sneaked out of the camp hoping that enemy agents or VC sympathizers nearby would not see us. There was only one road to Khanh Binh. I was so much scared. We knew so sure about the enemy tactics of

After almost forty years, Tony must have confused his John Wayne movies and/or when he saw that movie, because *The Green Berets* was released in 1968

464

attacking an outpost to strike the reinforcements. We were now the reinforcing units. I became paranoid, "They will attack us?" "But where and when?" Everyone looked so serious. No one was talking. Something was on their mind. I thought they were scared as much as I was.

We moved along the road slowly and carefully. We looked around for any signs of movement of any kinds. No boats in the river, no farmers, no civilian foot traffic, no birds were in sight. Lt. Sang said it did not look good, and we agreed. We returned to our silence and kept walking. We were about half way to Khanh Binh. All of the sudden, we heard the explosions of the howitzer shelling in the outpost's direction. Over the radio, we learned the Charlie launched another wave of attack on Khanh Binh. We could hear machine gun fires and small arm fires. The enemy attacked us before dawn? This was very unusual because the day would break very soon. It could also mean that they had a lot of men or their strength larger than a battalion to attack an outpost in daylight. We were getting closer and closer to Khanh Binh. A burst of submachine gun fire rung out from the point of our platoon. Shit! We took cover. Our lead men spotted the enemy and fired the first rounds. We exchanged fires. We realized that it was not an ambush. The VC of about a company size was advancing toward Khanh Binh as well, and they into us. Our men were expecting an enemy ambush; therefore, they detected the enemy movement the first hand. After about 10 minutes, too long for a skirmish, we did not have casualty. Lt. Sang and Taylor decided to split our element. Taylor wanted me and a half squad to stick with him. Our mission was to lure the enemy into believing that we were withdrawing and they would chase after us. By doing this, we would diverge the enemy forces and reduce the pressure they laid on the outpost. Before I could tell Taylor this was a fucking suicidal idea, Taylor already moved out swiftly. The CIDG's and I followed him. We spread out and started firing our automatic rifles at the enemy, leaving Lt. Sang and his men behind. As the enemy directed their firepower in our way and followed us, Lt. Sang and his men quietly moved out of their position and advanced toward Khanh Binh as planned. We fired, moved back, and took cover. The enemy tailed us for a while, and then they stopped. For some unknown reason, probably they thought we were taking them into a trap, they changed their direction. We paused for a rest then moved north to catch up with Lt. Sang's unit.

Lt. Sang radioed his unit reached the outskirt of Khanh Binh and spotted the enemy. On the move, we could hear the intensive gunfire, the medley of our M16's, M60 machineguns, grenade launchers, mortars, and artillery that overwhelmed the VC's AK47 and RPG machineguns. It was a good sign, I thought. For about 30 minutes we could not reach Sang's location yet. I felt we did not move an inch even we were walking very fast. The AK 47's fired less and less. The VC machinegun fired sporadically, indicating the enemy was withdrawing. Lt. Sang and his men dislodged the enemy from besieging the outpost. They were the first element to link with men inside. We rejoined them an hour later. Sang's unit had casualties. Medivac was on the way.

Taylor and I rushed into the outpost through the broken barbed wires, which were all messed up by the enemy B40 rockets and explosive. At least 10 bodies of the VC sapper team perched on the barbed wire around the perimeter. They tried to open a path for their men to move in. Not too far from the VC dead bodies, in the communication trench, our soldiers were sitting lifeless against the wall with the rifle in their hands. I saw five women, the soldiers' wives who followed the husbands everywhere, lying in the trench next to their beloved men. They died with their husbands while they helped them reloading the weapons. Gray smokes with the smell of flesh burning and gunpowder filled the atmosphere over the outpost. We rushed toward our bunker to find "Flash". He was expecting us. Still with a usual smile on his face, he looked very tired and old, but happy when he saw us. I made coffee for the team and we ate our C-ration for breakfast. "Flash" recounted the fighting last night.

We talked with the wounded, comforted them, and ensured them the dust-off was not too far away. We went to the outer perimeter and replanted the claymore mines that had been used in the fight. We also repaired the bunker, half of which was knocked down by the incoming rounds. We gave the rest of our C-rations to the CIDG's men before leaving for the camp before sunset. "Flash" was going back with us. On the outboard, he sat quietly. I did not know what he was thinking. On the way back, we prepared for a counter attack should an ambush happened. We only had some sniper fires but no one got hurt. We reached the camp safely.

It is hard for me to remember all details. I am sure that I miss to mention a lot of things, but basically I cover the incidents in which I took part. After we left Camp A-424, I went to work for the company. I heard that "Flash" was killed in an ammo re-supply trip. He was driving the truck, which was overloaded, and a heavy ammunition crate fell on him when he hit a bump on a dirt road.

Many Hoa Hao friends of ours died for the right cause and their belief. Many were imprisoned for a long time after the country collapsed. Many lost their families, wives and children, at sea during the escape for freedom. Our heroes died and sacrificed their lives for their now living friends. I owe them my life in the war. My family owes them the comfort they now enjoy. We owe them a lot of things...and we shall remember them as long as we live.

Respectfully yours,

Tony

(Tony) Trung P. Nguyen

Tony Trung was also deposed in 2005 for the trial, the twenty-two page deposition may be read in its entirety at www.ExpendableElite.com.

ARTHUR H. WEED
ATTORNEY AT LAW

1231 STATE STREET, SUITE 207
SANTA BARBARA, CALIFORNIA 93101

(805) 962-9339 (FAX) 962-2030

August 21, 2000

Robert Logan

[handwritten note, top right]

DAN - FYI

I WILL CALL JIMMY DEAN
WHEN I FINISH EDITING

POST CARD COUNT

TONY TRUNG   NO
JEAN PHAM   YES
VAN DANG   NO
PHO LE   NO

Dear Bob;

Sorry it has taken me so long to write this letter. The fellow I talked to about a month ago who apparently is the Secretary of the "Special Forces Association" was Jimmy Dean and he left two numbers when he called me: (910) 485-5433 and (910) 485-1041. I'm not sure which one I used to call him back.

The gist of what he said is that Col. Dan Marvin *used to be* a member of the Special Forces Association, but apparently is no longer welcome. Specifically he said his "book was a fantasy" and that the "camp never came under attack by the Viet Cong" and that Col. Marvin never went to "assassin school."

Jimmy Dean also told me that Col. Marvin apparently claimed the CIA contacted him "about an assassination" but that this did not happen. Col. Marvin also said a "Captain Vanak" (phonetic spelling) was with him during all this, but that he is now deceased. However, Captain Vanak is not dead and in fact he testified before the CID in Washington. In addition Captain Vanak would state he never even knew Col. Marvin, according to Jimmy Dean.

Jimmy Dean also stated "there would be repercussions" if you went ahead with the project, but I was careful to assure him that the last thing you wanted was to make a documentary about circumstances which did not happen.

I hope all goes well and that we will see the three of you out here for good next year (assuming there aren't any "repercussions".)

Sincerely,

ARTHUR H. WEED
Attorney at Law

AW:ns

An August 2000 letter from Arthur H. Weed, Esq to Robert Logan telling of a threatening phone call he received from "Jimmy" Dean of the Special Forces Association.

Lieutenant Colonel Daniel Marvin
United States Army Special Forces (Retired)
P.O. Box 538, Cazenovia, New York 13035-0538
TEL: UNLISTED ◆ FAX: 315-655-3056

4 September 2000   FILE:JD040900

James C. Dean
Secretary, Special Forces Association
Post Office Box 41436
Fayetteville, North Carolina 28309-1436

SUBJECT: False Statements made to Arthur H. Weed, Esq., in July 2000 by James C. Dean that impugn the credibility of and malign the character of the undersigned (Retired LTC Daniel Marvin, SSAN 320-26-5983).

Mr. Dean,

Reference is made to your July 2000 telephone conversation as Secretary of the Special Forces Association with Attorney Arthur H. Weed regarding your opinion as to the veracity of facts that I have made public relating to my personal experiences as a member of the United States Army Special Forces.

I understand that you spoke from your office telephone number (910) 485-5433 and spoke as Secretary of and on behalf of the Special Forces Association, not as a private citizen. Speaking with the weight of that office and speaking as an officer of an association representing thousands of present and former US Army Special Forces members, many of whom knew me and/or served with me during my years in Special Forces, your statements could (and would normally) be accepted as an honorable and candid representation of a well founded opinion based on a knowledge of the facts.

But most of what you told Attorney Weed was not based on fact, Mr. Dean. Of all those statements that I have been informed of as being the statements you made during your telephone conversation or conversations with attorney Arthur H. Weed, the only statements that were factually correct were two; one being that I *used* to be a member of the Special Forces Association and the other being that I was apparently *no longer welcome*.

Inasmuch as I have previously provided the Special Forces Association with documentation supporting the content of my 1988 manuscript titled, ***The Bassac Bastards*** , I will not be redundant in

LTC Daniel Marvin to James C. Dean - 4 Sep 00 - Page 1

LTC Marvin's four-page response to James Dean and the SFA, concerning the call from Mr. Dean to Robert Logan's attorney, Arthur Weed, which effectively stopped Logan's film project based upon this book.

again providing same to you. I will refer herein to specific letters from the undersigned to you in your capacity as Secretary of the Special Forces Association, which conveyed such documentation of proof and I will provide copies of same as enclosures to copies of this letter being provided Attorney Arthur H. Weed and the producer of documentaries who he represents. A set of same will be provided my attorney to use as a basis for a character defamation lawsuit should you refuse to recant your libelous statements.

I am appalled that you told attorney Arthur H. Weed "there would be repercussions" if the producer went ahead with the production of a documentary based on my experiences as written into the 1988 "The Bassac Bastards" manuscript. I assume the repercussions you alluded to would be against the producer of the documentary. If you indeed meant that there would be repercussions in the Special Forces establishment, then I would agree and I would believe that to be a positive thing, as much needs to be done to assure that recurrence of certain illegal activities is negated by a system of control mechanisms that would direct unconventional operations be conducted in accordance with U.S. and International Law.

Specifically, you told attorney Weed that my *"book was a fantasy,"* insinuating that *the Bassac Bastards* manuscript being used as the basis for the documentary was a product of my imagination. You also stated that my *"camp never* came under attack by the Viet Cong."

With exception of the massacre of unarmed civilians by a U.S. Helicopter crew near Camp Rach Gia on 26 December 1966, all other actions of significance included in my 1988 manuscript have been corroborated and I have audio tape or signed, written documentation to support what I have written from former ARVN Lieutenant General Quang Van Dang (Special Assistant to President Thieu and earlier the IV Corps CG), former ARVN Lieutenant Colonel Phoi Van Le (my counterpart at Camp Dan-Nam in An-Phu, South Vietnam), retired Major John E. Strait (XO of A-424), other members of my A team (James A. Taylor, Raymond J. Johnson, and Richard Sirois) and two of my former Vietnamese National interpreters at Camp Dan-Nam (both now detectives in a major metropolitan police force). General Dang, LTC Le and the two interpreters are now U.S. citizens.

In addition the Monthly Operational Summaries (Contact Shelby Stanton) contain verification of the many battles in our area against a numerically superior enemy force. With my letter to you dated 13 October 1997, I enclosed copies of photos, a battle map dated 19 May 66, the weapons, ammunition and equipment status report of 31 May 1966, Combat Statistics for Cam Dan-Nam for the period 1 January 1966, and the GRAPEVINE article *No Laughing Matter* which tells about the battles of mid-May 1966, the assassination plot against Prince Sihanouk, attempted CIA retaliation against my forces and my

11 month struggle to demand and obtain a complete investigation of false allegations against General Dang that resulted in his being issued a permanent entry visa on 7 September 1989. I personally brought General Dang into this country from Montreal, Quebec on 24 September 1989. All of these documents and information relating to the verbal corroboration of Strait and Taylor were provided the U.S. Congress as the primary evidence to base the investigation which cleared General Dang. When I spoke to General William Yarborough and Rudi Gresham on 2 October 1997, I informed both of what I had provided Congress, and in my letter to Rudi Gresham (I was asked to communicate with Gresham by General Yarborough) I enclosed copies of articles relating to both the AnPhu experience and the William Bruce Pitzer assassination and told of my contacts with former Green Beret John McCarthy and former CIA operative David MacMichael, both of whom were part of the CIA's three pronged plot to assassinate Prince Sihanouk in 1967 dubbed "*Operation Cherry.*"

In my letter to you dated 3 June 1998, I enclosed an *unlimited* "*AUTHORIZATION and PRIVACY WAIVER*" for use by the Special Forces Association in obtaining any information they so desired on my past and advised you that Senators D'Amato and Moynihan and Congressman McHugh were familiar with the investigation that cleared General Dang. Would I have provided the waiver if I had been wanting to hide anything?

Would the Special Forces Association be willing to request that General Yarborough, Rudi Gresham, and the former members of my A Team (Strait. Taylor, Johnson & Sirois) sign an AUTHORIZATION and PRIVACY WAIVER permitting unrestricted access to government records relating to these individuals by attorney Arthur H. Weed?

I do understand that my former team members have been asked to remain loyal to the Special Forces Association (as I also was asked by Rudi Gresham in my taped telephone conversation with him) and who, to a man, now refuse to talk to or correspond with the undersigned. Interesting in that each had already provided me with written or audio taped corroboration of what they knew of the events told about in the 1988 manuscript - each of them having been provided a copy of same prior to the 1988 Special Forces convention in Fayettevlle, North Carolina.

I am also providing Attorney Weed with an extract of my 2 October 1997 telephone conversations with General Yarborough and Rudi Gresham which includes the General telling me of CIA personnel involvement in the Special Warfare Center as "advisors for the faculty." Both gentlemen said that the William E. Pepper book "*Orders to Kill*" was a "blatant, sick lie. Interesting, in that the book and other testimony and evidentiary material (including information I supplied relating to SF involvement in allowing a significant number of weapons, even M1D sniper rifles, to be mailed to a black SF officer in

Detroit, Michigan from the 46th SF in Thailand) was used, in the November/December 1999 4 week wrongful death suit in Memphis, Tennessee to have the jury find Loyd Jowers liable for Martin Luther King Jr's death. Jowers was found by the jury to have been part of a grand conspiracy involving the U.S. Army, the FBI, the CIA and the White House of Lyndon Johnson.

It is interesting also to note, that during my telephone conversation with General Yarborough on 2 October 1999, the general said, referring to the assassination plots I had reported to him involving Special Forces personnel: if these things occurred it was due to "individuals operating outside their sphere of authority and confidence." He added that "they should be investigated." I wonder, Mr. Dean, what action has been taken within SF or SFA by retired General Yarborough to demand an investigation, particularly when he is knowledgeable that all of these matters have been reported to Congress?

Mr. Dean, I have requested from you and from Gerald Willsey (Chapter LXI of SFA) a copy of *THE DROP* that contains your notice of my having been removed from SFA membership, and have yet to receive a copy. PLEASE send me a copy without delay.

Most sincerely,

LTC Daniel Marvin
USASF (Retired)

No enclosures

Copies: Attorney Arthur H. Reed and the documentary producer with the following enclosures:
a.   2 Oct 97 record of telephone conversation segments
b.   10 Oct 97 letter to Rudi Gresham
c.   13 Oct 97 letter to Jimmy Dean, SFA Secretary
d.   27 May 98 letter from James C. Dean, SFA Secretary
e.   3 Jun 98 letter to James C. Dean, SFA Secretary
f.   2 Jun 98 AUTHORIZATION AND PRIVACY WAIVER
g   15 Jul 98 letter to James C. Dean, SFA Secretary
h.   19 Aug 98 letter from James C. Dean, SFA Secretary
i.   5 Sep 98 letter to James C. Dean, SFA Secretary
j.   15 Sep 98 letter from James C. Dean, SFA Secretary

SPECIAL FORCES ASSOCIATION
Post Office Box 41436
Fayetteville, North Carolina 28309-1436
Telephone: 910-485-5433 • Fax: 910-485-1041
http://www.sfahq.org
Email sfahq@aol.com

18 September 2000
Daniel Marvin
PO Box 538
Cazenovia, NY. 13035-0538

Mr. Marvin,

Reference your letter dated 4 September 2000, Subject: Alleged
False Statements made to Arthur H. Weed, Esq. in July 2000 by James
C. Dean.

I stand by any comments I have made, to anyone, concerning
false allegations you have made on Public Television and in Written
Articles.

The entire investigative file, to include but not limited to:
Statements and rosters of A-424, C-4, 46th Company, 6th SFG (A),
Special Forces Officer Course 2-64, and DA Records and Reports, are
now in the possession of our Attorney.

All future correspondence from you or your representative should
be directed to:
Attorney-At-Law
Bobby G. Deaver
3760 Bald Mtn. Rd.
West Jefferson, NC. 28694

F.Y. ,

James C Dean
James C. Dean
Secretary

cc: Robert Francis Logan
RFL Productions
C/O Arthur H. Weed, Attorney-At-Law
1231 State St, Suite 207
Santa Barbara, CA. 93101

The SFA response to LTC Marvin's four-page letter of September 2000. Dan
wonders to this day why Bobby Deaver did not bring the "entire investigative
file" mentioned in this letter to the trial to present as evidence for the jury to
consider.

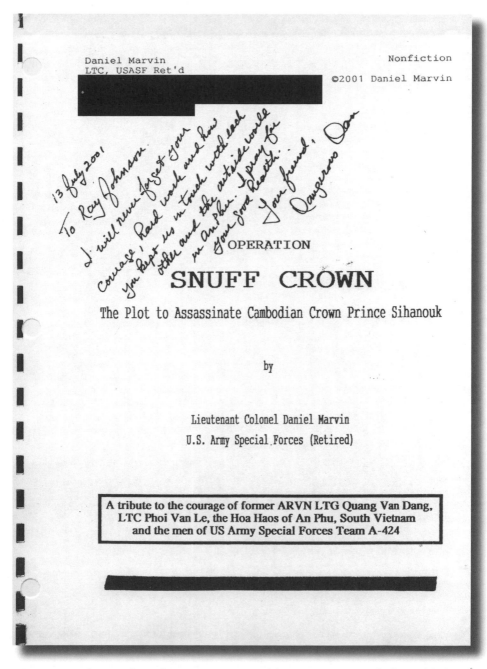

13 July 2001
To Ray Johnson,
I will never forget your
courage! Read work and how
you kept us in touch with each
other and the outside world
in Anphu. I pray for
your good health.
Your friend, Dan
Dangerous Dan

OPERATION

SNUFF CROWN

The Plot to Assassinate Cambodian Crown Prince Sihanouk

by

Lieutenant Colonel Daniel Marvin

U.S. Army Special Forces (Retired)

> A tribute to the courage of former ARVN LTG Quang Van Dang,
> LTC Phoi Van Le, the Hoa Haos of An Phu, South Vietnam
> and the men of US Army Special Forces Team A-424

Continuing his work on his manuscript and his campaign to find a publisher.
LTC Marvin retitles his book, adds information gathered from Ray Johnson, Jean
Pham, Tony Trung and others. Here is a copy—clearly labeled as nonfiction—of
the revised manuscript, then entitled *Operation Snuff Crown,* and inscribed to
Ray Johnson by Dan in July 2001.

© GLENN OLIVER & GEORGE HEIB JFK SW/SF MUSEUM PRODUCTIONS

6 Dec 01

Hi:

Have a merry Xmas & a happy new yr. and a great Xmas day. Hope you and all the family are feeling fine.

As for me I'm getting there slow but sure. Have to go to the hosp next month. but for how long SPECIAL FORCES I do not know. I still hanging in there. Marlene & the kids are great.

I sorry I could not help you out on your book. But I knew nothing about all this combat.

Take care & be well

Ray & Marlene

Dropping in to wish you a Merry Christmas

A very friendly 2001 Merry Christmas card to Dan Marvin from Ray Johnson.

2-06-2002 11:03AM   FROM PRESIDIO PRESS 415 898 0383   P. 1

505B San Marin Drive • Suite 300 • Novato • California 94945-1340
415-898-1081 • FAX 415-898-0383 • e-mail <mail@presidiopress.com>

February 6, 2002

By Fax

Lt. Col. Daniel Marvin

Dear Dan:

Thank you very much for working so hard with your re-write, but I am sorry to say that we are not able to make you an offer for your story.

I believe that every word you write is true. But because of the "spooky" subject matter, and your commercial presentation, I think you would be best served by having your book published by a mass-market publishing house such as Bantam, St. Martin's Press, Avon, Berkley, or Signet. I urge you to give one of those publishing houses a try.

I am sorry, Dan, that we couldn't connect on this. But out of about 1,600 submissions years, we only take on about 16 or so, so please don't feel too bad.

Thank you again for your good work, enthusiasm, and friendliness. If I can be of help please give me a call.

Sincerely yours,

E. J. McCarthy
Executive Editor

America's Foremost Publisher of Military History
on the web at www.presidiopress.com

One of the many rejection letters received by LTC Marvin. Note the sentences – "I believe that every word is true. But because of the spooky nature …" The Internet and desk-top publishing were changing traditional avenues, and Dan's book was published in May 2003 by TrineDay, a small publishing firm in Oregon headed by Kris Millegan.

♦ Website: www.ExpendableElite.com ♦ e-mail: ddm52@juno.com ♦
♦*A Born-Again Christian*♦

18 March 2003

Dear Ray,

Thanks so much for the chapter newsletter. I really appreciate it. I hope and pray that some day the people in charge of SFA will realize that what I am trying to do is to help the SF to stay strong and steer away from those things that are illegal. I would like to again be a member in good standing

How are you and Marlene doing? Kate and I are fine. I seem to have my diabetes under control and can even have ice cream once in a while...

The big news is that my book went to the printers on St. Patrick's Day. I should have the first batch here to sign in about 4 weeks. I'll mail yours as soon as get 'em.

I enclose a few pictures that will be in the book.
I still have to go thru the book one more time to make sure there are no goofs.

What do you think of this whole war situation? I think we should get out of the UN if they don't have enough guts to do what is right. Seems like every other nation, except Great Britain and Australia want our fighters to shed all the blood and then they will profit once the war is over.

Well, Ray, take good care of yourself and that sweet wife of yours...
I will be anxious until the day I mail you your copy of the book....

Your friend and comrade-in-arms,   Dangerous Dan

DAN:
Check PAGE 3
I have it underlined

PLEASE don't say anything
to J.F. about me
sending you the AT13
or the DROP.

REPORT FROM NATIONAL HEADQUARTERS

Jimmy Dean gave Chapter 1-18 an update on the Yard Land Project. SFA collected over $40,000.00 and with what STMP (Save The Montgnard People) collected, it came to a total donation of over $100,000.00.

Jimmy also briefed Chapter 1-18 on LTC(R)Dan Marvin and his book "Expendable Elite", which has been proven to be 100% lies.

A letter from LTC Marvin to Ray Johnson thanking Ray for sending Dan the note, and an article from the *Bugged Beer Can* a SFA newsletter. Together these items indicate the prevailing fear and the outright attacks against this book.

2 Jun 03

Hi Dan:
    Just a few lines to let you know I
rec'd your book. I just finished it yesterday.
Now I'm sending it off to my brother in
Fayetteville. He wants to see what the
"sneaky pete" were up too. After he finish
reading I well get it back.
    I hear Jimmy Dean got his
copy.
    As for your book its good & good
reading. But I can't remember alot of
what I did. first off. I was not there when
the fire hit an Phu. I got there after
the fire. I don't remember no C.I.A. Agent
or the blond lady. their is more but I'll
give you a call. To much writing to go
thru the whole book.
    I sending you 3500 dollars for the
book. If you have another copy send it too
me. My daughter wants one. Please send it
the cheapest way.

    Give my best to your family & hope
all is fine with them. As for me &
Marlene we are doing alright

        Please take care & be well

        Ray

I no good at writing any more. I make to
many mistakes as you can see.

A June 2003 two-page letter from Ray Johnson to LTC Marvin that tells Dan
his book is "good & good reading," and that Johnson wants to buy another for
his daughter. The same Ray Johnson who later sued Dan claiming $100,000 in
damages for defamation and libel from that same book. This letter is transcribed
on pages 394.

19 July 2003

TO: Fred Wayne Lawley, President, Special Forces Association

FROM: LTC Daniel Marvin USA Special Forces (Retired)

Mr. Lawley,

You received a signed copy of my nonfiction book "EXPENDABLE ELITE - One Soldier's Journey Into Covert Warfare" on 16 May 2003 according to official postal service records. Since that time I have been led to understand by members of the SFA and outsiders that your organization is actively discouraging the marketing of my book by different means.

I pray that I heard wrong and I would be pleased if you were to prove to me that SFA has actually promoted or endorsed my book.

I am just as certain, as others within your organization who have read my book from cover to cover are certain, IF you had read my book you would understand, particularly when it is known by you as the reader by way of the notes in the book, each detail of any significance, excepting only the massacre of innocent peasants discussed in Chapter Two, Massacre West of Rach Gia; have been corroborated in writing or by audio tape by former members of my team A-424 who are discussed in the book, Former CIA Station Chiefs Shackley and Polgar, former ARVN General Quang Van Dang & Colonel Phoi Van Le (both now US citizens), three South Vietnamese interpreters that are included in the book and copies of reports, covering that period (27 December 1965 thru 1 August 1966) such as SPOTREPs, SITREPs, and MOPSUMs, you would have endorsed the book as a true account of what took place in AnPhu, South Vietnam during the time I commanded A-424.

I ask that you read my book and then report your conclusions in THE DROP, providing me a copy of same. If you do not want to honor my reasonable request, please advise. I do not intend to let this matter of the SFA going against the truth stand without action on my part to let the world know what you are all about with respect for the truth.

Suffice it for me to write you as I wrote President George H.W. Bush in 1989 when I asked that he demand an investigation be conducted to clear General Dang of the heinous lies and harmful innuendo and that a permanent entry visa be issued General Dang. I provided President Bush a copy of the 1989 draft manuscript for this book as the sole evidence for his people to use to begin the investigation and I told President Bush that I would not quit in my struggle for General Dang until I died or the Lord returns and takes me home. President Bush ordered the investigation and General Dang was cleared of all charges, issued a permanent entry visa and I personally brought him into this country from Canada in September 1989. The attached letters from three of General Dang's children give you a picture of what they went through during these years

of their Father's horrible treatment at the hands of the CIA. My book tells the truth of how General Dang saved out lives - the men of A-424 and approx 400 of our VN SF and Strikers. IF it is your idea, your desire, your modes operandi to squelch the truth and to deny General Dang a world-wide readership to know the truth, I will fight that immoral and unjust approach to the truth in any way that I can legally and morally and will pray that you come to your sense in this matter and do what is right.

I would like to hear from you soon and I would encourage those who I have sent copies of this e-mail to be prepared to contact you personally by telephone at 910-485-5433 or by fax at 910-485-1041 or e-mail at sfahq@aol.com.

Most sincerely,   LTC Daniel Marvin USASF (ret)

A two-page July 2003 letter received by Wayne Lawley, SFA President from LTC Marvin concerning his now published book, *Expendable Elite*

Cazenovia Republican

Local resident authors book

by Janey Hurd

Lt. Col. Daniel Marvin, United States Army Special Forces (retired), has just had his first book published, called "Expendable Elite - One Soldier's Journey Into Covert Warfare." Marvin lives in Cazenovia with his wife Kate. He received 26 medals and commendations throughout his career and has been on many radio and television programs. Marvin also organized a support the troops rally in Cazenovia this spring.

Marvin shares his experiences and introduces readers to the people and places that left a strong impact on him.

"I started the book in 1984, and for 13 years beginning in 1990 tried to find a publisher to publish a book that I wanted to use to tell the people the truth of what you read, and to get others like myself to come forward, so that there may be an opportunity for the USA to rid itself of the worst of what evil runs this government," said Marvin. "It is the abuse of power and how it affects many."

Marvin was born in Detroit in 1933 in a cheap tenement apartment. His father left just after Marvin was born and Marvin didn't see him again until he was 21 years old.

Marvin's mother worked hard whenever she could find a job during the Depression. When he was 5 years old Marvin's mother moved him and his older brother Bill to Chicago. When Marvin was 11, he saw that high school gangs were robbing old ladies and stealing their groceries. Marvin formed a little gang called the "Blue Jackets" and they watched in their area on the south side of Chicago for the other gangs to attack women.

"We attacked them and went after them anytime we saw them, and never lost," Marvin said.

Marvin enlisted in the Army from Ithaca at the age of 18. Marvin said he enlisted because he wanted to be in something inherently dangerous and he had grown to love the military.

Marvin first served as an enlisted man in the U.S. Army, from recruit in June 1952 to sergeant first class. Commissioned a second lieutenant in the combat engineers at Fort Belvoir, Va., he went on to retire as a lieutenant colonel. A Green Beret, master parachutist and combat infantryman experienced in covert operations, he was a veteran of eight combat campaigns in the Korean and Vietnam wars and was thrice decorated for heroism.

Marvin was schooled as an unconventional warrior at the special warfare center at Fort Bragg, North Carolina, where he learned the fundamentals of special operations, including guerrilla warfare, special demolition, counter-terror, civic action, assassination techniques and psychological warfare operations from veteran Green Beret and CIA instructors.

"Secrecy was demanded during the many months of rigorous guerilla and counter-guerrilla warfare training," said Marvin. "Once we'd passed the rigorous training and had earned the right to wear the coveted Green Beret, we discussed little of what we'd learned with family or

July 23 to 29, 2003

friends." That secrecy fostered strained relations within family, non-SF friends and wives."

"As the wife of a Green Beret, it would be psychologically heart-wrenching for Kate to be ready at a moment's notice to bid me goodbye, not knowing where the mission was taking me, how long I'd be gone, or what danger was involved," Marvin said. "Duty demanded I tell her only superficial 'fluff.'"

"During my years of service as a commissioned officer in the US Army, I made it a practice to be somewhat distant, perhaps indifferent is the better word, from those whom I served with, whether senior or subordinate," Marvin said. "I did not want friendship or concern for a particular individual to affect my ability to lead or to make tactical decisions."

Marvin said that the reports he submitted to his headquarters in Vietnam appear in the book and he has corroboration to back up everything in the book except chapter two.

Marvin continues to campaign almost single handedly against government sponsored terrorism and assassination, spending countless hours daily to get what he says is the truth out.

JANEY HURD

Retired Lieutenant Colonel Dan Marvin is pictured outside his home in Cazenovia.

"This is the whole truth, the good, the bad, and the ugly of what took place during my tour of duty in South Vietnam, beginning in late December, 1965," said Marvin.

"There are few people who possess the courage to put their voice or their signature on the line as testimony regarding illegal, immoral or unsound actions ordered and, or perpetrated by the CIA or other agencies within the Washington establishment," said Marvin.

An article in LTC Marvin's hometown newspaper about this book.

8/8/2003 4:46 PM FROM: 760-3875 QTVS Quik Time Virtual Service TO: 3211190 PAGE: 001 OF 001

Page 1 of 1

Linda

From: "Daniel Marvin" <ddm52@juno.com>
To: <sfgwoa@hotmail.com>
Cc:

Sent: Wednesday, August 06, 2003 8:34 PM
Subject: Re: Message 7/20/03 To SFAHQ

Dear Wayne Lawley,

Reference is made to your rather vague and noncommittal e-mail of 25 Jul 03 which said in total "We are in receipt of your e-mail. You will hear from us in the near future. Wayne Lawley, President, Special Forces Association."

Please expedite your review of EXPENDABLE ELITE and your action on including your review in THE DROP.

It is extremely important that you do so as a friend of mine recently called me from Fort Bragg who had spoken with a number of young Special Forces sergeants - some of them at a firing range activity - and was told by more than a few that my name had been mentioned "as an enemy of the Green Berets". That is as far from the truth as you can get. I believe the US Army Green Beret is an undeniably valuable asset to this nation and the narrative of my book tells just how expert they are in what they do and how they are the ones who could have made victory the outcome in the Vietnam war. I understand, from an honorable person I know who is within your organization, that my provision of evidence that showed probable SF involvement in events leading up to the assassination of Dr. Martin Luther King Jr. led to negative action being taken against me by the SFA. What a shame, was it not? Read John 8:32 And ye shall know the truth, and the truth shall make you free.

It is the devious leadership that sometimes comes to bear in and above the SF commands that is the problem and a serious problem.

Please advise within three days when you will be completed with your review and in what issue of THE DROP your review will be included.

A man who honors the US Army Green Berets

LTC Daniel Marvin US Army Special Forces (Retired)
AKA Dangerous Dan

*If I answer this, his ASS is mine.
Deavers & you plus my input (words) 8/8/2003
if you need them.*

W

At the bottom of this fax of an email that was sent by LTC Marvin to the SFA is telling personal note, penned by SFA President Wayne Lawley. The document was produced during the discovery phase of the lawsuit.

SPECIAL FORCES ASSOCIATION

Post Office Box 41436
Fayetteville, North Carolina 28309-1436
Telephone: 910-485-5433 • Fax: 910-485-1041
http://www.sfahq.org
Email sfahq@aol.com

13 August 2003

Robert A. Millegan
Publisher
Trine Day
P. O. Box 577
Walterville, OR 97489

Mr. Millegan,

This letter is in reference to a recently published book by Trine Day titled "Expendable Elite —
One Soldier's Journey into Covert Warfare".

We are not aware of your vetting procedures for people such as Mr. Marvin, however, they
surely leave a dubious impression of credibility with us. At the outset, we find five statements
on the inside cover of the book to be false and misleading. We also find (in reference to the
book) Mr. Marvin's use of and his calling: "And ye shall know the truth, and the truth shall make
you free", to be insulting to the members of this Association.

In view of the honorable and truthful combat history of the "Silent Professionals", we are
offended by Mr. Marvin's fictional account of covert operations with us and insist that you, as
publisher, take immediate measures to change this book to "fiction by a dreamer" or remove it
from all avenues and sources of sales within the next 30 days of the date of this letter. Should
you choose to ignore this request, we will have no recourse other than legal action and the
publication of our documentation to disprove these published false statements.

Mr. Millegan, this is our clearly determined promise, that should you fail to believe our
challenge, we invite your inquiry of Warner Books or CNN about our resolve when the
truthfulness of U.S. Special Forces combat operations is at stake.

Mr. Marvin has been informed that he owes an unvarnished apology to U.S. Army Special
Forces to include Detachment A-424 members, and more importantly, he owes this great country
of ours. He owes us apologies for his prostitution of any truth found in his unworthy book.

Sincerely,

Wayne Lawley
President

James C. Dean
Secretary

The SFA's first threatening letter to TrineDay. Note the reference to the intimidation of CNN, discussed by Kris Millegan on page 413.

SPECIAL FORCES ASSOCIATION

Post Office Box 41436
Fayetteville, North Carolina 28309-1436
Telephone: 910-485-5433 • Fax: 910-485-1041
http://www.sfahq.org
Email sfahq@aol.com

September 22, 2003

Mr. Millegan:

More than thirty days have passed since our letter of 13 August 2003, requested (demanded) action on your behalf to correct the libelous accounts published by you in Dan Marvin's "Expendable Elite." You have elected not correctly to (portray or classify) the imaginary accounts of Dan Marvin and the Special Forces unit to which he was assigned as fictional.

Accordingly, we have no alternative to exposing your publication and Dan Marvin's writings as libelous to the members of the team who faithfully served Special Forces and their county at the times depicted by Marvin in his allegedly true accounts of his and their tours of duty.

Colonel Tuttle especially was accused of violating his oath of office, of conspiring with Marvin to subvert the official and stated policies of the United States *vis a vis* Cambodia, Of ordering or knowingly permitting Marvin to invade by artillery, mortar, and automatic weapons, including sending armed soldiers of two nations into a country with whom we were not and have not had hostilities, and cover up of the worst kind in relations to his duties as Marvin's commander, among other things.

He has made similar and equally libelous allegations against the members of A-424, and in addition has alleged in his book that these honorable soldiers committed treason and sedition in "siding with him" in refusing to obey lawful orders to close the camp and turn it over to other friendly troops, including conspiring to commit armed conflict with American and friendly forces who, according to Marvin, were en-route to attack the compound and kill them all. He named Sergeant Taylor and other named individuals as traitors and felons who violated general orders, special orders, international treaties and laws, and the Uniform Code of Military Justice. These men either have to live with these false allegations of criminal conduct which adversely affects their proud service to our country, or take such action as necessary to expose these allegations as false.

None of these men have ever shirked from what their consciences direct them to do. They have avowed not to start now. They feel that the attack on them is as vicious as Marvin's attack on Special Forces, CIA, and the Flag of the United States, which cannot stand. Marvin's expulsion from Special Forces Association was accomplished due to his lies while serving with the USA Special Forces in Ft Bragg, NC and Vietnam. That might be all that SFA can do legally. However, it stands ready, willing and able to assist

The September 2003 two page threatening letter from Wayne Lawley and James Dean of SFA to TrineDay. No "proof" was, or has ever been, provided. Kris Millegan posted this and the earlier letter at the book's Web site.

them, and other men who were impugned at various parts of his book as neurological and pathological killers of foreign nationals, as well as endangerment of fellow soldiers.

Accordingly, SFA will assist these libeled soldiers obtain counsel, obtaining true statements (already we have more than 20) of the duty and activities that contradict the fantasies of Marvin, and will do whatever we legally are permitted to do in defending the honor of Special Forces, the CIA, and the memories of those of our brethren who have made the ultimate sacrifice in upholding the honor and traditions of our proud individual units and our nation. The next communication will be from the attorney for those men named in the Secret Life of Dan Marvin.

Sincerely

Wayne Lawley
President

James C. Dean
Secretary/Administrator

Expendable Elite: It has been Association policy for the past five years that we will not accept publications or authors that demean the U.S. Army Special Forces with statements that are bald ass lies. This book, *Expendable Elite*, is one of the worst examples of what we have opposed since **William Pepper's** allegations concerning the 20th Group in his book "The truth about the murder of **Martin Luther King, Jr.**" In a letter to the publisher of this outlandish book, Mr. **Robert Millegan** of Trine Day, the Association demanded that *Expendable Elite* be taken off the market or a correction be made to claim this publication a work of fiction, not the truth, within 30 days or legal action would be taken. Neither Trine Day nor the author, **Dan Marvin**, believed we would keep our word. Now, by the time you have received this Winter *Drop*, a court action will have been initiated by seven members of A-424 and others named in this publication, against defendants Trine Day and Dan Marvin. The attorneys were obtained by the Association and full support will be given to the prosecution of this case.

Contributions: Several large donations were made this quarter that increased the Montagnard Land Project Fund and Memorials. Report in Spring 2004 *Drop*. ✄

A notice from the Spring 2004 SFA magazine *The Drop*

Juno e-mail printed Sat, 27 Sep 2003 08:55:10 , page 1

From: Daniel Marvin <ddm52@juno.com>
To: sfahq@aol.com
Cc:

Date: Sat, 27 Sep 2003 08:52:46 -0400
Subject: Wayne Lawley's and James Dean's purposeful attack on the truth of my book "EXPENDABLE ELITE"

Subject: Wayne Lawley's and James Dean's purposeful attack on the truth
of my book "EXPENDABLE ELITE"
Message-ID: <20030926.215918.868.7.ddm52@juno.com>

TO: Wayne Lawley, President of the Special Forces Association (SFA) and
the SFA Secretary, James Dean, other Special Forces personnel (active and
retired) and those others who are interested in this situation primarily
due to their high regard for the truth.

FROM: Lieutenant Colonel Daniel Marvin, US Army Special Forces (retired)

President Lawley and Secretary Dean, in your 13 August 2003
letter to publisher Robert A. Milligan of Trine Day Press you accused him
of publishing "Marvin's fictional account of covert operations" as a
nonfiction book and threatened "legal action" if Mr. Milligan did not
take "immediate measures to change this book to 'Fiction by a Dreamer."
President Lawley and Secretary Dean, you should understand you
are also accusing those who corroborate the facts of my book (documented
in the NOTES section of my book) of being "false and misleading." Do
you recognize that fact?
I know in my heart that those in all parts of this world who
admire Martha Raye (Colonel Maggie) will want to believe that this book
(Expendable Elite), which Colonel Maggie wrote the Foreword to after
reading the first draft manuscript in 1988, measures up to her high
standards of integrity Martha Raye is rerspected by people of all
nations and has been friends with thousands of Special Forces and visited
them in combat areas as well as their training environment. If my book
were not true in her mind's eye, why would Martha Raye ask to write the
Foreword to my book? Please see attachment that is a scanned copy of
Martha Raye's computer printout Foreword with a personal note to me. Also
see attachment that show Martha Raye with myself, John Strait and Richard
(Bac-si) Sirois in July 1988 at the SF Convention.
In addition to casting aspersions at Martha Raye, you did so to
General William C. Westmoreland, Lieutenant General William Desobry, ARVN
Lieutenant General Quang Van Dang, ARVN LTC Phoi Van Le, SF Major John E.
Strait, SF CSM Richard E. Sirois, SF SGM James A. Taylor, SF SFC Raymond
Johnson, Interpreter Trung P. Nguyen and Frances Dinkelspiel.
I'll go into detail regarding Martha Raye only: On the 12th day
of January 1966 Martha Raye, who we all knew as Colonel Maggie, visited
my team in Camp An-Phu, South Vietnam and first met me and my men at that
time. See details of her visit in pages 90 and 91 of the book. As you
will read in my book, She risked death coming into An Phu and her first
action was to help the team medics in the medical facility treat wounded
CIDG fighters. We only had the pleasure of visiting with Colonel Maggie

LTC Marvin's September 2003 two-page email answer to the SFA concerning their threat to sue.

for forty minutes, but the memory of her visit would last forever. In early 1988, after receiving her copy of the first draft manuscript for this book and prior to that year's U.S. Army Special Forces Summer Convention, she called me to reflect on her visit to An Phu. After reading the manuscript, she said she was "compelled" to ask if she could write the Foreword to my book. I said yes, honored that she wanted to and even more pleased when she told me, during the 1988 SFA Convention, that it would be the only book she would write a Foreword to.

On 20 February 1988, Colonel Maggie mailed her signed computer print out of her Foreword to LTC Marvin with a personal note to me. Check it out - a copy is attached.

Those who have read my book and who have known me for years wonder if it would be a good idea if you were to read my book before casting stones at me and my publisher? I don't know of any other book that captures the full role of an A Team in an counterinsurgency and military government role.

Inasmuch as you threaten a courageous publisher with legal action and inasmuch as members of SFA have told me of your ongoing actions to assassinate my character and discourage others from buying my book, I am gathering the truth together of our past interaction - particularly your action to kick me out of the SFA when you learned of my sending a copy of the US Army investigation that told the truth of SF gunrunning in 1967 that was potentially linked to the infiltration of Black Militant organizations by SF personnel and which reported the overt actions taken by MI Officer LTC Robert Bartelt to squelch the truth, to Attorney William E. Pepper who successfully represented the King family in the Memphis trial that found the US government to have acted with complicity in the assassination of Dr. Martin Luther King Jr..

Let all who receive this be the judge, but only after reading EXPENDABLE ELITE..

LTC Daniel Marvin USASF (ret) AKA Dangerous Dan

Galations 4:16 Am I therefore become your enemy, because I tell you the truth?

AO 440 (Rev. 8/01) Summons in a Civil Action

ORIGINAL FILED

UNITED STATES DISTRICT COURT

District of _____ South Carolina

MAR 2 5 2004

LARRY W. PROPES, CLERK
CHARLESTON, SC

William B. Tuttle, Jr., Raymond J. Johnson, George H. Kuchen,
John E. Strait, Richard Sirois, William Menkins and James A. Taylor

V.

Daniel Marvin, Trine Day, LLC., and Chicago Review Press,
Incorporated

SUMMONS IN A CIVIL ACTION

CASE NUMBER:

2 04 0948 18

TO: (Name and address of Defendant)

Daniel Marvin
Trine Day, LLC
Chicago Review Press, Incorporated

YOU ARE HEREBY SUMMONED and required to serve on PLAINTIFF'S ATTORNEY (name and address)

an answer to the complaint which is served on you with this summons, within ____20____ days after service of this summons on you, exclusive of the day of service. If you fail to do so, judgment by default will be taken against you for the relief demanded in the complaint. Any answer that you serve on the parties to this action must be filed with the Clerk of this Court within a reasonable period of time after service.

LARRY W. PROPES, Clerk

MAR 2 5 2004

CLERK

(By) DEPUTY CLERK

DATE

We are served with a summons.

11.   Plaintiff George H. Kuchen is a citizen and resident of the State of North Carolina. Plaintiff Kuchen was a Medical Sergeant assigned to Detachment A-424 during the period between November 1965 to March 1966, and was under the command of Captain Marvin. He is the Sgt. Kuchen to whom Defendant Marvin referred in his book "Expendable Elite". In the book, Sgt. Kuchen is alleged to have conspired and committed various violations of his oath to his country, including several violations of the Uniform Code of Military Justice, sedition against his country, treason, failure to obey a direct order, and violating international law and the standing general orders of the Departments of Defense and Army not to cross over into or fire weapons into a friendly nation, Cambodia.

27.   Plaintiffs were libeled and slandered nationwide by the Defendants, injuring the Plaintiffs' reputations as a result of the publication of said book. Plaintiffs also continue to be slandered by Defendants in national events promoting this work. The said falsities in the book "Expendable Elite" are defamatory as it has subjected the Plaintiffs to hatred, ridicule, and contempt, by including but not limited to, readers of the book nationwide and their friends, family members, and fellow and veteran members of the United States Army. The defamatory statements seriously impute criminal conduct by Plaintiffs, and portray Plaintiffs as "loose cannons" in the eyes of the Plaintiffs' fellow United States citizens, including those in the State of South Carolina.

28.   The statements made by the Defendants were libelous and slanderous per se, constituting a false imputation of felonious criminal conduct, giving rise to a general presumption of damages by law not required to be proved by evidence.

2.   grant each of them judgments for damages against all Defendants, jointly and severally, for each claim for relief sought herein in amounts in excess of $100,000 each as compensatory damages;

3.   allow a jury to award punitive damages in favor of Plaintiffs in amounts to be determined by the jury, against all Defendants, jointly and severally'

The "charges" against us. Shown are the offenses alleged by George Kuchen. There were a similar charges pressed by each of the seven plaintiffs. The plaintiffs' expenses and attorneys were provided by the SFA.

B STAR-NEWS | SUNDAY, APRIL 4, 2004

Vietnam vets resist renegade tag in lawsuit

By Ken Little
Staff Writer

A U.S. Army Special Forces "A" team detachment commanded by Green Beret Capt. Daniel Marvin waged an unknown war in Vietnam in 1965 and 1966. Among its top-secret missions was to carry out a CIA-sponsored assassination of Cambodian Crown Prince Norodum Sihanouk.

Mr. Marvin, who retired from the service in 1973 as a lieutenant colonel, recalled his gripping experiences in a book published last year titled *Expendable Elite: One Soldier's Journey Into Covert Warfare*.

There's just one problem, according to a lawsuit filed last week in U.S. District Court in Charleston, S.C.: The book isn't true.

The civil suit was filed by six men who served under Capt. Marvin in an encampment near the Cambodian border, and his Special Forces commander. They are represented by Wilmington lawyer

SEE SUIT | 6B

6B

SUIT
CONTINUED FROM 1B

Benjamin Deaver. "I think they would like to get their reputations back," said Mr. Deaver, who served as a Green Beret in the 1980s and sometimes represents the interests of Special Forces organizations.

Promotional copy for the book on the Internet site of its Oregon-based publisher, TrineDay, promises Mr. Marvin's account will acquaint the reader "with the unique nature of special operations forces" and how covert operations are "masked to permit – even sponsor – assassination, outright purposeful killing of innocents, illegal use of force and bizarre methods in combat operations."

The lawsuit seeks compensatory and punitive damages in excess of $100,000 for each of the plaintiffs, who it says were "libeled and slandered" and portrayed in the book as "loose cannons." TrineDay and the book's distributor, Chicago Review Press, are also named as defendants. Mr. Marvin, reached by telephone Wednesday at his upstate New York home, said he wasn't aware of the lawsuit, but stuck to his guns.

"Almost everything in that book is corroborated by those same people," he said. "Everything in the book is true."

Plaintiffs include three Fayetteville-area residents – George H. Kuchen, Raymond J. Johnson

> "They were proud of what they did, and this book portrays them as rogue warriors."
>
> Benjamin Deaver
> *Lawyer representing Vietnam veterans involved in a lawsuit over claims in a former colleague's book.*

and James A. Taylor. Mr. Marvin's commanding officer in Vietnam, William B. Tuttle, now lives in South Carolina, where the lawsuit was filed. The other plaintiffs live in California, Michigan and Texas.

All take pride in their service with the Special Forces, Mr. Deaver said.

"These men are really the heroes. They were the fathers of the Green Berets, actually," he said. "They were proud of what they did, and this book portrays them as rogue warriors."

In his book, Mr. Marvin wrote that he and his men were working with a Buddhist sect called the Hoa Haos near the Cambodian border when the CIA hatched a plot to assassinate Prince Sihanouk, the country's leader. In the lawsuit, Mr. Tuttle denies he gave Mr. Marvin any orders to cross the border or warned him he would be on his

own if captured.

Mr. Marvin, now 70, wrote he pulled the plug on the mission because the CIA didn't come through on a promise that President Lyndon Johnson would make a public statement condemning the presence of the Viet Cong in Cambodia.

Book publisher Kris Millegan said Wednesday the Special Forces Association was trying to use its influence to prevent sales of the book, which was rejected by mainstream publishers. It has sold about 2,000 copies to date.

"I absolutely stand by the content," Mr. Millegan said. "They're trying to diminish the book," he said, because "it makes Special Forces look bad. This is harassment."

Mr. Marvin, who refers to himself as "Dangerous Dan," said he did not go public with information about his tour in Vietnam until after becoming a practicing Christian in 1984. That experience, he said, compelled him to tell the truth.

Mr. Marvin was interviewed in the 1990s British-produced television documentary, *The Men Who Killed Kennedy*, about the assassination of President John F. Kennedy. In it, he claimed he was approached in August 1965 by the CIA to "terminate" a naval officer serving at Bethesda Naval Hospital who may have been in possession of a 16mm movie film of President Kennedy's autopsy. The man was found dead the next year of a gunshot wound to the head, officially ruled a suicide.

GET CONNECTED StarNews
Call 343-2391 or 1-800-222-2385 to subscribe

Ken Little: 343-2389
ken.little@starnewsonline.com

The Secretary provided an updated concerning the book *"Expendable Elite"*. The Summer issue of **The Drop** has a two page report on a complaint, dated 5 March 04, by 6 members of A-424 and the C-4 Commander (VN 65-66) against Dan Marvin, Trine Day, LLC and the Chicago Preview Press, Inc. The complaint charges that the book, alleged by Dan Marvin to be a truthful account of his tour with Detachment A-424, contains false; libelous; defamatory; embarrassing and humiliating accusations of the actions, conduct, and military services of the plaintiffs. We will keep the membership updated as the case progresses.

The article above is by Ken Little of the *Star News* and the inset at the lower left hand corner is from the Fall 2004 SFA's magazine *The Drop*

**IN THE UNITED STATES DISTRICT COURT
FOR SOUTH CAROLINA
CHARLESTON DIVISION**

FILE NO. 2 04 0948 18

WILLIAM B. TUTTLE, JR.,	)
RAYMOND J. JOHNSON,	)
GEORGE H. KUCHEN,	)
JOHN E. STRAIT,	)
RICHARD SIROIS,	)
WILLIAM MENKINS and	)
JAMES A. TAYLOR,	)
Plaintiffs,	)
	)
v.	)
	)
DANIEL MARVIN,	)
TRINE DAY, LLC., and	)
CHICAGO REVIEW PRESS, INCORPORATED,	)
Defendants.	)

AFFIDAVIT OF GENERAL (*RET. ARVN*) QUANG VAN DANG

I, General Quang Van Dang, on oath and having been duly sworn, hereby depose and say:

1.   In 1966, I commanded all South Vietnamese Armed Forces in the IV Corps area as a Lieutenant General.

2.   Attached hereto, as Attachment "A", is a true and complete copy of a personal letter I wrote to Lt. Col. (LTC) Daniel Marvin (USASF Ret.) while I was in Montreal, Quebec.

3.   I sent the personal letter of Attachment "A" to LTC Daniel Marvin on or about November 10, 1988.

4.   LTC Daniel Marvin has informed me that the personal letter of Attachment "A" was one of a number of documents independently forwarded and/or submitted by LTC Daniel Marvin, during that time period, to George H. W. Bush in connection with LTC Daniel Marvin's

Two page April 2005 affidavit supplied and signed by General Quang Van Dang in support of LTC Marvin case. The plaintiffs' attorneys objected to this evidence and were able to keep it from the jury.

request for further investigative undertakings by the U.S. State Department to facilitate an immigrant Visa grant for my person.

5.   An immigrant Visa was issued to my person on or about September 7, 1989.

6.   I make this affidavit because my health is poor, and I want to memorialize, under oath, my recollections of that time period with particular specificity to the letter of Attachment "A".

Signed under the pains and penalties of perjury this 28 day of April, 2005.

Quang Van Dang
Quang Van Dang

==

On Wed, 28 Dec 2005 06:57:05 -0500 "Thomas Polgar" <▓ writes:
> From Tom Polgar: Your book arrived December 37. Thanks and
> particularly for the inscription dated December 20. I only wish I
> could have done more.
>   On page 322 your refer to the April 1973 meeting of President
> Nixon with President Thieu in San Clemente, California. They met
> several times during Thieu's visit. I was present at one of those
> meetings. I remember distinctly the promises President Nixon gave,
> in the presence of Secretary of State William Rogers, the incoming
> American Ambassador Graham Martin and others.
>   The betrayal of South Vietnam was the bitterest and most
> traumatic experiences of my life. It should be noted that the
> Americans working in Vietnam, including Ambassador Martin and
> myself, were betrayed, too. We were never advised that the policy of
> supporting South Vietnam has changed. President Thieu was never so
> advised. Had we been told, we might have been able to embark on a
> different course of action prior to the North Vietnamese attack and
> perhaps found the means toward a more dignified exit. I could not
> bring myself to believe that we would betray and abandon the country
> we created. That we did so, soured my views toward government
> service and was a big factor in my voluntary, early retirement.
>   Thanks again. Although I was in Vietnam later than you, the land
> and the people were the same. the many pictures in your book brought
> back memories.

Bottom half of page: An email from former Saigon CIA Station Chief Thomas Polgar that corroborates the fact that our nation betrayed and abandoned the South Vietnamese.

The Register-Guard

SECTION **F**

SUNDAY, DECEMBER 18, 2005

Team Editor • Ilene Aleshire
338-2377 • ialeshire@guardnet.com

Business

Money and Technology

THOMAS BOYD / *The Register-Guard*

Kris Millegan *runs Trine Day Press out of his home near Walterville. The press is being sued by the Special Forces Association, a fraternal group that disputes stories told in a Vietnam memoir by retired Air Force Lt. Col. Daniel Marvin.*

Soldiers association sues independent publisher over Vietnam book

BATTLE FOR A WAR STORY

BY KAREN McCOWAN
The Register-Guard

WALTERVILLE — A tiny publishing house here is in the cross-hairs of a $700,000 lawsuit backed by the Special Forces Association, a fraternal organization for current and former U.S. military special operatives.

On the one side are Kris Millegan's Trine Day Press and one of its authors, retired U.S. Air Force Lt. Col. Daniel Marvin, who have been targeted in the case. On the other are seven men who served with Marvin in Vietnam during 1966 and 1967.

They contend that Marvin's book "Expendable Elite: One Soldier's Journey Into Covert Warfare," provided a "false, libelous, defamatory, embarrassing and humiliating" account of their activities at An Phu near the Cambodian border. They seek $100,000 each in general, special and punitive damages.

Millegan said the case already has racked up nearly $50,000 in legal expenses, and it could bankrupt his small press, which has published just eight books and sold a total of 40,000 copies since its creation four years ago.

But he declined to agree to the men's demand that he reissue the book as a work of fiction. He stands by Marvin's account, saying that some of the defendants verified it on tape at Marvin's request after he sent them early drafts in 1988.

"I have audio tapes from the people who are now suing me, not only confirming Col. Marvin's story, but saying he could use their names," Millegan said.

His willingness to challenge the lawsuit has won admiration from other small, independent publishers, said Teresa Kao, owner of Our Town Publishing in Portland and

former president of the Northwest Association of Book Publishers.

"Small publishers typically can't afford to carry liability insurance," Kao said. "If someone decides to sue you, there just isn't money for this sort of thing.

"Too often you see people say, 'I'll take this book off the market if you'll make this lawsuit go away,' " Kao said. "But Kris sees this really as a kind of quest. He is just going ahead with it because he believes it needs to be done."

A South Carolina U.S. District Court jury began hearing the case on Halloween day,

but a mistrial was declared two days later after one of the plaintiffs' attorneys suffered a medical emergency.

Judge David Norton has scheduled a new trial to begin Jan. 23.

In their opening statement, the plaintiff's attorneys, Ben and Bobby Deaver, acknowledged the audio tapes, but say their clients thought they were being asked to "vet" a work of fiction.

At particular issue are Marvin's contention that he was assigned to assassinate Cam-

Please turn to **PUBLISHER,** *Page F4*

WAYNE EASTBURN / *The Register-Guard*

Trine Day's *books often include allegations of conspiracies, such as linking Yale's Skull and Bones society with drug running.*

SUPER BOWL SET
Steelers overpower Broncos in Denver;
Seattle defense pounds Carolina. **Sports, 1C**

The Post and Courier
THE SOUTH'S OLDEST DAILY NEWSPAPER

January 23, 2006 · Charleston · North Charleston, S.C.   **MONDAY**   Founded 1803 ★ 50 cents

Briefly

THE POST AND COURIER
FRIDAY, JANUARY 27, 2006.**3B**

Libel trial over book continues

Ex-Green Berets trade charges

BY SCHUYLER KROPF
The Post and Courier

Like the Vietnam War, a closely watched libel trial over a book about the Green Berets is going on longer than most people predicted.

Jurors probably won't start deliberating until Monday over whether allegations in a book on the elite Army troopers are fact or fiction.

The four days of testimony so far at the U.S. District Courthouse in Charleston over "Expendable Elite: One Soldier's Journey into Covert Warfare" has brought a series of

No leads yet in oting death

oudy Sunday, a few n the open garage of w Street, while others the driveway. , it appeared to be a ernoon. But inside, led the house to offer dolences.

" said Cassandra Bai- ar-old Robert Bailey, lled at about 9:30 the let likely intended for

Authorities were still searching for the gunman Sunday and had yet to receive a solid lead, North Charleston police spokesman Spencer Pryor said.

Robert was killed while at home with his family watching television. He was in the living room with his 4-year-old sister watching the Disney Channel. His parents, Cassandra and Richard Bailey, were in another room watching "America's Most Wanted." An older brother and sister were not at home at the time.

A ruckus outside caught the boy's attention. Curious, he pulled back a thin

Please see ROBERT, Page 5A

BAILEY FAMILY
Robert Bailey, 11, was killed Saturday after being shot by a stray bullet while he was in his house.

alliance hurdle for U.S.

Book's claims to go before judge

Plot to assassinate foreign leader alleged

BY SCHUYLER KROPF
The Post and Courier

The book's dialogue reads like the script from "Apocalypse Now."

"You want us to assassinate Crown Prince Sihanouk?" the Green Beret asks.

"Yes," answers an alleged CIA man.

"Your job," the agent continued, "will be fo bring about his death and make it appear to have been done by the Viet

There was considerable coverage of the trial by the local Charleston newspaper. Reporter Schuyler Kropf wasn't in the courtroom for the initial playing of the plaintiffs audiotapes, but was there for some of the subsequent audiotapes. And although the tapes were a crucial part of the trial, they were never mentioned. And as can be seen by the headline below the paper trumpeted the "spin" version of the outcome of the trial, even though LTC Marvin and TrineDay were the clear victors having been compelled to defend themselves in court and prevailing.

The Post and Courier

Inside GMLc
What's to know about sweetgrass? Actually, a lot. **2B**

LOCAL & STATE

Index
Business 9B
Obituaries 4,5B
Weather...........14B

Tuesday, January 31, 2006   On the Web: charleston.net   Section B

Green Beret suit ends in draw

Jury decides neither side defamed the other in legal fight over book

BY SCHUYLER KROPF
The Post and Courier

A $700,000 defamation lawsuit over a book that says U.S. Green Berets illegally fired into neutral Cambodia in 1966 and nearly committed mutiny during the Vietnam War ended in a draw Monday.

A jury of four men and four women ruled that neither side in the legal fight over the book "Expendable Elite" defamed the other.

The book's author claimed victory for the truth, while lawyers for the Green Be-

rets said their fight might not be over.

After deliberating for 2½ hours, a jury at the U.S. District Courthouse in Charleston said the seven Green Berets who sued retired Green Beret Lt. Col. Daniel Marvin over his portrayal of their actions failed to prove that his written words defamed them.

In tandem, the jury said Marvin failed to prove his claim the ex-soldiers defamed him when they made public statements that his book is "100 percent lies."

Both sides had different interpretations of the outcome.

"This is a big victory for these guys," said Chris Ogiba, lawyer for Marvin and his publisher, Trine Day Press, which also was found not liable.

Marvin said the verdict vindicated his story that Americans were fighting in Cambodia early in the war, that the Green Berets were poised to help assassinate Cambodian Prince Norodum Sihanouk, and were ready to fire on friendly forces rather than surrender a base and put a tribe of allied Vietnamese natives into jeopardy.

"I'm glad to see the victory of truth over evil," Marvin said through tears.

Charleston lawyer David Collins said Marvin's claims remain in doubt because the jury didn't rule whether his book was true, only on whether the seven ex-Green Berets were defamed.

During his closing argument, Collins said Marvin's account doesn't mesh with the historical record, and that the area around An Phu was mostly quiet and peaceful in 1966. He called Marvin the "Walter Mitty of Vietnam" because, as a quartermaster in charge of supply and logistics, he never would have been exposed to such daring military actions, Collins said.

Like the fictional character Mitty — a henpecked husband with extravagant daydreams— "everything he (Marvin) saw in day-to-day life was blown totally out of proportion," Collins said.

Marvin published his story in 2003, saying it detailed how covert operations are "masked to permit, even sponsor,

Please see BOOK, Page 3B

The cover of Daniel Marvin's book.

Cazenovia Republican

Volume 200, No. 6
Feb. 8 to 14, 2006

Home of Ben Wightman

75 CENTS

cnylink.com

Cleared

Dan Marvin returns home victorious

BY WILLIE KIERNAN

LTC Dan Marvin is famous for not going down without a fight. After being accused of defamation of character and libel by seven ex-members of the Green Berets, he went to trial and proved his case. A jury found him not guilty and his personal saga for truth continues.

Marvin, a retired lieutenant colonel and a resident of Cazenovia, is also an author. He wrote a book called, "Expendable Elite: One Soldier's Journey Into Covert Warfare" in which he detailed some of his missions in Vietnam, including how the CIA asked him to assassinate the Cambodian crown prince. After he ultimately refused, the government ordered an attack on his camp. A South Vietnamese general intervened and Marvin lived to write about it. However, he was accused of printing false claims, and went to trial in the Federal Courthouse in Charleston, SC.

"The CIA does not like the book because I accused them of trying to kill me and my men," said Marvin. "Everybody, with the exception of my publisher, thought I was going to lose. I feel vindicated that my book can now be internationally known as the truth."

Marvin had endured 13 years of 120 rejections and a $40,000 debt when he received a phone call from Kris Millegan, the publisher of TrineDay Press in Oregon.

"My background, besides being a songwriter," said Millegan, "is my father was branch chief of the CIA in Asia in the 40s and 50s. He left in 1959 when all the drug running started. My parents were telling me lies since I was four years old. So now I don't always believe them when they tell me a cover story."

Claiming that "truth is the first casualty of war," TrineDay's intent is to bring suppressed views and works to a wider audience. The manuscript, which began as a military diary, was rejected over and over, not because of its inauthenticity, but because of its nature.

"I have another book coming out," said Marvin. "It's going to be called "Devious Elite" with details about Martin Luther King's assassination and who killed Kennedy. That's the real reason they're coming after me."

Marvin claimed the Special Forces Association, membership of roughly 10,000 ex-Green Berets, was funding the case to keep his books off the shelves. They used the trial to bleed the author and publisher of their assets.

"Although my company was named in the charge," said Millegan, "I could've gotten out of it. But I figured my understanding of covert warfare would be helpful. He was carrying the burden for quite a while. We developed a very interesting relationship, sometimes sharing motel rooms together. The colonel is quite a man, with a long list of achievements. Something else for someone who didn't graduate high school."

The jury deliberation lasted only two hours including time for lunch.

"I knew all they could sue me for was publishing top secret information and naming a CIA operative," said Marvin. "And if they did, they were admitting the truth."

Marvin has a wife, three children, 11 grandchildren and two great-grandchildren. One of his grandsons is stationed in Iraq.

"I'm still a patriot. We have the best government, the best military, the best special forces; but there are some evil people in powerful positions," said Marvin. "It's important to get out the fact," said Marvin, "that this book is true."

Retired LTC Dan Marvin nurses one of his cups of coffee at Common Grounds

PUBLISHER WINS CASE

Embattled publisher Kris Millegan of Walterville sent a message this week that his company TrineDay and author retired Lt. Col. Daniel Marvin were found not guilty of libel and defamation in a South Carolina U.S. District Court.

"This verdict was reached after extremely long and complex jury instructions by Federal Judge David Norton," says Millegan. The jury was unanimous after two hours of deliberations, he says, and "the jurors all asked to have their exhibit books signed."

A counterclaim against the plaintiffs was also decided by the jury, but not upheld. Millegan says he hopes through the courts to recoup some of his $100,000 in legal fees.

The $700,000 suit was filed by seven men who served with Marvin in Vietnam. They objected to his book, *Expendable Elite: One Soldier's Journey Into Covert Warfare*, saying the book provided a "false, libelous, defamatory, embarrassing and humiliating" account of their activities in the war.

"We won the case," says Millegan. "Our defense was truth."

The plaintiffs, backed by the Special Forces Association, have threatened to appeal the verdict, says Millegan. — *TJT*

News stories in LTC Marvin's and Kris Millegan's local papers

IV Corps S.F. combatants get cash reward

Saigon Daily News 7 June 66

SAIGON, June 6 (VP)— Lt. Gen. Dang Van Quang commander of the IV Corps last Saturday morning visited a number of outposts near the Cambodian border, in Chau Doc province.

On this occasion Gen. Quang presented a reward of VN$64,500 to outstanding soldiers of the Den Nam Special Forces camp in An Phu district.

The commander of the camp briefed Gen. Quang on the achievements of the Special Forces combatants from May 19 to May 23. During this period the combatants drove out approximately three VC battalions who attacked Khanh An, Khanh Binh and Binh Thien outposts. The Forces killed 170 VC and captured 47 others, along with four crew-served and 18 individual weapons. Besides, nearly 200 other VC either dead or wounded, were reported carried away by their comrades.

This visit was a part of an inspection tour of various outposts along the Cambodian border.

Accompanying the IV Corps commander on the trip were Brig. Gen. Lam Quang Thi, commander of the 9th Infantry Division and Major Nguyen Thanh Chuan, commander of the Special Forces in the IV Corps.

VC Attack Border Posts

S. Post 21 May 66

SAIGON MAY 20 (AP) — Viet Cong troops attacked two Vietnamese outposts Thursday near the Cambodian border about 110 miles (177km) west of Saigon but were driven off by combined air ground, and artillery fire, a Vietnamese spokesman said.

The posts North of An Phu, were manned by Vietnamese militia.

The spokesman said 59 Viet Cong were killed in the fighting which he described as intense. Vietnamese casualties at each post were listed as light.

The government militiamen captured a large stand of arms including machineguns, submachineguns and individual weapons among them one rifle of Russian make. Four Claymore mines also were seized together with 89 mines of other types, the spokesman said.

He said the Viet Cong were seen carrying many wounded from the field.

Contemporary news accounts from Saigon newspapers about some of the events of *Expendable Elite*. The plaintiffs' attorneys objected to this evidence and were able to keep it from the jury.

TOP SECRET

B. (TS) JCS PLANNING   1

   1. (TS) In October 1965, the Joint Chiefs of Staff requested   2
a study be made on US policy and alternative US courses of action   3
to deal with Cambodian support of the Viet Cong. As a result of   4
the study, the JCS concluded that certain courses of action   5
were appropriate and necessary for immediate implementation in   6
dealing with the problem. One of these actions provided for the   7
covert paramilitary operations in Cambodia to reduce the infiltration 8
of personnel and material and to collect intelligence information.*   9

   2. (TS) While higher authority, in early 1966, had determined   10
not to seek a policy decision for conducting this type of para-   11
military operation, it was considered prudent that planning pro-   12
ceed in the event less serious undertakings should prove ineffec-   13
tive and the problem with Cambodia grew.**   14

   3. (TS) CINCPAC, in providing a concept for these paramilitary   15
operations, emphasized the need of organizing and equipping forces   16
and assets to face the growing problems of the use of Cambodia   17
as a sanctuary by the VC and the NVA. CINCPAC proposed that   18
besides intelligence agents, approximately 16 reconnaissance teams   19
and small exploitation forces (four companies) should be organized   20
without delay. These units would be deployed against targets de-   21
veloped by the tactical maneuvering of US forces in areas bordering   22
Cambodia. Until events required deployment in Cambodia, it was   23
determined that they could be fully employed in SVN. CINCPAC   24
also envisioned that fast, shallow draft boats and motorized   25
units, operating from a base in the Gulf of Siam, be used in   26
Cambodian waters for the purpose of agent infiltration, sabotage,   27

---

* (TS) JCSM-812-65 dated 12 November 1965   28
** (TS) JCS Msg, 250001Z Jan 1966   29

                                                                          30

A TOP SECRET planning paper from the Joint Chiefs of Staff of the US Military that states unequivocally, "One of these actions [based on an October 1965 JCS study] provided for the covert paramilitary operations in Cambodia to reduce the infiltration of personnel and material and to collect intelligence information." The plaintiffs' attorneys objected to this evidence and were able to keep it from the jury.

1. General Situation: Intelligence reports received on 7 May, indicated that a VC meeting had taken place on 24 April to discuss and formulate plans for attacks against outposts in An Phu district, Chau Doc Province, during the rainy season. Participants in the meeting consisted of the Chau Doc Province Commissioner, An Phu District Commissioner, 364th VC Battalion Commander (AKA 521st Bn), and the 264th VC Battalion Commander (AKA 261st Bn). Intelligence reports continued, indicating that an attack would occur in the immediate future. On 18 May current intelligence strongly indicated that two VC battalions, the 364th and 261st, would attack CIDG FOB's and PF outposts at Khanh-An, Phon-Hoi, Phu Hum and Don Ki that night. Based on this accumulation of intelligence, all CIDG and PF units in the area were placed on a 100% alert. An ambush force, consisting of one platoon CIDG, 1 platoon PF, 1 VNSF and 2 USASF, was dispatched to guard a vital bridge along the main supply routes to the FOB's and OP's, and also to act as the initial reaction force for units in the northern protion of the district in the event of a VC attack.

2. Concept of Operation:

   a. At 0325 hours on 19 May, the 261st VC battalion reinforced by the 367th VC battalion with an estimated strength of 700, launched an attack against the CIDG company at Khanh Binh and completely surrounded their position. The VC force employed 81mm mortars, 60mm mortars, 57mm recoilless rifle, 3.5 rocket launcher, LMG and small arm fire, and conducted "Human Wave" type assaults every 15-20 minutes. Simultaneously the PF outpost at Khanh An, manned by a platoon of PF and the reconnaissance platoon from Camp An Phu, came under attack by an estimated force of 200 VC from the 512th VC battalion. The 512th Bn employed 81mm mortar, 57mm Recoilless Rifle, LMG and small arms fire during the assault. Anti-aircraft guns were also employed upon the arrival of a "Puff" ship over the area. At 0530 hours, the ambush force at the bridge site ambushed a VC demolition squad attempting to blow the bridge. At 0340 hours on the 19th, the PF outposts at Khanh Binh, Phu Hum, Phon Hoi, and Don Ki came under harrassing small arms fire, which continued for approximately two hours at each location.

   b. At 0515 hours, a reaction force of 3 platoons CIDG, 2 VNSF, 1 USASF and the VN Camp Commander departed An Phu, linked up with the ambush party at the bridge then proceeded to Khanh Binh to relieve the pressure on the surrounded CIDG company. By the time the reaction force reached Khanh Binh, at 0700 hours, the VC had penetrated and were occupying 10 meters of the outer perimeter defensive trench. Effective heavy fire was placed on the VC lines by the reaction force, forcing the VC to withdraw from Khanh Binh into Cambodia. From their sanctuary in Cambodia the VC continued to place 81mm mortar and LMG fire on the CIDG positions until 1030 hours. At 1100 hours, the VC broke off the attack on the Khanh An OP and withdrew north approximately 2 kilometers.

   c. On 20 May at 0300 hours, a company of VC launched a second attack against the PF OP at Khanh An. The OP at this time was being supported by a company of Regional Force troops, causing the VC to be unsuccessful in their attack which they broke off at 0320 hours. A second attack against the CIDG company (now reinforced) at Khanh Binh was initiated

The 31 July 1966 Inclosure 13 to Section II to "Operational Report on Lessons Learned" corroborates details of the five-day battle in the Khanh Binh and Khanh An areas of An Phu District.

by an estimated 500 VC at 0130 hours on 20 May. A second reaction force consisting of 3 platoons of CIDG, 2 VNSF and 2 USASF departed An Phu at 0500 hours. An 81mm mortar, manned by 2 VNSF and 2 CIDG, was set up approximately 1800 meters from the battle area to give supporting fire while the remainder of the reaction force moved into contact with the VC who had once again surrounded the CIDG positions at Khanh Binh. The VC broke contact at 0600 hours and once again withdrew into Cambodia. At 0700 hours, the CIDG company was withdrawn from Khanh Binh and replaced with a company of fresh troops. Although the VC had withdrawn from the CIDG positions at Khanh Binh, the PF OP, 2 kilometers north, was still surrounded and receiving harrassing fire. A relief operation for the OP was requested from Province headquarters, but was not approved. However, a CIDG force moved to the OP and cleared the immediate area.

d. A third attack was launched against the CIDG post at Khanh Binh by an estimated 200 VC at 2045 hours, 20 May. This assault was limited to MG and small arms fire which indicated that the VC had spent their crew served weapon ammunition or were preparing for a large scale assault. A flare ship and a gun ship arrived over the area approximately 25 minutes later giving illumination and fire support. Under heavy suppressing fire from the "Puff" ship, the VC were forced to withdraw, limiting their actions to the south side of the CIDG positions until finally breaking off the attack at 0300 hours on 21 May.

e. On 21 May, a temporary FOB was established at the Don Ki II outpost, consisting of 1 platoon of PF and 2 USASF. An 81mm mortar was mounted, with the capability of supporting both Khanh Binh and Khanh An. At 2000 hours the VC launched a fourth attack against the CIDG company at Khanh Binh with an estimated strength of 200. A "puff" ship arrived over the area at 2200 hours, providing illumination and fire support, but was greatly hampered by .50 caliber MG fire from a Cambodian outpost approximately 2 kilometers from Khanh Binh. The VC broke off the attack at 2210 hours, but continued to harass the CIDG positions with 81mm mortar fire until 2345 hours.

f. A fifth attack against the CIDG at Khanh Binh was launched at 2030 hours on 22 May by an estimated 200 VC, supported by 60mm mortar and MG fire. The CIDG forces were supported by 81mm mortar fire from the temporary FOB at Don Ki and 155mm howitzer fire from An Phu. The VC attack was broken up and they were forced to withdraw at 2110 hours.

g. On 24 May, a multi company search and destroy mission was mounted to clear the VC from the area thus preventing them from gaining a foothold. Friendly elements consisted of 1 company Mike Force, 1 company of KKK, 1 company of CIDG, 2 VNSF and 2 USASF. The operation was initiated with 155mm howitzer and 81mm mortar concentrations being fired into the area. Upon entering the operational area the Mike Force established heavy contact with the VC at 0910 hours. An airstrike was received at 1055 hours, covering the area with rockets, napalm and strafing runs in close support of the attacking ground forces. At 1325 hours, contact with the VC was lost and the operation was terminated.

h. Throughout the entire period of 19-24 May, CIDG and PF forces in the northern half of An Phu district were in continual contact with the VC.

INCLOSURE 13 TO SECTION II to Operational Report on Lessons Learned (RCS CSCFO-28 (R1)) 31 July 1966

2

3. Conclusions

a. The intelligence net employed in An Phu district was a well organized and highly effective force, providing extremely accurate information in a timely manner.

b. The CIDG and PF forces maintained a high state of morale and fighting effectiveness throughout the period and defended their positions in an outstanding manner.

c. Had the ambush party not been sent to the bridge site on the night of 18 May, the VC would have successfully destroyed the bridge, causing a lengthy delay in the reaction forces reaching the battle area which could have resulted in a decisive victory for the VC.

d. Air support that was received was exceptionally well executed and proved highly instrumental in the defense of the FOB and OP's, however air support was lacking in quantity as indicated below:

TYPE	REQUESTED	APPROVED	DISAPPROVED
Flare Ship	3	2	1
Gun Ships (Helicopter)	2	1	1
TAC Air	2	1	1
MED EVAC	4	1 (US)	3
TOTAL:	11	5	6

INCLOSURE 13 TO SECTION II to Operational Report on Lessons Learned (RCS CSGPO-28 (R1)) 31 July 1966.

3

The table at Page 497 shows graphically that Dan Marvin commanded/advised more CIDG, RF and PF fighting forces in the IV Corps than any other A-Team Commander. The plaintiffs' attorneys objected to this evidence and were able to keep it from the jury.

1. GENERAL — IV CTZ

DET	LOC	COORD	DATE STARTED	VNSF CO	NO. VNSF	USASF CO	DMO/USASF	CIDG	RF	FF	WPNS ISS	CCAP TNG	LIKE FORCE	MISSION
C-4	CAN THO	VS843116	JAN 63	MAJ CHUAN	17/43	LTCOL DALLAS	12/44	1/166						CC
B-41	MOC HOA	XS030909	FEB 65	CPT HUAN		MAJ CONN	9/15							CC/S
A-411	BINH HUNG	VQ848818	JUN 65			CPT HARRINGTON	2/10		7/820	2/140		113		CIDG/SPS
A-412	CAI CAI	WT562076	APR 65	LT NGHI	3/10	CPT HEDEGAN	2/11	2/149			75			CIDG/BS/SS
A-419	BINH THANH THON	WT868032	NOV 64	CPT TAN	3/7	CPT O'CONNELL	2/10	5/721	1/110	9/342				CIDG/BS/SS
A-414	MOC HOA	XS028899	JAN 64	CPT HUAN	5/13	CPT BRIDGEWATER	2/10	4/465	2/284	10/420				CIDG/BS/SS
A-415	TUYEN NHON	XS273773	APR 65	LT AN	3/11	CPT VAT	3/11	5/541	1/87	4/163	151			CIDG/SS
A-416	KIEN QUAN II	VS974757	OCT 65	LT GIANG	3/13	CPT MARDECK	3/11	4/367	3/326	9/171	29			CC/S/SS
B-42	CHAU DOC	WT131842	APR 65	MAJ KIEM	4/13	LTCOL BRENER	8/14	4/436 46	9/1637	68/1616				CIDG/BS/SS
A-421	HA TIEN	VS437447	APR 65	CPT NOI	3/8	CPT HUDSON	2/7	3/526	1/138	3/122	11			CIDG/BS
A-422	VINH GIA	VS762612	AUG 64	CPT NAM	4/11	CPT SMITH	2/9	4/533	71	16/543	36			CIDG/BS/S
A-423	TINH BINH	VS953712	APR 64	CPT SON	3/10	CPT HOWELL	2/7	4/563	3/336	17/525				CIDG/BS/S
A-424	AN PHU	VB105945	OCT 64	MAJ PHOI	10/10	CPT MARVIN	2/2	6/766	4/435	23/834	99			CIDG/BS/S
A-425	THUONG THOI	WS313955	MAY 66	MAJ DANH	3/9	CPT MC COY	4/12	4/526	4/435	20/584		128		CIDG/BS/S
A-426	TRI TON	WS005518	MAY 65			CPT THACKER	1/8		5/595					SS
A-427	PHU QUOC	US867295	FEB 65	MAJ KIEU	3/9	CPT SLOKA	2/11	4/507	5/526	3/82				CIDG/SS
A-428	TAN CHAU	WS291936	MAY 65	CPT KICH	2/5	CPT MILES	3/10	1/231		24/901				CIDG/SS
A-429	BA XOAI	XS956628	JAN 66	CPT KAPP		CPT KAPP	3/11	5/735			18	102		CIDG
A-430	DON PHUC	WT524004	JAN 66	CPT BAUL	3/16	CPT TOPP	3/12							HF
TOTALS:					69/188		69/225	56/7298	44/5644	208/6443	419	343	409	

Postscript
Bobby Deaver, Esq.

It was once written, "When men and women of good conscience arise in search of truth, all things are made equal and whole once again."

Evil men and organized criminal gangs have always existed in the human experience. Paraphrasing the sentiments of Saint Augustine in *The City of God*, "They ruled by sheer force of will with impunity. It was discovery of their evil deeds that did them in, when the light of truth showed into the void of darkness they had created."

So it was on that fateful day of reckoning for Bobby Deaver and the Special Forces Association at Federal District Court in Charleston, South Carolina, during mid-January 2006. Bobby Deaver, a former Special Forces warrior and an experienced lawyer, was carrying the water in a futile libel suit against LTC Dan Marvin over his book *Expendable Elite*, a true tell-it-all, about how our brave soldiers may come to fear forces within our own government more than any enemy.

Living in hell is a specialty acquired by those men who are trained to be our nation's very best, those willing to lay down their lives for the "national destiny," freedom, and the common good.

"War is Hell, and Hell is War. There is no equal in human cruelty." These words were uttered by my uncle, former Sgt. Ernest Whigham, who served for an eternity on the front lines in World War II under "Old Blood and Guts," General George Patton, a merciless old warrior who lived his life in search of a battlefield.

The horror my uncle Ernest never overcame was his inability to control his own men from raping and murdering innocent citizens of captured cities and villages, and the infamous orders from General Patton to execute all German prisoners, in direct violation of the Geneva Convention. Uncle Earnest returned home to America a wild man, who would never forget the whites of their eyes, their tears, the sight of them down on their knees, begging for a mercy that would not come from the end of his revolver.

Upon his return home, he would often take his rifle and disappear for days, deep into the silence of the woods, hunting Germans and hiding from unseen ghosts who he believed were out to kill him, to silence him and his conscience once and for all, fearing if he talked of our crimes against humanity and our barbarity, surely the nation would suffer.

Maybe, that's what Bobby Deaver and the plaintiffs had had in mind when they entered the courtroom at Charleston for the first round back in October of 2005. But soon, Deaver was confronted with damning testimony by Dan's own men, the plaintiffs now forced by their shiftless leaders to live in fear, to recant all that they said was true in the tell-all book.

Did Deaver, faced with the prospect of having to stare down the truth before this jury, simply walk away and head out the door to Roper Hospital? At Roper he checked himself into the emergency room for treatment of what he would later describe as an upper-GI problem.

After an hour-long telephone conversation with Deaver a few weeks later, it seemed to me that it had been a desperate attempt to avoid facing that jury and having to choke on the truth for lunch. As an experienced heart patient, I can share my speculations with you.

By his own admission, Deaver had suffered a silent heart attack in the mid '90s, and every time he gets an EKG, it shows that he's had or is having a heart attack. Given this history and/or presentation, any good ER physician is going to keep someone overnight for observation. And, according to Deaver by phone with me, there he was, in the hospital, until checking out at 7:00 A.M. the next morning.

Deaver knew all too well that Colonel Marvin and his publisher were stretched financially by attorneys' fees, hotel rooms, flights and meals for witnesses, etc., and by checking himself into the emergency room of Roper Hospital at Charleston, and then not returning to the courtroom that next morning, he effectively forced the judge to declare a mistrial, one that would cost Colonel Marvin and his publisher another round of expenses that they might not be able to bear: defeat by lack of resources.

It's a trick as old as the legal profession itself, and after talking with Deaver, who I think feared disbarment over the tactic if discovered, I became convinced that this is what he had done. Bobby Deaver promised he would fax me a copy of the Roper Hospital admission and discharge summary-report.

It never came, but at least Bobby Deaver and the people who manufacture darkness have lost at trial. They lost to the light of truth shone by Colonel Dan in this exciting book.

John Caylor
Investigative Reporter
Editor of *Insider-Magazine.com*

Jaded Tasks
Brass Plates. Black Ops, & Big Oil - The Blood Politics of George Bush & Co.
BY WAYNE MADSEN

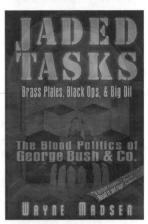

This investigative account details how America's economic and intelligence associations with Saudi Arabia and Pakistan led to the devastating September 11 attacks and illustrates the role that private military companies are playing in George W. Bush's "new world order." Based on personal interviews, never-before-published classified documents, and extensive research, this examination details the criminal forces thought to rule the world today—the Bush cartel, Russian-Ukranian-Israeli mafia, and Wahhabist Saudi terror financiers—revealing links between these groups and disastrous events such as 9/11.   Paperback: **$19.95**, 320 Pages, 5.5 x 8.5

Fixing America
Breaking the Strangehold of Corporate Rule, Big Media, and the Religious Right
BY JOHN BUCHANAN, FOREWORD BY JOHN MCCONNELL

An explosive analysis of what ails the United States
An award-winning investigative reporter provides a clear, honest diagnosis of corporate rule, big media, and the religious right in this damning analysis. Exposing the darker side of capitalism, this critique raises alarms about the security of democracy in today's society, including the rise of the corporate state, the insidious role of professional lobbyists, the emergence of religion and theocracy as a right-wing political tactic, the failure of the mass media, and the sinister presence of an Orwellian neo-fascism. Softcover: **$19.95**, (ISBN 0-975290681) 216 Pages, 5.5 x 8.5

Ambushed
Secrets of the Bush Family, the Stolen Presidency,
9-11, and 2004
BY TOBY ROGERS

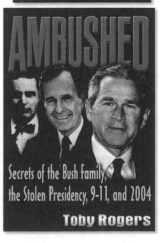

A searing examination of the lies and intrigue that brought the Bush family to power
Based on more than a decade of research, this exposé presents troubling information about America's first family and its second member to become president, George W. Bush. Revealed are the Bush administration's deceptions about the September 11 terrorist attacks and the resulting cover-up, the role of long-time Bush family friend Charles W. Kane in tampering with contentious Florida ballots, and the details behind Prescott Bush's stint as the managing director of a Nazi bank. The Bush family's ongoing association with the mysterious Skull and Bones society is also explored. This alternative history sheds light on the darker side of the powerful Bush family that has been ignored by the mainstream media.
Softcover: **$14.95** (ISBN: 0972020772) • 150 pages • Size: 6 x 9

Dr. Mary's Monkey
How the Unsolved Murder of a Doctor, a Secret Laboratory in New Orleans and Cancer-Causing Monkey Viruses are Linked to Lee Harvey Oswald, the JFK Assassination and Emerging Global Epidemics
EDWARD T. HASLAM (AUTHOR), JIM MARRS (FOREWORD BY)

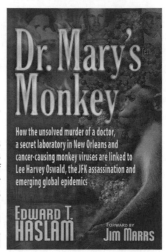

Evidence of top-secret medical experiments and coverups of clinical blunders

The 1964 murder of a nationally known cancer researcher sets the stage for this gripping exposé of medical professionals enmeshed in covert government operations over the course of three decades. Following a trail of police records, FBI files, cancer statistics, and medical journals, this revealing book presents evidence of a web of medical secret-keeping that began with the handling of evidence in the JFK assassination and continued apace, sweeping doctors into coverups of cancer outbreaks, contaminated polio vaccine, the arrival of the AIDS virus, and biological weapon research using infected monkeys.

Softcover: **$19.95** (ISBN: 0977795306) • 320 pages • Size: 5 1/2 x 8 1/2

Welcome To Terrorland
Mohammed Atta & the 9-11 Cover-up in Florida
BY DANIEL HOPSICKER

Drug-trafficking, an FBI cover-up, silenced witnesses, and other reasons why the true story has never been told.

This in-depth investigation into the associations of Mohamed Atta and other terrorist pilots in Venice, Florida, as they prepared for the 9/11 attacks discloses that the FBI led a massive postattack cover-up designed to conceal their knowledge of the terrorists' activities. Unreported stories about the rampant drug-trafficking of the financier behind the flight school the terrorist pilots attended are fully discussed, with attention to the stunning evidence that the CIA was aware that hundreds of Arab flight students were pouring into southwest Florida. This examination of the conspiracy behind the 9/11 investigation and the CIA complicity in the illegal activities that allowed the known terrorists' activities to continue offers truth behind the "official" story of the attacks.

Hardcover: **$29.95** (ISBN 0970659164), • 408 pages • Size: 6 x 9

a MADCOW PRESS book

Without Smoking Gun
Was the Death of Lt. Cmdr. William Pitzer part of the JFK Assassination Conspiracy?
BY KENT HIENER, FOREWORD BY DANIEL MARVIN

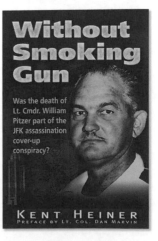

This shocking account of intrigue, lies, and governmental complicity provides inexplicable evidence that suggests a larger conspiracy behind JFK's assassination. Three years after Kennedy's assassination, Lieutenant William Bruce Pitzer, who was reputed to have film that refuted the conclusions of JFK's official autopsy, was found dead in his office at the National Naval Medical Center in Bethesda, Maryland. In 1995, a retired special forces captain claimed that a representative of the CIA recruited him to assassinate Pitzer. Revelations of a possible conspiracy within a conspiracy raise larger questions of the measures taken to suppress the truth and the potential dangers of a government that operates outside the law.

America's Secret Establishment

An Introduction to the Order of Skull & Bones

BY ANTONY C. SUTTON

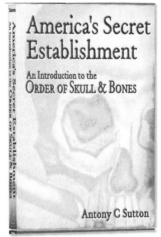

The book that first exposed the story behind America's most powerful secret society

For 170 years they have met in secret. From out of their initiates come presidents, senators, judges, cabinet secretaries, and plenty of spooks. They are the titans of finance and industry and have now installed a third member as United States President George W. Bush. This intriguing behind-the-scenes look documents Yale's secretive society, the Order of the Skull and Bones, and its prominent members, numbering among them Tafts, Rockefellers, Pillsburys, and Bushes. Far from being a campus fraternity, the society is more concerned with the success of its members in the post-collegiate world. Included are a verified membership list, rare reprints of original Order materials revealing the interlocking power centers dominated by Bonesmen, and a peek inside the Tomb, their 140-year-old private clubhouse.

ANTONY C. SUTTON was a research fellow at the Hoover Institution at Stanford University and an economics professor at California State University, Los Angeles and is author of 21 books, including *Wall Street and the Rise of Hitler.*

Hardcover: **$24.95** (ISBN 0972020701), Softcover: **$19.95** (ISBN 0972020748) 335 pages • Size: 5 x 8

Fleshing Out Skull & Bones

Investigations into America's Most Powerful Secret Society

EDITED BY KRIS MILLEGAN

An expose of Yale's supersecretive and elite Order of Skull & Bones

This chronicle of espionage, drug smuggling, and elitism in Yale University's Skull & Bones society offers rare glimpses into this secret world with previously unpublished documents, photographs, and articles that delve into issues such as racism, financial ties to the Nazi party, and illegal corporate dealings. Contributors include Antony Sutton, author of *America's Secret Establishment*; Dr. Ralph Bunch, professor emeritus of political science at Portland State University; Webster Griffin Tarpley and Anton Chaitkin, authors and historians; and Howard Altman, editor of the *Philadelphia City Paper.* A complete list of known members, including George Bush and George W. Bush, and reprints of rare magazine articles on the Order of Skull and Bones are included.

Hardcover: **$32.95** (ISBN 0972020721), Softcover: **$24.95** (ISBN 0975290606) 720 pages • Size: 6x9

The Octopus Conspiracy

and Other Vignettes of the Counterculture
from Hippies to High Times to Hip Hop and Beyond ...

BY STEVEN HAGER

Insightful essays on the genesis of subcultures from new wave and yuppies to graffiti and rap.

From the birth of hip-hop culture in the South Bronx to the influence of nightclubs in shaping the modern art world in New York, a generation of countercultural events and icons are brought to life in this personal account of the life and experiences of a former investigative reporter and editor of High Times. Evidence from cutting-edge conspiracy research including the real story behind the JFK assassination and the Franklin Savings and Loan cover-up is presented. Quirky personalities and compelling snapshots of life in the 1980s and 1990s emerge in this collection of vignettes from a landmark figure in journalism.

STEVEN HAGER is the author of *Adventures in Counterculture, Art After Midnight,* and *Hip Hop.* He is a former reporter for the New York Daily News and an editor of *High Times.*

Hardcover: **$19.95** (ISBN 0975290614) • 320 pages • Size: 6 x 9

Sinister Forces
A Grimoire of American Political Witchcraft
Book One: The Nine

BY PETER LEVENDA, FOREWORD BY JIM HOUGAN

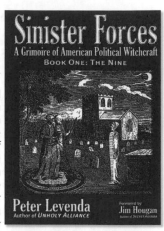

A shocking alternative to the conventional views of American history.
The roots of coincidence and conspiracy in American politics, crime, and culture are examined in this book, exposing new connections between religion, political conspiracy, and occultism. Readers are taken from ancient American civilization and the mysterious mound builder culture to the Salem witch trials, the birth of Mormonism during a ritual of ceremonial magic by Joseph Smith, Jr., and Operations Paperclip and Bluebird. Not a work of speculative history, this exposé is founded on primary source material and historical documents. Fascinating details are revealed, including the bizarre world of "wandering bishops" who appear throughout the Kennedy assassinations; a CIA mind control program run amok in the United States and Canada; a famous American spiritual leader who had ties to Lee Harvey Oswald in the weeks and months leading up to the assassination of President Kennedy; and the "Manson secret.

Hardcover: **$29.95** (ISBN 0975290622) • 396 pages • Size: 6 x 9

Book Two: A Warm Gun

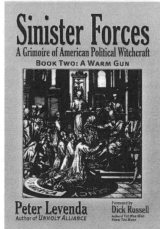

The roots of coincidence and conspiracy in American politics, crime, and culture are investigated in this analysis that exposes new connections between religion, political conspiracy, terrorism, and occultism. Readers are provided with strange parallels between supernatural forces such as shaminism, ritual magic, and cult practices, and contemporary interrogation techniques such as those used by the CIA under the general rubric of MK-ULTRA. Not a work of speculative history, this exposé is founded on primary source material and historical documents. Fascinating details on Nixon and the "Dark Tower," the Assassin cult and more recent Islamic terrorism, and the bizarre themes that run through American history from its discovery by Columbus to the political assassinations of the 1960s are revealed.

Hardcover: **$29.95** (ISBN 0975290630) • 392 pages • Size: 6 x 9

Book Three: The Manson Secret

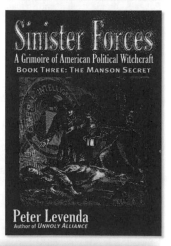

The Stanislavski Method as mind control and initiation. Filmmaker Kenneth Anger and Aleister Crowley, Marianne Faithfull, Anita Pallenberg, and the Rolling Stones. Filmmaker Donald Cammell (Performance) and his father, CJ Cammell (the first biographer of Aleister Crowley), and his suicide. Jane Fonda and Bluebird. The assassination of Marilyn Monroe. Fidel Castro's Hollywood career. Jim Morrison and witchcraft. David Lynch and spiritual transformation.The technology of sociopaths. How to create an assassin. The CIA, MK-ULTRA and programmed killers.

Hardcover: **$29.95** (ISBN 0975290649) • 422 pages • Size: 6 x 9

Trine Day
P.O. Box 577
WALTERVILLE, OR 97489

ORDER BY ONLINE OR BY PHONE:
TrineDay.com
1-800-556-2012